The Spirit of the Game

Gustav von Hertzen

The Spirit of the Game

Navigational Aids for
the Next Century

FRITZES

CE Fritzes AB is a subsidiary of Liber AB · Wolters Kluwer Sweden

Address:
CE Fritzes AB
Box 6472
S-113 82 Stockholm, Sweden

Orders:
Fritzes
S-106 47 Stockholm, Sweden
Telephone: +46 8 690 90 90, Fax: +46 8 20 50 21

THE SPIRIT OF THE GAME
Gustav von Hertzen
1st edition
ISBN 91-38-92227-4
© 1993 The author and CE Fritzes AB

Jacket Design: Grafisk Studio RING
End papers: Albrecht Dürer (1471–1528)
Self-Portrait at 13, drawing 1484, and *Adam and Eve,* etching 1504 (front);
St. Jerome in his study, etching 1514, and *Melencolia I,* etching 1514 (back)

Composing in Sweden by KK Grafiska AB, Stockholm
Printed in Sweden by Graphic Systems AB, Göteborg 1993

This book is dedicated to

Eric Rhenman (1932–1993)
a progress dynamo
if ever there was one

Acknowledgment

As I worked on and off for twenty years with the manuscript of this book, numerous people have given me help which must regrettably remain unacknowledged. I should however like to mention my son Thomas who read an early version and encouraged me to go on. The first drafts were written in Swedish and a rough translation was made by Nancy Adler. Later on I undertook to rewrite the whole book in English; not much is left of the original manuscript. I am heavily indebted to John Calton of the University of Helsinki for the final language check as well as for many valuable suggestions.

I should also like to thank Professor Rolf Wolf and his group of postgraduate students at the Gothenburg Research Institute for their important contribution to the final version of the book. The presence of Professor Sten Jönsson added weight to the discussions.

I dedicate this book to Eric Rhenman, founder, president and chairman of the Scandinavian Institute for Administrative Research (SIAR, now SIAR-Bossard). He gave me his unwavering support during the long gestation period right up to the time of his unexpected death. The generous contribution of the SIAR Foundation has made publication of the book possible.

My last and most sincere thanks go to my wife who has stood by me for more than forty years. Without her this book would never have been written.

Table of Contents

Dear Reader

Now as you start reading – take heart. This is not meant to be a pleasure trip so do not be discouraged if you do not understand everything immediately. Just read the short summaries, skip the difficult parts and go ahead. The story will take hold if you are of the right stuff. Mankind is off on the greatest adventure ever undertaken and you are, like it or not, personally involved. During the next century, we will either make it or break it.

This book poses an intellectual challenge. By applying the core of mathematics and the natural sciences, including biology, I have mapped out our present situation against the backdrop of natural and human history. Above all, I have tried to extract a sense of direction from the philosophical and religious muddle of our times. I do not pretend to offer any final truths but I do try to expose manifest nonsense and help you in defining your own framework of values – your personal truth.

As for the organization of the text, the main train of thought is interspersed with short illustrative passages. These can be bypassed but, more often than not you will find that they offer some respite from the hard cerebral slog. True to life, the different subjects have not been neatly separated but are interwoven in an organic structure, as it were. The cross-references in the margin together with the index should be helpful in finding your way around the book.

The Opening Gambit (Chapter 1) gives you an overview but then you are on your own. Initially, the shifts in perspective may be somewhat confusing but sooner or later you will perceive the continuity of the argument as the various pieces fall into place. My aim is to provide navigational aids for our joint voyage of discovery, and whatever the quality of the chart, the only compass we have is our deepest sense of fair play, the search for meaningful truth – the Spirit of the Game.

1.   Opening gambit

> This whole book is but a draught – nay, but the draught
> of a draught – oh Time, Strength, Cash and Patience!
> *Herman Melville*
>
> Only fools and charlatans know all and understand all
> *Anton Chekhov*
>
> I am not interested in erecting a building, but in seeing
> clearly before me the foundations of all possible build-
> ings
> *Ludwig Wittgenstein*
>
> What I can't create, I don't understand
> *Richard Feynman*

A bold pursuit

I began work on this book in the late Sixties as a protest against the intellectual
and political follies of the time. Those particular delusions may have lost their
appeal but, time and again, the thread of common endeavour seems to get lost in
a maze of incommensurable opinions. And no wonder, since agonizing uncertainty is the inescapable companion of cultural advance. All the more important then that we make an effort to rise above the fray, striving for a coherent
world-view and a superior orientation.

My book is an entreaty to people of good will, people who retain a feeling of
responsibility beyond their personal sphere of interest. My main concern is our
Western culture, which, for better or for worse, dominates the world. All our
hopes and fears are tied up in this joint venture; never have the prospects been so
exciting and yet so threatening. The future of humanity, of everything we
believe in, is at stake.

The wisdom of the ages has been packed into our genetic code, offering
unique opportunities in the game of life. We should roll up our sleeves and try to
justify the good fortune of being born human. All along we must make fateful
choices, fully aware of our inherent fallibility which tends to lead us astray as
we strive to distinguish truth from falsehood, good from evil, right from wrong.
The ultimate in uncertainty must be absorbed as we opt either for a living God
or for the Nietzschean position that God is dead.

Whatever our convictions or dispositions may be, we are now on the verge of
a great discontinuity. We will soon be able to influence our genetic set-up and

thus in a profound sense select ourselves. This rapidly increasing self-reference will lead to a sudden expansion in our scope for play and introduce an almost divine freedom of action. The question is: can we cope with this challenge? Do we dare to desire such unlimited emancipation, such an expansion of consciousness? A new creation is in the offing – for which we had better be prepared.

In aspiring to a great goal, we cannot avoid error; meaningful mistakes are the true source of new insight. Truth is the sublimate of false hypotheses and abortive experiments, failures and frustrations, rejects and refuse. Thus, let us trust in the spirit of the game and move boldly ahead running through the whole gamut of human enterprise as best we can.

Man and his world

We start out by clarifying *The Nature of Reality* (Chapter 2) as it has been interpreted by our finest minds. Advances in mathematics and science in particular have shown that the world cannot be caught in a net of deductive thought. No language can express its own truth criteria; no "truth machine" can ever be built. The laws of nature do not, in general, allow accurate prediction, while philosophy, at best, can only provide some pointers for our searching intellect: "Every honest philosophy is self-destructive" (Ludwig Wittgenstein).

To cope with the enormous complexity of existence, I have introduced the game metaphor and I shall look at the whole world – particles, proteins, people and societies – as an interactive game process, governed by a hierarchy of comprehensible rules. The world is not a being but a becoming – a great game. As for the players, man is by far the most successful in sight, even if he has a predilection for futile zero-sum games. Sustained plus-sum play can be achieved only if we submit to a set of overriding meta-rules, the fundamental values of human coalitions. The game still permits innumerable creative moves but there is always a list of don'ts – forbidden moves which give the game its meaning.

It all began with a Big Bang about fifteen billion years ago when the elementary particles commenced their self-organizing play. Quantum physics articulates the rules of that game and has finally brought us into contact with the core of reality. At the quantum level the particles have retained a minimum of freedom; they betoken a shadow of an individual choice. One way or the other, this quality is transformed into consciousness in the human brain. Sentient beings are, after all, the ultimate proof of the reality of existence.

To proceed with our exploration, we shall need a better understanding of *The Nature of Man* (Chapter 3) as he appears in the light of evolution. Merciless Darwinian selection has made us clever survival artists, internally directed by innate rules which program us for primitive group solidarity. Beyond that tribal level, human co-operation is an unstable affair, wholly dependent on arbitrary conventions and a fragile ethics. Since prehistoric times, man has been his own prey and predator: *Homo homini lupus* – man is the wolf of man.

Like all life forms, man is subject to the mechanisms of molecular evolution. Although genetic determinism seems to hold all creation in its iron grip, cultural preferences can sometimes initiate far-reaching genetic change. The break-throughs of human evolution may well have been achieved by marginal groups, tottering on the brink of extinction. Language and consciousness are probably the by-product of such mortal challenges.

Brain research is, for sure, the most direct route to knowing ourselves. Even if neuroscience is still in its infancy it can provide some clues to the nature of creativity – one of my main themes. At its most basic, thinking is the art of making mental mistakes, and creative work reiterates this game at a higher level. Only by testing and discarding ideas, conjectures, prototypes, do we make real progress; the worth of creative work stems from all that is thrown away. But the decisive factor is the largely implicit framework of values, or value frame, which gives direction to the process.

At the heart of it all lies creative self-reference. Touching infinity, it loosens the grip of iron determinism. Be on the lookout, it will surface in many disguises.

The culture of man

The Culture Game (Chapter 4) takes us deeper into the play of human interrelations which is further expounded in *The Economic Game* (Chapter 5), *Political Games* (Chapter 6) and *The Games of Science* (Chapter 7).

A culture is in essence a vast superorganism with its own quasi-genetic inheritance. Values are the chromosomes of culture which direct the intricate plus-sum play from the wings. The family is the core of culture. Only in the intimate family context can the vital cultural heritage be transmitted, principally by persistent motherly indoctrination, to coin a phrase. Breakdown at this basic level will have slow but very serious consequences.

Culture is a collective learning process where the dead time, the delay between cause and effect, can be very long indeed. Accordingly, learning (and unlearning) becomes increasingly arduous as we work our way up from technical, economic, political and scientific games to the ultimate value frame. Whatever we do, the game proceeds regardless. Either we go on absorbing painful, invigorating lessons or we settle for drawn-out decay and death.

Stagefright has become endemic just as the material conditions for a sustained cultural advance are finally within reach. The prevailing mood seems to call for gloomy cultural defeatism which absolves us of any responsibility for the future. Crying wolf at every turn, we have swung from a starry-eyed belief in progress to equally ignorant and fashionable prophecies of doom. It is difficult to accept the obvious – that the future is open and depends on us.

Man can, within limits, be a law unto himself but in making use of this restricted freedom we would do better to keep our humble origins in mind. Intellectual arrogance prepares the ground for the greatest follies: pride goes before a fall. Destructive minus-sum games – wars and insurrections – have been the hallmark of human history while lasting economic cultivation has rarely found fertile ground.

The modern market economy is a self-adjusting plus-sum game, a prodigious provider of wealth. It is unjustly blamed for our economic and ecological woes, the majority of which are due to self-inflicted market failures. Economic disgrace is the consequence of political shortcomings and, at root, of human greed and spite. Our extended prehistory has imprinted communal sharing on the human mind. This "epigenetic" rule is in permanent conflict with the accumulation of private property – at heart we are all socialists.

Democracy is a continuous learning process which depends on the calibre of the citizenry. The belief in the good will and the good sense of the common man is our specifically democratic utopia, disparaged by extremists on the right and left. While democracies have shown unexpected tenacity under threat, they are vulnerable to the poisons of prosperity. The greatest, in fact the only danger comes from ourselves, from our ingrained preference for short-term satisfactions, for pleasant lies as against unpleasant truths – the ever-present temptations of foul play.

Democratic rule is not a self-propelled progress machine. It merely provides a shell for human aspirations, a set of means without specific ends. Unlike socialist utopias, it does not require angelic citizens but neither will enlightened self-interest suffice. We need a minimum of civic virtues, some sense of purpose, a grain of faith and love to maintain the social coalition and sustain the plus-sum play. The market economy and democratic rule both economize on such "love", which is always in short supply: "Man's moral capacity makes democracy possible but also makes it indispensable" (Reinhold Niebuhr).

The task of science is to discover and make explicit the rules of all the ongoing games, heightening our self-reference; as such it has a key role in the cultural interplay. Science is no "truth machine", but depends wholly on its own implicit rules and the integrity of scientists. As it stands, the scientific community could well act as a paradigm for human self-organization. Technical prowess, the market economy, political democracy and scientific advances are all of a piece – they sink or swim together.

Our Western culture is the outcome of breathtaking collective creativity which amounts to a very vulnerable game. Successful cultural play should not be taken for granted. My thesis is that values – the meta-rules of the game – are the decisive factors which make or break the plus-sum play. Values ultimately direct all human co-operation, be it within the family, in business or for nations or entire cultures. The quality of the values decides the future: the meta-rules are the main competitive weapon for a culture, a country, a company – for human communities of whatever scale.

Values are notoriously difficult to pin down. There are no proofs or refutations in questions of value; the outcome is clear only in the light of extended hindsight. The value frame has real substance only to the extent that it influences the actual mode of play, repelling fallacies and promoting creative advance. The ubiquitous parasites and free-riders of society – the cheats and the cynics – must in any case be beaten off to provide sufficient scope for honest progress dynamos who take on the everlasting task of reforming society.

Cultures, like countries and companies, tend to become victims of their own success. Cultural advance depends on the hidden rules of social self-organization, which we recognize only when they have gone by the board. Then and there, society returns to the not-so-blessed state of nature where all culturally-imposed inhibitions evaporate and only family and tribal bonds remain – man, once again, becomes the wolf of man.

The value universe

Before we can talk about the elusive *Spirit of the Game* (Chapter 9), we must first gain a proper understanding of the limits of *Language Games* (Chapter 8). There is certainly cause for caution here. Treacherous word play has lead generations of philosophers astray – "every word is a prejudice" (Friedrich Nietzsche).

Our very existence depends on hard-won information which is encoded in every cell and directs all the life processes. We now understand the genetic alphabet and the basic syntax, but the immensely rich semantic content can never be significantly reduced. The vernacular, too, is virtually irreducible; the sense is wholly dependent on the overall context.

In contrast, the abstract language of, say, number theory is based on a minimum axiomatics and a crystal-clear syntax. And yet, it too displays astonishing, self-referential creativity, expressing undecidable mathematical propositions which can neither be proved nor disproved. Computers are restricted to the deducible aspects of mathematics; every general-purpose computer can, given enough time, compute everything which is computable.

The marvel of the human mind makes conscious plus-sum play possible but it also, inevitably, introduces lies and deceit; semiotics has been defined as the science of whatever can be used for lying. Our ordinary language certainly fills the bill: everything can be discussed but nothing can be proved. The mother tongue is immensely flexible; it embraces and defines all professional languages, which should be sufficiently circumscribed to make stringent reasoning possible.

At every level of language the meta-problems – the questions of truth and meaning – can be approached only by way of a superior metalanguage. Engaging art languages provide such superordinate platforms and can serve as conduits to the essence of existence. Art is information in immediate action. Nothing is explicitly explained: a work of art is the sole witness to its own truth. Honesty is the touchstone of great art: " He who does not lie, who dares to refrain from lying is already original enough" (Ludwig Wittgenstein).

Our behaviour and misbehaviour, our words and deeds are the key to the future. During the last centuries we have been living precariously on accumulated capital and are now approaching a state of spiritual impoverishment. All investments eventually wear out; the greatest truths have to be re-created and re-formulated. Without the support of genuine faith we are hurled back and forth between scepticism and fanaticism, susceptible in our irresolution to a miscellany of modern superstitions.

Through acts of faith we have created a steadily expanding value universe which knows no limits. For this arduous voyage of discovery, we need the support of a cultural credo, a shortlist of prohibitions endorsing freedom, frugality and fair play. The only categorical imperative is the aspiration to plus-sum play, which is the measure of morality. The outcome should exceed the stakes; creation should be enhanced.

Absolute truth is out of this world even if lies and fallacies can be exposed. The notion of God is even more elusive. Nevertheless, there is a chasm between believers and unbelievers which most of us try to straddle. Personally, I think that everyone must, in the end, make their choice between the long and the short term, between meaning or no meaning, between God or no God. "Everything is allowed if God is dead" (Fjodor Dostoyevsky).

Rejecting God, man has presumed total independence but, in the final instance, timid humanism cannot stand alone. To escape inanity, man must be seen in a superior perspective. He will always seek a higher mission – or descend into bestiality. My personal credo enshrines the strivings of a progress dynamo. He or she wants to enrich the world, to be both strong and good, adroit and honest – in short, to heed the Spirit of the Game. A prodigious but not inhuman programme, well worth failing.

2. The nature of reality

2.1 Mathematical truth

No interesting language, not even mathematics, can explain itself; at every level of language the central meta-problems, the questions of truth and meaning, must be tackled from above. It follows that most of mathematics is beset by undecidable propositions which can neither be proved nor disproved. This very fault allows the wonderful play of mathematical self-reference, thus creating models for all possible worlds. But the world, as it stands, cannot be explained by logical or mathematical deduction; the abortive efforts to that end originated in a gross overestimation of the power of formalised mental processes.

The impotence of logic

The young Ludwig Wittgenstein (1889–1951) opens his *Tractacus Logico-Philosophicus* (1922) with the phrase "Die Welt ist alles was der Fall ist" ("The world is all that is the case") – an elegant piece of self-reflection which indicates the limits of logical argument. Subsequently he shows that self-verifying propositions, i.e. absolute truths, are tautological and have no real content; in themselves they say nothing about the world. There is no base on which an absolutely valid system of ideas can be built. Our real problems cannot be handled in irrefutable terms. On the contrary, the fundamental concepts of logic and mathematics themselves have to be defined in the vernacular.

These insights dispatched the long-held hope of a unitary and axiomatic deduction of mathematical truths from first logical principles; Bertrand Russell's (1872–1970) and Alfred North Whitehead's (1861–1947) ambitious programme in their *Principia Mathematica* (1912) was reduced to an empty gesture. Instead, Kurt Gödel was able to prove (1930) that every "interesting" axiomatics can generate propositions which are undecidable: their truth or falsity cannot be deduced from the axioms. Ordinary arithmetic is the best example of such an "incomplete" Gödelian system. Multiplication and addition are sufficient for the creation of "interesting" mathematics. Restriction to one or the other mode eliminates any self-reference and reduces arithmetic to a

cf. 39; 279

cf. 33; 328

completely calculable and trivial game of numbers, yielding no undecidable propositions.

cf. 388   Advanced arithmetic is built on simple, logical symmetry breaking. When we add, +1+1 = +2 and −1−1 = −2; so far, so good. When we multiply, +1 · +1 = +1 but −1 · −1 is also equal to +1 and $\sqrt{-1}$ becomes non-existent, imaginary. Double positive is even more positive but double negative is also positive in most languages. Why is that so? Because it makes sense in our everyday language game. Negation is not just the opposite of affirmation; which leads to meaningful mathematics, too.

Explicit and universally valid procedures (algorithms) are not generally available for solving interesting mathematical problems. The textbook formulas for solving equations of the second or third degree soon come to an ignominious halt: no algorithm can be deduced for equations of the fifth degree.

cf. 328   Since the mid-seventeenth century, every generation of mathematicians has battled with Pierre de Fermat's (1601–65) "great" theorem: "the equation $x^n + y^n = z^n$ has no Diophantine roots for $n > 2$", i.e. no combination of integers for x, y, z satisfy the equation if n is greater than 2. Fermat himself proved his theorem for n = 4, and Leonhard Euler (1707–83) found the proof for n = 3. Subsequent mathematicians have pushed the proof to ever higher exponents; by 1992 it stood at n = 4,000,000. In 1988, Gerd Faltings proved that the number of roots must be finite. The general case remained a veritable perpetuum mobile of number theory until, in 1993, a very credible, 200-page long proof was presented by Andrew Wiles. Provided that no faults can be found (thousands of earlier "proofs" have been proved wrong), Fermat's great theorem can now be laid to a well-earned rest.

Further progress in meta mathematics and semiotics has confirmed that no interesting logico-mathematical language can establish its own truth. The power of self-expression is dependent on this apparent drawback which opens up the development of the game, leading it through internally verifiable relationships into an infinite variety of unverifiable mathematical structures. No consistent system of thought can contain a limited number of insoluble problems; in short, mathematics is inexhaustible.

Conceptual undecidability

cf. 281   In his intuitional mathematics, L.E.J.Brouwer (1881–1966) denies the autonomous and transcendental existence of mathematical concepts and relationships. Rather, mathematical objects are intuitively comprehended mental constructs intimately related to man's perception of personal time, the intrinsically dualistic relation of before-after. In this perspective, undecidable theorems are not only indeterminable but indeterminate. In a progression towards infinity, uncertainty cannot as a rule be reduced to zero. Thus the "either *a* or *not a*" of logic, the law of the excluded middle, does not necessarily hold when the number of alternatives increases without limit. This allows a third agnostic type of truth; the solution is not only out of reach, it is also literally unknowable. The analogy with the fuzzy logic of quantum mechanics and Werner Heisenberg's

cf. 34; 62; 379   (1901–76) famous uncertainty principle is worth noting.

Gödel's theorem does not apply to supernatural numbers beyond infinity, which are

defined by introducing the negation of Gödel's theorem as a new axiom in arithmetic. *cf. 329*
The mathematical manipulation of such transcendental entities comes up against remarkable limitations. Depending on the notation system, the quantities can be either added or multiplied, but no formalism permits the use of both types of calculation – again the spectre of the uncertainty principle looms.

The problem of computability raised its head once it became clear that vast areas of mathematics are non-computable and out of bounds for straightforward logical deduction. In 1936 Alonzo Church introduced a sweeping definition for "effective calculability". It included all stepwise mathematical procedures covered by well-defined rules and was shown to correspond to the well-known class of general recursive functions. In the next year Alan Turing (1912–54) came up with his machine-like computation model, a third assault on the limits of computability. Soon it became apparent that Turing's notion of the "mechanically calculable" tallied with the earlier, more abstract concepts.

> The Turing machine allows thought experiments modelled on an exactly defined but only virtually existing computer. The input is an endless tape where the problem is presented as a string of binary code (O:s and 1:s). The machine can read the tape, move it one step at a time in either direction and add, change or erase information. The unlimited supply of empty tape provides room for intermediate calculations and memory storage. When the problem is solved the machine stops and the result appears on the tape in binary code (everything else is erased).
>
> All specific Turing machines are preprogrammed according to given algorithms. For each and every one of the finite number of machine states, the hard-wired program prescribes in detail what the machine will do in response to the tape input, including a possible change of state. A universal Turing machine can in principle imitate the operation of all these special-purpose machines. The sophisticated hardware can be properly programmed according to any algorithm (coded on the tape as software) which will operate on the problems presented further down on the same tape.

The universal Turing machine, though cumbersome, is a finite and fully transparent design; nevertheless it can, in principle, compute everything which is computable. (Surprisingly enough, this quality is shared by all general-purpose computers which are constrained only by their finite memory space.) The machine stops when the problem is solved or when the input is contradictory and generates inconsistencies. If the problem happens to be undecidable, the machine will continue its calculations *ad infinitum*. Unfortunately, there is no general method to find out in advance if the machine will stop. The Turing halting problem is logically undecidable in concurrence with the general principle of Gödelian uncertainty. *cf. 32; 333*

cf. 328; 329; 333; 381

Chaotic intractability

Theoretical computability does not guarantee that the problem can be solved in practice. If the burden of computation increases exponentially with the number of elements or moves involved, the problem soon becomes intractable. *cf. 112*

> Many interesting board games such as chess and the Japanese game of Go belong to this category, i.e. it is not generally possible to calculate the "right" move. However, in the game of Nim (and all its variants) a winning strategy can be formulated, since by a *cf. 45*

mathematical trick of the trade the number of calculations can be kept from increasing exponentially.

Mathematical intractability does not *per se* preclude arbitrarily exact approximations by an incremental search strategy. But this procedure, too, comes up against formidable difficulties.

> The classic three-body problem is mathematically intractable. To be sure, the interaction of three dot-like objects under the influence of gravitation is covered by well-known differential equations, but they cannot be solved. The mathematics is non-recursive and hence no explicit algorithm is available. The best one can do is to guess at a future state and calculate the error, closing the gap by successive iterations. With modern computers any degree of accuracy is achievable in handling the 21 independent variables of the three-body problem, but if the number of variables is increased to thousands (or even millions as required by astronomy), the simulation will outstrip the capacity of any conceivable computing machinery.

More baffling is the appearance of deep unpredictability in totally deterministic systems. Such chaotic dynamics defy even the approximate pre-calculation of any long-term trajectories.

> Hill's reduced model of the three-body problem assumes that the mass of one of the bodies is negligible. This particle will not influence the movements of the two heavyweights, which will steadily turn around each other following a stodgy, periodic choreography. In contrast, the negligible speck of dust seems to have lost its bearings. It does not settle into a stable track but is drawn into a dance of non-repetitive, aperiodic perturbations. The slightest variation in the initial conditions or minuscule outside disturbances will throw the particle off its calculated course. Simulations with different makes of computer produce progressively diverging trajectories because of the differing ways of rounding off the last digit.

cf. 62; 66; 74 The hallmark of chaotic dynamics is the rapidly increasing divergence of states which initially were almost identical. Classical physics or mathematics is insensitive to small perturbations – vanishing causes have vanishing effects. Chaotic dynamics on the other hand put even mathematical causality into a new perspective.

Simple mathematics (and physics) is linear; any two solutions can be added and superimposed on each other. Linearity holds generally for differential equations of the first degree, which can be easily integrated. Now, the mathematical coupling of only three non-linear variables can cause a chaotic breakdown of predictability, even if the system is completely deterministic in principle. Computer simulation may bring out strange attractors, underlying patterns which describe the dynamic behaviour of the system without divulging the details of specific trajectories.

> The first to identify a strange attractor was Edward Lorenz in 1963 (see figure 2.1). The Lorenz attractor is produced by the following group of non-linear equations:
>
> $$dx/dt = -10x + 10y; \quad dy/dt = xz + 28x - y; \quad dz/dt = xy - 8z/3$$
>
> At any instant in time, the three variables fix the location of a point in Cartesian space. The chaotic trajectory never intersects or repeats itself but goes on tracking new paths

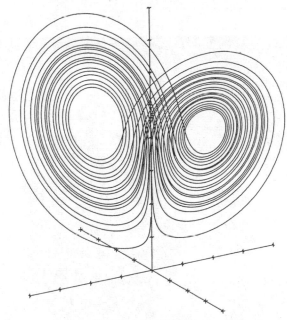

Figure 2.1 The Lorenz attractor (See Gleick, 1988)

forever. When infinitely drawn out, the trajectory acquires a "fractal" dimension of 2.04 – slightly stouter than a plane.

Normal, well-behaved mathematical functions usually approach clearly defined attractors, be it a point, a line, a periodicity, eternity or any other explicit mathematical entity. Random chaos, for its part, is completely featureless and does not develop in any way: it has no attractors. Quasi-chaotic interplay is distinguished by strange attractors which have a recognizable shape, but cannot be pinned down by mathematical deduction; they are infinitely convoluted and rich in detail. Strange attractors are highly fractured structures which elude the strict dimensionality of ordinary mathematical objects. Such entities are called fractals.

cf. 70

cf. 32

Chaotically interacting gravitational forces have produced the rich regularity of the solar system, with its planets, satellites, comets and asteroids, the intertwined rings of Saturn, the mysterious moons of Jupiter, Uranus and Neptune as well as the strange links and resonances between widely scattered heavenly bodies. Venus, for instance, rotates once round its axis in precisely two-thirds of the earth's year. To top it off, the inner planets – classic models of strict Newtonian conduct – evidently constitute a weakly chaotic system, excluding the predictability of their relative positions in the very long term.

Abstract creativity

On closer examination both logic and mathematics reveal themselves to be empirical sciences, in which research proceeds by means of subtle mental exper-

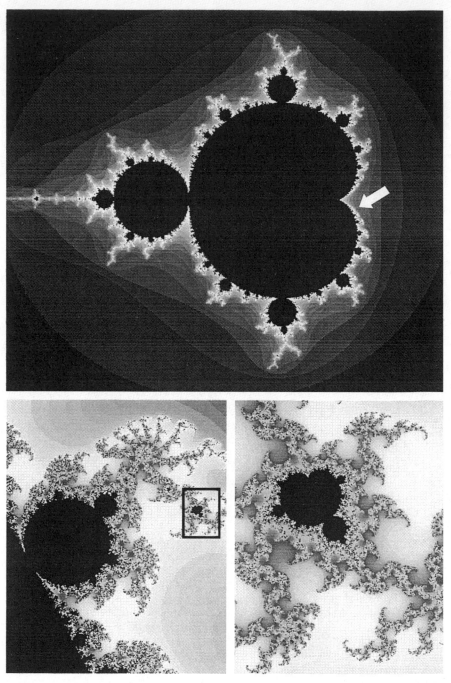

Figure 2.2 The Mandelbrot set with two successive magnifications (by courtesy of the Institute of Mathematics, Helsinki University of Technology).

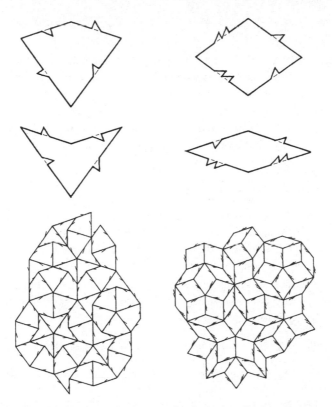

Figure 2.3 Two pairs of "Penrose tiles", each of which will tile only non-periodically; the lower figures show regions of the plain tiled with each pair (Penrose, 1989)

iments, nowadays supported by computer simulation. Only tautological systems are completely self-verifying since there is no substance, nothing of "interest" to uncover. But simple iterative systems can display astonishing creativity when the argument is self-referentially replaced by its function over and over again.

The Mandelbrot set, discovered by Benoit Mandelbrot in 1979, is the most complicated mathematical object (or should we call it a subject?) so far discovered (Figure 2.2). In essence, it is produced by the iterative squaring of a complex number X + iy, always adding a constant C (i stands for the square root of –1, the base of imaginary numbers). The borderline of the Mandelbrot set is a strange attractor for the parameter values which are on the verge of pushing the iteration towards infinity. The endlessly incised boundary is nowhere differentiable, but nevertheless it is fully connected: the boundary has the fractal dimension of two. Under magnification the curve never repeats itself despite the recurrence of similarly curled seahorses and indeed a profusion of miniature Mandelbrot sets, each one with its own slightly divergent features. Infinite variety unexpectedly emerges as a straightforward mathematical process plays itself out on the computer screen, probing ever finer details of its fractal domain.

Penrose tesselations, named after the mathematician Roger Penrose, (figure 2.3) are   cf. 73
the geometrical equivalent of algebraic self-revelation. A combination of only two different shapes can tile an infinite plane in a non-periodic mode; no pattern will ever repeat itself on any scale. Yet nature goes one better in three dimensions. Snow crystals

are built up from simple symmetric water molecules H\O/H but the crystals never repeat themselves.

Mathematicians have had a penchant for those special circumstances which allow the truth of a proposition to be rigorously deduced from the premises – from the inside as it were. However, such shortcuts are the exception that proves the rule. In the general case, one has to step out of the given axiomatic framework and literally look around its external structure, empirically discovering and investigating the often outrageously chaotic facts.

A hierarchy of languages

Like infinity or the microcosm of quantum physics, the inmost substance, the "reality" of mathematics cannot be strictly defined. At the basic level we can articulate reasonable rules of the game within a formalised language. But the introspective capacity of a self-referential idiom is necessarily limited: no interesting language can explain or justify itself. A higher-order language may put the basic idiom into perspective but is even more opaque and impenetrable due to the broadened axiomatic base.

The capability of a special-purpose Turing machine increases tremendously with the number of states it can assume. The biggest number the machine can print out (and halt) is one yardstick for the computing power. A 4-state machine reaches number 13, a 5-state machine at least the number 1915, and we will probably never know the maximum number which can be printed out by a 6-state machine. Higher state machines achieve numbers which are effectively non-computable and increase faster than any conceivable mathematical function. Thus a universal Turing machine (with a huge number of states) will accept all recursively enumerable languages and can formulate in its own code an arbitrary number of undecidable propositions which the machine, of course, cannot solve! But there is a maximum number, this side of eternity, which even a universal Turing machine cannot transcend.

cf. 33

cf. 381

These inherent limitations of mathematics are fundamental to all deductive thinking. No interesting language, not even mathematics, can explain itself, its own foundations or consequences. In one way or another they all come up against the classic liar paradox – "this proposition is not true" – which was *cf. 328* refined by Gödel with the help of the most sophisticated tools of his trade. In the same vein the mature Wittgenstein suggested that ordinary language can be perceived as an open-ended, self-organizing game. The relationships between the different word-moves create a pattern which to the trained player conveys *cf. 41; 347* real but mostly rather inaccurate information.

We will return (in section 8.2) to the questions of mathematics and language. Suffice it to say that in the hierarchy of language games, the vernacular bears the highest rank. Here nothing can be definitively proved; stringency is sacrificed to flexibility and significance. Even so, all our special languages have been worked into delicate instruments for the human intellect by the simple expedients of the mother tongue which thus comes to grips with its own limitations. But at every *cf. 310; 331* level of language the central meta-problems, the questions of truth and meaning, must be tackled from above. The world cannot be explained by logical or mathematical deduction; abortive efforts to that end originated in a gross overestimation of the power of formalised mental processes.

2.2   Scientific veracity

The natural sciences have gone from strength to strength and, thanks to quantum physics, elementary processes are rather well understood. Even so, the more complex manifestations of matter eschew scientific predictability. Most dynamic systems are inherently unsolvable and can be approached only by extensive computer simulation. As for human oriented sciences, they still grope for the right paradigms. No clear-cut scientific method will deliver a tenable explanation of man and the world. But an honest confrontation with reality cannot disregard our best scientific traditions. On the contrary, it must depend on the very same values which underpin our wavering quest for scientific truth.

From Carnap to Popper

We shall be studying the relationship between reality and science in greater detail below (Chapter 7). However, a brief analysis of the universal claims of science is called for at this stage. The impressive achievements of the natural sciences indubitably suggest close contact with the essence of reality. Consequently, it has been widely assumed that these insights must be based on a set of axiomatic truths which would constitute the rational grounds for our faith in science. Following Pierre Simon de Laplace (1749–1827) and Ernst Mach (1838–1916), the logical positivists, with Rudolf Carnap (1891–1970) in the *cf. 279* van, made frantic efforts to realise this programme by applying rigorous scientific reasoning – all of which sounds very much like Baron Munchausen's method of pulling himself up by his own bootstraps.

These endeavours have scarcely affected practising natural scientists who have generally been content with a pragmatic empiricism. Those with an epistemological bent have probably adopted some version of Karl Popper's critical rationalism as put forth in *Logik der Forschung* (1934) and the *Postscript to the Logic of Discovery* (1981–2). According to Popper, a scientific theory can never be finally verified but an ill-conceived theory can be falsified by experiments and rejected or improved upon. A doctrine which cannot be falsified, at least in principle (psychoanalysis is a much quoted example) is void of meaning and will, one way or another, succumb to circular argumentation; it achieves self-immunization by excluding any error.

Although Popper states that the truths of the natural sciences mirror characteristics of the material world, he asserts that scientific findings can only be granted provisional validity. All knowledge is partial; no truth is the whole truth; formal systems can always be made more effective and provide greater economy of thought. Popper's philosophy of science is both pragmatic and principled, in keeping with his endorsement of political pluralism.

Hermeneutic pragmatism

Even Popper has not gone unchallenged among natural scientists. Critical rationalism seems to be inadequate in the early, exploratory stages of research when scientists still hardly know what they are talking about. For all the clarity and freshness of Popper's philosophy of science it is still reminiscent of philosophizing about art: the reasoning may be correct in itself but represents little more than retrospective wisdom. The "explanation", if any, is seldom a valid prescription for creative work.

> Michael Polanyi (1891–1976) attacks (in *Personal Knowledge*, 1958) the traditional scientific notions from a hermeneutic standpoint. In his view, genuine knowledge is a form of capability or skill; "pure knowledge" has no meaning. Scientific orthodoxy is maintained and developed by a small number of connoisseurs who master the subject. Polanyi's approach has a lot in common with William James' (1842–1910) pragmatic philosophy. According to James, only the well-functioning, the useful, the practicable and effective implies real insight; everything else is empty speculation. This train of thought has close links with Wittgenstein's ideas on the working of language.

Every piece of knowledge is based on conviction and is really an act of faith. In most cases we have to fall back on trustworthy authorities; within our own profession we rely on hard-won internal experience (Polanyi's "tacit knowl-
cf. 286 edge") which does not require explicit validation. Facts that do not fit into an otherwise convincing and aesthetically attractive whole are simply disregarded. In creative thinking the insight precedes the proof; later on, incisive self-crit-
cf. 111–118 icism will separate the wheat from the chaff.

Thus, when all is said and done, nothing can be fully revealed, explained or irrefutably proved. Every act of real understanding is, on the other hand, an irreversible process. A familiar pattern, a meaningful structure, will always be "re-cognised" but isolated facts and linear-logical reasoning have limited power of persuasion. They often lead to paradoxes which tell us something about the obscure nature of the particular language game.

The aspirations of science

All science starts with the forming of mental structures by proper naming, a
cf. 112; 281; 342 primary hermeneutic challenge. After this initial orientation phase, scientific interest concentrates on summarizing and simplifying the observed data, reducing observable events to rules of the greatest possible generality. The lure of reductionism is a natural result of man's "scientific need", his longing for insight and understanding.

The natural sciences derive their formidable strength from the close interdependence of all their ramifications. Together they constitute a unitary system, in which the different branches of science employ the same concepts, mutually reinforcing one another. The credibility of physics, chemistry, astronomy and molecular biology does not primarily depend on quantitative mathematical models, which are often available, and even less on some scientific method which no-one has yet succeeded in clearly defining. The decisive factor is that the same invariant rules of the game apply over the whole field of material phenomena.

A consistent feature of our world equation seems to be the absence of any strict dividing-line between the forbidden and the permissible. The tunnelling effects of quantum physics do permit, although with low probability, "impermissible" border-crossings. When it comes to the individual process, determinism has lost its grip but, by the same token, the mathematical formalism of quantum mechanics has made triumphant progress in describing elementary particle play.

> The dimensionless fine-structure constant, (roughly 1/137) is a measure of the coupling (the strength of the interaction) between electrons and photons. It is one of the fundamental quantities of physics and is equivalent to $\dfrac{2\pi\ e^2}{hc}$ where h is Planck's action quantum, e is the charge of the electron and c the speed of light. This value can now be measured to within less than 1/10 million (seven significant digits). The theoretical calculations of quantum-electrodynamics have so far stood up to the increasingly accurate measurements. Thus, there is good reason to assume that all fundamental modes of the electron play are completely covered by the mathematical formalism. For the first time our mathematical language game seems to have established immediate contact with "the thing in itself". *cf. 74*

Einstein's general theory of relativity has not yet been fully confirmed, but it has so far stood up to all available tests. In combination with the well-known rules of quantum physics, it allows dizzying insights into the mysteries of uttermost time. Although complete self-understanding is beyond our reach, the natural sciences are revealing a comprehensible cosmos in the chaos of apparently unrelated cognitive input. Beyond the clearly visible levels of games upon games, we can glimpse a general Heisenbergian uncertainty, strangely broken supersymmetries and collapsed strings of multidimensional realities – perhaps the very grounds of creative order in a stunning manifold of universes.

The limits of reductionism

Reality is the outcome of a large number of processes proceeding in parallel or in interaction with one another. When the actors (e.g. atoms or molecules) are independent members of a large population, the behaviour of the system can often be described by a set of linear differential equations which reflect the rules of the collectivist game at a high level of abstraction. Individual occurrences are then completely irrelevant.

cf. 61; 70 The molecules in a gas collide randomly with one another. As a result of their irregular "Brownian" zigzag motion, a given dense assemblage will gradually spread into the surroundings. In such complete chaos, the route of the individual molecule has no effect on the diffusion process; on average the distance from the starting-point is always proportional to the square root of the time elapsed.

Perfect, statistically predictable randomness is rather an exception in the real world. It was selected by early physicists only for the sake of intellectual expediency; science is, in the words of the biologist Peter Medawar (1915–87), the art of the soluble. Strictly valid scientific generalizations are available only in special cases: most dynamic systems are inherently unsolvable.

By fate or good fortune the world has been forced into some sort of intelligible order. Gravity is a ubiquitous restraint which has organized matter in many *cf. 25* unforeseeable ways. When the full, completely random chaos of Brownian statistics is suitably constrained, the resulting quasi-chaotic interplay can produce new, information-bearing patterns despite (or rather because of) its mathematical intractability.

If the haphazard route of Brownian thermal motion, projected in a single plane, is not allowed to cross itself (which in physical terms corresponds to the polymerisation of amino acids into proteins), intractable non-linearities creep in. The complexity of the interaction is equivalent to that of a universal Turing machine (or a general purpose *cf. 23; 298* computer) which cannot be described in any simplifying terms.

Paradoxically, complete freedom from constraint spawns trivial predictability while the imposition of rules creates an unpredictable game. The ensuing discrete dynamics is amenable to computer simulation if the basic rules of the game are known; yet we are very far from the slick, explicit "solutions" which used to be the emblems of scientific truth.

The stringent rules governing the elementary particles leave little scope for play, but the room for individual manoeuvre increases as we scale the ladder of evolution to macromolecules and living organisms.

Two-dimensional cellular automatons which play around on a limitless chessboard provide us with rough but reasonably realistic models of creative interplay. If every cell can assume x different states and can interact with y neighbouring cells, the number of applicable game rules is $_xx^y$. In 1948, John von Neumann (1903–57) anticipated the reproductive mechanism of life in his conception of a self-reproducing and self-repair- *cf. 337; 401; 419* ing automaton. Such a device would require, according to von Neumann and Stanislaw Ulam, no more than about 200,000 cells, each one interacting with four of its neighbours while assuming 29 different states. This "organism" could structure its play in $_{29}29^4$ alternative modes, each one offering unfathomable variations of the particular game. More recently, E.F. Codd has come up with an equivalent design (the Universal Computer Constructor) employing only eight different states.

The monotonous drift of a process close to equilibrium is scientifically accessible and predictable. It proceeds without external support in contrast to creative play, which is contingent on a sufficient supply of outside energy. In the best of circumstances some of the energy may then be preserved as new, useful information, but the surplus is normally wasted in an extravagant display of *cf. 67* haphazard moves.

The slow flow of a gas or a liquid is laminar, and obeys well-known equations of fluid dynamics. If the pressure gradient is increased, the flow suddenly becomes turbulent in an irregular pattern of emerging and disappearing vortices. This is the classic example of how smooth uniformity is turned into chaotic change by the excessive dissipation of energy. In the same way, the influx of solar energy keeps the atmosphere of the earth in a highly turbulent state. Accordingly, long-term weather forecasting presents an intractable scientific problem, exceeding the power of even the fastest computers. *cf. 66*

We can achieve a profound understanding of the fundamental rules of the game, but the unfolding of complex reality is largely buried in (pseudo)chaotic unpredictability. Yet the development of corresponding language games does allow the mental or computer-aided representation and simulation of actual play, which in most cases remains the only way to track down obstinate realities.

Interim audit

In logic and mathematics we are omnipotent, and should be omniscient since this is a universe of our own making. But in the previous section we have shown that such is not the case. Rather, pure abstractions seem to possess a surprising creativity. Similarly, the elementary particles exhibited new capricious attributes in the initial seconds of the emerging universe. Were such phenomena predestined, "determinate", or governed by pure chance? or were they the outcome of a creative search process? These questions return with increasing alacrity as the molecular complexes evolve into multiform life, finishing up as distinct individuals and conscious personalities.

In mathematics, a few additional rules for multiplication convert a trivial addition game into exuberant arithmetics, and a similar giant step is taken when *cf. 21; 327* proceeding from propositional to predicate calculus. This progress is illustrated by the non-computable effects of increasing the number of states in a Turing machine. *cf. 28*

M.W. Green has shown (in 1964) that for an infinite number of states the increase of *cf. 283* just one additional state in a Turing machine (from n to n + 1) increases its potential power (the maximum printable number for instance) by a factor which is bigger than any function of the original number of states, n. Cumulative exponentiation, for example (n over n; n times), is woefully inadequate for expressing the growth in the powers of play.

The addition of a single axiom can significantly enrich the scientific discourse, but great caution must be exercised in making such a move; after all, empty prejudice is all too easily smuggled in by the back door. An additional rule *cf. 301* should strike at the core of the game. The new invariance must invoke a deep discipline, which enhances our thought economy while preserving the perceived scope for play. Newtonian and Einsteinian gravitation; the atomic structure of matter; the preservation of mass, energy and momentum; Darwinian evolution through natural selection; the Planck action quantum; and Heisenberg's uncertainty principle – they are all great examples of creative axiomatic constraint.

cf. 39; 61; 285; 344 Quantum mechanics has been called the most successful scientific theory of all time. The Schrödinger wave equation (named after Erwin Schrödinger, 1887–1961) expresses the basic invariance, which looks deceptively simple:

$$\frac{ih\ d(\psi)}{2\pi\ dt} = H(\smallint G)$$

ψ (psi) is the amplitude distribution of the wave function and H is the Hamiltonian operator which renders the energy of the system in terms of the positions and the quantified momenta of the particles.

The Schrödinger equation describes the evolvement over time (t) of any particle assemblage in the world of electromagnetic interaction. The presence of i, the square root of -1, indicates that we are once removed from immediate reality. Indeed we have to square ψ to get at the probabilities of the particles' appearance. In any particular instance it remains an open question as to how the complex wave function will "collapse" and which of the many superimposed states will take part in a real process.

In the case of a single photon or a single electron, the wave function reduces to the Maxwell and Dirac equations respectively. A solution can be found for the hydrogen atom (one proton + one electron), and approximations are within reach for other simple systems. But when the numbers of particles increase, the mathematics become intractable and we have to fall back on classical physics and chemistry.

The Schrödinger equation is deterministic, and any future state could be exactly calculated (in principle) if we knew the initial state at t = O. But this is not possible, and the equation cannot be fully focused as to location and momentum at the same time. The formalism of matrix algebra, developed by Max Born (1882–1971) and Werner Heisenberg, clearly points to the fuzzy nature of quantum mechanical reality and occasioned the famous uncertainty cf. 22; 62 principle.

The "correct" interpretation of quantum physics is still a hotly debated topic. Does it tell us everything which is knowable or are there, as Albert Einstein (1879–1955) suggested, some cf. 75; 379 hidden variables which assure the absolute predictability of the ways of the world? Personally, I prefer to side with Nils Bohr (1885–1952) and the majority opinion which regards quantum physics as a complete but underdetermined theory. It allows the unforeseeable which even God cannot know.

At present the natural sciences work very well although nobody quite seems to know how or why. The situation becomes more controversial when we put man under the magnifying glass. In the social sciences, not to speak of the humanities, reliable and comprehensive paradigms are conspicuous only by their absence. Continuing specialization has simply caused a malignant fragmentation of the body of knowledge.

The great forerunners of the social sciences were consistent in proclaiming the need for a holistic approach to the understanding of the human condition. Max Weber (1864–1920) for one claimed that sociological and historical research neither could nor should be kept apart, although he preferred to believe that a scientific, value-neutral sociology was possible. Latterly, exaggerated reductionist zeal has driven these "soft" sciences towards laboured imitation of natural-scientific methodology, which robs the scientific work of its relevance. Despite many brilliant suggestions, most positivistic social science barely deserves acknowledgement.

Full understanding of the phenomenon of *Homo sapiens* seems to be unattainable in practice, and is probably precluded in principle; witness the self-devouring snake. No clear-cut scientific method can adequately elucidate man and his world. For all that, the escalation of complexity obviously calls for a circumspect broadening of the axiomatic base. Moreover, an honest confrontation with reality cannot disregard our best scientific traditions; on the contrary, it must depend on the very same values which underpin our wavering quest for scientific truth.

2.3   Philosophical explications

The history of philosophy is a tale of human fallacies, subsequently exposed by later generations. We have now finally come to understand the limits of language and philosophy, i.e. of explicit, analytical thinking. Since classical times a supreme repose, harmony and balance had been a self-evident attribute of all basic truths. Whitehead's process philosophy takes the opposite track in its strictly dynamic approach. The world is not a being but a becoming; at every moment it is created anew, although in accordance with statistically immutable rules.

Greek overture

Philosophy, the love of wisdom, is in essence thought about thought. The ambition of this self-referential "science of sciences" has always been to present a consistent and unassailable picture of the world and of life, based on first principles. In view of what has been said above, the continual frustration of these hopes should hardly come as a surprise. It is all too easy for philosophical and metaphysical expositions to degenerate into empty language games, disconnected from reality. Even at best, they largely reflect the existential prejudices of the particular thinker in an abstruse idiom.   *cf. 82*

Almost all the philosophical leitmotivs were struck between 600 and 400 B.C. as Greek speculative thought approached its apogee. Thales, the first of the philosophers, had studied marine fossils and declared with great conviction that *water* is the origin of all things, while his disciples, Anaximander and Anaximenes, adopted *infinity* and *air* respectively as the point of departure for their rival cosmologies. Heraclitus regarded *fire* as the real original substance, in- *cf. 305* terpreting existence as a dynamic interplay of creative elements. He was contradicted by Parmenides, who insisted that life and motion are only illusory ripples on the surface of things – the deepest reality is *eternal repose*.

Meanwhile Pythagoras, the first idealist, had consecrated number and geometrical form as the ultimate origin of reality, and his followers foreshadowed Friedrich Hegel (1770–1831) in propounding a dualistic dialectic of opposites as the creative principle. Xenophanes, a contemporary of Pythagoras, advocated philosophical monism in defiance of the polytheist tradition. He was also the first sceptic, expressing his doubts in no uncertain terms.

> A famous fragment by Xenophanes is worth quoting: "No man has perceived certainty, nor shall anyone perceive it, about the gods and all whereof I speak; for however perfect what he says may be, yet he does not know it; all things are a matter of opinion."

Anaxagoras, tutor to Pericles, moved towards a scientific epistemology by proclaiming material substance indestructible. The changes we perceive are just fluctuations of form; nothing ever disappears. Leucippus and his pupil Democritus followed up this programme and presented a thoroughly materialist philosophy, embodied in an inchoate atomic theory.

cf. 301
> The unchangeable attributes of the atoms have their origin, according to Democritus, in their specific geometrical forms – round, triangular and so on – and since they are provided with "hooks", they are capable of producing all the combinations which we observe in the variety of the real world. The soul is made out of the most delicate atoms which also mediate the sense impressions, the sole source of knowledge.

Protagoras, a pupil of Democritus, coined the phrase "man is the measure of all things" and introduced an almost modern pragmatism while Zeno of Elea formulated several of the most striking paradoxes of all times. His exact coeval, Empedocles, anticipated the theory of evolution in his didactic poem on the origin of species by way of natural selection. Finally, with Hippocrates and Socrates, a practically effective and philosophically self-conscious humanism appears as a historical highlight. But Hellenistic society failed to respond to this theme and over the following centuries was disabled by defeatism – a resigned aftermath, lacking both hope and faith.

Classical coda

The great Peloponnesian war (431–404 B.C.) and the death sentence of Socrates in 399 B.C. mark a turning-point in the Hellenic feel for life. An exuberant game full of possibilities was succeeded by laborious intellectual construction work. This resulted in the most remarkable philosophical monuments of all time, purporting to offer a safe refuge from painfully aggressive facts. The polemically infected agnosticism of the Sophists; Plato's (427–347 B.C.) grand but reactionary and nigh on totalitarian idealism; the frozen heroism of the Stoics; the value relativism of the Cynics; and the refined hedonism of the Epicureans – they all denote different escape routes from an unacceptable reality, an attitude quite alien to earlier generations.

> Boethius (ca.480–524 A.D.) represents the last gasp of antique philosophy and prefigures the main themes of medieval scholasticism. Waiting for his execution, ordered by the Ostrogothic emperor Theoderic, he writes *De Consolatione Philosophie* (The Consolation of Philosophy), the gripping epitaph of a whole age.

The blind alleys of thought are both unavoidable and instructive. The classical thinkers charted vast but barren intellectual realms; in the process they supplied navigating instruments for inquiring Arabs and newly-awakened Europeans, eager to sail into unfamiliar waters. Plato's idealised Golden Age has spawned countless mental miscarriages while the contrarious, eclectic-descriptive realism of Aristotle (384–322 B.C.) misled many an adept into a mire of self-immunising language games.

> Aristotle's stature as a philosopher and pioneer of rigorous logical speculation did not save him from serious lapses in the natural sciences. He was good at descriptive biology but his physics lost itself in circular argumentation. Solids have an inherent need to fall to the ground, fire naturally soars upwards due to its heavenly origin, and all earthly motion ceases of itself since the natural state of all bodies is to be at rest – as everyday observations and common sense strongly suggest.
>
> Aristotle's thinking is flawed, not by erroneous conjectures but by intellectual hubris. Starting from his own encyclopaedic erudition, this paragon of rational reasoning seriously strived for an all-embracing conclusion to all science. Aristotle virtually blocked any further investigation into the workings of the world for nearly two millenia. Not until 1664 A.D. could Isaac Newton (1642–1727), then 21 years old, claim with equanimity: "Plato is my friend, Aristotle is my friend, but my best friend is truth".
>
> Despite Aristotle's strenuous efforts to avoid confusion in his word play, the blundering starts at the linguistic level. Sweeping but empty generalisations bury the deeper structure of the game and make it inaccessible to critical analysis. For example, Aristotle provided a superficial formulation of the second law of thermodynamics – all motion-energy does in fact tend to be transformed into heat-energy – but unfortunately this does nothing to illuminate the main principles of mechanics.

We can still perceive echoes of Aristotle's pseudoscientific arrogance in the never-ending supply of flimsy "scientific explanations". Much of modern psychology and sociology is flawed by a self-immunizing vocabulary. *Homo sapiens'* conduct is "explained" by reference to a set of drives or "needs". For every mode of human behaviour a corresponding need is postulated, be it for food, for sex, for social contact, for love, for religion and so on. But we rarely hear anything of man's scientific needs – the psychologists seem to enjoy super-human motivation.

European polyphony

The Christian doctrine was confronted in its early days by all the subtleties of Greek thought, and for several centuries found itself wrestling with a fatal contamination of Neo-platonic ideas. The Fathers of the Church, from Ori- *cf. 420* genes (182–251) to Augustinus (354–430), came up against almost insuperable problems in linking together the eruptive revelation of Jesus Christ with Greek reason. Their theological disquisitions had serious philosophical flaws, and became the fateful seeds of extended ecclesiastic conflict.

Thomas Aquinas (1225–74) tried to follow Augustinus' famous dictum that "the true philosopher is the lover of God". His pursuit of a comprehensive Aristotelian system of theological thought became the mainstay of Roman Catholic orthodoxy but other, more portentous themes reverberated in medieval scholasticism. Already in the early twelfth century Abélard (1079–1142) presented a doctrine of self-critical rationalism that in due course was deemed heretical by two Councils of the Church. Over the following centuries the

Franciscans with Bonaventura (1221–1274), Roger Bacon (?1214-1294), John Duns Scotus (?1265-?1308) and William of Ockham (?1300-?1349) in the forefront, struggled to combine mystical insight with rational thinking. Ockham's razor – plurality is not to be posited without necessity – is still as trenchant as ever in cutting through inflated language games, and Cusanus' speculations on natural philosophy anticipated both the principle of relativity and a boundless universe.

Nicholas of Cusa (1401–1464), known as Cusanus, is a brilliant exponent of the dynamism of the Late Middle Ages. Passionately involved in ecclesiastical politics and the reform movements of his times, he became absorbed in theology, mathematics, geography, medicine, the natural sciences and art. Cusanus produced a pioneering analysis of the Koranic texts, and in astronomy he was the first to revive the heliocentric world-view of Aristarchus; in due course, his work inspired Nicolaus Copernicus (1473–1543). Furthermore, Cusanus established that the atmosphere has weight by directly demonstrating the fact that plants take up a substance (carbon dioxide) from the air.

cf. 301

Cusanus' philosophical discourses were inspired by Meister Eckehart (1260–1327), the greatest mystic of the Middle Ages, who taught that man's inner universe mirrors the creativity of God and all creation. God cannot be named: we can speak of Him only in paradoxical extremes where opposites coincide and illuminate one another – a first version of Bohr's principle of complementarity. With wonderful intuition, Cusanus expresses ancient and ultramodern epistemological wisdom: "The learned man is aware of his own ignorance"; or "The search for truth is like squaring the circle". He must be regarded as the progenitor of semiotics: "We cannot know the things, only their signs"; "The first science is the science of signs, that is language."

Later philosophers have produced a unique series of ambitious self-reflections. Francis Bacon (1561–1626), René Descartes (1596–1650), Baruch Spinoza (1632–77) and John Locke (1632–1704) displayed their own personal view of life as well as the spirit of their time in commensurate intellectual constructions. The fallacies of the preceding doctrine are exposed in ever more stringent analytical language until David Hume's (1711–1776) radical scepticism and Immanuel Kant's (1724–1804) philosophical self-analysis put a stop to naively objectifying speculation.

cf. 350   Kant set out "to expose the illusions of a reason that forgets its limits" but his unattainable "thing in itself" presupposes a static core of existence – a good example of the prejudicial influence of the language game. Since classical times a supreme repose, harmony and balance had been a self-evident attribute of all basic truths. Differentiation and multiplicity, the restlessness of the life process, were obvious signs of a flawed ancestry.

Newton's absolute time and space rest within this Platonic tradition whereas Wilhelm von Leibnitz (1646–1716) saw all reality as a string of occurrences: "Quis non agit, non existet". In Leibnitz' view only action is real – it precedes time and space, which are merely useful conventions.

The cock-a-hoop philosophers of the Enlightenment isolated in deistic fashion the rationally regular clockwork of the world from its rather unpredictable Creator. Later, the creative aspect of existence was to receive more attention.

For Johann Gottlieb Fichte (1762–1814), an individual-psychological process, which he called *Anstoss,* was the crucial reality. Related notes were struck in turn by Arthur Schopenhauer (1788–1860), Sören Kierkegaard (1813–1855) and Friedrich Nietzsche (1844–1900), while Henri Bergson (1859–1941) introduced a rather gratuitous *élan vital* into the equation of life. Hegel for his part, had developed a personal pantheism, contending that the world as such is the embodiment of divine reason expressed in the dialectic progress of history. Consecutive efforts at a grand synthesis ended up with the phenomenology and existentialism of Edmund Husserl (1859–1938), Martin Heidegger (1899–1976) and Karl Jaspers (1883–1969).

Meanwhile Wittgenstein had shown, rather convincingly, that every honest philosophy must be self-destructive. Rational thought cannot measure itself *cf. 290* without recourse to some subtle self-deception. Driven out of this fool's paradise, post-Wittgensteinian philosophy had to lower its sights and gradually eschewed all value judgements as well as metaphysics. This self-inflicted checkmate has driven philosophers to put ordinary language – the very medium of thought – under scrutiny and forced them to investigate a few very instructive dead-ends.

Time sets the tone

In the philosophical turmoil of the times, the distinguished mathematician Alfred North Whitehead stands out. Chastened by the impasse of his venture into metamathematics, he arrived (in *Process and Reality,* 1929) at a consistent *cf. 21* and radically dynamic metaphysics. In his panentheistic process philosophy, God is both imminent and transcendent, both part of and external to the world.

Whitehead's rather convoluted train of thought is presented here in a simplified and slightly modified version. The basic idea is that change is the only reality. The world is not a being but a becoming: all substantives dissolve into *cf. 72, 376* verbs. The relative stability of our universe is conditional on a multitude of exactly co-ordinated replays, self-repeating resonances whose life-spans though very long are not unlimited.

> The lasting nature of all structured particles of matter (the hadrons) depends on internal *cf. 34* exchange processes, a constant juggling of mesons and gluons between quarks, protons and neutrons. The unstructured leptons are incapable of playing internal games and can therefore be stabilized only by interaction with their own external fields. An electron (and positron) continually exchanges either real or virtual photons with its surroundings: this interplay constitutes the electric field. A "naked" electron deprived of its field would imply an infinite electric charge – a metaphor for the impossibility of pure being. *cf. 74*
>
> The lifetime of the neutron is fairly short (c. 10 minutes), while the proton was previously regarded as completely stable. However, the calculations of quantum chromodynamics now suggest a half-life of between 10^{32} and 10^{34} years – very long but not *cf. 67; 378* infinite. Long-lasting particles can be regarded as standing waves, self-sustaining but timebound resonances. No interactive process and thus no observable reality is possible without a temporal framework in which it literally takes place.
>
> Energy packets with zero rest mass are isolated "naked" processes that literally cannot take place; for them the only existential solution is pure self-repetition. In the

case of photons, electric (position) and magnetic (motion) energy are unceasingly transformed into each other. This wave-motion reproduces itself at maximum velocity in four-dimensional space; the frequency of its self-reflection is proportional to the energy transfer. A photon is a pure, immaculate process; it has no perception of time. For the photon there is no before-after, and it must seek refuge from this "impossible" position in the speed of light and the consequent obliteration of subjective time.

The "thing in itself" is thus a chimera, one of philosophy's many pseudo-problems. At every moment the world is being created anew, albeit in accordance with statistically immutable rules. Only this process of continual recreation is real; all stability is transient, all unchanging particles are subjective extrapolations justified on the grounds of our thought economy but devoid of any ultimate reality. According to Brouwer, even mathematical relationships *cf. 22* exist only in a timebound conceptual world; they are virtual processes. (Whitehead, incidentally, put mathematical abstractions in a separate, transcendental *cf. 388* category of eternal "Platonic" entities.)

At relatively low temperatures, selected self-stabilizing structures – atoms and molecules – attain an existential respite and may develop on the strength of their intrinsic creativity. Our human consciousness is the most striking display of the innovative potential of these fundamental processes, and should provide sufficient grounds for assuming that even the simple building-blocks of matter possess a rudimentary creative capacity, a certain scope for play.

2.4.   The great game

At this stage, I shall introduce the game metaphor to evince the hidden dynamic structure of all existence. The world is displayed as a string of interacting processes, governed by comprehensible rules. The Great Game ranges from the highly repetitive quantum jumps of elementary processes to the singular questions of faith which give direction to our cultural play. The good games are open, interesting, unrestrained but self-disciplined, anticipating unbounded plus-sum play. Their unobtrusive rules turn out to be deep, dynamic truths which give free rein to individual creativity without sacrificing meaningful co-operation at a higher level.

Persuasive redefinition

"Game" in a narrow sense usually refers to idle but captivating and time-honoured pastimes; the Indian epos Mahabharata (ca. 1000 B.C.) tells us how the Pandava brothers lost their entire kingdom in a fateful game of dice. In the year 1397, a law was passed in Paris to curb the passion for cards; Lord Byron

(1788–1824) maintained with some justification that gambling is man's favourite vice.

Nowadays we speak in a derogatory sense of political play, and war games are part of normal military staff work while ordinary people play the stock exchange or innocent bingo. In most languages there are several other connotations; besides poker we play the piano and actors play Shakespeare on the stage. Furthermore, we all engage in role play according to the prevalent social conventions; we play together in the football team or the management group and, finally, we should not overlook child's play.

> It was a stroke of genius when Ludwig Wittgenstein depicted our linguistic communication as a game in which words are handled like chessmen. Every word has an identity   *cf. 28; 347*
> and, like a chess-piece, follows certain prescribed and relatively simple rules. An orderly
> interplay between the word-pieces can produce innumerable combinations of meaningful utterances but an even greater number of expressions are forbidden by the grammar.
> A spoken sentence corresponds to a series of moves, in which the symbolic values
> become integrated into comprehensible statements. This dynamic approach to linguistics launched a new direction in semantics and philosophy; it also caused a profound
> change in what is meant by games.

Any further extension of the game concept is naturally open to criticism. All definitions which deviate from common usage should be met with mistrust; abuses are legion. An ancient rhetorical trick is to identify one's own hobbyhorse with certain highly esteemed concepts, while vilifying the antagonist with abominable imagery.

> Linguistic cheating has a venerable ancestry; good examples of such persuasive redefini-   *cf. 358*
> tions are easy to spot in Plato. According to Karl Marx (1818–83), the "real value" of a
> utility is equated with the related input of manual labour; the "surplus value" – the
> compensation for other production factors – then becomes sheer robbery. Thus, at a
> single blow, the whole market economy and the concept of profit has been persuasively
> redefined as accomplished theft and betrayal. The air has been thick with misinformation about what is "really" meant by democracy, freedom, human rights and so on. In
> *1984* George Orwell (1903–50) parodied this technique; witness the perverted Ministries of Truth and Peace.

There is no harm in persuasion provided the persuader candidly shows his hand. The game metaphor adequately reflects the hidden dynamic structure of all existence. It imparts a legitimate linguistic development, husbanding mental resources in the contemplation of a complex world. What is more, it provides useful tools for discussing not only human co-operation and contest, but also the basic existential and ethical options facing man.

Preceding players

There is of course nothing new about the game metaphor: Wittgenstein's language games were developed in the 1930s although his *Philosophical Investigations* only appeared posthumously in 1953. The Dutch historian Johan Huizinga (1872–1945) examined, in his *Homo Ludens* (1938), fashions and forms of social intercourse in the Middle Ages, regarding them as a ritualised game with definite rules; Roger Caillois (1913–78) has later used a similar approach in scientific sociology. Herman Hesse's (1877–1962) famous novel *Das Glas-* *cf. 374* *perlenspiel* (The Glass Bead Game) was published in 1943. It describes a fictitious society in which the main activity is a contrived art game, a *l'art pour l'art* of extraordinary refinement.

John von Neumann and Oscar Morgenstern's (1902–77) pioneering work, *Theory of Games and Economic Behavior* (1944), was specifically aimed at practical utility. Game theory has since found applications in academic treatises as well as in some less erudite contexts, but the immense potential of this approach has not yet been convincingly demonstrated. Fernand Braudel, for one, concedes in his monumental historical survey (*The Wheels of Commerce* 1979): "It might be fun to try and write the history of capitalism within the parameters of a special version of game theory."

In 1948 Norbert Wiener (1894–1964) introduced the concept of cybernetics to embrace an important group of communicative game processes with feedback. More recently Manfred Eigen and Ruthild Winkler have used the game of probabilities as the point of departure for an eminently accessible and initiated analysis of the thermodynamics of life processes *(Das Spiel*, 1975). J.C. Polkinghorne (*The Particle Play*, 1979) methodically applies the game metaphor in a popular work on the elementary particles, while Steven Brams uses fully fledged game-theoretical models in his attempt to analyse the way the cards fall when we play against *Superior Beings* (1983). Finally, Geoffrey Brennan and James Buchanan in *The Reason of Rules* (1987) call for systematic reform in the political game of democratic self-government.

The concept of dialectics has more venerable roots. Aristotle cherished this type of verbal acrobatics which the medieval schoolmen perfected. Although the dialectics of Hegel, Marx, Friedrich Engels (1820–95) and Herbert Spencer (1820–1903) may be granted a dynamic process interpretation, they nevertheless retain the doctrinaire nature of their forerunners. All these abstract schemes represent impoverished modes of play and the underlying rules of the game ensnare even the gifted player in his or her own, self-serving modes of thought.

> Marxist dialectics, amply spiced with Freudian depth psychology, has left a long trail of philosophers-cum-literary pundits who tirelessly define and redefine the correct Parisian cut of the fashionable intellectual garb. To keep up with this spectacle is a signally
> *cf. 370*   unrewarding exercise.

Without rules no game can be played, and human give and take is reduced to pure anarchy. A lack of checks and balances opens the door for spurious double-dealing while all-too-prescriptive rules result in boring replays. Ponderous statements of the obvious can then be blown up into pretentious self-immunizing doctrines, justifying any human folly. The good games are open, interesting, unrestrained but self-disciplined, anticipating unbounded plus-sum play. Their unobtrusive rules turn out to be deep, dynamic truths which give free rein to individual creativity without sacrificing meaningful collaboration at a higher level.

Commitment to change

Quantum physics assures us that the core of reality is a composite of stepwise occurrences, a display of distinct interacting processes. In accordance with Whitehead's metaphysics, the world can thus be viewed as an evolving game of creative self-organization carried out by innumerable players of varying apprehensions and appetites, talent and ambition. A selection of fortuitous advances has been carefully preserved as life on our planet: the wisdom of past generations has been successively imprinted on the genetic code. Each and every false move results in negative feedback – the lesson has to be relearned time and again. The same laborious learning pattern is repeated in human play but at a swifter pace. Technical errors are generally discovered fairly quickly, economic feedback operates more slowly, and decades may pass before a political lesson is hammered home.

Science accounts for insight into the nature of the rules of the game, preferably in mathematical form. In turn, the very act of acquiring scientific knowledge involves patient participation in a superordinate culture game. This, again, is directed by axiomatic values, faith-related meta-rules, which are quite insensitive to the feedback from an indifferent or even hostile world. Questions of faith must stand the test of distress and adversity over many generations. The choice between detached withdrawal and commitment to change has been one of the great dividing lines of human history.

> Gautama Siddartha (?563–?483 B.C.), more familiarly known as Buddha, started out with a dynamic hypothesis about the state of the world: "there is no eternal, everlasting, unchanging, permanent or absolute substance". In truly Platonic fashion he found serious fault with this state of affairs and in due course became the visible symbol of timeless Nirvana – the ultimate negation of change.   *cf. 113*
>
> Jesus of Nazareth, too, was convinced of the transience of all things. "Heaven and earth shall pass away: but my words shall not pass away". Only his message was not concerned with ineffectual harmony: "Suppose ye that I am come to give peace on earth? I tell you Nay, but rather division."

Interactions devoid of any kind of game relation, statistical or otherwise, cannot be comprehended rationally; in fact they resemble parapsychological phenomena and belong to a separate metaphysical category. But we should not, a priori, deny the possibility of such events occurring. Singularities such as the Big Bang suggest that it may be impossible to capture existence in its entirety in a coherent network of game rules. Unfortunately, in all empirical investigations the odd irreproducible observations are weeded out. They simply do not possess scientific relevance, and the only recourse is to fall back on our fundamental metaphysical hypothesis – the universal order of play in an intelligible world.   *cf. 307*

cf. 310

Playing the game

At this point a brief recapitulation may be called for. Logicians investigate the fundamental and "self-evident" rules of thought while mathematicians examine the unfolding of "interesting" games based on well-defined axiomatic assumptions. At best the natural sciences yield definitive rules for the interplay of particles in explicit mathematical terms. However, we generally have to content ourselves with looser formulations. In chemistry, for instance, the complexities of the game still defy accurate prediction.

Electrons and other leptons are well-defined and (so it is believed) non-composite particles, but they have nonetheless retained a minimal scope for play. The hadrons (protons, neutrons, mesons), on the other hand, have a clear internal structure, and the atoms already appear as separable isotopes. They are sometimes subject to individually unpredictable radioactive decay, depending on weak interactions – one of the well-known games of elementary particles alongside electromagnetic interaction and the strong interaction within and between nucleons. The synthesis of these disparate games into the single consistent set of rules of a Grand Unified Theory (GUT) serves as a superb challenge to theoretical physicists. If the ultraweak but all-pervasive force of gravitation could be included, we would arrive at a supreme "Theory Of Everything" (TOE).

As we proceed to the macromolecules and enter the world of biology, the specific skills of the actors become evident. The rules applying to elementary particles are still enforced in toto; the force of gravity affects all mass, and total *cf. 63* entropy increases inexorably in all real processes. Nevertheless, the game is beginning to acquire meaning and become highly competitive; life is at stake. The players make their increasingly independent moves against or with one another in a variety of coalitions, playing all the time against the merciless rules of the surrounding environment.

With man a new dynamic emerges; the almost inconceivably slow changes in the fundamental rules of the game are supplemented by fully-fledged and freely-generated cultural play. The genetic base still defines a number of restraints on human behaviour but the actors have become very flexible and cunning; above all, they are now clearly conscious. The game derives its distinct value from the rules of social interplay. While static societies are exhaustively described by the totality of explicit norms, creative cultures get their bearings from a small set of fairly abstract values.

Sooner or later even a vigorous cultural tradition will outlive itself. Consequently, the crucial problem is the capital rule that changes the rules for changing the rules of change . . . The final derivative always has the last word, unless – and it is a big "unless" – the process is prematurely terminated. But what is this terminal rule or derivative? Here we come up against a fairly common phenomenon in the language game. The largely implicit frame for thought cannot support itself but has to be intuitively buttressed by articles of faith – the inexpressible spirit of the game.

2.5   Elementary game theory

Zero-sum games are purely distributive exercises and imply vacuous contest while minus-sum games represent destructive infighting. Only constructive plus-sum play adds value to this world of ours. Confrontation and misinformation are at the core of zero-sum play whereas successful plus-sum games build on co-operation through trusting communication. Just the same, all players are confronted with the problems of dynamic stability, the proper balance between positive and negative feedback which is the special concern of cybernetics.

King of parlour games

Before discussing game theory as such we should take a look at a specific example in order to examine the concept of games in somewhat greater detail. Chess, the king of parlour games, is a conventional game clearly defined by a set of wholly transparent rules which, for the seasoned player, represent only the most trivial of constraints. The purpose of chess, and above all of what is called chess science, is accordingly to gain greater insight into the hidden and implicit rules that underlie successful play.

> Opening theory, pawn formations, knight tactics and the like are the somewhat elusive terms for heuristic procedures reflecting the dynamics of chess. There is certainly food for thought here: a simple game for two players with 32 pieces on 8 × 8 squares, with crystal-clear rules and perfect information has for hundreds of years confounded an assortment of the finest human brains. Chess is a whole microcosm in which established truths are regularly overturned by heterodox innovators. The goal of chess theory is to demonstrate the optimal, unbeatable strategy; with the help of powerful computers this is not a wholly unrealistic aim. But by that stage, chess as a game would have lost its point.

We have noted that the elucidation of simple, open games may be not only impracticable but outright impossible. Closed games such as chess are mathematically completely determined and predictable, but can be quite refractory in practice. Even a minor increase in its complexity, such as the introduction of a third dimension, would probably be enough to put the analysis of chess beyond the reach of any realizable computer.   *cf. 23* *cf. 53*

Zero-sum games

The simplest possible game has two players, each of whom can make one of two alternative moves. An elementary example is the game of Matching Pennies. The players simultaneously show a coin revealing either heads or tails according to their own choice. If the outcomes are identical, player A is the winner; if not, player B wins.

Matching Pennies can be fully described by the following diagram which presents the outcome of the game in matrix form (figure 2.4).

Player B

		Heads	Tails
Player A	Heads	+1	−1
	Tails	−1	+1

Figure 2.4

Each square represents a certain combination of moves and is designated in terms of A's payoff; B's payoff bears the opposite sign.

> What is the best game strategy for Matching Pennies? By randomly choosing heads or tails, the maximum loss is minimised (von Neumann's minimax theorem). This gives a certain 50 per cent payoff and is the optimal strategy against your opponent's best (i.e. identical) play. The main point is to avoid giving your opponent any information at all about your own intentions, but obviously this safe strategy fails to exploit your opponent's deviations from the dead-sure minimax strategy.

In Matching Pennies, as in all the usual parlour games, the total value of the game is unaffected by its resolution. The sum of the game, the aggregated outcome of all the players, is a constant (in this case zero). Thus constant-sum games neither create nor destroy value; they are purely distributive exercises. The overall payoff is wholly determined by the premises; it is not influenced by the mode of play.

The constant payoff of the game can also be perceived as concealed information which must be extracted from the opponent. If there are just two alternatives with equal probabilities (as in Matching Pennies) one round of play *cf. 65* is equivalent to one bit of information. Accordingly, the most efficient way of gaining insight in a state of complete ignorance is to reduce the uncertainty *cf. 112* stepwise by 50 per cent, acquiring one bit of information at every step.

> In playing Twenty Questions you should take full advantage of this principle the like of which was conscientiously observed in classic gunnery procedure. First the target was confined within a wide fork which was successively subdivided down the middle, until the correct range was established.

cf. 277 Futile zero-sum play is transcended when we play such games against nature, disclosing its secrets by perceptive questioning. We gain knowledge but the opponent is not losing anything – except perhaps its mysteries.

Plus-sum play

A normal business deal is a good example of a plus-sum game: merchandise changes hands only if the product is more desirable to the buyer than to the seller. The value added by the transaction is then equal to this difference in desirability. Our example (figure 2.5) shows in matrix form a plus-sum game, in which the maximum value of the game is 1; a payoff occurs only if the product changes hands. The aggregate outcome thus depends on the mode of play (the distribution of the profit is of course a typical zero-sum problem). The corresponding minus-sum game (figure 2.6) arises in situations of potential conflict.

		Buyer	
		Buys	No buy
Seller	Sells	+1	0
	No sell	0	0

Figure 2.5

		Party B	
		chooses peace	chooses war
Party A	chooses peace	0	−1
	chooses war	−1	−1

Figure 2.6

Only through a mutual desire for peace can destruction be avoided, although the aggressor always counts on his opponent footing the bill.

The frame of reference often determines the status of the game. Chess can be regarded as a typical zero-sum game, since the aggregate value of both players' results remains constant. A win for one party is offset by a loss for the other; a draw gives neither of them anything. In poker the situation is even more obvious; there is no change in the quantity of money, although coinage is constantly changing hands.

In broader terms chess can be perceived as a plus-sum game. The score for which the players are battling represents an added value of its own, proportionate to the originality of the play and measured in terms of the stimulus and recreation experienced by the antagonists. Then the most important thing is not to win but to play a good game. But in an even broader perspective we could regard chess as a minus-sum game, in which huge amounts of thought, time and tobacco are consumed to no sensible purpose.

Game strategies

In game theory the emphasis is on the principles of rational play, that is strategies which will guarantee the optimal result even against the best defence (i.e. your opponent's optimal strategy). In a zero-sum game it is primarily a question of minimizing your opponent's potential gains and preventing dangerous counter-moves. Misleading your opponent or at least withholding information becomes a key issue. The upper hand can be gained only by peeping at your opponent's cards or by exploiting his mistakes, which is often risky, particularly if you yourself fail to remain poker-faced.　　　　*cf. 57; 225 cf. 48* For good reason the ancient Chinese strategist Su-Tzu (who lived in the fourth century B.C.) gives deception top priority in his treatise on the art of war. In a minus-sum game, disinformation carries the highest premium. A computer can be programmed to beat most human opponents in Matching Pennies, if the use of a randomising procedure is forbidden. The computer gradually identifies a pattern in the human action and, in the end, achieves a result somewhere around 60–65 per cent – which just goes to show how difficult it is for us to behave in a completely aimless way.

To achieve the optimal outcome in a pure plus-sum game, good communication and collaboration are called for. In real life, a sizeable zero-sum component is usually present, and additional information can then be a mixed blessing. A firmly stated and credible threat, for example, affects the bargaining position of the threatened party to their disadvantage.

Let us now consider a more intricate type of game called the battle of the sexes. Husband and wife have decided to spend an evening out and have the choice of boxing or ballet as entertainment. Most of all the couple wants to be together but are, of course, in two minds about the programme. The payoff matrix then takes the form given in figure 2.7.

Husband

		boxing	ballet
Wife	boxing	+1, +3	−1, −1
	ballet	+1, +1	+3, +1

Figure 2.7

The wife's payoff is designated by the first figure and the husband's by the second in the respective squares. Togetherness has a value of two while watching one's preference makes for one unit of pleasure. Watching the spouse's preference has a nuisance value of -1.

There is obviously a conflict of interests here, which induces mutual arm-twisting. If each party tries to impose his or her will on the other, the end result is a poor return (both pick their preferences) or zero-sum play (both stay at home). The maximum plus-sum is four; the problem is how to share this common good. For a single occasion, no rational resolution is available but if the event can be repeated, the obvious thing would be to agree on a mixed strategy. Wife and husband alternate as decision-makers and both gain their fair half of the value of the game. Co-operation is thus the key to success in a plus-sum game whereas confrontation is at the core of such zero-sum play as Matching Pennies, where the optimal strategy also results in a draw.

Cybernetic feedback

Every independent system, be it mechanical, biological or social, must maintain itself in harsh or outright hostile surroundings. The dynamics of such self-regulating processes is the concern of cybernetics, which studies interactions of the type presented in figure 2.8.

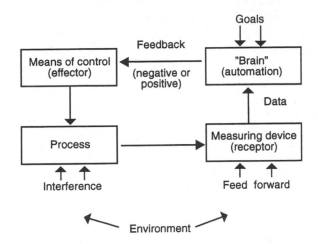

Figure 2.8

The process may involve, for example, a machine, a production line, an organism, a company or a society and is subject to interference from an unstable environment. The receptor indicates changes in the process and the environment – temperature or concentration, material or cash flows, friends or enemies, threats or opportunities. The preprogrammed "brain", for its part, intelligently weighs this information against previously accumulated experience, and handles the available effectors in accordance with the goals.

Stagnant homeostasis implies the passive maintenance of existing favourable conditions. Every deviation is perceived as unfavourable and is met by auto-repressive *negative feedback*: an action intended to eliminate the deflection of the receptor. Autocatalytic *positive feedback* is, on the other hand, exploited in the aggressive maximization of production, offspring, wealth and suchlike, or the minimizing of external threats. Such goal-setting calls for dynamic reinforcement of favourable trends, which in turn requires quite sophisticated strategies. Accordingly homeostatic regulation assumes a mere supportive function; checks and balances will generally be subordinated to growth-oriented and often risky activities. And yet, a complex, interactive system may run out of control and the maintenance of a modicum of internal equilibrium then acquires the highest priority.

Stability is a central problem of cybernetics. Even the simplest control circuit may become unstable, oscillating from one extreme state to another. Mathematical criteria for stability are available but, in most cases, heuristic rules of thumb must suffice. Early telltale signals from the environment can be captured and utilized in a feed-forward mode to expedite the necessary feedback action. Delays or discrepancies in signal reception and transmission are always detrimental. Every extension of this dead time between the occurrence of the disturbance and the activation of the effectors will increase instability and reduce the viability of the system.

cf. 202; 394

Human beings and other living creatures generally function with astonishing purposefulness, but social organisations are endemically plagued by inadequate self-regulation. The same can be said of many human artefacts; sophisticated computers, for example, always produce a number of surprises at the prototype stage. In principle complete *ex ante* control is possible by simulating the operation on a more powerful computer but the supercomputer will be exposed in *cf. 333* turn to even more severe childhood complaints .... Undaunted, the cyberneticists have made further verbal advances in the classification of self-stabilizing processes. Systems capable of developing new self-regulating modes of play are called "ultra-stable" and possess freedom of manoeuvre within an "ergodic" field. We shall later return to both ultra-ergodic and multistable systems.

> Sometimes system theory, information theory and game theory are all thrown in under the heading of cybernetic sciences. Be that as it may, a narrow cybernetic approach thrives on linear continuity in contrast to the highly non-linear step-functions of game theory. The latter stand for the independent choice of the players, as well as for the discrete dynamics of our quantized world.

cf. 407 Extreme cyberneticists see existence as a closed, fully understandable and deterministic process – an obviously self-destructive supposition. True cybernetic insight into these putatively absolute rules of the game would necessitate the never-ending re-examination of the resulting, enriched meta-games. On the other hand, frivolous illusions of freedom will, paradoxically, keep us within predetermined patterns of play.

2.6　Partners and opponents

Elementary game theory throws new light on the age-old problems of human co-operation. While trusting collaboration would be in the best interest of all, selfish defection seems to be the rational option for the individual player: foul play is safe. Game theory appears to preclude fully rational decision-making, except in the simplest of circumstances. Any meta-rules that might be agreed upon, as a matter of expediency, will be torn by self-contradictions and burdened with profound inconsistencies. The search for "objective" norms for human behaviour is in vain – we must always absorb a great deal of personal uncertainty.

The prisoner's dilemma

The idea of a "rational" decision-maker pervades most systematic arguments about human behaviour, especially in economics. It is generally assumed that every individual actor is aiming at maximum payoff, at least in the long run. In game theory, however, selfishly optimizing strategies quickly come up against striking paradoxes. For historical reasons the classic example has been dubbed "The Prisoner's Dilemma".

Two people have committed a crime together. They are apprehended by the police and cross-examined separately. If one of them squeals, he gets off scot-free while his accomplice takes the rap. If both keep quiet they are kept in custody but must eventually be released. If both talk they will get a reasonable sentence.

"The prisoner's dilemma" has a payoff matrix of the type shown in figure 2.9.

Player B

	collaborate	defect
collaborate	+2, +2	−1, +3
defect	+3, −1	0,0

Player A

Figure 2.9

For both players the order of preference is: (a) I defect, you collaborate; (b) we both collaborate; (c) we both defect and (d) I collaborate, you defect. An outsider will immediately see that honest collaboration (2+2=4) is a reasonable strategy for both parties. The game-theoretical dilemma appears when we realise that selfish rational considerations inevitably lead to zero-sum play. This is because defecting is a dominant strategy; it always gives a better payoff than honest collaboration, regardless of the choice made by the opponent (3 against 2, and 0 against -1 respectively). As the same argument applies to both sides, the potential plus-sum game deteriorates into a profitless and uninteresting zero-sum confrontation – foul play is safe.

If the game can be repeated over and over again it becomes a supergame, and there will be an opportunity for mutual learning by way of confidence-building or retaliatory play. The player making the first move has four strategies at his disposal, namely:
- always collaborate
- always defect
- imitate his opponent's moves (tit for tat)
- go against his opponents play (tat for tit).

The second player has a choice between sixteen meta-strategies, but only three result in a stabilised pattern of moves. Two of them are collaborative strategies, while the third locks the parties in permanent conflict. Further exponential expansion of strategies is useless, because it can be shown that in an n-person game (in this case 2-person) an analysis of n strategic levels is enough to provide all possible information about the nature of the game.

cf. 59; 338

The Prisoner's Dilemma clearly incorporates a severe temptation to cheat. Experiments with test subjects (see Morton Davis: *Game Theory*, 1970) have shown that collaboration has its problems even in fairly clear-cut co-operative set-ups. Let us consider the payoff matrix in figure 2.10.

Player B

	collaborate	defect
collaborate	+6, +6	+4 +7
defect	+7, +4	−3, −3

Player A

Figure 2.10

A collaborative strategy seems the obvious one, but about half the subjects made moves in accordance with the risky defection alternative. In the game matrix of figure 2.11, the envy rationale comes out in the open.

		Player B	
		collaborate	defect
Player A	collaborate	+4, +4	+1, +3
	defect	+3, +1	0,0

Figure 2.11

The players still chose defection with a frequency of about 50 per cent, and this tendency was accentuated as the game was repeated. Man appears to have a strong inclination towards irrational decision-making; the opponent's loss is more important than one's own certain profit. In the absence of any long-term collaborative platform, the competitive aspect dominated *ad absurdum*.

> Admittedly, the experiments reflect an artificially isolated environment, although the payoff was in cash. They were carried out mainly with university students in the USA; a comparative study in different countries and involving different strata of society could be highly revealing.

Spoiling the game for the opponent provided an incentive which was obviously worth its price and kept boredom at bay. This grudging preoccupation is even more patent in purely emotional wrangles. The all-too-human tendency towards conflict escalation, quarrelsomeness, cupidity and vindictiveness has its roots in such consumptive spite. Hurting your adversary becomes the overriding concern; any gain to the other party is felt as a painful personal loss.

Zero- and minus-sum games are worthless in a higher perspective and do not merit any sacrifice. But when the game creates value, risk-taking becomes both unavoidable and attractive. Only by means of bold initiatives and generous leads can the plus-sum component be realized, slumbering resources utilised, the forces of nature or society mastered. Indeed, only by such acts of faith can life be filled with meaning.

Rudimentary coalitions

When there are more than two players in a game, a new interesting variable appears – the formation of coalitions in various constellations. In the simplest case all the players coalesce into two coalitions and once more we find ourselves in a two-person game, such as an industrial dispute.

A typical wage conflict can be reduced to a "chicken" type of game matrix (figure 2.12). The total added value of 12 units is easily destroyed if both parties are playing "macho".

		Employees	
		demand 10% wage increase, no strike threat	demand 20% wage increase, strike threat
Employer	Pays wage increase	1 11 (settlement)	0 12 (pushover)
	Refuses wage increase	2 10 (status quo)	−5 0 (strike)

Figure 2.12

We have assumed that:
- sales revenues = 170 per cent of the original wage sum
- fixed costs = 50 per cent of the wage sum
- profit before any wage increase = 20 per cent of the wage sum

The order of preference in this game of chicken is: (a) I stall, you give in; (b) we both give in; (c) I give in, you stall and (d) we both stall. No optimal strategy is available for either party, but it is quite clear that the players should avoid the lower right-hand corner (both stall) at all costs.

On such occasions a strategy of threat or blackmail presents itself, despite the fact that – or rather because – a realised threat often counteracts its own aim. (An old chess maxim declares that "the threat is stronger than its execution") But the nature of the game changes if it is repeated over and over again. "Softening up the opponent", "setting an example" and the like are then included as part of a long-term meta-strategy in an extended supergame. If threats are not carried out at irregular intervals, they will in due course be dismissed as bluff.

Once again we come up against the paradox that super-rational players who strive aggressively to optimise their payoff, may produce wholly irrational consequences for all participants. Less high-powered but peaceful actors do better, but if the disparate elements are mixed, the hawks will first defeat the doves and then recklessly spoil the game for one another. Arguments of this kind led Marx to prophesy the impending breakdown of the capitalist system which he perceived as a banding together of utterly self-seeking individuals. Such "evil associations" are mired in mutual distrust and do, indeed, lack long-term cohesion, but Marx did not realise that the citizens of democratic societies are willing to make considerable sacrifices in the interest of fair play.

The core of the game

In 1912 Ernst Zermelo (1871–1953) demonstrated that all finite two–person zero-sum games with perfect information are determined. In other words there is an optimal strategy for both parties, although the optimal sequence of moves may be buried deep in labyrinthine complexity. Absolutely correct play at chess, *cf. 45; 330* for example, must always lead to the same result: either a draw or a victory for white or, improbably, a victory for black.

As we proceed to multi-person plus-sum games, the degrees of freedom increase exponentially. For rational coalition building, one obvious goal is to find the joint strategic optimum which maximises the value of the game, i.e. the total payoff for the "grand coalition" of all the players. The permutations of play which fulfil this criterion constitute the core of the game.

Assume a game with three participants, A, B and C. None of them can do anything on their own, but in a grand coalition (ABC) they can together earn, say, 3 units. The coalitions AB and AC can each earn two units on their own, while BC can only manage one. Obviously, all three players must collaborate to stay within the core. The situation is diagrammatically expressed in figure 2.13.

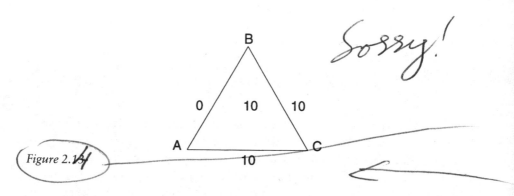

Figure 2.13

A distribution A 3/2, B 3/4, C 3/4 , for example, is within the core while 1, 1, 1 is on the borderline, because AB or AC can earn as much in pairs as they can in the grand coalition. Given a distribution A 2, B 1/2, C 1/2, BC will be the subcoalition which fails to gain any additional value from the grand coalition. In these borderline cases the rational self-interest of some of the players approaches zero and so does the strength of the coalition.

The core represents the area of maximal common interest in the plus-sum game. (In a zero-sum game the core is always empty.) It indicates the bounds for fruitful collaboration, but gives little guidance about a just or even a reasonable division of the joint payoff.

Settlement criteria

The grand coalition includes all the players who can contribute to the game. It thus maximises the total outcome but is generally exposed to latent conflicts of interest. Key players or whole groups may rise in rebellion, and blackmail may be rampant. But a fragmented set of players cannot utilize the full value of the game, and so the search for collaboration begins anew.

Game theorists have tried to produce objective, mathematically stringent criteria for a fair settlement between the parties. A basic requirement of stability is that no individual player or subcoalition can find a more profitable alternative on their own. In other words it is imperative to stay within the core of the game. As early as 1906 Wilfredo Pareto (1848–1923) presented a similar criterion. In a Pareto-optimal situation no-one can get more out of a game without someone else losing at least the same amount.

L.S. Shapley has designed a settlement model in which it is assumed that every player's legitimate payoff is equal to the average marginal utility which he contributes to the coalition when it is formed in all possible sequences, with players joining one at a time.

An example of Shapley's model:

To each of players A, B and C separately the value of the game is zero
To the coalition AB its value is also zero
To the coalition AC its value is 10
To the coalition BC its value is 10
To the grand coalition ABC the value of the game is also 10.

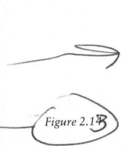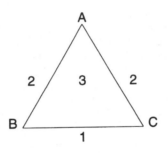

Figure 2.14

Shapley's values are then: A = 5/3; B = 5/3; C = 20/3 Total= 10. Note that by sharp bargaining C could achieve an even better result, close to the value of the game.

Shapley's distribution appears impartial but can sometimes lead to unreasonable results. Thus the entire marginal utility may fall to a new player joining the coalition, which does not seem fair. J.C. Harsanyi has amended the Shapley model by taking into account the contrapuntal weave of threat and counterthreat. All players are regarded simultaneously as participants in all possible syndicates (subsets) of players. The individual payoff is calculated by adding all the returns (some of them negative), that would have accrued to the player through the diverse syndicates. Even in the absence of any positive contribution an outsider has a nuisance value for the grand coalition if he has access to an effective threat.

In real life most constructive play is based on the separation of plus- and minus-sum games. Threats are neutralised by a corresponding capacity for reprisals. Only when the participants have acknowledged approximate parity in wreaking havoc can they start to discuss the fairness of alternative collaborative arrangements.

Even the most sophisticated settlement models are simplified constructs. Accordingly, von Neumann and Morgenstern had to accept a multiplicity of competing "solutions" to most multiperson plus-sum games. They bravely postulated that at least one contradiction-free set of superordinate rules, ("a constitution") would be available for all games. Still, no watertight proof could be found, and in 1967 W.F. Lucas invalidated one of the fundamental assumptions of classical game theory by constructing a ten-person game with no contradiction-free "solutions".

cf. 212 For some time, biologists have been looking for stable evolutionary strategies in the competitive interplay within animal species. Extensive simulations of such games exhibit, at best, multiple points of stability; any determinate "solution" dissolves into thin air.

cf. 315 The widely endorsed Bayesian theory of rational choice presupposes (among other things) that the decision-maker can assign to each of the presumptive outcomes a discrete number to serve as a measure of its desirability on a one-dimensional scale of value. A complex or, at worst, contradictory value system obviously puts paid to such a procedure. Thus game theory precludes cf. 59; 111; 238; 266 fully rational decision-making, except in the simplest of circumstances.

In *Morals by Agreement* (1986) David Gauthier has made a fresh attack on the problem of rational morality. He is intent on showing that the Prisoner's Dilemma can be resolved and a liberal societal order constructed by purely rational, contractarian argumentation. His guiding principle of "minimax relative concession" is a refined version of Shapley's and Harsanyi's schemes. Gauthier concedes that his model is not optimal: genuine altruism is more efficient precisely because it is not derived from calculated self-interest. More devastating is that the empirical evidence points the other way – intellectual acuity does not diminish conflict, quite the contrary. Moreover, the model does not explain itself: that is the author's own very sympathetic moral commitment.

It seems safe to conclude, that the search for "objective" norms for human behaviour is in vain. Any meta-rules that might be agreed upon, as a matter of expediency, will be torn by self-contradictions and burdened with profound inconsistencies. The practical application of grand principles therefore always calls for personal risk-taking and the absorption of uncertainty, that is, faith.

2.7   Exemplary play

To test the unifying aspect of the game metaphor, I shall apply it to a sampling of palpable reality. Chance plays an important part in both mundane operations research and esoteric quantum physics. The competitive world market comes across as a huge plus-sum game whereas life is engaged in an equivalent though more ferocious struggle for reproductive success. Altruistic animal behaviour introduces a game-theoretical quandary which culminates in human ethics. Rationality and transcendence are complementary concepts; without some intimation of eternity the accumulated reserves of mutual trust become depleted and society falls to pieces.

Monte Carlo and the market

Despite the limitations of game theory, interest in game-mathematical applications has spread considerably since the Second World War. International conflict-resolution and military strategic simulation have received most of the attention but a good deal of work has also been done in analysing social, political and business play. Unfortunately, the explication of a lengthy sequence of moves with several players and many alternative courses calls for an exponentially increasing input of computing capacity. It is therefore understandable that advanced game-theoretical considerations have so far had little impact upon businessmen, managers or politicians.

When we play against chance or nature the situation is different, since the opposing moves are at least statistically predictable. Probing the way towards thermonuclear fusion, von Neumann and Ulam pioneered a game-orientated simulation method, called Monte Carlo, which has been extensively applied in both scientific and operations research.

> First a mathematical model is constructed according to the explicit, statistically valid rules of the game. The independent variables are then given a set of values according to pure chance or perceived probabilities. Finally the game is played on a computer, i.e. the variables are allowed to interact within the framework of the model. The implicit rules of the game are thus obtained by empirical means and it is possible, for example, to find the value of a difficult integral, to analyze the behaviour of high temperature plasmas, to *cf. 110* assess the risk of overloading an electrical or communications network and to estimate the likelihood of poor harvests or military setbacks.

Unequivocal odds for roulette, dice or poker can be mathematically calculated and belong to the stock in trade of every professional gambler. However, success in more complicated games is based on an arcane skill in the Monte Carlo mould. When faced with difficult decisions, financiers and scientists, statesmen and artists probably use such semi-intuitive simulations in evaluating alternative moves. *cf. 218; 353*

> The available plus-sum provides the impetus in all business transactions but head-on competition brings in an element of warfare concomitant with minus-sum play. The complexities of strategic business decisions thus often defy rational calculation and the seasoned executive must rely on a deeper percipience. Personal experience and competent staff work will provide the essentials for a rough simulation model; the obvious profit yardstick must usually be complemented by assessing the Bayesian desirability of assorted imponderables. Then the Monte Carlo game can be played, by varying all the independent variables according to their inherent probabilities. The vagaries of the market-place can generate particularly noxious outcomes and deserve special attention in the final trade-off between risk and profitability. And finally, the self-contradictions of the value structure must somehow be dealt with . . .

Plain bargaining is a zero-sum game and requires another type of skill. As we have seen, no additional information should reach the opponent and a good *cf. 47* poker face is immensely valuable if the players rely on bluff ("I can't pay more than so much"), or if they want to exert pressure ("I won't buy from you again"). But deadpan inscrutability can become a severe liability if the protagonists, by an exertion of good will, make a turn to collaborative strategies ("Let's put our cards on the table and go 50/50").

In games involving several independent buyers and sellers, in other words a market, the profitability of price-haggling evaporates and a more or less defined market price punctures the two-person zero-sum game. Subtle aspects of quality, delivery time, transport distance and customer relations take precedence. In a well-functioning market all the players participate in a distinctively plus-sum game. The aggregate value of the transactions is constantly maximized and the *cf. 184* zero-sum components remain in the background.

> In special cases, the simple pair game can assume a markedly plus-sum character; for example if a unique invention can be exploited by one organisation only. Nevertheless, the first impulse in such a case is to look for alternatives in a rudimentary market, precluding monopolistic blackmail by the other party. Courtship, love and marriage, on the other hand, represent phases in a high-risk, quasi-monopolistic plus-sum game, in which any reference to the "market" will destroy the value of the game.

The individual player in a present-day market economy gets an impressive return on his rather modest input. The gigantic plus-sum game of global commerce provides enormous leverage by the extensive division of labour. New participants enrich the game as well as themselves, and all countries are thus drawn irresistibly into the grand coalition of the world market.

The reproduction game

Since immortality is not of this world, the primordial self-confirming rule of the evolutionary game is the propagation of one's own genes in coming generations: the whole surplus of the metabolic process is usually reinvested in new life. If animals compete in an unstable environment, logic prescribes that the available investment capital shall be disseminated over the greatest possible number. This opportunistic "r-strategy" is so called because it relies on the *rate* of increase of the population. A vast number of "cheap" progeny is produced and any passing opportunity can be quickly exploited, maximizing the probability of encountering a suitable habitat.

Long-lived animals in stable environments favour the diametrically opposite "K-strategy", so called because the carrying capacity of the environment constitutes the population-restricting factor (*Kapazitet der Umgebung*). The rules of the competitive game then favour efficiency and the careful husbanding of resources. Maximum dispersion is of lesser importance; the available resources are concentrated instead on a few descendants, who are cared for and protected over an extended period.

> The apes are the outstanding example of the K-strategist; the female chimpanzee conceives every fifth year, and the total number of her offspring does not exceed five or six. The fertility of *Homo sapiens* is much higher, and this may have been a decisive selection factor when early hominids were in direct competition with the apes. Still, care was not traded for fecundity. On the contrary, man is a pronounced K-strategist, since not only parents but also close relatives and even distant kin may support the young.

Ultimately the whole tribe and the nation loyally participate in a coalition whose task is to assist in the upbringing of children to ascertain the continuation of society.

Altruism of a sort is discernible already at the early stages of evolution, for example in slime mould colonies. That is to say, the individual reduces its own reproductive chances to the advantage of close relatives. However, in such cases the group acts as a strictly controlled super-organism, and defectors have no hope of surviving outside the community.   *cf. 132*

At a higher evolutionary level we find ourselves in a game-theoretical dilemma. How can altruism ever gain a foothold in a species with limited individual interdependence, and why is "sacrificial" behaviour not eliminated by internal competition? What forces can maintain a willingness to collaborate and prevent a relapse into short-sighted egoism?   *cf. 97*

Using a computer, Richard Dawkins has simulated the following interesting (and here somewhat modified) evolutionary experiment *(The Selfish Gene,* 1976). It is assumed that mutual grooming considerably improves the chances of survival by removing harmful parasites. Such behaviour will then give a certain competitive advantage to a small isolated group in which it is genetically entrenched. When the group multiplies, the purely statistical probability of relapse also increases. Any individual who fails to reciprocate will accrue a relative advantage, and the cheating genes of the free-rider will inevitably spread. At this point Dawkins introduces resentful "grudgers" who insist on fair play. A grudger grooms all his comrades at the first meeting, but refuses on subsequent occasions unless the individual concerned has reciprocated (a tit-for-tat   *cf. 51; 338* strategy). Single grudgers cannot cope in large groups but a small gang of them can gradually drive the cheats out of the co-operative.

Over the ages some kind of group selection has obviously rewarded small collaborating coalitions of dissenters at the expense of a quarrelsome majority, but competitive pressure from the outside is required to keep altruism (i.e. cameraderie and group loyalty) intact and internal rivalry in check. This del-   *cf. 86* icate balance becomes precarious as the population grows beyond all bounds, because the increasing internal competition tends to disfavour loyal plus-sum players.

Societal interplay

Rational democratic decision-making presupposes, strictly speaking, that people can agree on a welfare function, a meta-rule which integrates the individual preferences of all the citizens in a common order of priorities. Alas, in 1951 Kenneth Arrow showed (in *Social Choice and Individual Values*) that such a function cannot avoid internal contradictions; inevitably the coalition gets into logical conflict with itself. The problem of unassailable arbitration has only two   *cf. 56; 238* consistent but absurd solutions: absolute dictatorship or full vetoing rights for all participants.

For similar reasons, ethical self-contradiction must permeate the opinions of every   *cf. 408* conscientious and rationally thinking individual. The American philosopher Sidney Hook puts it as follows: "Our agony of choice results from the realization that right conflicts with right, good with good and sometimes the right with the good ... We want to be loyal, but if we are, we can't be truthful, and vice versa. We want to be free to live our life but find that we cannot do so except on the ruins of another's life."

Game-theoretical considerations support the following far-reaching conclusions:

☐ Democratic rules can be effective only against an implicit backdrop of common values, otherwise the polity will be torn asunder by disparate egoistic goals.

☐ Widespread discontent is unavoidable in authentic democracies; some people are dissatisfied with everything, most of them with something.

☐ To some extent, contradictory and "irrational" decision-making must be accepted; it is the price that has to be paid for the unity of the coalition: if opinions differ greatly, this price may be quite high.

All societies are encumbered by their own inconsistencies: concord cannot be guaranteed solely by enlightened self-interest. Some of the syndicates will always try to improve their own payoff by unfair means, like blackmail or threats of secession. To stabilize the social interplay, common-sense considerations must be complemented by "transcendental" influences. A democratic society is a voluntary meta-coalition, which can exist only by force of commonly embraced, superrational and emotionally entrenched meta-rules.

cf. 403

The expansion of democratic polities should therefore be undertaken with some caution. The assimilation of new citizens is never easy and can deteriorate into an unredeemed minus-sum game, in which allergic rejection mechanisms and parasitic exploitation mutually reinforce one another.

> The United States with its wide open spaces has, so far, worked admirably as a melting pot for successive waves of immigrants whereas in overcrowded Europe poor aliens have generally been unwelcome. The social integration of gypsies has proved particularly difficult. Their roving way of life certainly had its historically valid roots, but it was generally based on semi-fraudulent transactions. Once the credulity of people in the immediate neighbourhood was exhausted, it was high time to move on and establish a new set of transient trading contacts. The population in general, the "godje", or yokels, was viewed as an exploitable resource of a lower order than the "rom", which means
>
> *cf. 90*   "man" in Romany. Moral scruples were reserved for the tribe and the family; external social relationships were short-term and exclusively directed towards a profitable termination of the game.

Long-term commitment is the decisive factor. Genuine plus-sum games ultimately presuppose an infinite sequence of moves; otherwise, the paradox of the Prisoner's Dilemma rears its ugly head again. After all, it is always worthwhile to cheat on the last move. And once the players have grasped this fact, then the same argument must be applied to the penultimate move, and so on. The winner is the one who cheats first; the game deteriorates into bluff and deception, as a callous preparation for the finishing move when one's own reputation loses its value, and the fate of the other party ceases to matter.

If death is perceived as imposing a definitive term on all human striving and responsibility, it tolls the knell for every rationally acceptable ethic. In Fjodor Dostoyevsky's (1821–1881) well-known words: "Everything is allowed if God is dead". The societal plus-sum game is inexorably undermined by the coldly calculated moves of sponging zero-sum players. Material, biological and spiritual reproduction will be neglected; capital erosion will prevail; childlessness and high pensions are the logical but ultimately incompatible stations along the path of collective descent.

Without forbidden moves, no game has any meaning; but the rational grounds for the restriction of freedom – the "truth" of the game – can never be definitely proved. Rationality and transcendence are complementary concepts, petty self-interest must be voluntarily subordinated to meaningful meta-rules. Without some intimation of eternity the accumulated reserves of mutual trust become depleted and society falls to pieces.

Quantum games

Around the turn of the twentieth century the best minds of the day, including James Maxwell (1831–79), Ludwig Boltzmann (1844–1906), J.W.Gibbs (1839–1903) and Einstein, were busy investigating the rules of the random billiards game of freely moving gas molecules. They all agreed that the interplay itself was deterministic and calculable, in principle if not in practice. *cf. 2.2.6*

> The theory wears very thin indeed, even according to the science of the time. Calcula- *cf. 265* tions showed that the gravitational disturbance of a single electron, moving around on the other side of the universe, would crop up on earth after only 56 molecular collisions.

This "classical" approach proved fruitful in describing pure being – self-repetitive games in which nothing of consequence happens. Likewise, it adequately described processes which, deprived of their creative potential, fall monotonously back into the Nirvana of eventlessness equilibrium. But no explanation for the obvious wealth of creative variety in our world could be given: it took the arrival of quantum mechanics to restore the claims of physics to scientific universality. *cf. 66*

> According to the principle of correspondence, quantum physics should include the regularities of classical physics as marginal cases. The law of least action, formulated as early as 1744 by Pierre-Louis Maupertois (1698–1759), highlights this intimate relationship. Action is the product of energy and time (mathematically expressed it is equal to $\int mvdx$, where m is the mass, v the velocity and x the distance). Maupertois stated that bodies in motion always follow a route which minimises this quantity. In 1900 Max Planck (1858–1947) discovered that electromagnetic radiation follows Maupertois' rule only if the action is a multiple of a very small unit, i.e. Planck's universal action quantum 6.626×10^{-27} joule second. During the 1950s, Richard Feynman (1918–88) brought the formalism of classical and quantum-physical action together in his description of the motion of the electron as the appropriately weighted sum of all the theoretically possible classical trajectories. The result tallies exactly with the quantum mechanical calculations. *cf. 74; 109*

The quantum principle both restricts and extends the freedom of the game. The repertoire of moves is limited to a selection of relatively well-defined quantum jumps but the elementary process is left more or less open. Although particle assemblages behave statistically with great regularity, each separate move retains a certain indeterminacy.

The quantification of reality introduces a basic stability, because it avoids the chaotic escalation of infinitesimal perturbations which would otherwise play *cf. 24* havoc with any complex dynamic system. This collective order is enriched by a tiny amount of individual discretion – the inevitable consequence (or the cause) of Heisenberg's uncertainty principle.

Complementary aspects of elementary particles cannot be established simultaneously with arbitrary accuracy, since they reciprocally restrict the expression or materialisation of one another. For example, exact information on the momentum of an electron implies that we cannot obtain any knowledge of its position: it can pop up anywhere. The product of the uncertainties of complementary quantities always exceeds a fixed value. To put it mathematically:

cf. 22; 343; 285; 344; 379

$$\Delta P \cdot \Delta x \geq \frac{h}{2\pi} \text{ or}$$

$$\Delta E \cdot \Delta t \geq \frac{h}{2\pi}$$

where ΔP and ΔE are the uncertainties of momentum and energy, Δx and Δt are uncertainties of position and time, and h is Planck's action quantum.

There is no way of precisely pinpointing an elementary particle; we have to be content with the exactly formulated probabilities of quantum mechanics. The particle is really neither here nor there: it maintains an irreducible scope for play. Thus, in principle, every individual move is elusive. An exact energy-difference, for example, would presuppose total stability and the initial state of the process would persist indefinitely – in itself a self-contradictory postulate.

The ways of the world show that, despite the statistical cogency, a rudimentary freedom must be built into our very existence. Unlike chess, the game played by the elementary actors cannot be reduced to a set of individually binding directives. Rather, there is an incessant creative advance, a conception of superordinate rules which, by cybernetic feedback, modifies events at lower levels and encourages unpredictable plus-sum play.

In chapters three and four we shall try to pursue these fortuitous processes, which culminate in the co-operative performance of cultural games. But before tackling human affairs we should first take a closer look at the basic elements of matter, and try to conjecture how their ordered interplay can achieve that astounding feat – human consciousness.

2.8   Thermodynamic transitions

To recognize the unity of creation, we have to delve deeper into the nature of physical reality. Our evolving world appears as a vast, open-ended trial, driven by the dissipation of the original energy eruption (the Big Bang). The arrow of time is defined by the steady progress of the world towards greater disorder. Providentially, the rules of quantum physics allow the build-up of locally ordered structures which, when the earth was young, were folded into self-propagating information packets. It has taken life 3.5–4 billion years – roughly the remaining duration of steadfast solar activity – to reach its present degree of complexity.

Energy and entropy

In the preceding pages the world has been described as an ongoing process, a grand game hierarchy in which the individual moves – time-bound quantum jumps, resonances, vibrations, absorptions, emissions and so on – represent the only ultimate and concrete reality. By means of definite rules, chance and necessity are established; a structured universe emerges out of chaos. Tiny faults in the fundamental symmetries and slight probabilities of "forbidden" energy transfers provide opportunities for enriching the game.

The laws of statistics suggest, however, that an increase in aggregate disorder is inevitable in the universe – in marked contrast to our version of the world as a system evolving creatively towards an ever greater variety of well-informed play.

> Energy is indestructible but access to energy varies greatly. Electrical energy is pure *exergy* (free energy) and can theoretically be applied with complete efficiency. Thermal energy without temperature differences is useless, wholly randomised *anergy*, in which the energy is uniformly distributed, statistically speaking, over all available molecular energy states. In a closed system, Total Energy is always equal to Exergy plus Anergy. The exploitable exergy tends to be degraded into inaccessible anergy; the quantity remains the same but the average quality continually degenerates.

Entropy is a rather abstract concept, conversely related to the quality or accessability of energy. It is a precise measure of disorder which generally increases with temperature.

> Entropy can be defined in a number of ways. A particularly lucid one runs as follows: "the entropy of a system is equal to the logarithm of the number of quantum states accessible to the system".

Basically, entropy can be regarded as the principle of weakening and atten- *cf. 368* uation, decay and deterioration, disrepair and dilapidation, death and dissolution. Quality is the opposite of sloppy negligence; the pursuit of quality is equivalent to fighting entropy.

The second law of thermodynamics asserts that the entropy of a closed system never decreases and actually will increase during any "useful" processes. This is tantamount to the impossibility of a perpetuum mobile of the second order (a machine using the attenuated energy of its environment). By the same token, all energy differences tend to level out, and perceptible changes are irreversible.

> Within a closed system we can never revert to a previous state: we have to accept a continual increase in disorder or stay put. The world appears to be moving inexorably towards "heat death" by which point all matter will have turned into background radiation and the temperature will be uniform throughout the universe. Then all macroscopic movement will have ceased and entropy will have achieved its absolute maximum.

All real processes which change the world are accompanied by an increase in entropy. For example, every measurement is theoretically irreversible, information must always be paid for by an increase in entropy and disorder. There seem to be profound links between information exchange, changes in entropy, and Heisenberg's uncertainty principle, which bring out the dynamic nature of reality, the all-pervading aspects of time and the priority of process.

Entropy is a statistical concept and it applies, strictly speaking, only to large assemblages. How it can be related to individual elementary particles or the antagonistic force of gravitation is not altogether clear.

> Nothing can be isolated from the attraction of gravitation, a peculiarity of space-time which brings disoriented matter together and has squeezed part of it back into black holes. (Many galaxies, including our own, probably have a black hole at their centre.) The entropy of a black hole grows in proportion to its surface, which, according to general relativity, effectively contains even light as well as any other kind of electromagnetic radiation. The only exception is an extremely weak Hawking-radiation, due to quantum-mechanical tunnelling. Accordingly, black holes will very slowly lose energy and finally dissipate (after approximately 10^{117} years). So entropy has the last word, provided that the whole universe does not collapse in a final implosion – the Big Crunch.

cf. 380 In our cosmic epoch, entropy can, in any case, be used to define the arrow of time. In a closed system a state exhibiting greater entropy must be later in time. If there is no entropy difference, then time stands still locally; nothing meaningful is happening despite the continuing thermal motion of the molecules.

The law of entropy represents a strong argument against all self-sustaining cosmologies, but remains difficult to relate to the Big Bang. At that moment a tremendous amount of energy came about, begetting matter, time, space and information.

> In contrast to the very high entropy of black holes, the original Big-Bang singularity must have been conceived in a highly ordered state with low entropy. Roger Penrose has suggested that this was due to a very low value for the Weyl-tensor (after Hermann Weyl, 1885–1955) in the equations of general relativity. In the Big Bang, the Weyl-curvature of the gravitational field should have been close to zero, whereas it ought to be infinite in a Big Crunch. Thus the flow of time would be established as an absolute fact and the awkward paradoxes of time-reversal would disappear.

The present incompatibility between general relativity and quantum mechanics, between the gravitationally governed macrocosm and the free-wheeling microworld ought to find its resolution in a grand theory of quantum gravity (the TOE) which, if it can be achieved, may well incorporate intriguing non- *cf. 380* computable aspects.

Intrinsic information

The amount of information in a structure or in a message is linked with mea- ningful organization, and is not to be confused with meaningless repetition. It *cf. 361* increases with the improbability of the configuration, and is thus the exact opposite of entropy.

> The basic unit of information is a bit (*binary digit*,) and it corresponds to the reduction of uncertainty from 0.5 (50/50) to zero in the choice between two equally probable alternatives. The measure of information has the same dimension as entropy (energy divided by temperature), but naturally has the opposite sign; a bit corresponds to the *cf. 46; 419* entropy -1.38×10^{-23} joule/degrees Kelvin (Degrees Kelvin are counted from absolute zero which is close to $-273°$C).The energy equivalent of an information packet thus depends on the temperature of the environment. At higher temperatures the noise of thermal interference will be stronger and more energy will be required to carry a certain amount of information.

Information can be regarded as a form of temperature-dependent superexergy of the highest purity. The equivalence between mass and energy should there- fore be supplemented by an energy-information equivalence. Accordingly, mass can be comprehended as exceptionally compressed information stowed away in a complex, self-sustaining process.

> Every proton contains in principle a message corresponding to around 2×10^{11} bits at room temperature. Consequently, the proton loses its identity at about10^{13} °K and is transformed into more massive manifestations of matter. By audacious extrapolation we arrive at the Planck temperature (10^{32} °K), which allows the total mass of the universe to coexist within the Planck length (10^{-33}cm) for the Planck time (5.3×10^{-44}s). This represents the supposed Big Bang-conditions when all the fundamental forces, including gravitation, were unified. At that moment the universe was a single undiffer- entiated primordial atom, containing one bit of explicit information which involved the decisive choice – to be rather than not to be!
>
> The cost of creating matter was extremely high in terms of entropy. For every single *cf. 384* baryon (proton or neutron) left over in the Big Bang ca. 10^8 were annihilated by antimatter and dissipated as radiation in the expanding universe. This tremendous outpouring of wasted energy still pervades all space as the ubiquitous background radiation which has cooled down to 2.7 °K.

The expansion and cooling of the primordial atom broke up the absolute uniformity of creation and made possible the emergence of information-bearing structures. The world has proved a prodigal entropy-producer, but theoretical- ly the build-up of "pure" information implies only a small, exactly calculable reduction of entropy which must be offset by at least an equivalent increase in entropy elsewhere. This is an extraordinarily interesting relation, demonstra- ting one of the few rules that apparently apply to games of all types.

> In the nineteenth century Maxwell invented the following, fictitious experiment. Sup- pose that you fill a container with a mixture of gases, consisting of two types of

molecules. The container is divided into two parts joined by an extremely narrow duct. A fictitious character, "Maxwell's demon", is supposed to act as a gatekeeper, regulating the passage to provide a one-way track for each type of molecule; traffic in the opposite direction is turned back by operating a perfect valve. The absurd result would be that the gas components would separate by themselves. The entropy of the system would have diminished spontaneously, thereby contradicting the second law of thermodynamics.

The interrelation of information, entropy and energy supplies the theoretical explanation as to why such perpetuum mobiles cannot exist. In order to do his work the demon must extract knowledge about the identity of the approaching molecule and store it in short-term memory. This information then has to be obliterated for the re-use

cf. 333   of the memory, which requires energy equivalent to one bit of information, exactly balancing the exergy production of the fictitious machine.

Dissipative processes

The law of entropy implies certain strict and general constraints on all real, time-bound processes but, like other laws of nature, it does not prescribe the individual moves. A local increase in the amount of information is allowed as long as a supply of "order capital" is available from the outside. However, the thermodynamics of information-bearing structures remained a puzzle until Manfred Eigen and Ilya Prigogine recently found a plausible solution to the

cf. 61   problem.

The enigma was that every physical state strives towards equilibrium, i.e. maximum disorder, and the probability of a spontaneous increase in the amount of information seemed vanishingly small. Providentially, this condition only applies close to the thermodynamic state of equilibrium. Information-sustaining structures can arise if the system is far from equilibrium and contains considerable potential differences or energy

cf. 24   flows. Such a dissipative state is pseudo-chaotic: developments can be extremely sensitive to the initial conditions and the first moves in the game. Autocatalytic non-linearities cast around for their strange attractors and under such circumstances the probability of self-selective generation and storage of information can become significant.

Unlike the classical approach, quantum mechanics allows for a "disproportioning" of the available supplies of free energy. In the presence of a surplus, the evolving system can generate cumulative information by "feeding" on its environment. To protect the original investment. the highly organised subsystem must establish an ergodic space

cf. 50   through rigorous cybernetic self-control. Ingenious autocatalysis and intricate feedback loops are effective means to that end.

The phenomenon of life is the most impressive example of self-organizing structures but many everyday phenomena – the shaping of clouds, the waves breaking at sea, lightning and thunder – are vivid expressions of transiently organized dissipative processes.

In Thomas Mann's (1875–1955) novel, *Doctor Faustus,* young Adrian Leverkühn is shocked by the demonstration which his uncle puts on for his benefit. First, innocuous alum crystals are added to an ordinary jar of water. Then the precipitation of aluminium hydroxide leads to the formation of membranes, and the osmotic pressure causes water to be absorbed through the membranes into the interior. This generates an abortive crawling phenomenon – a homunculus frivolously created by the intervention of man.

The discharge of exuberant exergy tends to be consummated in a shower of   *cf. 32*
intermediate stages. Under favourable conditions, suitable bits can be folded
into self-stabilizing information packets but the forces of attrition are perpetually at work. Thermal noise is omnipresent, distorting the transcription and
disturbing transmission. Information too, despite its abstract character, is a
time-dependent actuality. It cannot be preserved for ever but has to be actively
maintained or, at higher levels, literally re-created.

Not even the proton, our most reliable information packet, is altogether
trustworthy. Even its concentrated self-knowledge can, presumably, on rare
occasions escape from its narrow confines to vanish irretrievably into the
boundlessness of the universe. But it is just such minute flaws that, in all   *cf. 39*
probability, endow matter with its reality and creativity.

The creativity of matter

Creation, to the best of our knowledge, goes back to the Big Bang about 15
billion years ago. Originally propounded by George Gamow in 1948, it has
now been corroborated beyond reasonable doubt. Our evolving world appears
as a vast, open-ended trial, driven by the dissipation of the primordial energy
eruption. At every stage, "Darwinian" self-selective processes produce new
information and beget game-enriching axiomatics. Whatever the mechanics,
the pervasive pull of gravity called into being stars and galaxies, and finally the
supernovas which produced all the heavy elements of our solar system. In the
sun, nuclear fusion has kept up a steady energy flow, which transiently structures our terrestrial atmosphere and elicits the elusive skywriting of the northern
lights.

It has taken life anything between three and four billion years – roughly the
remaining duration of steadfast solar activity – to reach its present degree of
complexity. The greater part of this time was spent on forging fundamental
autocatalytic processes, stabilized by a system of sophisticated biochemical
feedback loops. The tough competitive game eventually produced survival
artists which could secure a limited scope for personal play. Determinism was
gradually weakened and life was granted an expanding autonomy.

> Particularly in Marxist brands of philosophy, cybernetics has become the sheet-anchor
> for those who preach absolute determinacy of the life processes. According to this view,
> a spurious freedom of choice arises within a well-defined ergodic space where life-
> promoting homeostasis is upheld by negative feedback. Within these limits the orga-
> nism is free of external material necessities, and can thus influence its own life situation.
> But it is assumed that individual priorities are based on an objectively existing value
> system; freedom is ultimately a chimera, since it is exploited according to a prede-
> termined and "objectively" established scale of values. Everything that happens must
> happen in accordance with the deterministic models of classical physics, and the result is
> furthermore objectively "correct" and "scientifically" foreseeable. Human values are
> thus "analytical" concepts which can be ranked along a neutral scale, derived from
> pristine principles which . . . are just hanging in the air.

Instead of trying to force the phenomenon of life into a deterministic scheme, we should accept that its chief guiding rules are not laid down in advance, nor can they be clearly distinguished even in retrospect. The cybernetically definable ergodic space may be a measure of the degree of emancipation of different systems, life processes, people and societies, but the actual development of the game is unpredictable in principle.

In an unmitigated Darwinian selection game the survivors have tautologically authenticated themselves. Human competition certainly includes the survival aspect but for sentient beings bare subsistence is not enough: we yearn for a complementary set of rules. The evidence supports the view of Hume, Kant, Wittgenstein, Weber and G.E. Moore (1873–1958), that value judgements are synthetic, a priori, or axiomatic – depending on the philosophical jargon.

Our self-awareness is the most immediate and inviolable fact known to us: *cogito ergo sum* (I think, therefore I am). René Descartes rejected the connection between body and soul, convinced of the purely mechanistic and soulless nature of matter – a position which is no longer tenable. We would be wiser to recognize the unity of creation and grant even the simplest components of the universe a rudimentary creative capacity, extrapolating backwards from our personal actuality. Great complexity can have quite humble origins, as the *cf. 27* Mandelbrot set so eloquently testifies. Still, human consciousness appears as an inexplicable display of corporeal creativity, a stark reminder of the recondite nature of temporal reality.

2.9   Human consciousness

I posit that consciousness is brought about by incessant cerebral self-reference which fractally transcends our four-dimensional existence. Thus we gain a restricted overview of all reality, including ourselves, and can discern the world from the outside. Our consciousness knows no bounds; it expands inexorably with the accumulation of external and internal experience but, like our physical universe, we can only watch it from the inside. Still, in rare moments, we may somehow conceive the connection of all things and capture a glimpse of the vision of God.

The game of self-awareness

It is difficult to conceive of a time when the mystery of consciousness has failed to attract philosophical speculation. The strict separation of body and soul has, historically, been the prevailing prejudice and can still muster some distinguished support.

John C. Eccles, the venerable brain physiologist, applies quantum mechanics to prop up his dualist approach to the mind/matter problem (*Evolution of the Brain: Creation of the Self*, 1989). In strict consequence he invokes supernatural intervention at an early stage of human development "... each soul is a new divine creation which is implanted into the growing foetus at some time between conception and birth".

William James, the doyen of American psychology, was the first to perceive consciousness as a process, and later on it has generally been regarded as an epiphenomenon of complex brain activities. This assumption does not, however, promote facile solutions – if anything, it is the other way round. Our self is indeed insubstantial. In *The Concept of Mind* (1949) the philosopher Gilbert Ryle (1900–76) compared the soul to a university: we can point at the buildings, the curriculum, the dons and the students but we cannot pin down the university proper – it is nowhere and everywhere.

We are thus in search of a "concrete abstraction", a glaring oxymoron were it not for quantum physics, by which we have grown accustomed to such apparent self-contradictions. The quantum aspect seems, indeed, to offer novel opportunities for a rational understanding of human consciousness.

Henry Stapp has presented a sensible quantum model of brain activity, based on a Whiteheadian ontology (*Consciousness and Values in the Quantum Universe*, 1983). He correlates the mind to an aggregate hypercomplex wave function, a highly connected quantum-mechanical prodigy. The Heisenberg uncertainty of the micromolecular world is holistically sustained by the intricate neural network of the brain and transferred to tangible macrophysics. The collapse of numerous competing wave-forms into a single mental move is equivalent to a conscious choice and becomes an act of self-referential free will.

cf. 379

In *The Emperor's New Mind* (1989) Roger Penrose presents a strong case for the non-algorithmic nature of brain processes. He evokes a longitudinal gravitation which precipitates the quantum mechanical wave function into a real event, when matter in the range of the Planck mass (approximately 10^{-5} g) becomes involved. Penrose believes that only a breakthrough in quantum gravity will bring us closer to an understanding of consciousness.

cf. 109

Despite the lack of empirical evidence, the quantum interpretation of brain processes has considerable attraction. It relieves us of a whole load of well-worn metaphysical contradictions but has not so far provided a platform for discussing the different levels of animal and human awareness. Anyway, the leading lights of brain research have, so far, preferred to manage without quantum effects.

Gerald Edelman, who has championed neural Darwinism, has in *The Remembered Present* (1989) come forward with a model for the development of consciousness, based firmly on synaptic interaction patterns. The key concept is "re-entrant signalling", which, in diverse configurations, penetrates the cerebral field and facilitates a multitude of self-referential processes. Primitive consciousness is produced by the proactive superposition of past and present. At the top of the evolutionary ladder, language makes possible the conscious manipulation of conceptual entities and thus entails full consciousness. Although Edelman conjectures at a matter-of-fact level and eschews all metaphysical speculation, his reasoning is not incompatible with (and might even be complementary to) the aforementioned quantum physical notions.

cf. 99; 103

> Daniel Dennett's *Consciousness Explained* (1991) is a rather comprehensive descrip-
> tion of consciousness. The explanation seems to be that we do not need one because
> standard neurology and computer science suffice. Dennett pushes at many open doors
> but cleans out a lot of accumulated garbage in the process.

Reality can be adequately surveyed only from the outside: to immediately
comprehend a two-dimensional existence calls for three-dimensional creatures.
Similarly the validation of mathematical truth requires a meta-mathematical
value frame to provide the indispensable superior perspective. Consciousness
implies that we possess a certain overview of our own four-dimensional existence, as the mind plays with itself in ever-changing self-reference. Thus, we
must postulate a higher dimension to which man and possibly also other advanced species have some access.

> Higher dimensions are close at hand for religious thinkers; Karl Heim (1874–1958), for
> instance, has launched the idea in a theological context. More interesting is the appear-
> ance of hyperspace in the natural sciences. As early as the 1920s, Theodor Kaluza
> (1885–1954) and Oskar Klein (1894–1977) demonstrated that if we give the general
> theory of relativity a five-dimensional formulation, Maxwell's electromagnetic wave
> equation appears spontaneously in the four-dimensional case. The Kaluza-Klein ap-
> proach has proved fruitful in the latest attempts to construct 10-dimensional unified
> *cf. 379*   field theories.

Our self-awareness is coupled to brain activity, an incredibly complex physico-
chemical process. The brain's self-programming requires interaction with the
environment; the neonate is barely aware of itself although all the brain cells are
in place. Without a stream of sense impressions the brain cannot exploit its
potential, explore reality, identify patterns, work out the rules of the game.
Devoid of social contact the "I" cannot become aware of itself; our latent
identity, entrenched in the cerebral processes, remains closed within its objectively four-dimensional actuality.

Fractal dimensions

We may speculate casually about higher dimensions, but such loose ideas must
be set within a tangible framework. The fractals – dimensional quantities in-
tervening between the integers – offer an attractive mathematical model for my
cf. 25 present purpose.

> The concept of fractals derives from the infinity mathematics of Georg Cantor (1845–
> 1918). In 1890, Giuseppe Peano (1858–1932) could demonstrate that an "infinitely
> complex" curve can fill a plane if it is extended without limit. The Brownian, thermally
> randomised motions of microscopic particles represent the physical equivalent of a
> *cf. 32*   Peano curve. But a curve may also be constructed such that its dimension is a fractal,
> something between one and two.

A simple fractal can be obtained by envisaging the development of an equilater-
al triangle analogous to a snow crystal. The diagram in figure 2.15 makes this
clear:

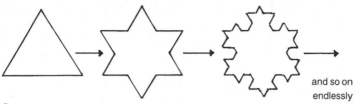

and so on
endlessly

Figure 2.15

The circumference of the snow crystal is multiplied by four thirds at every stage. By infinite extrapolation the resulting Koch snowflake (after Helge von Koch, 1870–1924) becomes a self-similar fractal, a curve which is continuous but non-derivable at any point. Its extension transcends infinity, in a manner of speaking, and intrudes partially in the second dimension. The dimension of the resulting fractal is mathematically defined as log4/log3 = 1.2618, something between a line and a plane.

> Fractals may arise for example from the iteration: $x_n+1 = f(x_n)$ where $n \to \infty$. (The Koch-curve emerges when $x_n+1 = 4/3x_n$). Many of these self-generative functions tend to run away towards well-defined attractors while others unfold in a chaotic mode with successive terms exhibiting wild swings in an indeterminate manner. Whereas the Koch curve is rigidly self-similar, the convoluted borderline of the Mandelbrot set is infinitely varied and displays new riches of detail down to any depth of analysis. *cf. 27*

A fractal dimension presupposes infinite continuation of the convolutions of the curve or the irregularities of the surface, as the scale approaches zero. This is in accordance with the modern conception of the nature of reality. The elementary particles are not well-defined points, where the grainy nature of matter comes to an end; instead they can be described in terms of statistically prescribed processes. The uncertainty principle excludes exactly defined positions and trajectories; even the vacuum is far removed from absolutely unstructured emptiness.

> The vacuum, the total absence of all reality, has proved quite problematic in terms of quantum physics. The blame for this, or rather the credit, can once again be traced back to Heisenberg's uncertainty principle. An exactly-defined zero energy is not permissible; thus, with miniscule probability, energy must arise randomly out of nothing. Even a complete vacuum is therefore laden with uncertainty and "virtual energy", a mixture of positive and negative energy states (antimatter can, indeed, be perceived as a mirror realm of negative energies). The amount momentarily "borrowed" from the vacuum multiplied by the time of "debt" must be smaller than or equal to $h/2\pi$. Although the average energy is equal to zero, a peculiar "graininess" does arise even in empty space-time. Every particle induces in the surrounding vacuum an aura of "virtual" *cf. 380* partners, wave packets and antiparticles, which call forth even more elusive playmates and interactions in an infinite regress. *cf. 75*

The wealth of variety in the world does not disappear as space and time scales approach zero. Material interfaces are therefore qualified for interpretation according to the fractal principle; they are always somewhat "wrinkled" and possess a certain "sense" of a higher dimension. Any real surface is not only irregular down to the last atomic detail; the ambiguity is further enhanced by the creativity of empty space. A three-dimensional particle has, by virtue of its process nature, an analogous depth contact with the fourth dimension of time; *cf. 39*   pure being appears to be a metaphysical impossibility.

Consciousness – a hyperfractal?

Imaginative computer simulation has brought forth a whole hierarchy of fractals. They range from the relative simplicity of the Koch curve, through the multifractals characteristic of turbulent flow to the completely non-repetitive superfractal of the Mandelbrot interface. I postulate that human consciousness is coupled to an intense cerebral variability which conceives a hyperfractal, capable of penetrating into a fifth dimension. Four-dimensional space-time can then, to some extent, be surveyed and embraced by the incessantly scanning brain function. In cybernetic terms consciousness is an ultra-ergodic system; the same state is never repeated. Not only does every brain diverge, but every conscious moment of a single human brain generates a new and unique experi-
cf. 100   ence unlike anything that has gone before. Only thus is there a guarantee of continuing "ruggedness" in the boundary of space-time, providing contact with a higher dimension.

cf. 378   Whitehead's process philosophy postulates that reality is totally time-conditioned; every event requires a time greater than zero. The above argument, too, presupposes the existence of a minimum time unit, a time atom. The perfect continuity of time would sanction limitless accuracy in its measurement, which in light of the uncertainty principle would presuppose infinite levels of energy. The same fundamental principle that forces the quantification of other aspects of reality, should also work for time (and distance). The aforementioned Planck time, 5.3×10^{-44}s, is one candidate for the time atom. The quantification or the "graininess" of gravity and space-time (in essence the same thing) remains an open question, but a change in its topology at sufficiently small
cf. 65; 378   dimensions close to the Planck length (1.6×10^{-33}cm) appears increasingly plausible.

Strange attractors are fractal structures, which embody the implicit rules of
cf. 25   quasi-chaotic play in the appropriate hyperspace. Accordingly, consciousness could be interpreted as a superstrange attractor, emerging out of incessant self-simulation at the hyperfractal intersection of concrete and abstract actualities. Our mental processes thus become the metaphysical proof of the fuzzily quantified structure of the world.

cf. 389   A hyperfractal state is not compatible with completely deterministic machinery. Its prerequisites are an infinite wealth of variety, self-repetition without self-similarity, a meaningful unpredictability, or in other words individual freedom. An injection of random disturbances does not increase the latitude of a determined system; on the contrary, connectedness suffers and the result is just a less efficient machine. Living organisms utilise extensive homeostatic feedback to control such disorder, tenaciously defending the integrity of their ergodic space – the freedom of choice.

Speculating about computer consciousness is a fascinating exercise, and not the
cf. 99   sole reserve of science-fiction writers. The description and adequate programming of an activity always presupposes a higher intelligence than is involved in

direct implementation. Consciousness is an excessively dense language game transcending even the high cardinality of the vernacular. Thus the construction of "beings" with genuine self-awareness calls for superhuman overview and insight as well as a hypothetical hyperlanguage, which removes conscious computers to a far-off and perhaps unattainable future.

cf. 353

cf. 99; 105; 335

Between mind and matter

We are heavily indebted to our animal ancestors for key elements of our mental machinery. The feeling of absolute reality is, for example, an indispensable animal dimension of human consciousness. Left to its own devices, consciousness is trapped in a vacuous void. So where should we draw the line for conscious behaviour? This is very much a question of definition. Chimpanzees recognize themselves in a mirror while monkeys do not, but it would be imprudent to jump to conclusions on the basis of such isolated observations.

cf. 78

> Donald R. Griffin has presented a comprehensive survey of intelligent animal behaviour (*Animal Thinking*, 1984; *Animal Minds*, 1992). Based on numerous examples he makes a strong case for conscious planning among warm-blooded animals, but he does not make a proper distinction between animal consciousness and complex instincts and reflexes.
>
> *cf. 423*
>
> The following experiment seems to set at least the amphibians apart. If the optic nerve of a frog is cut, turned through 180°, and sewn together again, the nerve fibres will spontaneously establish contact. The frog now sees the world upside down and it will snap consistently in the wrong direction whenever an insect comes within sight and reach. The frog never learns from experience but mechanically repeats the mistaken reflexes for the rest of its life.
>
> The optic nerve of a mammal will, on the contrary, refuse to connect properly. Evidently, differing synaptic states are immediately established and the nerve fibres do not "find" one another after the cut. On the other hand, man soon learns to reprogramme his visual impressions. A test subject wearing glasses which turn the world upside down can learn to function without much difficulty after only a few days. But when the glasses are removed his world will again stand on its head for a while.

The frog resembles a well-programmed self-repairing automaton while the mammalian brain has to pay for its creativity with the inability to repair damage, although considerable cortical reserves can be brought into play.

The scattered data presently available do not carry much weight. Systematic investigation of neural activities in different species combined with imaginative mathematical modelling could, conceivably, bring the fractal hypothesis of consciousness within the realm of testability.

> Penrose has conjectured that meaningful synaptic patterns are akin to his non-repetitive tesselations. A new and orderly configuration must take into consideration the overall situation; it cannot be achieved locally, step by step. Such wide-ranging, macroscopic but quantum-mechanically directed processes might correspond to non-algorithmic mathematical insights and human creativity in general.
>
> *cf. 27*
>
> In another vein, the neurobiologist William Calvin (*The Cerebral Symphony*, 1990) has proposed a Darwinian model for the emergence of thought in the neuronal network. Thinking is placed on a par with a competitive game, which pits different combinations of thought fragments against each other, always selecting the fittest according to some

cf. 112 superordinate criteria. This scheme neatly avoids the need for explicit programming, but does not in itself connect mind with matter.

It might be possible to produce a comprehensive model of the amphibian type of brain but human self-awareness is probably inherently non-computable even if we could find a fractal measure for consciousness *per se*. All new experiences and insights (including internal perceptions) expand our consciousness, which knows no boundaries. But like our physical universe we can only watch it from the inside.

The oceanic experience

The brain operates in a metastable state of dissipative biochemistry, and the mathematical treatment of analogous physical phenomena may therefore further illuminate our subject matter.

cf. 39
cf. 71
cf. 61
cf. 31

We have previously alluded to the infinite charge of the "naked" electron. This induces a similar, infinitely strong opposite charge in the immediate surroundings which is teeming with virtual photons and electron-positron pairs. By means of Feynman-diagrams the complex interplay can be analyzed and, by good fortune, the ensuing mathematical series is convergent (the infinite number of higher terms can be neglected). Hence the real charge of the electron can be calculated with a high degree of accuracy as the minuscule difference between virtual infinities. Such computer-based "renormalisation" is equally indispensable in the analysis of many macrophysical phenomena when, on the verge of chaotic change, infinities appear in the mathematical models. Examples of this are fluids close to the critical point and magnetic material at the Curie temperature. Most typical are metastable states bordering on large-scale quantum phenomena like superfluidity and superconductivity.

Dissipative and chaotic states are relatively indeterminate. A minimal and almost imperceptible move in the microdimension can make the whole macroscopic system change course in a cascade of cumulative self-realization.

cf. 24; 320

The minutest difference between the starting points of a chaotic process can cause significant macroscopic bifurcation. Computer simulation of one realistic mathematical model started with an initial difference of 10^{-12} and yielded an amplification of 10^{13} after only 50 iterations. Quantum mechanical uncertainties can thus easily create completely different outcomes for the same game, given that the process is charged with dissipative energy. There is no lower limit for the proximity of the points that predestine divergent developments; it is not a distance in the usual sense since it has a fractal dimension of less than 1.

In the typology of physical state equations, a characteristic entity is the number of dimensions in which changes must be taken into account. The interesting point is that if the dimensionality should exceed four, it would be possible to avoid the complicated renormalisation procedure, and the much simpler classical field theories would apply. We can take this to mean that the slightest transgression of four-dimensionality generates a general and comprehensive juxtaposition of the elements within a system. Bypassing infinity, all its several parts are brought into continual and immediate contact with one another; they, as it were, "feel" one another.

David Bohm (1917–92) arrived at similar conclusions by way of his unorthodox interpretation of quantum physics. He postulated that subatomic particles do have definite positions, but with the awkward consequence of non-locality – non-mediated action at a distance. Everything becomes holistically bound up with everything else.   *cf. 34; 379*

The oceanic experience of the mystics springs to mind. Cut off from everyday trivialities, human consciousness occasionally enters an abnormally high fractal dimension and for one blissful moment of concentrated introspection experiences the connection of all things, beholds the meaning of existence and captures a glimpse of the vision of God.

3. The nature of man

3.1 Nature or nurture

Man is the product of his animal ancestry, the *summa summarum* of living experience upon our planet. Accordingly, not only our bodies but also our behaviour and temperament, our vices and virtues are conditioned by inherited mechanisms. The dominance of the genes does not exclude a certain freedom of action and thus most of the fuss about "nature or nurture" is beside the point. What is important is to identify the limits of our freedom of manoeuvre as individuals and as groups. To that end, we need a better insight into the innate rules which direct human interplay.

Genetic predestination

Before taking on the whole array of cultural games, we must try to understand the character of the key player *Homo sapiens*. The conditions of human creativity deserve special attention; the creative impulse is the quintessential quality of our race. The obvious malleability of human behaviour has consistently led the self-appointed reformers of mankind astray. Our psyche is not an empty slate on which high-handed directives can be freely engraved. Nor can the nature of man ever be nailed down in cogent detail. What we *can* look for are the ethologically binding rules that define and circumscribe the latitude our species actually enjoys here and now.

Man is undoubtedly in the frontline of evolution, irrefutably facing the future. On this earth at any rate, we are the provisional front-runner in the self-organizing game that life has been playing with both possibilities and impossibilities over the last three or four billion years. Most of the countless innovations have been rejected but this torrent of negative feedback has produced a positive print-out – the smooth-running machinery of collaborative enzymatic processes which form the conservative foundation for all life on our planet.

Upon this cellular base, intricate enough in itself, an increasingly complex superstructure has been erected. For millions of years the hominids were quite inconspicuous until, suddenly, human development stepped up a gear. About

50,000 years ago *Homo sapiens* ceased to be just one species among many; he ate of the tree of knowledge and took the plunge into cultural, self-generating evolution. Since then his innermost nature has hardly changed. The answer to the question "What is man?" must be sought in the genetic constitution which pushed and pulled him over the threshold out of Eden.

> Over the eons our genetic heritage has been preserved and enriched by and through the whole animal kingdom – the phylum of Chorelata, the subphylum of Vertebrata, the class of Mammals and the order of Primates. Man is protected against parasitical intrusion by a highly discriminatory immunological defence, and a cascade of nervous and endocrine feedback co-ordinates all the major functions of the body, including the process of maturation as well as ageing and death.

The crowning feature is our brain, the centre for external information-processing but almost equally sensitive to impulses from the inner universe of instincts, emotions and the play of the intellect. In this turmoil of competing influences, the subject itself emerges with an incessantly growing scope for play. Human consciousness entails a knowledge of life and death exclusively reserved for our species.

Limited autonomy

Before going any further we should remind ourselves of the mental schemes which we have inherited from earlier forms of life. A new breed of psychologists is now excavating the evolutionary roots of human foibles and fears.

> The dread of snakes and spiders is deeply embedded in our genetic heritage while the attraction of the panda, the koala and the teddy bear stems from their soft, childlike proportions. Campfires that died down long ago still exert their attraction as we gather round an open hearth. Much older are our inborn geometrical insights, the ability to cope in a four-dimensional world has been reinforced by the stereoscopic vision bequeathed to us by tree-climbing ancestors.

cf. 73 We must also assume that our sense of the absolute actuality of existence was programmed into our predecessors at the very onset of neural development.

> Perception of reality can be gravely disturbed, for instance in severe schizophrenia or as a result of cerebral injuries. Many survivors of the "Spanish flu" of 1918 suffered from viral sleeping sickness (encephalitis lethargica) with accompanying damage to the substantia nigra of the middle brain which, in turn, led to an extreme form of Parkinson's disease. Oliver Sacks tells us in *Awakenings* (1974) how patients who had been passive and immobile for years were able to renew normal communication after receiving modern medication (L-dopa compensates in part for the disturbed brain functions but, regrettably, the effect is transient). When one patient was asked why she had spent so many years without moving, the reply was: "I had run out of space to move in". Before treatment, several of the more serious cases had exhibited pronounced regressive symptoms. One patient was unable to drink normally; she lapped up liquids like an animal. This indicates the presence of a complicated co-ordination of muscular functions which became accessible as a result of brain damage. Thus, the lapping function must be filed away deep inside the brain together with a lot of other useless inherited traits.

Anxieties and phobias, compulsions and obsessions, the heritage of tens and possibly hundreds of millions of years are waiting to take over, should the superimposed neural structures lose their viability. Meanwhile, we enjoy the pick of this collective wisdom, unaware of its broad foundation. The ancient pantheistic notion of the unity of creation finds clear corroboration in the universality of the basic life processes; man is the *summa summarum* of living experience upon our planet.

The cerebrum is the seat of the intellect but our personality and individual character are prescribed by the "old-fashioned" parts of our brain. These we *cf. 82; 100; 391* have certainly inherited, root and branch, from countless preceding generations. It is unlikely that the basic infrastructure was affected by the latest evolutionary spurt, when the hypertrophy of the cerebral cortex became the measure of man's humanization.

Identical twins provide the most striking proof of the pervasive influence of the genotype not only in physical appearance but also in terms of the disposition of the personality. They exhibit a remarkable congruence in talents and inclinations, regardless of whether they grow up together or apart. Psychological studies of children have demonstrated the persistence of some early characteristics such as independence, the ability to concentrate, perseverence and suchlike. Those with a sunny disposition really do seem

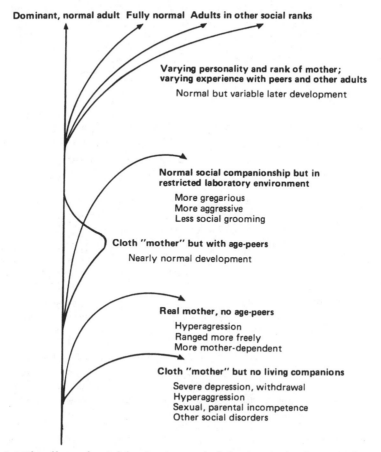

Figure 3.1 The effects of social deprivation on the behaviour in the rhesus (Wilson, 1975)

to have been born with the gift of good temper; they exhibit helpfulness and a positive view of life, independent of external circumstances.

The dominance of the genes does not exclude the influence of the environment. In particular, we should be on guard against early deprivations which are linked to deeply buried genetic programmes.

> Only recently it became clear that immediate bodily contact between a mother and her newborn infant is important in eliciting the affective bond between mother and child. Our present cultural crisis may stem in part from the neglect of such basic epigenetic rules. Figure 3.1 summarizes the result of experiments with rhesus monkeys and high-lights some additional pitfalls of the maturation process.
>
> An impassive "cloth mother" seems to be an acceptable substitute for the real thing but the absence of playmates in the same age group has severe implications for the adult monkey. One shudders at the impact of all the unsound instruction which, under the banner of "scientific opinion", has been heaped upon unsuspecting parents.

Our culture seems imbued with a supreme contempt for the inherited rules of the game. Man's exceptional adaptability has created the illusion that human nature is like putty in our hands. Such claims are all part of a desperate attempt to flout determination at the moment of conception. Our quest for freedom has led to insolent pride and pointless rebellion against the very foundations of life. Yet genuine scope for play is conceivable only under the aegis of genetically stabilized rules, and greater insight into these innate directives is urgently needed if we are ever to improve our understanding of ourselves.

Burdens of inheritance

Man should not boast of his freedom of choice, least of all in the deceptively simple options of everyday life. Our best intentions come to grief when they are faced with deep physiological directives which slyly appeal to our pleasure-seeking senses.

> Man's outward appearance is genetically well defined. The widespread problems of obesity remind us of the presence of persistent regulatory mechanisms, persuasive urges which are hardly accessible to volition or rational thought. Our food habits are no bad measure of the limits and possibilities of free will, especially if we are carrying an hereditary surplus. Customary weight reduction schemes usually fail, but the over-weight disappears if the gratification of the senses is thwarted by serving up totally tasteless food.
>
> cf. 100; 394
>
> In simplistic terms, hunger and satiety are controlled by two separate centres in the hypothalamus; in cases of morbid slimming (*anorexia*) the hunger stimulus fails to operate and all food intake becomes repellent. In our modern society, far more people suffer from the putative malfunctioning of the satiation centre. But the ability to accumulate fat in times of plenty has been an important asset, especially for females who have not been expected to shine in physical performance. The grotesque obesity of most Palaeolithic female statuettes and the innate tendency of bushwomen to accumulate layers of fat around the buttocks (steatopygia), suggest that excess fat is a fairly normal attribute, for the fairer sex at any rate.

We are, by and large, at the mercy of the endocrine system, which becomes painfully evident during serious emotional disorders, such as manic-depressive psychosis. Our hormonal balance is directed by polypeptides, secreted by the pituitary gland which, for its part, is regulated by neurosecretions from the hypothalamus. Here the track is lost for the time being; our volition remains submerged in the perpetual play of the neuronal network.

> A thorough understanding of the sexual differentiation process goes some way to explain the immense variability of human inclinations. To cut a long story short, the masculine-feminine aspect of our personality is largely determined by the excretion of masculinizing hormones (chiefly testosterone). Testosterone treatment can have uncanny consequences, especially in young girls; excessive muscle development is accompanied by changes in vocal pitch and personality. It is less well known that even quite small deviations from endocrine normality reveal themselves in behavioural changes. Boyish girls, for example, show a slight surplus of testosterone, and similar aberrations have been observed among political extremists of both sexes. A systematic study of successful sportswomen or female chess champions could be worthwhile, but apparently next to nothing of the sort has been undertaken.
>
> Overt homosexuality is caused by the same hormonal mechanism. The inchoate brain is predisposed for female behaviour; the dormant masculine traits must be activated by the testosterone production of the foetal testes. Consequently, hormonal malfunction during pregnancy will cause the imprinting of the converse behaviour pattern. The search is now on for the genetic roots of sexual deviation.

Sociobiology has been the catchword for an evolutionary approach to the development of behaviour and has already achieved considerable success in the study of animal communities. The sociobiological approach comes closer to the truth than the predominating schools of psychology, sociology, economics, jurisprudence and other human-oriented studies with their scorn for the inconvenient input of the natural sciences. Sociobiology places man in his evolutionary context, and saves him from becoming a compliant object for arbitrary speculation or well-meaning but irresponsible utopians. Unfortunately, its message has been marred by a rather self-serving attitude.

> Edward O. Wilson's impressive survey of *Sociobiology* (1975) touches on humans only in the concluding remarks. He presumes, somewhat rashly, that within a century complete sociobiological knowledge will have pushed scientific development to the point of destroying any possible ethical basis for mankind. In *On Human Nature* (1978) he explains with supreme hindsight all human behaviour in terms of genetically determined adaptive behaviour. In *Genes, Mind and Culture* (1981), written together with Charles Lumsden, his stance has softened. It is assumed that genetic control is *cf. 415* executed by a set of inherited epigenetic rules which appear spontaneously in response to the social environment and decisively influence human preferences in the choice between alternative moves in the cultural game.
>
> Irenäus Eibl-Eibesfeldt has presented a balanced view of the human condition in his work on human ethology (*Die Biologie des menschlichen Verhaltens*, 1984). Without jumping to unwarranted conclusions, he compiles a comprehensive list of well-documented inborn traits of *Homo sapiens*. While staunchly defending the reality of epigenetic rules which strongly influence most aspects of social interaction, he concentrates on broad generalizations, applicable even to the most diverse groups of our species. The finer gradations, exposing connections (if any) between heredity and cultural development, would be even more interesting but may be beyond the resolving power of objective scientific investigation.

We have to admit that not only the bodily functions, but also our temperament, is controlled by primordial mechanisms. A lifelong leaning towards optimism or pessimism can be traced back to the same source. The professional as well as the amateur philosopher tends first to make unconscious but fundamental *a priori* assumptions about the evil or virtuous nature of man and the world, about the meaning or meaninglessness of existence. Then he spends the rest of his life deducing these predetermined opinions from the simplest possible premises and principles. Our most daring intellectual superstructures are hanging from invisible but tenacious threads of affection.

cf. 35; 100; 129; 391

In life we are all dealt certain cards but how we play them is a matter of personal discretion. General tendencies can only refer to statistical averages, and collective rules are never binding on the individual personality. Most of the fuss about "nature or nurture" is therefore beside the point. What is important is to identify the limits of our freedom of manoeuvre as individuals and as groups.

Psychosomatic parity

The acute interdependence of body and mind suggests that influence works both ways. By persistent training, man can indeed acquire surprising control over otherwise autonomous organs.

> The practitioners of Yoga are famous for this ability but they have been outdone by a Californian boy named Hansen who, motivated by a suspected heart disease, learnt to exert complete control over his heart-beat at the age of thirteen. Conversely, the synchronization of the menstrual cycle among women living in close proximity implies effective though unconscious socio-physiological feedback mechanisms.

Everybody has experienced how a strong affect reduces sensitivity to pain. Stigmatization dramatically proves the transubstantiating effect of pious exaltation while hypnosis and acupuncture demonstrate the susceptibility of our faculties to outside manipulation.

> The placebo effect is a measure of human suggestibility which is thought to explain about 30 to 40 per cent of the efficacy of drugs. In a comparative experiment it was found that twelve weeks of placebo therapy cured 70 per cent of patients suffering from stomach ulcers while two types of medication cured 84 per cent and 87 per cent respectively. The deception contains a remarkable element of auto-suggestion; 13 out of 14 neurotic patients began to improve after taking what they knew to be plain sugar pills. The doctor still possesses the aura of the medicine man, and his prescriptions evidently carry the healing powers of the talisman.
>
> Conversely, evil spells have a malignant effect on the believers. Mortality rose significantly when the barely measurable but heavily reported cloud of Chernobyl radioactivity passed the United States in early May 1986. Any radiobiological influence is out of the question; the induced fear obviously pushed some sick people prematurely over the brink.

Exorcists of diverse extraction have always, for better or worse, found ways to exploit our essential gullibility. A chaotic world devoid of meaning and pattern drives us to despair; the absence of any superordinate values inevitably leads to

a sensation of the absurdity of life. We clutch at any straw; superstition is the   *cf. 293*
easy way out of an existential deadlock.

> Occultism is widespread in our culture, constantly resurfacing in new guises. The still   *cf. 368*
> fashionable pendulum magic was scientifically refuted as early as 1812 by the French
> chemist Michel-Eugene Chevreul (1786–1889). Slight, unconscious finger movements
> produce the "correct" swing only if the "medium" knows how the pendulum should
> move. A blind test immediately exposes the illusion. The same mechanism is at work in   *cf. 307*
> water-divining and related, fairly harmless self-deceptions.

Self-emolliating escapism can be vanquished by youthful daring which often
silences even ordinary common sense. Stimulation and excitement may be more
important than security and survival – boredom is sometimes a fate worse than
death. Our passion for the game provides a loophole in the pitiless determinism
of the evolutionary game – here a power-enhancing lever can be inserted. We
can, by hook or by crook, modify our conduct, moderate our impulses, systematically developing desirable dispositions.

The discord between animal reflexes and human self-awareness has been a
perpetual theme of the philosophers and religious founding fathers; more recently Sigmund Freud's (1856–1939) over-simplified model has become a tired
platitude. Later psychologists have tackled the problem with greater subtlety,
and the following scheme should reflect mainstream opinion, compressed by
the game metaphor (figure 3.2).

Game level	Fundamental rules of the game	Payoff	Field of play
Child, parent bond	Unambiguous discipline, unquestionable authorities	Primary needs: self-preservation, nourishment, security	Family
Teenager, gang bonding	Group loyality, conformity-based authorities	Social needs: sexual acceptance, group identity	Kin, peer groups
Youth, individualism, community bonding	Duty and principles, legalistic authorities	Self-centred needs: stimulus, ambition, self-realization	Organization, business, politics
Mature human being societal and cultural bonds	Arbitration by the conscience, transcendental authority	Spiritual needs: creativity, harmony, meta-motivation	Science, philosohy, art, religion

Figur 3.2 Hierarchy of the mind

Human maturation is divided into four stages, which correspond to the physiological and evolutionary development of man. As we move up the scale, superi-
or levels of play gradually complement the deep structure, preparing the way for
individuation and even some spiritual freedom. In general, primitive needs must
be at least tolerably satisfied before higher ones can be expressed but the rank
order is not absolute. In war, the group identity can supplant self-preservation,
and martyrdom proves that the feeblest of existential forces can overrule the
powerful urge to live – a victory of weakness.

3.2   The emergence of homo sapiens

Man is the sole survivor of his genus because he became the chief agent of his own change. Superior coalition-building gave *Homo sapiens* a decisive competitive edge. Effective communication paved the way for long-term co-operation in complex cultural games. Tribes and nations evolved into vehicles of solidarity and evoked a cascade of positive feedback, which imbued the human plus-sum game with unquenchable vigour.

Circumspect genesis

For every distinct form of life, the existential directives are embodied in a cluster of genes, each one characterized by its own specific DNA-(deoxyribo*n*ucleic *cf. 92; 320* acid) sequence. By way of DNA-hybridization it is possible to evaluate quantitatively the total deviation between the genomes of different species. Thus for the first time we now have a reliable picture of the phylogenetic relations between currently existing primates (figure 3.3).

> For the chimpanzee and the gorilla the time of separation from the Homo-lineage is still disputed but the given sequence of events conforms to the most parsimonious evolutionary tree. It is remarkable that although Homo diverged from the apes at least five

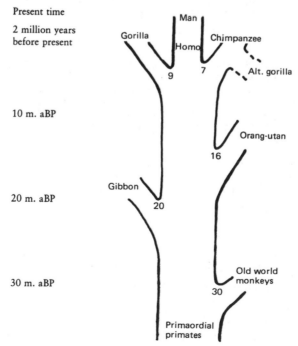

Figure 3.3 The pedigree of the primates

million years ago, the DNA of humans and chimpanzees are still 98.4 per cent identical, although there are significant differences in the chromosomal organization.

Homo sapiens is the sole survivor of his genus: the deep roots of human physiology and behaviour are therefore still the subject of diverse speculation. To throw in a new idea, let us assume that hominization was initiated between five and ten million years ago by isolated groups of primaeval apes who became specialized foragers of small but nutritious seeds. This would explain the remarkable differences between the apes and the hominids in the design of the hand and the masticatory apparatus.

> In such a scenario, the impediment in food intake was the cumbersome chewing of each individual seed, and the use of stones for crushing the grain constituted a decisive competitive advantage. This started a chain of positive feedback between tools, adroitness, intellectual ability and nutrition potential. The gradual freeing of the hands from mundane perambulation – two-leggedness and an upright posture – was certainly an integral part of the process.
>
> Four-leggedness is very effective for locomotion but precludes carrying burdens back to camp. Early hominization might have been preceded by the strengthening of family bonds, which compelled the males to support their mates and offspring with food from distant sources. This conjecture is in line with the doctrine of culture-induced evolution but is, of course, very difficult to verify. *cf. 95*

Whatever the merit of this scheme, we should assume a gradual strengthening of social bonds. The sharing of resources within the family or troop became a condition of survival and has remained the very basis of human solidarity. *cf. 231*

Social conditioning

Five to six million years ago, a major climatic change caused the desiccation of the Mediterranean. In Africa, desert and savannah expanded to the detriment of the forest. The environmental instability fostered social collaboration which in the long term made scavenging and hunting profitable for the early hominids. Long stalking bouts favoured hairlessness as a means to avoid overheating in a warm climate.

> The central nervous system of *Homo sapiens* expends about 40 watts which corresponds to almost half of our basal energy requirement. Considering the temperature sensitivity of the brain, the additional heat load certainly brought the cooling problem to a head. Hairlessness could thus be a necessary consequence of an expanding intellect, phylogenetically speaking that is!

Good hunting and success at war called for leadership and discipline. Primitive *cf. 150* submission reflexes were refined to allow co-operation in larger bands; social organization evolved into the supreme weapon in the struggle for lebensraum. Frail, redundant elders were transformed into imposing chiefs or awe-inspiring shamans – venerated repositories of tribal values.

> Serious violence is actually quite rare within primate groups; like the apes, we turn instinctively to less dangerous ways of resolving conflict. The standard forms of conflict resolution are dominance, submission or comradeship. Approval is often gained by asking for advice or for some minor service – an intelligent variation on the submission

theme. Even so, dominating father figures have an advantage in politics. Elderly men generally possess the economic and political power; only dramatic cultural upheaval opens the way for more youthful talent.

The viability of the female until long past the menopause is uniquely human. Evidently the input of grandmotherly experience and care more than offsets the lack of reproductive capacity. Childhood was extended to match the need to learn, which favoured family formation and the differentiation of the sexes. The foundations of sexual morality were laid down at this early stage; eventually, incestuous intercourse became strictly taboo.

> The bias against inbreeding has deep phylogenetic roots; it has been found in frogs and even banana flies. Female mice show a marked aversion to closely related males, and chimpanzees possess similar barriers to copulation "in the family". Our revulsion against incest has very good reasons. A Czechoslovakian study found severe mental or physical defects in 40 per cent of incestuous children as against 5 per cent of children born to the same mothers fathered by non-relatives.
>
> The genetic instructions cannot be read literally, but they respond to relevant clues in the environment. In the kibbutzim, for example, playmates are perceived as brothers and sisters, since all children grow up in the kindergartens in intimate contact with one another. As a result, marriage (or sexual intercourse) is very rare within this closely-knit group. Significantly, all the famous incestuous characters of world literature turn out to have been separated from their subsequent partners at an early age.

The enhancement of female eroticism and visible sexual characteristics kept the men emotionally tied to their mates, increasing the inclusive fitness of both sexes. The hunters felt a strong pull to return to base where the women maintained the old gathering traditions. Close collaboration during the chase and in defence modified the sexual rivalry of the adult males, and may have imparted survival value to homosexual leanings.

cf. 59; 145; 152   The inclination of male youngsters to cluster into gangs is evident among most primates and provides yet another thread in the complex network of archetypal instruction. Fraternities of aggressive juveniles at the fringes of society have always operated as an innovative counterweight to the conservative, security-related values of the adult establishment. However, adolescent self-assertion is tempered by group solidarity. This is an inborn human response, particularly in young males under external pressure, and it is a prerequ-

cf. 86; 158   isite of organized collaboration in peace and war.

> In his *Divina Commedia*, Dante Alighieri (1265–1321) relegated traitors to the deepest, ninth circle of hell. For him, betrayal was infinitely worse than plain murder (the seventh circle) or theft or forgery (the eighth circle). A strong taboo still prevents boys from telling on their pals, and "scab" remains a four-letter word of the utmost opprobrium.

The hominization process certainly involves a loosening up of predetermined instinctive responses. Cameraderie competes with sexual envy, affections fight egotism; by and by a minimum of intellectual freedom begins to germinate in the push and pull of rival epigenetic rules.

Burst of competition

Superficially the hominids remained for millions of years a less than successful group of animal species. *Australopithecus* may have used a variety of tools as well as baskets and nets; *Homo habilis* certainly did. *Homo erectus*, the fore-runner of *Homo sapiens*, extended its territorial range from Africa to most of Eurasia. It commanded fire, communicated by language, dressed in animal skins and mastered a diversified set of tools.

The evolution and radiation of man has been the subject of much unsound

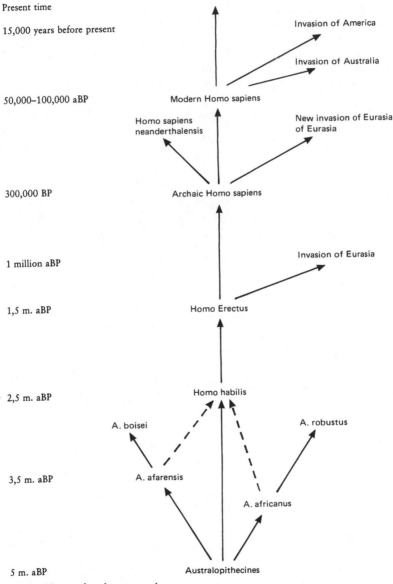

Figure 3.4   *Homo development chart*

speculation. Recent advances in paleontology and genetics provide some reliable building blocks for human prehistory (see figure 3.4), even if the exclusively African origin of *Homo sapiens* is still hotly debated.

The nodes of progression have, in the customary way, been placed at the several validated species. Cladistic analysis indicates, however, that these well-established types may not be direct ancestors of man. Rather they were temporarily successful branches which eventually became extinct. Our true progenitors were probably very thin on the ground, poor relatives of the dominant stock. Evolution seems to proceed by roundabout routes; one step back, two or three ahead.

cf. 97; 339

The Quaternary Period was initiated by a series of ice-ages which started 2.5 million years ago. The dramatic fluctuations in climate, particularly in high latitudes (see figure 3.5), put a premium on adaptability and resourcefulness ,which intensified cultural competition. Less than definite mitochondrial studies indicate that the emergence of modern *Homo sapiens* took place in Africa around 200,000 aBP in a very small population. The breakout from the African homeland was supposedly accomplished 60,000 to 70,000 years ago by tiny groups of perhaps only a few hundred individuals; the population bottleneck seems to have persisted for around 10,000 years.

The notorious *Homo sapiens neanderthalensis* is probably just one of many dry branches of hominid evolution. He established himself in Europe and the Near East less than 100,000 years ago with a relatively varied culture, probably including religious

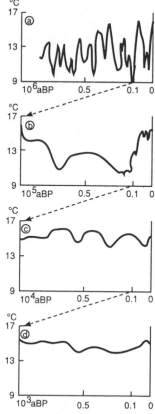

Figure 3.5 The mean temperature of the Northern hemisphere on four different time scales, down to 850,000 aBP (top chart) (Clark, 1982)

ideas and burial rites. Barely 50,000 years later the Neanderthals had vanished. The concomitant upsurge of *Homo sapiens sapiens*, as witnessed by breakthroughs in technology and art, is certainly no pure coincidence.

During periods of heavy glaciation, sinking sea levels uncovered landbridges facilitating the migration of intrepid hunter-gatherers. Australia was colonized 40,000–50,000 aBP while the Americas may, on scant evidence, have got their first human inhabitants 25,000 years ago. Widespread human presence is substantiated from ca. 15,000 aBP. We are now living in a warm interglacial which started about 12,000 years ago and brought destructive floods, still retained by our collective memory.

What happened over the last 50,000 years when modern man moved over to the fast track and overtook all his rivals? A radical genetic revolution is out of the question. Instead we must postulate the evolution of human culture to a point where the cultural heritage became the decisive competitive weapon. Verbal competence, social coherence and technical know-how produced a self-supporting and self-perfecting web of rules for the game of social co-operation. Fierce intraspecies competition intensified the fight for survival and triggered a steady acceleration in the pace of innovative moves and countermoves, which has endured to this day. Less successful groups found difficulty in establishing an ecological niche appropriate to their way of life because the superior culture easily adjusted to new and less attractive territories.

The contest certainly involved warlike combat but basically it was enacted as a battle for vital resources – primarily food. Under such conditions genetic isolation is an unstable state of affairs and the cohabitation of genetically distinct populations becomes problematic.

> Gause's law was formulated in 1934 by the Russian biologist G.F.Gause. His Competitive Exclusion Principle proclaims that two (or several) species with identical strategies for survival cannot co-exist in the same habitat for any length of time. When food becomes scarce (as it will sooner or later), one of them will always come out on top by however slim a margin, and drive the others to extinction or out of the contested niche. This logic seems to hold for economic competition as well and could thus have been highly relevant for early human evolution. *cf. 97; 178; 188; 218*

Man emerged as his own chief environmental variable, and he is thus both the cause and the effect of accelerating cultural evolution. This vicious feedback obliterated *Homo erectus*, *Homo sapiens neanderthalensis* and probably several related subspecies from the face of the earth in a relatively short time. Unless preventive measures are taken, slightly deviating groups such as Australian aborigines, pygmies, bushmen, Khoisan (Bushmen and Hottentots) and Amazonian Indians will probably go the same way. *cf. 173*

Genetic fine-tuning

No genetic revolution was needed to bridge the gap between *Homo erectus* and *Homo sapiens*; rather, the age-old principle of building on strength was switched from muscular to intellectual power.

> The growth of the brain in the hominid line is the fastest ever achieved. The slow but

steady increase in the relative weight of the mammalian brain provides an interesting perspective.

Geologic period	Prey	Predator
Early Tertiary (60 mill. aBP)	0.18	0.44
Middle Tertiary	0.63	0.76
Modern mammals	0.95	1.10

The numbers represent the encephalization quotient. The mean of modern mammals is arbitrarily assigned a value of 1; *Homo sapiens* then stands for about 10.

Obviously the predator must outwit the prey which in turn tries to go one better, locking the antagonists in an extended competitive race. Now, I have just pointed out that man has long been both his own prey and predator, putting the highest possible premium on cerebral development. The internal politics of the group emphasized the cerebral nature of competition. To get the upper hand, it was necessary to penetrate the opponent's psychological position and beat him at his own game. The ubiquitous contest between fair and foul play has certainly had a share in sharpening the human intellect.

cf. 105; 158

The cortex, in particular, developed at a maximum rate and the mastery of language broadened the base for cultural progress. This evidently compensated for greater vulnerability, an extended childhood and difficulties in childbirth caused by the excessive volume of the foetal brain.

cf. 103

The burst of human intelligence is coupled with a specific adaptation of the vocal apparatus. The construction of the palate in the apes precludes the articulation of human speech, and Neanderthal-man seems to have been subject to similar limitations. *Homo sapiens sapiens* has a lower larynx and a wider pharynx, which facilitates a rich vocalization while an intricate swallowing reflex prevents food from finding its way into the easily accessible respiratory tract.

Long-term co-operation in complex cultural games presupposes genetically prescribed and emotionally actuated group loyalty; in practice, rational argument about its utility is of minor importance. The aptitude for social interplay and coalition-building gave our strain of the genus *Homo* a decisive competitive edge.

cf. 60; 97

cf. 359

Native tribes generally consider only themselves as humans while foreigners are on a par with beasts. Ethnocentrism is the technical term for our deeply engrained bias against aliens and the idolization of one's own people. This parochial outlook has a linguistic dimension; "man" is often synonymous with the name of the tribe excluding everyone else from humanity. Civilized people show the same leanings; in ancient China "han" meant both man and Chinese. Curiously enough, modern English lacks an appropriate word for a human being – a mensch.

Tribes and nations are the super-extended family of the individual. They became vehicles of solidarity and sources of ambition, stimulating the cultural interplay. A cascade of positive but often painful feedback imbued the human plus-sum game with a new spirit.

The well-documented naivety of some isolated tribes is probably typical for our not-so-distant ancestors. The inevitability of death remained unacknowledged and every fatality was ascribed to demons or magic spells. Nor was the causal connection between sexual intercourse and childbirth properly understood. The realization of the fundamental facts of life and death signified a traumatic change of world-view – an irreversible step along the thorny path towards modern man.

In the end we made contact with the supreme game, that conglomerate of emotions for which we have but one poor, abused word – love. Love has always been in short supply but for that very reason it is a fitting measure of the emergence of man. Our selfishness has become conscious, and deep down we crave for an antidote – some charitable spirit in the game.

Love and consciousness raise human dignity and induce self-control, opening new vistas of creative play. The ability to control some instinctive responses does not, however, justify a disregard for human nature, our rich biological birthright. Thus, before we take on human creativity, we had better have a look at the evolution of life and its most spectacular outgrowth, the human brain.

3.3　Self-selective evolution

There are good grounds for assuming that evolution is triggered by changes in behaviour which, again, may be initiated by cultural choice. Radical evolution always happens behind the scenes, carried by a small population, desperately struggling for survival in a different way. When it succeeds, such a group can autocatalytically create its own genetic environment. Man has unconsciously exploited this opportunity but to make the most of our gradually increasing scope for play we must thoroughly understand the irrefutable rules of the game. Only then can we select – within bounds – our own evolution.

The genetic pool

Before examining our human ventures in greater detail, we should first try to come to grips with the spontaneous dynamism of the fundamental life processes. In essence, the base sequence of the DNA in a gene directs the synthesis of *cf. 320* the appropriate protein; mutations in the DNA are generally reflected in the protein structure. Molecular biology has recently revealed many of the moves in *cf. 321* the evolution game (see figure 3.6).

> Cytochrome C is a crucial metabolic enzyme, common to all higher organisms from yeasts to mammals. It is formed by a string of 104 amino acids and, in the course of evolution, no less than 30 mutations have occurred without upsetting the basic function of the enzyme. Cytochrome C is one of the most conservative proteins; the substitution of one per cent of the amino acids takes 20 million years. The rate of genetic change of the globins (haemoglobin and myoglobin), for example, has been more than threefold. Human haemoglobin is dominated by a normal form but systematic screening has revealed around 500 variants, most of them viable. Only 25 of the 287 amino acids of normal human haemoglobin appear to be invariant in all vertebrates and vital for the oxygen-carrying capacity of the protein.

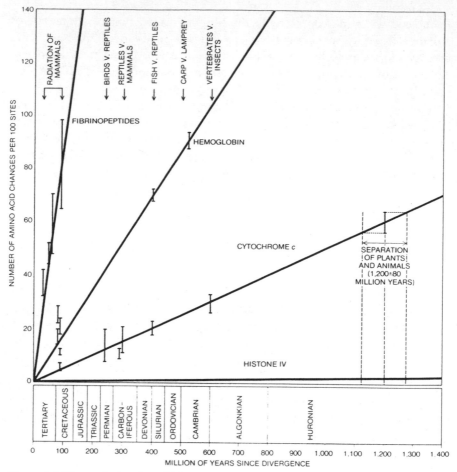

Figure 3.6 The evolution four different proteins (Dickerson, 1972)

The human genome is by no means compliant. A single deviation on a crucial point can cripple the corresponding protein. But many mutations cause only minor or no disturbances. Most human proteins are polymorphs, that is they appear in two or more modifications. These are not morbid divergencies; rather it is a question of normal (or perhaps we should say neutral) heterogenicity, which makes every person unique even at the primitive protein level.

Neutral mutations go a long way to explaining the surprising variegation of the genetic material within a species. New mutations are continually produced, and can be "kept in reserve" over long periods, so that diversity is maintained despite the unceasing selective pressure. Hybridization by way of sexual reproduction, and the accompanying recombination of the genes (meiosis, crossover) effectively mixes the cards and multiplies the potential for differentiation. Non-beneficient genes can be kept in check since they are generally recessive, in other words they do not manifest themselves when paired with normal genes. Genetic polymorphism is often strongly correlated with improved competitiveness because it opens the door to endless permutations, many of them displaying heterozygotic superiority.

> A well-documented example is the human sickle cell anaemia, caused by a point mutation in the haemoglobin gene. (The deoxygenated red blood cells are deformed and look like sickles.) The illness is endemic in malarial areas, and in primitive conditions leads to the early death of homozygotes (when the deleterious gene is inherited from both parents). Heterozygotes, on the other hand, are more resistant to malaria than normal individuals. This potentially lethal gene is thus important to the survival of the population as a whole.
>
> If 40 per cent of the population are heterozygotic carriers of the defective gene, then on average:
> – 16 per cent of the children will be very anaemic and barely able to survive;
> – 48 per cent will be slightly anaemic but relatively resistant to malaria; and
> – 36 per cent will be normal but will have low resistance to malaria.

Genuinely hereditary diseases depend on a definite genetic defect, often coupled to enzyme insufficiency (there were about 5,000 recorded instances by 1990). Proneness to many or perhaps most human infirmities is also genetically conditioned. Rheumatism, infantile diabetes, multiple sclerosis, blood-vessel disorders, dementia and many cancers are substantiated cases while schizophrenia, manic depression, alcoholism and even criminal behaviour appear to be clearly implicated. The concepts of "health" or "normality" are quite fuzzy; our built-in weaknesses keep the options open in the evolutionary plus-sum game.

> The value of diversity in the gene pool is dramatically highlighted by the reaction of the   *cf. 125*
> banana fly to mutagenic radiation. The vitality of the radiated population increases in
> comparison with an untreated reference group. An increase in the exposure to mutagens
> may thus strengthen the species in the long run.

Natural selection remains the final disciplinarian of genetic change. The redundancy of the genetic code allows nucleotide substitutions which do not affect   *cf. 321* protein synthesis. These are two to three times as frequent as efficacious mutations. The life process generally insists on veracity in the duplication of immemorial prescriptions but in many of the finer details it can be rather forgiving.

Protean variability

Thermophilic "archaebacteria" are apparently the oldest surviving forms of life. They gave rise to the fairly uncomplicated prokaryotes (bacteria and blue algae) as well as the more sophisticated eukaryotic organisms. Despite, or perhaps because of their simple streamlined design, the prokaryotes are still full of vigour, displaying unparalleled adaptability.

> In the prokaryotes, the greater part of the DNA is located in a long thread but DNA also
> occurs in the form of plasmids – ring-formed self-replicating structures. Plasmid genes   *cf. 322*
> can be exchanged between bacteria and can even be transmitted from one species to
> another; plasmid-programmed enzymes have proved to be key factors in the quick
> adaptation of pathogenic bacteria to antibiotics. Extraneous pieces of DNA can easily

cf. 324 be incorporated into the plasmid ring, a fact which is exploited in the laboratory controlled introduction of alien genes into micro-organisms.

The genome of the prokaryote Escherichia coli, a familiar intestinal bacterium, consists of about 4,000 genes, most of them mapped in detail. This "primitive" organism incorporates sophisticated cybernetic feedback: at least 100 different proteins are involved in regulating motility, metabolism, membrane transport and the like, according to the inputs from the environment. The complexity of genetic play is accentuated in the higher organisms where the genome is concentrated in a clearly distinguishable nucleus. These eukaryotes – yeasts and moulds, fungi, protozoa and all plants and animals – are still in many ways *terra* cf. 323 *incognita* for the geneticists.

Surprisingly, most of the DNA of eukaryotic cells seems to consist of inactive and apparently useless genetic ballast or padding (introns and pseudogenes). Some regions of the genome are stuffed with highly variable sequences which act as personal hereditary imprints but serve no identifiable purpose; elsewhere useless information may be repeated thousands of times. The self-reproductive expansionism of the genes has been invoked as an explanation but it is still a mystery why natural selection has accepted such persistent luxury. One possibility is that the correct expression of the functional cf. 323 genes requires an extensive set of spacers. Be that as it may, the eukaryotes seem to command a good deal of anonymous genetic material of no specific destination – blank pages as it were.

The genome does not hold enough information to prescribe a fully-fledged organism in all its particulars. The intricate process of embryonic differentiation and growth are particularly difficult to account for in terms of molecular biology. One way out is to interpret the morphology and survival strategy of a cf. 24; 99; 320 species as a coherent set of strange attractors, a complex but well-ordered outcome of a quasi-chaotic interplay between the proteinaceous actors.

This conjecture may look strained but some support can be drawn from straightforward computer simulation. Michael Barnsley (see *Fractals Everywhere*, 1988) has constructed a sequence of increasingly fern-like structures just by playing around randomly with four basic transformations of the plane. The end result is an accurate rendition of the black spleenwort fern! (see figure 3.7)

In a similar vein the spots and stripes of many mammals can be traced back to a simple genetic program, which is played out over time and stopped at a preselected stage. The pattern evolves from the single streak of the badger to the composite striping of the Zebra and the rich patchwork of leopards and giraffes.

Figure 3.7 The emeergence of a black spleenwort fern (Gleick, 1988)

We should be wary of attaching any sort of utilitarian design to the incredibly efficient mechanisms of life. Nevertheless, shorter feedback loops may exist than those conventionally embodied in Neo-Darwinian dogma.

> Our immune response is conditioned to tolerate "self" by an early process of self-extinction (reverse Darwinism). Later on, the orchestrated hypermutation of immunoglobulin genes can produce a profusion of antibodies to find the right match for an alien antigene. This response takes a few days but remains imprinted for life in the fine-tuned immunological memory. The behavioural adaptability of animals is equally remarkable. Dogs can adopt new inheritable behaviour within ten generations, and blackcaps (Sylvia atricapilla) have recently come up with a remarkable shift in their hereditary pattern of migration.

There is mounting evidence for some sort of short-cuts in the acquisition of inheritable information in eukaryotes. The signs of extragenetic learning and recollection are especially intriguing. The search should be on for a short-term memory, with narrow access to the ultra-conservative DNA code.   *cf. 323*

> Cancerous cells are convenient objects for study, because they are "immortal" in the sense that they reproduce without limit in a suitable growth medium. Treatment with cell poisons like metotrexat will kill most of the cells but the survivors develop resistance, due to small fragments of DNA called "double minutes" (DM) situated within the cell nucleus but outside the chromosomes. DM carries the genetic program for an enzyme which enhances the synthesis of new DNA, and counters the cytostatic action of metotrexat. Initially the resistance is reversible and the DM disappears if the poison is withdrawn, but if the challenge continues for several months DM is permanently established in the chromosomes of some cells, and resistance becomes inheritable within these particular cell lines.
>   A metotrexat challenge may also cause a doubling of the gene responsible for production of a detoxification enzyme; gene doubling in malignant cell lines is not uncommon during long-term treatment of cancer patients with cytostatic agents. Furthermore, it has been shown that the incidence of "useful" mutations in Escherichia coli can be significantly higher than the random background rate. This does not necessarily infer "directed" mutations; the driving force could be a generalized stress-induced increase in mutagenicity, fervently probing for a life-saving exit.

Genetic change may not depend exclusively on capricious chance but can be the outcome of adaptive cellular learning. Easily transferable chromosome pieces, (called transposons) further increase the versatility of the genome. As mentioned above, prokaryotic cells apply similar stratagems in building up resistance to a multiplicity of drugs. The logic of life does not, even at a primitive stage, rely solely on luck, but acts in adversity with purposeful resilience. Such self-direction does not contradict Darwinism *per se*; deep down the adaptive mechanisms have always been learnt by trial and error.

Culture-induced evolution

It would seem that particularly among birds and mammals, the central nervous system allows for an abundance of internal representations, each one simulating an alternative mode of action. We may safely assume that germinal creative responses can guide this dissipative system in unpredictable directions. An individual, and consequently a species, is thus part of an open process in which even the weakest impulses can be followed up in many different ways instead of being channelled towards a stable and predetermined solution of the existential game.

> Tools have always been regarded as a human prerogative but animals, too, sometimes employ aids extrinsic to themselves. Egyptian vultures use stones to crush ostrich eggs, and sea otters apply a similar technique to open abalone mussels. Such behaviour is largely genetically determined but many predators, such as wolves and killer whales, have to learn to hunt; they are only vaguely programmed for collaboration in groups. Apes, and in particular chimpanzees, exhibit locally deviating subcultures. Among birds, mocking of a new predator species is quickly induced and can persist over several generations even in the complete absence of adverse experiences.
>
> The most spectacular case of documented animal acculturation started off during the Second World War when some blue-tits in south-west England hit upon the idea of piercing the seals of milk bottles left by the milkman on the doorstep. This innovation gradually spread throughout Western Europe, until at least 20 species of birds had adopted it. Socializing titmice were particularly quick at learning while the response of solitary species, like robins, was slower.

There are good grounds for assuming that evolutionary metamorphosis is triggered by changes in behaviour, spurred on by incessant intraspecific competition. This pathfinder function has not escaped the attention of some of the leading lights of the scientific community (Karl Popper, Konrad Lorenz, Edward and Allan Wilson to name but a few). Behavioural traits show a remarkable phylogenetic plasticity compared with morphological characteristics. Accordingly, cultural fluctuation may be the kernel in the seed of evolutionary change. Almost imperceptible collective, or even individual preferences can release a self-reinforcing process of adaptation into the environment.

> Darwin's Galapagos finches, for example, may originally have evolved subcultures adapted mainly to the varying sources of food on the different islands. Favourable leads then started a long process of self-selection from within the available genetic material. Amended by new mutations, it brought out considerable differentiation of the beaks, in particular, and also induced the use of thorn tools.

Cultural choice gradually establishes a frame of "values", which modify the rules of the protracted game of morphological adjustment. A pervasive culture can, over time, autocatalytically create its own genetic environment. Evolution may thus, occasionally, acquire a purposeful direction, freeing itself from meaningless repetition in some genetic cul-de-sac.

In the world of molecular biology, too, the old nature versus nurture argument is beginning to appear rather passé. If blind genetic variability allows a broad repertoire of behaviour patterns, cultural choice will soon be able to pick up a suitable set of self-selected action programmes. Commendable conduct *cf. 105* will then become genetically entrenched in Darwinian feedback processes. Without stumbling into teleological argument, we could go even further and surmise that the genome of higher organisms incorporates rudimentary simulation models of the struggle for life. Some kind of slowly accumulated foreknowledge, an implicit representation of crucial existential rules, would then endorse new developments of the genetic game.

Concealed innovation

Classical evolution theory focuses on the main driving-forces – selection and chance mutations – but neglects the weakest and perchance the most important one: individual preference, personal latitude, the almost foredoomed attempts of the deviant group to survive in a different way. The interplay between genetic variation, epigenetically determined behaviour patterns, and local cultural differences generates an evanescent chain of feedback which transmits the steering impulses of relatively free and flexible behaviour to the slow process of morphologically manifest genetic change.

Large populations with intensive gene exchange are almost bound to stagnate or to fall into the trap of excessive specialization. The severe internecine struggle drives piecemeal optimization but precludes innovative leaps and sometimes produces evolutionary oddities. The tendency towards segregation among *cf. 90; 325; 361* many animal species is thus of some moment. A conservative dependence on territory, particularly during the reproductive phase, preserves the cultural and genetic heritage of marginal groups. The result is differentiation; new races and *cf. 191* species emerge with novel adaptive concepts.

> The logic of competition, as expressed in Gause's law, can force speciation by a mecha- *cf. 89* nism called character displacement. Normally, the genotype of a species adheres to the mean but if the environment is more effectively exploited by a mixed strategy, the fringes may profit from a window of opportunity. The middle ground is then squeezed by excessive competition while the deviants enjoy more room for manoeuvre. In the end the original species is neatly split in two, each one occupying distinct parts of the expanded niche.

The runaway successes naturally dominate the fossil material at the expense of progressive transitional forms. Radical evolution always happens behind the scenes, carried by a small population. The decisive advances have probably been achieved by seriously endangered species and allopatric minigroups tottering on the edge of annihilation, their strength born of desperate weakness. *cf. 88; 136; 156; 178; 339*

> Unselfish behaviour goes against the grain of evolution despite its potential value to the species. Reciprocally altruistic behaviour has some staying power but, to gain the upper *cf. 339* hand, it must be embraced by at least a substantial minority in the group. Only in a small *cf. 59* population can the critical frequency for the altruistic gene be exceeded, triggering off the mechanisms of group selection. Surviving "selfish" genes will, nevertheless, hang on as free-riders, evading the personal costs of self-sacrifice. Without persistent negative feedback, such as unpleasant consequences for bad behaviour, selfishness will sooner or later win the day and cause a breakdown in the collaborative game.

So was Jean Baptiste de Lamarck (1744–1829) right after all? He was certainly wrong about the actual mechanisms involved. Mercifully, we do not carry on the acquired vices of our forebears. Imposed behaviour is certainly not inherited, however hard Trofim Lysenko (1898–1976) and Joseph Stalin (1879–1953) may have tried to tell both maize and men how to behave. Or, as Martin Luther (1483–1546) put it, "good deeds do not make a good man". But a good man does perform good deeds. By spreading the good tidings he can penetrate

the minds of his fellow-beings, setting off a cascade of cybernetic feedback and affecting the very core of the dissipative process we call spiritual life, with
cf. 417 possible repercussions for the genetic code itself.

We have no yardstick for this extremely weak primary interaction, but we would be wise to listen to Luther and beware of overestimating the strength of its influence. For the seed to germinate, it must fall on good soil where it can
cf. 178 initiate open and evolving processes. By its inherited causality, predestination holds all creation, including man, in its iron grip. Only by respecting the inescapable rules of the game can we realize ourselves and exploit our unparalleled cerebral capacity, making the most of the gradually increasing scope for
cf. 418 play. Only then can we select – within bounds – our own evolution.

3.4   Creative brainpower

Our hypertrophic cerebral cortex represents a tremendous increase in creativity. An impressive array of parallel connected hardware extracts successively higher levels of abstraction from the raw input data. As the concepts broaden, more dispersed synaptic networks are brought into play. Sense perception and muscular commands have their given places in the cortex, but memory, reasoning, imagination – "thinking" in short – seem to be realized in widely distributed, hologram-like patterns. Although human intelligence is genetically determined up to about 70 per cent, heritability is much weaker since extraordinary intelligence is connected with rare gene combinations, which usually come apart in the next generation.

Human head start

In the previous pages we have been probing the complexities of the evolution game, with particular emphasis on the main actor, *Homo sapiens*. Over the ages successive seals of approval have literally inscribed life-promoting rules of human conduct onto our genetic code. Conservative elements were gradually pushed into the background by the evolving brain, and man became the chief agent of his own change. The sudden intensification of evolution is the result of ferocious cultural competition.

Our hypertrophic cerebral cortex constitutes the physiological basis for a tremendous leap forward in creativity. It is the seat of intelligence, of consciousness and of linguistic capacity; here the drama of man is played out in all its abundant variety. The human brain consists of at least 100 billion nerve cells or neurons, each one invested with anything up to 10,000 connections called synapses. About 90 per cent of the brain cells are situated in the cerebral cortex.

Every neuron is an independent microcosmos: it can make or break synaptic contacts which inhibit or excite each other by firing off electrochemical signals, either slowly or in bursts of up to 1,000 times per second. The hypercomplex electrochemical network is constantly rewiring itself in a self-instructive mode. Furthermore, the brain is supplemented by a variety of hormonally active neurotransmitters. About one hundred have been characterised to date but the number of these neuropeptides may be much greater. To complicate matters, *cf. 425* the brain has many features of an analog computer; the strength of synaptic interaction is continuously variable.

> The human brain is the culmination of molecular and cellular self-organization. The theoretical capacity of our brain is about 10^{15} bits, rivalling the content of all the books ever written. Like other meaningfully complex systems it possesses the ability to surpass itself. The opportunities for play are generally far richer than the rules of the game; human thought is immeasurably more complex than its material base. Gödel has put it as follows, reasoning from his own undecidability theorem: "... the description of what a mechanism is doing in certain cases is more involved than the description of the mechanism (itself), it requires ... higher types". The wiring diagram of the brain relates *cf. 73; 105* to thinking in the same way as an exquisite instrument relates to the music performed on it.

Even though around half of the human genome is dedicated to the nervous system, it falls far short of any precise blueprint. Instead the genetic message probably consists of general directives regarding the overall architecture, enhanced by pertinent instructions about the microstructure. *cf. 94*

> Explicit data can often be compacted into a fraction of its apparent volume; the decimal expression of π has no bounds but it can be calculated to an arbitrary number of digits by applying a short computer program. The key element in such a directive is the final command "and so on", which can generate an endless string of "new" data. The logical depth of such numbers is quite high but their complexity is low, since the latter depends on the amount of information enbedded in the generating rule. *cf. 389*
> The Mandelbrot set is a wonderful example of the power of simple iteration when applied in an imaginative way. Similarly, the genome directs a hypercomplex game which arrives at a set of non-computable strange attractors – the highly individual neural network of the brain. Conscious thought, the actual play of this supercomputer, is twice removed from the rules of neural recombination, and entails another loop of irreducible complexity which will forever defeat our powers of prediction.

The central nervous system of the foetus evolves at an accelerating rate, starting with the phylogenetically oldest structures. The cerebral cortex is completed in one last amazing spurt. At birth the child's brain is numerically complete; few if any new nerve cells are formed later on and some have already been weeded out. Cell-formation clearly exceeds needs; during maturation, the surplus neurons are unable to make a sufficient number of purposeful contacts and perish in a well-directed competitive game. This is an instructive display of Darwinian *cf. 69; 103* self-organization which recurs in human learning processes. For neurons as well *cf. 112; 184*

as for humans, the only game plan is to make sense of confused perceptions,
cf. 109; 112 clutching at any attainable meaning.

Brainy design

The architecture of the brain is basically hierarchic but the diverse processes are strongly interactive and the chains of command are frequently bypassed. Younger structures, with the cortex at the top, dominate the limbic system and the hypothalamus, which in turn regulate the endocrine system through the
cf. 80; 394 pituitary gland.

> We have already noted that the more primitive parts of the brain exert a strong influence on the intellectual functions, and we may well wonder who is ultimately in charge? The cortex certainly chooses the means but the limbic system, which is presumed to be the
> *cf. 82; 391* site of the emotions, is heavily involved in setting the aims.

Like the rest of the body, the brain exhibits a right-left symmetry, but most information from the senses travels diagonally. Thus, the right hand is governed by the left frontal lobe and the sensation of touch follows the same cross-connectional pattern. The left-hand field of vision is mapped onto the right occipital lobe and the right ear reports mainly to the left auditory cortex. With this proviso, the location of the nerve inputs in the cortex follow fairly clear geometrical mapping principles. Particularly sensitive organs such as eyes, lips, tongue and fingertips are allowed to command a correspondingly disproportionate share of the data-processing capacity. Sense impressions generally pass first to the cerebral cortex, reaching lower levels only after evaluation by ingenious data-processing. The sense of smell is an exception; it is linked directly to the limbic system. Olfactory and taste sensations thus carry an immediate impact.

> Despite the abundance of neural connections in the brain we ought to look for economic principles in cerebral processes. After all, the complex behaviour of a bee is programmed by no more than 50,000 neurons. In an elegantly written essay (*Vehicles*, 1984) Valentino Braitenberg presents a series of speculative, cybernetic automatons as models for the evolution of the brain and the mind. Starting from simple fundamental elements and easily comprehensible feedback, he conjures up a whole series of purposeful behaviours right up to a general guiding principle, a self-realising "*Zweckoptimis-*
> *cf. 393* *mus*" (expedient optimism) – Ernst Bloch's (1885–1977) "*Prinzip Hoffnung*" in its most primitive version.
>
> In cybernetic terms, mental activities are aspects of an ultra-ergodic process, meaning that the interplay of self-organising synaptic clusters is non-transparent and never
> *cf. 72* repeats itself. Such neural networks can sustain both superimposed and self-completing modes of play. Intensive training quickly recruits half-employed neurons into an expanding syndicate of co-operating members. By amassing neural data-handling capacity, the acuity of sensory input and motoric control can be greatly enhanced: reliable
> *cf. 335; 407* performance can be extracted from rather unreliable components. A single neuron can play many roles simultaneously, and take part in a multitude of evolving structures each of which can severally retain, integrate or retrieve distinct information, as the case may be. Hence the hologrammatic decentralization, the powers of association and classification, the flexibility and the robustness of the human brain.

The cerebral cortex is, physiologically speaking, an extremely introverted thought machine. Less than one per cent of the synaptic contacts of the cortex are available for communication with sense organs and the rest of the brain. By far the greater part of its data-processing activity is literally spent reflecting on itself.

> The onslaught of new experience calls for continuous reprogramming of the synaptic network. According to Francis Crick (*What Mad Pursuit*, 1988, together with Graeme Mitchison) we dream in order to get rid of pseudo-memories: meaningless associations, parasitic modes of eduction, false connections as it were. Dreams are collections of computational garbage which, if retained, would clog the data processor and prevent the fixation of long-term memory. The Australian hedgehog seems to be the only mammal which does not dream; accordingly it is burdened with an inefficient, oversized brain. Getting rid of our daily misapprehensions might be the chief function of dream-producing REM-sleep. This mishmash is a scrambled projection of human fears and desires, obsessions and frustrations – as such an inexhaustible source of unconventional ideas.

By painstaking research the first stages in the processing of sensory signals have been charted. An impressive array of parallel connected hardware is extracting successively higher levels of abstraction from the raw input data. As the concepts broaden, more dispersed synaptic networks are brought into play – an important functional principle of the brain. Still, these are early days: for instance the organization of short, medium- and long-term memory is known about only in very general terms.

> The cerebral mechanism of information retrieval is still mysterious, at least in its details. The successive stimulation (by an electrode) of a distinct point on the cortex can evoke quite different recollections while the same remembrance can be recalled in a separate location. Faults in the short-term memory produce ludicrous effects when people, while perfectly articulate, immediately forget what they are saying. But too much remembrance has similarly debilitating consequences. A.R. Luria (1902–77) reports the astounding feats of a mnemonist who possessed a faultless and ineradicable recall of the most trivial things. His computer-like mind could not forget anything and was thus incapable of real understanding or the slightest creative effort.

For the present, we must be content with a rather crude and sketchy account of our brain processes. Nevertheless, our limited knowledge may provide some pointers for our inquiry into human creativity.

Mental asymmetry

In contrast to animals, the human cerebral hemispheres exhibit considerable differentiation while the interaction between the left and right halves is remarkably sparse. Lobotomy – severing the connecting nerve tissue – certainly affects the personality but nevertheless seems to be of surprisingly little consequence.

> Electroencephalography (EEG) and, more recently, magnetic resonance imaging (MRI) have revealed the presence of highly chaotic states during epileptic seizures. Before the advent of suitable drugs, a lobotomy was the only available remedy because it decreased connectedness and thus suppressed chaos in a crude manner.

The availability of lobotomized patients created a new branch of brain research which revealed a striking specialization between the two halves of the brain. The right hemisphere cannot, for example, verbalize its intelligence or even name the simplest object but it has a remarkable capacity for spatial problem-solving. Muddled speech is not, after all, necessarily equivalent to muddled thought.

At least the following faculties exhibit a clear right-left partiality:

Left hemisphere	Right hemisphere
Linguistic skills	Musicality
Logic manipulation	Multidimensional perception
Information analysis	Empathy
Deduction	Intuition, imagination

The left half, which controls the right side of the body, is markedly intellectual while the right half is more emotionally orientated and shows much less differentiation. Almost all (99 per cent) right-handers exhibit clearly delimited centres of speech and verbal understanding on the left side (Broca's and Wernicke's areas). The exceptional ability to learn languages is a specific human talent, equivalent to the acoustic radar of dolphins or bats.

> In one case out of three, the language centre of left-handers is located in the right hemisphere. If right-handedness is enforced on this substantial minority, the verbal message must first be transferred to the left hemisphere before it can be written down. These covert left-handers show a remarkable aptitude for writing in mirror script – the most famous example being Leonardo da Vinci (1452–1519). The mirror conversion makes for a direct connection to the right side, facilitating linguistic articulation.

Speech centres are of course indispensable to verbalization but this does not mean that we actually speak with the Broca-Wernicke areas. The undamaged brain is an integrated whole; we express ourselves by applying all the available cerebral capacity. Sense perception and muscular commands have their given places in the cortex, but memory, reasoning, imagination – "thinking" in short – seem to be realized in widely distributed, hologram-like patterns.

> Using new techniques, like positron emitting tomography (PET) and magnetoencephalography (MEG), it is now possible to study quantitative changes in brain activity under different kinds of stimuli. Intellectual tasks activate quite specific patterns in the left half of the brain while emotional commitment triggers off more indefinite reactions on the right side. Women generally show less differentiation between the hemispheres than men (which may explain why women compete separately in cerebral sports, like bridge and chess, as well).
>
> Written Japanese provides an opportunity to check human symbol-handling procedures. Unsurprisingly, the analytic *Kana* signs for syllables and single letters activate the speech centres of the left side while the *Kanji* symbols, which designate whole concepts, are primarily processed by the right half of the brain. (Sometimes homophonic Kanji-signs are traced on the palm of the listener's hand to ensure proper communication.)

At every step, brain research is confronted by apparent inconsistencies. The distributive working mode is contradicted by a host of observations which have been made on the effects of localized lesions.

> Strokes often cause selective physical disablement but more surprising is the accompanying, often highly specific impairment of our intellectual abilities. Problems of recognition and/or naming can appear in weird combinations. Prosopagnosia, the inability to recognize faces, is caused by brain damage to a small, clearly defined locus. Aculcalia, arithmetic incapacitation, may preclude counting beyond the number four; writing can be restricted to the consonants only – all without serious loss of other human faculties. Intense training tends to compress the corresponding brain activities to a minimum space which might account for the selective loss of these deeply ingrained capabilities. The most disturbing (but merciful) lesion is anosognosia: the inability to recognize or acknowledge your own mental deficit – a very, very common affliction.

cf. 150

It has become commonplace to link creative work to the right hemisphere and to ascribe a critical-analytical function to the left, but this is an oversimplification. Creativity calls for whole-hearted commitment, which mobilizes the entire brain as well as the endocrine system.

Cerebral learning

At birth a human infant is completely helpless; a few atavistic reflexes such as grasping and rudimentary walking disappear within days or weeks, and have to be laboriously relearned at a more conscious level. Even the most primaeval skills call for intensive training of the central nervous system.

> Visual data processing must be laboriously learned in early childhood. Diffuse light will not do the trick: the synapses of the visual cortex will not connect properly without adequate stimulation. Likewise, the movements of a newborn are completely uncoordinated because several nerve fibres compete in activating the same bundle of muscles. Motoric competence is acquired only through extensive exercise by the painstaking elimination of contradictory nerve contacts.
>
> Once our motoric responses have become second nature they are relegated to servant status, to be summoned at our will and whim. Curiously enough, our impulse to move can be recorded a fraction of a second before we become conscious of our intention, putting another question mark behind the enigma of free will?

cf. 69; 99

Language learning, too, calls for intensive practice and the concomitant neural conditioning. Children are spontaneous players of the language game, soaking up the rules according to preprogrammed principles. It is just a question of evoking an existing but latent proficiency.

cf. 355

> "Nurture" proponents have devoted considerable energy to teaching chimpanzees and gorillas to talk but they have never broken through the three-word barrier (e.g. mummy, daddy, food), maybe because the anatomy of the anthropoid apes inhibits the requisite formation of sounds. Attempts to develop sign languages have been more successful, although it is difficult to draw definite conclusions. A real symbolic function, related to conscious internal representations (thinking) is still very much in doubt. Communication with animals is an ancient dream but apes lack the Broca-Wernicke areas, and this fact alone should serve to cast doubt on the somewhat overblown expectations.

cf. 90

Generally speaking, our inborn aptitudes provide a creative potential, but active tutoring is critical; adverse conditions can seriously block normal development. Unfortunately, a "superenvironment" does not seem to do very much for the genetically underprivileged, although the flexibility of the human brain is rather impressive. Severe brain damage can be made good, at least partially, with the help of systematic mental training. In a young child the whole speech centre can be transferred to the right half of the brain which then acts as a reliable stand-by.

Our imperfect intellect seems to be in need of recurrent challenges to retain its elasticity. Some chessmasters, scientists or artists fail to live up to their early promise, but plenty of examples of the opposite prove that this is no law of nature. The loss of brain neurons, which accelerates with age, may simply mean that the nerve cells are giving up and pass away after waiting in vain for a meaningful mission.

Genetic democracy

We must not close our eyes to the perhaps unpalatable fact that cerebral capacity is inherited more or less in the same way as physical appearance. Paradoxically, the genetic game of chance guarantees a certain measure of intellectual equality in the population. If the social setting were decisive to the development of intelligence and creativity, then a rigid class society would be the only stable political structure. Slight variations in external circumstances would irresistibly amplify themselves in every new generation. The presumed end result would be the complete segregation of the gifted from the rest.

Many superficial characteristics, such as eye colouring, can be traced back to a single gene pair or a few linked genes which follow strict Mendelian rules. Intellectual ability, however, depends on the interplay of numerous factors, and the mathematics of heredity becomes exceedingly complex. Extraordinary intelligence is connected with rare gene combinations which usually come apart in the next generation. The consequence is that the children of both gifted and untalented persons alike tend to be closer to the average than their parents. It is in the very nature of the genetic game to redistribute and equalize the odds.

Ever since the early days of Alfred Binet (1857–1911) the idea of measuring intelligence has attracted social technologists. To quantify unequivocally the intellectual capacity of the individual, to place every cog in its right position in the wheels of society was an irresistible idea! But enthusiasm has waned since numerous discrepancies began to disturb the polished surface of impartial quantitive investigation. Cultural bias is a persistant problem and to crown it all the tests suggest a ranking order between the races with yellow at the top and black at the bottom (the Japanese have an average intelligence quotient of 111). On the other hand, the standard deviation in intelligence quotient in the USA between sisters and brothers (11) is of the same order of magnitude as that in the population as a whole (17).

Intelligence testing has produced an endless stream of contradictory results. It is apparently very difficult to sort out these sensitive relationships in a cool scientific manner. The strong correlation between the results of classical intelligence tests and pure speed of reaction offers a suggestive starting point. Quicker action increases the performance of a computer, and it seems reasonable that the intellect can be sharpened in the same way, other things being equal.

The gift of comprehension is genetically determined up to about 70 per cent, even if heritability is much weaker, as explained above. Despite the unsettled genetics of intelligence, evolution has succeeded over the ages in producing the central nervous system of *Homo sapiens*.

> The very plasticity of intelligent behaviour drives the genetic selection (the Baldwin Effect). As newborn babies, we are all equally stupid but individuals closer to the optimum brain structure will learn quicker and have a survival advantage. Once again we see how the human race has created its own selection pressure. Even if some crucial behaviour patterns may become hard-wired over time, intelligent flexibility carries the highest premium and makes for accelerating evolution. *cf. 90; 96*

Systematic attempts at intellectual "breeding" would come up against formidable difficulties – even disregarding our ethical apprehensions. Eugenics is a scientific and political minefield in which most people are happier to fudge the issues. What we could and should try to do is to avoid negative selection, and even this calls for the greatest caution, considering the superficial state of our present knowledge.

Our limited experience with lower forms of life shows us that while some specific characteristics can easily be added, deleted or enhanced, the resultant organisms inevitably suffer a loss of vitality. Wild forms are generally superior in an open environment where the continual trial and error of natural selection successively upgrades the species. Unless we want to degrade man by turning him into a domesticated animal, unfit for independence, we must remain very cautious in the deliberate amendment of human intelligence.

> Our brain is much more than a specimen of highly-refined computer power, but even in computer terms it is probably approaching the limits of the possible. Mathematical stability criteria affirm that increasing complexity must be compensated for by a decrease in connectedness; otherwise a self-generated internal catastrophe will occur. Indeed, systems on the edge of chaos can perform the most complex computations. Genius is seldom far from mental aberration; chaos is the cybernetic neighbour of creativity. *cf. 101*

The distinguishing feature of *Homo sapiens* is his ability to observe himself, to step outside his own condition, to question both inherited and social directives. Conscious manipulation of our own genetic make-up is a logical extension of this creative self-reference – an enticing lure beset with misgivings until we have recognized our innermost limitations and really understood the basis for our own creativity. *cf. 73; 99; 335; 418*

3.5　　Charting creativity

The baffling act of creation does not lend itself to an exhaustive analysis. In total ignorance, random trial and error is the only available research strategy, but intelligent beings, men or animals, are rarely placed in such incomprehensible situations. We instinctively look for illuminating features, always working towards a holistic interpretation where the new knowledge will fit in. Only the totality of existence is utterly inaccessible to comprehensive conceptualization; it transcends every intellectual framework.

An intellectual bind

We take great pride in the capability of the human brain, and yet man's technological achievements pale before the marvels of biology. A single eukaryotic cell surpasses all human machines and factories many times over in efficiency, economy and dependability. A certain measure of humility is thus called for. Human inventiveness, our conscious ingenuity, appears rather trite when compared with the continuing biological miracle which is the prerequisite of our existence.

cf. 105　　Surveying creativity presupposes some kind of meta-creativity – a paradoxical situation which also faces us when we talk about language or think about thought or try to find out the truth about truth. Any attempt at an exhaustive analysis stems from pure intellectual vanity, a pointless urge to trivialise creative play.

> Sociological "structuralism" vividly illustrates this tendency. The efforts of Vladimir Propp (1895–1970) and Claude Lévi-Strauss to force folktales and myths into dogmatic schemata (Propp suggests 31 plots and seven characters) may perhaps yield a dividend in terms of conceptual convenience. The related effort to conjure up a supersemiotics as a common denominator for literature and art – indeed for every aspect of human culture
> *cf. 297; 349*　 – is proof of incredible hubris.

Behaviourist psychology exhibited a similar contempt for the creative spirit, *cf. 307* scantily disguised as scientific rigour. In the heyday of behaviourism innumerable rats were made to suffer in protracted tests where the only way of solving the given problem was to apply a stochastic search strategy, a blind fumbling for an electric switch or the right way out of a maze. Once the rat had solved the puzzle, subsequent runs went faster and faster. So what have we discovered from all this abuse of trial and error? Simply that "he who seeks, will find", and that "practice makes perfect". Perseverance and industry are indubitable components of creativity but the behaviouristic pursuits were an affront to common sense.

In total ignorance, random trial and error is no doubt the only available research strategy, but intelligent beings, men or animals, are rarely placed in such incomprehensible situations. The precisely-defined experimental conditions of the behaviourist typically exclude any kind of sensible response and diverge radically from real life. The gestalt psychologists soon reacted against this barren approach and started to investigate the innate ability of man and the higher animals to grasp complex relationships by using internal representations of the real world. In other words they allowed the subjects to think: to learn by making meaningful mental mistakes.

> In his classical experiments on chimpanzees (1917), Wolfgang Köhler (1887–1967) showed that apes can use tools intelligently. After considerable thought and a few unsuccessful trials, the chimps managed to use the rods at hand to get at some bananas which were beyond their normal reach. Later studies in the field and in zoos have confirmed the inventiveness of the apes and of chimpanzees in particular.

Human beings are normally able to take in their surroundings and assess alternative strategies; above all they are in a position to consider whether it is worthwhile tackling the problem at all. Only the totality of existence is utterly inaccessible to comprehensive conceptualization; it transcends every intellectual framework and can reduce men to the state of disorientated rats, each one trapped on his own personal treadmill.

Ingenious bisociation

The creative process seems to be exceedingly erratic and unpredictable – something of an outrage to methodical minds. There has been no lack of heroic attempts to get a hold on creativity. The most famous example is Hegel's dialectic scheme whereby thesis and antithesis are welded into a creative synthesis. Hegel himself was convinced that he had dialectically deduced the basic truths of the Christian creed from first principles. His ideas do not lack a certain grandeur, but they have been vulgarised and pushed to absurd lengths by followers on both the right and the left, the most notable instance being Marx .

Arthur Koestler (1905–83) has, in the *Act of Creation* (1964), enriched the Hegelian system with Bergsonian ideas. According to this Koestlerian dialectic, the core of the creative process is bisociation, that is to say the combination and overlapping of disparate or previously unrelated elements.

A simple joke can be elegantly analyzed with the help of Koestler's scheme.

> A well-meaning visitor to a mental hospital watches one of the patients fishing, with great concentration, in the swimming pool. He says: "How's your catch been today my good man?" The patient looks at him with obvious disgust and counters his question with another: "Have *you* ever caught any fish in a swimming pool?"

Humour is quite rightly perceived as an original display of human creativity. Charlie Chaplin's (1889–1977) brilliantly constructed gags have cinema audiences clutching themselves in agonised laughter – with tears in their eyes. An author like Thomas Mann saw himself first and foremost as a humorist, and

Franz Kafka (1883–1924) was sometimes unable to suppress his mirth as he read aloud from his early drafts to a circle of friends. Laughter is the soundest of reactions to a quasi-logical but literally non-sensical state of play, the ever-present absurdities of life.

Parody and caricature have always been employed to cut exaggerated preten-sion down to size, and during the Middle ages the court jester could achieve the position of a licensed truth-teller. But more often than not the joke is an act of aggression. Schoolchildren apply crude mockery in their jostling for position in the pecking-order, and adults all too easily indulge in egotistical self-assertion by making fun of others. Malicious double exposure of human frailty readily produces tragic as well as comic effects. The butt gradually becomes a victi-mized laughing-stock, and the joker turns into a clown bringing ridicule on himself – a primitive defence mechanism resembling the gestures of submission employed by men and animals alike.

Koestler regards self-aggrandizement and self-denial as opposite poles with physiological counterparts in the endocrine system. The argument is extended to a vast panorama of creative activity, from harmless puns and venomous satire through objectifying scientific activities to highly-strung artistic creativity and mystic contemplation.

> The gulf between the intellect and the emotions assumes, in Koestler's view, patholog-ical proportions and he sees this chasm as the source of all evil. His conclusion is drastic; we should try to control irrational aggression by administering appropriate drugs on a massive scale, thus restoring the spiritual harmony which has been disturbed by the hypertrophy of the intellect. This cure might be worse than the disease; anyhow Koes-tler has few equals in his quest for a grand synthesis of humanistic and scientific ideas. The outcome is sociobiology on a lofty, speculative level.

The Koestlerian scheme can be expanded into a network of successive bisocia-tions but it would remain a gross oversimplification lacking in explanatory power. The polyphony of creation can hardly be reduced to lucid series of ingenious binary operations. Koestler has admitted as much and left the back door open for "the intervention of extra-conscious processes". Fair enough. A painstaking analysis by retrospective deduction must not be mixed up with the baffling act of creation.

Re-creative learning

Man, with his inbred optimism, tries to master an intractable whole by looking for feasible sub-solutions. During the 1920s, John Dewey (1859–1952) pro-posed a scheme for creative action whereby the problem is first defined, then broken down into manageable parts and finally attacked with the proper ana-lytical tools. Unfortunately, Dewey's direct approach fails from the start, except in the simplest of cases. More often than not, the appropriate demarcation of our concern is the most demanding phase of the creative act. Once we know *exactly* what we want, the problem is almost solved or we can see that it is unsolvable. Dewey has thus hardly touched the core of creativity but he did improve our understanding of the learning process.

> Learning passes through at least two phases. To begin with, material is accumulated and memorized in a weakly organized form. Subsequently the bits fall into place and the process becomes irreversible as the mind takes hold of its new intellectual property. The empirically observed alternation between rapid learning stages and plateaus void of visible progress confirms this interpretation.

Self-tuition implies a restricted form of creativity. The risk-taking, the uncertainty, the cosmic chill of the unknown is eliminated; you can always enter the safe house of knowledge by familiar backdoors. Nevertheless it is a matter of re-creating the original inspiration, albeit by easy short-cuts. The learning process should thus be a good guide when we try to close in on creativity.

> Polanyi and Penrose (among others) recount that when studying a lucidly presented but exacting mathematical proof, they rarely feel convinced after a first reading. After repeated scrutiny, the overall picture gradually emerges in a broader context. Only then can the final result be accepted and the inevitability of the proof recognized. Not even mathematical truth can be logically enforced; the application of algorithms cannot be reduced to an algorithmic process.   *cf. 69*
>
> Feynman tells us that he did not understand the official version of quantum mechanics in the available textbooks, and so for five years he concentrated on re-creating the whole theory. From these tribulations he acquired an almost visual simulation model of the relevant physics. His mastery grew to the point of intuitive insight, and he could then promptly advance towards a breakthrough in quantum electrodynamics. With proud   *cf. 61* humility he declared on his death bed: "what I can't create I don't understand".

Our inborn sense of the multidimensionality of life is connected with a deep scepticism towards linear-logical arguments. We instinctively look for illuminating features, always working towards a holistic interpretation where the new knowledge will fit in. One has to see through the whole maze of complex relationships: seeing is believing.

> The common denominator of many mental disorders is the impairment of ordinary perception. The patients may have difficulties in discerning a familiar picture or pattern against a somewhat unruly or disorganized background. They are bewildered by the meaningless "noise" of the surroundings and unable to delineate a significant form, the "gestalt", from the mass of irrelevant information impinging on their senses. The   *cf. 278* mentally deranged cannot see the wood for the trees – a diagnosis which, taken in earnest, would put away most of the population.

Clear perception is acquired in early childhood, when our cortex learns to make sense of the rather chaotic visual influx. Language learning provides another *cf. 100* example of such eclectic creativity. The human infant has an astounding proclivity to utilize increasingly sophisticated linguistic tools, and new linguistic experience can continually enrich the vocabulary well into late middle age.

There are strong grounds for assuming that language learning offers a paradigm of creativity; the human brain is especially well-equipped for hermeneutic-linguistic play. But we know, too, that the speech centres are narrowly circumscribed in the cerebral cortex. The suggested analogy must therefore be interpreted in very broad terms to retain its relevance.

Heuristic problem-solving

Outsiders often regard mathematics as a purely deductive science based on algorithms, that is to say unambiguous and computer-compatible problem-solving schemata. We have already dealt with this particular fallacy; the application of and especially the search for new algorithms is often a creative challenge of the first order. Even if a solution exists, it may not be deducible in the usual analytic way. For example, most differential equations can, if at all, be solved only by a series of qualified guesses, a groping towards the correct shape
cf. 57 of the corresponding integral. Once the solution has been found, it can be easily checked by applying unequivocal derivation rules. This is an example of the class of "trapdoor" functions, which are served by straightforward formulas in one direction, but which in their inverse form present a formidable mathematical problem.

> The multiplication of integers is among the simplest mathematical routines, but there is no generally applicable algorithm for the reverse operation, namely factor analysis. We can only make tentative exploratory moves or apply brute calculating force: to find the factors of the product of two 200-digit primes, for example, would take untold years of computer time.
>
> This trapdoor function provides the key to an elegant and well-nigh unbreakable coding method (a cluster of powerful computers in parallel might, in the end, do the job). The sender uses the receiver's public code number which is the product of two huge primes. The encrypted text can be decoded only by applying the secret prime factors, known to the receiver. The message has been neatly dropped through a mathematical trapdoor and it can only be reclaimed with the help of confidential information about the construction of the lock.

cf. 112; 302 Faced with mathematical intractability, men have since Antiquity turned to heuristic methods of mathematical problem solving. Pappus (around 300 A.D.) recommends systematic experimentation in seeking proofs for mathematical hypotheses, and in modern times George Polya (1887–1985) and Imre Lakatos (1922–74) have further developed these ideas. Heuristics is concerned with laying down certain rather loose guiding principles with no pretentions to generality or infallibility. The result is a set of empirical rules-of-thumb for the problem complex under investigation.

> Henri Poincaré (1854–1912), a giant of mathematics and the father of chaos theory, makes the point that a heuristic "guessing" represents the pre-eminent working method of mathematicians. After a lengthy period of fruitless labour comes the moment of inspiration, the conviction that "it must be so", which generates sufficient energy for the often tedious work of proving the point rigorously. Carl Friedrich Gauss (1777–1855), perhaps the greatest mathematician of all time, once said: "My results have been ready for a long time, but I don't know how to reach them yet". His intuition usually hit the mark, *inter alia* a clear outline of non-Euclidean geometry, while the bold hypotheses of ordinary mortals usually turn out to be the fruits of wishful thinking. A few withstand both proof and disproof; some of them may in due course join the class of hypotheses which can be proved to be unprovable.

Herbert Simon has (together with Allen Newell in *Human Problem Solving*, 1972) analyzed the heuristic search process in well-defined problem situations. They abandoned the traditional, algorithm-orientated search for the best solution and introduced "satisficing" conditions to measure what is "good enough". More recently Simon has developed Subjective Expected Utility (SEU) criteria for economic decision-making but he hastens to deflate the utility of his model: "(Human beings) have neither the facts nor the consistent structure of values nor the reasoning power at their disposal that would be required".   *cf. 56; 335*

Fair enough. We need the best tools we can lay our hands on but the routine application of any explicit method can only produce intrinsically self-evident data.

> Art criticism long ago abandoned a normative attitude to the objects of its study. The   *cf. 367*
> old prescriptions for writing the perfect novel, painting a faultless picture or composing
> an impeccable sonata appear completely irrelevant today. Once the roots of a particular
> style have been revealed by discerning critics, the artist is bereft of his raison d'être.
> Unlike the artisan, he should after all map new territories and interpret unknown
> realities.

The swelling stream of publish-or-perish research is a symptom of scientific elephantiasis; a lot of the publication explosion is simply unnecessary ballast. Professional recognition should be attainable by competence in pursuing inherently interesting but risky research ideas. The publication of negative results is often of greater scientific value than the safe harping on about adiaphora – matters of supreme indifference.

3.6   The creative process

The initial state of incubation is always indeterminate or indeed chaotic; the situation is perceived from the inside, so to speak. At least a tacit value frame is indispensible if we want to give shape to a difficult problem and hold chaos at bay. In general, creative work must be paid for by a string of ruefully rejected hypotheses. Only after such a passage through purgatory, can we rise above the subject matter and clearly perceive its multidimensional connectedness. The fumbling in the dark is over, and deceptive sub-solutions no longer tempt us to terminate the task before time.

Seminal prelude

Every act of creation is preceded by an incubation period during which unstructured information impinges on the unprepared personality. The creative opportunity is not apparent, or if so only in a hazy form. During incubation scattered facts and ideas are weakly organized into preliminary structures which lack a common denominator but act as precipitous points of departure. During this early self-organizational stage the causal connections are inaccessible to analysis; we might even postulate an analogy with the origins of life itself.

cf. 319; 323 In the early stages of evolution we must assume considerable variability in the DNA (or more probably RNA) and the corresponding proteins. Only a small part of the proteins produced "on trial" self-aligned into useful spatial structures. But, under intensive competition, the most viable ones combined to form functional systems with survival value.

cf. 74; 99

cf. 350 In much the same way we float innumerable threads of thought which interlock randomly to form myriads of unique structures, neural patchworks as it were. When we face a creative challenge, tentative search processes are triggered off; all the retrievable thought molecules take part in a Darwinian elimination tournament. The inane babble is edited out in favour of understandable utterances, indefinable concepts conjoin to form the embryo of a meaningful shape. The fitness of the survivors is enhanced by the absorption of "interesting" bits and pieces from the vanished set-ups. A vague idea eventually appears in the midst of pointless noise, but the arbiter of taste in this beauty contest remains in the dark.

Perception gradually improves during the random reconnaissances of the incubation period. Even so, extrapolation of this method rarely results in acceptable solutions despite a disproportionate input of labour and time. Instead, we must be brave enough to stop at some suitable point and venture a preliminary hypothesis, a provisional draft, an idea, a sketch. This first attempt naturally depends on the initial conditions and it is sure to be misdirected – if not totally, then in part. But as Francis Bacon noted many centuries ago: "Truth comes out of error more readily than out of confusion". A fair guess or a conjecture, to use *cf. 30; 110; 281* a finer phrase, marks the beginning of a manageable creative process.

cf. 23 Random guessing is like looking for a needle in a haystack – a very inefficient way of gaining information. Accordingly, a stochastical, non-deterministic (guessing) computer is exceedingly complex; its number of states is of the order 2^n if n is the number of states of an equivalent deterministic machine. There is no way optimizing such a computation, and it is also impossible to find out how well one is doing. One might find the best procedure by a lucky guess but it is impossible to prove its optimality.

cf. 46 In a manageable search process, the solution can be tracked down by partitioning the search space, preferably down the middle. To stay with the haystack simile, a detector would tell us in which half of the haystack the needle is located.

Creative guessing falls into an intermediate category. We do not start out in total ignorance but neither, in general, do we know precisely what we are looking for. Lacking a dependable chart and compass, we navigate by dimly-perceived preferences – inarticulate private values.

cf. 100; 282 The generation of values is a higher art of guessing, a generally neglected aspect of creativity which incorporates the self-approved rules of the game. At least a tacit value frame is indispensible if we want to give shape to a difficult problem, weeding out meaningless suppositions and holding chaos at bay. We might take the value scale for granted in solving predetermined problems like crossword puzzles or examination posers, but purport and priority, significance and relevance are less obvious when we tackle open-ended scientific, social, business, or artistic games. The emphasis on values and the concomitant absorption of uncertainty reaches a maximum in religious messages.

> The Buddhist doctrines represent an extreme explication of the top-down approach. *cf. 43*
> First we must start with the right vision, which means that the sufferings of life can be
> expunged only in Nirvana. Then, only with the right intention, the right words, the right
> conduct and way of life, the right aspirations and mental awareness, and finally through
> the right kind of meditation can we achieve a higher and truer vision until, ultimately,
> the rising spiral leads to full enlightenment. On the threshold of Nirvana we perceive
> that reality is an illusion and we are freed from the eternally revolving wheel of rein-
> carnating life. Buddha "guessed" that the world is a meaningless zero-sum game, and so
> the solution to the mystery of life must involve a highly-qualified suicide. Naturally
> neither this idea nor its converse can be verified but Hamlet's cardinal question – to be
> or not to be – reflects our basic existential alternatives.

A creative hyperheuristic

The essence of creative play is to find a fruitful game, anticipating the axiomat- *cf. 367; 377*
ics and groping for clarifying rules and directive values. The end result can be
verified, at least tentatively, but in order to reach the goal we must enter an
arduous Darwinian process of creation and ruthless selection. When we try to
circumvent convoluted trapdoor functions, we sometimes fumble almost blindly for solutions which, once revealed, emit a self-verifying glow. Again and
again we have to guess the answer before we get at the right question.

Caution will lead us nowhere, we might as well throw our well-founded
doubts to the winds and try out a hypothetical hyperheuristic, a hermeneutic-
iterative model of creative activity like that exhibited in figure 3.8. Its practical
value should not be exaggerated but at least it could contribute to the understanding of the creative process.

The initial state of incubation is always indeterminate if not chaotic; the
problems are perceived from the inside, as it were, and generally lack structure.
Locally well-organized regions can provide natural starting points but they may
also lead the global solution down the wrong path. Sooner rather than later we
should throw ourselves into the creative spiral outlined above.

> The following commentary provides a few, rudimentary signposts.
>
> *The creative phase*
> Formulate preliminary hypotheses, seek to discover meaningful patterns and structures,
> ramble about and mull over ideas, exploit free associations or daring analogies.
> *The value-generation phase*
> Develop yardsticks and test procedures for assaying different hypotheses, pay conscious
> attention to personal and subjective values and try to define their content. What do you
> really want to achieve? What is the ultimate context? Refine your taste!
> *The critical phase*
> Compare the available alternatives, analyze their consequences, try to falsify the start-
> ing-points and identify gaps in information and deduction, pose concrete and practical
> questions, consider quantitative models.
> *The information-collection phase*
> Trace relevant information, pay heed to problems of reliability and varying frames of

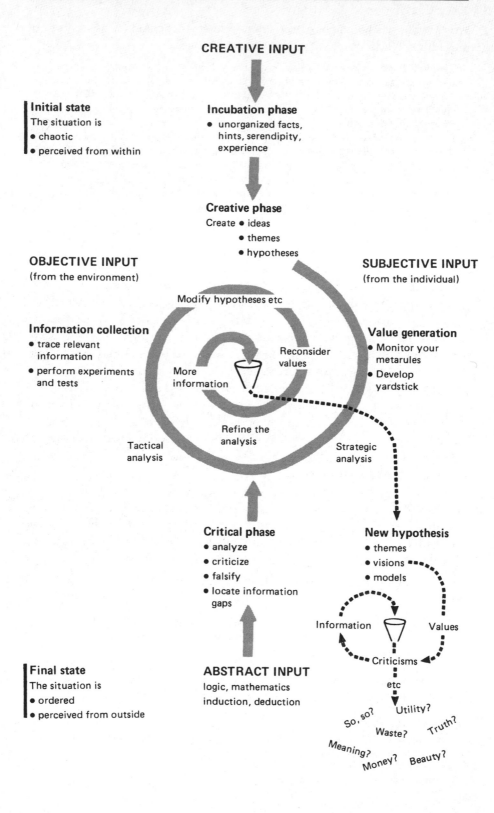

CREATIVE INPUT

Initial state
The situation is
• chaotic
• perceived from within

Incubation phase
• unorganized facts,
  hints, serendipity,
  experience

Creative phase
Create • ideas
       • themes
       • hypotheses

OBJECTIVE INPUT
(from the environment)

SUBJECTIVE INPUT
(from the individual)

Modify hypotheses etc

Information collection
• trace relevant
  information
• perform experiments
  and tests

Reconsider
values

More
information

Value generation
• Monitor your
  metarules
• Develop
  yardstick

Refine the
analysis

Tactical
analysis

Strategic
analysis

Critical phase
• analyze
• criticize
• falsify
• locate information
  gaps

New hypothesis
• themes
• visions
• models

Information   Values

Final state
The situation is
• ordered
• perceived from outside

ABSTRACT INPUT
logic, mathematics
induction, deduction

Criticisms

etc

So, so?   Utility?
      Waste?   Truth?
Meaning?
      Money?   Beauty?

reference, carry out experiments or simulations, ponder the results. Did you ask the right questions?

After the first round, we should:
- modify the hypotheses
- re-appraise the values
- critically evaluate the conjecture
- identify further gaps in knowledge
- seek new relevant information
- rejuvenate the process with modified hypotheses, and so on.

Whenever there is a strong negative reaction, the process should take a short-cut and return to the creative phase in search of a better hypothesis. Even so, the iteration usually generates a sense of frustration. When the end of a blind alley is in sight, most of the previous work must be scrapped and the situation ought to be tackled again from other, possibly opposite or converse points of view. New openings are at a premium and adventurous lateral thinking comes into its own in generating new ideas for later, rigorous evaluation.

Chess and language games

Before going any further let us test our heuristic on the decision-making that takes place in chess, a process which provides a simplified model of creative activity.

cf. 345

> According to Adrian de Groot (*Thought and Choice in Chess*, 1965) a playable move (but often not the best move) is arrived at after the following considerations:
> - first the position of the pieces is taken in, and several alternative moves are briefly reviewed, (incubation and creative input);
> - a hypothetical move is selected for closer consideration, (the basic hypothesis);
> - evaluation starts in light of the general perception of the situation, for instance in the dimensions offensive/defensive, safe/risky or checkmate combination/position reinforcement (performed in the light of the player's chess-value system);
> - next comes the critical examination of potential changes in the balance of forces on the board, control of the centre, pawn position, threats and ties, line domination etc. (a tactical analysis where the immediate effects of the hypothetical move are evaluated in more detail);
> - the process ends with an empirical follow-up of the chosen sequence of moves, exploring the ramifications as far as possible (final exhaustive testing of the intended move to expose unexpected pitfalls); and finally
> - whenever there is negative feedback the process is retracted and starts again with a new, hypothetical move.

By the stated heuristic a large number of tentative moves can be examined within a limited time span. Thus, the detailed analysis of alternative move sequences does not start the process (as it does for a beginner) but comes at the end as a final confirmation of the soundness of the planned move.

Our model can also be tested in a linguistic context. We have all, on occasion, experienced difficulty in recalling the right word, or a striking phrase. There is of course no deductive method for reaching the solution; instead we must try to create and test a variety of hypothetical alternatives. Once the apposite expression has been retrieved through the trapdoor of memory, it is immediately recognized and the game of hide-and-seek is over. The construction of whole sentences may involve multiple experiments, despite the fact that most of us are actually quite accomplished language players.

> Demanding translations conform equally well to our model. First, a number of "strategic", value-ridden problems must be solved (for instance, do we prefer foreign loan-words or new terms in our own language, literal translation contra idiomatic expressions and so on). Only when preliminary standards have been established is the time ripe for a critical evaluation of the first draft. Identifiable gaps in information can be filled by consulting reference books, by studying dialects and comparing idiolects; new expressions can be tested out with the help of selected experts or target groups. After this preliminary round we may be ready to draw up a new and possibly rather different set of hypotheses, value judgements and so on.

Liberating hypotheses

Cognitive competence is based on a set of habitual conjectures which can make *cf. 103* sense of even the faintest visual clues. At every moment we routinely recreate our sensory and conceptual worlds, hardly aware of any dilemma except when confronted with ambiguous figures of the classic type shown in figure 3.9.

Figure 3.9 Hare or duck?

> The observer swings between two equally plausible hypotheses (hare or duck), without finding any firm ground for a definite stand. He looks assiduously for a pattern, postulating an intent and looking for hidden cues. In other words he behaves in a creative way albeit on a banal or downright animal level. The classic Rorschach inkblot test (named after Hermann Rorschach, 1884–1922) systematically exploits our innate capacity for structuring visual material, the tendency to see a meaning in even the most random relationships.

We are in similar straits when we are in the midst of the creative process, beset by false starts and dead-ends. The final solution often appears as pure serendipity but as Louis Pasteur (1822–95) once remarked "chance favours only the prepared mind". Once the liberating hypothesis – our personal truth – is in sight, the answers begin to emerge and the first durable structure takes shape.

From then on the setbacks are only temporary and persistent work will fill in all the necessary details.

> A liberating conjecture is recognized by its ability to act as an autocatalyst, organizing available data and previous mental experience in a surprising and wholly convincing way. This usually takes plenty of time. The theory of evolution is a classic case in point. The decisive insight of the *Origin of Species* (1859) came to Charles Darwin (1809–1882) only after a long incubation period, and after that he toiled for 20 years to strengthen his case before being pushed into publication by A. R. Wallace (1823–1913). *cf. 314* But sometimes the solution appears with the force of a revelation, perhaps even in a dream-like state of clairvoyance (Poincaré, Pasteur, Kekule), or like an eruption of creative power in the shadow of death (Mozart, Galois, van Gogh, Nietzsche). Wallace had hit on natural selection in a fit of fever on the Moluccan Islands.
>
> Creative minds avoid any dogmatic fixation on given symbolic schemes; they think mainly in pre- or protolinguistic terms, groping for shapes and images which establish direct contact with realities. When Einstein tried to describe his own creative process, he spoke of manipulating image flows, of an active internal vision. Maxwell consciously used concrete visual analogies as the mental scaffolding when working on his highly abstract electromagnetic wave theory.

Apparently the holistic approach of the right half of the brain dominates during hypothesis-formation while the evaluation and articulation of the multidimensional structure is the task of the left hemisphere. During periods of intensive creative activity we have to assume a constant interplay between profoundly committed but disparate cerebral centres. The iterative spiral revolves at vertiginous speed, discarding an enormous number of defective alternatives.

The ordeal of creation

The rewarding termination of a creative game usually comes within reach only after a number of hypotheses have been ruefully rejected and the passage through purgatory properly paid for by a string of mental miscarriages.

> Marcel Proust (1871–1922) points out that the value of a work of art stems from what has been sacrificed and abolished, and Ernest Hemingway (1899–1961) advised a young and hopeful author that the more bloody good material he left out, the better his novel won be.

Most rough drafts, sketches, abandoned themes, rejected manuscripts, *cf. 178; 309* scrapped models or wild business ideas are never put on the record; they land on the scrap-heap of history together with unsuccessful financial speculations and perpetual motion machines of all kinds. Supreme achievements are built on the ruins of foiled expectations. Johannes Kepler (1571–1630) performed literally *cf. 301* millions of futile calculations in his search for mathematical regularities in the movements of the planets, and Einstein formulated his general theory of relativity only "after endless toil, and tormented by self-doubt".

In our model the creative input is iteratively condensed, finally emerging as a question mark. Sometimes the dead end is self-evident and the result falsifies itself. More often it takes a hard decision to reject a malformed brainchild and write off considerable investment in time and emotion. In any case the value, the true information content of the finished work is in some sense proportional to the waste involved. Mediocrity is the outcome of premature closure but how good is good enough? There can be no objective answer to that question. Periods of furious activity have to give way to meditation when setbacks are silently digested, experience reorganized, questions reformulated. Precious time must be invested in storing up strength for a fresh attack on the problem.

cf. 377; 389 (margin note)

At the beginning of 1917 Jean Sibelius (1865–1957) wrote to a conductor friend before a planned concert: "I am deeply unhappy. It was a tough job, composing my fifth symphony for my fiftieth birthday (1915). And so I've been reworking it radically over the last year but – I'm not satisfied. And I *cannot,* I simply cannot, send it." In his diary he wrote: "I must forget (the fifth symphony) and go on working. Perhaps the sun will shine again." After an exhausting struggle the symphony acquired its ultimate triumphant form in 1919.

The final solution may suddenly strike with the clarity of lightning; normally, however, repeated and intensive efforts gradually lead to a hermeneutically heightened understanding. The problem-solver has gained in self-reference, raised above his object, and achieved a balanced perception of the goals, the means and the possibilities as well as the risks and uncertainties. This state is marked by a subjective sense of comprehension and clarity which does not necessarily imply detailed knowledge. Intuitive mastery of the problem complex has been achieved and its multidimensional connectedness can be clearly perceived. The fumbling in the dark is over, and deceptive sub-solutions no longer tempt us to terminate the work before time.

Johann Wolfgang von Goethe (1749–1832), that natural genius, wrote his first version of Faust in his youth and put the finishing touches to the drama at the age of 83 – surely the longest conception process in the history of literature. Together with Wilhelm Meister, Dr. Faust personifies his creator while also reflecting a fundamental impulse in our culture. In the fever of discovery Faust stops at nothing; eternal damnation is a small price to pay for a stimulating life full of restless activity. As an old man, his great dyke and drainage project completed, he is reprieved by the panentheist Goethe on the grounds that "Wer immer strebend sich bemüht, den können wir erlösen" (he who strives always to the utmost him can we save). Goethe's greatest wish was, in fact, to see the Suez and Panama Canal projects realized before he died.

cf. 345; 354 (margin note) The self-perfecting, laborious and often painful iterative process described above generates a set of mental rules which define and circumscribe a dynamic simulation model. An internal imagery has been created, providing a means for examining and manipulating all the relevant interacting elements at will. We are viewing at a superior level, as when two almost identical and decidedly flat photographs are visualised in the convolutions of our brains as a three-dimensional stereoscopic reality. The outcome can be a scientific insight, a technical invention, an innovative business strategy, a potent theme or a personal style – at any rate a truth which in its own peculiar way reflects upon the nature of the Great Game.

3.7 Creative play

In creative play, our refined intellect must soil itself with subjectivity. We must select our values and absorb considerable uncertainty – in other words perform acts of faith. But once the pieces of the puzzle are in place, the solution is charged with its own conviction. Creative people are seized by a passion for truth, a yearning for perfection, an innate aversion to convention, platitude, sham or indeed any kind of false play. Thus, the only way to promote creativity is to permit it.

Passion for the game

The pull of creative play is well-nigh irresistible to inventive and independent minds. The challenge of the unknown will not be gainsaid, despite the ingratitude that will almost certainly be its reward. During the incubation phase the driving-forces rarely take aim at a specific target; instead they reveal themselves in an indeterminate sense of responsibility, a tension that produces thoughts like: "I've got something to contribute", or "there's something odd about this", or simply "this is an interesting sort of problem to work on". The true genius possesses a visionary ability to pose the fertile question, to strike a worthwhile seam. Often only the clear light of hindsight will distinguish him from the crank or the monomaniac, obsessively chasing his empty goal.

> As a schoolboy Einstein was already fascinated by the idea of an observer chasing a ray of light or descending in a steadily accelerating lift, but years of unremitting labour were needed before he arrived at the special and general theories of relativity.

By definition, creative acts are moves in a plus-sum game; the absence of innovation is a symptom of introverted, self-contradictory and sterile values. Conversely, fruitful effort humbly intimates the fertility and the underlying meta-rules in every sphere of life. *cf. 275; 317*

> Creative processes in science and art, technology, commerce and politics reveal striking similarities – an isomorphism illustrated by the applicability of the game metaphor. The mathematician elucidates the self-induced interplay of axiomatic abstractions while the natural scientist plays an empirical game of questions and answers, unravelling the rules of nature. Technicians, businessmen and politicians all play for high stakes and sometimes gamble against desperate odds. Countless language games are the basis of all human communication; art languages try to penetrate the innermost nature of man. Lastly, philosophers and theologians seek desperately to play against God.

In creative play we must first choose our game. Then we must learn or create the fundamental, explicit rules and, finally, we should play the game skilfully, constructively and above all with passion. In any case, we are far removed from the abstract world of grand ideas where, in Friedrich von Schiller's (1759–1805) words, our thoughts play so amicably together, and much closer to that concrete reality in which things inevitably collide. Creative work means getting something new and untried to function, be it a mathematical deduction, a chemical synthesis, a machine, a business idea, a theatrical performance, a composition, or a social institution.

The old adage about the ingredients of artistic creation – 1 per cent inspiration and 99 per cent perspiration – applies to all creative activity. Only intense practice at the self-elected game will advance our understanding beyond the trivially explicit towards mastery and superior judgement.

> *cf. 107*
>
> Thomas Mann wrote 5,000 words every day without corrections whereas Charles Dickens (1812–70), Leo Tolstoy (1828–1910) and James Joyce (1882–1941) re-wrote parts of their novels at least fifteen times. Chaplin had to labour doggedly at the movies which appear so spontaneous, discarding whole sequences which would amount to masterpieces. After long consideration, Ludwig van Beethoven (1770–1827) sometimes rejected up to fifty themes before tackling the composition proper. And the modest, almost self-effacing testimony of Johann Sebastian Bach (1685–1750) was "I have been forced to work hard; anyone who works as hard can achieve as much."

Economy is one of the key elements in the iterative process. The first round in the spiral sequence *hypothesis – evaluation – critical analysis – information collection – improved hypothesis* presumably occurs beyond the reach of self-control. Even the subsequent more conscious cycles must pass fairly quickly. A massive input into the embryonic phase inevitably binds the work to its capriciously chosen inception, impeding the creative process and proffering mediocrity.

Options cannot be kept open for ever. Sooner or later we must embark on a definite train of thought which inevitably prefigures the outcome. Innumerable ways of playing the game are eliminated without much ado. Thus, in creative play the key decisions must be taken early on and always involve a major element of risk. Time, money and reputation are at stake in varying proportions, and the final consummation of all the effort may forever remain an elusive mirage. If and when the goal is reached, the haunting doubts should evaporate, at least in the ideal case. The newly-created code should lay bare the secrets of the enigmatic trapdoor function: the solution to the problem is charged with its own force of conviction. Once the pieces of the puzzle are in place, no further proof is necessary.

The beholding eye

The grandmasters of chess are a well-defined élite of eminent personalities, and they can serve as a suitable test for the conjectures presented above.

> *cf. 345*
>
> de Groot has compared the performance of chess players at different levels. The masters excelled above all in the almost immediate and exact grasp of the game situation. An exposure time of three to five seconds sufficed for a practically faultless depiction of the positions of the pieces on the board. The grandmaster does not possess an eidetic memory which achieves exact reproduction. Rather, he grasps in holistic fashion the dynamic tension of the chessboard, the web of threats and opportunities. Given this deep insight, the actual moves can be sketched out with optimum economy of thought and time.

The chessmaster has laboriously learnt the right intuition, he sees through the superficialities of the position, dismisses barren ideas and senses the hidden opportunities. Artists like William Shakespeare (1564–1616) and Bach *père* could produce masterpieces at very short notice; they, too, were grandmasters of their crafts.

> Explicit verbal reasoning is a blunt tool in creative work because it produces a distance, an isolating layer of abstraction which excludes immediate contact with the intricacies of the game. The requisite concepts and categories will always outnumber the available vocabulary, and mastery can be retained only by playing directly with the cerebral representations of perceived reality.

cf. 117; 345

Creative tension arises in the conflict between the short-term, the given or the practicable on the one hand, and vague ethical-aesthetic priorities on the other. If the feasible and effective is perceived as displeasing, then either our skill or knowledge are incomplete, or the economic resources are insufficient – or our concept of beauty may be superficial and misleading.

cf. 301

> Chess games and chess problems can take part in actual "beauty contests" in which the entrants are assessed by an impartial jury. Stuart Marguelis has tried to disclose the norms applied by asking chess experts to judge pairs of single moves. He came up with some quite unequivocal rules which can be condensed under the following headings:
> – surprise (avoid the conventional, violate heuristics)
> – economy (a minimum of means, a maximum of utilization)
> – consistency (employ themes, be consistent)
> – clarity (contrivance is counter-productive)
> Even this simple set-up reveals deep aesthetic principles which show a close affinity with our self-verifying trapdoor functions.

Creative work is ultimately guided by its own aesthetics, by "taste" in an extended sense. Given sufficient extrapolation, "right" and "beautiful" should converge. However, it is in the nature of things that our spontaneous self-satisfying insight becomes less dependable as the complexity of the game increases. Overwhelming unanimity on some current problem in politics or philosophy is always suspect whereas in art, truth and beauty may become one.

Creative collaboration

The ability to act in unclear and risky conditions distinguishes creativity from mere intellectual acumen. Even the keenest intelligence is the slave of its own built-in system of rules.

> An advanced computer can be regarded as a highly-specialized artificial brain which commands an extensive memory, faultless logic and a heuristic appropriate to the problem in hand. But this intellect has a severely restricted outlook; it cannot step outside the framework of the problem and redefine the game by accepting new rules, risks and responsibilities. Fresh ideas or viewpoints are thus excluded, and new paradigms or radical re-evaluations are entirely out of bounds.

cf. 337; 351

How, then, are fruitful hypotheses created? Outstanding proficiency in the form of a thorough acquaintance with the subject matter can be an indispensable prerequisite but may also act as a barrier to revolutionary insights. Falling back on the subconscious simply moves the problem downstairs without further illumination.

> The creation of creativity would certainly be a profitable operation, and many consultants have established themselves in this line, pushing their patent prescriptions. For a brief period brainstorming was all the rage. It has now been replaced by a variety of other techniques that dislocate our prejudiced opinions, promote imagination by analogies, and facilitate the associations of new ideas. This kind of systematization may be helpful in the mundane tasks of product development or advertising but a real breakthrough in creative thinking is not on the cards, despite all the hype.

Far-reaching trains of thought start only in the privacy of an individual study although, objectively speaking, the final result is always a collective creation. The seminal moves of a unique personality can take their proper place only in subordination to the cultural game; in any case creative effort has to be financed one way or another by the surplus of routine workers.

cf. 123   Team-work is the rule rather than the exception in modern technological, economic, scientific and even some artistic enterprises. Well-functioning working groups coalesce into veritable superbrains, cohesive coalitions, in which the pleasure of playing is the principal payoff. Nevertheless every product-development group or research team or theatre company needs a competent authority – a manager, director, team captain or coach. There is normally little latitude for supreme soloists even if opportunities sometimes arise for genuine star performances.

> In the public eye, Neil Armstrong and Edwin "Buzz" Aldrin played first and second fiddle respectively in man's landing on the moon. They were honourable figureheads in the greatest PR project in history, supported by tens of thousands of patient extras. It was of course a tremendous feat of engineering but the truly original accomplishments were in the project management and the politics.

Advanced computer technology is the product of a continuing explosion of creativity, and should thus provide valuable clues for the organization of inventive activity. The lesson we have learned so far is that the innovative methods of today can only solve the problems of yesterday. There is no surrogate for human meta-motivation, stimulated by youthful enthusiasm and keen competition. In order to participate in creativity our refined intellect must dirty itself with subjectivity – selecting values, absorbing existential uncertainty, performing acts of faith.

When goals are clear and means are available, professional management should be enough. But genuine creativity cannot be commanded nor is it responsive to administrative procedures – it can only be permitted. It is a matter of personal involvement merging into collaborative commitment. Most magnificent team efforts depend on a few pivotal if inconspicuous actors who set an example by their quiet but essential contributions, selflessly enhancing the level of play.

Creative effort rarely has a definite end. A positive solution triggers off a spate of less demanding work; the viability of an innovation ultimately depends on the details, the proverbial habitat of the devil. What is more, a creative breakthrough changes our outlook: a self-amplifying cascade of unforeseen opportunities is released, opening up new vistas of cultural advance and raising the level of our existential plus-sum game.

Visionary ventures

The only effective way of promoting creativity is to give full rein to individuals, leaving their circles undisturbed and leaving them to get on with their game. Creative people are vulnerable and not very good at pursuing their own in- *cf. 161* terests. They can exhibit an almost childlike innocence or playfulness, sometimes spiced with shrewdness or infantile self-absorption. But at bottom there is always a fundamental sincerity and humility, a passion for truth, a yearning for perfection, an innate aversion to convention, platitude, sham or indeed any kind of false play.

> Wolfgang Amadeus Mozart (1756–91) and Charles Darwin are among the best documented cases of such compulsive percipience which takes over the whole personality. Mozart conceived many of his works in a state of clairvoyance; "Then my soul is on fire with inspiration. The work grows; I keep expanding it, conceiving it more and more clearly until I have the whole composition finished in my head though it may be long." Late in life Darwin for his part lamented over his obsession with scientific thinking. He complained that his mind had become a machine for generating generalisations out of masses of scattered facts and that he had completely lost his capacity for enjoying music and poetry.

The labours of creative efforts may produce only stillborn issue; massive personal stakes may all be lost when the game is up. The element of risk and the differences in playing strength are proportional to the level of the game. Poor players are likely to spoil the game – in science and business usually for themselves, in politics often for their fellow-beings as well.

> How the quest for fair and beautiful play incites unique acts of creation is largely beyond our understanding. Men of genius follow their own rules but they are all *cf. 366; 371* possessed by the same irrepressible determination to win, which draws the resources of the personality together in a focus of white-hot intensity. Deep down we may assume some sort of irritant, a flaw, a fight against a fault, or at any rate a grain of discontent to be encased in layer after layer of shimmering pearl.
>
> Creative forays imply confrontation with authorities, internal and external, and succeed only by passionate commitment. No group venture, however well-organized, can compete with the total subjection of one single mind to the task at hand. Once mastery has been achieved, work may indeed proceed in an effortless manner even if few are so blessed or damned that life and deed completely coincide – a state which the dying Mozart summed up in the words: "I compose because it tires me less than resting."

In its finest expression artistic creation may verge on the force of religious revelation and attain that visionary generation of values which is the supreme form of creativity. Alas, the world is full of false prophets, paranoics, charlatans and imposters, and it is therefore only too tempting to play it safe, to stay on the sidelines and opt for the passive role of the sceptical spectator. But no-one can avoid taking part in our joint human adventure. We are all producing accomplished facts, irrevocable moves in the great game of existence in which everything is at stake.

Creative endeavour is a self-imposed hardship, sometimes a self-assertion bordering on insanity in the eyes of rational and reasonable people. Sören Kierkegaard succinctly exposes the vulnerability of the creative spirit as against the cautiously calculating cynic: "There are two ways: one is to suffer, the other is to become a professor of the fact that another suffers". Kierkegaard never flinched from this *Enten – eller*, "either – or".

3.8   Cultural interplay

Natural selection is always at work, with or without our approval. Every change in the rules of reproductive play has far-reaching consequences. Has natural selection gone into reverse? Can the flood of unrestricted human procreation be stemmed? If the high-fertility populations become permanently dependent on the birth-controlling strata, we can expect severe instability. Equally menacing is the self-righteous myth about the "natural" virtue of humankind. This fallacy perverts our most precious aspirations and spawns the articles of a false faith.

Genetic assets

Can we maintain our cultural creativity or will we fall victim to our own successes like so many other cultures and species? Or to put the question differently, how is human evolution functioning today? No precise answers can be given to these somewhat vatic questions but there is a widespread unease in the air, an indefinite feeling that the forces of evolution are out of gear or have even gone into reverse. One conspicuous sign is the persistent negative correlation between earning power and birth-rate.

Are these questions legitimate? They seem deceptively simple but immediately put us in a quandary. To assess human evolution we must apply a value frame which seems to imply that such questions are forbidden! Come what may, we should not silence such embarrassing inquiry.

> Palaeontology has supplied countless examples of degenerative development; evolution does not proceed in a straightforward manner. Quite unconcerned, we postulate a value scale embracing "lower" and "higher" forms of life. We speak incautiously of "enriching" or "impoverishing" changes, placing ourselves indisputably at the top of the pile. Quotation marks have recently become fashionable fig leaves which should hedge against any indecent exposure of anthropocentricity. But man tries in vain to wriggle out of his role as law-maker and supreme judge – although this does not mean that *Homo sapiens* is a finished or faultless masterpiece.

How is our genetic capital affected by obvious changes in the rules of the survival game? Despite massive medical intervention, there is little risk of an insidious increase in inherited deformities, thanks to the high mortality rate at the embryo stage.

> According to somewhat divergent assessments, on average between 50 and 70 per cent of human fertilized egg cells are aborted at an early stage, mainly due to genetic defects. An increase in, say, ionizing radiation and the concomitant rate of mutation would be largely offset by this sifting mechanism. The incidence of spontaneous dominant mutations is less than 10^{-5}–10^{-6} per gene and no significant increase has been observed, not even among the descendants of the survivors of Hiroshima and Nagasaki.   *cf. 93*

Environmental influences, with the exception of an all-out nuclear war, do not constitute a serious threat to the genetic heritage of the human race. Ambient factors, such as mutagenic chemicals and radioactive radiation, have always acted on our genetic substance. Even a well-advised programme of eugenic intervention would be of marginal significance only. However, selection is at work, with or without our approval; every change in the rules of reproductive play has far-reaching consequences.

The scope for play

The transition from opportunistic hunting and gathering to monotonous agriculture certainly was the cause of great mental stress. Husbandry calls for hard and persistent labour, the rigid systematization of female gathering chores – certainly a most unpleasant kind of life for inveterate hunters and fishermen. The resulting process of selection, lasting several thousand years, must have left an indelible mark on our genetic inheritance. Unlike the primitives of today, we are the heirs of hardy, toiling peasants. The parsimony and pronounced territoriality of the farmer are transformed into local patriotism and nationalism; rustic behaviour patterns reappear as ordinary middle-class virtues.

The discovery of intoxicating drinks has been credited with speeding up the evolutionary process. According to this argument, the production of alcohol added a new dimension to natural selection. Obviously the excessive drinkers were soon eliminated, and this may have correlated with a genetically-based activation of the surviving population. Recent experience of the effects of alcohol on aborigines has shown that at least the liquidation effect is real, and there is clear evidence that some populations have developed specific protective mechanisms.

> Orientals have a comparatively low tolerance of alcohol. Two Japanese out of three react with palpitations after quite moderate drinking. Poisonous acetaldehyde, the primary oxidation product of ethanol, accumulates in abnormal quantities and evokes typical symptoms of hangover after a relatively small intake. This condition depends on an inherited deficiency of the enzyme aldehyd-dehydrogenas: the low incidence of alcoholism in Japan is thus caused by an inborn antabus reaction. Alcoholics in Japan (and probably in other countries too) generally show an elevated level of aldehyd-dehydrogenas activity.

Deadly diseases have no doubt affected evolution in analogous ways, and today

drugs constitute yet another agent of selection. Apart from the countless individual tragedies behind the abstractions so airily tossed around, we have to
accept an inestimable and irretrievable loss in the interim account of man. Our
genetic variety is continually being curtailed while new traits are emerging in a
game of impenetrable complexity.

Inherited epigenetic behaviour patterns provide the foundation for all our
social relations, but do not prevent us from aspiring to self-selected meta-rules
for human interplay. Further studies of the feedback between cultural values
and our biological heritage should thus be given the highest priority. We are
gradually achieving a meaningful frame of self-reference, and are thus approaching one of the decisive turning points in the history of mankind and
cf. 418 perhaps of life itself.

The confusing multiplicity of cultural forms and the evident plasticity of
human nature are enough to deter even the boldest minds. Our hesitation is
increased by a vague feeling of impropriety; are we not implicitly pursuing the
mechanization of man? Still, the success of the natural sciences has shown that a
surprisingly simple and profound regularity can be concealed behind the apparent jumble of transient observations, none of which has in any way diminished
the wealth of variety in our universe or cast doubt on its creative potential.

Reproductive surplus

Unlimited propagation is generally regarded as the foremost rule of the evolutionary game but there are many examples of quite effective self-regulation
among species subject to severe population pressure.

> Tadpoles secrete a pherom which, at high enough concentrations, prevents eggs from
> hatching, and in adverse circumstances many mammals simply abstain from mating, or
> re-absorb the foetus, or cannibalize their young.

Homo sapiens' reflexes are ambivalent on this point. The law of the jungle
should be unrestricted procreation, but a number of primitive people exercise
adequate birth control.

> Infanticide, sometimes combined with cannibalism, has been fairly common in tribal
> communities but more sophisticated methods are well-documented, too. Among the
> Australian aborigines, an operation was performed on young men at the initiation
> ceremony whereby the spermatic duct (the *vas deferens*) was opened so that the sperm
> would not enter the vagina during intercourse. When a child was desired, a finger could
> be held over the opening. In Africa there is no sign of a population explosion among the
> Kung! bushmen, in glaring contrast to the surrounding Bantu peoples. Years of breast-
> feeding combined with a high incidence of relatively mild venereal disease, particularly
> gonorrhoea, reduce female fertility. An early adaptation between man and micro-
> organism may have curtailed reproduction.

In ancient cultures, the widespread use of contraceptive techniques remains
substantiated. However, abortion was certainly practised and the exposure of
deformed or otherwise unwanted children has worked as a safety valve among
many if not most civilized peoples. In Antiquity, large-scale and publicly sanc-

tioned infanticide may have been a contributory factor in the regression of the Greek and Roman cultures.

> In Rome, girls were particularly at risk, and an incongruous preference for boys recurs   *cf. 137*
> in most cultures – not least in modern China and Korea. In Europe, the custom of
> abandoning unwanted infants of both sexes persisted throughout the Middle Ages and
> led to the establishment of foundling hospitals in many of the larger cities. The mortality
> rate was excessive to put it mildly; in eighteenth-century London and Paris it was at least
> 90 and sometimes close to 99 per cent. This did not diminish the popularity of public
> care. Jean Jacques Rousseau (1712–78), that self-declared spokesman for humanity,
> cheerfully used the system to absolve himself of the responsibility for each of the five
> babies he sired.

The endemic overpopulation of countries such as India and China proves that human procreation is following its own rules. Both the high fertility in poor countries and the low reproductive rate in the Western world has been ascribed to socio-economic feedback. Social security certainly plays an important role.

> In traditional societies, the care of the old falls upon the children, a practice which in
> many cultures has been underwritten by reverent ancestor worship. Accordingly, the
> survival of enough offspring is still indispensable in the developing world. In the welfare
> state, children are economic liabilities, at least for the better off. The tab for old age is
> conveniently foisted onto somebody else.

Economic factors notwithstanding, the baby boom after the Second World War indicates that deeper, socio-psychological causes cannot be neglected. Even more puzzling is the well-documented tendency for a higher proportion of male births after periods of war. Hitherto unexplored mechanisms are obviously at work.

> About 99.9 per cent of the spermatozoa are neutralized by the woman's immunological
> system before they reach the ovum. This may not happen completely at random and
> could be influenced by the mother-to-be's state of mind (only one rape out of 600 results
> in pregnancy). The speed and direction of evolution may have been decisively affected
> by such covert, maternal self-selection.

Birth control promotes ecological balance but may also cause cultural stagnation, and invites encroachment from surplus areas. Even if contraceptive techniques were to be applied worldwide, there would always, without the strictest enforcement, be individuals or groups reproducing themselves in excess of the "norm". A high nativity rate is perfectly acceptable, provided that the people involved take full responsibility for their offspring. But if the high-fertility populations become permanently dependent on the birth-controlling strata, we can expect severe instability and attendant socio-political convulsions.

Some pertinent questions

The age-old quest for the putatively static character of human nature is certainly misguided. We should rather try to lay bare the sources and fundamental rules of the dynamic interplay between the individual, the group and material reality. Among the profusion of such approaches we have philosophers like Hegel,

Nietzsche and Marx, historians like Oswald Spengler (1880–1936) and Arnold Toynbee (1889–1975), psychologists like Freud and Carl Jung (1875–1961), a biologist like Ernst Haeckel (1834–1919) and an anthropologist like Lévi-Strauss, just to mention a few prominent figures. Regrettably most of them start from too narrow a base and suffer from what could be called "the great leap syndrome". With a powerful sleight of hand, a single flash of insight, they seek to reveal the hidden mechanisms of man and his society.

This off-hand intrusion into our human game is rather irritating, to say the least. We react with justifiable anger at being reduced to puppets bound by the "inexorable laws of history" or the "commands of the unconscious". Instead we should think in more dynamic terms such as emotional economy or moral deficit. But neither must we forget our dependence on human heredity and the mundanities of our immediate surroundings. Here too we should brace ourselves for the possibility of coming down on the wrong side in controversial issues.

Why did the first advanced civilizations emerge in subtropical areas whereas Western culture seems strikingly attached to the temperate zones? Charles Louis de Montesquieu (1689–1755) already speculated on these relationships in his theory of climate, and Ellsworth Huntington (1876–1947) has tried (in *Civilization and Climate* 1915 and *Mainsprings of Civilization*, 1945) to track down the correlation between climate and prosperity in a systematic way. He traces the decline of Graeco-Roman culture to a gradual climatic change which, combined with the destruction of the forests, resulted in water-logging and endemic malaria throughout much of the Mediterranean.

Successive improvements in the control of our environment have gradually transplanted the cultural centres towards cooler and more challenging areas. Huntington could point to an astonishing correlation between "climatic energy" and economic development in the early twentieth century. Although his analysis is open to criticism, it is at least broadly plausible and deserves further consideration. At least we can, with some trepidation, establish that corruption in human societies increases roughly in proportion to the distance from the poles.

cf. 136

Brilliant ideas and assiduous studies are easily wasted in the quest for immediate, total and final knowledge – futile attempts to close the game. Every mental model that restricts and impoverishes our play as measured against historical reality must be false. On the contrary, authentic insight into the hierarchy of games should enhance human emancipation by unmasking muddled thinking and fraudulent utopias.

One of the most disagreeable features of our modern world is its bloated expectations, its grandiose resolutions, its endless speechifying about inalienable human rights (rarely obligations), and its belief in a never-never land where we can have our cake and eat it. We should be more concerned about the decay of our internal environment than about impending ecological disasters which, after all, can be avoided once the human mind has come to terms with itself.

The price of freedom

My intention in the preceding pages has been to show that we cannot and should not ignore the rich heritage that evolution has provided. We should strive for mastery over destructive forces, and cold-bloodedly learn to exploit all available energies. Modest additions or minor modifications of the ground plan are feasible, but to go against our genetic grain is pure folly and delusion. Such acts of self-exaltation are bound to fail; man falls victim to his innate desires and limitations while his reason twists itself inside-out trying to explain away the mess.

> Our instinctual impulses evolve into sentient feelings in the incessant information-processing of the cortex, the arrogant upstart of the brain. All the same, the volatile hopes and fears, appetites and aversions are securely seated in the older cerebral structures which are in pretty good command of the underlying rules. Anonymous affective charges hide behind the hubris of the intellect, making a mockery of logic and rationality.
>
> *cf. 82; 100*

Man can think sensibly but is controlled by his passions, he can rise to heights of altruism and yet behaves with cynical ruthlessness and bestial cruelty to his neighbour. All this and more lurks under the smug surface and should evoke ceaseless soul-searching. The most zealous flagellants denounce man as a universal pest, only fit for extinction. More menacing is that the self-righteous myth about the "natural" virtue of humankind is taking hold. Vital impulses such as the longing for stimulus, identity and purpose are dismissed, aesthetic and religious yearning denied. To fill the gap, an indiscriminate "goodness", a spontaneous benevolence towards all other human beings is rashly postulated. These misconceptions pervert our most precious aspirations and spawn the articles of a false faith.

> Common sense together with an expanding body of scientific investigation should provide some understanding of the phenomenon of *Homo sapiens,* but the innermost nature of man will always elude our inquiring mind. Yet we daily respond to that riddle in our thoughts, our words and our deeds. Here, at the core of our personal identity the truth and falsity of mankind is concealed; here, for better or for worse, the rules of human interplay are determined.

Giving free rein to human desires spells disaster. Inhibitions are the key to all organized co-operation: in the circumspect choreography of genetic expression; in the complex interplay of the neuronal network; even in the accommodating discipline of our language games. Like good upbringing, ethics excels in saying "no": only apposite restraints will give personal and cultural self-organization a chance.

Fortunately, in our culture human values have gone a long way towards allaying the ruthless Darwinian game of natural selection. The price of this freedom is faith, an unconditional acceptance of axiomatic meta-rules, a set of self-imposed restrictions in the scope of play. Man is still bound by matter and the primordial survival imperative. A direct breach of these rules is inconceivable, since it presupposes an arbitrary universe excluding any creative play. Agony, sorrow and evil are the inevitable by-products of the very rules which give life its value. These sacrifices grant access to the great stage where we can follow the example of the mature Wittgenstein and embrace the world from within.

4. The culture game

4.1 What is culture?

Culture implies some kind of ordered collaboration, and in many insect societies the genetic directives of social organization are laid down with diabolic precision. Ruthless selection has, over the eons, engrafted some rules of good behaviour on our genome, too. In a shorter perspective, persistent historical feedback continues to transform our cultural and genetic heritage. Along the way, human creativity – toil and enterprise – has produced new technologies which form the very basis of human culture.

_____

Programmed collaboration

In the foregoing chapter I maintained that cultural development is the ultimate driving-force of evolution; the rules for successful existential play are gradually imprinted on the genetic code. Dramatic breakthroughs ensue when essentially disparate forms of life combine their strengths.

> The emergence of eukoryote cells about two billion years ago can be traced back to a symbiotic collaboration between sophisticated organisms, which were short on energy, and primitive prokaryotes which could serve as "power stations". This evolutionary hypothesis is strengthened by the fact that the mitochondria, which produce most of our cellular energy, apply a slightly deviating DNA alphabet in their independent reproductive system. Chloroplasts and ribosomes, too, are probably based on early imports of prokaryotic material. All these organelles are located in the cell plasma and are thus propagated only through the maternal egg cells.
>
> The mitochondria feature aerobic oxidation, which is eighteen times more efficient than anaerobic processes. Available energy sources (e.g. oxidation of sugar) are converted into user-friendly _Adenosine Triphosphate_ (ATP). ATP is a highly convertible energy resource. It can be stored and is utilized by most cell structures including the nucleus, which otherwise has to fall back on its own rather inefficient anaerobic metabolism.

cf. 186

The symbiosis between many plants and nitrogen-fixing bacteria is a nice example of a cultural plus-sum game played across strictly-drawn genetic boundaries. Corals and lichen-forming fungi cannot survive without the support of highly-specialized photosynthetic algae while endosymbiotic bacteria and protozoa act as subcontractors for fermentation services in the cattle rumen. We could even look at the whole biosphere as a loose coalition consisting of reciprocally adaptive subcultures, called species.

cf. 321 The adverse interaction between parasitic intruders and host defences generally leads to extended co-adaptation and co-evolution which, in a few selected instances, has resulted in new, symbiotic forms of life. Viral infection, for example, might have provided the springboard for decisive leaps of evolution among higher organisms (computer simulations have confirmed the feasibility of such a mechanism). Sexual recombination was probably the apposite response to excessive viral infiltration of the genome. There are ample grounds for Mephisto's lamentation in Goethe's *Faust;* whatsoever the evil cf. 388 deeds he tries, he cannot but take part in God's work of creation.

Embryonic development offers a more convincing model of close collaboration between at least semi-autonomous cellular entities, and we can easily reverse our language game and regard every differentiated individual as a supercultural organization. The dividing line between multicellular individuals and closely collaborating cell communities is, in fact, fuzzy enough.

The Portuguese man-of-war (of the genus *Physalia*) is a remarkable pelagic organism. The newborn cells first roam freely in the upper layers of the ocean but soon combine into a closely interconnected and highly diversified cellular coalition with specialized organs for feeding, digestion, defence, reproduction and so on. This "commonwealth" has achieved a degree of differentiation resembling that of many non-vertebrates, albeit by a roundabout route. Physalia is the evolutionary outcome of successive progress in the co-operative interplay between originally autonomous individuals.

In extreme cases, the directives for social collaboration are laid down with a precision equalling embryonic development. Among many insects, particularly of the order Hymenoptera (wasps, ants, bees), the division of labour is rigorous- cf. 59 ly controlled.

This can be explained by the fact that Hymenoptera are haplodiploids; the males emerge from unfertilized eggs and are thus homozygotic. Both the egg-producing queens and the sterile workers are heterozygote females emerging from fertilized egg cells; consequently, all the "sisters" in a colony share three-quarters of their genes. Normally only half the genes of the closest kin are shared, and this relation also holds for mother and daughter among the Hymenoptera. For a female playing a rational reproduction game, investment in the care of her sisters offers the best genetic odds. Her inclusive fitness is optimally enhanced by supporting the society and foregoing the production of progeny of her own. The powerful impulse towards an altruistic social organization among Hymenoptera can thus be traced back to genetic egotism, pure and simple.

Some of the ant and bee communities appear to have reached their high social organization about 100 million years ago, and have apparently arrived at one of evolution's innumerable stalemate positions. All new leads would worsen the outcome; the only solution is to mark time in a narrow circle of self-repeating moves.

Artificial "ant societies", created by computer simulation, highlight the particulars of the Darwinian learning process. Random "mutations" impinge on the ants' "genetic" program with a low frequency. "Evolution" takes place when suitable survival criteria select the fittest for self-propagation. The "species" quickly optimizes itself to the simulated environment, and can adjust to moderate change, but the original unmod-

ified ant program possesses superior adaptability. As a rule, unlearning is slower than
the accumulation of new information.   *cf. 219; 278*

All the same, most species of the order Hymenoptera are not particularly social,
and the ant-colony type of organization is highly developed among the termite
order (Isoptera) which has a normal distribution of genetic material between
the sexes. The naked mole rat of East Africa (Heterophalus glaber) is the
outstanding mammalian example of self-sacrificing social differentiation, with
a queen for exclusive breeding, non-reproducing workers, and so on. The
genetic logic does not predestine evolution *per se*. Cultural learning will, in the
long term, become engrafted on the genome – the only out-and-out guarantee of
correct social interplay.

Applied technology

Specially gifted species naturally fall back on their own innate techniques: the
spider spins, the beaver builds – each in its own genetically prescribed way. In
comparison, man's gradually increasing technical control over his environment
is of very recent origin and marks the successive epochs of human development.
Tools and ceramics; farming and husbandry; weaving and writing – all serve as
suitable designations for the level of cultural play. Only when ideas and knowledge are reduced to practice do they become entrenched and may, in the end,
influence even our common databank – the genetic code.   *cf. 98; 146; 278;*
                                                                                         296; 308; 417

> Mathematics (including logic) is the most abstract of sciences, regarded by the Greeks
> from Pythagoras onwards with almost religious reverence. In Antiquity, profane appli-
> cations were sporadic at best. The impressive mathematical achievements were never
> tied down to profitable, down-to-earth activities; even before the barbarian onslaught
> they had largely dissolved into thin air.
>
> An abundance of practical applications is a necessary condition for sustained pro-
> gress in the science of mathematics. Only when logarithms, spherical trigonometry and
> differential calculus were put to productive purposes could the great mathematicians of
> the eighteenth and nineteenth centuries penetrate new regions of symbolic interplay.
> The present enormous upswing in computer technology has already born fruit in
> brand-new mathematical exploits.

Learning and repetition mould our technical applications into highly reproducible pieces of mental property which constitute the very basis of all the other
human games – economics, politics, science, and art. The condescending dis-
missal of technology as a banausic exercise reveals an astonishing intellectual
arrogance and a lack of historical perspective. Hieroglyphs and alphabets, the
very stuff of refined thought, were developed by eminently practical men with
quite mundane objectives.   *cf. 190*

Man's predecessors were "technicised" long before the emergence of *Homo
sapiens*; the tinder-box and tools of stone are evidence of a notable technological standard. Our present shying away from the challenges of the nuclear age
reflects previous agonizing on the threshold of cultural discontinuities. This is
by no means the first time history has been thrown off its tranquil course – by
bow and arrow, by the plough, the pen, the wheel, by copper, bronze and iron,

and by ever new incarnations of Promethean fire. Our forefathers courageously chose the new and the necessary, leaving the illusory safety of repetitive games to the pusillanimous.

> The technology of the future will be based on novel and almost unlimited sources of energy (nuclear fission and fusion power, solar and geothermal energy etc). Computers will provide ample information-processing capacity for any foreseeable needs while new illuminating insights into the life process open up captivating vistas. The consuming power of combustion and the amazing strength of a piece of forged steel must once have roused similar emotions – alternating between hope and fear.

Every technological breakthrough calls for a substantial measure of ordinary pluck. We are all born cowards in the face of the startling and the strange; hence the deep-seated taboo-reaction which was triggered off by the advent of nuclear power. In the faint-hearted view, harnessing nuclear forces constitutes a blasphemy which dangerously disturbs the universe; for the brave, technical progress contains the seeds of its own salvation.

Meaningful work

The systematic application of technical skill in the service of long-term goals is equal to plain, everyday work. Persistent heavy labour was imposed on man only when he switched from hunting and gathering to farming and husbandry.

> The story of the Creation is a gripping metaphor for man's reluctant but mandatory adjustment to the drudgery of agriculture. "In the sweat of thy face shalt thou eat bread", runs the immutable edict. No alternative is given but it is plain enough: starvation and death.

Deep down we still feel a nostalgic yearning for the sanguine lifestyle of our freely roaming forefathers – bygone chores become fashionable games of pleasure. Today affluent males go hunting and fishing with a frenzy worthy of better ends. By contrast, work is a systematic, often drab but always purposeful repetition of familiar plus-sum games. It is a self-elected sacrifice towards a meaningful purpose.

> In a well-known psychological experiment, workers were told to move barrow-loads of sand from one heap to another. When they were ordered to return the same sand to the first pile they began to grumble, and when the process was repeated several times they refused to co-operate any more. The utter pointlessness of the job made it an almost unbearable torment, for which no normal wage could compensate. But mediaeval masons, who knew that they were building a cathedral, could put up cheerfully with dangerous and unremitting labour for years on end, and the floorsweeper at Cape Canaveral who was asked by President Kennedy what he was doing gave the dignified answer: "I'm sending a man to the moon".

Of course, men work with a keen eye for bettering their own lot. Without such a carrot the stick remains the sole means of forcing human cogs into the production machinery. Work becomes fundamentally acceptable only if we have a reasonably clear idea of how and where it fits into a broader context.

In most societies the daily grind has been regarded as a necessary evil, suitable only for slaves or serfs. Martin Luther and Jean Calvin (1509–64) made a lasting impression on our culture when they proclaimed work as the fulfilment of life – a personal service to God. Idleness was perceived as the fount of vices, and our daily toil became regular instalments towards paying off the burden of guilt. Communism, the ultimate extension of Calvinism, dressed the protestant work ethic in its most radical garb. The words of St. Paul, "If any would not work neither should he eat", endowed Marxism with much of its force.

cf. 252

Confident enterprise

Tools and language, the everyday aids of hand and mind, have led mankind much further than the boldest neolithic utopian could dare to have imagined. Even so, high cultures rarely appreciated their inventors. In Mediaeval Europe, too, technical improvements stayed out of the cultural realm, a legacy of Antiquity's indifference. All the same, a more prosperous future was patiently prepared during the Middle Ages by anonymous entrepreneurs, often lay brothers and sisters who seized every opportunity to improve technology.

> Alongside the impassioned theological debate, matter-of-fact Benedictines were harnessing horses and putting them to plough in the heavy clay soils of Northern and Western Europe. Windmills were beginning to turn, and thousands of waterwheels were not only grinding grain, but also driving the treadle for making clothing, hemp, linen and paper, as well as bellows and the smithy's hammer, water pumps and saw-mills. (The Doomsday Book of 1086 A.D. recorded 5,264 water mills in England.) On the distaff side, the spinning wheel (originally a Chinese invention) provided the base for a growing textile industry while knitting was the product of indigenous female ingenuity.

Private enterprise flourished despite, or rather because of, the political fragmentation of European culture. This is born out especially in comparison with the contemporary, highly-centralized Chinese Empire. The time value of money was established on a financial market, despite the indignant protests of the Catholic Church.

> The relatively good supply of risk capital during the High Middle Ages is quite striking. Lombard traders and Jewish moneylenders were gradually outflanked by commercially organized guilds and wealthy banking dynasties, all equally ready to finance prodigal princes as well as bold entrepreneurs. In the year 1450 a Mr Fust, lawyer and venture capitalist, betted another 800 Gulden on a new idea: printing by means of moveable type. The inventor, Johann Gutenberg (1394–1468), could not deliver in time and was forced out. No matter, the first printed Bible was published in 1455 by the house of Fust and Schöffer, signalling the dawn of a new age.

The gradual accumulation of wealth facilitated risky long-term investment in mining syndicates, trading companies and voyages of discovery, but the growing confidence in the established rules of the political game was equally important. This became clear when England embarked on the Industrial Revolution: successful innovation could, besides riches, also bring social status.

> A hundred years after the birth of Christ, Hero of Alexandria demonstrated a working steam turbine, and probably designed the *aeolipile*: a steam-driven device for manoeu-

vering temple doors. Obviously no ancient businessman jumped at the invention, and it was not until the early eighteenth century that Thomas Newcomen's (1663–1729) steam engine was set up to pump water out of the Cornish tin mines. The real break-through for machine power was due to James Watt (1736–1819), who took out his basic patent in 1769. To encourage Watt, Parliament extended his patents in 1775 by 25 years. Watt was duly incited to pursue aggressive commercialization in companionship with Matthew Boulton (1728–1809) but later in life declined the baronetcy offered to him.

An attitude of Faustian entrepreneurship fostered engineering prowess. New materials, better tools and more accurate instruments dovetailed to produce a cornucopia of technical innovations, which again was a precondition for the advance of empirical science. Even today, complete technological transparency is the exception; the proper scientific explanation can generally be found only in *cf. 278* retrospect.

> The inventor is driven by his immediate interest in the game, a desire to master in-tractable matter and to make it serve his purpose. The result should be tangible and useful but often ignominious failure is the only payoff for incredible labour. No amount of book learning or theorizing can conceal the shortcomings of practical work. Unlike the psychoanalyst or the priest, a technician or a physician always runs the risk of a public fiasco.

Enterprise is a show of self-confidence, a bet on uncertain prospective profits. It calls for bold endeavour and the postponement of our infantile craving for instant gratification. In all cultures, such plus-sum play has prepared the ground for advances in pure, disinterested knowledge. Our understanding of the games *cf. 204* of nature is now growing by the day and most basic problems – say the supply of energy – can be charted, analyzed, and certainly also solved by applying sound science. Unfortunately, this does not guarantee a satisfactory resolution. Tech-nical accomplishments depend, in the long run, on the cultural climate and presuppose corresponding progress in economics, societal organization and values – that is, faith in the future.

Historical tuition

The astonishing cultural variety among humans may or may not be related to differences in the genetic make-up. In any event, a culture creates its own self-selective processes but of this bewildering interplay we can only make bold *cf. 415* conjectures– so far we know next to nothing.

cf. 128   Huntington, for one, has dared to take up this sensitive subject, and he invokes the
cf. 97   Parsees, the Jews, the Icelanders and the New England Puritans as instances of highly-efficient group selection. The Icelanders, for example, were driven repeatedly to the edge of annihilation by a variety of national disasters; dire necessity led even to eugenic intervention. In 1644 the French geographer Isaac La Peyrère (?1594–1676) noted that beggars risked castration or execution, and that marriage was forbidden unless the parties could support themselves and their children (this last stipulation was also sometimes applied in Central Europe). The material poverty was counterbalanced by an astonishingly high level of general education, manifest in a widespread interest in history and literature. La Peyrère reports, "They are great chess players, there not being

a peasant in the country, but what he has a set of it". Iceland still prides itself on a highly disproportionate number of grandmasters.

We may not yet be ready to explore without prejudice the ongoing genetic evolution of *Homo sapiens*. Even so, we can safely state that the historical feedback, its admonitions and reproofs, constitutes a strong formative influence. It leaves an indelible imprint on our cultural and genetic heritage.

> Around the middle of the thirteenth century Russian society fell under Mongol rule, which lasted several hundred years. Despotic centralized power was combined with total disregard for human suffering. In order to prevail, the Muscovite princes had to adopt the policies of the Master Race *in toto*. Russia never had citizens: its inhabitants were more like cattle in the personal possession of the Mongol khan or the Russian tsar. The continuous social mobilization kept the overweening machinery of government intact, regardless of the particular regime in charge.
>
> The last century has been particularly grim. George F. Kennan has pointed to the successive negative selection of the First World War, Revolution and Civil War, Stalin's purges and finally the Second World War.

The Russian experience has always been that might is right, a primitive rule derived directly from the amoral struggle for life. The sufferings of the Jewish people constitute a complementary experience.

> Despite traumatic pressures and enforced flexibility, the Chosen People have always held fast to their faith – the law of God. This set the limit on compromise; the eschatology was the common denominator of all the conflicting factions. Despite repeated rebellions followed by bloody reprisals, the Romans finally granted the Jews dispensation from the obligatory worship of the emperor – an unparalleled religious concession. Even in the Diaspora the community was able to maintain its self-imposed values which prefigured what later came to be known as bourgeois virtues. These included hard work, thrift, truthfulness and care of the destitute. Adultery was an abomination, the monogamous family was, in sharp contrast to the surrounding peoples, devoted to the tender tutelage of all children, God's most precious possession. It is hardly surprising that the Jewish communities grew in numbers and wealth; they may, at times, have run up to 10 per cent of the population of the Roman Empire.

cf. 127; 140

The obsessive adherence to a precarious but profoundly self-stabilizing tradition preserved the identity of the Jewish people and the most sacred source of our Western culture. Thanks to the Jews we have maintained contact with an authority superior to any self-righteous and overbearing temporal potentate.

But the fight against external oppression can and must be waged with success on other fronts too; in the fourteenth and fifteenth centuries this point was not lost on the Swiss, who fought vehemently for their independence.

> The peasants in the original cantons had always been accustomed to manage their own affairs in a democratic way. A conflict with domineering feudal lords was unavoidable and, quite unexpectedly, the Swiss emerged as the victors after a series of spectacular battles at Morgarten (1315), Sempach (1386), Morat (1476) and Nancy (1477). The Swiss soldiery evolved into a formidable military machine, until the defeat at Marignano (1515) put an end to their ambition. Nevertheless, internal strife persisted and was aggravated by the religious tensions of the Reformation. Only centuries of distressing experiences could persuade the individual cantons to relinquish their regional chauvinism, and to integrate themselves into a single confederation. There has been no clash of weapons since that year of 1848.

It took over 400 years of reluctant learning to persuade the Swiss to bury the hatchet and extend local principles of justice to an inter-cantonal association. The result is a polity which is highly decentralized but for this very reason firmly established. It has remained a surprisingly disregarded model for democratic decision-making. The countries of the European Community were more than a century behind when they began to emulate the Helvetic confederation.

4.2   The core of culture

The rules for human collaborative play have to be recreated by every new generation. Basic values and good manners are imbibed with the mother's milk; the distinction between fair and foul is laid down in the home. A culture is definitely crippled if female self-indulgence ever gets the upper hand. Voluntary everyday offerings maintain the morality which keeps the cultural coalition together. The cumulative plus-sum play is based on a kind of moral capitalism: the profit stands in direct proportion to the spiritual investment.

The basic rules

cf. 39; 44 In an earlier chapter I affirmed that all reality can be comprehended as a twisted bundle of time-bound and essentially transient processes. With reference to the phenomenon of life, and of culture in particular, such a statement verges on the trivial. Cultural games have to be continually replayed or they are lost for ever.

The first commandment is adequate biological reproduction. A viable culture is capable of assimilating alien elements but discontinuity in the genetic base involves a grave risk. Systematic neglect of this vital point implies a breach of fundamental rules, a betrayal of the very process of life. Irresponsible overproduction is almost as destructive. Children cannot be launched upon the world like human spawn without undermining social solidarity and, in the end, paralysing all feeling of shared humanity.

A stable material and economic base is the next challenge in the game of life. Backsliding through negligence or overexploitation brings its own inevitable punishment, and will in the worst case wipe out the carriers of culture. More often there will be a painful and genetically selective adjustment to the new, self-wrought realities. Ecological balance of a kind has so far been achieved only through total commitment to tradition – otherwise our gluttonous appetites easily get the upper hand.

> Man is not alone in heedlessly undermining the conditions of his own existence. The over-grazing by domesticated cattle in the Sahel region has its counterpart among the wild reindeer of Western Greenland. When the natural increase in numbers exceeds the carrying capacity, the food – mainly the slow-growing reindeer lichen – is literally eaten

away, which causes a precipitous crash in population. The cycle is repeated at 60-year intervals. The ravages of contagious diseases follows similar patterns which become quite commonplace, as we work down through the biological hierarchy.

Environmental degradation is not an inevitable feature of high cultures. We certainly possess the knowledge and the material resources to preserve the ecological balance and to avoid any runaway catastrophes but this presupposes good housekeeping: our investment in the future should always exceed the necessary depreciation.

The collaborative play of the cultural coalition has to be re-created by every new generation. Our character settles early in life; we imbibe of the basic rules of the game with our mother's milk. We should therefore take a look at family life, that most common and significant of cultural processes.

Family culture

Pairing among animals ranges from hurried copulation to long-term bonding. A team of two, bound by a life-long contract, ought to be the most effective unit in the competitive struggle for existence, and yet this constellation is the exception rather than the rule. (Hermaphrodism should be even more competitive and would certainly assure sexual co-equality, but for some reason it did not catch on among vertebrates.)

The development of stable monogamy comes up against substantial evolutionary obstacles. The male's attempts to impregnate as many females as possible is the prevailing masculine strategy in the genetic contest. Accordingly, physical domination or elaborate fitness displays are at a premium. Once estab- *cf. 260* lished, such a trend reinforces itself because any female will try to mate with the most seductive male, thus increasing the attractiveness of her sons and enhancing the propagation of her own genes.

> The runaway evolutionary effects of female prejudice sometimes assume absurd proportions. Only the relative absence of competition and predation has allowed the indulgence of male peacocks and birds of paradise in their excessive finery, but the consumption of sexual luxury is conspicuous in most polygamous species.

Stable pairing exemplified by swans and geese generally goes together with an almost unisexual appearance (but not vice versa), and intimate group collaboration among mammals is also linked with a similar lack of external sexual characteristics.

> The sex differentiation of the lion illustrates a borderline case. The magnificently maned male (or more often two co-operating brothers) is unique among cats in dominating his pride. Yet he exercises no real leadership, and the females account for most of the hunting. Instead a new lion ruler, which on average appears every third year, methodically kills the offspring of his predecessor in a recurring Slaughter of the Innocents while most of the females spontaneously abort current pregnancies (among Amazonian Indians, Yanomami stepfathers engage in similar practices). Territorial struggles are exclu- *cf. 170* sively a male affair with the pride as passive spectators, in glaring contrast to the female-dominated hyena packs.

Homo sapiens occupies an intermediate position. Sexual dimorphism is obvious but not extreme, and the behaviour of the average husband is a compromise between the autocratic airs of the lion male and the all-out commitment of the he-swan. Our uneasy vacillation between monogamy and polygamy reflects the precarious genetic control. The family is, nonetheless, a basic institution in all human societies. Kinship relations are the original warp of our social fabric and the corresponding rules are often worked out in the minutest detail.

> The anthropological literature overflows with examples of the significance of common ancestry. Suffice to say that the Falashas, the Ethiopian Jews of Gondar recently transferred to Israel, counted relatives down to seventh cousins.

While familial cohesion has been a matter of course in the privileged strata of high cultures, self-employed farmers had to fight tooth and nail to preserve their identity. In most places it was a losing battle: poverty and feudal oppression inexorably eroded the traditional bonds of lineage among the peasants. The ascendance of the nuclear family as a close coalition is associated with the emergence of an independent middle class in pre-Renaissance Europe. The prospects of a family business in a competitive and insecure environment were tied to the appropriate upbringing and training of the heirs.

> The famous artist and humanist Leon Batista Alberti (1404–72) was a scion of a long line of respected Florentine merchants. Like Dante he became a writer in exile and expounded familial bliss and the bourgeois virtues of thrift and circumspection in his *Libri della Famiglia*.

The Reformation can be regarded as a reaction against the sloth and moral laxity of the late Middle Ages. It brought a decisive resurgence of family life by endorsing a frugal life-style and stressing the father's familial obligations. Religious conversion should, first and foremost, imbue the believer with responsibility for his or her closest dependants. In the family circle children were taught industry, veracity, a sense of duty, self-control, and other Old Testament vir-

cf. 137; 251 tues, which have supported subsequent cultural development.

Affectionate demands

At all times, the personal rules of conduct constitute the very pith of society, and these must be passed on from generation to generation by the unremitting indoctrination of family life.

> D.C. McClelland (*The Achieving Society*, 1961) demonstrates fairly convincingly that high performance standards – the prerequisites of cultural development – are due to affectionate but consistent parental goal-setting. He pinpoints a causal relationship between prevailing values in upbringing, and cultural dynamics 50 years later. The case studies range from Golden-Age Greece to nineteenth-century England and suggests a strong correlation between the number of "achievement images" in the available educational material, and economic growth two generations later. More recently, Paul Ken-
>
> cf. 227   nedy has, in *The Rise and Fall of the Great Powers* (1988), elaborated the obvious: economic clout is indispensable for global military might. Thus the humble self-discipline of family life ultimately projects its values onto the world stage.
>
> In *Generations* (1991) William Strauss and Neil Howe present a semi-quantitative

model of socio-psychological cycles based on a thorough, albeit selective, analysis of American history. Four generational types – the idealist, the reactive, the civic and the adaptive – alternate in 88-year periods; the average sway of each generation is 22 years. Each type exhibits peculiar characteristics and confers an endowment – positive or negative – on the young. During a complete 88-year cycle, society works itself through a spiritual awakening as well as a secular crisis, both of which are sandwiched between bouts of distressed scepticism and self-seeking cynicism.

When child-rearing is resolutely handed down to doting subordinates – tutors or household slaves, nurses, nannies or governesses – irreparable damage is done to the most sensitive links in the chain of culture.

During the eighteenth century the French upper classes neglected their offspring to a horrifying extent. Babies were often sent at birth to wet-nurses in the countryside; sometimes they did not see their parents again before puberty. The French revolution was a natural reaction against the failure of the élite to live up to its responsibilities. The meaning of *noblesse oblige* must be introduced right in the nursery.

Nothing can replace the profound commitment of parents and grandparents to their descendants. The decline of families, classes, nations and whole cultures can be traced back to domestic negligence. Our extra-genetic spiritual heritage has been laboriously assembled over centuries and it must be carefully grafted on to the budding shoots: neglect of this pivotal process will be punished literally up until the seventh generation.

Olympian sex roles

Most societies and all high cultures have been patriarchal, which means that men have generally taken care of the political decision-making in society. But of all human relationships, that between mother and child is the closest. Although the *paterfamilias* has formally been the highest authority, the mother has at all times had a decisive influence over the most intimate rules of the socialization game. Basic attitudes and values as well as good manners and decent behaviour are established at home. Here the distinction between foul and fair is laid down, here on her own ground woman is the final arbiter.

In all ages the rules of proper conduct have borne the stamp of feminine approval but little has been heard of female contributions to material culture. It is a safe conjecture that patient and gifted women were the driving force behind the pivotal development of agriculture, pottery and weaving.

Sexual role differentiation has its direct counterpart in the world of religious ideas. Since time immemorial, the fertility of the soil has been tied to the female principle. Mother Earth is a universal mythological entity, tolerating a motley crew of local and even semiprivate divinities. Conversely, the gods of pastoral peoples are, almost without exception, imposing male characters, often with strong monotheistic leanings. A peaceful co-existence with rival potentates is then out of the question. The God of the nomadic Hebrews, of Abraham, Isaac, Jacob and Moses, was intensely jealous of his position, and Mohammed (570–632) consistently preached the strictest monotheism to his Bedouin warriors.

The ascendancy of high culture seems to require a strong paternal initiative, vehemently demanding religious exclusivity. Its hallmark is an intrepid creative offensive built on bold positive feedback. Men ache for heroics, a legacy of big-gamehunting forefathers. Life-preserving homeostasis, the cautious negative feedback of maternal care, is relegated to the background and vested in feminine cult objects with a popular appeal. To many Christians, icons of the Virgin Mary complemented by relics and saintly images have long represented the intimate substance of piety.

The Reformation revived the supremacy of Yahweh at the expense of the emotional and therapeutic elements of the Christian faith. In the twentieth century we have gone the whole hog, idolizing the intellect and submitting to pitiless ideologies or their even less human personifications. It is hardly surprising that the female side of ourselves reacts with panic-stricken escapist reflexes: drugs and hippy cultures. The green revolution represents another attempt to return to the bosom of motherly protection.

The tension between masculine intellectual self-assertion and feminine emotional realism is a stimulating irritant in the dialectics of social and family life. In this interplay the male is the weaker vessel. His genetic make-up is ambivalent and less adapted to the routines of modern civilization, which in many ways suit the specifically female need for security.

Desertion by the father or uninhibited patriarchal dominance both upset the delicate balance of family life with dire consequences. Either the loss of dynamism leads to matriarchal cultural stagnation, or the women are ruthlessly exploited by frustrated family fathers. The masculine lust for power then loses contact with the essentials of ordinary life, finally crashing into destructive minus-sum games. The implications are even worse if the foundations of maternal morality are shattered. Bad masculine manners are certainly distasteful but a culture is definitely crippled if female self-indulgence ever gets the upper hand.

Fatal failures

High cultures are enduring miracles, always vulnerable and insecure in their puffed-up self-sufficiency. They do not advance with the inevitability of a natural force, but are in constant danger of exhausting the original fund of spiritual equity whereupon collective creativity gives way to purely repetitive replays, sometimes *ad absurdum*.

The culture of ancient Egypt spanned a period of roughly 3,000 years, but by about 2600 B.C., at the beginning of the Old Kingdom, it was already past its prime. A rigid canon stifled artistic expression; the famous pyramids constitute eloquent evidence of cultural elephantiasis – an absurd apotheosis of Egyptian values. Most of the material surplus was channelled into outstanding pieces of real estate, which served as a guarantee for the eternal life of the top executives and their retinue.

cf. 192; 234

The same theme recurs in countless variations throughout history. Triumphant cultural coalitions develop their co-operative play with supreme skill, only to fall back with depressing regularity into a tangled undergrowth of legitimized faking and cheating.

The foundations of Chinese thought were laid during the turbulent periods of Spring and Autumn (770–476 B.C.) and Warring States (475–221 B.C.). Kung Fu Tzu (Confucius), Lao Tzu, Mo Tzu, Chuang Tzu and Meng Tzu (Mencius), among others, played over a vast philosophical register with a passion approaching the intellectual excitement of their contemporaries in Greece (there may even have been a Greek link by way of India). Subsequent cultural developments show an impressively broad sweep. Remarkable were the many technical innovations: the wheelbarrow and the harness; paper and printing; deep drilling and gunpowder (it *was* used in warfare); the compass and the abacus – all were discovered and developed by practically-minded Chinese. Many of the ideas probably drifted all the way to Europe, nucleating the inchoate technological progress of the Middle Ages. Natural gas was used for heating while paper money, mass production, and an efficient system of water transport stimulated the economy.

The promising start eventually gave way to cultural stagnation which can be traced back to the rather obscure realm of culture-specific meta-rules – a resigned adherence to tradition; a tolerant hedonism; a lack of religious commitment – in other words a deleterious deficit of bad conscience. Without this the inherent dynamics of the technical insights did not come into full play. The common man never had any say. Instead all power was invested in the Emperor and a vast bureaucracy was created whereupon society petrified in parasitic hypercentralisation, interrupted by spasms of destructive anarchy.

cf. 146; 400

In European minds the decline and fall of the Roman empire has remained a momentous event. Originally, Roman administration relied on the support of local notables, who were tied to their clients by mutual obligations. This social structure was gradually disrupted by the venality of a bloated bureaucracy and the predation of local military commanders. Prefiguring a feudal society, farmers went into bondage seeking the protection of powerful landlords. The ever-increasing numbers on the dole in Rome and later in Constantinople became a severe drain on imperial finances. In the end, emperors were so impotent that they could not muster even a minimum of defence against roving marauders.

In 363 A.D. parts of Tripolitania in North Africa were pillaged by Bedouin tribes. Count Romanus, the Roman commander, arrived with his army but began on the spot to blackmail the poor inhabitants and retreated when they could not pay up. In 367 an inquiry was authorized by the emperor Valens to investigate the case but Romanus was well connected and bribed his way out. The two local leaders who had taken a stand had their tongues torn out for their pains.

Prompted by the approaching Huns, the Vandals and Alans, among others, marched over the frozen Rhine (December 3, 406) and swept through Gaul and Spain. When the Vandal army crossed the straits of Gibraltar in 429 it was no more than 20,000 strong; yet the Vandals easily subdued the province of Africa and finally sacked Rome in 455.

The decaying empire was a carcass which attracted vultures from far and wide. Large areas were in the hands of brigands and permanently out of administrative control. The government was unable to fulfil any of its duties and barbarian rule was, in many cases, preferable to the graft of imperial warlords and tax collectors.

Vigorous cultures are based on cumulative plus-sum play, a kind of moral capitalism in which the profit stands in direct proportion to the spiritual investment in coalition-building. Particularly in its Protestant-Calvinist version, *cf. 173; 251* our western culture is – or at least has been – moulded by the idea of accumulation, based on the strength of the work ethic and individual responsibility. Other cultures imbued with similar values, above all the Sino-Japanese, seem particularly disposed to embrace and exploit at least a part of the cultural heritage of the West. The Japanese transformation after the Meiji revolution serves as a spectacular example of a radical development of the cultural game, *cf. 206* supported by an almost intact value frame.

The marrow of culture

A creative culture is an exceptional, self-organizing supercoalition which is constantly facing threats from without and conflict from within. It is punctuated by a never-ending series of crises but instant contact with the meta-rules maintains social coherence, even under severe stress. In periods of consolidation, successful responses are systematically woven together into a hierarchy of repetitive feedbacks. Ultimately this creeping bureaucratization reaches the very marrow of culture. Even the obligations of faith are delegated to specialists whose task is to maintain contact with the divine powers. The professional performance of prescribed rituals guarantees every paid-up member of the creed the maximum allowance of eternal bliss in return for a minor ceremonial *cf. 400* contribution – religion has degenerated into high-powered superstition.

> With great efficacy Tibetan wind or water-driven prayer wheels used to repeat the Tantric formula "*Om mani padme hum*" – Ah, the divine wisdom in the Lotus. Most faiths can boast a good deal of prayerful activity, albeit none on quite so mechanical a level (if we dismiss the "In God we trust" on the American dollar bills). The standard form of the Muslim prayer, the Jesus Prayer of the Orthodox, and the rosary-recollected Ave Marias and Paternosters of the Roman Catholics all impart autosuggestive spiritual therapy, but they undermine the silent prayer of our daily deeds – the genuine sacrifice of the self.

The abdication of a personal faith amounts to corruption at the core. Instantaneous personal satisfaction is maximized at the expense of fellow citizens and the future of the community. The outcome is an anarchic playback towards more primitive social states where loyalty does not extend beyond the limits of instinctive tribal solidarity. The integrating, axiomatic rules of the game reveal themselves through their absence, and the whole edifice crumbles when an indefinable frame of reference fails to invest each constituent with sense and purpose.

We would surely like to take time off from the painful challenge of creativity, to rest on our laurels, silence our consciences, enjoy a little hard-earned vacation – isn't this after all a duty to ourselves? One thing is clear: we are and remain in debt, we live off our forefathers, their accumulated capital, their material and intangible investment, their toil and sweat. The great inspirers, the founders and prophets of faiths, have certainly created crucial roles, but in this context ordinary people are the main actors. The unceasing re-creation of common values by voluntary everyday offerings sustains our internal truth, the means and ends of the cultural coalition.

4.3   Culture reproduction

High cultures lack the buttressing of tribal solidarity. Accordingly, family upbringing must be supplemented with the state-sponsored transmission of good citizenship in whatever guise. The overt preaching of even the most convincing creed would certainly be counterproductive but our youth needs some inoculation against seductive superstition and the most prevalent intellectual fallacies. Only then can they capitalize on their family upbringing, re-create fundamental values and internalize the rules of our human plus-sum game.

The chromosomes of culture

The core of culture, discussed in the previous section, corresponds to the nucleus in the cells of eukaryotic organisms. This site of inheritance steers the exceedingly complex cultural game by a set of inconspicuous meta-rules. High cultures lack the buttressing of tribal solidarity; their cultural chromosomes are unstable and the maintenance of the crucial message requires an organized effort. Accordingly, family upbringing must be supported by the state-sponsored transmission of good citizenship in whatever guise it may take.

Unruly adolescents are not very receptive to the arguments of common sense, or enthusiastic about patient long-term toil. For this reason every community has to emphasize the authority of elders and find ways to institutionalize the process of maturation. In most hunting and gathering societies, boys in particular undergo harsh initiation ceremonies, underlining the magic rebirth of the untamed youngster as a responsible member of the clan or tribe. Modern school grades and academic examinations correspond fairly well to the rites of primitive peoples – they are a gateway into the adult world.

The internal value system, the very kernel of a culture, is not amenable to explicit verbal articulation, nor can it be adequately understood by the inexperienced mind. Young people often have a sound aversion to ideological force-feeding, but they make easy victims for unscrupulous manipulators who cynically exploit their innate drives.

> Nothing captivates the male adolescent more than the right to armed self-indulgence. The schoolboys of Sparta and Nazi Germany, of Palestine, Iran, China, Cambodia and Somalia have all thrown themselves into an orgy of legitimized violence with the same unmitigated enthusiasm. *cf. 86*

We should not expect too much of systematic education. The template for cultural reproduction must be inherent in the whole upbringing; the meta-rules should be so unobtrusive that they can be re-discovered and thus become part of the personality. Many laudable ends are not attainable by a formal curriculum which often counteracts its purpose. Education for peace, for example, quickly degenerates into sanctimonious self-deception. Every culture represents in itself a holistic attempt to utilize our limited resources of goodwill; peace is simply a by-product of successful play.

Classical models

All high cultures have set great store by the education of an élite. Imperial China stands for the most impressive attempt at self-stabilization by systematic instruction.

cf. 400   Filial piety; respect for authority; loyalty to the state; idealization of immutable harmony – all these came together in the teaching tradition of Confucianism to produce the Chinese version of the gentleman. The mandarins, the end product of the educational machine, had passed through exacting competitive examinations and enjoyed enormous prestige. From the Tang period (618–907) onwards the imperial administration depended entirely on the existence of a reliable bureaucracy, recruited mainly from the ranks of the mandarins. But the introverted self-sufficiency and risk-aversion of the intelligentsia drove education into a dead-end. Under the Ming rulers (1368–1644) the syllabus had been focused on the humanities, China's much revered classic literature. All subjects with a practical orientation, including mathematics and the natural sciences, were conspicuous by their absence. The striving for the final completion of the cultural game reached its peak with the publication of the greatest encyclopaedia of all time, which ran to 11,000 volumes, issued in only three copies!

cf. 252 Despite great achievements, Chinese history illustrates the futility of even extreme efforts to conserve a spiritual heritage. The Graeco-Roman culture had a more open and speculative attitude to life and the world but like China it was handicapped by a lack of respect for the daily round. Empirical methods were not rarefied enough for the noble intellect of the Greeks; new insights could not
cf. 133; 143 entrench and enrich themselves by practical applications.

For all that, ancient Greece has been the model for the integration of youth into modern societies. The military exercises of young men were complemented by physical and intellectual training in the Greek gymnasia which extolled the principle of the harmony of body and soul.

> The same means can easily be adapted to quite different ends, as illustrated by the brutal Spartan practices of the time. Even in Plato's ideal Republic the education of the young was based on almost totalitarian authority. Every man was indoctrinated to discharge the obligations of his pre-ordained class; family ties were prohibited as subversive to the state. Women were generally an irrelevance to the Greek philosophers, although Plato himself did adopt a more liberal attitude towards the end of his life.

The Middle Ages inherited from classical Antiquity an excessive belief in logical analysis and deduction which became juxtaposed with the conceptions of Christian theology. The result was an orthodox canon, reflecting a well-organized universe in which God, men and beasts all had their allotted place. In the rigid class structure of the Middle Ages, Plato's Republic dominated Christ's Kingdom of God by stealth.

We could look upon the dawn of the modern age as a renaissance, not only of Greek art and thought but of the Gospels as well. It was a revolt against the straitjacket of scholasticism, set off by the ordeal of the Black Death in the middle of the fourteenth century, when Europe lost 25 million, about one third of its population. The naive mediaeval *Homo ludens* stumbles into an adolescent crisis of identity involving a re-evaluation of all values – a condition we have not yet overcome. The diverse attempts at pedagogic reform have all been undermined by the ambivalence of our value system.

> Heinrich Pestalozzi (1746–1827), the pioneer of modern teaching, tried to put the lofty ideas of Rousseau's "Émile" into practice. He personifies the conflict between the ambitious ideals of philanthropy and the intractable limitations of human nature. Pestalozzi started as a successful substitute father for destitute pupils, but his Yverdon institute soon became something of a fashionable boarding-school for the children of prosperous "progressive" parents. Although persistent strife among the teachers was to lead to the collapse of the school, its founder's ideas more than survived the fiasco. Pestalozzi strongly emphasized the paramount importance of upbringing and moral teaching but failed, as so many others, to systematize this process in a school context. At the end of his life he declared resignedly, "Life itself is the teacher".

The quantitative goals of the early reformers have been achieved and surpassed but the dream of individual guidance and ethical training has evaporated. In the nineteenth century, perfectionism was pushed to such lengths that a French minister of education boasted of knowing at any given moment exactly what was happening in every schoolroom in the country. Despite the onslaught of good intentions, official or unofficial education policy continues to stifle far-reaching innovation in teaching.

Vicious deduction

Elementary education in reading, writing and arithmetic generally works quite well. But further up the learning ladder we are trained to solve problems under the following rather unrealistic conditions:

-all the necessary information is available;
-little or no superfluous information is offered; and
-there is one and only one correct solution to each problem.

No wonder that our conditioned reflexes are poorly adapted to the real world. The intellectual cripple is often at an advantage in the abnormally simplified situations where deductive thinking celebrates its greatest triumphs.

> Straightforward logical problems can cause a good deal of difficulty to people of average talents. We are given the following advance information about the inmates of a prison with four cells:

cell	1	2	3	4
	man	*woman*	*black*	*white*

> We are faced with the proposition: "All men in the prison are black". The question is: "Which cells must you examine, to ascertain the truth of this statement?" Only about 4 per cent of normal students can cope with an intelligence test of this type. And yet there is a 60 per cent probability that people who have received shock therapy for serious

brain damage in the right cerebral hemisphere will manage the test successfully. The electric shock has put the right half of the brain out of action and allowed the left to function with great logical clarity, undistracted by any flights of fancy.

Cells 1 and 4 are those which should be checked. Cell number 3 is irrelevant because the proposition does not state that "all blacks are men", which seems to be taken for granted by ordinary common sense.

Normal people have considerable difficulties in inducing a state of computer-like stupidity when it is called for, keeping rampant creative impulses in check. The ability to think logically is by no means a sufficient or even a crucial element of creativity, but it is indispensable when we check the final outcome, looking for errors and omissions.

The dilemma of the pedagogue stems from the difficulty of evaluating, let alone teaching creativity. As said before, all we can do is to permit it. But the deeply entrenched and exaggerated respect for analytically precise models of problem-solving unintentionally produces adepts attuned to bureaucratic and security-oriented paradigms. This reinforces the values behind the educational policy and may lead to a vicious circle of ever-increasing regimentation and risk avoidance.

> In primary school the child is in the safe hands of a single teacher but as soon as the subject matter becomes more abstract and demanding it is carved into fragments. Just as the children enter puberty, the authority of the teacher is seriously eroded. Would it really be impossible for gifted children from higher grades to work alongside the subject-specialist teachers? Is it unrealistic to advocate a broadening of competence throughout the teacher's working life? Must knowledge really be hacked into mince-meat and made unappetising to youngsters still lacking the ability to digest dismembered information? Could the courses not be grouped together around some meaningful theme, such as the evolution of the universe, of life, and of man, which would then be penetrated in ever greater depth at higher levels of education?

Our hypertrophic educational system must find ways of augmenting the analytical problems of the textbooks with personal challenges calling for a creative response. Demanding laboratory exercises and practical fieldwork have a liberating effect as students confront tangible reality. Otherwise they are only too likely to come off the academic conveyor belt with a false notion of how the world really works.

Re-creative learning

Most of the criticism presented here is old hat, and the many commendable attempts to break out of the vicious circle have no doubt had an impact. But the essence of the argument is that despite a lot of lip-service, cultural reproduction has been largely relegated to travelling second class. Our best minds seem to shun this area; the dearth of innovation shows up in the drabness and lack of dynamism in education.

cf. 152   In the best Confucian tradition, Japan, South Korea, and Singapore stand out as paragons of didactic diligence. Competition for the top schools has become so fierce that there are (in Japan) cramming schools for gaining entrance to the cramming schools which prepare pupils for the entrance examinations to the most prestigious institutions. Conversely, educational laxity obtains in the West; the learning by rote, still prevalent in the East, has been traded for a commiserative dearth of discipline and a wishy-washy curriculum.

Teaching, in particular, should be geared to handling a continual process of self-improvement, liberating the intellectual resources of pedagogues, pupils and parents. Set against this we have to accept a reasonable level of inequality and inconsistency, disorder and plain mistakes; otherwise we will never attain rising standards of general education. A radical unfettering of teaching activities would attract both new talent and some risk capital; it would go a long way towards improving the status of the educator and enhancing the reproduction of our culture.

> To achieve these ends, educational vouchers have been introduced in many places, but   *cf. 210*
> this is just the beginning. A real market with risks and opportunities, profits, and losses
> must be created even if the public acts as the major paymaster. Only when rectors and
> headteachers are awarded full managerial responsibility, will failures become fruitful
> and innovations get off the ground. Only then can outstanding methods propagate and
> beget better and better ideas.
>   Computer power should at last come into its own, starting at an early age when the
> childish predilection for playing new language games can be utilized to the full. Later on
> pupils should learn to understand and apply the rules of nature, as they have been
> revealed by our keenest brains. Finally they should try to master the superabundant
> material of the humanities and to grasp the historical context, guided by a minimum of
> prejudicial principles.

Stereotypical liberalism is steadily diluting our cultural inheritance and, despite everything, we should beware of vacuous value-neutralism. The prevailing allergy towards value judgements drives our students into the desert of value nihilism, and forces upon them a premature absorption of existential uncertainty. After all, young people are only too prone to swing between blasé scepticism and cocksure self-confidence.

The overt preaching of even the most convincing creed would certainly be counterproductive; imprinting values by rote works only in the nursery. The fundamental problem is to transmit to future generations the fluid and impalpable truths of the cultural game using practical skills and explicit knowledge as expedient receptacles. The youngest members of our cultural coalition need some inoculation against seductive superstition and the most prevalent intellectual fallacies. Only then can they capitalize on their family upbringing, re-create fundamental values and internalize the rules of our human plus-sum game.

4.4   Social subcultures

The cultural game is maintained by a whole network of subcultures, countless semi-permanent groupings linked by ideals or interests. Access to such a diversity of often contradictory influences allows for a sense of genuine loyalty vis-à-vis superordinate structures. At all times, spontaneously-forming, self-organized groups have spearheaded the great breakthroughs of our culture. Every authoritarian attempt to interfere in this self-regulating play has a stultifying effect: no bureaucratic restrictions can be imposed on those who seek the truth.

The social fabric

Mammals exhibit a wide range of cohabiting arrangements, from the single female with her young to structured communities of wild dogs, hyenas, dolphins or killer whales. Hunting efficiency is greatly augmented by teamwork, and man has made the most of this incentive. Innumerable chases and skirmish-
cf. 85; 231   es have inscribed a predilection for partnership in our genetic code.

Anthropological studies suggest that the inherent stability of human associations declines as the size of the group increases. At a population level of around 300 to 500, splintering occurs spontaneously, even in the absence of compelling
cf. 170   external causes. A similar phenomenon can be observed in industrial and military organizations. Man is basically a tribal primate: the maximum size of this fundamental in-group is defined by the number of realizable personal relationships.

cf. 103   As innate experts on human physiognomy, we can reliably identify, at most, about one thousand individuals. These form our personal ambience, and can unhesitatingly be distinguished from the multitude of unknown faces. The rest are vaguely differentiated strangers. It is therefore difficult for any close-knit community to expand beyond a given limit.

A tribe can keep its grip on an expanding population by invoking common history and language. Nations, too, must exploit such primordial tribal impulses to keep the coalition together. We cannot feel immediate solidarity with millions of people; the nation, and certainly the culture as a whole, remains an abstraction. Even ordinary cities generate anonymity roughly in proportion to their size. The inhabitants develop a basic indifference to the fate of their fellow-citizens, with appertaining self-defensive or even aggressive attitudes. Were it not for our identification with smaller reference groups, we would be atomized into wholly interchangeable constituents of the much-heralded "masses".

The cultural game is maintained by a whole network of subcultures – workshops, companies and organizations, trade unions, political and religious associations, teaching and research institutions, sports clubs, societies and coteries – countless semi-permanent groupings linked by ideals or interests.

> In the United States there are 131,250 (1986) associations in the realm of trade and industry alone, including the American Society for Association Executives with over 18,000 members. It has been calculated that the average American needs only four or five intermediaries in order to make contact with all his fellow countrymen. Even taking into account a redundancy factor, this implies only 100 – 200 human contacts per individual. In Finland with its population of barely five million there are about 80,000 active registered associations. The average Finn belongs to at least half a dozen different, formally organized groups. These figures may be something of a world record; anyhow they confirm the enormous complexity of the cultural tapestry.

The access to such a diversity of often contradictory influences, information channels and personal contacts leaves the individual a certain latitude in both judgement and action, and allows for a sense of genuine loyalty vis-à-vis superordinate structures. Total identification with a single subculture – be it employer, party, church or secret society – entails the delegation of personal responsibility to the upper échelons of the dominant group and is an ominous simplification of the cultural game.

Business settings

No subculture, least of all a business, can thrive without the invisible support of a broad set of integrating rules, which sustains a lasting plus-sum game. The rapid growth of the Japanese economy would, for instance, have been inconceivable without the well-established value system. The link between the basic rules of the social game and economic prosperity is even more visible in the opposite case of stagnation.

> In many (if not most) less-developed countries, verbal usage is basically insincere, and not only in politics. Every utterance outside a circle of intimates is just another makeshift in the everlasting jockeying for position. Worthies of various degrees seek to enhance their status by making grandiloquent promises while the people try to protect themselves with great verbal virtuosity against oppression, extortion and exploitation. The whole language game is thoroughly politicized, giving unbridled expression to lofty intentions or to humble subjection, as the case may be. The connection with any genuine undertaking or concrete action is more or less accidental and is open to constant revision.

In a bazaar environment, investments are necessarily opportunistic and short-term; every business becomes a string of isolated transactions since any lasting commitment would be suicidal. The only enduring relationships are based on the family, kin or the tribe. Loyalty to superordinate rules is almost non-existent; a man as good as his word is not a pillar of society but rather an anachronism, ready for the madhouse.

> Centuries of systematic abuse can be halted by injecting fresh credibility into the business game under the umbrella of impartial political and legal rules. Hong Kong is the outstanding example of the fertilization of a barren island by decent government, admittedly including a shot of opium trade for starters. English detachment and sense of

fair play complemented Chinese industry and thrift to produce an unprecedented economic success. The departure of the English in 1997 will make for a very interesting econo-political experiment.

Emulating the success of Hong Kong, the other small "dragons" (Singapore, South Korea, Taiwan) have enlisted traditional values to serve as the requisite societal cement. The enlightened dictatorship of Lee Kuan Yew in Singapore comes close to the Confucean ideal of benign and propitious government which unfetters entrepreneurship but upholds the political tutelage.

cf. 148; 403

Tightly-knit secret societies did evolve as protection against arbitrary exaction particularly in China, providing a framework for long-term business relations. More often than not merchant guilds or professional corporations have come out into the open and tried to organize society to their exclusive advantage. Occasionally, powerful trade organizations have even managed to impose an order of their own over large areas.

> In the Middle Ages, North Italian merchant cities – Pisa, Genoa and Venice – were the masters of Mediterranean trade, extending their rule over long stretches of coastline. Meanwhile the Hanseatic League dominated large tracts of Northern Europe, particularly around the Baltic. Later, the various East India companies vehemently struggled for the hegemony of the Far East.

In the long run, syndicalist coalitions lead to restrictive practices and to the suffocation of the innovative impulse. Remote control by commercial self-interest, howsoever astute, lacks the legitimacy that is indispensable to any durable administration. Government requires deeper roots if it is to provide an adequate framework for sustained economic progress.

Over the ages, high civilizations assigned all drudgery to slaves and serfs or, at best, to day labourers. The rigid class structure entailed economic stagnation, and was bound to create severe social stress which has pervaded the better part of human history. In our culture, the abhorrence of slave labour has been instrumental in forcing technological development which is now running away at breakneck speed.

Thanks to mechanization and automation, we are now returning to a more varied work setting, in which our original hunting and gathering instincts can find an outlet. At the same time our proclivity for working in groups is being utilized; economic co-operation crystallizes into born-again tribal allegiance. Profit-seeking enterprises, from the smallholding to vast multinational organizations, constitute distinctive coalitions which confer an identity on their members, and endow the intrinsically boring economic game with meaning.

Creative fellowship

Modern business administration tries, as best it can, to take advantage of our predisposition for collective play. Work teams and project groups are matters of course while the most progressive managers make a point of encouraging the manifold informal networks within the company.

cf. 86   Imposed intimacy generates remarkably strong social bonding. Male adolescents are especially susceptible to such chemistry; a shared classroom or military service can leave an indelible imprint.

Whatever the merits of a good organization, the full flourish of human interplay is evoked only by voluntary association around common interests – philately or football, bird-watching or philosophy. Science could survive without its colleges, its universities, fraternities and specialized associations but it would not last long without the spontaneous interaction of committed enthusiasts.

> Perhaps one half of scientific information is disseminated by some 40,000 traditional journals worldwide. They pick and choose in blissful confusion among the material on offer, each according to its system of peer review or the idiosyncrasies of its editorial board. A quarter of all communication is conveyed via *ad hoc* congresses and symposia, and the rest – which is probably the most significant part – is passed along by personal contacts, correspondence and talk. The creative process sorely needs free discussion and the spontaneous criticism of trusted fellows. The roundabout route via the professional publications causes delay and deprives the message of its freshness, but it fills the indispensable need for widespread documentation and the accumulation of personal merit.

Creative team-work builds on a shared frame of reference: reality is perceived in   *cf. 122* similar categories, albeit from slightly different angles. A stimulating challenge releases ingenious argumentation which eventually puts the problem in proper focus. Once the group has learnt to master a common language, the creativity of the members is synergetically utilized.

Most epoch-making cultural achievements have stemmed from such exquisite intellectual plus-sum play. Vienna at the turn of the twentieth century furnishes a striking example of locally concentrated intellectual fertility. The Hapsburg capital produced a veritable fireworks of spectacular performance, covering all aspects of culture.

> The author and journalist Karl Kraus (1874–1936) was the central figure in one of the key groups. His uncompromising call for sincerity and disdain for epicurean affectation was the common denominator of the diverse personal creeds. Such a Tolstoyan ethos provided a springboard for Ludwig Wittgenstein, Arnold Schönberg and Adolf Loos, the fathers of modern philosophy, music and architecture respectively. The novelist Robert Musil, the dramatist Hugo von Hofmannstahl, the poet Rainer Maria Rilke and the painter Oscar Kokoschka were influenced by Kraus. Ernst Mach, together with Theodor Herzl and Ludwig Boltzman, were among the household gods of the group but Freud was a dirty word: according to Kraus, psychoanalysis is the very disease that it claims to cure.
>
> During its last decades the Hapsburg monarchy was a cultural hothouse bursting with exotic plants including composers like Gustav Mahler and Alban Berg, and authors like Franz Kafka, Franz Werfel, Hermann Broch and Elias Canetti. The philosopher Franz Brentano influenced Edmund Husserl as well as the psychologists Karl Stumpf and Alfred Adler. The famous economists Joseph Schumpeter, Ludwig von Mises and Friedrich von Hayek have their roots in Vienna: Karl Popper was born there and so was Peter Drucker, one of the pioneers of practical business philosophy. Equally famous are the logical positivists of the Vienna circle, which included Moritz Schlick, Otto Neurath, Rudolf Carnap and Kurt Gödel.

The Vienna groups are by no mean unique. Niels Bohr and his informally managed Copenhagen institute played a decisive role in the mid-1920s, when modern quantum mechanics was launched in a few years of hectic discussion by Werner Heisenberg, Erwin Schrödinger, Paul Dirac, Wolfgang Pauli, and Louis-Victor de Broglie, with Albert Einstein, Max Born and Paul Ehrenfest as inspiring but somewhat dumbfounded mentors. Meanwhile the Cambridge-Bloomsbury group, gathered round the philosopher G.E. Moore and the writer Lytton Strachey included such incandescent minds as Maynard Keynes and Bertrand Russell, Virginia Woolf and E.M. Forster.

> Farther back in history, we can perceive Pericles and Socrates as centres of intellectual brilliance, attracting fresh talent from far and wide. Almost two millenia later, the rebirth of Greek thinking was accelerated by the illustrious group that gathered round the *primus motor* of the Florentine Renaissance, il Magnifico, Lorenzo de' Medici. And at the turn of the eighteenth century, the Industrial Revolution was catalyzed by the Lunar Society in Birmingham, where Erasmus Darwin, Joseph Priestley, Josiah Wedgwood and James Watt were the most prominent actors, with Adam Smith and David Hume in the wings.
>
> The nuclear age, too, was initiated by a team of dedicated enthusiasts. In almost euphoric delight, the Los Alamos gang under Robert Oppenheimer rolled out the atomic bomb in minimum time. After the war, the exploit was repeated when Edward Teller and Stanislaw Ulam directed the construction of the hydrogen bomb in a somewhat less exuberant atmosphere.

Man is a social animal and thrives on intellectual plus-sum play. We could not do without the hermits of the human spirit but genuine originality comes into its own only when immersed in the rich interplay of kindred souls.

Self-organizing games

Major scientific (not to speak of artistic) achievements grow out of the rather chaotic interplay of self-directed actors. The outcome is a strange kind of world market bordering on anarchy. People, ideas and institutions ferociously compete for publicity and available material resources. The virtually blindfolded search is a cogent exposition of high-level Darwinian discovery in the making. *cf. 377* Really a glorious muddle, it is yet a vast and successful plus-sum game.

Every authoritarian attempt to interfere in the self-regulating play has a stultifying effect: no bureaucratic restrictions can be imposed on those who seek the truth. To do so just invites self-deception, prejudice, superstition and conceit. Free inquiry and free flow of information is the breath of life, not only for science but for all culture.

cf. 218
> The same optimum conditions hold good for the more mundane economic games. Michael Porter shows in *The Competitive Advantage of Nations* (1990) how highly diversified clusters of freely-interacting companies have attained global prominence. Intense rivalry *and* collaboration has, to take a few examples, raised German printing presses, American patient monitoring equipment, Italian ceramic tiles and Japanese industrial robots to worldwide renown. The entertainment industry offers even more convincing evidence; Hollywood is an exemplar of creative economic self-organization.

The global scientific community stands as a model of fruitful cultural interplay. Injustice and the abuse of power are the exception and do not call for constant

counter-measures; recurring waste and the duplication of effort is a small price
to pay for reinsurance against doctrinaire thinking and lack of self-renewal. *cf. 313*
Although the inherent rules of the scientific game presumably make the best of
the situation, scientists cannot altogether steer clear of the fashions and pre-
conceptions which permeate our culture.

> The study of the genetic base of different populations or the discussion of eugenic
> problems, even in purely scientific contexts, have been thoroughly discredited by the
> Nazi scam. Such issues are certainly not "in", they are "sensitive", and are mostly
> weeded out at the conceptual stage quite apart from the problems of adverse publicity.
> We simply do not want to hear about such things, content as we are with the dogma of
> human immutability. More ominous is the steady increase of bureaucratic interference. *cf. 310*
> At the National Institute of Health in Washington, a posse of Protocol Implementation
> Review Committees (PIRCs) is charged with the responsibility of stopping "contro-
> versial" research. Now a second tier "panel to review research further" has been added
> to quash any unpalatable proposals that may have slipped through the PIRCs.

Is some knowledge so potentially dangerous that we should banish it for fear of
its incontestable force? Such self-censorship would be a fatal error. Where are
the high priests who could define the limits of judicious ignorance, and what
would ensure that despite everything the genie was not let out of the bottle,
either openly or in secret? We must trust both ourselves and our fellow-beings in
the dauntless acceptance of reality.

> At the beginning of the fifth century B.C. the Pythagoreans strove to carry on the
> master's work by pursuing secret mathematical knowledge based on the mystical in-
> terpretation of numbers. According to the prevailing doctrine, natural numbers and
> their rational relations (the fractions) provided the key to the enigma of the universe.
> However, the mathematicians soon realized that the diagonal in a square cannot be
> expressed in an exact numerical relation to its sides, or as we would put it today, $\sqrt{2}$ is
> an irrational number. At this time the Pythagoreans occupied a leading political posi-
> tion in the Greek colonies in Southern Italy (Magna-Graecia), and when Hippasus, a
> member of the fraternity, brought this mathematical scandal into the open, legend has it
> that he was drowned for his audacity. The Pythagoreans were soon swept away by a
> popular uprising, and their considerable scientific achievements evaporated, thanks to
> the self-imposed exclusivism and pretentious pipe-dreams of a secret society.

If we want to call off the quest for truth we can only do so by appealing to some
explicit superordinate criteria, man-made idols as it were, which distinguish
once and for all between right and wrong, true and false. Thanks to the absence
of such authoritarian intervention, natural science especially has gone from
strength to strength. In recent times artistic activity has by and large enjoyed
similar advantages. Only posterity will tell whether the outcome is equally
impressive.

4.5   Individual game plans

The viability of a society depends on the quality of its custodians. The self-propelled reformers or progress dynamos are the leaven of culture. They orient themselves to the ethical fields of force, nucleating selflessly co-operating fraternities. The greatest threat comes from cheating cynics who seek their own advantage by infringing the rules of the game. They must somehow be restrained even though the ultimate problem of guilt remains unsolved. The dedicated progress dynamo faces a daily challenge of spiritual renewal and intellectual honesty. His or her success is a necessary and, perhaps, sufficient condition for a self-enriching cultural game.

Fair language play

Cultures are borne along by individual actors, each operating according to his own lights and following a private strategy. These personal rules of the game are established early in life when social competence is instilled by family upbringing. The actual interpretation of the norms depends on both individual rectitude and the cultural context. The purport of the commandment "Thou shalt not bear false witness" may apply only within the immediate family circle, or it may be extended to a limited subculture of friends, acquaintances or colleagues before achieving ultimate universality in its Judeo-Christian version.

> Since the beginnings of language, truthful speech has certainly facilitated co-operation and imparted selective advantage at the group level. Shrewd lying may, on the other hand, improve individual fitness by providing a free ride. A bad conscience is the evolutionary safeguard against such perfidious behaviour. Fortunately, we seem to possess an inborn, albeit weak respect for truth, and a small tightly-knit community can easily identify and castigate its free riders. Conversely, such defectors thrive in large, anonymous societies; the requisite minimum of morality increases with the size of the relevant social grouping.

cf. 97; 216; 219; 271

Even if we audaciously take truthfulness for granted, serious misunderstandings can arise due to differences in usage or cultural background.

> If you ask a Japanese politely and cautiously in English "I suppose it isn't possible to carry out the project?", the answer will be a puzzled "Yes". Although the Japanese appreciate the indirect form of address, they do not use negative interrogatives which will be handled by the English-speaking Japanese with strict logic. If you put your question directly and aggressively, "Is it possible to carry out the project?", you will never get a curt "No". The Japanese are said to have seventeen ways of indicating a negative response but the word "no" is never used in practice since it would evoke an unbearable confrontation and lead to a breakdown in the communication process. The lack of enthusiasm will instead be indicated by a string of less offensive signals. In Japanese all concepts tie together organically and are torn apart by our quest for clarity. When insisting on straightforward answers, the Westerner just creates awkward tension.

Differences in tacit frames of reference or ideological convictions can obstruct the exchange of information, but even sharply diverging positions are no absolute obstacle to understanding. With some good will on hand, at least a modicum of communication should be attainable. In the language game there is no substitute for fair play which entails subordination or at least accountability to some kind of higher authority or arbitration. Otherwise truth will be the victim of polemic and the game spoilt for honest players.

Cynics and reformers

Human beings will always be tempted to infringe the prevailing norms in order to gain personal advantage: lying is just the first step down a slippery slope. Wily parasitism without the slightest regard for the other players or for a joint purpose marks the end point of moral degradation. In his *Gulag Archipelago* (1974) Alexander Solzhenitsyn denounces these cheats, self-serving opportunists and wanglers, who always come out on top when ethical standards totter and values are at a discount.

At bottom it is a question of our relation to the rules of the game. If we apply as a parameter individual attitudes to the mostly unwritten rules which structure human collaboration in all associations and societies, we arrive at the human typology presented in figure 4.1.

The personality type	Does not develop . . .	Develops . . .	The rules of the game
Respects . . .	Passive conformists	Dynamic reformers	
Does not respect . . .	Cheating cynics	Revolutionary fanatics	
The rules of the game			

Figure 4.1

Timorous conformists (top left) exhibit a passive and "bureaucratic" loyalty; they form the majority and maintain a low profile whereas the other groups are seeking influential positions. The conformists' lack of commitment can be offset by active, enthusiastic, rule-enhancing reformers (top right). These modern knights are the agents of self-organization and act as self-propelled progress dynamos, interpreting and enhancing the meta-rules of the community. They orient themselves to invisible ethical fields of force, efficiently transforming the available brute energy into purposeful action. Reformers are creative culture-builders, prone to forming plus-sum-playing fraternities which are committed to the often thankless task of modifying even the most sacred prepossessions of the group.

Revolutionary fanatics of diverse hues, including anarchists and nihilists (bottom right), aim at a wholesale transformation of the game and ostentatiously flout the prevailing rules. Their very frankness may eventually bring about the conversion to a more constructive approach. When it comes to the future of the company, the community, the country or the whole culture, the greatest threat comes from the cheating cynics (bottom left), who seek their own advantage by disingenuous infringement of the rules without any intention of improving them.

> We have all encountered this sort of behaviour, often in others and sometimes in ourselves; striking examples from school, military service, the football team or the night-shift suffice. As a moral corrosive the cheats may seriously weaken the fabric of any social body and, accordingly, we have developed an allergic reaction to disloyalty
>
> *cf. 86; 90* and duplicity. Deceit has, for its part, become ever more artful; the parallel evolution of social hosts and parasites goes on and on.

The cheat deceives not only his superiors: he also misleads his friends and betrays the common cause by indulging in conspiracy, intrigue, innuendo, flattery – wangling of every kind. The cynics are ruthless careerists, self-centred, unprincipled opportunists. They are the poison of all communities, and are generally bent on taking over affluent, easy-going organizations while cunningly avoiding real challenges.

The response to the unwritten laws of the language game are particularly revealing. The cynic deliberately distorts the intention of his opponent, and the
cf. 354 contaminated information packet is played back with a will to mislead.

> For long we became accustomed to massive feats of falsification by the several ideologies which impudently placed themselves above truth. But we must also look out for the more insidious contagion which seeps through the core of our cultural establishment; bluff and imposture can prevail at the very top of linguistic self-analysis. Paul de Man (1919–83), the fixed star of "new" American philosophy and literary criticism, made a virtue of barefaced obfuscation. He painstakingly concealed his collaboration with the Nazis, which may well have left him in a state of despondent value nihilism. Incredibly, a whole generation of arts students has been taken in by this intellectual
>
> *cf. 293; 374* confidence man, the godfather of deconstruction.

A moral verdict can never be one-dimensional and is rarely self-evident: who wants in any case to set themselves up as judge? We are all human, and in real life most of us hold residence in all four boxes. When the chips are down, each one of us must ultimately answer for his own actions – but to whom?

Here we come up against the boundaries of tolerance. Systematic spoilers of the game must somehow be restrained or eliminated from the coalition, even though the ultimate problem of guilt remains unsolved. Otherwise, parasitic modes of play take over and the community falls into a deadly tailspin of decay.

Cynical derailment

cf. 50 The cheats' spontaneous response in games like the Prisoner's Dilemma amounts to the callous exploitation of the good will of the other players. No superordinate guidelines are operative; for the cynics the primitive passion for play has taken over. What remains is a fundamentally trivial and paltry game in which the inflated ego is regarded as the only piece of importance. As Oscar Wilde (1854–1900) so adroitly observed, the cynic knows the price of everything and the value of nothing.

Armed organizations are relatively immune to cheats because of clear-cut rules and rather unequivocal competence testing. The exceptions are all the more illuminating.

> General K had distinguished himself as company commander during the Second World War. He was very ambitious and decided to advance his career by all the means at his disposal. He passed out of the Finnish military academy with honours by using "sick leaves" for swotting before the major exams, by familiarizing himself with the terrain before "surprise" manoeuvres, and similar devices. Things went so far that his expulsion was considered but a vote went in his favour. At the end of the course his instructors reported: "K is outstanding, ambitious, wilful, and ruthless. His ambition might lead his decisions astray and to difficulties in adjusting to realities."
>
> As unit commander he trained his men to perform well at exercises where his superiors could observe them, at the expense of proper training. As major-general his political connections and his undeniable qualities unexpectedly won him the appointment of commander-in-chief of the armed forces. Despite some positive initiatives, the morale of the officer corps in particular declined sharply under General K; he constantly played to the gallery and fussed about minor details. His main interest was success in the army skiing competitions; the age-handicap rules were altered so he could win, and soldiers were sometimes commandeered to clear the tracks of pine-needles to improve the glide. After several instances of minor misconduct and incautious public statements, General K had to resign under threat of public scandal. He later received a mild sentence for "abuse of rank". General K never expressed any regret and regarded himself as a victim of envious machinations.

The cynic operates at the infantile zero-sum level, desperately pushing his luck. He reduces life to a game of chance, and one which he is bound to lose in the end as death always makes the last move. When emotions are stunted and contact is *cf. 233; 293* lost with the innermost meaning of life, playing the game becomes a lunatic end in itself which justifies all the available means. Human co-operation is then bound to collapse: a football match becomes a brawl, national rivalry blows up into war – unbridled self-assertion is the chief source of destructive minus-sum play.

Even a fairly unequivocal identification of the game-wrecker as the very incarnation of evil naturally suffers from problems of interpretation. And what can be done if the adjudicators themselves are corrupt? From this point of view a free pluralistic society seems to be the only viable guarantee of human dignity. Dogmatism does not then have the last word; the condemned can always appeal and demonstrate their worth in a new context.

An essential prerequisite of a free society is unceasing dynamism; the frontiers of the possible must be constantly extended to provide scope for honest but unorthodox players who cannot or will not adjust to the existing establishment. A static condition is a terrible obstacle when it comes to the creative channelling of our biologically conditioned restlessness.

Moral infirmity

The reformer has always had a difficult time in the political game. A tender conscience and all-embracing concern rarely bring their own reward, and few only are granted the laurels of the statesman. Political discord often deteriorates into unrestrained polemics and mud-slinging. The breakdown of communication prepares the way for destructive strife; brutal minus-sum games have, globally speaking, been the rule rather than the exception. Standards of value become deranged in the concomitant process of institutionalized lying; the self-perpetuating delusions of the victorious establishment may virtually lock out any and all conscientious objectors from society.

> Peter Grigorovitch Grigorenko was a much-decorated major general in the Red Army, chairman of the cybernetic section of Frunze's military academy. The revelations of Stalin's reign of terror had shocked him, and he reacted strongly against the gradual return to Stalinist practices in the early 1960s. This led to clashes with the authorities, culminating in prison sentences and finally (in 1969) to committal for "care" in the infamous Serbski Institute of Forensic Psychiatry. Grigorenko was diagnosed as being "mentally ill", and a short extract from his dossier is worth quoting:
> "Reformist ideas have assumed a stubborn character that determines the patient's conduct. Furthermore the intensity of these ideas increases in connection with various external circumstances, which have no direct relation to him, making him uncritical of his own words and actions... the patient must thus be regarded as being of unsound mind." It hardly needs adding that when Grigorenko was deprived of his Soviet citizenship and moved to the West (in 1974), professional psychologists were unable to find any sign of paranoia, schizophrenia, or any other mental disorder.
> Thus sincere idealism and a sense of personal responsibility – the very qualities that distinguish the reformer – were obviously regarded as attributes of abnormality in Soviet society. Grigorenko interfered without any obvious selfish, professional or other motives in matters which did not concern him. He would not yield despite rejection, harsh reprisals, degradation, and imprisonment – the only possible explanation of such behaviour was that terrible mental disorder known as chronic reformism!

Linguistic cheating, consistently applied, poisons the powers of reasoning and ends up as a sacred lie, a palliative for the people. As in Dostoyevsky's *The Brothers Karamasov*, the Great Inquisitor always bears the heaviest burden. He has to maintain the illusion, coldly exploiting the baseness of man while absolving the faithful for deeds performed in the harsh service of historical necessity. Voluntary withdrawal from such a dead-end is very difficult, if not impossible. The easy solution is to let the ultimate goal – the millenium, the world revolution, the rule of the universal church – justify all the dirty means.

> Under Adolf Hitler and Joseph Stalin, Idi Amin or Pol Pot, no constructive opposition was possible, but the indomitable spirit of humanity reappears when oppression becomes less absolute. People like Andrei Sacharov (1921–89) and Alexander Solzhenitsyn have shown what courageous individuals can accomplish when the authorities feel some constraints on their freedom of action. They are in fact the best servants of the regime which half-consciously honours the debt.

For the average person of good intentions there are few options in a highly repressive society. He has no access to the concessions given to exceptional personalities of international stature and any attempt at organized opposition provokes violent countermeasures. The choice seems to lie between ingratiating dissimulation, meaningless tilting at dangerous windmills or passive resignation in a kind of inner exile. Most people choose to reserve their loyalty for the intimate family circle and for their kindred, friends and workmates. They try the best they can to hibernate in their everyday existence and keep the wheels turning, in hope of better times.

The progress dynamo

The reformers are progress dynamos, cultural catalysts who propitiously direct the ever-changing dynamics of the social process. They represent a life-enhancing will for renewal, and convert time-worn meta-rules into new, revitalizing impetuses. It is a matter of combining respect for well-tried structures with fresh enterprise and audacity while resisting the temptations of perfectionism, the Fata Morgana of dazzling utopias.

A list of reformist virtues would sound naive and inflated, and would anyway miss the point. Our powers of expression seem to falter before blameless heroes while cautionary examples are immediately convincing. In Shakespearean parlance: "Men's evil manners live in brass; their virtues we write in water". Even so, I want to single out an allergic reaction to passive conformity, the rejection of revolutionary posturing, an aversion to futile zero-sum games which, despite all the wearisome compromises, still marks the genuine reformer. He is a *cf. 123; 428* meta-capitalist, always trying to improve and enrich the world, producing much more than he consumes.

> Politics is a rather dirty game which taints many if not most of the participants. Yet the US presidents Woodrow Wilson (1913–21) and Herbert Hoover (1929–33) were both men of impeccable credentials. They pursued noble aims by practical means but came to grief at the end of their careers. Wilson's fate is particularly heart-rending. He died, a broken man, after failing to push through his visionary post-war policies against the diehard opposition of conservatives at home and abroad. To heap insult on injury, condescending psychoanalysts reduced his idealism to a self-seeking "Christus complex", the ominous forerunner of Grigorenko's "reformism". In the final analysis, we obviously needed the lessons of the Second World War to realize the fatuity of American isolationism and petty-European nationalism.
>
> Thomas Masaryk (1850–1935) became the first president of Czechoslovakia, a country which was a somewhat flawed product of Wilson's principle of national self-determination. He was a self-styled protestant in the Wilson and Hoover mould, and set himself the ideal "pravda vitezo" (living in truth). Recently, the Czechs had the nous to elect another upright figure, the dissenting playwright Vaclav Havel, as head of state.

The viability of a society depends on the quality of its custodians. This does not refer to just a few particularly exposed individuals but to the overall standard of the responsible élite in business, politics and science, in the civil and military services, education, and the judiciary. Peter Drucker has claimed that the one quality indispensable to leadership is integrity. The utterly honest person will uphold the values which attract capable colleagues. He will retain their loyalty by refraining from unnecessary intervention, and he will not poison the atmosphere with the petty problems of his own ego.

Enterprise is a fundamental condition of the market economy, and our impressive economic surplus is due to the fact that progress dynamos of varying eminence have been left pretty well at liberty to realize their technical inventions and profit-seeking ventures.

> David McClelland (*The Achievement Motive*, 1976) has studied the attitude of entrepreneurs to different game situations and showed that, compared with the controls, they preferred play in which both luck and skill are needed; games of pure chance or requiring only a lot of practice were rejected as uninteresting. Successful businessmen exhibit a certain kinship to our pragmatic progress dynamos. Men like John D. Rockefeller, Andrew J. Carnegie, Alva Edison, George Eastman, Pierre J. Dupont, Henry J. Ford, Alfred J. Sloan and Tom Watson (looking only at the USA) were certainly no paragons of virtue; they were driven by strong personal ambition and often applied ruthless methods. Nonetheless, their personal values proved superior compared to the money magnates of other cultures. To them wealth was not so much an end in itself as a means to creative self-realization; it was a question of measuring up to a self-imposed yardstick. Or as Tom Watson Jr. of IBM puts it, quoting Oliver Cromwell (1599–1658): "If you stop being better, you stop being good".

Prosperity seems to correlate with tolerant attitudes on such issues as race and faith. Societies which have given refuge to persecuted minorities – Huguenots, Jews, Armenians – have generally witnessed a subsequent upswing, not least in wealth. Even more evident is the correlation between oppressive regimes and economic stagnation.

> In 1492, when Columbus sailed for America, the capture of Granada had just sealed the fate of the Muslims on the Iberian peninsula and all Jews and Moors were expelled from Spain by royal decree. This marked the culmination of several hundred years of national ascendancy. The empire no doubt waxed for another hundred years, sparkling in the splendours of precious metals brought in from the New World. Two resounding national bankruptcies at the beginning of the seventeenth century exposed for all the world the waning caused by the centralizing pull of an authoritarian government and the spiritual conformity imposed by the Inquisition.

Established high cultures regularly react to both internal and external ferment with haughty self-sufficiency. Imperial China rejected for hundreds of years anything more than the most superficial contact with the "foreign devils". Strangely enough, such arrogance reaches its apogee at the moment when the need for radical change should have become self-evident.

> The Chinese Emperor Ch'ien-lung's snub to the British trade mission in 1793 is a good example of inveterate self-aggrandizement: "I have no use for your country's manufactures. Therefore . . . it behoves you . . . to display even greater devotion and loyalty in future, so that by perpetual submission to our Throne you may secure peace and prosperity for your country." Only after the disastrous opium war (1839–42), was a bureau for foreign affairs established in 1861 but its name "Tsungli Yamen" (Office for General Management) still reflected the traditional view that no real powers could exist outside of China.
>
> In Japan, the Tokugawa Shoguns demonstrated how to isolate an entire culture from alien influence. In 1614 Shogun Iyeyasu officially condemned Christianity, which had been introduced by Portuguese Jesuits and counted 300,000 Japanese converts. Under

his successors Iyemitsu and Bakufu the terror was intensified, and thousands of faithful proselytes suffered systematic torture and a futile martyr's death. In 1638 all contact with the outside world was finally and categorically broken off. Japanese returning from abroad were to be promptly executed – a law that applied even to storm-driven sailors. The only exceptions were two strictly guarded trading posts in Nagasaki, one for Chinese and one for Dutch merchants.

A self-assured central power can easily crush tentative reformers and keep profit-hungry businessmen at bay, but the simplification of the game costs dear in terms of cultural impoverishment. The most valuable production factors will fail to renew themselves when the rules of the game have been fixed once and for all. Open and tolerant societies, on the other hand, are characterized by ethical ambivalence; goals are constantly redefined and fundamental values called into question. The dedicated progress dynamo thus faces a daily challenge of spiritual renewal and intellectual honesty. His and her success is a necessary and, quite possibly, sufficient condition for a self-enriching cultural game.

4.6   Law and order

The law of the land is only the pinnacle of a submerged structure. Political and social order is not upheld by the legal framework as such, but must fall back on our intrinsic sense of fairness – a tacit support for the reasonable rights of fellow-citizens. At regular intervals, absolute justice has been visited upon our culture, and every time it has led to unprecedented violence and injustice. Faced by our all-too-human frailties, we have to be content with the limitation and mitigation of the most glaring inequities. No rules are better than the people who support them. We, the people, are obviously fallible and must, in the last instance, seek validation from a higher authority.

The credibility of law

Within the intimate circle of family and relatives we can rely on innate social reflexes and patriarchal authority to keep cheats in check. Extending these controls beyond the tribal community requires law enforcement backed by central administrative power. A viable society is ratified by the maintenance of its monopoly on coercion. The alternative is the unblessed state of natural anarchy – blood feuds or plain banditry. Short-sighted plunder then replaces long-term tilling as the dominant survival strategy, and it can take centuries of careful conditioning to foster renewed respect for the rules of plus-sum play.   *cf. 143; 274*

The function of the judiciary is to interpret and implement the explicit rules of societal interaction. The laws themselves may be outdated, self-contradictory, or even absurd. But if their application is consistent and thus sufficiently predictable, confidence in legality will be maintained. Here tradition and custom often play a part at least as important as explicit statutes.

> In his memoirs Alexander Herzen (1812–70) describes the confusion caused in Vjatka, a remote corner of north-eastern Russia, by the arrival in the 1830s of a zealous young official. An honest village elder who wanted to compensate him for his services in the customary manner was thrown in jail and threatened with the letter of the law. Delicate diplomacy was required before a miscarriage of justice was averted and everything could revert to the reliable old ways.

Arbitrariness in any form is the undoing of a legal system; court proceedings must not offer too many unpleasant surprises. Justice should work in a foreseeable fashion; only then can it be further enhanced and expanded. Sweeping resolutions and ineffectual laws deplete the always meagre funds of credibility and act as obstacles to genuine reform. No amount of legislative diligence can substitute for the autonomy of the judiciary, the impartiality of court procedures, and the guarantees against police excesses. At least since Montesquieu, these rules for supervising the implementation of the rules of law have been the real touchstone of judicial propriety.

Legislative quandaries

How far can we get by extending and refining the codified rules of human intercourse? Let us once more turn to chess, an exemplary model of law and order.

> Chess is completely defined by explicit rules which should ensure equity. The clock accurately measures the expended time; black and white alternate between the players; all controversial situations such as the repetition of moves, stalemate and so forth are fully covered by unequivocal rules and precedents. For world championships a complicated ritual has been devised. Procedures for choosing the locality, dealing with disturbances, illness and the like, are all specified down to the last detail. The game and its framework and a series of further encircling frames are all clearly established. Even so, insuperable differences of opinion can still arise in the aggressive atmosphere of professional chess tournaments; the unprogrammable judgement of a referee cannot be dispensed with.
>
> As a cerebral sport, competitive bridge is almost on par with chess. Until recently, it mainly relied on the good behaviour of the players until a series of scandals revealed that cheating had crept in at championship level. Stricter rules have been adopted but presumably bridge is still, at a pinch, regarded as a game for gentlefolk.

Legal statutes are only the pinnacle of a submerged structure. They ultimately rest on a tacit code of honour – our intrinsic sense of fairness. An inherent quandary of jurisprudence concerns this foundation: where does one draw the line between illegality and the merely immoral?

cf. 403   In the Western world, the notion of illegality has suffered considerable swings. Bad habits like swearing or card-playing or coffee-drinking have been outlawed; meanwhile the case of tobacco-smoking is, once again, pending. Adultery is still a crime of sorts in many places while, quite recently, prohibition comprised not only drugs but alcoholic drinks as well. The deeper questions of guile and mendacity or sin and shame are even more refractory. Generally they have been met with benign neglect but perjury and contempt of court are serious offences, at least in the United States.

Experience has shown that the proliferation of written law is ineffectual. Some superficial symptoms might be curable but the indefinable core of human conduct is out of reach. Any attempt to control it will come to grief, causing fatal inconsistencies and insuperable difficulties in interpretation. The legislature inevitably stumbles at the ambivalent rules of the language game, and   *cf. 346* prosecution becomes counterproductive. The gap widens between the letter of the law and our ordinary sense of justice, once again reducing the credibility of the legal system.

> A sweeping solution to this problem, popular with totalitarian régimes, is to define illegal conduct in vague, all-embracing terms such as "subversive activity likely to damage the reputation of the state". The citizen is thus exposed to the arbitrary judgement of those in command. Disinterested investigation is replaced by a callous power game, reducing the judiciary to a collection of dummies.

In continental Europe, justice is based largely on comprehensive legislation while Anglo-Saxon law puts more emphasis on judicial precedent and the discerning powers of judge and jury. Anglo-American jurisprudence gives priority to the protection of the individual, calmly accepting the acquittal of sundry criminals whereas the Roman tradition, obtaining in most of Europe, is more authoritarian: *the raison d'état* is never completely disavowed.

In Japan, the introduction of Western law did not seriously undermine the traditional reconciliation procedures. A clear verdict should be avoided at all cost because it would involve a horrible loss of face for the losing side. The Japanese are suspicious of abstract justice and rely mainly on reciprocal community relations. In the West, litigation is less traumatic and the paternalistic   *cf. 228* notion of state responsibility incites regulatory excess. We are haunted by the mirage of perfect justice, which would enforce our happiness by unrestrained legislation – bliss by decree.

A sense of fairness

In most civilized countries, respect for the rule of law is still deeply entrenched despite many absurdities inherent in the administration of justice. A mute injunction makes us uneasy when contemplating illegal acts. The likelihood of discovery and punishment has something to do with it, but does not generally play the decisive part. This stock of loyalty is gradually whittled away in a thicket of pernickety bills and regulations. As Montesquieu remarked: "When it is not necessary to make a law, it is necessary *not* to make a law".

> In the United States, dropping litter is, in general, heavily fined – to little avail. An American business friend of mine once unthinkingly threw away a cigarette butt at the railway station in Zürich. When he turned around, he noticed an elderly Swiss gentleman picking it up and putting it in the trash bin. My friend said to me: "I have never been so ashamed in my whole life".

Social control is much more effective than any judiciary in maintaining a reasonable level of security and holding the cynics in check. This requires a strong sense of community, something which has come under severe strain as a result of extensive urbanization and the accompanying atomization of communal bonds. For the common man, justice is all about perfidy punished and honesty rewarded. When the administration of law is perceived as arbitrary or grossly unfair, a breach of the explicit rules becomes quite acceptable while the exploitation of legal loopholes is denounced as fraudulent.

> The abuse of the defendant's right to a fair trial is widely resented and is draining the respect for the law. At home we learned that any misdeed should be promptly confessed to, whereas in court bare-faced lying pays off handsomely.

The Mafia syndrome, the several manifestations of organized crime, shows the vulnerability of large democratic societies to vindictive gangs who have the insolence to impose their own perverted morality on the hapless victims of intimidation and extortion.

> In a residential area, rife with robbery and burglary, it seems natural to organize a self-defence force if the police are either unable or unwilling to maintain order. Anyone who refuses to join or pay his way may be subject to reprisals, and so the groups of vigilantes gradually fall into the protection and blackmail racket. Demonstrations of brutality persuade unwilling clients of the foolishness of suspending payments, and rival organizations watch jealously over their territories. Commendable civic initiatives can degenerate into cancerous exploitation; the Sicilian mafia was originally a popular resistance movement against oppressive Spanish overlords.

While the army should protect the nation against outside enemies, the police is the executive organ of its immunological defences. They must be invested with the exclusive right to use physical force against offending citizens in order to maintain internal peace.

> Oddly enough, the police are generally met with suspicion if not open hostility. The enforcers of abstract, impersonal rules rarely elicit sympathy when they clamp down on illegitimate human interest. An atavistic reflex inhibits identification with the cops even
> *cf. 86*   if we grudgingly assent to their indispensability.

What if the establishment usurps power and becomes malignant, selfishly optimizing its own game? What happens if the executive refuses to implement the decisions of the court, or if our elected representatives choose to extend their mandate for life and supplement their numbers by co-option? Even the best constitution is a pragmatic patchwork which can be eroded from without or corrupted from within. Political and social order is not upheld by the legal framework *as such* but must fall back on indefinable funds of good will, a tacit support for the reasonable rights of fellow-citizens.

Tragic justice

Justice should follow both the letter and the spirit of the law, without regard to inconsequential circumstances. We all agree that personal relations or social position should not be allowed to affect the verdict, but how do we stand vis-à-vis the basic philosophical problem of jurisprudence – the personal responsibility of the criminal, his freedom of action and objective guilt? What does "unaccountability" or "diminished responsibility" mean in the eyes of the court; what allowance should be made for upbringing, education or genetic handicaps? Which extenuating circumstances are really consequential?

If the explicit code of law has been broken, then a crime has been committed and legal action must follow. Only the severity of the sentence leaves room for discretion. The final verdict often reveals a bizarre or even tragic aspect of justice.

> During the early 1960s the sedative thalidomide was freely available in Europe. Thalidomide proved a potent teratogen and many women, who had taken the drug during early pregnancy, gave birth to children with severely deformed limbs. Some of the mothers were driven to desperate measures, and a woman in Belgium was tried and sentenced for the murder of her thalidomide baby. In her plight, had she the right to take the life of the malformed child? Had the court the right to convict a despairing mother as a common criminal? The juridical aspects of euthanasia can be – and have been – endlessly debated but there seems to be only one consistent decision in such a case. Though the mother's action may have been morally defensible, it was still a punishable offence. She sacrificed herself for her child, but the court upheld the vital rules that obtained. Both sides may thus have been in the right.

The tragic conflict arises in the disastrous confrontation of incommensurable or incompatible plus-sum games. When the good is doomed to destruction because of its inherent limitations, major meta-rules stand out in sharp relief against a sombre background. Jurisprudence alone cannot eliminate innocent suffering or iron out the twists of fate. Inconsistency is ineradicable, regardless of the proliferation of clauses. In the end, we must humbly accept the tragic dimension of the human condition.

The confrontation of primitive people with superior Western culture often ends in drawn-out tragedy. In retrospect we easily indulge in moral masochism, thoughtlessly posturing for the prosecution. History, however, frequently shows that even the best intentions can go dreadfully wrong.

> Captain James Cook (1728–79) was a discoverer of irreproachable character who took exceptionally good care of his crew. (He was the first to use limes, lemons, oranges and sauerkraut as protection against scurvy.) Yet his first expedition to Tahiti in 1769 triggered off a process of decline, even if we discount the prevalent myths of paradisial islands. After half a century of internecine strife and social turmoil, civic order was finally restored on Tahiti by the heavy-handed efforts of puritanical missionaries. *cf. 170*
>
> Even more instructive is the case of the Jesuits in South America who, from 1611 onwards, assumed responsibility for the welfare of the indigenous peoples covering a vast area, centring on present-day Paraguay. The Indian communities were virtually cut off from the rest of the world and were benevolently governed by a highly motivated paternalistic theocracy. When, in 1768, the Jesuits' rule was abrogated, the Indian population was totally disoriented. The cities crumbled, agriculture fell into disarray, artisan skills evaporated; the whole social fabric wasted away in a few decades. Later, Paraguay plunged into a series of disasters, and its population was for long incapacitated by iron-fisted caudillos.

It is not easy for an impartial observer to set himself up in judgement of the intruders or to find tenable alternatives leading to a happier resolution. Of course we can insert shock absorbers, keep violence to a minimum, avoid outrages and ameliorate suffering. In the long run, it is impossible to keep human beings in a game reserve; we cannot protect them from temptation – that is, from themselves. Aborigines should not be treated as endangered animal species. To do so is, *de facto,* to deny them their dignity as humans.

There is no legitimate court of appeal for the trial of such cases; the clash of cultures lies outside the jurisdiction of any legal authority. Legislation can resolve conflicts only within the coalition of an organized community.

The highest authority

Ever since Hugo Grotius (1583–1645), men of law have tried to derive definitive legal principles from clearly expressed "self-evident" ethical principles. Unfortunately their ambitions are bound to fail. The law must reflect explicit rules, and for this very reason it can never become the supreme norm.

> In *A Theory of Justice* (1971) John Rawls tries to place law and justice on an entirely rational foundation. He has produced a magisterial work; infallible in its logic, excelling in scholarship, and bursting with scientific methodology. The goal is to prove how certain simple axiomatic assumptions, pursuant to the principle of fairness, lead to a number of indisputable inferences which should thus provide the only acceptable basis for legislation. Rawls' conclusions do not differ much from our ordinary sense of justice. That is hardly surprising as the author's foremost ambition obviously was to present "scientific" grounds for his own by no means unattractive prejudices. The point, however, is his unprecedented claim to scientific generality and total objectivity. Ostensibly abstaining from value judgements, the author skilfully applies circular argumentation, and tries by strict logic to convince anyone holding "rational" values. Of late, Rawls has tried to make amends in *Political Liberalism* (1993), but this partial retraction does not betray a change of heart from the belief in full-blown rationality.

At regular intervals absolute justice has been visited upon our culture, and every time it has led to unprecedented violence and injustice. Nothing and nobody then escapes the vigilance of the legal machinery; all denunciations are plausible, no punishment too severe when it comes to obliterating sin or – most important of all – eliminating the depraved opponents of the glorious Millennium. But the argus-eyed guardians of orthodoxy soon lapse into corruption while the cynics ineluctably advance to the top.

Faced by our all-too-human frailties, we have to be content with the limitation and mitigation of obvious injustices. An adequate level of collaborative play can be maintained only by leaving benign reformers reasonable scope for their constructive moves. The legal structure has to be constantly re-examined in open debate and under constant confrontation with all related philosophical and ethical problems. In the course of the political process our deliberations may gradually produce beneficial changes in the codified rules of the game. Sometimes this takes so long that the judiciary quietly allows antiquated legislation to fall into oblivion.

> Many of the witch trials of the sixteenth and seventeenth centuries were strictly legal pageants. The jurists of the time took broomstick rides and the evil eye very seriously,

and the accused were often fully convinced of their guilt. The rapid spread of syphilitic infection fanned the witch-hunters' hysteria. The virulent new spirochete strain, probably originating in the New World, caused fearful ulcerous sores all over the body, and the shameful nature of the disease exacerbated the latent misogyny of the times. By the early eighteenth century witchhunts had fallen into disrepute and the laws ceased to be enforced. Good old witchcraft was deftly re-diagnosed as superstitious delusion which, in some cases, was shown to be caused by a poisonous mould parasite on rye (ergotism).

Howsoever we pursue higher levels of justice, the problem of ultimate vindication remains. Is it invested in the supreme court, the parliament, the president, or the all-powerful people themselves? No rules are better than the people who support and respect them but we, the people, are obviously fallible and must in turn seek validation from a higher authority.

4.7   Destructive games

Our genetic controls proscribe violence only within the family and tribe. Physical assault therefore provides the "natural" move in any proliferating conflict between larger units. War does not call for any detailed explanations and needs no peculiar motive. On the contrary, it is peace that must be justified by referring to the obvious advantages of plus-sum play. Where there is neither referee nor sanctions, the initiative will sooner or later slip into the hands of the most vindictive players. The probability of armed conflict can only be reduced by making war sufficiently unpleasant even for megalomaniacs and inveterate gamblers.

War and culture

Since relations between autochthonous tribes or sovereign states fall outside any jurisdiction, the not-so-enlightened self-interest of the peoples or their rulers is the highest standard of value available. Unfortunately, it has all too often been opportune to channel ambition or discontent into aggression towards an outside enemy. Every community has its own collective memory in which the impression of ancient wrongs is lovingly preserved, and often reinforced from generation to generation.

> In 1914 a certain Mr Pretorius was ordered to exterminate a herd of 140 elephants in South Africa, but after his best efforts 20 of them survived. In 1930 the area became a national park but the distant recollection remains; the present fourth-generation elephants are still abnormally shy and aggressive towards human beings.

Homo sapiens for sure has at least an elephant's memory. There is always some long-standing grudge to fall back on when a favourable opportunity for military assault presents itself. Defence of one's own territory, on the other hand, is a firmly established social reflex, and so the stage was set for all those episodes of war that have marked the passage of human history – and no doubt of prehistory as well.

> The many signs of physical assault on ancient fossilized skulls betray use of weapons against his fellow men among *Homo erectus*. Indeed, warfare is not a prerogative of the human race but raises its ugly head among many other mammals. The popular perception of peaceable beasts killing only out of necessity is badly misplaced. Male chimpanzees occasionally go for all-out warfare; particularly repulsive is the practice of devouring the young of roving alien females.

cf. 167

> The myth of the peace-loving savage has shown remarkable staying power despite a wealth of evidence to the contrary. Among the Red Indians, the matrilineal and matriarchal Iroquois of New England were infamous for their belligerence as well as for their torturing habits. Nevertheless the Yanomamis of the Amazon basin probably hold the American record for aggressiveness (inevitably, this state of affairs has been blamed on white intruders). All the same, warfare seems (until recently) to have been directly responsible for almost one third of male deaths. Every village was at war with its neighbours, killing men and capturing women with the same gusto. As soon as the population exceeded a critical limit of about 150 individuals, the community split spontaneously into new factions.

cf. 139; 150

cf. 191

> Polynesians are renowned for their affability but Hawaiians and the Maoris of New Zealand were both notoriously warlike, and when Captain Cook arrived in Tahiti for the third time he found that bloody war was in the offing against Moorea, a neighbouring island. Vicious feuding has been a fact of tribal life in many areas of Melanesia, New Guinea, North and South America and Black Africa. In those regions European colonization actually introduced a modern version of the ancient Pax Romana.

By and large, cultural progress and the spread of civilization have reduced the horrors of war, even if the separate events have become more spectacular. Alas, a high level of culture has been no guarantee against invasion or civil war. On the contrary, the rising spiral of agricultural productivity and population increase has called down calamities at regular intervals.

> China's long-term population record reflects a series of setbacks connected with eruptions of violence. Time and again, the decay of highly centralized government brought down the same misfortunes; famine, peasant rebellion, warlordism, pillage and plunder. The breakdown of internal order vies in destructiveness with the extended periods of occupation and foreign rule. (see figure 4.2)

National demarcations came to dominate our social identity as they provided a stable institutional setting for enduring cultural development. The very existence of nation states has eliminated endless tribal feuds but, at times, rampant chauvinism degraded the fatherland into an object for adulation which violently ruptured higher-level cultural patterns. Such idolatry can lead to nothing but evil, as we have learnt to our cost.

cf. 256; 309; 398

Civilization versus barbarism

Religious and ideological wars are particularly destructive, as are collisions between different cultures. As they expand, high cultures in general (and Western culture in particular) tend to crush or to assimilate more delicate structures. Combat is limited to isolated incidents; reverses are temporary but victories all the more decisive. The exploitation of the American continents is an extreme

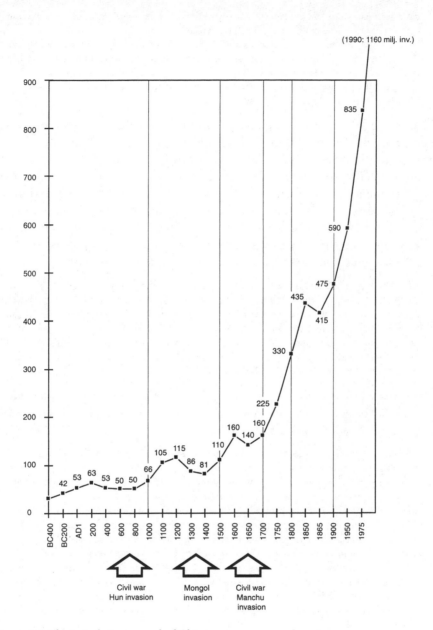

Figure 4.2 The population record of China

example of the confrontation between widely differing cultures. Great empires tumbled down like houses of cards while primitive tribes offered protracted but, in the end, equally futile resistance.

A decisive factor here was the unintentional intervention of biological weapons, in the form of epidemics of various kinds. These afflicted both sides but the Indians were more vulnerable. The greater part of the active population was wiped out within a few decades. Surviving children and old people were demoralized and incapable of carrying on the cultural game in the face of such desertion by the gods.

It is worth noting that both Athens and Rome were ravaged by "plagues" during the Peloponnesian and Punic wars respectively, and similar epidemics in the second and third century A.D. erased up to one third of the population of the Roman provinces. The apparent displeasure of the divine powers certainly undermined the self-confidence and long-term viability of the societies involved.

Historically, the incessant expansion of European culture constitutes a great exception; usually the boot has been on the other foot. With discouraging regularity, the annals tell of the invasion of civilized countries and kingdoms by primitive barbarians, bent on looting, murder and destruction. Prehistorical Jericho, founded some time before 8000 B.C., was repeatedly devastated by bellicose nomadic tribes, and the same story can be told of Sumeria, Egypt, India, China, Meso-America and Ancient Rome. During the tenth century Vikings and Hungarians were still devastating vast areas of Europe and in 1242 the West avoided the iron heel of the Mongol hordes only by a quirk of fate.

After the swift subjugation of Russia and an irresistible rampage through Poland, Austria, Hungary and the Balkans, the Mongol commander Batu withdrew his forces to the lower Volga when news reached him of the death of the Great Khan Ogadai (all major chiefs convened to elect a successor, and the presence of loyal troops was certainly needed to confer credence on the candidacy). Timerlane's Mongol reign of terror at the end of the fourteenth century was the latest and probably also the last manifestation of such primitive military power.

Crude barbarians no longer have any chance against well-organized national armies and sophisticated weaponry. In fact they never had, provided there was sufficient cohesion in the cultural coalition.

The victories of the Greeks over the Persians at Marathon (490 B.C.) and Salamis (480 B.C.) are textbook examples of what decisiveness and solidarity can achieve against superior numbers. However, the conventional emphasis on the miraculous nature of these feats gives a false picture of the relative strength of the combatants. The Greeks were fighting on their home ground, and their tactics and weapons were both superior. Above all their morale was of quite a different calibre. Every Greek soldier was a free man and was commanded by elected *Strategi* under self-imposed discipline. The martial art of the Hellenes was refined in the course of the Peloponnesian wars (431–404 B.C.) when soldiery became a profession: before long, Greek mercenaries formed the back-bone of the Persian army. Guided by Alexander the Great and his pothos – a passionate missionary zeal – Macedonian cavalry and Hellenic hoplites amazed their contemporaries (and posterity) by conquering most of the then known world within a span of nine years (334–325 B.C.).

The borders between culture and barbarity are inherently unstable. On the frontiers, weakly defended settlements prove an irresistible lure for tribal pillaging which, in turn, provokes punitive expeditions and pacification campaigns. *cf. 143* A high culture is compelled to expand, otherwise it will implode ignominiously.

The barbarians of tomorrow cannot succeed by brute military force but only by striking subversively at our weakest points. Accusations and threats will, in familiar fashion, alternate with appeals for peace and forbearance; vengeful extortion will be interchanged with mealy-mouthed entreaties. If we lose our nerve, any dictator armed with a few nuclear devices could, by bare-faced intimidation, hold the strongest nations to ransom. In such a confrontation some old-fashioned virtues like valiance and fortitude will, once again, be in strong demand.

Frames of reference

War sweeps away most of the accepted rules of human interplay. The residual norms which are nonetheless observed by the combatants provide an acceptable yardstick for assessing the vindictiveness of warfare. Hostilities can range in severity from regular, sportsmanlike border disputes, over various intermediate forms ("civilized" wars with Geneva-type conventions), to unrestrained attempts at mutual destruction in an orgy of minus-sum play.

> The Pentateuch provides horrifying documentation of war from the victor's point of view. To begin with, the sons of Jacob slayed all adult male Schemites after a spurious peace settlement. Later Moses, in the name of Yahweh, declares the holy war of extermination on the indigenous inhabitants of Canaan: "thou shalt smite them and utterly destroy them; thou shalt make no covenant with them, nor shew any mercy unto them". Heedless of the Lord's command, the chosen people were content to massacre the men while taking the women and children as slaves.
>
> Rig-Veda provides a similar picture of the Aryan infiltration of north-western India in about 1500 B.C. The same theme must have recurred throughout history but we lack documentation of, say, the Bantu expansion which swept through most of Sub-Saharan Africa about 2,000 years ago, wiping out Pygmy and Khoisan peoples in the process. *cf. 89* The exploits of Shaka, the Zulu king (c1787–1828), is a late episode in that migration of peoples. In the 1820s, he laid waste to most of the present-day Natal province in South Africa and precipitated turmoil in the interior. This struggle for lebensraum (called *Mfekene,* the Crushing) left about two million dead on the ground and when the Boers entered in the 1830s on their Great Trek, they moved into an almost empty land.
>
> The latest spasm in this history of African genocide took place in 1972 when the ruling Tutsi minority in Burundi dispatched most of the rising middle class of the putatively inferior Bahutu tribe. Around 100,000 people were cut down while world opinion barely frowned at the blood-letting (since then the tables have been turned and the Tutsis are now the underdog).

In Moses's interpretation, Yahweh's commandment "Thou shalt not kill" obviously had no reference to Canaanites or Philistines; it was intended purely for domestic use. Surprisingly, the Babylonians, and even more notably the Persians, behaved with comparative chivalry towards the conquered Jews. Some implicit convention favoured conciliation and made amicable cohabitation possible.

> The complex irrigation system based on the Euphrates and Tigris was kept more or less intact for thousands of years through all the fortunes of war, but decay set in after the Arab occupation in the seventh century. The final blow was delivered by invading Mongols (in 1258) who annihilated the peasant population to secure more pasture for their horses. The destruction of society's infrastructure brought life-supporting maintenance work to an end, and the arable land declined into semi-desert.

In spite of ominous barbarities, the participants in the Second World War were nonetheless subject to certain inhibitions. The rapid return to peaceful intercourse after the unconditional surrender of the losers shows that the state of war was only a gory parenthesis.

The temptations of war

Our genetic controls proscribe violence only within the family and tribe. Physical assault therefore provides the "natural" move in any proliferating conflict between larger units. War does not call for any detailed explanations and needs no peculiar motive. On the contrary, it is peace that must be justified by referring to the obvious advantages of plus-sum play. Overarching social structures are inherently artificial, and therefore require constant self-justification. No wonder nation states can be aggressive; a common enemy makes for an irrefutable *raison d'être*.

> Games and sports are the innocent prototypes of martial encounter; self-initiated division into two camps easily arises even in a perfectly homogeneous group. Man's passion for combative play is highly visible in the ice-hockey rink, on the football field and at the chessboard; it is equally apparent in the rivalries of business and politics. Despite fierce controversies, the infliction of grave bodily harm is taboo and outside the arena even the most ferocious antagonists adjust without much difficulty to normal civilized behaviour. Violent aggression involves an escalation of the means and a brutalization of the rules of competitive human interplay. Ultimately the participants lose all common cause and concentrate exclusively on destroying one another.

War is a terrible simplifier; it lifts moral responsibility from our shoulders and minimizes internal zero-sum games by supplying a comprehensible public objective, an inviolable identity and clear hierarchic order. War is a deceptive short-cut to the fulfilment of latent social needs and legitimizes many of our worst inclinations. Patient but often rather boring everyday toil is replaced by the exciting hazards of battle; enemy losses give much more satisfaction than our own gains. Personal disappointments and feelings of inferiority find an outlet in the brutal power play of the war machine, and the victors can unilaterally dictate the rules of the endgame.

> Many entrenched class structures can be traced back to the suppressive policies of conquest. The helot system in Sparta, India's caste distinctions, and South African apartheid are obvious examples. Political and economic privileges became firmly established by self-perpetuating socio-economic feedback.

According to Karl von Clausewitz (1780–1831), war is an extension of politics by other means, but the converse is equally pertinent. Classical foreign policy is warfare by peaceful means, or to cite Su Tzu: "the supreme art of war is to subdue the enemy without fighting". Clausewitz puts it as follows: "the conqueror loves peace; he would rather invade without encountering any resistance."

cf. 48

The prestige of great powers is indispensable in the build-up of bluffing capability. Cold war is a matter of manoeuvring for an advantageous striking position, just in case. Parades of strength are meant to frighten the enemy into subjection at little cost to the aggressor, but they easily become the first moves in a poker game which calls for an flurry of ever-increasing stakes. Finally, all jointly accepted rules of the game are discarded and the grim logic of elementary game theory claims its own destructive due. In an atmosphere of mutual mistrust, both parties want to enjoy the benefit of the first blow.

> With cool acumen Thucydides declares (around 400 B.C.) "the most genuine but least mentioned cause of the Peloponnesian war I consider to be that the Athenians had become powerful, thus inspiring fear in the Spartans and driving them to war". The Athenian side was moved by a similar apprehension. "Events themselves compelled us to advance to our present position of imperial power, principally because of fear . . . and then it seemed too dangerous.. to take the risk of letting that position go".   *cf. 249*

Although by its very nature warfare is an obvious minus-sum game, successful wars have often brought profit to the winning side. In developed societies, natural resources and markets or compliant tax objects have been the main items on the income side. Under primitive conditions the booty – goods, cattle and, above all, land and slaves – was certainly not to be despised.

Well-armed peace

Should we then turn to radical pacifism, fighting unflinchingly against war and working for total global disarmament? The advocates of these policies disregard the fact that whatever the content of the well-meaning proclamations, their influence is restricted to the genuinely peace-loving parties.

> Inspired by Alexander the Great, Chandragupta Maurya set out to found the first Indian empire in 325 B.C. The Mauryan dynasty reached its peak under his grandson Asoka, who ruled over the whole subcontinent except its southern tip. Disgusted with the ravages of war, Asoka converted to Buddhism, abolished conquest and announced a policy of eternal peace. His basic creed, dharma (the principles of the right life), promulgated honesty, truthfulness, compassion, mercifulness, benevolence, non-violence, non-extravagance, non-acquisitiveness and so on. It was put down in numerous inscriptions and was propagated by emissars to all neighbouring countries. For all that, the empire began to crumble after Asokas' death (232 B.C.) under the assault of voracious aggressors. In the year 185 B.C. Bhadratha, the last of the Mauryans, was assassinated by his commander-in-chief: politics had reverted to business as usual.

Where there is no referee and no sanctions, the initiative will sooner or later slip into the hands of the most vindictive players. Anybody can start fighting on his own but peace always has to be the work of many. The probability of armed conflict can only be reduced by making it sufficiently unpleasant, dangerous and unprofitable even for megalomaniacs and inveterate gamblers.

> The disasters of the Second World War are generally blamed on Hitler, Mussolini and their like, but equally guilty were the starry-eyed pacifists of the 1930s who created a military vacuum in Western Europe and extended an open invitation to aggression. Not without reason has "appeasement" become a dirty word, a symbol of almost criminal stupidity, naivety, short-sightedness and cowardice.

Resolutions can never exterminate war; this can only be achieved by intrepid, practical co-operation in which the plus-sum gradually gain ground as a common goal, and the meta-rules are honoured with sufficient candour. As trust grows, the weapons will be laid aside, one by one, but absence of arms is no guarantee for tranquility. If the basic concord is shattered, Balkanization or Lebanonization ensues and the necessary weaponry materializes out of thin air. Then the vicious circle of destruction grinds down the social structure, leaving the antagonists at one another's mercy.

Potential aggressors must not be lead into temptation. Relative safety can be assured only by making the risk-gain relationship sufficiently discouraging for even the most sanguine warmonger.

> The mushroom clouds over Hiroshima and Nagasaki filled men's minds with awe, and many were those who foretold the end of the world. In 1945, as a 15-year-old school-boy, I wrote a composition which ended with the far-from-original prophecy that the mutually deterrent effect of nuclear weapons would probably save us from another world war – so far, so good!

A major nuclear exchange would, quite simply, be an unprofitable affair. No rational decision-maker would expose himself to the risk of devastating nuclear, or perchance still worse chemical or biological reprisals. We may assume that even psychopathic dictators do not differ from the rest of mankind in taking a strong interest in self-preservation. But neither a balance of terror nor a Great Power accord or even a unipolar world provide lasting guarantees against a global massacre. Our continual awareness of the threat of disaster is the very price which has to be paid for relative safety. Even and especially in this extreme case, security is the most perilous of illusions.

4.8   The culture coalition

Cultural dissolution is a spontaneous process. Without a constant injection of rejuvenating creative impulse – cultural exergy – the grand structure of human interplay will disintegrate. Now as our Western culture becomes universal, we are left with many disturbing questions. Can the core of culture survive when it is transplanted to alien soil? Will we see vigorous hybridization or only devious decay? The most fateful question for our culture and, indeed, for all mankind is: how can we renew the funds of spiritual energy? How can we secure lasting access to morality and love, the scarcest of resources? How to stay in touch with the ultimate rules of the game?

Collective creativity

Unlike polities of whatever order of magnitude, cultures are not held together by any explicit rules or institutionalized authority. The culture game is the outcome of innumerable individual considerations, moves and countermoves.

Its players are only half-consciously involved in a coalition which effortlessly unites myriads of men in a self-organized plus-sum game.

I am thus defining culture as collective creativity which enhances and rejuvenates past performance, relentlessly striving for deeper self-orientation. The core of culture consists of slowly evolving but inalienable values, axiomatic articles of faith comprising the whole register of philosophy and ethics – from the meaning of existence to the moralities of ordinary human relations.

> In the seventeenth century tiny Netherlands was at the forefront of European culture. In *The Embarrassment of Riches* (1987) Simon Schama unravels the fabric of Dutch culture into its separate strands. Calvinist faith and humanist concern, military prowess and commercial cunning, bourgeois luxury and care for the destitute, enjoyment of life spiced with worry about indigence or infirmity and a nagging fear of invasion or inundation – all this was part and parcel of Dutch ascendance. General education, academic research and workaday technology flourished amidst a profusion of newspapers, popular prints and genre paintings. The upshot was a fiercely independent and highly decentralized, democratic and affluent welfare society, reasonably tolerant of foreign creeds (particularly the Jews) and a sanctuary for free thinkers, domestic or alien. Spinoza and Descartes found refuge in Holland, and many of the Mayflower pilgrims had temporarily settled in Leyden before embarking for North America. The diminution of creative tension in the Netherlands during the following century lacks adequate explanation. Perhaps the sting of fastidious embarrassment had faded away.　*cf. 252*

Deep-seated convictions are major determinants of conduct, while explicit creeds play only a minor role. Controversies regarding the Christology or the Holy Communion have little relevance in themselves but have served as disguises for basic disagreements over existential if not political priorities.

The separate economic, political, scientific and even artistic games can, up to a point, be isolated and observed but the cultural game in its entirety is inaccessible to exhaustive analysis. We are riding together on the crest of a wave which once began beyond the vanishing horizon of the ocean of time. The swell exists solely by virtue of its motion and cannot be halted for scrupulous examination; its impulse can only be sensed through resistance or reinforcement.

Personal commitment

In cybernetic terms, a vigorous culture represents a combination of ultra-stable systems which, in themselves, can develop freely within the ergodic space. *cf. 50* Such "multistable" totalities are naturally extremely unpredictable but there should nonetheless be some deep-seated reason for the more striking disparities between different epochs and cultures, societies and communities. External conditions such as geography, natural resources, and climatic changes cannot be disregarded, yet their explanatory power is hardly sufficient. Neither should *cf. 128* the erratic fluctuations in man's intellectual and ethical capabilities be ignored, although our innate moral infirmity certainly is fairly constant in general. The answer to the riddle seems to lie in a set of extraordinarily sensitive feedbacks which amplify the inspired achievements of small groups or even individuals, endowing them with decisive impact.　*cf. 82; 97*

cf. 24; 66; 98
To achieve creative change, a society must be in a metastable state, far removed from homeostatic equilibrium. It can be compared with a supersaturated solution which appears placid on the surface but is open to sudden change in different directions. A single seeding crystal will then release the stored energy and steer growth in accordance with its innate template. In the same vein, a grain of corn can shape solar energy, water, carbon dioxide and various minerals according to its own hidden image. Similarly, a spiritual seed, a grain of mustard or a leaven, may direct the course of history by its imminent powers of persuasion.

An inverse relation between the importance of human achievement and its incubation period might be conjectured here. It may take decades, centuries or even millennia before significant insights bear fruit. Noble deeds are done in silence, and the highly acclaimed leaps of mankind have been preceded by the labour and self-sacrifice of innumerable men and women, long since forgotten. Our marginal personal freedom has at least this chance to manifest itself in adding value by honest but unpretentious moves in the human interplay.

Every founder of a new creed builds on old foundations, but upon these he sets a personal and comprehensive though vaguely formulated hypothesis about the conditions of human existence. Naturally most of these preposterous gambles, like so many other evolutionary experiments, are destined to die a sudden death or to flow out into the desert of lost opportunities.

The prophet Mani was duly crucified in 276 A.D. but his disciples were apparently deprived of a Pentecost. Just the same, Manichaeism long remained a serious rival to Christianity, and its fundamental ideas lived on in many mediaeval heresies. The last orthodox Manichaeans can be traced to late thirteenth-century Chinese Turkestan.

The miracle of faith is difficult to comprehend, even in the partial light of hindsight. What did the odds look like on Calvary? Almost two thousand years later we are still unable to proclaim a final verdict: the case is open, the jury is still in recess.

The only available criterion of success is that the game goes on, with ever-increasing stakes financed by the accrued interest of the players, losers and winners alike. The failures may look like a complete waste but they form the cf. 117; 377; 389 indispensable seedbed for the right moves. Despite (or because of) the lack of a clear destination, the rules of our human game have to include an element of visionary faith which maintains an open value universe – a precondition for creative collaborative play.

Unflagging reformation

The fiery revolutionary has been hailed as the historical driving-force *par excel-* cf. 245 *lence*, but he has generally been the victim of his own emotional shortcomings. Exaggerated self-esteem and wounded vanity find their outlet in conspiratorial fanaticism, richly spiced with idealistic rhetoric. The rebel is a fireraiser who gets his kick out of blasting and burning – demolition by word and deed. Dramatic advantages can be extracted from such revolutionary poses and under extreme provocation they may be understandable, but their historical significance has been much exaggerated. Revolutions are unnecessary when they are possible but unfortunately impossible when they are necessary.

cf. 249

> Superficially, the recent, highly encouraging developments in Eastern Europe seemed to give the lie to this maxim; in fact they illustrate the former part of the sentence. The authority and self-confidence of the governing communist clique was undermined to a degree which made peaceful liberation possible; underground conspiracy and violent revolutionary struggle became redundant. The virtual absence of bloodshed and destruction demonstrates the reformist nature of the events.

cf. 255

The constructive course of history is set by considerate reformers both in the ordinary application of worthwhile rules and in the bold inception of new cultural elements. Our anonymous protagonist works loyally for reform even if he must expect growing opposition from established interest groups. His plus-sum game enriches the coalition but there are always losers in strong positions who should be weakened or won over at least to tolerate the good cause. Improvements in the rules have to be "sold" and sometimes the sales resistance is so fierce that the reformer, like Luther, finds himself in an unwanted revolutionary situation.

> While the rebel indulges in proud self-righteousness, the reformer has to temporize and make concessions. His childhood faith and youthful idealism are diluted; the "illusions" are lost. This is of course a recurring predicament for decent human beings. How well have I traded my talents? How did I compromise my soul today? These are disturbing questions which eventually may fade away leaving only depressing inanity – the treadmill of life.
>
> The armchair radical, who does not have to answer for his deeds, can afford to sneer at the very idea of squaring with his conscience. Even so, he tends to fall into the trap of the prevailing intellectual, artistic or political fashion. The progress dynamo does not jump onto the nearest bandwagon; on the contrary, he detests easy shortcuts and abhors playing to the gallery.

Reformist zeal cannot aim for decisive victory nor does it guarantee moral indemnity. On the contrary, the alternation between belief and uncertainty, hope and despair is a characteristic of cultural advance. The very success of a trustful breakthrough will provoke unexpected reverses and necessitate a period of retreat and introspection until the time is ripe for new fruitful expansion.

This deep learning (and unlearning) process applies to individual human beings as well as to organizations, nations and whole cultures. A decentralized pluralistic community draws its strength from internal competition which should be both fierce and fair. Then individual blundering does not matter while replicable accomplishment acts as a guide to future play. The unavoidable relapses are symptomatic of our imperfect mastery of the game but if we are good apprentices they ultimately become irrelevant – a part of the price of life.

Cultural self-criticism

In theory, past cultures should provide material for studies in social pathology and in many cases we have access to a wealth of information, particularly about the last stages before the breakdown. Unfortunately, almost any model can be verified by a suitable sifting of the data. We cannot carry out a reliable post-mortem of extinct societies, and our conclusions about past civilizations are bound to depend on ingenious empathy.

Cultural criticism has always been a popular pastime; nor has there been any lack of philosophers of culture with claims to professional status. The most plausible of their analyses have a clearly pessimistic bias.

> Giovanni Battista Vico (1688–1744) was perhaps the first confident "philosopher of history". A self-taught professor of rhetoric in the University of Naples, he acknowledged in his *Scienzia Nuova* the animal origin of mankind and predicted cyclical relapses into bestiality when man turns completely cynical or, in Vico's words, becomes "a coward, an unbeliever, an informer, hiding his evil intentions behind flattery and hypocritical wheeling". Vico attributed the rigid class society to imperfections in religion, and so alienated not only the bigoted clerics but also the ardent believers in unceasing progress. He coolly defied the leading intellectual lights of the day, discounting their new-fangled rationalism with dictums like "Man became all he is without understanding it". Goethe was one of the earliest admirers of Vico, who has gained renewed relevance in our post-Auschwitz and post-Gulag age.

Pessimism is basically a sound reaction while cultural chauvinism, particularly in institutionalized forms, is an indication of decadence. Marxism for example disseminates blatant scientistic superoptimism: the world is an automatic progress machine, guaranteeing the triumph of the just. The Leninist-Stalinists consistently practised an ironical re-interpretation, closer to the laws of nature – *cf. 404* the triumphant are always right!

Societies of ideological purity and monolithic structure should be very interesting to the outside observer. The inbred self-insulation offers that almost ideal object for scientific investigation – a fully determined, isolated but nevertheless observable system.

> Alexander Zinovjev has (in such works as *Bright Future*, 1978) rendered a vivid picture of Brezhnevian socialist reality. Sycophancy and obsequiousness are rewarded; all creative play is systematically suppressed; cynical careerists have the upper hand; the entire social machinery is bogged down in disillusioned dogmatism. Public lip-service is a cover for cheating, wangling and sponging at all levels; the facade of propaganda conceals the cracks but can't deceive the insiders who recognise that fraud and fakery are integral to the system. Steadfast idealists must be effectively excluded from positions of influence. Lowly progress dynamos might be tolerated at subordinate levels but only complete cynics can enjoy the confidence of the leaders: dog will not bite dog.

Socialism has, at least in theory, adopted the concern of the Christians for the weak and underprivileged; a host of authors in exile paradoxically attested to the inherent creativity of socialist humanism. The logic of communist doctrine drove the rest into inner exile and Russia to the brink of economic collapse. Zinovjev's merciless criticism was at the time dismissed as libel. The refusal to listen to prophets of doom or to question the established rules of the game is in itself a grave symptom of decline. Token deeds and dictatorial ways take the place of real substance while the cultural game gradually becomes a caricature of its own best intentions.

> The Soviet perestroika was a belated reaction to the economic and cultural sclerosis of a

one-party state, which stood in glaring contrast to the dynamism of despised capitalism. The Zinovjean analysis was courageously adopted, but the attempts at reform tried to spare the old-fashioned political structure which was the undoing of the whole effort. A ruling coalition can hardly cure itself while in government but for a Leninist party the relinquishment of power amounted to total self-denial and, as it happened, outright suicide.

The rejection of the realities of socialism does not imply unreserved approval of our own way of life; quite the contrary. For good or ill, Marxism is a vital part of our cultural heritage, and we should watch and learn from this vast social experiment in which an explicit and in many ways seductive rule system was applied without any consideration for traditional values. A sober analysis will disclose familiar features of our Western culture in its reckless efforts to solve the equation of human coexistence once and for all. Criticism of Communism, Fascism and suchlike is always cultural self-criticism.

The grand coalition

Cultural dissolution is a spontaneous process. Without a constant injection of rejuvenating creative impulse – cultural exergy – the grand structure of human interplay will disintegrate. Like life, human culture is incessantly reorganizing itself by creating new information, but its genetic base is weak and must be reinforced by steady ethical innovation. Traditional values are exposed to continuous wear and tear; the exergy of creative joy and self-fulfilment eventually degenerates into the worthless entropy of stereotype and self-indulgence.

> World history abounds in splendid visions of the ultimate Millennium, which should obliterate all social ills and thus justify all available means. Such endeavours soon fall into a tangled web of self-deception, hypocrisy and cheating. The new rulers invariably establish themselves as an even more unforgiving and oppressive upper class.
>
> Philosophers, the lovers of truth, may be fallible but their sincerity is not generally in doubt. Georg Lukács (1885–1971) seems to be a notable exception. He won international acclaim for his sharp intellect which he put in the service of Marxist totalitarianism. The young Lukács stood model for "Naptha" in Thomas Mann's *The Magic Mountain*, and made his "pact with the devil" in 1919 when he became minister for culture and education under the notorious bolshevik Bela Kun. At the end of his career the faithful servant of the party was installed once again as minister for culture under the ill-fated reformist Imre Nagy. He cunningly resigned one day before the Soviet invasion in 1956 and was duly restored to favour in 1957.

The fateful question for our culture and, indeed, for all mankind is: how can we renew the funds of spiritual energy? How can we secure lasting access to morality and love, the scarcest of resources? How are we to stay in touch with the ultimate rules of the game?

According to St. Matthew Jesus says "Ye are the salt of the earth: but if the salt have lost his savour, wherewith shall it be salted?" Everywhere and at all times free-riding wanglers tend to oust the constructive players, just as surely as substandard money drives sterling coin out of circulation.

> The self-delusions of our intellectual élite have brought these questions into renewed focus. Julian Benda (1867–1956) took the spiritual imposters to task in *La Trahison des*

Clerques (The Treason of the Intellectuals, 1926), and in the same year André Gide (1869–1951) exposed the omnipresent counterfeiters in *Les Faux-Monnayeurs* (The Counterfeiters). In Albert Camus' *La Peste* (The Plague, 1947), the highly contagious moral deprivation endangers all society.

cf. 410 While ends have proved delusive or downright diabolical, the only feasible solution has always been to fall back on immaculate and irreproachable means, purpose-sanctifying rules which provide a rich though unpredictable yield in an uncertain future. With an approach both simple and practical, Moses' ten pragmatic commandments (or prohibitions), Socrates' sceptical search for truth and the New Testament's Sermon on the Mount launched our Hebraic-Graeco-Roman culture on its bold trajectory.

Western civilization is in the process of incorporating all humanity in a grand coalition, a worldwide decentralized meta-culture. The moral responsibility for various abnormalities thus falls to some extent on our doorstep, although we can gently refute enforced obligations at a global level. Our first duty is to put our own house in order but, concurrently, we are bound to work and missionize for better rules and better play, giving further form to those values which have stood the test of time. This process should help us to clarify our faith while constructing the proper tools for shaping a worthwhile future for mankind.

In the following chapters we shall examine in greater detail the rising hierarchy of economic, political, scientific and artistic games, returning at last to the supreme meta-rules where ends and means converge. One point deserves to be mentioned here and, indeed, repeated. Any attempt to formulate these overriding aspirations explicitly and definitively is bound to fail. Our greatest plus-sum game, the free and open community of man, can be kept intact only by unwritten and imperceptible rules. The ultimate meaning of our stumbling moves remains inaccessible to the pure intellect.

5.   Economic games

5.1   Praxeological principles

The hard core of economics, called praxeology, is rooted in the plain logic of life. Physico-chemical and biological processes serve as models for the praxeological rule system: the struggle for survival is, in essence, naked economic competition. This is illustrated by Gause's law: two or more species (companies) cannot co-exist in the same habitat (market) if they have the same survival (business) strategy. One species (company) will be at least marginally stronger and come out on top, exterminating the others. Hence the incessant speciation and differentiation in nature and economic life. Our vast economic plus-sum game depends on super-ordinate rules, but no norms can eliminate the zero-sum component – the conflict between the self-interest of the competing players and coalitions.

Precious information

In the previous chapter we tried to elucidate some crucial aspects of culture. Now the time has come for a more systematic examination of the social fabric. The economic game builds a bridge between technological means and political ends; it represents an ordered interaction between human appetites and productive capabilities. Enterprise, labour, capital and technological know-how are channelled into the fulfilment of perceived needs, thus providing the material means for higher-level political, scientific and artistic play.

All these processes are, of course, intimately connected. The economy does as much, and as little, to determine social structure as it is itself circumscribed by the available technology, which in turn is governed by what we call the laws of nature. Lower levels of play always constrain the development of higher-order games; technical and economic advances introduce new degrees of cultural freedom while receiving guidance and stimulating impulses from above.

> Economics is concerned with the exchange and allocation of scarce resources. If the supply is unlimited, then even vital utilities such as air and water will have no subjective value. Thwarted human needs and desires incessantly compete for satisfaction and constitute the driving force of the economic game. The price which clears the market,

whether by barter or cash transaction, measures the value of any utility in comparison with alternative offers. The price for postponement of gratification and thus the value of time in human affairs are reflected in the prevailing interest rate, a prime determinant of capital accumulation.

The basic logic of economics is rooted in universal human preferences. It has been subsumed by Ludwig von Mises (1881–1973) under the concept of praxeology, a set of irrefutable invariances which constitute the axiomatic foundation of the economic game. They cannot be disregarded any more than engineers can ignore the laws of physics or chess-players the elementary rules of their pastime. Praxeology expounds the forbidden moves but leaves open a universe of opportunity. Praxeological tenets have been compared with the basic theorems of geometry, for which it would be futile to seek empirical confirmation.

> "Capitalism" is praxeologically an inept designation of the market economy. The accumulation of capital is, of course, a *sine qua non* for all economic development. It is hotly pursued particularly by socialist countries – their dismal failure notwithstanding.

In conditions of extreme poverty or strict uniformity – as in prison, the slums or the army – man's basic needs can be foreseen with reasonable accuracy and the exchange process can be conducted by administrative fiat. As economic freedom grows, planning goes haywire due to a lack of reliable information. Following Friedrich von Hayek (1899–1992), the praxeologists confidently claim that consumer preferences, the hidden database of economics, can be decoded only with the help of self-organizing market forces.

> The free play of the market mimics a Darwinian selection process. Most tentative connections between buyer and seller fail at the outset but eventually a pattern is established which incorporates most of the information gained by unremitting trial and error. Even so, explicit knowledge always carries a price; if the peddlers of information were to display their wares to the full, it would amount to a gross giveaway. Therefore the information market and, *mutatis mutandis*, all other markets must remain imperfect and retain some measure of zero-sum play.

cf. 58; 99

cf. 227   The market mechanism transforms countless individual decisions into a reliable read-out, and any meddling in the market constitutes unacceptable interference from the praxeological point of view. And yet such a purist attitude is unrealistic as it isolates the economy from the superordinate level of political play. For good or ill, certain extra-praxeological rules will always be imposed on the economic game. Thus, the collection of taxes is probably the oldest and certainly the most detested distortion of the economy, without which the political framework would collapse along with trade and industry. The acceptance of praxeological axioms is a necessary but not a sufficient condition for advanced economic interplay.

Economic catalysts

Praxeological regularities are often isomorphic with well-known laws of nature. The relation between supply and demand, for example, can be illustrated in terms of the physico-chemical law of mass action which prescribes the proportions of the chemical reactants in a state of thermodynamic equilibrium.

> A physical system at equilibrium is self-stabilizing and strives to oppose or to moderate any imposed change. This principle, named after the French physicist Henri-Louis Le Chatelier (1850–1936), is manifest in the law of mass action. It defines a stable, reversible equilibrium of the reactive system, a state in which time is out of action, the free energy (the exergy) has reached a minimum and no further net reaction occurs. A disturbance of the balance – say a change in the pressure of one of the reactants – provokes an immediate chemical reaction which consumes the excess and restores the equilibrium. This idealizing condition can be approximated by applying a suitable catalyst.

cf. 63

A fully reversible chemical reaction mimics a perfect market. It presupposes instant catalysis whereby the system reacts promptly to all external changes of supply and demand so that equilibrium is immediately restored. Such cases are pretty rare in chemistry, and the perfect market has the same scarcity value in economic life (although it has been widely invoked as an academic fiction).

Imperfect information is the main cause of market irreversibilities. Stock exchanges almost eliminate this "stickiness" by minimizing the gap between sell and buy quotations, but even there intelligence has a price, as reflected in brokerage fees. In other contexts, information can carry immense value: smart inventions may open up undreamt of sources of wealth.

> In biology the role of brokers and businessmen are played by enzymes, ubiquitous and highly specific biocatalysts (a single enzyme molecule can accomplish up to 10,000 conversions per second). Creative entrepreneurs, too, have their biochemical equivalents. A great innovation occurred about two and a half billion years ago, when primitive algae, with chlorophyl as the crucial catalyst, began to utilize the energy of sunlight for the assimilation of carbon dioxide from the primordial atmosphere. This economic revolution in the bioeconomy led in due course to the depletion of carbon dioxide and the creation of an oxygen atmosphere, which in turn opened up new sources of energy by the combustion of organic material.
>
> All higher animals and most moulds and fungi depend on this oxygen economy but bacteria and yeasts utilize with great alacrity quite modest potential differences, such as the anaerobic fermentation of sugar into alcohol. Only scrupulous sterilization can restrain nimble micro-organisms from taking advantage of existing organic material for their own ends, and even inorganic reactions are vigorously exploited. Specialized bacteria combine hydrogen and oxygen to produce water, and others gallantly oxidize sulphur to produce sulphuric acid. I have myself seen a solution of a trivalent arsenic salt polluted by a large colony of bacteria, which obviously managed its energy supply by oxidizing the trivalent arsenic into its quinquevalent form.

Economic life depends on its own middlemen, its traders and jobbers, profiteers and speculators. Even the slightest economic incitement can be utilized by hyperactive businessmen, distinctive catalysts of the market economy. Only exceptional measures can prevent the exploitation of tempting profit potentials; drug pushers, bootleggers and other racketeers are the equivalents of pathogenic bacteria. Despite its imperfections, the self-regulating allocation of resources proceeds with smooth efficiency, reminiscent of the enzyme-directed processes of the biosphere.

The limits of growth

The fundamental rules of praxeology share their logico-mathematical roots with the natural sciences. Accordingly, the biological analogy can be extended to business competition, innovation, capital accumulation, and so forth. Money, our most liquid asset, also has its equivalent in biochemistry.

cf. 131   Sugar, in its various incarnations, is the most important energy source for plants and animals but the glycogen in muscle and liver tissue must be "exchanged" against an equivalent amount of oxygen in a combustion process, analogous to bartering in trade or clearing settlements in the world of finance. Spontaneously reactive ATP is the universally viable form of biochemical energy, a freely convertible currency which can be immediately utilized in most of the innumerable transactions of cell metabolism.

Unrestrained organic and economic growth are logically equivalent and obey the same mathematics. Under constant external conditions, the growth of both living organisms and capital investment follows the calculation of continuously compounded interest.

Mathematically the following relations obtain:

$Q_t = Q_o \cdot e^{pt}$ where

Q_o = quantity at time zero

Q_t = quantity at time t

p = interest rate (as a fraction)

e = Neper's number ~ 2.71828.

If p is greater than zero, then after an initial phase whose length depends on p, Q_t will move quickly towards infinity. Thus exponential growth sooner or later comes to a sudden stop.

Evolutionary pessimists like to refer to this perilous piece of mathematics but in practice it has little relevance. In life as in business, the limits of growth are determined by factors such as competition, the depletion of resources, parasitism and the problems of waste. No trees will ever reach the sky regardless of whether there are any absolute constraints on the development of the game.

A bronze-age economist could have predicted the end of civilization with reasonable accuracy. Deposits of easily accessible copper and tin were soon depleted. Tin, especially, became very scarce by the end of the third millennium B.C. when the Near East temporarily reverted to the chalcolithic (copper + stone) stage of tool development. Our paleoeconomist would probably have scornfully condemned any attempt to produce a surrogate based on readily available iron-ore. Tough bronze was superior in almost every respect to brittle and rust-prone iron while the problems of steel technology must have looked insurmountable.

Around 1300 B.C. early iron objects from Anatolia were used as jewellery and commanded a price, forty times their weight in silver (many other useful materials like copper, ceramics and glass found their first use as objets d'art). A century later innovative entrepreneurs had developed competitive steel products – a creative response to the first raw material crisis in history. In Egypt, with its ample supplies of bronze, the iron age arrived some 300 to 400 years late and in China the delay was even longer. This indicates that the supersession of bronze had little to do with its inferiority as a material; it was dependent on local variations in the praxeological balance.

The evolution of life and the history of mankind both exhibit a series of

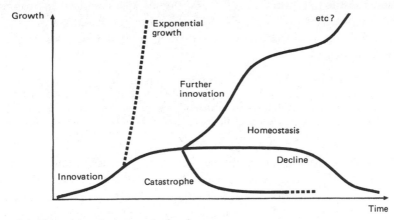

Figure 5.1 Alternatives in economic development

unpredictable quantum leaps, which have opened up unknown sources of nourishment and energy as well as virgin space for new generations.

The "normal" growth process is usually visualized as an S-curve: first comes a slow innovative phase, followed by exponential expansion which is gradually arrested and slowly fades into homeostatic saturation. Other plausible scenarios (see figure 5.1) could be some sudden catastrophe, a gradual decline, or further innovations. Homeostatic repetition possesses no ultimate stability and will sooner or later conjoin the innovation or, more probably, the decline scenario.

The choice between innovative ascent on the one hand and decline or catastrophe on the other is not dependent on the laws of praxeology but rather on the cultural environment. Consistent neglect of the market feedback leads into a labyrinth of dead-ends and the squandering of scarce resources. In extreme cases the market signal becomes perverted, so that decreasing prices increase the supply or vice versa.

> Falling grain prices have sometimes compelled the farmers of North America to extend the area under cultivation, thus temporarily increasing macroeconomic instability. Nor do higher food prices necessarily mean an increase in supply. In the absence of consumption opportunities or in times of political instability, the peasant may prefer to stockpile or to fallow his fields rather than serve the market. If disorder is severe, he may even refrain from cultivation and fall back on bare subsistence. Such a reaction to the economic distress caused by Joseph Stalin's policy of rapid industrialization gave the Soviet leader his excuse to launch the brutal collectivization of agriculture.

The economy depends on the political frame of reference; the promising growth spiral has all too often been disrupted by instabilities in the political game.

Economic evolution

The Darwinian struggle for survival reveals striking analogies with what we might call higher-order praxeology. Evolution is, in essence, the outcome of continuous economic contest in an entirely apolitical and amoral environment.

cf. 89; 218 An illuminating example is provided by the aforementioned Gause's law. If several companies compete in the same markets with identical business ideas, only one will survive.

> Gause conducted his decisive experiments with small protozoans. In the initial growth stage, when food was abundant, two similar species could coexist but when it came to the crunch the weaker strain was annihilated. However, some species could establish a stable balance of terror by settling in different parts of the tank and excreting mutually toxic chemicals.

In head-on competition, marginally weaker companies are bound to lose out. Either they perish, or they take refuge in differentiated niches with distinctive conditions for success. Every viable company, like every species, must have some superior competence and enjoy some competitive advantage in its own line of business.

Game-theoretical considerations of this kind can be extended to explain many, if not most, of the peculiarities of competitive self-organization. Stable and nourishing biotopes, such as rain forests and coral reefs, will produce a highly diverse flora and fauna while the unsteady and meagre conditions of biological and economic deserts can sustain only a few, less differentiated life forms.

Aggressive emigration is an ancient dynamic response to Gause's law, and cultural change is often transmitted by migratory pressure waves.

> The historical evidence generally reflects events from the point of view of the higher civilizations. For instance, we can only guess at the background to the extensive raids of the "sea people" in the Eastern Mediterranean around 1200 B.C. or the recurring exploits of Central-Asian peoples; Huns, Avars, Mongols and Turks. Phoenician, Greek and Polynesian colonization, on the other hand, appears fairly legitimate in our eyes while we have more mixed feelings about the Vikings' eminently praxeological expeditions for purposes of trade, plunder and conquest; their immensely successful Norman postscripts seem more respectable. Subsequently, the subjugation of Siberia and the North-American West has entered the folklore of the societies involved.

Nonetheless, entrepreneurial expansion has been the exception rather than the rule in the permutations of history. Resigned adherence to bare survival has been the standard reaction of *Homo sapiens* to economic challenge. In their longing for placid homeostasis, established cultures have generally reinforced this tendency and thus strangled innovative impulses.

Only in an imperfectly organized society, which retains some degree of freedom, may the roof seem too low and the hut too cramped. Rather than remain trapped in a hopeless zero-sum game, the weaker and/or more enterprising party may embark on a new venture, seizing the chance of staking out a territory of their own. The evolution of our economies is critically dependent on these *cf. 221* agents of change.

> Innovative enterprise is fraught with hazardous complications and calls for a lot of hard work. Consequently, the typical manager is not tempted so much by the prospect of increased profitability, as spurred on by the dread of being overtaken by the competi-

tion. The oft-quoted profit motive has a necessary complement in the fear of being out-manoeuvred or overplayed. Disturbing innovation often originates in marginal organizations which can teach the dominant actor a lesson whenever he becomes complacent.

The praxeological approach emphasizes the inherent logic of economics, the unyielding invariances in the structure of the game. Such value-deficient insights fall short of explaining the all-important variations in economic performance under outwardly very similar conditions. Real understanding can only be achieved by taking account of the tacit meta-rules of the economic game. The plus-sum character of economic life depends on these superordinate aspects, but no system of rules can eliminate the zero-sum component – the conflict prevailing between the self-interest of the competing players or coalitions.

5.2   Economic emancipation

Lasting technological progress and a sustained increase in prosperity comes up against deep-seated genetic blockages. Either the establishment ruthlessly appropriates the surplus, or it is wasted in an avalanche of popular shortsightedness and spite. How, then, can we explain the present cornucopia? Are we to achieve a continual increase in standards of living or will a gradual decline or a sudden collapse be our lot? Freedom from toil and want appears attainable at last – but only if we refrain from enjoying it! We must thoroughly understand this paradox in order to counteract the blindly antagonistic forces which time and again have destroyed the economic game.

Neolithic prelude

Advantageous exchange is certainly as old as mankind itself. We tend to regard the market economy as a modern invention, but a "world market" for flint and obsidian evidently existed already in Palaeolithic times. The distribution patterns suggest trade agreements, resale, or other special commercial relationships, all of which bear witness to the surprising sophistication of the Palaeolithic economy.

The transition to the Neolithic age in about 10,000 B.C. marks a deep crisis in the economic game. The invention of the bow and arrow along with other advances in hunting techniques led to unthinking mass slaughter. The end result was the extermination of a good deal of the most desirable prey.

The mammoth, the woolly rhinoceros and the giant deer disappeared from Eurasia, and many of the large carnivores, such as the cave bear and the sabre-toothed tiger, became extinct as well. Unaccustomed to humans, the endemic megafauna of Australia and the Americas was virtually wiped out upon the arrival of nomadic hunters. Around 12,000 B.C. approximately 75 per cent of the big mammals (those weighing over 40 kilograms) suddenly disappear from the American fossil record. Indigenous mammoths and mastodons, camels, rhinoceroses, horses and deer perished together with their superstructure of highly specialized predators. The same story repeated itself when remote islands were originally colonized in the first millennium A.D. Madagascar lost its giant lemurs and elephant birds, New Zealand the giant moa, and Hawaii the flightless geese.

The sudden extinction has been blamed on climatic change, which may have been a contributing factor, but on the whole it is a far-fetched explanation. The almost simultaneous development of agriculture and animal husbandry in many places was forced upon man by the breakdown of the Palaeolithic hunting homeostasis. Seeds, roots and fruits had always been an important source of nourishment, but it was the collapse of the hunting culture that started the long march towards the controlled production of food and the hierarchic organization of society.

The economic revolution of the Neolithic era involved a remarkable emancipation of man's intellect, leading in due course to an open-ended chain reaction. Specialization through trade and an archaic barter economy paved the way for social co-operation, irrigation and large-scale agriculture. Newly-founded towns organized the flow of information, stimulating imaginative thinking and technical progress.

cf. 133   The development of written language is an excellent example of the dynamics of the times. Small, concisely shaped tokens of clay symbolizing the various necessities of life (cattle, grain, cloth etc) were originally used for the purpose of simple arithmetic and primitive book-keeping. When traded goods were dispatched to distant customers, passing through the hands of many middlemen, delivery was documented on a "bill of lading" consisting of an appropriate set of symbolic clay tokens. The next stage was to pack the tokens in a hermetically-sealed capsule of fired clay, to avoid any tampering with the message. The capsule could be conveniently stamped with the sender's and/or recipient's seal; the remaining problem was that the middlemen were unable to check whether or not the document agreed with the delivery. The solution was to impress the distinctive shapes of the tokens on the outside of the capsule. Around 3000 B.C. written language in its cuneiform version had arrived.

The cultural dynamism of the Neolithic period involved a leap in the dark, and must have generated widespread anxiety. Torn between ancient emotional impulses and a dawning rationalism, *Homo sapiens* began to play his own game. He had eaten of the tree of knowledge, lost his innocence – the clear-cut genetic program – and was expelled from his pristine if not pastoral paradise. Even today we show a propensity for escapist relapses. We are sorely tempted to evade the chill of our new-won rationality in favour of totalitarian utopias which proffer the primitive warmth of universal solidarity – "mankind as one great family". Emotionally we are still living in the Palaeolithic age, painfully alienated from the self-evident rules of the kindred group but inevitably yielding to the incentives of the economic game.

The curse of stagnation

A first generation of high cultures appeared about 8000 B.C., based on the agricultural potential of the Fertile Crescent in the Middle East. Later, the peoples of the Huang Ho and the Indus valleys followed suit. The wholly independent developments of Mesoamerica and the Andes pursued a similar course, albeit with an additional time lag. But high cultures were the exception after all; in Australia, for example, development seems to have come to a complete standstill. The cultural game apparently requires a critical mass of interacting individuals in order to realize its inherent growth potential. Like biological evolution, economic interplay does not generally achieve genuine optimization: in the absence of fierce competition good enough solutions will prevail.

> On Tasmania anthropologists have found clear evidence of cultural regression. The earliest inhabitants supported themselves by fishing, but about 4,000 to 5,000 years ago the population began to decline, returning to a gathering economy with shellfish as the main source of food. When the Europeans arrived, the 5,000 strong Tasmanians used only a minimum of tools and had descended to the lowest level of culture ever observed. They soon died out, victims of ruthless colonialism and their own ineptitude.
>
> In Polynesia the level of human activity – the potency of a society – generally increased with the size of the territory and the population; New Zealand was clearly the most vigorous place. R.L. Carneiro has found a striking correlation between population *cf. 170* size and the complexity of the cultural web (figure 5.2).
>
> A similar relationship obtains between the size of a clearly-defined habitat (say an island) and biological diversity. Species formation requires a certain segregation but *cf. 97* total isolation breeds only stagnation.

The initial steps of a high culture must necessarily involve the evolution of an economic plus-sum game. These embryonic stages remain forever obscure while we know all the more about later, relatively static periods. Creative enterprise is almost invariably followed by bureaucratization and exploitation

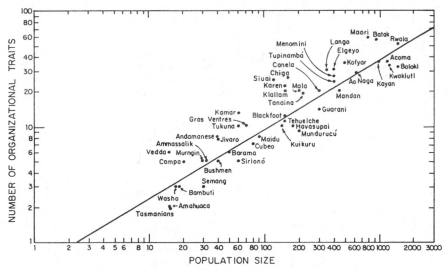

Figure 5.2 Cultural complexity as a function of population size (from Wilson and Lumsden, 1981)

by the ruling class or special-interest groups. Economic zero-sum games preponderate and the flagging primary product is redistributed with increasing
cf. 233 arbitrariness and largely according to non-economic criteria.

> In repressive societies, the lack of economic self-regulation necessitates bureaucratic intervention at every stage. Soviet socialism succumbed to an ever-increasing complexity of decision-making, which made for delays upon delays until the economy was approaching *rigor mortis*. Similar mechanisms can be blamed for the rigidity and downfall of many ancient, overcentralized states. Typically, the élite channelled dis-
> *cf. 142*   proportionate investment into imposing building projects. The pyramids of Egypt, the ziggurats of Sumer and Babylonia, the great wall of China and the temples of the Mayas all served the self-justification of the ruling nomenclatura – repression by monuments.

Despite internal stagnation a culture can continue to expand in population and geographical extent, borne along by its inherited fund of spiritual and material
cf. 234; 393 capital. Such successes are illusionary. Routine self-replication is not enough; time will irrepressively distort the cultural programme. Without strenuous self-renewal, the graft and greed of well-connected power-brokers will, sooner or later, corrupt the rules of the economic game; autonomous farmers have regularly been reduced to impotent serfs. But even the most oppressive oligarchy must maintain a minimum of decorum; otherwise the rulers will be reduced to wielding pick and shovel themselves.

Epigenetic interference

Primitive societies exhibit a heavy and suffocating superstructure, a complex web of ritual rules in marked contrast to the harsh game of pure economics. The fruits of individual effort generally belong to the extended family, if not to the whole tribe. In the less developed countries, a prosperous man easily falls victim to this archetypal group solidarity; a horde of "distant relatives" suddenly descends on him demanding a slice of the common cake. In imitation of Pierre Proudhon (1809–65), the father of anarchism, they contend that clinging to personal property is equal to theft.

> A somewhat unexpected consequence is the widespread nepotism and corruption in many developing countries. The least that an influential politician owes his kinsmen is a post within the administration; similar pressures are then brought to bear on the newly appointed civil servants as well. In Papua New Guinea the "wantok" system of social insurance depends on the right of any clan member to claim support from an affluent clansman after "one talk". Similar customs reverberate in the more advanced societies. After a political swing, the habitual spoils are regularly redistributed among the victors and an "old boy" network can mobilize considerable energy to find a position for some less gifted member of the unofficial brotherhood.

cf. 232; 274 Like an unconditioned reflex, a similarly misguided loyalty affects much of our public debate. A subconscious epigenetic undercurrent exerts its irresistible pull – at heart we are all socialists.

> Populous society, indeed all mankind, is seen as a single homogeneous mass. The needs of countless separate individuals have to be satisfied; their well-being seems to depend entirely on the planning and meddling of political opportunists or academic gurus. Such

lack of respect for other people's ability to manage their own affairs defeats all common sense.

The division of labour through free commerce involves a rational and self-organizing interplay between people, reaching far beyond the instinctive and genetically rooted norms of the kin group. The rules of the game are and must be different from those in the family, the parish or the political party. Thus, the coldly calculating undertone of business transactions is in constant conflict with ingrained epigenetic directives.

In 1840 Louis Blanc (1911–81), the French socialist leader, coined the battle cry, "From each according to his abilities, to each according to his needs." The first to respond on a practical level was Otto von Bismarck (1825–98), who became the somewhat incongruous father of state-sponsored social security. Old-age pensions and indemnities for accidents at work were introduced in the period 1883–9. The retirement age was set at 65 mainly for economic reasons: at the time only a few per cent of the workers lived long enough to become eligible.

I have touched on these sociobiological considerations in order to put the analysis of our economic problems in perspective. Technological progress accompanied by a general increase in prosperity has never been an automatic or continuous process because it inevitably comes up against deep-seated genetic blockages. The economic stagnation in former high cultures can hardly be blamed on some "objective" cause such as the exhaustion of natural resources; the carriers of culture probably lost their way in a maze of social and political conflict. The economy imitates nature; it is always in dynamic, praxeological balance, and unless we are capable of actively advancing the game it will slide back under the weight of very natural human indolence and ruthlessness, ill will and spite.

The dichotomy of economics

Since the rise of socialism, nations and trading blocs have been divided between planned economies, with centralized allocation of resources, and market economies which rely on free exchange between independent actors. Although neither have ever existed in a pure state, and the differences are increasingly blurred, it is of some interest to compare various aspects of these cybernetically contrasting models. It comes as no surprise that our Western education and health care faithfully reflect the characteristics of a socialist planned economy.

Aspect	Planned economy	Market economy
Values	Society-oriented	Citizen-oriented
Social framework	Monolithic	Pluralistic
Rules of the game	Many and detailed, explicit orders	Few and general, implicit guidance
Key players	Politicians, bureaucrats	Entrepreneurs, consumers
Key moves	Administrative directives	Business transactions
Game inputs	Primarily physical production resources	Primarily money
Key problems	Mainly supply side, materials, vendors, production	Mainly demand side, cost price, customers, marketing
Co-ordination	Centralized, bureaucratically integrated	Decentralized, integrated by the market
Control parameters	Central supervision, compulsion	Profitability, competition
Dynamic elements	Planned goals, quantity	Enterprise, innovation, quality
Price formation	Artificial, regulated	Free
Taxation	Differentiated purchase tax, low income tax	Standard purchase tax High and progressive income tax
Links with world market	Weak	Strong
Intensity of play	Low	High
Security and stability	High	Low
Motivation	Primarily non-economic	Primarily economic
Rewards	Power, status, preferential treatment	Money

The planned economy cannot in fact operate without a market function but its performance is degraded by political and ideological elements at all levels. Praxeologically-motivated decisions are regarded as provisional concessions, until the egotism of the economic game is finally eliminated by a deft combination of material abundance and human solidarity. In principle, every problem is politicized, each one involves state intervention; instead of crumbling away, the state becomes absolute.

> The strictly-planned economy works reasonably well in a state of mobilization. But the difficulties escalate as consumers acquire more freedom of choice. Nothing can replace the trial and error of market communication which accurately reflects the demand for goods and services. The dynamics of the supply side are almost equally perplexing. Trivial technical development might be foreseeable but genuine invention or innovation, not to speak of significant scientific discoveries, elude any kind of quantitative prediction.

While planned economies strive to disqualify the economic game, a market economy aims for the maximum scope for economic play. State meddling in the market game is seen as a temporary expedient requiring exceptional justification. Crises and wars tend to derange the economy; scarcities and clear-cut national goals transform the consumer from master of the market to servant of the state, and many typical features of the planned economy suddenly appear. Once things return to normal, there is a general sigh of relief. Rationing, queues and compulsory service are relegated to the past, and money regains its position as the universal measure of material value.

Economic emancipation

Even a reform-minded figure like Michel de Montaigne (1533–92) could see only a zero-sum in economic competition: "It is clear that one country can only gain if another loses". The worldly-wise Francois de Voltaire (1694–1778) stood for the same idea: "one man's advantage can only mean another man's loss". This obsession with zero-sum play was overcome by Adam Smith (1723–90) who perceived how the wealth of nations was created by the competitive struggle within a set of rules ensuring fair market play.　　　*cf. 228*

In a game with a constant sum, the focus is on the problems of redistribution. Capital accumulation and affluence can obtain only at someone else's expense, and every fortune thus has to be based on qualified robbery. Obviously, such a stance cannot be seriously maintained but it elicits the response of collective spite, so exhaustively analysed by Ludwig von Mises in *The Anticapitalist Society* (1956).

> The resentment of the less well-to-do assumes a spurious scientific guise in the myth of the zero-sum nature of the international market economy (see for instance Frantz Fanon (1925–61) *Les Damnés de la Terre*, 1961: The Wretched of the Earth). The soothsayers of the radical left have claimed, in earnest, that the poverty of the developing countries is the result of economic exploitation on the part of the developed world – after all, its wealth must have come from somewhere! If that is the case, why have Afghanistan, Ethiopia and Liberia remained so poor? And why has African socialism inexorably drifted towards bankruptcy?

Our bodily needs, like the highest of human strivings, are of an absolute kind. Hunger, thirst and sexual drives can be completely if transiently satisfied while religious revelation and artistic experience draw their value from inexhaustible sources. But a position in the hierarchy, for example, can only be comprehended on a relative scale and is always the cause of envy. The competition for prestigious satisfactions generates a distinctive zero-sum game in which covetousness plays a crucial role.

> The value of the Order of the Garter would be drastically debased by widespread distribution, and if everyone were to drive a stretched limousine, it would simply mean overcrowded parking lots. National self-assertion also builds on facetious zero-sum emotions. As group members, we can experience by proxy an imaginary superiority over the rest of the world – a helpful palliative for the petty failures of our daily lives.

As long as opulence retains its considerable status value (quite a while), dissatisfaction with the unequal outcome of the market-economic game will persist. Consequently, the indecent displays of affluent societies are heavily censored. A new economic order is called for, to ensure a fair allocation of scarce resources and to avert, or at least postpone, ecological deterioration. Such moves would just drag us deeper into the mire because they would involve a terrible waste of our most precious assets – billions of human opportunities for independent economic plus-sum play.

> Without the constant prodding of external competition, the self-proclaimed "Socialist bloc" would in no time have slipped into quasi-homeostatic decay. Even China, the remaining citadel of socialism, is now vesting its hope in a market economy, that prodigious provider of wealth. Only bigoted environmentalists still think in terms of a global zero-sum game: economic gain can in their eyes only be achieved by robbing pristine nature. Nevertheless, the greens are right to include the environmental impact in the cost calculation. We must truly try to enrich the world and take into account all externalities by discounting the adverse as well as advantageous side-effects of our human endeavours.

How, then, can we explain the present cornucopia? Can we achieve a sustainable increase in standards of living or will stagnation and stratification, a gradual decline or sudden collapse be our lot? The final economic emancipation of man, freedom from toil and want, appears attainable at last – but only if we *cf. 251* refrain from enjoying it! This paradox is part of the secret of our success, an enigma we must thoroughly understand in order to counteract the blindly antagonistic forces which, time and again, have destroyed the economic game.

5.3   The market game

The market economy is a huge self-organizing and self-adjusting plus-sum game, a rather chaotic interplay which, like the weather, is subject to occasional instabilities. A modern market economy is incompatible with static homeostasis; the system itself plays havoc with stability, inducing a stream of disturbing innovations. Even so, swings in the business cycle depend, first and foremost, on ill-advised decision-makers. Human greed and gullibility promote unsound speculation which is bound to defeat itself. For want of "correct" information, we must accept that the market is always wrong, but at least it is constantly busy seeking its own truth.

The world market

Our modern world economy is essentially a gigantic market game, played according to straightforward but unwritten rules. There is no referee nor any institutional framework as such, and yet everybody wants to be in on the act – a sure indication of its plus-sum character. The only sanctions are the counter-moves of the other players. If one nation "makes itself impossible", it is simply frozen out for a while. No-one wants any dealings with the defaulter who is caught in an offside position.

Despite attempts to give a head start to economically backward countries by development aid (soft credits or preferential trade agreements) the world market functions with cool, Pareto-optimal perfection; all kinds of goods are sup- *cf. 55* plied with irrefutable objectivity and a minimum of friction. Highly-specialized traders and businessmen effectively exploit any price gradients for their own livelihood. The least disturbance in supply or demand causes readjustments which serve to clear the market. Corrupt practices certainly affect the game in some places, as do an assortment of national trade restrictions and international treaties, raw material pacts, cartels and the like. The cards are then stacked against some players but such distortions are easily accounted for by the market mechanism.

> The world market, with its almost perfect catalysis, is a striking example of praxeological balance. It is in many ways a blessed state of nature governed by inviolable laws and untrammelled by any value system. Meddlesome bureaucrats, susceptible politicians and fidgety public opinion all remain within the national borders: the world market has no bias.

As we cross the trade barriers that define the borders of individual countries or regional trade blocs, we enter a different atmosphere. Inexorable economic rules are replaced and/or complemented by a multiplicity of special regulations. Much of this legislation is due to special pleading, which invariably claims to speak in the national interest. If we discount the specious arguments, there remains a legitimate need for the protection of certain national or regional values and objectives. A few basic themes recur in various disguises:

☐ Internal solidarity prevents the cold-hearted rules of the world market from deciding the fortunes of large segments of the population. Duties and levies, export charges and subsidies still abound despite the progress of free trade; government intervention is buttressed by many less visible obstacles.

☐ In its lengthy eliminating rounds, the world market game may generate extremes of specialization and mutual dependencies which the Great Powers in particular find unacceptable. The fear of economic blackmail and the threat of war are the main justifications for autarchic aspirations. At bottom, it is a question of national sovereignty.

☐ The most respectable motive for national trade barriers is the need to protect the national economy from the impact of violent price fluctuations. We will return to the problem of stability later. Protectionist measures increase, in any case, the susceptibility of the world market to price swings by reducing the market volume.

The complete isolation of national markets is certainly unwise but cautious cushioning may be in order. In the long run, the economic optimum probably coincides with the whole-hearted acceptance of the rules of the world market.

No government has yet dared to take the plunge without a string of reservations; every nation tries to place the onus of free trade on its neighbours (witness the protracted GATT negotiations). The ever-increasing volume of world commerce shows, however, that we are slowly heading for a truly global economic community.

Excessive self-criticism

Although the plus-sum game of the market economy has no equal when it comes to efficiency, flexibility and innovation, it has nevertheless attracted fierce and sometimes well-founded criticism. If we disregard purely demagogic arguments, the following flaws have drawn most of the fire.

☐ The inequality of opportunity. A few players start out with a lot while most have little or nothing. This can lead to ruthless power play which breaks even modest standards of fairness. Radical demands for equality call for the abolishment of the "commutative justice" of market forces.

☐ The selfishness of the economic game. Business is often condemned as morally degrading and inimical to the loftier aims of mankind. Another version of this criticism emphasizes the stress which can be caused by the great intensity and relative insecurity of the market game.

☐ The instability of the market economy. Fluctuations in the business cycle, overproduction (or underconsumption), and unemployment are symptoms of deep-seated contradictions. This pragmatic criticism carries the greatest weight, and has been the source of considerable concern to advocates of the system.

The equality argument can be dealt with briefly. Economic inequality can be largely offset by income transfers in order to approximate the "distributive justice" of political processes. The market economy can bear high levels of taxation, albeit with some awkward repercussions. The question of ownership has been emphasized out of all proportion. In fact it doesn't seem to matter much whether the economic players are physical persons, limited companies or publicly-owned enterprises, provided they all stick to the same rules and the game is refereed by an impartial umpire.

> We could envisage a modern market economy as a huge corporation with decision-making delegated to "lease-holders" (or "owners" if we prefer the term) who retain what is generally a modest share of the revenues as profit. This seems a low price to pay for the initiative and long-term responsibility of people left to administer the common property as their own.
>
> According to the customs of the Germanic peoples, inherited property was not freely disposable; rather it was in the custody of its current holder, to be managed in the best interests of his heirs. This restriction on ownership certainly facilitated the emergence of capitalism, and the endowment motive is still at work in the amassment of fortune.

The moralizing argument can be dismissed even more summarily. Nobody has ever lost his soul by engaging in fair play. The intellectual stimulus and personal involvement should more than outweigh any symptoms of stress.

The stability problem

The national economy can be regarded as a system of cybernetic interactions. Planned economies are based primarily on macroeconomic feedback which calls for the comprehensive physical planning of consumption and production. The market economy relies mainly on a self-regulating price mechanism which co-ordinates the actions of the countless individuals involved. These consumers and producers, debtors and creditors, inventors and entrepreneurs certainly cannot be described as unwaveringly rational decision-makers, but the imperfections should normally cancel out without causing any runaway upheavals.

> A modern market economy is incompatible with static homeostasis. As a result of what Joseph Schumpeter (1883–1950) calls creative destructiveness the system itself plays havoc with stability, inducing a stream of disturbing innovations in product development, production technology, distribution, marketing, financing, organizational structures and so on. At the same time the market game has to absorb the repercussions of social change which, to a large extent, represent the political feedback of its own successes. Meanwhile natural disasters, wars and other external crises may exert additional strains on society, increasing the turmoil. Notwithstanding all these excuses, the market economy is at times plagued by inherent instabilities.

Why is it, then, that our decentralized market system sometimes lets us down? How can a successful plus-sum process suddenly deteriorate into a severe depression, an arena for lost opportunities? In the first place we should remember that the market economy, by its very nature, is a weakly chaotic interplay of independent actors. Its spontaneous self-organization must, like any genuine learning process, produce some disorder or even setbacks.

> Chaos theory has, with some success, been applied to stock markets. The price movements follow the shape of a pile of sand which is fed by a steady flow of grains from above and corresponds to the slowly accumulating "real" value of the market. The height of the pile, which reflects the apparent value or price, develops in a chaotic manner despite the stable input of sand grains. Gradual increase is interrupted by sudden, unpredictable crashes.

The appeal of a "mixed" economy lies in its, largely illusionary, stability and sense of direction. To beat government planners at their own game, the economic players must learn how to anticipate the consequences of each other's moves. Managers and investors are often gripped by the herd instinct. Fashion gets the better of business acumen, and when politicians and union bosses join the fray, bad decisions accumulate in an overheating economy.

Poor performance is ultimately punished by bankruptcy, but in a severe downturn, penalties are not restricted to a few unskilled or unlucky players. A substantial minority (or even a majority) is set to lose and this causes a general outcry for more government intervention. One way or another, swings in the business cycle depend first and foremost on ill-advised decision-makers; their collective misjudgements depress macroeconomic performance.

> The economic boom creates a euphoric sense of success; it seems so easy to earn money – just make a bold gamble like everybody else! During a recession, all those misdirected moves have to be quietly written off while pessimistic apprehensions rapidly spread in the community. Man, even the toughest businessman, seems to live in the present,

submissively swimming with the tide. Political memory is said to last six months; business memory lasts a little longer but in a few years' time the whole sad story tends to repeat itself. It is difficult to make countercyclical decisions, to invest when business is sluggish and to reap the harvest when it revives.

What then can be done to improve the game, to increase the skill of the players and the level of play? Massive nationalisation is best forgotten, and improved education is no panacea either. Inevitably, business schools are long on mathematical models and case histories but short on life experience and mature judgement; on balance they have become part of the problem. Practice is the best and possibly the only teacher, but even its lessons seem sadly evanescent.

Candid speculation

The problem is that even if we rationally understand the situation, we are emotionally bound to what we can perceive in front of us. It takes a hardened, professional gambler to go against the received wisdom of the day, to believe in the always doubtful intellectual analysis, coolly mastering the two-headed monster of greed and fear. Such calculated audacity is in short supply but is sorely needed; willy-nilly we are all involved in speculation when making major business decisions.

> Everywhere market liquidity is maintained by speculators who act as transactional catalysts, utilizing the price dynamics of currencies, commodities, stock markets and so on. Their operations should prevent or, at least, soften disruptive swings but these very market-makers are nevertheless blamed for the extreme movements in price. A moment's reflection should show that a speculator can make a profit only if his actions have a moderating effect on price fluctuations. Those who go too far in their speculations in a bull or bear market will lose out. One of Baron Nathan Rothschild's (1777–1836) favourite maxims was "Leave the last 10 per cent to the next man", and when John D. Rockefeller was asked how he had earned so much money, he answered: "I always sold too early".

Speculators go their solitary way boldly anticipating price movements at their own risk. This gives the marketplace a forewarning which increases the stability of the cybernetic feedback by reducing the "dead time" between a change in the fundamentals and corrective action. Apart from this admittedly very important effect, speculation is a zero-sum game, and we have to ask ourselves if, on average, professional speculators must make a profit, who are the losers? The answer is: the amateurs, in particular bureaucratic organizations and "ordinary" buyers and sellers who want to play it safe, but inadvertently speculate in the preservation of the *status quo*. They wake up too late and react in a panic.

The worldwide deregulation of the financial markets has introduced new instabilities caused by the huge amounts of money sloshing around in the marketplace. Meanwhile, unscrupulous tycoons have found sufficient ammunition for their raids on the sitting ducks of business, stretching the accounting rules and deceiving gullible investors in the process. We need more discipline, mainly by disclosure, to castigate uncandid speculators who enjoy the advantage of amorality connected with "the last move".

cf. 60

The pros and cons of company raiding are widely debated. At any rate, an international comparison shows that economic efficiency is not dependent on aggressive cornering or hostile takeovers. In Japan, a merger or a takeover is possible only with management approval and in Germany, too, unfriendly approaches are the exception. Money is not necessarily the measure of all things and, oddly enough, such restraint seems to be conducive to making more of it.

Thanks to constant speculation on the currency market we are kept abreast of the relative values of various legal tender. The drawback is the lack of short-term stability in an unregulated market. Far from neglecting the anticipated moves of fellow-players, the reckless speculator fails to consider anything else. Realities recede into the background as feverish gambling carries a market to implausible extremes and everybody plays at "beggar my neighbour".

John Maynard Keynes (1883–1946) once said that "the art of speculation is to antici-pate what average opinion expects average opinion to be" and he went on to analyze speculation of third, fourth or even higher degrees. The great tulip craze in Holland in 1636–37 is the classic example of such systematic second-guessing. During a three-year period, prices of tulip futures rose sixtyfold; at the height of the boom the price trebled every week before the inevitable crash. In the eyes of public officials money was running amok, and the magistrates soon intervened to forestall another debacle. The first unregulated paper market (Windhandel) thus came to an inglorious end.

cf. 221

Human greed and gullibility promote unsound speculation which is bound to defeat itself. Whether fixed but rather fictitious official rates of exchange are preferable to speculative market pricing remains a matter of debate. By way of compromise, the "correct" value of a currency could well be supported by central banks in open market operations on a profit-making basis. For want of "correct" information, we must in any case accept that the market is always wrong; but at least, as Georg Soros puts it in *The Alchemy of Finance* (1987), it is constantly busy seeking its own truth.

5.4   Playing and betraying the economic game

There is usually a wide gap between the economically desirable and the politically feasible. We are in for real trouble when strong pressure groups insist on bending the rules in their favour. Such false play results in major imbalances. Capital formation stagnates as the state becomes the nanny of emasculated citizens and the insufficient investments cannot provide enough work at the overblown costs of labour. The outcome is first inflation, then stagflation and finally widespread unemployment and economic crisis – something has to give. By industry and thrift, the losers in the Second World War have consistently outperformed the winning side. The Japanese, in particular, have clearly succeeded in optimizing the plus-sum game of the market economy – albeit at a price.

Managing instability

We neglect the fundamental praxeological tenets only at our peril, but these laws of logic must be supplemented by a suitable set of complementary man-made conventions and regulations. Society is, after all, the sum total of this political superstructure which will bend but cannot break the iron rules of pure praxeology. Man has always lived in a mixed economy in which basic public services such as defence and the judiciary are regularly supplied by the state. The list of such "public goods" has recently been greatly extended, and the amount and degree of state intervention is one of the major controversial issues of our time.

One of the tasks generally assigned to government agencies is the elimination or at least the amelioration of instabilities. As it happens, the national economy is an unwieldy and little understood multiperson game, in which well-intended but clumsy interference may prove ineffective or even counterproductive.

> The crash on the New York stock exchange in September 1929 was aggravated by government action which led to a substantial reduction in the supply of money and thus precipitated the worst depression of all time. Some dampening would have been appropriate a couple of years before, but once the crisis had become acute the squandering of capital on poor investments was already a fact. The disastrous intellectual collapse of managers, businessmen and speculators had occurred earlier, well before the dive on the stock market.

cf. 49; 394 In economics the dead time between regulatory action and its measurable effects can be very long, sometimes several years. In combination with powerful external disturbances this causes serious steering problems.

> When an inexperienced person adjusts the feedback parameters in a process, saddled with cumbersome cybernetics, the control loop begins to swing from one extreme to the

other with a frequency close to the dead time. The standard solutions to this problem   *cf. 49*
are to:
- reinforce the system's self-stabilizing properties;
- eliminate or attenuate grave disturbances;
- measure important but ungovernable disturbing factors and use this data as input for
  auxiliary control devices (feed forward regulation);
- break down the process into manageable parts by measuring and regulating intermediate variables (cascade control);
- reduce feedback, or refrain from it altogether; and
- have patience – do not force the issue.

The simplest cure is time. Economic crises tend to blow over by themselves in a
year and a half while it may take eighteen months of intensive care to achieve a
worse result. The clever use of feed-forward action is the hallmark of the skilled
macroeconomist, while the impetuous use of feedback courts disaster.

Stagflation

Leading economists now seem to have got the stability problem fairly well
under control – or so they think. However that may be, recession has not
recurred on the scale of the early 1930s. Instead we find modern market economies struggling with more or less chronic stagflation, a combination of stagnation, unemployment and inflation. Hasty but popular cosmetic actions are
legion while politicians compete with one another in the noble art of making an
omelette without breaking eggs. The voters have little understanding of the
economic game, hence the sometimes enormous gap between the economically
desirable and the politically feasible.

The world has seen many cases illustrating the plight of societies which refuse to accept   *cf. 225*
economic realities. For much of the present century Uruguay was the model democracy
of Latin America, bankrolling its expanding welfare state with income from the boom-
ing meat market. When the downturn came after the Second World War, the country
was left with an expensive social support system and low efficiency, which led to the
downfall of democracy and the establishment of a harsh police state. Argentina's recent
history exhibits the same pattern, one which may be in store for many of the newly-rich
oil nations. Good fortune appears to be an affliction rather than a boon.
  I have studiously refrained from strengthening my case with numbers but just this
once a small dose of statistics is in order.

Argentina	*1930*	*1989*
Per capita output (U.S.-89 $/year)	3700	1800
World ranking	7th	70th
Inflation rate (%)	2	5000
Government spending (% of GNP)	11	45

Struck by economic success, people mostly expect too much too soon. Politicians cynically oversell the business boom, increase public spending and end up
hopelessly in debt. The voters are treated as election fodder incapable of understanding basic economic issues. Nonetheless it is only a question of simple cause
and effect, certainly not beyond the grasp of the ordinary citizen.

Switzerland provides an encouraging instance of a more widespread understanding of the economic game. All important economic decisions are in the hands of the electorate, and yet the Swiss economy could well serve as an example to us all. This shows that what we call economic problems have very little to do with the manipulation of the economy but all the more to do with political maturity.

Japan is another, much celebrated model of economic success but, despite all the lip-service, Western haughtiness has largely inhibited the assimilation of the Japanese lesson. When Professor Naoto Sasaki started a series of lectures on Japanese management methods at the London School of Economics, the first question from the audience was: "Why are you here instructing your very competitors?" His mischievous response, "You would not do it anyhow", has been used as a caption for the Sasaki seminars ever since. The least we could learn from the Japanese is how to learn from other people.

cf. 136   We have already noted that there are no definite technological constraints on material progress, and the praxeological imperatives should not overwhelm the intellect of economists. Thus a weak economy is symptomatic of serious distortions of the political process, a collective delusion. People do not want to *cf. 278; 369* adapt, they prefer to live a lie.

The reproduction rate (number of children per fertile female) should remain at around 2.3 in order to maintain a constant population in the long term. In most European countries it fluctuates between 1.5 and 1.8, which means that we are shamelessly exhausting our living capital. A substantial proportion of the prevailing unemployment is directly caused by the low birthrate. A certain over-supply of man- and especially woman-power is hardly surprising considering that the labour-intensive care of children and pensioners is transiently at a minimum. This kind of self-evident reasoning seems to be anathema to the politicians of the day, who prefer to wallow in economic escapism.

Treatment is usually administered only by fits and starts; painful withdrawal symptoms soon induce the adoption of quick fixes. In this respect, expanding budget deficits are an example of a remedy that will produce new waves of instability. The spectre of stagflation still haunts many market economies, and we should therefore consider a few of the traps that the Swiss and the Japanese have so happily avoided.

Disruptive power

The abuse of economic power had been widely disparaged long before Marx. The greedy usurer and the wicked exploiter are archetypes in the folklore of all high cultures. An ideal market economy leaves no scope for such racketeering, but unfortunately reality is far from perfect. In the market game, disruption in the balance of power between the major actors is not the exception but the rule.

In North America the power of business grew steadily from the mid-nineteenth century onwards. As companies merged to form dominating trusts, they were able to set the manufacturing margins at their convenience while manipulating politicians and civil servants in the process. Antitrust legislation brought some spectacular successes, but neither the trustbusters nor the fragmented trade unions could check the feverish ambition of businessmen. The growth in consumption was abnormally low in relation to the rising wave of investment, which finally collapsed in 1929 in the greatest stock market crash of all time. The Great Depression is the most telling example of instability generated by the unrestrained pursuit of profits, big, quick and certain – a highly unstable set-up.

The industrial barons of the early twentieth century left a legacy of almost permanent overcapacity and unemployment which affected a whole generation of economic thinkers. They all agreed with Keynes that consumption should be encouraged, and were thus ill-equipped to tackle the later scourge of stagflation which reflected a reversal in the balance of power. Now it is the wage-earners who stridently demand employment for all at a level of wages and benefits set by the trade unions and their political allies. By the 1950s this coalition had gained *de facto* control over the supply of labour and the related legislation, defying all the rules of the market place – wages could only go up.

In our modern market economies, widespread unemployment is a direct consequence of the cartelization of labour and the concomitant suspension of market forces. The legitimacy of the trade unions became problematic the moment they attained a dominant position. From such a vantage-point it is always more attractive to dictate the terms than to adjust to realities. Disruption and unemployment will persist until the abuse of power is righted and the price of labour once again reflects supply and demand.

Inflationary intoxication

Rising prices do not, as such, signify inflation but may be due to under-supply, caused by natural disasters or a depletion of resources. The inflationary spiral establishes itself only when wages are raised to preserve an unrealistic level of consumption "by force". A similar picture emerges if the process is set off by runaway wages or government banknote financing: the inflated purchasing power chases an insufficient supply and triggers off an automatic price reaction, which is then offset by further wage increases. An attempt to keep prices down artificially implies a continuous waste of capital – an invitation to national bankruptcy, acceptable only in a siege economy.

> Many experts claim that a "moderate" level of inflation has a stimulating effect on the economy. Empirical evidence suggests that this is so; the mechanism involved is fairly easy to grasp and also quite illuminating. Particularly in its initial stage, inflation gives rise to big capital transfers; savers, pensioners and other disorganized and politically powerless groups are gradually robbed of their property and incomes. Consumption falls off while credit-based business expansion is favoured, especially if the real rate of interest remains negative. Consumption has thus been converted into capital which, as we all know, is one of the preconditions for rapid growth – the market-economy version of Stalin's ruthless industrialization campaign.

You cannot fool even ordinary people all the time. Inflation ceases to stimulate growth when the flight to real values, index-linking and so on, puts a stop to capital transfers. Instead the country is stuck with persistent and "paradoxical" stagflation where once again a lot of poor investments have to be written off.

The public sector's growing share of the national product adds another aspect to the psychology of inflation. It is so easy for the wage-earner to forget all his indirect benefits: shorter working hours, education, health care, pension schemes and so on. Cradle-to-grave insurance has to be paid for and the price is high, due to the inherent inefficiency of publicly-run redistribution systems. Despite some recent successes in the fight against inflation, numerous well-organized groups continue to grab what they can for themselves whenever the occasion arises.

> Recently this game of one-upmanship has been upgraded by fashionable altruism. Despite the plunging savings rate, public opinion is easily incited to support additional spending on medical care, social welfare, education, cultural activities – all good causes in their own right. This plethora of "responsibilities" turns into flagrant irresponsibility when fiscal excesses are consistently covered by deficit financing. Consumption on credit usually invites trouble, and we are in for big trouble when rich societies meet the expense of their foreign aid by going on a borrowing binge, driving up the real interest rate for everybody else in the process.

Inflationary pressures will not go away, as long as a community tries to live beyond its means by transcending the laws of praxeology in a quest for un-assailable positions, incomes and social security. Sabotage of the market only results in a loss of work motivation, escalating debt, misallocation of capital and, in the end, falling living standards. The finely-tuned economic game has been betrayed; the sum of rational microeconomic decisions results in a minus-sum game for the national economy.

The Japanese model

The Second World War swept aside many outworn social conventions; it razed political power centres, released substantial forces of production and promoted previously unheard-of research and development efforts. An abnormally high rate of investment combined with minimal consumption laid the foundations for the boom of the post-war years, despite (or perhaps because of) the previous destruction.

It is remarkable that the greatest and most lasting upturn occurred in countries which were psychologically prepared by defeat and devastation for extremely low consumption during the initial take-off stage. This proves, once again, that what we call tangible capital is of less economic importance than technological skill, national solidarity and the postponement of material gratification. The losers in the Second World War have remained relatively unaffected by stagflation, a condition which has mainly afflicted the former victors.

Japan started from scratch – burnt-out cities, foreign occupation, near starvation, no raw materials – and has ended up bankrolling the rest of the world. The disgrace of the lost war made the Japanese receptive to radical change and was a spur to the most successful learning process of economic history.

> An extensive land reform was executed by general Douglas McArthur (1880–1964) without much ado. Legislation, including the major rules of the market economy, was taken over wholesale from the United States but applied with a Japanese twist. The

mighty conglomerates (zaibatsus) were broken up while industrial democratization was pursued with gusto. In the major corporations the principle of lifelong employment was extended from top management to all employees. In the factories, all visible signs of the class society, like separate entrances and cafeterias, were abolished and university graduates had to start their careers on the shop floor. This drive for equality has greatly contributed to the spectacular rise in productivity. President Goto of Daihatsu personally cleans the toilets every morning at 6 am. This gives him reliable feedback on the morale of the workforce, he says.

Amae, a feeling of mutual dependence and obligation, is the cornerstone of human relations in Japan: individual arrogance must be suppressed at all cost. Intensive communication is accordingly the keynote of Japanese management at all levels. Even if decisions are actually made at the top, custom requires that they must be acceptable to everybody concerned. Traditional honorifics serve as a counterweight and thwart any abuse of the system. Additional support is found in the Samurai tradition, another mainstay of Japanese society. The reciprocal loyalty of master and servant is embodied in the consensus-craving working team.

Trade unions are generally organized on a company-by-company basis, and many corporate executives have emerged from their ranks. The end result is a system of close and frequent consultations between industry, labour, research institutes, the administration and politicians, which provides all parties with the maximum amount of information. Unofficially, companies often co-ordinate their plans and sometimes the whole process has an air of official approval about it.

> None of this in any way reduces the pressure of competition, either at the corporate or the individual level, but the zero-sum element in the market game is substantially reduced. Japanese companies are surprisingly open. As a rule, large corporations publicize their long-term plans, and market share data are freely available. MITI (Ministry for Trade and Industry) makes in-depth studies of the various industries, and then presents its recommendations. Several industrial crises were successfully managed by way of such "administrative guidance", but official growth strategies have often misfired or been politely ignored.

Economic growth was regularly given top priority over wage increases, pollution, and the urban environment. But "Japan Inc." now has sufficient resources to maintain economic growth while tackling environmental problems, and allowing for a high standard of living. Despite murky politics, the Japanese have clearly succeeded in optimizing the plus-sum game of the market economy – albeit at a price.

> The typical Japanese employee is a male workaholic with few interests outside his workplace; workers and staff are all committed to the company, body and soul; the women are, in general, confined to the home or have menial jobs. The Japanese have been forced to amalgamate Western values with domestic tradition and the concomitant stress is taking its toll. The inherent ambivalence has been reflected in dirty politics but now the youth are increasingly reacting against the ingrained corruption. They feel constrained by the social straitjacket and opt in growing numbers for a freewheeling life style. How this will affect the fabric of society remains to be seen.

The Japanese work ethic has its roots in the village, which carried the joint responsibility for cultivating and mending the communal rice paddies. The Japanese employee is a born team-player, bent on beating the competition by perfecting products and working methods. The value system is pervaded by a Confucian sense of duty against a background of tolerant Shintoism and introspective Zen-Buddhism.

> Over centuries of enforced frugality, the Japanese have acquired an almost religious abhorrence of waste or extravagance. "Mottainai" is the derogatory expression for such abuse which is regarded as close to blasphemy. Akio Morita, the founder and chairman of Sony, tells how he had to rescue a Japanese friend from a small hotel room in New York, where his dread of "Mottainai" led him to pile up old copies of the *New York Times* until he was practically crowded out.
>
> The high savings ratio (well above 30 per cent) is sustained by thrifty housewives who are habitually in control of family finances. Such in-built parsimony is counterbalanced by a national passion for gambling. The gaming pachinko halls attract huge crowds, and lately the Japanese penchant for speculation has driven both the real estate and the stock market to giddy heights and an inevitable crash.

Once producers of shoddy consumer goods, the Japanese obsession with cleanliness and due process now supports a quest for quality. Any complaint, neglect, breakdown or imperfection in general will fatally disturb the heavenly harmony and fill every employee with shame.

> By an ironic quirk of fate, the main guru of Japanese quality control is the American professor W. Edwards Deming, who introduced the key concepts in the 1950s. The practical success, however, builds on conscientious self-inspection; the shopfloor worker is the unsung hero of Japanese productivity. Anyhow, the Deming prize is the highest award for quality in Japanese industry.

This rampant perfectionism may obstruct creativity, which in its early stages always goes against the tide and strikes a startling discord. Thus far Japanese industry has not been a source of great innovation; its strength has been the skilled application of available knowledge amounting to superb execution. Recently, investment in both basic and applied research has increased dramatically. Japanese diligence and ingenuity could well have an even greater impact on future technology.

5.5 Developing the economic game

While money is doubtless a human invention, private property has deep roots in our evolutionary ancestry. To avoid the cost of constant infighting, a mixed "bourgeois" strategy has evolved among many species. Scarcity of resources leads to the division into distinct preserves; you defend your territory but do not invade your neighbours'. By the same token, our extended prehistory has imprinted tribal solidarity on the human mind. In large communities these epigenetic rules are in permanent conflict – at heart we are all socialists. In my view, long-term plus-sum play can be assured only by educating the public in the rules of capitalist perseverance, thus broadening the base of players with a capital stake in the game.

The role of government

Political interference can often be an obstacle to economic growth whereas sound policies stimulate techno-economic progress, and set off a rising spiral of prosperity. Governments must certainly stand by the fundamental rules and look after the basic infrastructure, but they should also refrain from clumsy intervention.

> In most countries, central government has traditionally assumed the main responsibility for the key modes of communication. The postal system, for example, is almost everywhere a state prerogative. Public agencies are common in telecommunications and railway transport; major roads are built and maintained with tax money. Waste disposal, energy and water supply, too, generally fall within the public domain. Furthermore, health care and education are, at present, mostly in the custody of the state.
>
> The success of these endeavours has been very mixed. In many notable instances spirited civic concern has sustained communal institutions over long stretches of unselfish service. Sooner or later, public administration seems to impair efficiency and inventiveness; petty power games proliferate within the safe enclosures of bureaucratic procedures and government budgets. Public bodies are rarely forced to admit mistakes: accordingly they do not learn. In the absence of sheer terror, only a competitive threat can shake up an overprotected organization and revive the creative impulse.

A good administration should act as an umpire, directing and supervising the entire economic game at one remove. In the optimal case, the gain to the players ought to stand in direct proportion to the plus-sum value of their inputs, allowing for some politically motivated boundary conditions.

Rather than assuming that people are incapable of managing their own affairs, governments should trust the economic competence of their citizens. If *cf. 270, 275* our inborn penchant for economic play were activated, say by means of the school syllabus, the social safety net could be designed for the minority of constitutionally destitute. Now a substantial portion of the national income is recycled by political processes through government agencies. A higher level of self-risk is clearly indicated – the state should only be the provider of last resort.

> The savings rate has suffered a precipitous decline in most industrial societies, with a few notable exceptions such as Japan and Switzerland. In both countries government has largely eschewed outlays for personal insurance and pension plans: consequently its share of the gross national product is relatively low. Scandinavia seemed, for quite a while, to offer convincing counter-evidence to the evils of public overspending, but disillusion is now setting in.
>
> For half a century Sweden was the outstanding model for "democratic socialism". More than 50 per cent of the GNP was taxed away and redeployed in a plethora of welfare programmes. The clearly expressed aim was to equalize not only the outset but the very outcome of the economic game. The relative success of these policies can be traced back to the long tradition of societal rectitude among the Swedes, once the paragons of Lutheran probity. Recently, Swedish workers claimed the world record in absenteeism, misappropriating sick pay on a huge scale. Honesty is increasingly thrown to the winds as the moral capital runs out. At long last, a political reorientation is now underway.

State intervention is intrinsically suspect since it increases the concentration of power and interferes with the proper task of government; the burden of proof should always rest on the advocates of extended public involvement in the economic game. A much-heralded compromise is to let profit-seeking enterprises provide, say, health and educational services while the government pays for
cf. 149 them with a voucher system. But an unholy combination of state intervention and private profiteering can become the worst of all possible worlds.

cf. 263
> In the United States, the health sector currently absorbs 14 per cent of GNP, and its share is still rising. The efforts to improve productivity by administrative gimmicks or profit incentives have so far proved unsuccessful, partly because the real problem lies beyond economics. In an ageing population, the potential demand has no upper limit; to curb it, one way or the other, takes painful political decisions.

Standards of value

Since Croesus, King of Lydia, had his profile minted on a piece of gold (ca. 550 B.C.) the portraits of rulers or the insignia of sovereign states have appeared on the face of legal tender as a mark of reliability. Coins of gold, silver or copper provided a trustworthy standard of value, supplemented in primitive societies by such items as cocoa beans, mussel shells or tobacco. In practice, any object of a certain rarity or utility can act as a common denominator of scarcity and a catalyst of exchange. For pastoralists, cattle has been the self-evident measure of value while able-bodied male slaves represented the current coinage for long periods in West Africa. In most of its variants, however, money is just a social convention, based on confidence in the prevalent currency.

Money should function as the incorruptible gauge of economic value but even precious metals are occasionally subject to severe depreciation.

> During the sixteenth and seventeenth centuries the easily-won wealth of the New World, gold and above all silver, flooded Spain and all Europe in a long inflationary wave. Over a period of 150 years prices and wages rose between 100 and 300 per cent, a

neat testimony to the validity of the quantity theory of money, so eloquently advocated by Milton Friedman.

Not so long ago the price of gold fell by half and the price of silver by 80 per cent in the course of a few months while other "eternal" measures of value, such as diamonds, have lost a good deal of their glitter. Paper money, on the other hand, is always at the mercy of politicians. During one year (1923), the German mark depreciated to less than a billionth of its former value. Since the Second World War, economic self-discipline has begun to waver even in the strongholds of the market economy; inflation has at times assumed pandemic proportions.

Not even a strict monetary policy can entirely guard against a decline in the value of money. Quite apart from global disasters, even relatively minor disturbances such as local military conflicts, raw-material cartels or crop failures are capable of undermining the purchasing power of the strongest currency. Prudent central banks should therefore consider a flight to real values, gradually replacing a substantial part of their monetary reserves with some of the major commodities and semi-manufactures.

> Flexible stocks of coal and oil, grain, soya beans, sugar, fertilizer, cement, pig iron, and non-ferrous metals, wool, cotton, cellulose and suchlike represent real utility, especially in an emergency, and such warehouse receipts could partly replace the reserves of convertible currency and bars of gold in the vaults of the central banks. At the same time the self-regulation of chronically unstable commodity markets would be improved, and our vulnerability to econo-political disturbances would be markedly reduced.
>
> The efficient buying, selling and financing of these buffer stocks represents an intriguing problem. Inherently the operation could be both rational and self-supporting. A co-operative network of central banks would have all the advantages of a dominant player. Unlimited sources of capital should make it an invincible speculator, if the influence of economic "policy makers" or self-serving lobbyists can be resisted.

Although goods of immediate utility are the only concrete source of security, certified documents are and will remain the rational means of payment under normal conditions. Oddly enough, human affirmations are on the whole gladly accepted at face value. Every promissory note, bill of lading or deposit receipt implies confidence in the debtor, or at least in the legal machinery which, if necessary, will enforce the creditor's rights. Similarly, ephemeral paper money symbolizes the continuity of business and the stability of the social order. If a currency becomes debased, the core of productive performance has been corrupted. Inflation is a measure of collective self-betrayal and of our inability to play fair in the economic game.

Proprietorial responsibility

While money is doubtless a human invention, private property has deep roots in our evolutionary ancestry. A game-theoretical analysis of animal rivalries will serve to place our economic and political quarrels in a biological perspective. For a member of a successful species, the main competitors are its own kin. Besides driving speciation, fierce internal strife has, in many cases, induced a sense of ownership which makes for a moderating rule of the game.   *cf. 56*

In the terminology of John Maynard Smith, the pioneer in the field, hawk-like aggressiveness (fight to the finish) and dove-like docility (avoid open confrontation at all costs) are the two pure strategies in competition within a species. Just the same, mixed strategies often serve the best interests of the individual. Retaliators, for example, fight only against hawks while bullies exclusively attack doves.

The territorial instinct is the epigenetic expression of a mixed strategy aiming at contest avoidance. The defender of a territory has a strong psychological advantage, a "right" to the area or "property" over which it has taken possession. This "bourgeois" instinct minimizes the cost of conflict and imbues the struggle for existence with a plus-sum character.

Aggressive hawks attack indiscriminately and soon tear one another to pieces while timid doves are always giving way or wasting time in inconclusive confrontations among themselves. The bourgeois plays the hawk in his own territory; otherwise he plays the dove. This strategy brings some order into the competition among bourgeois players. Isolated hawks and doves may survive in a bourgeois society but their internal conflicts degenerate into minus-sum games. The generally acknowledged property rights constitute a self-stabilizing rule of the social game under a wide range of conditions.

Private property is not an arbitrary human contrivance but a logical, deeply ingrained reaction to increasing population density: scarcity leads to a division into distinct preserves. To the individual his home is his castle, and to a country geographical borders are inviolable. Societies must nowadays also try to guard air and water, once the most abundant of utilities. "Common goods" are always squandered, since they are nobody's responsibility.

The potency of totem and taboo was certainly enhanced by the need to cast a protective spell on collective property. The introduction of divine possessions ruled out the misappropriation of sacred sources, groves or game, and acted as a safeguard against over-exploitation.

In a state of nature man exploits "unearned" resources; he gathers but he does not sow. His growing command of the environment permits untrammelled expansion which eventually actuates a "bourgeois" charting of ownership rights and responsibilities. The alternative would be (and has been) continual impoverishment and ecological disaster.

Unrestricted slash and burn agriculture is currently destroying huge tracts of tropical rain forest which at present trends will disappear within a few decades. Deforestation is blighting in other areas too; today only three per cent of Ethiopia is covered by forest against 40 per cent in the year 1900. Besides local disruption, the excessive burning of biomass causes an exacerbation of the impending greenhouse effect.

Ancient cultures heedlessly devastated the mountain forests of the Mediterranean region and primitive people can be equally unconcerned about their environment. Easter Island was an attractive woodland when the Polynesians arrived in about 400 AD. Twelve hundred years later the Europeans encountered a society, barely surviving on a deforested island and plagued by memories of social strife and internal warfare, slavery and cannibalism.

Besides private property, the market economy allows for a richly varied proprietorial structure which includes the state, the municipality and, in particular, independent associations of every kind – companies, co-ops, trade unions, not to mention a plethora of non-profitmaking organizations.

> Many of our environmental problems obviously require some form of global co-ordination, but the establishment of clear-cut ownership has generally proved much more effective than any international agreements. The much decried "plunder of the oceans", when many coastal states extended their territorial rights up to 200 nautical miles offshore, seems to have engendered a sense of responsibility based on enlightened self-interest.

Revisions in the rules of the territorial game should be very circumspect. We are touching here on status-ridden instincts, the very foundations of human identity and long-term motivation. The legal transfer of tenants' or squatters' *de facto* rights against some reasonable compensation rarely causes any problems, but sweeping property transfers in a flush of revolutionary zeal are generally destructive for all concerned.

> Between 1968 and 1970 Peru's sugar industry was "nationalized" by the revolutionary military junta, and turned over to the workers. Decay promptly set in; maintenance was neglected, investment funds dissipated – all decisions were geared to immediate gain. This cannibalization of the industry was accompanied by astounding examples of human exploitation. The owner-workers began to use the desperately poor and jobless to do all the work for a pittance. These latter-day neo-capitalists never dreamt of transferring even part of their ownership rights to the proletariat; rather they were bent on exhausting this marvellous source of wealth which a twist of fate had suddenly thrown their way.

It is easy to redistribute money that others have earned but much more difficult to teach people to manage their newly-won capital. "Easy come, easy go" was one of the earliest insights of elementary economics – it still holds good.

Accumulation and redistribution

Whatever the merits of private property, a modern society cannot be allowed to become the battleground of a few powerful capitalists. No fortune is based exclusively on the efforts of a single enterprising individual, on his gifts or his labour (leaving aside ruthlessness and luck). The creation of capital depends on the contributions of many active collaborators, and on the state-financed infrastructure. This fact has been exploited to the hilt as justification for punitive tax rates – a political reaction to the praxeological distribution of income and wealth, which is invariably perceived as grossly unfair by the majority of the population.

A continual increase in the supply of capital is a prerequisite of lasting prosperity, and one of the great controversial issues of our time has been: who should have command of these assets which ultimately represents a collective postponement of need-satisfaction? How can we avoid over-consumption and the squandering of capital while also allowing for the fair redistribution of material resources? Long-term plus-sum play can be assured only by educating the public in the rules of capitalist perseverance, thus broadening the base of players with a capital stake in the game.

> In Switzerland a farmer once took pity on a tramp who, despite certain misgivings, was treated by the housewife to food and drink. His desperate economic condition was the subject of lively discussion, and every possible way of making a decent living was looked into. In the end the farmer could think of no alternative to the very last, desperate expedient: the tramp would have to dip into his capital!

We must resolve the fateful combat between selfish owner-interests and politically-inspired punitive taxation. If close to half of personal income is regularly diverted to the public purse, the economy will sooner or later degenerate into a fiscal farce in which the cheats always come out on top. Ordinary people lose their motivation to work, and the dynamism of habitual overachievers is drastically curtailed at the expense of society as a whole.

> Inflationary mechanisms have been given a powerful boost by obsolete tax regulations. Tax on individual expenditure rather than on income would modify the tendency to excessive spending, encourage savings, and promote the widespread accumulation of capital. Under a comprehensive system of consumption tax, people living off the retained earnings of their forefathers would no longer enjoy a position of fiscal privilege. A personal fortune is a desirable reserve fund but it should not provide a long-term substitute for the active acquisition of a livelihood.

Children are the greatest investment of the average couple. No-one should be surprised to find that the willingness to invest in this way is fading in the developed world; the tax regulations do little or nothing to alleviate the financial sacrifice of responsible parents. If the rules of the economic game remain inimical to child-rearing, we will soon have made fatal inroads into our basic human capital.

> The proletariat of today consists of nuclear families with two or more offspring. However well-educated, gifted and hard-working the parents may be, their standard falls far below that of childless couples of similar background. At present only the asocial can avoid disproportionate additional burdens; sometimes they even make money out of procreation.
>
> A substantial transfer of resources from the childless and from higher age groups to the parents of young children is essential. One way of achieving this would be to scale pension contributions in reverse proportion to the number of dependants. After all, well-brought-up children are the best guarantee for the viability of national pension funds.

Creating prosperity

In the long run, only an increase in the supply of goods and services will stabilize the economy and protect the value of money. To achieve this goal, the inclination to secure privileged and unproductive enclaves in the economy must be firmly resisted. If business or union practices become predatory and fixed games abound, only strong moves – old and new – will break the hold of the monopolists.

☐ If the market is rigged, trade unions, co-operatives or even the state or the municipalities could establish competing enterprises on equal terms. In most cases the very threat of such action would probably be sufficient to restore fair play.

☐ Working hours, vacations and so on should be adapted to business conditions. Any bias against part-time work or flexible working hours should be overcome.

☐ Security of tenure could be reduced all along the line, so that not only politicians and managers but also academicians and civil servants would share the risk of losing their jobs. The number of losers would not increase but the vigour and value of the game should be greatly enhanced.

☐ Much primary education, health care and social work could be undertaken by companies or co-operatives on a contractual basis. The principal (state, municipality, church or other association) should regularly control performance.

☐ Local monopolies could be contracted out or auctioned off for limited periods. Corrupt practices, sloppiness and featherbedding would be greatly reduced but ingenious accounting procedures are mandatory to forestall short-term exploitation.

Last but not least, widespread administrative overregulation should be dismantled. This usually flies in the face of entrenched parochial interests. More often than not, the authorities are met with clamorous demands for more meddling which are not always easy to dismiss.

> Cab services in big cities should, in theory, provide a good example of a free, self-regulating marketplace. In real life they are heavily regulated almost everywhere. The casual relationship between vendor and customer precludes the discipline of long lasting relationships and fosters all sorts of abuse. In the public eye the threat of "unfair competition" and "disordered markets" seems to justify a lot of awkward bureaucracy.

To relieve the political pressure, which tends to pervert the economic game, the interests and anxieties of the common man should be integrated in the market system. The ultimate aim is to broaden the base of players with a capital stake in the game:

☐ Profit-sharing could be extended to all permanent employees who in effect would become partners. A system of suspended shareholding would foster co-responsibility within the company while contributing to the general savings rate and social security.

☐ Large organizations should try to delegate most of their daily operations not only to subcontractors but to capable intrapreneurs and distance workers, thus transforming themselves into fairly loosely-knit agglomerates. The central unit could concentrate on innovation, information-processing, financial management and marketing.

☐ Tenancy could generally be transformed into ownership; the rent for a city house or flat would then be converted into an instalment payment by this urban variant of land reform.

☐ Direct and indirect external costs – environmental pollution above all –

should be rationally allocated to companies, communities and consumers alike on a causation basis.

☐ "Pollution rights" could be issued as a separate currency to stress the incommensurability with other production factors. Permits for global pollutants like carbon dioxide could even be traded internationally on commodity exchanges.

In the developed world, we may slowly be moving towards fair economic play but serious global inequities will remain. The best favour we can do ourselves, as well as the economies of the less developed countries, is to accept some painful changes and co-operate in a new worldwide division of labour. Our most effective tool in fulfilling this ambition is the market economy, epitomized by the activities of much-vilified multinational companies. Adroit, profit-seeking organizations act unwittingly as economic missionaries, preaching the praxeological gospel of productivity.

5.6   Games of enterprise

In a sensible economic game, the lodestar for strategic deliberations should be the macroeconomic plus-sum effect. Every company ought to become a unique partner in an implicit, plus-sum playing coalition, thus justifying its independent existence. A good entrepreneur generates unflagging energy and inventiveness, propelling human energies into an almost religious fervour of purposeful activity. Every leader holds his coalition together by impregnating its activities with meaning. Without such a link with superordinate meta-rules even the best organization will wither away. In the end, the value system will stand out as the main competitive weapon, be it at the level of the company, the country or the culture as a whole.

Struggle for survival

Companies are islands of careful economic planning in the agitated and treacherous waters of uncontrollable market flux (this striking metaphor was coined by my late friend, Eric Rhenman). The justification for the existence of a company lies in the relinquishment of individual play in favour of the common gain for the corporation. Awkward business transactions and time-squandering haggling are superseded by a firmly controlled internal plus-sum game. The productivity potential generally rises as size increases, but so do the moral *cf. 156; 219; 271* demands on the members of the organization. The market economy is constantly searching for the optimum balance between planned co-ordination and incorruptible market forces.

We have already stated that in a well-adjusted economy the profit of a business should fluctuate in proportion to its macroeconomic utility. Corporations naturally look for profit but the instinct for self-preservation is an even stronger urge. Bankruptcy is the dreaded final verdict, indispensable to the integrity of the game. Risk-free expansion thus flouts the market principle and corrupts politicians, civil servants and entrepreneurs alike.

> In many countries well-meaning but ill-advised agricultural policies have created surplus mountains and lakes of intrinsically valuable foods. The world record was secured by the European Community when it recycled surplus milk powder as cattle feed in an agri-political *perpetuum mobile*. The perfectly understandable desire to guarantee a modest income for livestock-owning smallholders backfired because efficient large-scale producers exploited the bias in the rules, increasing their own production while eschewing any responsibility for marketing their produce. Similarly, European trade unions are in true monopolistic fashion squeezing the market for all it is worth while shrewdly shifting the cost of the soaring capacity – unemployment that is – onto the public purse. Farmers or workers in healthy competition? Heaven forbid!

Guaranteed sales at guaranteed prices, the mainstay of the socialist economies, sounds like an extremely convenient arrangement but it inevitably leads to absurdities. Traditionally, such semi-socialist corporatism has aroused considerable sympathy when invoked in the name of poor farmers or downtrodden workers but a return to fair play is imperative. Economic as well as biological progress can only be induced in a race between competitors which, like Lewis Carroll's queen of hearts, must run hard to stay put.

On the brink of a technological breakthrough, private enterprise really comes into its own. A crowd of entrepreneurial companies happily throw themselves into the fray, jostling for position. After many turbulent elimination rounds, a few tried and tested approaches pay off as profitable businesses: the rest go bankrupt or are absorbed along the way.

> The mushrooming and selective extinction of, say, electronics or biotechnology companies, has its counterpart in evolutionary history. The Ediacara-formation of Western Australia has preserved a peculiar Precambrian world which flourished between 600 and 700 million years ago. It is replete with soft-bodied life forms which, with few exceptions, suddenly disappear from the paleontological record. Later on, in the 500 million years old Burgess shale, we can observe a stunning variety of experimental design in early arthropods (hard-shelled invertebrates). Of 30 basic body plans only three became established, but these have enjoyed continual success as highly diversified insects, spiders and crustaceans. The first vertebrates, too, played around with the number of fingers and toes before arriving at a five-digit standard.

Every company has to cut out a livelihood for itself in the market-economic mêlée. The manner in which this struggle for survival is conducted is decisive for the future of society.

Concordant strategies

In their day-to-day operations, individual companies are linked in a competitive struggle which leaves little room for manoeuvre. In strategic decision-making,

on the other hand, management enjoys considerable leeway as conventional
cf. 57; 353 economic yardsticks become sadly insufficient. In a sensible economic game the
lodestar for these deliberations should be the macroeconomic plus-sum effect.
Any deviation from this course means waste and decreases the value of the
game. A bigger cake means a better chance of a worthwhile slice for everyone. It
is obviously in the interests of all that the game should be transparent so that
these difficult strategic choices could be based on maximum information.

Competition is necessary and inevitable but not an end in itself. A head-on
combat between organizations with the same business idea and similar cost
structure is a deadly affair with at most a single survivor. A percipient company
should try to avoid such waste by striving for excellence in a narrow field of
competence, creating, conquering, developing and defending the relevant market niches.

> Naked competition easily deteriorates into a minus-sum game, when the losses inflicted
> on the adversary become an end in themselves. Vicious price cutting is the result of
> stagnant business conditions combined with substantial overcapacity (this is a game of
> *cf. 53* chicken, which should be easier to resolve than the prisoner's dilemma). Protracted
> industrial infighting often leads to government interference by heavy-handed restruc-
> turing or a convoluted quota system, all in clear violation of the market ideology. But
> insistence upon uninhibited competition just speeds up the establishment of the dreaded
> *cf. 89; 188* monopoly. This paradox of the market economy highlights Gause's law as the determi-
> nant of cut-throat competition both in nature and business.
> *cf. 154* Keen competition can be fierce *and* constructive if the combatants succeed in differ-
> entiating their products or services at least in a superficial way. Heavily promoted trade
> marks serve this purpose very well; the raging battle between Coke and Pepsi benefits
> *cf. 224* both adversaries by greatly expanding the market for soft drinks.

A company should act as a node in the networking of diverse but reconcilable
interests. It should be a unique partner in an implicit plus-sum coalition, thus
justifying its independent existence. The strategic vision must include the future
actions and reactions of both customers and competitors, not forgetting other
key actors. These hard choices define the profit potential of the business and
circumscribe the external efficiency of future operations. They should ensure a
certain competitive advantage but profits will be realized only by way of internal efficiency – professionalism and productivity. The company must be a
good player at its chosen game.

Strategic decisions are always taken under conditions of great uncertainty.
Hence mistakes and failures are unavoidable, since the available information is
incomplete and unreliable. Moreover, a corporate strategy geared to making a
distinct contribution to the common good should be reasonably successful, if
the economic game is well conceived. The sum of all good corporate decisions
will then make up a dynamic national economy with a minimum of waste from
poor investments or futile competition. It pays all players to have a look at each
other's cards but this presupposes the "Japanization" of a good many written
cf. 206 and unwritten rules. Only then will the excessively selfish actor, who attempts
to get the upper hand by stealth, find himself in a well-deserved losing position.

Corporate culture

A modern business enterprise provides an attractive arena for the collaborative efforts of energetic and gifted people. Not only are primary material needs fairly well satisfied, but the individual also acquires a sense of identity, a source of stimulus, an outlet for his creative impulses. Here our hallowed progress dynamos can find a rewarding base for their endeavours. A well-run company under competitive pressure can bring out the best in its crew, restraining envy and promoting a healthy self-esteem. Semi-suppressed atavistic propensities for hunting and fighting, for tilling and cultivating and, above all, for playing exciting games find a structured outlet in business organizations. We don't risk our lives, only our money; serious mistakes lead not to death but merely to bankruptcy; friendship is confirmed not by blood sacrifice but in a joint effort to solve problems and cope with all kinds of reverses.

> Such a rosy picture should of course be tempered by recalling the many boring and repetitive tasks that are still part of production and transport, trade and administration. This menial work belongs to a transitional stage. Heavy manual labour has been virtually eliminated in modern factories. Routine chores requiring no judgement, creativity or human contact are increasingly delegated to robots and computers. The relative number of rewarding jobs in installation, maintenance, planning and salesmanship are multiplying while the concept of management is acquiring new dimensions in areas such as market studies and research projects. Work and play are blending together: the corporation becomes a resource for the individual and a vehicle for the values and aspirations of the staff.

Every company is a microcosm with its own unique history and code of honour, its internal politics, control system and decision processes, its successes and setbacks – in brief, its own culture. The market economy is a wide-open testing ground where various corporate values can show their real worth. Bad luck or incompetence frequently bring the game to a premature conclusion, but sweet success can also lead to fatal self-gratification. At worst, the company becomes the hapless prey of unscrupulous top management.

> Negative feedback can take an awfully long time to sink in. General Motors indulged in their incestous management style for decades, before the moment of truth arrived. Lately, even IBM has been driven into a strategic loss position by nimble-footed competitors. Once the organizational cancer becomes evident, the whole company is infiltrated by metastases.

Large organizations are inherently vulnerable to management inertia; you can always blame somebody else. Unlearning is exceedingly slow as top executives *cf. 133; 278* remain insulated from customer contacts. Internal relations take precedence over market information while efficiency becomes overly dependent on company morale – which is always in short supply. In small companies, administrative *cf. 156; 216; 271* controls can be kept at a minimum because cynics are easily exposed and evicted. Successful growth, however, presupposes additional funds of ethical capital to keep the expanded organization efficient.

Durable company structures yield pertinent models for the self-renewal of human coalitions – tried and tested prescriptions for a long span of life. In the end, the value system will stand out as the main competitive weapon, be it at the level of the company, the country or the culture as a whole.

> Continuous adaptation has become a condition of survival, especially for big, unwieldy companies; "the learning organization" is a favourite buzzword among progressive top executives. To make people productive, conflicts of interest must be amicably resolved and disparate value frames reconciled. Such management by values will draw on the skills of a coach, a mentor, an arbiter or even a sage. Teaching and tutoring faculties will become the source of authority; emotional maturity must in any case take precedence over intellectual brilliance.

Participative management and employee ownership is gaining ground while the traditional rift between owners, managers and the workforce shrinks into insignificance. People are already the most important asset of a modern corporation and, on average, more than half of company funds are nowadays reserved for "soft" investments in research, process and product development, market penetration and above all human competence: training and tuition. The organization is kept together by the finely-tuned rules of an invisible contract, which are supplanting union power and managerial dictate. In many industries the majority of employees are directly exposed to the stimulus of the commercial game and are constantly involved in learning and retraining. Instead of tedious routine, an excess of excitement and variety may become a cause of alienation.

Where there's a will . . .

What actually motivates our company managers? Most of them are probably strongly averse to risk. They manoeuvre cautiously and introduce radical changes only under severe pressure. The essential irritant is provided by self-styled progress dynamos, creative risk-takers who enjoy unlimited self-confidence and an almost missionary zeal for making money by investing, expanding and creating.

Every investment in new markets or in new products or technologies, indeed any substantial investment at all is a gamble; disaster always threatens despite meticulous analysis and painstaking planning. Most great innovative advances are preceded by a wearisome thirsty stretch where hope perpetually beckons in what may prove a barren desert.

> Generally, the lead times for substantial innovations are long indeed. I was personally involved in the conception and development of xylitol, an anticariogenic sweetener which is now widely used in confections such as chewing gum. The rocky road to success took twenty years to tread, and it was scattered with stumbling blocks such as a worldwide cancer scare, a misconceived factory and a problematical joint venture.

Behind every innovation there lies an intense passion for the game, a craving for outstanding achievement. Fresh resources, human and financial, are always attracted by new ideas and interesting ventures, even against overwhelming odds. The typical entrepreneur has supreme confidence in his ability to handle unforeseen developments, to cope with crises, to get himself out of trouble. But he is not a gambler relying mainly on his luck; rather, he prefers games in which

he can influence the end result by his own resourcefulness and tenacity. To the   *cf. 4.5.10*
genuine entrepreneur, no situation is hopeless: he will not stop looking for at
least a lateral chance to turn adversity to advantage.

> The following test (inspired by Martin Gardner) puts our sagacity on the spot. Three
> test subjects are wearing caps which may be either the right way round or back-to-front.
> The subjects can all see the other caps but not their own. The instructor says: "Anyone
> who can see a cap back-to-front, raise your hand." Three hands are raised. He then
> asks: "Who can tell me first whether his own cap is the right way round or back-to-
> front?" Some minutes pass, and there are no answers. You see two caps back to front.
> How do you react?
>
> This quiz obliges the passive person to give up, the rebel condemns the game as
> pointless, and the cynic furtively looks round for a reflecting surface. The progress
> dynamo assumes there is a genuine solution and starts playing around with different
> hypotheses and their implications. He can see two caps back-to-front but what about
> his own? Gradually the silence tells him something. That his own cap is the right way
> round becomes successively less plausible, and in the end logically impossible.
>
> His own cap must be back-to-front too. Otherwise the situation would be immediate-
> ly given away to the two who could see one cap the right way round. The lengthy silence
> following the experimenter's question eliminates this alternative, which ascribes only a
> minimum of reasoning power to the participants. The same line of thought will work
> with four or even five subjects, but then presupposes a higher level of logical sophisti-
> cation in the group.   *cf. 201*

The single-minded pursuit of his purpose is the outstanding characteristic of the
successful businessman. Occasional sharp practices may be part of the picture
but moral fibre is decisive in the long run. The passion for play must bend to
restraining rules for worthwhile ends to be achieved.

Values in competition

Self-advancement is an indispensable driving force in the creation of economic
value and many entrepreneurs strive for success at any price, ending up among
the destructive cynics. Like a chessplayer, the typical businessman is a born   *cf. 315*
fighter while the progress dynamo is constrained by an artistic or scientific
streak. The latter always tries to make authentic contributions, guided by the
rules of fair play. The problem is to distinguish genuine competence from
cynical self-promotion.

> Jean Paul Getty (1892–1976) once acquired a fairly large but badly-run company. He
> called its twelve top ranking executives together and told them how he intended to
> tackle the problems. Nine of those present agreed eagerly with every word he said, two
> were silent. Only one produced a clear and carefully motivated criticism of the new
> owner's plans. Getty had (or so he tells) intentionally presented an oversimplified and
> distorted programme. His critic was made managing director with the silent members
> of the meeting as assistants. The yes-men had to leave the company, wiser for the
> experience.

Much hinges on this process of selection; if it is misguided, the machinery of
management will eventually break down. Adversity is the best and probably the
only reliable sifting device. Success breeds complacency and arrogance; only
unpleasant misfortune will unambiguously endorse the right stuff. After their

passage through purgatory, the real progress dynamos can advance with a deeper self-reliance, unencumbered by illusions of infallibility.

The selfish element in entrepreneurship is deeply entrenched in human nature, and the eternal problem is to exploit it constructively and achieve a plus-sum game for the community as a whole. In this sense every society gets the entrepreneurs it deserves.

cf. 162

> Historically, the social and political environment has usually precluded innovative investment and locked the economy into a futile zero-sum game. At worst, a minimum of self-employment had to be propped up by draconian measures: in mediaeval Russia free peasants were forbidden to sell themselves as slaves, which was their only way of avoiding a crushing tax burden!

cf. 224

A good entrepreneur feels strongly about, one might even say he loves his core business. Given a suitable environment he generates unflagging energy and inventiveness, propelling human energies into an almost religious fervour of purposeful activity.

> In 1909 the brand-new trams in Osaka made a strong impression on the 15-year-old Konosuke Matsushita (1894–1989). He immediately envisaged a whole society transformed by electrical machines. This was the start of the Matsushita Electric Company, a corporation with about 200,000 employees and a turnover of 61 billion dollars (in 1992). Matsushita has described his version of the progress dynamo in no uncertain terms: "Everyone here is motivated to do his work on his own initiative. There is no compulsion and no orders from above ... I realize that I must have been running all the time at high speed over many, many miles. Yet I ran on my own steam. Nobody pushed me". One of his employees has emphasized Matsushita's humble capacity to learn: "Chairman Matsushita always told us to have an impartial and open mind, to listen sincerely and modestly to what others have to say." Behind all this there is a longing to improve the world: "I decided that the mission of the manufacturer is to fill the world with products as cheap and abundant as water so as to bring a better life to all."

At present, the action is shifting from hardware production to services, reflecting the pressures of consumerism and the needs of the information society.

> Sam Walton, the founder of the retail chain Wal-Mart, became the richest man in the United States through his emphasis on thrift and customer value. The whizz kids of the computer age are, for their part, driven by the vision of a world where overflowing information is within easy reach of each and everyone. When Steve Jobs of "Apple"- and "Macintosh"-fame was deprived of his brainchild, he relentlessly went on to create "Next". Bill Gates is an even more spectacular example of the new software-entrepreneur. In 17 years, the Harvard drop-out has catapulted his company, Microsoft, from next to nothing to a turnover of $2.8 billion (1992) and a market capitalization of $23.8 billion, surpassing IBM's.

Entrepreneurship is not restricted to the founders of private companies. A reformer or a progress dynamo will express himself in similar ways in any position of responsibility, provided he has the requisite freedom of action and is subject to some kind of market feedback. He must convincingly define a mission, integrating the efforts of his crew with the outside world. The leader holds the coalition together by impregnating its activities with meaning. Without such a link with superordinate meta-rules, even the best organization will wither away. Dissension will flourish as insoluble conflicts of interest and loyalty generate moral schizophrenia, producing a house divided against itself.

5.7   Meta-rules of the market economy

The market is intrinsically amoral and without purpose: everything depends on the overarching rules of the cultural game. Nature has now become a scarce resource which must be integrated into the market mechanism. Basically, it is a question of sufficient supply of energy and, for the first time, almost unlimited sources are in the offing. Given enough energy, problems of pollution or raw material shortages can always be solved by human effort, knowledge and capital. We should thus be striving to create an abundance of all these. The meta-purpose of economic activity is to add more value, to swamp ourselves in money in order to provide adequate scope for play, at least for the great majority of mankind.

The customer is king

Unlike all other animals, man appears to have an almost insatiable appetite. His desire for goods, toys and pastimes has not yet reached its limit except for a privileged few who, with varying success, battle with the curse of excessive affluence. Collectively, man's needs will always be boundless. The productivity of labour is thus a key issue in all economies, albeit temporarily obscured by the explosive development of superproductive technologies. Stimulated by a sensible rule system, our passion for the game has been surging into commercial life, creating an abundance of material utilities for the consuming masses, and making money all the time.

The market economy requires some slack in its self-regulating mechanisms, some leeway in the shape of overcapacity and oversupply which allows the smooth adjustment to ever-changing realities. There should always be a surplus of utilities in relation to disposable cash; accordingly, sales become the bottleneck to any business operation. The salesman is the missionary of the market; the customer is the centrepiece of activity, the king of the game.

> A good salesman humbly puts himself in the buyer's position and argues his point from there. Here, in the mind of the consumer, the choice is made between countless alternative acquisitions. In comparison with this evaluation, the opinions of business leaders and bank directors are of little import; the customer always has the last word.

The cultural legacy of Europe has an aristocratic bent, and in contrast to Americans, Europeans are still somewhat bewildered by the fact that the likes and dislikes of the common man now pull the economic levers and steer the production process. Intellectuals of all shades are agreed in condemning the vulgar appetites of the masses. Surely it must be dangerous to put too much money into the hands of ordinary people?

cf. 218

> The occasional excesses of trade mark advertising can be pinpointed as blatant examples of market-economic waste. What eludes the critics is that the ads as such significantly contribute to consumer satisfaction. Coke and Pepsi thrive on an oxymoron: the real illusion of well-being induced in juvenile minds. Likewise, the haute couture of Cartier or Rolls Royce used to instil more blasé snobs with a specious feeling of superiority.

Freedom of choice permeates the market economy; we acquire and consume the products we deserve and, more often than not, we unconsciously connive at any double-dealing. By and large, a successful business must build upon consumer confidence, a point which is reflected in the enormous value of many trade marks. The supreme challenge is to create the customer. Her trust will soon be the only really valid capital when key production factors – money and manpower, market information and technological know-how – are freely available.

Capital formation

Since the customer is by definition infallible, sooner or later the businessman will, despite all his market research, pay the penalty for being in the wrong. The collusion of competitors or plain cartelization can temporarily distort the market balance, but does not alter the producer's fundamental dependence on the often confusing and contradictory demand signals. The inherent fallibility of the capitalist is one of the meta-rules of the market economy: every company has the right to make its own mistakes. The microeconomic disasters of unsuccessful risk-taking are a necessary consequence of the freedom of trade. Without a losing option, no information is gained and no plus-sum play can be cf. 377 sustained.

cf. 222

> Not so long ago, the scarcity of capital evoked a strong reaction to suspended payments; the debtors' prison was an instrument of economic retribution. In ancient Babylon and Greece, families were pledged as security (in China this custom persisted well into the twentieth century). A debtor first sold his children and then himself into slavery in order to satisfy the creditors. Later on the sanctions for default were wisely relaxed. When Solon (638–559 B.C.) repealed debt bondage in Athens in the year 592 B.C., he released the city-state on its path to economic, political and cultural take-off.

If bankruptcy is the stick, then profit is the carrot in the market game. Profit is the renumeration for successful risk-taking and should accordingly be understood as the surplus in capital revenues compared with some minimum risk investment, for example the interest on government bonds.

> For surprisingly long periods this basic rate of return has stayed in the range of 2–4 %

per annum in real terms. Very low interest rates may indicate economic stagnation, a slackening of the innovative spirit and lack of business opportunity. The contrary case is, however, a more ominous danger signal. Insufficiency of capital formation signifies a grave disturbance in the socio-economic machinery. This basic tenet was succinctly spelled out by Karl Marx: "Accumulate, accumulate, this is the golden rule of the capitalist!" Alas, we now seem to have lost most of our capitalist acumen.

Even if poverty is not exactly a sin, the deterioration of an economy is a certain sign of moral depravity. Wishful thinking has superseded prudent judgement when people try to take longer and longer advances on the future. Saving has been supplanted by short-sighted gambling, lotteries, sweepstakes or purely speculative investment. Success in these zero-sum games is contingent on misleading or deceiving your co-players, which makes for a state of collective *cf. 47* economic disgrace. Only symbiotic information-sharing and fair competition will sustain and extend the scope of the plus-sum play.

If we are unable to induce saving and unwilling to reward risk-taking and hard work, we lose the lever of economic enterprise. Competitive tension will evaporate and motivation is bound to fail. Sloth and sloppiness will spread when society loses its capability to promote by ability and the economy slips into permanent decline. An inflated bureaucracy will take over the government, haggling over the remaining spoils with militant and well-organized pressure groups. This gloomy picture may sound like an exaggeration of the dangers of excessive taxation and red tape, but the continuous expansion of the "grey" economy in most countries testifies to both the incompetence and the oppressiveness of the welfare state. History, moreover, abounds in examples of such economic and cultural backsliding.   *cf. 203; 271*

> China is a case in point. Confucianism took a dim view of trade and industry; again and again the endeavours of manufacturers and merchants were obstructed by the bureaucracy which clamped down jealously on any independent source of wealth and power. Already by 119 B.C., the production of salt and iron had become state monopolies. Later on, the art of making porcelain, paper and powder was kept secret for centuries while experiments with telescopes and submarines were simply forbidden. The central government nipped new technology and free enterprise in the bud, lest it should become a threat to the established order. The famous Wall of China served not only to keep enemies out but to keep potential emigrants in.

Many if not most past civilizations seem to have been strangled by their own safety nets, skilfully created by a risk-aversive élite. Such expedients seem less offensive when the beneficiaries belong to the lower social strata, but the free supply of the necessities of life to a politically influential populace eventually undermines the self-respect and allegiance of the ordinary citizen.   *cf. 264; 274*

Constant anxiety and concern for the future, the accumulation of capital when the going is good and painful adjustment in adversity are all vital attributes of economic as well as biological life. In the name of civic solidarity we must try to soften the blows of fate, but the onslaught of supplicants must not be allowed to corrupt the core of human enterprise – our only truly renewable resource.

The scope for economic play

Ever since the days of David Ricardo (1772–1823), economic structuralists from Léon Walras (1834–1910) and Wilfredo Pareto to Wassily Leontief have mapped out the basic economic metabolism of industrial society. The mechanics of exchange have thus been thoroughly analysed, and the first successful forays into business dynamics are now underway. Even so, our understanding of real-time economics is still in its infancy.

Beyond strictly verifiable praxeology, there can be no absolute rules for the economic game. Diverse value systems necessarily generate incommensurable policies which can be applied and criticized only in terms of their own axiomatic assumptions or boundary conditions. Every so often, prescriptive economists – unwittingly or deliberately – entangle the unremitting praxeological mechanism with party politics or purely personal prejudice. This opens the door for foul practices, poisons scientific impartiality and reduces the scope for sound economic play.

cf. 304; 314   Not without justification, economics has been called the dismal science. Complex man has been reduced to a simple Homo economicus, a fully rational (and sometimes even fully informed) model of callous self-promotion. This distorts reality beyond recognition: a society of pure-bred economic men could not survive for any length of time. The meta-scientific nature of economics is, at least implicitly, admitted by most economists. Nevertheless, most of them proudly prefer to be exactly in the wrong instead of getting it roughly right. Now a change of heart is in the air. In *The Moral Dimension* (1988) Amitai Etzioni challenges the neoclassical paradigm by elaborating the obvious influence of normative-affective factors on our economic behaviour, which can be properly understood only by taking account of culture-dependent values.

More important than professional skill is the desire to play fair, the recognition of inherent values beyond personal interest, and the profit motive. The self-organization of the marketplace is bound to break down unless the silent majority supports the spirit of the game. Cheats will gradually oust progress dynamos; escalating controls and government intervention will simply shift the foci of corruption. Deprived of personal responsibility people are reduced to the status of dependent serfs, incapable of managing their own affairs and unable to accept the risks and worries pertaining to the humblest capitalist rank.

Even under the best of circumstances, a fully-fledged market economy becomes problematic in a primitive setting. It clashes with untempered epigenetic rules and is thus subject to strong culture-specific repression. Sophisticated corporate arrangements such as profit centres, project organizations or matrix structures often flounder on similar impediments. Without individual initiative and accountability, greater freedom will lead to anarchy or apathy rather than to proficient plus-sum performance.

Floods of ink have gone into affirming the impending breakdown of our technology-based production system. Provided the population explosion can be checked (a big proviso), such panic-stricken reactions are unwarranted. Despite all the real and imagined crises, we have never been so well-off and the economic prospects should be the brightest ever. Our worst enemy is complacency. We *cf. 422* need all the warnings we can get – and there are plenty of them.

Paul Kennedy has recently extended his prediction of the downfall of the United States   *cf. 140*
to encompass the whole world (*Preparing for the Twenty-First Century*, 1983). The list
of woes is long but remedies are in short supply – Kennedy offers none. Population
increase stands, as it should, at the top of the list. Here modern biotechnology could
come to the rescue. A free supply of "abortion pills" to the poor women of the world
would change the situation dramatically. Typically, the problem is not technical or even
economical but purely political. Crucial rules of the cultural game must be adjusted and
a lot of ingrained prejudices overcome.

   Nor are the environmental problems to be belittled; ecological calamities have become a real threat, especially in the backward regions of our planet. The grim outlook is
not a consequence of techno-economical limitations. We can, for instance, only blame
ourselves for favouring outdated energy sources and their attendant pollutants. Obnoxious oxides of nitrogen or sulphur can be removed from the smokestacks but the
blanket of carbon dioxide will continue to enhance the greenhouse effect which constitutes the most formidable long-term threat to our environment. Disaster could, all of a
sudden, strike the Northern hemisphere if the sensitive system of ocean currents would
reverse, shutting off the Gulf-stream as has happened in the past.

Ensuring the ample supply of energy is the pivotal factor in the creation of
widespread prosperity. Now, for the first time, almost unlimited sources are in
the offing. Fission energy is a fact, fusion energy is within reach while solar and
geothermal energy may soon become competitive. Given enough energy, problems of pollution or raw material shortages can always be solved by human
effort, knowledge and capital; we should thus be striving to create an abundance of all these. The meta-purpose of economic activity is to add more value,
to create more capital, to achieve a superabundance of money in order to
provide adequate scope for play, at least for the great majority of mankind.

The institutional context

An orderly market is, in essence, a self-organizing super-game in which the
competitive interplay creates in Darwinian fashion new interesting information. At the same time, the market game co-ordinates the self-centred interests   *cf. 184*
of the participants and automatically resolves any conflicts which might arise.
Such a favourable result is contingent on the return of the same players over and
over again. Then a moderate measure of morality is sufficient to uphold the
long-term self-interest of the parties, evading the trap of the prisoner's dilemma
and implementing the rules of fair market play.   *cf. 275*

   At the beginning of the nineteenth century Scottish retailers began to squeeze the local
   competition in British West Africa. The outsiders were soon accused of unfair methods,
   but an investigation showed that the Scots were simply sticking to sound business
   principles, avoiding prevalent shady practices and thus attracting an increasing number
   of customers.

Ideally the economic game should operate as an open learning process of fairly
modest interest, a self-improving social metabolism regulated by countless
internal feedbacks. As ascertained above, no insurmountable technological
obstacles to economic growth are within sight. The market, however, is in-

trinsically amoral and without purpose: everything depends on the superordinate rules of the cultural game.

The conviction of the ordinary man that he can ultimately better his lot by dint of his own honest efforts is the deepest driving force of our economic plus-sum game. Economic competition is a stimulating surrogate for the struggle for survival, but an institutional setting is required to avoid short-sighted overexploitation or the brutal lawlessness of the jungle. Like overregulation, *cf. 269* political underperformance, too, poisons economic play. Either way business becomes a political game which ends up in poor politics and a wretched economy.

cf. 195 As it happened, Adam Smith wrote *The Theory of Moral Sentiments* seventeen years before his seminal work, *An Inquiry into the Nature and Causes of the Wealth of Nations,* appeared in 1776. In the latter book he espouses the well-known tenets of economic liberalism but he never loses sight of man's social accountability – the moral imperative which underwrites the viability of a fair market game.

The *Wealth of Nations* had an immediate impact, partly because the underlying ideas had been circulating for a considerable time. One of Adam Smith's sources was the thousand-page tractate *De Jure Naturae et Gentium* by the Swedish social philosopher Samuel von Pufendorf (1632–94). The illustrious Swede also inspired the Finnish clergyman and economist Anders Chydenius (1729–1803) who eloquently advocated a full-blown market economy as early as 1766 (*Den Nationella Vinsten – The National Gain*).

A complex market economy cannot function without an influx of old-fashioned morality. The indigence of totalitarian socialism has left different breeds of market-oriented societies to contend for the laurels of economic championship. Unexpectedly, the American philosophy of self-seeking individualism seems to lose out against Japanese-inspired models of corporate loyalty. Ethics is coming into its own as the chief competitive resource of the national economy.

In Japan, commerce relies largely on unwritten compacts. Japanese corporations are managed for the benefit of a tacit coalition of influental stakeholders – the shareholders do not necessarily belong to this category. Among themselves, companies establish extensive co-operative networks; the most prominent *keiretsus* centre around the big banks and trade houses. New business contacts are kept on hold until the credentials of the newcomer have been substantiated – which may take several years. Once established, both company and personal relations become long-term assets, sustained by the minimal turnover in the higher ranks of the hierarchy.

cf. 165 The United States is, as we all know, the promised land of the lawyer: there are 300 lawyers per 100,000 inhabitants (compared to the Japanese figure of 12). Legally enforceable contracts are a mandatory insurance against crooks who enjoy substantial freedom of action in a libertarian society. The anonymity of a vast, turbulent and multiracial country necessarily entails a comprehensive judicial superstructure. Morality is largely consummated by litigation which has evolved into a fine art.

For the sake of domestic peace, every organized community must begin – sooner rather than later – to tamper with the merciless rules of praxeology. The explosive growth of wealth is only fuelling the demand for highly automated solidarity on a national, regional and even a global scale. An apparently insatiable thirst for social security threatens to overload budgets and pension schemes everywhere.

cf. 274

Unfortunately, economic efficiency seems to presuppose a certain amount of inequity in the community; the prevailing inequality is one of the prime movers of the market economy. A clear and realistic formulation of the overriding political goals is therefore needed before we can design rational mechanisms for meddling with the praxeological outcome of the game. This is easier said than done. Private ownership and tribal solidarity are in perpetual conflict in our minds.

> Irrespective of the merits of political horse-trading, we must not forget that social stability is an economic value in itself. Fear of the breakdown of law and order is the strongest economic disincentive. Every productive investment in property, education or children springs from confidence in a better future and a reliable world order, upheld by legitimate authority. When people, companies, banks or nations stand surety for one another, they are giving voice to a common credo, mutually guaranteeing their economic viability. The ultimate collateral is, after all, the conviction that the economic game will preserve its vitality as the generator of shared prosperity.

Man does not live by bread alone but without his daily bread he soon loses any interest in higher activities. Cultural progress is dependent on a strong economy and has regularly followed in its wake, albeit with some delay. Wealth sometimes turns to greed, becoming an end in itself, but it also creates the necessary resources for social and health care, for education and for science, and – most important of all – for aesthetic and ethical development. In the end, only an affluent society can defend itself and solve its ecological problems, or feel concern for the underprivileged or provide patronage for drama, ballet, opera, art and music. The virtues of poverty are easily come by; only the wealthy can afford the financial consequences of a bad conscience.

The dynamism of the cultural game depends on smoothly running economic plus-sum play, but even a self-optimizing market economy cannot run for long under its own steam. The decisive meta-rules of the economic game must be sought in the political dimension and in spheres beyond. And so we must now leave the economy, with its Euclidean rectilinearity, to enter upon the crooked relativism of political play.

6.   The political game

6.1   The advent of democracy

Any hope of attaining a perfect and definitive social order should have
been dispelled long ago. We are doomed to grope in semi-darkness in a
sequence of miserable or, at best, mediocre moves. Democracy offers us
a broad and generally acceptable framework to support this collective
learning process. Its system of instrumental rules facilitates the orderly
resolution of conflicting interests and social tension. Historically, democracy has proved its value in spite of all the false starts and relapses. It
does not guarantee progress, security or prosperity, but it does provide
the opportunity for free self-organization – a prerequisite for personal
self-realization.

Tribal solidarity

In small and isolated groups of humans, the dictates of the environment damp-
ens down internal dissension. The political game is in its infancy and fair play is
secured by a tribal loyalty which is genetically entrenched. Survival depends on   *cf. 84; 192*
food, and a fair division of available supplies has certainly been a major factor
in human evolution.

> Among the Bushmen of the Kalahari desert, fruits, nuts and roots are generally gathered
> and consumed within the family whereas animal booty is shared within the whole group
> as reciprocal gifts (chimpanzees, too, share meat with one another but rarely plant food
> – a habit they share with New York stockbrokers!). In a sense even personal property
> such as weapons, household tools and jewellery are held in common. If a group member
> persists in demanding a "gift" of this kind, he cannot be refused in the end. But a moral
> credit has been established which must be redeemed at a later date. The feeling of guilt
> when we fail to return a service is an evolutionary adaptation; the golden rule was
> inculcated upon the human mind early on.   *cf. 150; 264*

In civilized societies the rule of reciprocal favours still obtains, albeit in a less
binding form. Presents are frequently exchanged, especially in Japan, and our
feasts and banquets, weddings, funerals, confirmations and Bar Mitzvahs fall
into the same category. The emotional grip of Christmas gifts stems from a
nostalgic yearning for the bosom of the ancient extended family. In real life,

such primaeval communities stunt individual initiative and encourage insolent
cf. 192 sponging.

> During the 1830s, Charles Darwin visited Tierra del Fuego at the southern tip of
> Patagonia. He was intrigued by the aborigines who turned out to be incorrigible thieves.
> When thwarted, they begged insistently for gifts, keeping up a constant ritual whine
> which was phonetically rendered by Darwin as "yammerschuner". Surrounded all
> night by the rhythmical throb of the begging chant, expedition members were often
> unable to sleep.
>   Darwin's narrative is included in his *Journal of Researches into the Geology and
> Natural History of Various Countries Visited by H.M.S. Beagle,* (1839). As late as the
> turn of the twentieth century, Captain Joshua Slocum (1844–1909) was tormented by
> the same endless "yammerschuning" when he passed the Strait of Magellan on his
> solitary voyage (*Sailing Alone Around the World,* 1899).

The insistent call for solidarity reflects the expectations of the kinship group
with regard to mutual support and equality. Elementary justice is exercised
when the rich foot the bill in proportion to their wealth, as they did at the ritual
potlatch feasts of the American Indians of the North-west. Such "democratic"
behaviour patterns are prescribed by an archetypal morality which guarantees
tolerable collaboration while arresting social evolution.

The administration of justice is no problem in small tribal groupings; punishment is meted out promptly, according to ancient precedent. As society grows
larger, tensions arise between families or clans, ethnic groups or denominations, which may be resolved in various forms of ritualized revenge. Blood feuds
can then persist over many generations of Montagues and Capulets, Serbs and
Croats, Christians and Muslims, occasionally escalating into open warfare.

Hierarchical power

Large coalitions can be held together only by centralizing vital social functions
and by delegating a considerable amount of power to specialized bodies – in
other words, by way of political processes. But who defines the rules of the
political game, who takes action against transgressions and who is responsible
for fair play? Simple solidarity is not enough; it has to be complemented by
another ancient rule of the game, the hierarchical reflex of obedience and
loyalty to a leader.

> Under suitable conditions most higher animals establish a discernible order of rank.
> Organized leadership is less common, however, and is found mainly among flock-
> hunting mammals. *Homo sapiens* is certainly hierarchically programmed, and it is
> rather surprising that respect for the leader is fairly weak in contemporary populations
> at the Stone Age level. However, it may be misleading to compare twentieth-century
> primitives with our own remote ancestors. An early divergence of the pertinent epige-
> netic rules may have been one of the causes of cultural differentiation.

While the sense of belonging diminishes with distance, the strong leader can
operate from afar. Indeed, his authority may be considerably enhanced by
isolation from his subjects. The king or the High Priest is transformed into a
cherished symbol of the community; he is credited with divine inspiration, and

in extreme cases endowed with unlimited power exercised through persons of lesser dignity, aristocrats or bureaucrats as the case may be.   *cf. 429*

Tribal solidarity and respect for the chief are innate in human nature and as such are the mainstays of constructive political play. By and large, we have grievously misemployed these endowments. History is plagued by the seemingly insoluble conflict between élitist and egalitarian impulses. Again and again we have failed to reconcile freedom and order, equality and efficiency, fellowship and the practical division of labour. In such cross-currents good intentions have generally suffered shipwreck. Violence, open or concealed, has always been the decisive move in the political game.

> In naked power play the paranoiacs usually have a decisive advantage. They are always (on putatively good grounds) first with the dagger-thrust, the poisoned cup or the bullet in the neck. Tyrants and dictators are megalomaniac cynics who have established an unblemished track record in these merciless games of survival.

Whereas the kin group or the tribe can live up to an ideal of harmony and homeostasis, there seems to be no obvious model for human co-existence on a grand scale. To preserve social stability, our forebears had to sacrifice much of their human dignity. Arbitrary despotism and repressive bureaucracy have generally prevailed while glaring injustice and abject degradation was meted out to the great majority.   *cf. 192*

Charisma and bureaucracy

In primitive or impoverished conditions each day has to bear its own burden; mere survival is reward enough. Existential problems appear only when domination of the environment admits a wide variety of alternative moves. We have already affirmed that, devoid of value, personal freedom becomes a state of rational and emotional absurdity. Increasing prosperity both presupposes and   *cf. 159; 293; 420* promotes the generation of superordinate rules; but for the moment their content can be left open.

Value-generation is initiated by exceptional people, true or false prophets who, for reasons good or bad, have lost their sense of fallibility. As charismatic political leaders, they can dispense authoritative solutions for all societal problems, especially if the breakdown of established values has created a receptive market. To the common man, almost any conviction is preferable to the uncertainty of value nihilism. In a state of anarchy, the prospect of some sort of law and order can make even violent sales methods acceptable to the majority.

> Moses, Pericles, Lenin and Hitler delineate a wide spectrum of political charisma. Obviously mankind's universal yearning for emotional security and unequivocal meta-rules can, in the last resort, be satisfied even by preposterous fakes. When divine inspiration – the bread of life – is missing we eagerly devour insalubrious stones.

The charismatic capital is managed by expanding bureaucratic institutions which create theologies, establish dogmas, devise appropriate rites, and organize other more down-to-earth activities. After the death of the founding father, the freedom of action enjoyed by his followers is successively circumscribed until all positions of power are ultimately occupied by professional bureaucrats. The top posts become largely ceremonial while the real decision-makers play their games of palace intrigue behind the scenes.

> Originally, both spiritual and secular powers were invested in the king but, over time, his political influence usually waned until he was virtually confined to ceremonial duties. The prehistory of both ancient Athens and Rome reflect this pattern and more recent examples abound. In the eighth century, the Merovingian kings of France were unceremoniously dumped by their powerful Mayor Domos, and not much later the emperors of Japan were promoted to the status of living gods, all too exalted to bother about earthly matters.

The strength of the bureaucracy lies in conservation, systematization, routinization, in other words, in radical simplification. So even if the original vision has paled, the bureaucratic apparatus can be kept running for a long time by the forces of social inertia. But any serious strain will throw it off course, and a fresh dose of charisma will be needed to set it right. In the end, no administration can remain viable without intermittent injections of invigorating faith.

cf. 142; 192

Totalitarian aberrations

In the past it has only been possible to achieve political continuity and legitimacy under autocratic homeostasis. The price of stability has generally been stagnation; radical change has taken its toll in violence and retrogression while inducing the emergence of new and often more terrible forms of tyranny.

Totalitarian political systems, from the mediaeval Catholic church to contemporary socialist-state societies, have solved the stability problem by stiffening the social fabric with infallible dogma which amounts to a distorted reflection of the original revelation. The logical outcome is the absence of internal renewal, a dearth of creativity. The essentials are given, and all that remains is mundane interpretation and application, dignified by a suitable set of eschatological expectations. The future heaven upon earth provides the final justification for the most monstrous actions, atoning for every crime and absolving the individual from personal guilt.

> According to the Spanish philosopher José Ortega y Gasset (1883–1955), totalitarian movements really do represent the "masses" – irresponsible and regimented crowds lacking any cultural affiliations (*The Rebellion of the Masses*, 1929). In the name of the collective, these victims of social atomization are capable of committing atrocities which, as private citizens, they would find abhorrent. Disorganized crowds lose all sense of responsibility and unhesitatingly follow their basest impulses whereas a genuine social community raises its members above themselves in an auspicious ethical plus-sum game.

Bereft of all accountability the ordinary citizen becomes the hapless executor of his leader's delusions. Stimulating political interplay is replaced by passive submission and paltry performance. Individual responsibility evaporates and moral schizophrenia assumes epidemic proportions. Wherever omniscient ideologists usurp all power and establish a monopoly predicated on faith, progress dynamos will be alienated and their contribution wasted.

Any hope of attaining the perfect and definitive social system should have been dispelled long ago. We are doomed to grope in semi-darkness, blundering from one mistake to another, in a sequence of miserable or, at best, mediocre moves. All the grand pretentions and "final" social constructs of the past have been defeated by their own inherent impossibility.

The emergence of democracy

Joint decision-making is a natural aptitude of man, that coalition-builder *par excellence*. The popular assemblies of many of the classical Greek city states tried as best they could to recreate the original sense of tribal community, but even in democratic Athens less than one tenth of the adult male population enjoyed the franchise.

> For the ancient Athenians, democracy meant that all those entitled to vote had the same chance of exercising power in the name of the polity. The popular assembly was directly involved in all important decisions. The executive as well as the judiciary were chosen by lot; no-one was allowed to attain a politically privileged position. To the Greeks, our representative democracy would have appeared as a kind of oligarchy since the wealthy and/or influential are obviously over-represented in government. In classical Athens, eminent and ambitious citizens were often condemned to exile; only 6,000 votes were needed to bring about such ostracism.

The harsh realities of the slave society drove the Hellenistic polity towards oligarchy or dictatorship (the "tyrants" of old). Modern democracy is more indebted to the Roman republic which, over time, created a framework for containing political conflicts. But the *res publica* was heavily skewed in favour of the propertied classes and did not survive the strain of empire-building. Augustan self-sufficiency was Antiquity's political legacy to future cultures, and an enlightened despot became the best hope for a downtrodden human race.

> The Christian message was open, allowing a variety of interpretations, not least in the political dimension. The first Christian congregation in Jerusalem lived in a truly communistic community of common ownership, pending Jesus' early return. As it turned out they had to rely on the indefatigable Paul who stepped in with economic aid from other more practically-minded Christian congregations.
>
> Despite their superficial adjustment to the Roman social order, the followers of Jesus could not fail to be regarded as a challenge to the establishment. The refusal of the Jews to worship the emperor as God could be blamed on ancient customs and old-fashioned ideas, but there was no such excuse for the Christian converts who were busily spreading the Gospel far and wide. To Nero who ruled from 54 to 68 A.D. and Domitian (81 to 96 A.D.) the Christians may have been scapegoats for personal failure, but to Trajan (98–117) and Diocletian (285–305), they represented a subversive movement and a threat to the absolute authority of the emperor.

In the long run, brotherhood in Christ was incompatible with slavery, and many prosperous Christians discreetly extended the old Roman tradition of manumission by freeing all their slaves. It was only after the triumph of Christianity in the fourth century A.D. that the example of these reformists eventually became an ethical norm. Despite many relapses, slavery has never regained a permanent foothold in our culture, even if the barbarian invasions and the class structure of feudal society halted the progress of egalitarian ideals.

> Mediaeval city republics were generally controlled by powerful merchant families or craft guilds; only a select group of citizens enjoyed full civic rights. More convincing democratic self-government can be discerned in isolated, rural communities on the fringes of Europe: in the Frisian, Gothlandic and Icelandic peasant republics, in the sectarian Hussite movement and above all in the Swiss cantons, which provide the best *cf. 137* example of an unbroken democratic tradition.
>
> Independent protestant denominations have certainly played a significant role as seedbeds of democracy. Anybody in the congregation could raise his voice to explicate his personal version of the divine message. The chapel elected its own parson and took care of the infirm and destitute in its midst. The overt or covert ambition was to shine as a city of God amid the surrounding darkness.

During their ascendancy in the seventeenth century the largely Calvinist Netherlands became the first stronghold of modern democratic values – justice, *cf. 177* tolerance, free trade and scientific objectivity. In the following century, their role was taken over by England, and the movement culminated in the American revolution (the celebrated French revolution by and large flaunted the worst *cf. 247* sides of democracy).

The emergence of democratic ideals brought forth plenty of Cassandras prophesying doom. Appalled by the English revolution, Thomas Hobbes (1588–1679) elaborated on the inherent paradox of a self-governing people. The lack of any supreme authority must intensify party conflict to the intolerable point where the nation would inevitably tear itself apart. Later sceptics have, with some justification, pointed at exorbitant taxation and an end to the creation of personal wealth. Most pundits have concurred in the gloomy view that power in the hands of the populace could have nothing but disastrous consequences.

Democracy is sustained by a broadly accepted set of rules for resolving conflicts of interest. Above all it provides a dependable framework for a collective learning process which knows no end. Democracy, the voluntary coalition of responsible citizens, has proved its pre-eminence in spite of all the false starts and relapses, setbacks and aberrations. Democracy does not guarantee progress, security or prosperity but it does provide the opportunity for free self-organization, which is a prerequisite for personal self-realization.

6.2   Democratic play

Modern, large-scale democracy is, along with science, one of the unique features of Western culture. The details of joint democratic decision-making do not matter much, given a sufficient degree of circularity in political feedback. The governed must, in the last instance, control the governors. Equally important is that the might of the majority is balanced by the right of the minority and the individual. This is a tall order, but in democratic play society can embark on a virtuous circle with a relatively modest investment of morale. Once the community spirit has reached a critical point, the self-stabilizing process of accumulating ethical and material capital can get going.

Right is might

In the political game, might has in most connections been right. The coveted prize has been the power to make rules binding on all the members in the social coalition, or even the authority to intervene at will. Montesquieu certified that such power corrupts, and later experience has produced ample confirmation of his thesis. Corruption implies a breach of the explicit or implicit rules of collaborative interplay – the degradation of citizens to subjects.

The essence of democratic self-government is the circularity of authority, a broad-based but not necessarily universal suffrage and a secret ballot which transforms public opinion into political feedback. Majority rule does not, as such, exclude oppression and arbitrariness – Thomas Jefferson (1743–1826) called it the tyranny of the legislature. Popular prejudice may further exacerbate existing legalized discrimination.

> Alexis de Tocqueville (1805–59) was appalled on his American tour in 1831, not only by slavery but by the condition of the "free" negroes who in practice were denied the right to vote in the non-slavery states. He comments drily: "The majority claims the right not only of making the laws, but of breaking the laws it has made."

The marvel of modern democracy is that right becomes might, that personal privileges are at a premium. Power over other people is circumscribed by protective regulations transmuting the dominant rules of joint decision-making. Game-destroying violence is strictly taboo; the rules for changing the rules are sacred and often enshrined in special stipulations, requiring a qualified majority of votes. On concrete matters, however, the sovereign people may decide through their representatives as they think fit. Political decisions are ultimately accepted by even the most die-hard opposition; they are provisional and revocable in contrast to the fundamental framework of the game.

> Unlike the quasi-anarchic interplay of economic exchange, the political marketplace rests on a formalized structure, which calls for some hard choices. Election procedure is fraught with difficulties, starting with the practical problems of electoral registers,

delineating the constituencies, controlling the count, and guarding against undue influence or plain fraud. The real quandary lies in the voting process. Before any proposal reaches the final ballot, a series of polls must be held to eliminate all but two of the numerous options. Many alternative voting procedures are on offer for these eliminating rounds. One of them must be singled out – but under which voting procedure?

A referendum is a relatively simple affair but the variety of electoral methods adopted in parliamentary or presidential elections foreshadows a somewhat depressing conclusion: there is no generally valid and impartial system for selecting a set of representatives by popular vote.

> The nomination of electoral candidates is another complex problem. Militant minorities have always found unfair ways of pushing their favourites through, but the more democratic selection of candidates by preliminary voting is only a marginal improvement. General elections present the same vexing problem of fairness. The single-seat constituency seems straightforward enough but is open to gerrymandering and can result in minority rule. Proportional elections tend to fragment the political field: the outcome is often a hung parliament and a weak coalition government. By allowing two or more votes in one or several election rounds, accuracy in measuring the popular will can be improved. Even so, the ballot box remains at best an imprecise gauge.

We have to be content with rough approximations in reading the political barometer; absolute impartiality is unattainable. Fortunately, the sanctity of the election system does not depend on scrupulous objectivity. Apparent weaknesses do not justify a breach of the rules any more than mistakes or partiality on the part of the referee gives a soccer team the right to take the ball into their own hands.

Political articulation

The sacred character of the election procedure contrasts sharply with the pragmatism of everyday democratic politics, which is all too likely to sink to the level of factional strife or shameless log-rolling. And yet, in game-theory terms, parties and factions are the indispensable agents of representative democracy. Without systematic coalition-building, popular opinion would remain inarticulate. Voters clashing among themselves could cause endless commotion; shifting coalitions among voters and parliamentarians are the zest of political life.

> A good deal of necessary social conciliation takes place inside the modern party machine, which often leads to chronic conflict within the ranks. On being introduced into the British parliament by a seasoned colleague, a freshman opposition member gestured towards the government benches and exclaimed: "Ah! There's the enemy!" The veteran promptly corrected this misapprehension. "No," he said, "those are your opponents. You'll find the enemies on your own side."

We have already touched upon the impossibility of large diversified groups reaching rational agreement about a common welfare function, but even a small assembly trying to make a joint decision can find itself in a game-theoretical impasse. This is because most voting games have an empty core. The vulnerability of any complex voting procedure was rigorously proved by Kenneth Arrow.

cf. 56

cf. 59

This basic problem of psephology is best understood by referring to a simple example. Three voters (X, Y, Z) have to choose between three alternatives (A, B, C). Their individual preferences are given in figure 6.1.

	First	Second	Third
Voter X	A	B	C
Voter Y	B	C	A
Voter Z	C	A	B

Figure 6.1   Voters' preferences

Alternative A is preferred to B by voters X and Z; B is preferred to C by X and Y. C beats A by the same vote of two to one and the outcome is an insoluble stalemate. This paradox of the voting cycle does not appear if the alternatives operate along a single dimension, such as the size of a particular budget. It will inevitably arise as soon as priorities have to be set within a multi-dimensional frame of reference.

In opposition, shared discontent can sometimes hold a shaky coalition together but egotistical antagonism fails miserably in a responsible majority position. Long-term political collaboration requires more than rational grounds; enlightened self-interest is not enough. The inevitable inconsistencies and injustices have to be absorbed by the unrestrained exploitation of emotional factors – leadership, team spirit and expedient promises.

In the thick of things, the job of the politicians is to drum up support for some feasible compromise, often laboriously pieced together in a smoky backroom. Such machinations notwithstanding, parliament usually manages to reflect the mood of the electorate. In the political marketplace the current values of a nation are weighed and measured in unadulterated monetary terms. Budget debates are really crass disputations on democratic theology.

Much to the chagrin of action-oriented minds, democracy seems to beget mostly talk, talk and more talk. The drawn-out discussions fulfil an important function. Man has always resented decisions being made above his head. He has an ingrained desire to participate, to be consulted even if his input remains fairly nominal. The debates and disputes of modern democracies mirror the endless palavering around paleolithic camp-fires and produce the same beneficial effects: if not complete agreement then at least grudging acceptance.

It is easy to talk sweetly about compassion and human rights; it is a much weightier matter to increase the spending on medical care, pensions, the judiciary or education by raising taxes or perhaps by withholding money from traffic safety, environmental protection or a credible defence. At this point the demagogic approach evaporates; sweeping generalizations and wishful thinking have to yield to the *quid pro quo* of the practical trade-off. Here individual advantage must be weighed against collective benefit, the power of the majority against the rights of the minority, and the long term prospects against immediate gratification.

A genuine democracy is a transformer which converts the energy of popular demands and prevailing passions into coherent political action. The democratic mode of play articulates the largely implicit and multifaceted values of the electorate. A popular assembly will always be a lousy performer but parliament

is irreplaceable when it comes to defining the national credo in concrete, operational terms. Its mission is to maintain the frame for an ethical and moral
plus-sum game in which all citizens can participate according to their ability.

The verdict of the electorate

Despite certain possibilities for manipulating public opinion, the leaders in a
democratic society must keep a constant eye on the voters. But is the electorate
up to its job? Does it really enjoy the confidence of the power-brokers and the
ideological masterminds? The answer in many cases is "no", which means that
formal democracies are not impervious to rigged elections, coups d'état or even
cf. 271 a revolutionary volte-face.

In classical Greece, popular rule required referendums on all major issues, a
procedure retained in Switzerland to the present day. Nevertheless, representative democracy along Anglo-Saxon lines became the standard model, even if
direct representation was revived in the Puritan communities of New England.
With modern electronic information systems it would now be feasible to hold
plebiscites on all major issues, but are we really prepared to take the risk?

> In Switzerland the frequent referendums have reduced average participation in elections
> to well below 50 per cent. Indirectly the majority has thus delegated the decisions to a
> minority of particularly interested and presumably well-informed citizens. The figures
> show (surprise, surprise) that men over 50 are greatly over-represented among the
> active voters, with an extra bias towards the better educated and above-average income
> earners.
>
> In California, the citizens' initiatives of the early 1970s were instrumental in starting
> the tax rebellion which subsequently swept the Western world. But the proliferation of
> complex issues is, expectedly, turning away the less sophisticated voters and has in-
> duced a switch to the Swiss voting pattern.

The drawbacks of Gallup-democracy have become only too apparent and it
may not be wise to push people to the poll on every conceivable issue. The latent
political interest of the electorate will certainly come to the fore when it is really
needed in a crisis.

> An energetic élite, the aristocracy of action, will always remain responsible for the main
> social functions. In sports clubs or concert societies, in business enterprises or political
> parties – the initiators must always develop some measure of charismatic leadership.
> They have to generate enthusiasm among a clique of personal followers, absorbing their
> uncertainties and offering an opportunity for identification. The task of the common
> citizen is to develop his individual sense of foul and fair, and keep the hypocrites and
> sycophants at bay.

Democracy is certainly a risky venture. Elaborate proofs of its impossibility go
back to Plato's *Republic,* and they still appear pretty convincing. So why has
democratic rule, by and large, enjoyed considerable success despite ineffectual
phrase-mongering and inflammatory agitation? We always tend to overempha-
size the weight of discrete decisions, of material resources and prevalent skills
while undervaluing the importance of the learning process. A series of collective

mistakes may well constitute indispensable steps on the way to the right conclusions.

cf. 377; 389

The rules of the democratic game incorporate a series of sluggish feedback mechanisms. The most important control is imposed by the ballot box where for once the last have become the first. Modern democracy is the only political system which has succeeded in significantly reducing social tension; it has replaced violent coercion by patient negotiation, and has imposed egalitarian values on a dynamic society by empowering the poor. The outcome is not and cannot be definitive. On the contrary, the democratic game is and must remain open; goals and priorities are constantly called into question.

Querulous pluralism

In a national emergency the rules of democracy can be modified or even suspended, but they are resurrected once the crisis is over. The very life-blood of the community has been threatened; unlike totalitarian systems, democracy cannot thrive in a state of permanent mobilization. Nonetheless, the war potential of the democratic countries is impressive. In the face of an external challenge, internal conflicts are temporarily repressed by unifying and uniforming self-preservation; the communal adrenalin is given free rein.

cf. 273

> Prince Maurice of Orange (1567–1625), who commanded the army of the Netherlands against the Spanish, launched the "democratic" art of war. Ordinary men were transformed by continuous training into effective soldiers, held together by a conditioned reflex of loyalty. Lulls in the fighting were exploited for drill and digging defences. The first modern people's army was conjured up in response to the threat from Philip II's battle-hardened but pretty undisciplined mercenaries. The self-defensive fighting spirit of Swiss peasants and Bohemian Hussites was reborn at a higher organizational level, and achieved victory after an 80-year struggle against the might of imperial Spain.

After an exhausting war effort, democratic society reverts with remarkable ease to its normal state of querulous self-satisfaction. Supreme commands are dismantled more or less overnight, and the divisive political game goes straight into top gear. The concentration of power is replaced by diversity and pluralism in all areas of social life.

Democratic decision-making is usually a tedious and even sometimes sordid affair, marred by political bickering and backbiting. There are no indisputable solutions; democracy cautiously gropes its way ahead in Darwinian fashion. Progress is made by fumbling and stumbling from one compromise to the next through a thicket of blunders. And yet the fatal and irreversible errors are avoided.

> Since time immemorial political conflict could end only in the submission or ruin of the losing party; major shifts in power often led to the dissolution of society. In democracies, too, the losers stand down with much gnashing of teeth. Nevertheless they keep their lives, their honour, their property and occasionally even their political influence intact – an unimaginable extravagance in old-fashioned societies. A democracy is slow and inactive even in the face of violence, despite vociferous demands for prompt reprisals against undesirable elements.

Lawful obedience to the democratic rules can produce an astonishing political payoff. Democracy not only has an uncanny ability to neutralize or absorb deviating and even hostile groups – it positively exploits them. Everyone tries to further his own cause but nobody can actually direct the game. Hence the unpredictable but expedient meandering among the shifting shoals of public opinion.

A strong democracy enjoys almost unlimited confidence in its own internal stability and can allow itself a noise level, undreamt of in any other type of society. It can absorb its heretics, and grows miraculously stronger when acceding to its critics. A democracy can give way, change course, suffer defeat, and yet survive without losing its identity.

Supercritical value-generation

Deep political disagreements cannot be resolved by verbal confrontation or scientific analysis, but they can be worked out within the judicious frame of a smooth-functioning democracy. The only alternative is to fall back on the oldest and most convincing argument: naked force, war, death and destruction. Thus, for all its drawbacks, political democracy should be cherished as the womb of the future. Other types of society either prepare the ground for democracy, or are stuck in an evolutionary dead-end.

> This axiomatic premise cannot be logically deduced or proved beyond reasonable doubt. Unlike the economic game, the political rule system is fairly independent of the surrounding realities. Widely diverging models have proved at least temporarily feasible, and only broad historical experience can provide some empirical corroboration of our thesis.
>
> Since this book was conceived, democratic rule has gone from strength to strength though vast regions are still untouched by its spell. The dissolution of the Soviet empire opened the way for a democratization of sorts, but the incipient democratic game could well be smothered under an avalanche of frustrated expectations. The market economy is bound to disappoint if democratic capitalism is equated with greed, pure and simple.

Although democracy is the most exacting of social systems, it does not call for the impossible. People need not imitate the industry of the ant or the altruism of a saint to be good citizens. The civic virtue required is an aptitude for fair play; an accountable élite should be capable of rousing the majority in support of unpopular albeit necessary measures.

> Military service in democracies is, at least in wartime, based on conscription rather than voluntary or mercenary service. Likewise social security depends mainly on compulsory taxation despite the commendable activities of charitable institutions. Everyone accepts the personal sacrifice, provided the whole coalition follows the same jointly ratified norms. The collective ethic thus rises well above the average level of its constituent members.

The viability of democratic rule depends on its moral resources. The union of independent citizens should protect the weak, and must possess the power to curb any syndicate of evil strength in its midst. Respect for fair play must exceed a certain critical level if this political process is to become "supercritical" (to borrow a term from nuclear technology). A small surplus of civic morality then initiates a self-amplifying chain reaction which sustains the progress of democratic play.

> In a large community, not even the modest effort of voting can be justified as an act of self-interest in game-theoretical terms. It is obviously desirable that people vote but each individual's impact is negligible. In deciding to vote or not to vote we are thus taking part in a huge, multiperson game in which it is rational for every single person to pass the buck. This is perhaps the least pressing instance of the notorious free rider problem. Everybody agrees that somebody should pay the taxes, defend the country, take care of the destitute and so on, but volunteers are generally thin on the ground. What is in the interest of all is rarely in the selfish interest of any one individual.

The strength of a democratic polity is that society can embark on a virtuous circle with a relatively modest investment of community spirit. Once the critical point has been reached, the self-stabilizing process of accumulating moral capital gets going. Democracy is always imperfect, faulty, provisional and embryonic. We can only agree with Winston Churchill (1874–1965) that it is a terrible institution, but the best there is. Democracy is not primarily a mechanism for producing maximum material wealth; it is, above all, the vehicle for an incalculable range of free economic, political and cultural interplay.

> Describing the blessings of the future Communist society, Nikita Krushchev (1894–1971) spoke in the 1960s of "free homes, free food, free medical care, free transport". Everything was free, all needs satisfied according to prescribed objective norms. Where had we seen such a society before? Our cattle get the best feed, medical care, sleeping quarters and so on. No subjective preferences are accepted, and certainly no such unhealthy habits as alcohol, tobacco or coffee. Everyone is cared for with scientific precision; welfare is rampant and everything is free!

Politics has been defined as the art of preventing people from minding their own affairs. Under socialism existence tends to become totally politicized, and it is of the very essence of democracy that government intervention in the private sphere is kept to a minimum. Everyone should have the inalienable right to get unhappy in his own inexplicable way.

6.3   The anti-democratic mind

Only the democratic process can channel revolutionary fervour into constructive play; after all, democracy amounts to institutionalized revolution. The revolutionary urge and its total denial appear to be equally destructive, equally anti-democratic. If revolutions are indispensable they are impossible; the reign of terror that justifies the revolution also prevents its practical realization. If revolution is possible, then it is unnecessary because the regime is then open to change through moderate political action. Despite recent advances, we have no cause to crow. The rapidly multiplying majority of mankind has hardly started its march towards democracy.

Élitist deviations

In a democracy, every individual should have the opportunity to take part in the political game according to his own lights. Thus, the widest possible general education and a free supply of information is indispensable to every democratic society. Ideally, all citizens should become involved so that the available talent can be integrated into the democratic process. Even the angriest firebrands should be allowed to let off their surplus steam and become decent citizens.

> The democratic emphasis on broad discussion, consultation and compromise is sometimes seen as a barrier to true brilliance. The lack of decorum on the political stage naturally reflects the average level of the electorate, and it cannot fail to evoke a disgusted reaction from many high-minded souls. Indeed it was long *comme il faut* in progressive circles to dismiss the vulgar philistinism of the democratic process in favour of some immediate global reconstruction in the grandiose style of a Bakunin, a Nietzche or a Lenin. As we have already seen, this élitist deviation is rooted in mental instability. The personal superiority of such champions cannot stand the test of competition; it has to be defined axiomatically on grounds of racial affiliation, party membership or an exclusive world-view.

Man's innate emotional insecurity obstructs fair democratic play. We yearn instinctively for confident and infallible leaders, for streamlined decisions, a polished facade and at least cosmetic success in every sphere – man has a craving for agreeable illusions. Democratic government is doomed to disappoint. It offers party quarrels, incessant lobbying and horse-trading, ugly scandals, mistakes and miscalculations, regrettable weaknesses in people and institutions – in other words the undraped truth of human fallibility.

> By the end of the Second World War, the whole of Europe was threatened by a communist take-over. The Swiss economist and philosopher Wilhelm Röpke (1899–1966), one of my early inspirations, captures the mood of the times in the introduction to his *Civitas Humana* (1944). He recites the refrain of an old Greek folksong from the eve of the fall of Constantinople: "God's Will seems to be that the world turns Turkish."

On the face of it, all odds were stacked against wimpish democracy; very few of the self-appointed intellectual élite stood up to the totalitarian challenge.

Jean-Paul Sartre (1905–80) and Simone de Beauvoir are good exponents of the prevailing spirit of desertion. Of course there was some justification for their ultra-leftist views (when, after all, is radicalism not understandable?), but they never gave democracy a chance. Sartre's self-styled martyrdom appears especially repulsive in comparison with the real thing in the Soviet Union – the country of unreserved glorification. Alexander Sacharov and Jelena Bonner faced intimidation and isolation, and later fought the overwhelming power of the state with the feeble weapon of the written word whereas the French couple were merely indulging in intellectual arrogance. Nonetheless Sartre certainly needed democracy; his remarkable literary performance was possible only within the system he decried. Perhaps democracy also needed Sartre.

The revolutionary reflex is reinforced by that spontaneous sense of solidarity which is aroused by people in distress. The tenderest consciences, especially, are tempted to immediate action, dissatisfied with merely exposing the corruption of the social order. Any means of seizing power are justified by the noble aim of redressing intolerable inequity once and for all. The fervour is fanned by the fulminations of demagogues who easily arouse a response among the spoilt children of over-indulgent parents.

It is reassuring that the common man generally exhibits sounder judgement although democracies habitually treat their rulers with distrust. We make life difficult for our elected political representatives, although – or perhaps because – both policies and politicians faithfully reflect prevailing standards of morality. Every people gets the leaders it deserves.

> The charismatic chief mesmerizes his audience with the same tricks as the star performer on the stage. Roosevelt and Churchill as well as Mussolini, Hitler, Stalin and Fidel Castro, each in his own country personified the popular notion of a good show.

Professional revolutionaries

To obsessively self-exalted people, democratic haggling and petty compromise *cf. 178* is profoundly frustrating. If the game goes against them, they feel tempted to break the coalition, and to proclaim a revolutionary turn of stage with the role of führer cast for themselves. A totalitarian society, in which grumblers and whiners can be given short shrift, appears irresistibly attractive to excitable minds with an exaggerated idea of their own importance.

Democracies are fairly immune to serious insurrection because they are tolerant of innovative value-creation. This integrative capability is obnoxious to compulsive revolutionaries who, in desperation, labelled it "repressive tolerance". Conspiracy, the concealed coalition, has become an end in itself to latter-day terrorists.

> The paradigmatic figure in this genre is Sergei Nechaev (1847–82), Bakunin's disciple and leader of a small band of Russian anarchists. A habitual liar, Nechaev was also a callous murderer; he once had a member of his band executed simply to terrorize his gang into blind obedience. Mihail Bakunin (1814–76) disassociated himself from his follower, and Dostoevsky took him as the model for one, and possibly two, of the main

characters in *The Possessed*. Self-deification and total amorality characterizes such specimens, trash thrown up by human emancipation.

At some point the line must be drawn, beyond which tolerance does become repressive. Democratic teamwork must not be jeopardized to assuage the egos of a few extremists with a superiority complex. What matters to the professional revolutionary is not the professed ideal, but the actual assumption of power, scantily disguised under a cloak of self-immunizing eschatology. He strikes as the occasion offers, eliminating his more conscience-ridden rivals, disregarding all human consideration.

> Under the czarist régime, V.I. Lenin (né Uljanov, 1870–1924) was imprisoned and banished for his subversive activities; his brother had been executed earlier for the attempted murder of Alexander III. Lenin was exiled for three (!) years to Siberia where he lived in relative comfort with his wife, and pursued his revolutionary authorship. Once his sentence was completed he could leave the country.
>
> According to Lenin, "truth is whatever helps, strengthens and advances the party" – a blatant regression to atavistic amorality. During the First World War he was sitting in Switzerland busily preparing a revolution in that country. When it did not take off (the Swiss comrades hesitated at the prospect of any unlawful action) he self-assuredly predicted a revolution in Sweden, of all places. Lenin was completely taken by surprise in March 1917 (February according to the old-style Russian calendar) when the Czar abdicated and a democratically underpinned provisional government under Alexander Kerenski (1881–1970) took the reins.
>
> Lenin adjusted quickly, was passed along to Russia by the Germans and in July 1917 he promptly tried to seize power by force. After some initial distress he was allowed to resume his political activities. After their successful coup in November (October old style) the Bolsheviks showed no old-fashioned hesitation about liquidating their potential adversaries. When the dust had settled, Lenin remarked despondently: "there's an awful shortage of honest people".
>
> Adolf Hitler's (1889–1945) takeover followed a similar pattern. An unsuccessful putsch in 1923 led to nine months in prison where Hitler began to write *Mein Kampf*. Opponents of his rule, as we all know, later received less gentle treatment. Fidel Castro also had a bloody revolt and a surprisingly short detention (three years) behind him before he finally overthrew the weak and corrupt Batista oligarchy. His own way with the opposition is common knowledge.

cf. 289 Most democracies handle rebels with kid gloves – sometimes at their peril. In "revolutionary situations", when authority breaks down and anarchy reigns, the total lack of scruple gives the professional revolutionary a decisive advantage over less ferocious opponents. Paranoid ruthlessness and a cynical contempt for any rules of the game will carry the day. Only the democratic process can channel revolutionary fervour into constructive play; after all, democracy amounts to institutionalized revolution.

Vainglorious revolution

Absolute power has always been justified by the need to cut through short-sighted parochial interests, thus making room for universal welfare – the absolute good. However, such revolution from above carries an enormous democratic deficit and is bound to fail.

The pharaoh Amenhotep IV, called Akhenathon (1375–1258 B.C.) tried to impose on his people a new monotheistic religion (worship of the sun disc), a new art style (expressive realism), a new capital (Akhetaton, today Tell el-Amarna) and a reformed written language, based on the vernacular. Maat, the king's absolute truth, was to pervade all aspects of life. At bottom, Akhenathon's reforms were a vain attempt at self-deification: after his death everything reverted to the old ways.

Popular insurrections are equally ineffective. They rarely achieve lasting change and go down as futile demonstrations of the fact that neither rebels nor rulers can handle existing social realities.

Chinese history is replete with peasant uprisings, but up to and including the Tai-Ping insurrection (1851–1865) they achieved only devastation and excessive loss of life. Neither did the rebellion of the slaves under Einus (136–132 B.C.) and Spartacus (73–71 B.C.) do anything to change the direction of Roman society. The European peasant jacqueries of the late Middle Ages tell the same sad story, except perhaps in England.

In Naples, power was seized by a young fisherman named Masaniello in 1647. The insurrection was suppressed with great cruelty, and Southern Italy has remained one of the most backward regions of Europe ever since. The Pugatjov revolt in Russia (1773–74) met with initial success but was eventually crushed; it merely achieved a strengthening of the despotic regime. With the possible exception of Mexico, the only really successful popular revolution took place on Haiti during the Napoleonic wars when a slave uprising swept away the French and Spanish landowners. The result speaks for itself.

A fanatical and preferably ascetic intelligentsia provides the leaven necessary to an effective revolutionary process. A quasi-religious creed which denounces the existing social order is imposed on the cadres. The result is a collision between incompatible meta-rules; any joint frames of reference crumble and the only remaining forum for debate is the battlefield.

The English revolution of 1642 was supported by an enterprising puritanical middle class with a strong religious commitment to egalitarian principles. Oliver Cromwell was a fairly moderate Puritan, a man of common sense who sought to establish a compromise based on a constitutional monarchy, but it took several generations before a reasonably democratic structure emerged. These painful processes impressed a tolerant scepticism on the British national character; the market for high-flown revolutionary aspirations has remained remarkably restricted ever since.

When we consider past or present social abuses, we feel a spontaneous revulsion: the distress is heartbreaking, the injustice glaring, the arrogance of those in power intolerable. A cool analysis of the gains of earlier revolutions soon prompts restraint. At best (as in the British example) the traumatic experience may ultimately lead to a deeper democratic understanding, at worst to moral and material ruin.

In its very lack of revolutionary fuss the American revolution is a splendid exception granted that the move to a fully-fledged representative democracy appears manageable, at least with the benefit of hindsight. The glorious French revolution, on the other hand, was certainly a carnevalesque spectacle but a political disaster. The rule of the guillotine, which horrified contemporaries, could by modern standards be shrugged off as an aberration. But the result of all the magnificent gestures, the commotion and the frenzy, the bloodshed and the atrocities, was that one weak Louis (the sixteenth of that ilk) was cf. 236

deposed, only to be succeeded by another even more insignificant one (the eighteenth), while Europe fell under the reactionary yoke of the Holy Alliance. The serfs could surely have been freed and the Code Napoleon established with less turmoil by judicious horse-trading between sensible politicians.

The recent humiliating end of the Great October Revolution has certainly deflated much of the revolutionary fervour lingering in its wake. Nevertheless, we should not overestimate the upsurge of democracy which, so far, has been largely confined to the heartlands of Christianity.

> The Islamic world seems to be in constant turmoil, fanned by fiery fundamentalism. At its best, Sub-Saharan Africa pays only lip-service to democratic values, and Indian democracy is constantly teetering on the brink of disaster. The forceful example of Japan has had an impact in the Far East, but more than one billion Chinese are still kept on a tight totalitarian rein. Latin America offers more hope but, there too, the unrestrained propagation of the indigent could frustrate economic and political progress.

To proclaim the unconditional victory of democratic rule, as Francis Fukuyama has done (in *The End of History and the Last Man*, 1992), is foolhardy in the extreme. Many, perhaps most traditional value systems are incompatible with representative government. The rapidly multiplying majority of mankind has hardly started its march towards democracy.

Compulsive self-destruction

As we have seen, social coalitions between large numbers of people are fundamentally unstable constructs. Widespread individual creativity is not enough. On the contrary, the history of the Greeks, the Jews, and the Irish alone show just how difficult it is to keep together coalitions of gifted and overly self-confident men. Authoritarian rule can temporally put a lid on social unrest and redirect the pent-up aggression against outside enemies, but when it suddenly collapses, all the internal tensions are revealed.

> After the downfall of communism, we have been horrified by old tribal enmities flaring up in the Balkans and the Caucasuses. Even more instructive is the outcome of the First World War. In 1914, the autocratic states of Europe (Russia, Germany, Austria-Hungary) threw themselves cheerfully into the adventure of war, only to be dragged down by military defeat and revolutionary upheaval. The democracies – France, Great Britain and the United States – showed much less initial ardour but managed to win the war and to maintain their social order intact.

We have little evidence of modern democracies in defeat, but the available evidence suggests that they can take a lot of punishment whereas the towers of totalitarian strength come crumbling down.

> In the "winter war" of 1939–40, Finland stood its ground alone against the mighty Soviet Union. It lost ten per cent of its territory, yet retained both its independence and its democratic institutions through all the vicissitudes of the Second World War and its cold-war aftermath. The Baltic States (Estonia, Latvia, Lithuania) gave in without a fight (who can blaim them) but even there the brief moment of independent, semi-democratic rule between the world wars seems to have been an unforgettable experience.

Antique precedents are not altogether relevant but they show that democracies, too, can be brought down by their own follies. The struggle between Athens and Sparta was largely a consequence of Athenian hubris and the after-effects *cf. 175; 271* highlight a tragic moment in the history of mankind.

> After the trauma of defeat in the Peloponnesian war (431–404 B.C.), Athens was at the end of its tether. An oligarchic junta took over the government and within one year put to death a massive seven per cent of the Athenian citizenry. After the restoration of democracy, Socrates touched a raw nerve with his inquisitive humanitarian scepticism and arrogantly refused to bend to a political compromise (Socrates had, after all, been the tutor of Critias, the leader of the oligarchs). Socrate's death sentence (399 B.C.) confirmed the prejudices of the common man and thereafter the sovereign electorate gave short shrift to any inconvenient ideas. Political and moral reform was rejected and redistributive provisioning of the citizenry became the foremost imperative for politic-ians. (Allowances for public duties had been introduced by Pericles in 461 B.C.)

Every sincere moral impulse should be utilized as a trigger for self-examination and renewal even and especially in the face of popular prejudice. Political truth cannot be but impermanent and contradictory; the revolutionary urge and its total denial appear to be equally destructive, equally anti-democratic.

> The fall of the Weimar republic is the most depressing example of modern democratic failure. During the 1920s, Weimar Germany was a hothouse of scientific and artistic bloom but it lacked entrenched respect for the prevailing rules of the political game; true democrats were few and far between. Under the dual assault of communism and world depression, the German middle classes fell back on tribal politics: fascism amply spiced with anti-Semitism. A wave of primitive resentment washed over the German people, sweeping it along in a surge of blind emotional self-gratification – in the end an exercise in compulsive self-destruction.

To repeat: if revolutions are indispensable they are impossible; the reign of *cf. 179* terror that justifies the revolution also prevents its practical realization. If revolution is possible, then it is unnecessary because the regime is then probably open to change through moderate political action. To preach revolution in a democracy is not a crime but for that very reason it is incorrigibly stupid.

6.4   Learning and unlearning

By and large, truth is not much in demand; the lie is deep within us, crying out for confirmation. The "sovereign people" is often mistaken and may be completely in the wrong. If man fails in finding any fault in himself, genuine learning will cease and mismanagement will play havoc with all his possessions, including the precious environment. Willy-nilly, the voter has to discern the important issues and learn to become a responsible citizen; otherwise, those in charge will never improve their play. Political democracy is the only societal framework worthy of man, but whether man measures up to this dignity remains an open question.

The lie within us

The Old Testament subsumes human history in a single, all-embracing theme: the struggle between the people of Israel and the will of God as attested in the various ups and downs of existential experience. The protracted Darwinian game of trial and error entered a new phase when the primitive tribal God of Abraham and Isaac was reshaped by the successive insights of inspired prophets. Every affliction and every tribulation was perceived as a painful revelation of God's true nature. The Lord's chosen people were no longer right by divine dispensation, but merely by virtue of their own conduct.

> From its inception, Protestant preaching and politics drew heavily on Old Testament imagery to steer the flock away from original sin. The congregation was edified with the Exodus from the Fleshpots of Egypt, the Adulation of the Golden Calf, the Promise of Milk and Honey in Canaan, the Depravity of the Babylonian Whore and the longing for a Resurrected Jerusalem. Merciless retribution was meted out against the Amalekites and the Philistines of the day while domestic policies were invariably castigated for laxity and licence.

The repeated scourges visited by Yahweh on the tribes of Israel are a warning to any people which believes it can manipulate its future at will. Very unpleasant lessons may be forgotten in just a few generations. "Have not I held my peace even of old, and thou fearest me not?" exclaims the exasperated Lord in the words of Trito-Isaiah. Lately, historical memory seems to have become ever shorter, as impatient voters are tempted by treacherous shortcuts to peace and security, prosperity and happiness.

The ordeals of economic depression are forgotten as soon as times improve; once again the delusion of the Midas touch becomes contagious. Nobody acquiesces in a position below average, and the inevitable frustration raises the general yammerschuning to full pitch.

> The common good is usually blurred and widely dispersed whereas personal interest is sharply focused and may, thanks to shady practices, come out on top. Lester Thurow (*The Zero-Sum Society*, 1980) and Mancur Olson (*The Rise and Decline of Nations*,

1982) castigate the propensity of well-organized pressure groups to obstruct economic renewal and extract concessions at the cost of the public interest. When society is split into factions, which all clamour for a bigger share of the cake or dig in to protect established positions, the outcome is stalemate in a tedious zero-sum game. Excessive deference to vociferous lobbyists is equivalent to the tyranny of minorities; every constructive move is blocked by cynical extortionists. The deadlock can only be broken by a major crisis which cuts through the web of interlocking myopic interests.

We must stop blaming difficulties on external factors, and acknowledge that the fault is ours. The "sovereign people" is often mistaken and may be completely in the wrong. Appreciation of our fallibility is a precondition for any democratic learning: pride goes before a fall. The blunt language of reality with all its negative feedback should be accepted and correctly interpreted. The bitter medicine must be swallowed and self-complacent doctrines dismissed.

So far nothing has surpassed the wave of self-deception which engulfed the European intelligentsia on the subject of the Soviet Union in the 1930s.

One after the other the members of the cultural élite made the pilgrimage to Moscow and reported enthusiastically on the workers' paradise. André Gide, an early defector from the communist cause, was never forgiven by the domestic comrades for his scathing criticism in *Retour de l'URSS,* 1936 (Return from the USSR). In England, the disillusioned Bertrand Russell was simply ignored but when the journalist Malcolm Muggeridge reversed his stand and began to disclose the depressing realities, he was immediately attacked by Bernard Shaw (1856–1950), the illustrious Webbs, and the rest of the intellectual establishment which loved to hate their own imperfect institutions. More recently, Maoist fellow travellers were almost as credulous; not even the revelations of the domestic rulers have been completely effective in wiping out the illusions. At the time of writing, only North Korea and Cuba remain as wobbling cult objects for this kind of perverse self-identification.

Unfortunately the credibility of information does not depend primarily on the supporting facts or rational reasoning; rather, it is a function of preconceived opinions and deep emotional needs. By and large, truth is in little demand. The lie is deep within us, crying out for confirmation.

The sources of wealth

Human acquisitiveness is omnipresent but the striving for personal wealth has generally resulted in ephemeral zero-sum games. If cunning, greed and inventiveness alone were sufficient, the time of plenty would have arrived long ago. Capital has certainly been shrewdly managed but money itself was mainly seen as a means to status and an easy life. The wealth of the Western world is due to a set of new rules for individual play, introduced in the sixteenth and seventeenth centuries by adherents of radical reformation.   *cf. 140; 143; 196*

Max Weber was the first to suggest a connection between economic growth and religious conviction. The Protestant ethic, particularly in its Calvinist moiety, renewed the rules of the economic game. A direct personal relationship with God excluded any easy path to grace; the burden of sin had to be alleviated by virtuous daily toil; idleness was the source of all evil; man was guilty until proven innocent. The destitute were dutifully taken care of but even charity was suspect since it might support vice and delay

the inevitable assumption of personal responsibility. A life of luxury was inadmissable as vanity and worldly pleasure cut men off from salutory merit. Weber himself puts it succinctly: "Catholics sleep well". Bad conscience drove Protestants into a virtuous circle of saving and reinvestment in new, profitable business. Bourgeois morality was
cf. 177
born of a prosperous middle class; modern capitalism was on the march.

Weber's thesis has been hotly debated since its inception early in the twentieth century but the evidence looks convincing, at least to the prejudiced eye. In these matters quantification is at best problematic. Even so, the pre-eminence of Nonconformists in general (and Quakers in particular) as agents of the industrial revolution has been validated beyond reasonable doubt. By 1770, the Nonconformists made up 41 per cent of English and Welsh entrepreneurs against a 7 per cent share of the population.

Catholic and Orthodox regions of Europe long retained an economically under-developed feudal structure while "merchant" religions like Jainism in India embraced many strikingly protestant maxims. Recently the new "tigers" of the
cf. 146
far East have achieved an impressive economic take-off, supported by a paternalistic Confucean value frame.

An authoritarian political system has kept consumers and unions on a short leash, encouraged a high savings rate and skewed the market economy in favour of fast growth. Step by step dirigiste policies are being cautiously dismantled and the political straitjacket seems to be coming off, too.

Marxism, for its part, carried the egalitarian elements of the Reformation to absurd lengths. The work ethic, which the Calvinists imposed upon themselves, was replaced by a concentration camp mentality; Protestant admonitions became dictates of the state – material wealth was elevated from a mere by-product of probity to the supreme value. Marxism seems to be surrogate Calvinism; its impact is in inverse proportion to the previous impregnation of
cf. 135
society with Calvinist convictions.

Dizzy with good fortune we are beginning to confuse the role of worker and consumer. Work is no longer a duty but consumption is an inalienable right. Millions of unemployed, particularly in Europe, bear witness to our very human tendency to enjoy today the living standard of tomorrow. Unless we unlearn these bad habits and reverse present trends, prosperity will slip through our fingers and we will relapse into material and spiritual poverty.

Spiritual pollution

The extensive division of labour has brought unprecedented wealth, but expert opinion is not helpful for solving the all-important problems of human conduct and human values. In the prevailing turbulence, it is extremely difficult for an enlightened opinion to find its bearings and make effective use of existing insights. The borderline between faith and knowledge is unclear, and the confusion is compounded by the pedlars of modish illusion – itinerant soothsayers, diviners and wonder-workers.

The back-to-nature call rings out at regular intervals in our culture. Many of our middle-class "greens" unconsciously imitate the aristocrats of seventeenth-century France, with their passion for the innocent rural idyll of youthful shepherds and pretty shepherdesses. The "biodynamic" battle-cry could have been coined by Maximilian Bircher-Benner (1867–1939), the health-food prophet of the 1890s; our food must once again be instilled with "live" energy; "chemical" fertilizers and pesticides are anathema; nature should be left to follow its own course with the possible assistance of hack and hoe. But when it comes to their own reproduction, ardent ecologists change tack and hypermodern biostatic drugs are suddenly all the rage. The biochemical intervention in the hormonal cycle of female ovulation seems to be no cause for concern; woman is deemed to be devoid of delicate balances.

Ecological problems apart, there is little proof of serious health hazards from the environmental "poisons" of popular campaigns. Compared to the self- *cf. 358* inflicted scourges of smoking and drinking, drug abuse and overeating, those extrinsic threats fade into insignificance. What is more, the problems of pollution are accessible to scientific analysis and remedy; and yet nostalgic and blinkered environmentalists go on battering at the superficial symptoms of a vaguely perceived menace. Meanwhile the insidious changes in the rules of inter-human play fail to attract any attention. Like the Pharisees of the New Testament we are overly concerned with the cleanliness of our external environment while complacently assenting to inward pollution.

> New sexual mores have been hailed as heralding the liberation of mankind, without the slightest concern for possible and even probable repercussions in all spheres of individual and community life. Only the advent of AIDS has somewhat tempered this flight *cf. 260* into irresponsibility.

Paradoxically, our deepest doubts are directed at what we have mastered best. The safety concerns about nuclear power plants assume hypochondriac proportions and tiny doses of radiation fill us with horror, but, without qualms, we expose our children to the hazards of a substandard school system. When it comes to the study of people and their relationships, belief in science ranging from psychiatry and pedagogy to penology and politology is still in vogue.

> The environmental disasters of Eastern Europe are an eloquent testimony to the perniciousness of scientific socialism which poisoned the human mind in the first place. The conceited manipulation of men is mirrored in a corresponding disregard for nature.

To public opinion, the well-charted rules of the atomic nucleus involve unforeseeable and unacceptable risks whereas tried and tested *Homo sapiens* is considered safe at all speeds. If man fails in finding any fault in himself, genuine learning will cease and mismanagement will play havoc with all his possessions, including the precious environment.

Corruption of language

Without access to free information and an open debate there can be no structured political opinion, but, as it happens, this opens the gates for any amount of misinformation, slander, vituperation or plain lying. The level of journalism cannot rise appreciably above its readership: gossip and scandal are at the heart of human interest. This dilemma was stated succinctly by an exasperated de

Tocqueville: "Nothing is worse than a free press – except, of course, censorship".

Many of democracy's political problems stem from difficulties in the transfer of knowledge. The whole apparatus of information theory can be mobilized to investigate the causes of interference in the communication process but this is to miss the core of the problem. The difficulty lies deeper: we do not want to call things by their proper names. Language is habitually distorted by intellectual *cf. 358* dishonesty, a fictional double-talk of deceit and self-deceit.

> The undeveloped countries have graciously been climbing the promotional ladder, first to reach underdeveloped, then less developed, and finally developing status. Meanwhile, all shades of brown are nowadays by common consent deemed black. The linguistics of reverse racialism is appropriating everyone with a few drops of "blood". Not only has the negro disappeared; gone are all the nuances of racial intermediates which correlate with our rich human environment. To top it off, indecorous race has been substituted with politically correct ethnicity.
>
> The covert suppression of diverging views reaches its peak when the medium is systematically perverted by totalitarian censors. *Pravda* (The Truth), the organ of the communist party of the Soviet Union, has probably told more and bigger lies than any other newspaper on earth. George Orwell had such ready models in mind when he constructed "Newspeak" in his *1984*, with its total falsification of reality, supported by schizophrenic "double-think". The corruption of the very vehicle of communication is tantamount to collective and continual brainwash. The widespread abuse of words such as "freedom", "science" and "democracy" was once the hallmark of totalitarian socialism.

Unfortunately, our much vaunted freedom of information is no guarantee against persistent misrepresentation. A bit of pure invention can become a journalistic myth, taking on a life of its own and will remain largely unaffected by all attempts to quash it.

> According to leading American news media (Newsweek, NBC), the nuclear bomb was dropped on Hiroshima by the much-decorated Major Claud Eatherly who was later driven insane by pangs of conscience. Although this story was later repudiated – the undecorated Eatherly merely took part in a reconnaissance flight – and a film of what really happened was shown on the cinema circuits, most people still "know" that the man who bombed Hiroshima ended up in an asylum.
>
> The almost consistently skewed recounting of the Vietnam War had deeper causes and more serious consequences. A sense of being on a wrong-headed mission coloured the reports of most journalists. There was general agreement within the profession that the just end of opposing an unjust war justified the foul means in the form of slanted stories, the mispresentative selection of facts and the glorification of the enemy.

While the United States has from time to time suffered slight informational indigestion, the Soviet Union was a case of prolonged constipation. Glasnost made all the amassed dirt public in one shocking shove. The sordid facts about communist rule, well-known in the West, certainly had a cleansing effect but could not fail to undermine the regime.

Immunological learning

The crude struggle for power has always been dressed up in insidious hype. Words such as demagogy, agitation, polemic and propaganda refer to such forms of semantic double-dealing, which must be properly recognized if we are not to submit altogether to linguistic vice. A free society suffers convulsions every time a new epidemic of oversimplifications and half-truths breaks out. When weary voters are promised easy solutions to complicated problems, previous exposure to infection usually generates a certain scepticism and mitigates the course of the disease. But only the immunity provided by a severe childhood bout ensures effective protection against subsequent contagion.

> Since the Second World War the staunchest supporters of pluralist democracy have come from the rank of former communists. Arthur Koestler, Ernst Reuter (1899–1953), Willy Brandt (1913–92), Mario Vargas Llosa, among many others, had acquired intimate knowledge of totalitarian tactics from the inside, and would not be fooled by revolutionary rabble-rousing or sidetracked into spurious alliances.

Alas, effective learning is principally born out of distressing failures: most democracies have at some point gone through a traumatic revolutionary experience. The successful Puritan revolution evidently inoculated the British mind against further adventures of this kind. The democratic heritage found its final expression in the American Declaration of Independence. Its balanced humanism contrasts sharply with the inflammatory verbiage at the peak of the French revolution. Despite a few relapses, the French have never again allowed themselves to be intoxicated to the same extent by empty phrases and Utopian battle cries.

> The Nazi apocalypse seems to have transformed the Western Germans into model democrats overnight, and the trauma of total defeat appears to have had the same edifying effect on the Japanese. Inevitably, the seductive dialectics of Marxism found fertile soil in countries like Russia and China, where the people lacked immune protection and were traditionally prone to pretentious word-magic. But the toxins of self-deceit slowly paralyze society and the longer a cure is delayed, the more degrading the state of convalescence will be.
>
> Once external coercion disappeared, the communist power structure in Eastern and *cf. 179* Central Europe was dismantled almost overnight. The new-fangled democracies may be in for a few nasty surprises. Consensus-building is not an easy task once the enthusiasm of liberation has receded. The immunological reaction against totalitarianism should at least be fairly strong and serve as a guardian of political health.

Respect for the rules of the language game is wholly voluntary: an adversary can never be forced to admit that he is in the wrong. If he concedes defeat, it is out of a sense of shared loyalty to some higher interest. The success of the democratic game ultimately depends on such self-restraint. We must be ready to consider not only the strength of the opponent's power base but also the point of his argument.

The prominence of a democracy depends on the quality of the electorate, gauged by its immunological resistance to infatuating falsehood. Trust in the judgment of ordinary people is the singularly democratic version of utopianism which is scornfully rejected by élitist and totalitarian ideologies alike. Their scepticism is quite understandable; practising rulers have always agreed that the people do not enjoy the confidence of the government. The truth is that political democracy is the only societal framework worthy of man, but whether man measures up to this dignity remains an open question.

6.5   Hazardous freedom

Democracy has always been a risky business; anarchy and dictatorship lurk in the shadows. The social experiment at present underway is the greatest gamble of all. Under the onslaught of value nihilism, more and more people opt out of the cultural coalition and concentrate on short-sighted self-gratification. But democracy is, least of all, an endorsement of care-free happiness; it is more of a tough exercise in hazardous free-dom. On the face of it, the democracies have gone from strength to strength but the rot is working into the intangible framework. We must reject beguiling self-complacency and try to regain a modicum of humili-ty as we grope for the life-saving if unpalatable truths about ourselves.

Mandala politics

Liberty is always at risk. No amount of democratic erudition can protect us from exterior threats in a world which we cannot and do not want to control. Agreements, proclamations and resolutions have never acted as effective deter-rents to potential aggressors, and never will. Thus, precautionary measures against foreign attack inevitably require moral and material expenditures. Ex-treme pacifism necessarily represents a vote of no confidence in our basic values, since the sacrifices of self-defence apparently outweigh the right to play our own game.

> A resolute stand on defence certainly need not conflict with a long-term policy of international understanding and creative interplay between nations, regions and cultur-es. On the contrary, such efforts lose credibility if launched from a position of weakness. In order to repulse external aggression we must restrain our self-seeking individualism and reinforce integrity with strength.

A parochial outlook is the direct consequence of the very existence of the nation state, which has to emphasize the demarcation between itself and the surround-ing world. Domestically, constant readjustment and compromise is imposed on people, but beyond the borders the pent-up self-assertion can find an outlet in gloating over the faults and setbacks of neighbouring countries. Chauvinism *cf. 170* has always been a reliable anodyne for the agonies of domestic politics, and we ought to be wary of the resurgence of this unfortunate addiction.

The democratic learning process tends to concentrate mainly on internal relationships. Education in foreign affairs is sorely neglected, and the most delicate moves are frequently based on a lamentable lack of understanding. The gist of international politics has always been a Machiavellian zero-sum game. In pre-colonial India the mandala cosmogram was the traditional guide to foreign policy.

> The mandala is a Buddhist symbol of the universe, normally a square figure embracing a series of concentric circles. At its centre lies the home kingdom surrounded by its "natural" enemies, all waiting for a suitable opportunity to grab a bit of territory for themselves. In the next ring of states are our enemies' enemies, who are thus our friends; on principle the next ring must again consist of hostile states, and so on. Even numbers mean friendship, odd numbers conflict.

Until recently, foreign policy in Europe was subject to mandala thinking. Each country saw the success of an adversary in any sphere as a defeat for itself. National self-conceit assumed paranoid proportions forcing us back time and again to the level of atavistic family feuding.

> Since the Second World War the great powers have continued to revel in this game – witness China's support for the Junta in Chile, or the Soviet Union's for Idi Amin in Uganda and Marcos in the Philippines. Meanwhile, the Western powers unblushingly vetoed the expulsion of the Khmer Rouge from the United Nations in order to annoy the Vietnamese and their Soviet backers. Now (1993) Pol Pot, the worst butcher of recent times, might be set for a comeback under the United Nations umbrella.

History leaves no room for doubt: lasting gains cannot be achieved in foreign affairs by mandala methods, however astute. Self-centred *realpolitik* simply leads to losses for each and everyone. And yet when practical decisions are called for, short-sighted zero-sum play and the perverted logic of the prisoner's dilemma has in general won out.

Chauvinism suppressed

Democratic states rarely indulge in aggression, and modern democracies have never fought each other (the Anglo-American conflict of 1812 was the aftermath of the struggle for independence and does not really count). Naturally, democracies often fall into the zero-sum trap but sometimes astonishing feats of foreign policy are fulfilled.

> The diplomacy of the United States since the Second World War has not always been distinguished by far-sighted acuity: the stumbling and mumbling has earned a good deal of discontent, especially among its natural partners in Latin America. And yet Germany and Japan, bitter but defeated enemies, were transformed into dependable, if a trifle too successful allies. Not so long ago the humiliating American withdrawal from Indo-China left the adversaries at one another's mercy. The North Vietnamese had not realized that the best thing which can happen to a country is to lose a war against the USA! At long last, the USSR was decorously faced down; its remnants and former clients are now expecting their due.
>
> Nor was there any precedent for the liquidation of the British Empire after the Second World War. The retreat was not a military necessity; indeed in some instances it may have been premature or even irresponsible. But Britain's colonies had become an economic liability, and the country's post-war governments certainly interpreted pop-

ular opinion correctly when they promptly wound the whole thing up. France suffered
serious seizures as a result of the wars in Indo-China and Algeria. It barely survived as a
democracy whereas the autocratic regime in Portugal manoeuvred itself into an impossible position and vanished together with its colonial empire.

Rigid mandala-type moves rarely bring a country anything but misery and
deepening mistrust. The exceptional successes of foreign policy such as the
Marshall Plan in Europe or General McArthur's rule in Japan can be explained
only by the overt or covert intrusion of idealism into the sober diplomatic game.
But such democratic naivety can also lead to heedless pacifism and defeatism, as
the protracted indulgence of Hitler's political power-play clearly proved.

Today, after a rare demonstration of plus-sum play in foreign affairs, Western Europe has passed irrevocably beyond internal feuding. The democratic
core of the European Community has drawn the autocratic countries of the
Mediterranean into its orbit, and the wave of democratization is now spreading
all over the continent.

> The failure of *divide et impera* policies vis-à-vis the Community and the emergence of a
> credible alternative to the drab communist rule greatly catalyzed political transforma-
> tion in Central and Eastern Europe. Human rights was a victorious battle cry and has
> carried the day, backed up by military and economic muscle. All nations in the area
> want to improve their humanist credentials to become an eligible member of the
> European Community of nations. Once membership in the coalition showed an attrac-
> tive payoff, its pull became irresistible and increased with every new partner.

A good coalition has ample room for cultural, ethnic, economic and even
political diversity. Then individual freedom, standards of living and outward
security all support each other in a democratic integration process. National
identity will not disappear: solidarity with a subgroup or with a broader community need not detract from authentic patriotism. But the absolute, sovereign
state is no more, and the old jingoistic myths will wither away from lack of
nourishment.

Global accord

Human solidarity has its origin in the family, the neighbourhood, the village or
the township and can, by degrees, be transferred to overarching structures. The
nation states have, historically, usurped a disproportionate share of our civic
allegiance. Common economic interests, political integration and converging
values are now pushing at least the countries of Western Europe towards a more
natural, intermediate position in the hierarchy of loyalties.

> The responsible citizen must, in any case, stay rooted within a surveyable commonalty:
> the self-styled "world citizen" is unaccountable and has actually absconded from his
> civic duties. Mankind as a whole could well serve as the ultimate frame of reference but
> "humanity" may once again become the ideal cover for totalitarian persuasions, which
> recently turned the "State" and the "Party" into execution machineries. After all, the
> French Jacobins let the guillotine loose in the name of enlightened humanity.

Many intellectuals react to the steep increase in the means of violence and destruction by seeking refuge in some universal political construct. Others have taken cover in a submissive stance along the lines of "better red than dead". This is not a viable policy as several million red and dead Khmers could testify; capitulation has never been a guarantee for survival.

> The town of Tallin in Estonia, once a member of the Hanseatic League, recognized a more durable principle when its citizens inscribed above the entrance to their town hall "Wer nicht kämpft, hat kein Recht", "If you do not fight, you have no right".

The idea of a world state must be approached with extraordinary caution. We cannot and should not organize away all causes of conflict. The right to quit a particular coalition is a basic human prerogative. There could hardly be a worse political alternative than an all-powerful regime presiding over a static global society. Even the longed-for stability is a utopian mirage. Revolts followed by destructive civil wars and a reign of terror would be the probable consequences of a global state, not to mention the exorbitant price which certainly would have to be paid for its formation in the first place.

> The United Nations has generally been ineffectual in handling even minor disturbances of the peace. The outstanding exception is the recent crisis in the Persian Gulf when the Iraqi dictator managed to enrage virtually the whole world. Just the same, it fell mainly to the United States to take on the shoot-out with the bad guy.

As the spectre of a nuclear holocaust recedes, at least temporarily, incessant population growth and environmental problems seem to cry out for a world-wide solution. Political union cannot be the answer: we have good reasons to shrink back at the thought of a global plebiscite, where the firmly established democracies would be outvoted by a wide margin.

> The position of the developed countries is analogous to the much vilified white minority in South Africa (Israel might offer a different and perhaps less provocative analogy). How to visit the rules of democracy on a highly divergent population? How to avoid the swamping of values and standards, of precious freedom by a hostile or, at best, unconcerned majority? How to stem the deluge of impoverished migrants who threaten to overrun the borders?

We should hold on to a wide degree of decentralization in global affairs. Every nation must in the long term pull its own weight and be answerable for its own follies – otherwise we will never learn. What we could and should aim for, at this juncture, is a loose but world-wide coalition of perhaps a dozen democratic superpowers or confederations in a state of self-disciplined collaboration. A new international order can never provide full coverage against catastrophe but it could give us a flexible, pluralistic arrangement, sorely needed for ecological co-operation and open to unlimited cultural evolution. Closer integration by a global government would presuppose exalted, extra-terrestrial goals for mankind, such as the systematic colonization of space.   *cf. 419*

Subliminal risk-taking

People often claim to be horrified at the supposedly unjustified risks involved in much of our technological and scientific culture. We are indulging in an orgy of risk-elimination; at every step we are supposed to upset some known or unknown ecological balance. Of course there are always hazards which can turn out to be treacherous, particularly if they are neglected. These issues obscure the really critical problems of human co-existence. We cheerfully introduce radical changes in the internal rules of our human games without the slightest regard for the long-term consequences. Under the onslaught of value nihilism more and more people opt out of the cultural coalition and concentrate on short-sighted self-gratification.

> The rules of the sexual game are a crucial part of any cultural heritage although – or perhaps because – they have never been fully observed. Christian morality does, after all, go against the grain of human nature. The much vilified "double moral" of most civilizations conforms to an obvious evolutionary logic. Adultery does not, on the whole, promote female procreation whereas masculine philandering comprises a free reproductive ride. A cuckold has, on the other hand, been defrauded of his potential progeny.
>
> Wit few qualms, we have let go of our social mores and destabilized the family. The insistence on immediate sensual gratification is supplemented by the negation of any accountability. Fathers are with impunity running away from their responsibilities while motherhood becomes an oppression in the name of women's liberation. We could expect our scientific institutions to present an analysis of the social and cultural consequences of such radical changes in the rules of the game. The task is exacting but should have the highest priority. So far, scientists have shown little inclination to address these problems by bringing anthropology, historiography, sociobiology and psychology to bear. Studies in the style of the Kinsey report are not without value but they are only a beginning. More than 40 years and billions of dollars later the accumulating piles of irrelevant documentation have added little to our understanding.

cf. 139

cf. 253

We still know next to nothing about the intricate interplay within human societies. Apparently we do not want to know, preferring to persist in our ignorance. Knowledge may mean power but in this context it also means self-examination, responsibility and emancipation – in sum, the need to make painful decisions.

Threatening hubris

Impressive breakthroughs in technology, economics and science have launched us on the greatest adventure in world history. Democracy remains a risky venture; anarchy and dictatorship always lurk in the wings. The social experiment at present underway is the greatest gamble of all. Personal freedom of opinion and conduct, once granted only to a few, is now the lot of the many, even of the majority in some advanced countries. But will it not all end in disaster? Aren't the very foundations of the cultural game threatened by the mass demand for off-the-peg pleasures, simplified truths and instant solutions?

> Indeterminate anxiety is an unavoidable element of modern life. Premonitions of danger are natural and necessary to survival: for Heidegger, for example, worry or care (*Sorge*

in German) are at the heart of existence. Lack of concern is a certain portent of ruin, a negation of the very principle of life. An unspecified bad conscience constantly seeks some means of expression, but in times of change and reorientation much existential angst is worked off in pointless hustle and hypochondriac fretfulness.

The particular hubris of democracy is to accept its own average as the measure of all things. At all costs, we try to externalize our home-grown problems, suppressing the inference that the worst threat comes from ourselves. No amount of risk avoidance can protect us from our narrow-mindedness and impercipience. True insight is always the result of hard-won experience: "no pain, no gain", as the body-builders say.

> The mutiny on the Bounty (in 1789, the year of the French revolution) was spectacular news at the time, and the story has been reinterpreted over and over again. The most interesting aspect is the ultimate fate of the mutineers, isolated from the rest of the world on Pitcairn Island together with a few Tahitian natives of both sexes. Christian, the mutiny leader, had introduced democratic decision-making among the white crew whereupon a majority decided, despite his opposition, to appropriate all the women for themselves. This naturally created a good deal of tension. Christian and some of his men were slain by the Polynesian men who, in turn, were killed off by the rest of the crew with the support of the native women.
>
> The next crisis was caused by an innovation. A strong drink was produced from sweet potatoes by fermentation and distillation. All the men, except one named Young, abandoned themselves to excessive drinking. The women and children had to manage on their own, and finally withdrew altogether from the male community. As a result of internal fighting, accidents, delirium and clashes with the combative women, all the men died except Young and one of the drunkards called Smith. The two survivors destroyed the still and adopted a well-ordered life based on a mixture of biblical teaching and common sense. By the time the American whaler Topaz visited Pitcairn Island in 1808, Young had been dead for some years, and Smith was found ruling a happy extended family, teeming with small Christians, Youngs and Smiths.
>
> The Pitcairn experiment shows the democratic dilemma in a nutshell. In this particular case the abrupt sharing of power brought a disproportionate sacrifice; the survivors prevailed only by the skin of their teeth.

The learning capacity of democratic nations has exceeded all predictions, but our expectations, the list of what we regard as our inalienable rights, always seem to outgrow the gross national product. As demands on society continue to break all bounds, the existential yammerschuning reaches a climax. The most pathetic whine comes from a Swedish social democrat: "Our form of society has failed, since it has not made people happy".

Democracy is, least of all, an endorsement of carefree happiness; it is, rather, a tough exercise in hazardous freedom. In the end, you can only blame yourself – a most unhappy condition. Responsibility and discipline are not imposed from the outside; we rely solely on a broad framework of internally generated rules for political process. This machinery cannot create values, it can only channel them. The presumption that democratic rule in itself commands creativity or guarantees social and cultural progress is a dangerous illusion. The real content and meaning of the political game springs from deeper sources.

> In a remarkable study, *Making Democracy Work* (1992), Robert Putnam (with Robert

cf. 268; 273
0

Leonardi and Raffaella Nanetti) has tried to lay bare the grounds of good (and bad) government in the self-governing regions of Italy. After disproving all the fashionable causes – economic development, consensus politics, educational level, urbanization – he comes up with ordinary civic virtues as the only tenable reasons for the regional differences. Active interest in community affairs, mutual trust, tolerance – fair play for short – seems to be the necessary and sufficient precondition for a social plus-sum game. The pattern of "civicness" can be traced back to the city republics of the thirteenth century. Self-government is indeed a long learning process.

On the face of it, the democracies have gone from strength to strength but the rot is working into the intangible framework. Distrust of and disgust with politics and politicians has assumed alarming proportions; the electorate is becoming increasingly alienated from the political decision-making process. The impending threat must be tackled at a higher meta-political level. We ought to reject the incessant coddling of the media who consistently cater to our self-sufficiency. Instead we should try to regain a modicum of humility as we each grope for the life-saving if unpalatable truths about society and ourselves.

6.6   A new democratic institution

To facilitate the outrageously slow learning process, we need a new democratic institution – statutory Economic Institutes which would provide a dependable audit for the electorate. Their task would be to elucidate cause and effect in the economic game while preaching the simple gospel of practical praxeology and financial rectitude. We should not overestimate the effect of such thoughtful argument on the minds of a rather inconstant electorate. At least, the Economic Institutes could keep political windbags and racketeers at bay, providing more elbow room for sincere reformers.

Misguided voters

Elected office-holders are always subject to criticism; it is impossible to please everybody all the time. The government is constantly suspected of misrepresentation or outright deception. The public, understandably, resents being treated as ignorant election fodder, but we risk undermining the very basis of political authority and legitimacy with our democratic cantankerousness. We have only ourselves to blame when we repeat the same economic mistakes over and over again in slightly different guises. If we do not get our act together and try to improve the rules of the game, the democratic learning process will grind to a halt.

Democracy's weakest point is the election process, in which moral lightweights of all denominations often have a clear advantage. Whenever the voters cannot evaluate the effects of their verdict, the circuit of self-regulation breaks down for lack of well-considered feedback. The electorate deserves the best available information when called upon to form an opinion about their elected masters. Taxation, for instance, is an eternal political battleground where objective truth regularly suffers defeat. A bit of cool, scientific investigation would come in handy in keeping the citizens abreast of the acrimonious argument.

> There might be room for some new ideas even in this time-honoured traffic. How about a computer-calculated tax liability allowing for health, intelligence, age, education, maintenance obligations and inherited wealth? Earnings above the norm would then be tax-free. Extended loss of income due to unemployment, accidents and so on, could be covered by appropriate insurance policies. Perhaps high tax liability could even become a distinguished status symbol, rather like a golf handicap!

Maximum impartiality in the interpretation of complex reality can be achieved by introducing authoritative and independent expert bodies into the political process. To build on the pertinent but, admittedly, very soft sciences would appear to be ill-advised, to put it mildly (see sections 7.3–5). A bold approach might, nevertheless, be the smaller risk. To avert the danger of a slow demise we have to enter a higher-order learning process. Close interaction with practical problems should, anyway, serve to deflate at least scientific, if not political arrogance.

Trustworthy and apolitical Economic Institutes organized on national or regional lines would be a natural first step in such a strategy. The economic consequences of important bills and executive measures should be critically evaluated by the Institute on a statutory base. Political decision-making would thus benefit from access to the best available information. The voters, for their part, would have some solid grounds for assessing government policies.

Samaritans and free riders

There is a plethora of pressing economic problems lying in wait for the Economic Institutes. The demand for low price (or no price) public services is ever expanding, putting national and local budgets under severe strain everywhere. The problem is how to engage profit-seeking business in education and health maintenance. The insurance principle could certainly be applied here in more imaginative ways.

cf. 210

> The success of fire-insurance depends on precluding disasters by investing in preventive measures – installing fire detectors and sprinklers, improving processes, procedures and the attitude of the workforce. Similarly, health insurance should, regardless of the paymaster, be coupled to a life-long effort to preserve the health of the insured. Cost-effective medical examinations could support judicious self-medication, minimizing expensive hospital care. The greatest challenge would be to induce healthy habits and keep people from smoking, overeating, overdrinking and so on. The whole arsenal of the public relations and sales promotion community would be at the disposal of profit-making insurance companies – if they are prepared to take up the gauntlet. (In the USA, rapidly expanding health maintenance organizations (HMOs) seem to be on the right track.)

Besides educational and health policies, social welfare cries out for in-depth analysis which, nonetheless, is very thin on the ground. One reason may be that such attempts are bound to run into deep waters. Most difficult to assess is the impact on human meta-motivation, our rather overtaxed sense of civic duty.

Both political and moral reasons compel us to channel some of our affluence into underprivileged sectors of the electorate. But fundamental rules of fairness are overturned when material gifts are granted without reciprocity. Outside the immediate circle of family and friends, the recipient is placed in a false position. The end-result is the well-known resentment towards the donor – the Samaritans' dilemma.

cf. 231
> In workaday politics, the same mechanism works in constructive fashion. "Political debts" incurred during, say, electioneering must sooner or later be honoured, lest the fragile structure of political collaboration fall asunder.

When income transfers are conducted on a massive scale, the effects can be very serious and wide-ranging. Many recipients of social support feel that their human dignity and self-esteem is threatened by their becoming "a burden on the public". Unfortunately, an increasing number are overcoming these culturally conditioned inhibitions, and establish themselves as free riders while the growing social welfare establishment happily exploits its expanding market.

> Man does not have an inborn craving to work, although several of his innate impulses can be successfully exploited as work incentives. Regular daily labour appears to be specific to high cultures in general and to Western, Calvinist-inspired economies in particular. From primary school onwards, our children are (or have at least been) drilled in the elementary rules of work discipline. The entire system of upbringing and education is aimed at accustoming people to work, by making the available rewards conditional upon good performance. These fundamental norms keep the economic machinery running, and have generated unprecedented abundance.
>
> A social benefit, however justified, is a disincentive for the individual and may turn into a welfare trap. Eventually the free ride becomes a way of life. Every advantage is squeezed out of the commonality by the disoriented and disillusioned members of the B-team. Occasional earnings originate in the "black" economy, untouched by the taxman; outright crime is the logical end-station. The spread of such parasitism must, in time, bring the hapless host organism to its knees.

cf. 225 Strangely enough, it is less demoralizing to be regularly compelled to sacrifice a large portion of an honest income than it is to command unearned resources – be it public assistance, inherited wealth or a pools win. On a national level, the same can be said of large-scale aid to poor countries. When vulnerable groups are exposed to the international relief system, the end result may be the wholesale destruction of a culture.

> The huge refugee camps which absorbed dislocated Somalis from the 1970s onward severely undermined social values and have certainly contributed to Somalia's self-destruction. Once a nomadic tribe has become entangled in the deceptively secure and comfortable meshes of camp life, voluntary return to the barren and uncertain livelihood of the semi-desert becomes highly improbable.
>
> The resilient pockets of poverty in the big American cities present a similar stand-off. The ghetto culture has admirably adapted itself to public welfare. In the year 1987, 75 per cent of black babies in the inner cities were born out of wedlock. The roving underemployed men are haphazardly procreating while sponging on their latest live-in

partner who tenaciously trades upon her single parent status. Hardly a luxurious existence but a life-style which is perpetuating itself.

The solution to these problems is obviously way beyond standard economics. Non-profit making organizations working on very tight budgets have, in all respects, proved superior to government in managing human rectification.

> The churches and congregations; the Red Cross; the Salvation Army; the Boy Scouts; the AA movements – all depend on charitable contributions and the voluntary service of unassuming progress dynamos, stiffened by a paid skeleton staff (incidentally, the political parties depend on similar volunteering for their indispensable grassroots work). Success seems to depend on the proper identification of and attendance to a "market" which ensures the complementary interaction of benefactors and beneficiaries in a worthwhile plus-sume game.
>
> Peter Drucker tells us in *The New Realities* (1989) that in Florida, first sentence criminals are put into the custody of the Salvation Army. Three out of four are rehabilitated while actual imprisonment produced a 75 per cent failure rate. The Girl Scouts of the USA could point to similar results when it stepped up its activities in the inner-city ghettoes.

Some measure of reprocity, help to self-help, work or training, introduces an element of genuine exchange and avoids the emasculation of self-respect and personal initiative. To break the chains of fraudulent dependence is, at any rate, a formidable challenge to democratic societies.

Societal simulation

The time should now be ripe for the next development in our political game. A universal economic science must be modest however when it comes to practical application. General futurology is equally powerless, lacking a firm scientific basis. We should therefore seek to establish a new type of democratic institution, capable of acquiring profound insights into the economic game and related societal interactions.

Apart from the direct cost-effectiveness of any measures suggested, the proposed Economic Institutes will also have to consider the socio-economic repercussions. This is a daunting, meta-scientific task which can be mastered only as a slow, unpretentious learning process. Sweeping success is not on the cards; the economic game seems to be quite intractable even and especially in the short or medium term.

> The play of economics has many similarities with meteorology. There is a good chance that tomorrow's weather will not differ from today's. This primitive prognostication can be improved upon and the forecast horizon pushed a few days ahead by mobilizing ever-increasing amounts of input data and computer power. But strong non-linearities soon induce chaotic behaviour in the atmosphere, overwhelming every conceivable analytic tool. In principle, the wingbeat of a butterfly could, within a year, influence the global weather. Even so, some predictable pattern of rain and drought may be impressed upon the atmosphere; the el Nino oscillation is presently under intense investigation.   *cf. 61*

Short-term economic fluctuations exhibit chaotic unpredictability which is further aggravated by the effects of omnipresent forecasting. Partially chaotic systems may nonetheless be subject to an inherent long-range logic. By identifying a few deep variables we may be able to influence the economic climate and understand how it is forced in certain directions, regardless of the fluctuations of the economic weather.

The Economic Institutes ought to focus on practical problems and take a holistic perspective so as to get hold of a self-perpetuating learning curve. In the long haul, the aspiration would be to build a rudimentary but reliable simulation model of society, successively improving its powers of prediction; at best it could help in averting impending calamities.

> The distorted balance between individual rights and obligations will soon give rise to severe instabilities in our democratic polities. The rich tend to cluster in privileged districts or tax-havens while the poor adamantly insist on unearned income. Furthermore, the middle-aged are shamelessly pushing the burden of escalating public debt and high pensions on subsequent generations, not to speak of the cumulating ecological problems. To avoid the crisis, citizens must in concrete terms accept their debt to society, regardless of their whereabouts. No rights should, on the other hand, be established just by moving into a country as a refugee or otherwise.
>
> The onslaught of false play can be stemmed only by reintroducing inclusive economic feedback in individual decision-making. Pension and insurance instalments must increasingly be paid by the beneficiaries themselves. Students should bear the real cost of their education, and the parental investment in children must be properly recognized. A comprehensive analysis of the available options is urgently needed. If we do not tie citizens to the long-term consequences of their actions they will just walk away from their obligations. In the end, we will all go down in an orgy of irresponsible minus-sum machinations.

A penetrating economic analysis may offer durable solutions to quite refractory political problems. Above all, it should help to identify unavoidable uncertainties whilst reducing the attraction of political bargain sales that seduce the voter with bare-faced appeals to immediate self-interest. We could even envisage a regular audit of the public stewardship at intervals corresponding to the electoral mandate. The main purpose of the Institute would be to improve the transparency of the political process, the final decisions will always be left to the politicians.

Despite strenuous efforts to achieve impartiality, the links with superordinate game levels would remain problematic. The dilemma is that although an Economic Institute should beware of party politics, complete value-freedom would rob its work of any practical relevance. One expedient would be to define clearly the frame of reference for the particular economic game – a route that cf. 56 unfortunately is vitiated by almost intractable inconsistencies.

> cf. 412 The most favourable outcome for the largest possible number of coalition members is a maxim which comes close to the notion of Pareto-optimality. This version of utilitarianism, as developed by Jeremy Bentham (1748–1832) and John Stuart Mill (1806–73), is just one flattened projection of the current fuzzy and partly contradictory value frame. It reflects an expedient compromise of moral philosophy, and is no political panacea. As the weak and wretched tend to be neglected we hasten to put Darwinism into reverse and supplement Benthamism with an arbitrary dose of strictly egalitarian ideology. The

restrictions imposed will immediately circumscribe the opportunities for individual play, and may severely repress the productive self-realization of a gifted minority.

Explicit norms for political decision-making are likely to be misleading or downright repressive. A precarious, dynamic balance can be achieved only in the contest between competing and partially contradictory value systems. In the best of circumstances, the wide range of opinion contained in a democratic society merges into a complementary consensus, which provides a starting-point for collective problem-solving and would serve as an implicit value frame for the Institutes.

Promising knowledge

A number of existing organizations obviously cherish aspirations along the lines indicated. But the Economic Institutes should not be just another set of think-tanks. Besides the long-term build-up of practical experience and close links with enlightened sections of the electorate, such bodies require the authority pertaining to official status. At present the politicians can choose freely among countless instant prophets – political hucksters in economic garb who confidently deliver diagnoses and prognostications for all seasons. In the hullabaloo, the quiet voice of true knowledge is barely audible and the genuine expert has little chance of making his modest but valuable contribution to the democratic decision process.

> As guardians of the value of money, central banks would be natural seats for Economic Institutes. Monitoring the economy is anyhow part of their commission and some of them are already on the leading edge of economic research. The International Monetary Fund has, indeed, taken upon itself some of the duties of the proposed Institutes by policing the weakest economies and acting as a scapegoat for unpopular measures. (The proposed forerunner to a European central bank is called the European Monetary Institute – a sign in the sky?)

The nucleus of an Economic Institute must consist of eminent researchers, either co-opted or nominated by apolitical bodies. Membership of an Institute should represent the highest accolade of a professional career. It might seem tempting to let Institutes sit in judgement on politicians, calling them to account for inflation, tax increases or economic abuse. This would run counter to its role as a purely factual expert body. The electorate is the only arbiter of political conduct; in the end the Institute can earn the confidence of the people only within its own relatively narrow and clearly defined sphere of activity.

The Institutes should not be above criticism; on the contrary, objectivity and credibility are their only capital. There can be no question of monopolizing either economic expertise or the forecasting function. Institutes would simply represent statutory sources of economic comment, enjoying the trust of the electorate. They should at least free us from the talking heads who have cornered our talk-worn economic debate.

> While half-witted economic prescriptions for the political ills of society gain ample publicity, serious suggestions in the spirit of the proposed Institutes are passed over in

silence. In the wake of the student rebellion of the late 1960s, James Buchanan (*Academia in Anarchy*, 1980 with Nicos Devletoglou) has presented a comprehensive programme for reforming university education by the consistent application of simple praxeological rules. Education as a free commodity would be replaced by a price-governed marketplace, where excellence and efficiency are the common aims of teachers and pupils. The ultimate in economic rationality would be to give the educational institutes a stake in the future of their students, collecting small "dividends" from successful pupils throughout their working life. Alas, in education we are still wallowing in socialism.

An authorized investigative agency stands or falls by the relevance of the knowledge it commands. Academic qualifications are of little or no help against the healthy scepticism of pragmatic constituents. It may be doubtful whether economics has achieved a level of understanding which conduces to self-generating empirical learning, but at least a dependable analysis of current techno-economic problems should be feasible.

> Petrol-driven vehicles must, eventually, be phased out but electric cars are hampered by heavy and expensive batteries. Electric power could, however, be supplied continuously to cars by conduits embedded in the tarmac of the chief roads and expressways. The new infrastructure would necessitate some careful planning and a clear political decision to achieve the necessary system change – food for thought within Economic Institutes.

In any case, the economic field provides an attractive opportunity for testing the Institute idea. The combination of high social priority, an enormous database, and scientific erudition should, within the framework of an integrated institution, result in cumulative advances in our understanding of the game. A stream of meaningless pronouncements would, on the other hand, swiftly dispatch the pseudo-scientists back to their ivory towers.

Buckminster Fuller (1895–1983) once declared that the mark of real knowledge is that it can be utilized in improving a machine. The integration of economic expertise into the political machinery is thus a timely challenge and a natural development of democracy. If the economic experiment turns out well, other officially sanctioned brain trusts could be established to scrutinize the rules of the social coalition.

> The economic school of "public choice", pioneered by Warren Nutter, James Buchanan and Gordon Tullock, is trying to extend the principles of economic exchange (catallactics) and a rational *Homo economicus* to the analysis of democratic politics. One explicit aim is to prescribe improvements in the constitution by deft "political engineering", and thereby to optimize the politico-economical plus-sum game. The basic approach is to economize on the scarcest commodities, which are civic virtue and good will – "love" in general.

cf. 262; 273

We should not overestimate the effect of thoughtful argument on the minds of a rather inconstant electorate. Even so, our best if not our only hope lies in the power of attested knowledge over open-minded and concerned citizens. The new democratic institution could at least keep windbags and wise guys at bay, providing some room for sincere reformers. This is a necessary and maybe sufficient condition for the healthy development of the political game.

6.7   Meta-rules of the democratic game

Democratic meta-rules are imbued with an awareness of human fallibility, the fragility of institutions and the limitations of even the greatest statesmen. The real struggle for power is decided not on the political platform but in people's hearts and minds. There our values compete, there the cynic and the progress dynamo fight for supremacy – a troubled conscience is the most important prerequisite of democracy. The rules of the market economy and of political democracy reveal a remarkable congruity; the meta-rules of the self-organizing market game are a crude projection of fundamental democratic values. This supports the conclusion that modern democracy is a good model – perhaps the only one – for a sustained human plus-sum game.

The social coalition

The high and mighty have always tended to regard commoners as an exploitable resource. In contrast, a democratic society supplants crude power play with the inalienable rights of the individual, derived from the Christian concept of human value. Before God, all souls are equally valuable: the citizen thus transcends his instrumental utility as a mere subject.

> Everyone born into a modern democracy has become a member in a solidary social coalition, happily equipped with an enviable array of prerogatives. The obligations are usually restricted to tax liability for the prosperous, and at least the prospect of conscription in an emergency. While autocratic societies are held together by physical and psychological compulsion, the democracies rely on self-control by the intermittent feedback of the citizenry. All political conflicts should find a civil resolution in the context of such circular cybernetics.

The cornerstone of democratic society is a general belief in the ability of the individual, the family, the company, the city or the region to look after its own affairs. A set of minimum standards throughout society may be politically desirable, but the enforcement of all those "rights" can lead to administrative elephantiasis and orgies of cheating. This again entails an unacceptable degree of official supervision which clutters and clogs the mechanisms of government.

> The principle of subsidiarity has been unanimously accepted by the European Community, but will time and again be called into question both by the central bureaucracy and by articulate spokesmen for underprivileged groups. If the United States can be taken as a precedent, the pressure will be well-nigh irresistible. In Europe, though, old-fashioned nationalism and newly-awakened regionalism provide formidable counterforces which may yet save the day – if they do not blow up the prospective Union for good.   *cf. 228*

In democracies, opinions cannot be forced on people; they have to be sold amidst harsh competition. The customer profile is the decisive factor. If the consumers of the political message are ignorant or reckless, they will be bent on bad quality and buy defective policies.

> Shrewd appeals to factional interests represent the most insidious threat to the democratic polity. In the worst case, the voluntary social coalition splinters into mutually hostile syndicates. The pressure groups encroach on the rights of elected government, seizing the available funds of loyalty and undermining the capacity for compromise. In the end, ruthless group egoism destroys the keystone of all democratic collaboration, namely the agreement on the handling of disagreement.

In well-behaved democracies, riding roughshod over fairly small, respectable (or even less respectable) minorities is not considered good form. Secondary problems such as language policy are always accessible to solution, but fundamental convictions involving personal freedoms and rights can run on a destructive collision course. The Civil War in the United States (1861–65) seems to have been unavoidable even with the benefit of hindsight.

Voluntary political integration is a very time-consuming business, as the countries in the European Community have found to their cost. Democratic order is based on mutual respect, and must be allowed to expand slowly and organically, otherwise the political game degenerates into internal coercion and external empire-building.

> Despite the considerable cultural similarities between Sweden and Norway, the enforced political union of the two sister nations in 1814 caused so much ill-will on the Norwegian side that it was dissolved in 1905, after almost a hundred years of internal squabbling. If Sweden had taken to arms, this animosity would certainly have been aggravated and the inflamed situation could have become permanent. Today, there is a neighbourly relationship but political merger appears possible only in a broader European context.

Every country is subject to the challenge of change which, in the fullness of time, will expose even the proudest pillars of the political establishment. Free elections are important implements but, given the opportunity, people eagerly vote with their feet.

> The puncturing of the East German perimeter by way of Hungary in May 1989 was the beginning of a modern Völkerwanderung which in no time deflated the communist command. The haemorrhage of competent segments of the population generally bodes ill for society, albeit usually with a longer time lag.

Skilled as well as unskilled workers have always been responsive to wage differentials. Nowadays taxation, educational facilities, public order and the quality of the environment, too, weigh heavily when youngish professionals are settling down. Attracting the right kind of people (while dissuading the free riders) will become a key concern, not only for competing companies, but for communities and countries as well. This should be all for the good, since it will introduce a semblance of market feedback to the largely unaccountable public sector.

cf. 209; 275 The political reaction to the excesses of the welfare state has been slow in coming. New Zealand offers the most audacious example of the painful deconstruction process ahead. Successive governments of both the left and the right have consistently pushed deregulation and cut subsidies, reinforcing the market mechanism in the teeth of bitterly opposed interest groups.

In any coalition an increase in numbers will add to the potential gains but it also puts more strain on internal relations: the demand for "love" rises with the expansion of the polity. Growth means increasing complexity and more oppor- *cf. 156; 225* tunities for cheating and corruption. The only antidote to foul play is ardent decentralization, even at some cost to purely economic efficiency. The dispersion of power will ensure fewer but better rules for the political game, economizing on the precious commodity of "love".

Political fallibility

Feeling safe in the bosom of their tried and tested institutions, democracies, on principle, allow everything that is not specifically forbidden. Democratic societies thus enjoy maximum room for political manoeuvre. They may even decide to disenfranchise themselves by entering a compulsory socialist or fascist coalition. Unfortunately, aberrations of this kind are generally irreversible; liberty is easily forfeited. We may have acquired some immunity to those contagions but other fallacies lie in wait.

> The market principle is shamelessly applied to the value system which becomes heavily discounted – almost anything goes. A growing segment of the population eschews all civic duties, and kills time in blatant self-gratification only to complain bitterly of existential frustration. Eventually this exhaustion of intangible production factors will severely reduce the economic payoff, whereupon the blame will promptly be laid at the politicians' door.

Time and again we have seen brand-new democracies sink into a morass of *cf. 240* corruption, until they fall to the assaults of tribal egoism, party dictatorship, or military take-over. Could this also be the fate of countries which have enjoyed a long tradition of democracy? What would happen if a coalition of the non-productive – the students, pensioners, social welfare clients etc. – began to exploit their majority power at the expense of a hard-working minority? How would such a destabilized society react to extremist provocation? Must we brace ourselves for social convulsions, or will we perhaps fade away quietly as the bureaucrats provide for us from cradle to grave?

> The city state of Athens between 500 and 300 B.C. is a well-documented case of the rise and fall of a democracy. The lesson merits the attention of modern democrats. The terminal stage was reached around 320 B.C. when the all-powerful popular assembly voted in favour of equal pay for any service performed on a public body. This meant *cf. 249* that a substantial part of the population lived on welfare, in return for nominal participation in the affairs of state. Despite their remarkable artistic achievement and philosophical self-reflection, the Athenians were unable to see through the tangle of day-to-day politics and to get to grips with the core of their problem – the self-indulgence of the common citizen. This curse still haunts democratic rule everywhere. Ironically, the Greek predicament looks particularly grim.

In an affluent democracy money tends to lose its political potency although income and wealth remain important indicators of social position, and provide sanctuaries for independent opinion. Not so in conditions of ingrained poverty. In the developing countries, economic and political progress has repeatedly come to grief due to the resistance of crony capitalists and a bloated bureaucracy.

> In *The Other Path* (1989) Hernando de Soto describes how grassroot entrepreneurship is bogged down by vicious overregulation. To comply with all the procedures for the lawful registration of a modest, non-incorporated garment business in Lima (Peru), the proprietor has to approach the Ministry of Industry four times and the City Council twice while the ministries of Labour, Economy and Health as well as the Peruvian Social Security Institute are content with only a single supplication. In a field test, bribes were asked for on ten occasions; on two occasions the undercover agent had to pay up. In Peru, the adjudication of state-owned wasteland for building purposes takes 43 months of administrative paper shuffling in 48 government offices; the final building permit requires another 40 months of bureaucratic wrangling. Small wonder that a growing segment of the population opts for informal economic activities.

Democratic meta-rules are imbued with an awareness of human fallibility, the fragility of institutions and the limitations of even the greatest statesmen. The essence of democracy is enshrined in the small print; the judicial process and a punctilious polling procedure.

> The US congress has been a model for parliaments, especially in the Western hemisphere, but elections south of the Rio Grande have been rigged more often than not. In the United States too, the fairness of the electoral process has been wanting and is still the cause of much agonizing. The rules for campaign spending and financing become ever stricter while the air is thick with accusations of undue influence and outright bribery. The ethical guidelines for members of congress and the administration are certainly the strictest in the world; yet the struggle goes on and on to keep the head of the nation above the rising tide of corruption.

Easy optimism must be rejected. Our self-confidence must be moderated by scepticism and, yes, humility. Despite all its checks and balances, democracy is certainly not an automatic progress machine or a fail-safe insurance policy. Rather it is a vehicle for diverse values; its strength lies in an incessant concern for the cohesion of the coalition, in anxiety mitigated by a sense of mission. The basic rules are rather stable but, in a severe crisis, the polity has to reappraise the criteria for fair play by rallying to a common faith.

Crises of conscience

Whatever the mechanism, challenges will come from within or without. They may be ignored or concealed but, in the end, the ordeals cannot be avoided, however hard we try to deny or disregard the fundamental uncertainty of life. If the worst comes to the worst, tolerance must be temporarily set aside; democracies can be second to none in resolute ferocity.

> Geneva in the sixteenth century was a democratic city of God, somewhat in the style of the Iran of the Ayatollahs. The Calvinist faith was deemed infallible, and so every transgression of the precepts of the Bible, as interpreted by the Church Elders, was liable to the severest punishment. In the eighteenth century the city became a refuge for dissidents, but as late as 1602, when the Duke of Savoy laid siege to the town, the City

Council set aside democratic procedure to keep the citizens in line. Anybody who even suggested negotiations with the enemy was to be punished by summary disembowelment. *cf. 241*

In the face of an overwhelming external threat even democrats will toe the line, but democratic societies are not normally prone to excess even in self-defence. Political antagonists are free to blacken one another's reputations; the rough personal infighting takes place in the pitiless glare of publicity. Secretiveness is anathema, as it is deemed to indicate collusion against the public interest. Tough debate in a rich atmosphere of value pluralism is the sometimes foul breath of democratic life. Eccentric or downright destructive players are handled patiently and with kid gloves. The consequences of the present permissiveness are rather disturbing, to say the least.

> Tax dodging and benefit scrounging has become an art in the developed countries. Increasingly, drug addiction coupled to plain criminality is becoming a way of life. Public opinion is aghast but lacks proper guidance. The cultural establishment excels in futile hand-wringing while applying every conceivable argument to extenuate the free trips.

Ultra-liberalism ends in the abrogation of all the rules of the game – the antithesis of democratic freedom. By pushing the pleasure principle to unprecedented lengths we jeopardize the very foundation of a free society. In the words of Edmund Burke (1729–97), "men are qualified for civil liberties in exact proportion to their disposition to put moral chains upon their appetites." *cf. 420* *cf. 262; 268*

We must always brace ourselves for inevitable sacrifices lest we lose everything we possess. Tax money is not enough; other more precious inputs are required: moral courage, social service, maybe even life itself. We generally exhibit a craven aversion to shouldering responsibility when free-riders ought to be rebuked or contumacious coalition members censured. Endless indulgence is equivalent to moral cowardice, a refusal to distinguish between right and wrong.

> Italy's rather shaky institutions were incredibly feeble in dealing with the Mafia which, despite recent setbacks, still takes its heavy toll in the Mezzogiorno. As with economic ills, action was postponed until the very last minute when an electoral reaction changed the rules of the game. In Japan, too, the Yakuza (the local Mafia) has bought off many politicians who seem unable to clean up their own backyard. Now both Italy and Japan seem to be heading for a sea-change in political culture.

The real struggle for power is decided not on the political platform but in people's hearts and minds. There our values compete; there common cause is weighed against party politics; and there the cynic and the progress dynamo fight for supremacy. A willingness to put aside personal priorities, a receptivity to the signals of a higher-order game – in short a troubled conscience is the most important prerequisite of democracy.

Democratic despotism

The anarchist ideal is to abolish politics by leaving human interplay to be directed solely by market forces, ameliorated by the supposedly inexhaustible altruism of man. Confirmed democrats have generally been sceptical of such utopianism; politics and even morals can in fact be understood as a reaction to blatant market failures. "What is government itself but the greatest of all reflections on human nature" was the joint exclamation of Messrs. Hamilton, Madison and Jay (in *The Federalist*, 1787). And they went on: "The passions of men will not conform to the dictates of reason and justice without constraint". Neither did the founding fathers of the United States exhibit trust in the innate benevolence of magistrates, and they took considerable precautions to guard their fellow-citizens against power-hungry politicians and an entrenched bureaucracy.

The conditioned reflex of a politician is to expand the room for his political play at the expense of impartial market forces. The self-interest of every bureaucracy is, likewise, to increase its grip on society. Ultimately the cost of government may exceed the benefits and disintegration will be overdue.

> A business empire has lost its viability when the parts are more valuable than the integrated company. The head office is then directing a minus-sum game and will be obliterated by bankruptcy or a hostile take-over. The same logic is at work in the dissolution of political empires. The blows of external enemies never sufficed to destroy a great power like China, but an inept and overgrown bureaucratic superstructure has repeatedly crushed the Celestial Empire under its deadly weight. The same cancerous affliction, exacerbated by a steadily growing proletariat on the dole, was probably the bane of Rome, west and east. The downfall of the Mayas is still a mystery but one may surmise a similar chain of events leading to the evaporation of the societal plus-sum.

cf. 143; 163; 192; 225

cf. 229 Salvation by society has for almost a century been the tacit catchphrase of democratic politics. A slow reaction is now perceptible, but we are still perilously close to the state of subjugation described in apocalyptic terms by Alexis de Toqueville (*Democracy in America*, 1835):

> "I think that the species of oppression by which democratic nations are menaced is unlike anything that ever before existed in the world. ...[State] power is absolute, minute, regular, provident and mild. It would be like the authority of a parent if, like that authority, its object was to prepare men for manhood, but it seeks on the contrary, to keep them in perpetual childhood... [the government] provides for their security, foresees and supplies their necessities, facilitates their pleasures, manages their principal concerns, directs their industry, regulates the descent of property and subdivides their inheritance: what remains but to spare them all the care of thinking and all the trouble of living?"
>
> This is heady stuff but de Tocqueville goes on: "The principle of equality has prepared men for these things; it has predisposed men to endure them and often to look on them as benefits ... the supreme power ... covers the surface of society with a network of small complicated rules minute and uniform ... such a power does not destroy but it prevents existence; it does not tyrannize, but it compresses, enervates, extinguishes and stupefies a people, till each nation is reduced to nothing better than a flock of timid and industrious animals, of which the government is the shepherd." In one word, the state has become God.

de Toqueville exhibits an uncanny prescience of the excesses of egalitarianism   *cf. 56*
and the emergence of democratic self-indulgence. For sure, we should get oppressive government off the back of the people but what if the majority has
become so conditioned to the amenities of serfdom, that it refuses to be relieved
of the burden? Inordinate idolization of the benefactor state leads to democratic
despotism and can be overcome only by invoking superior values.

The limits of politics

Ideally the originators of binding political rules should remain unaware of their
individual starting positions within the coalition. The fairness of the game
would thus be ascertained behind a veil of ignorance, before the cards are dealt
to the players. A succession of social philosophers from Rousseau to Rawls has
tried, with limited success, to derive explicit and general rules for political
collaboration from this abstract precept. Alas, the clauses of the social contract
are stillborn constructs without any real political substance. The self-interest of
millions of people cannot be rationally combined into a self-sustaining legal
apparatus. The virtuous veil of ignorance is, in fact, a corollary to the ancient
golden rule and to Kant's well-known principle of reciprocity, but even such
illustrious antecedents fall flat in the absence of some higher legitimation.

Jesus' instruction: "Love thy enemy as thyself" is a cornerstone of democratic   *cf. 404*
co-operation. Unfortunately, even this lucid command can lead the literal-
minded down the wrong path.

> Extreme pacifists appeal to the clear Biblical instruction, as they smugly refuse to raise a
> hand against an enemy bent on destroying them or those they love. Their argument does
> not withstand closer scrutiny. If, unprovoked and perhaps in a fit of madness, I were to
> lay hands upon my neighbour, I certainly hope that somebody would be prepared to use
> violence to stop me. According to the golden rule of reciprocity, I should be able to
> render my neighbour the same service – thereby loving my enemy as myself.

The invocation of unlimited funds of good will is a vain attempt to abolish
politics, a childish escape from reality. Unfortunately we have to live with
original sin, our ineradicable self-interest. There is and always will be a severe
shortage of "love" which should accordingly be treated as the scarcest of
commodities.

The rules of the market economy and of political democracy reveal a remarkable congruity; the meta-rules of the self-organizing market game are a crude
projection of fundamental democratic values. This supports the conclusion that
modern democracy is a good model – perhaps the only one – for a sustained
human plus-sum game. In the words of Reinhold Niebuhr (1892–1971):   *cf. 119; 227; 317*
"Man's moral capacity makes democracy possible but also makes it indispensable."

> Max Weber was the first to perceive the link between political freedom and a free
> economy but the most convincing presentation of this case can be ascribed to Friedrich
> von Hayek (*The Road to Serfdom*, 1944). The widely differing cover stories of fascism
> and socialism conceal an identical collectivist core: contempt for individual liberty and

disgust with democracy. Hayek concludes with an almost clairvoyant conception of a liberal and decentralised Community of European nations.

Without the invisible hand of morally binding meta-rules the selfish moves of political actors will cancel out, precluding durable self-organization. To prevent political passions or crude selfishness from disrupting the social coalition, democratic forms must be filled with meta-political substance which creates and upholds a resultant plus-sum vector. The small residue of constructive intentions will then prevail and our better selves can find scope for play in the ingenious application of the spirit of the political game.

cf. 397   The mediation of the meta-rules must take place behind the scene. Any ideological notion of infallibility will poison democratic procedure. Direct interference of religious conviction is inadmissable because it disrupts the political game, just as arbitrary political intervention dislocates the market economy.

Although we have barely succeeded in formulating even the most crucial rules of social interplay, the fact remains that our democratic institutions have contributed to unparalleled individual and collective creativity. Profound and reliable knowledge has in many areas replaced superficial observation or pure superstition. Complex social interactions have, so far, escaped trustworthy analysis. For the time being, we can improve our societal competence only by circumspect trials and errors, played out in fair competition between different
cf. 377   modes of the democratic game.

The mind of man seems to be locked behind at least seven seals. Nevertheless, the final arbiter of our dissensions has to be sought in the scientific elucidation of human interplay. The desperately utopian goal is to obtain sufficient information about the condition of man, to gain reliable self-knowledge which would unite us in understanding and thus alleviate our political problems. Then, and only then, will democracy have come of age.

7. Games of science

7.1 What is science?

Science is a superordinate game dedicated to the elucidation of all the other games. Surprisingly, the rules of this science of science remains a muddle. Karl Popper's critical rationalism (or fallibilism) is the most attractive doctrine but, in the main, it explains discoveries only after the event. Like most creative undertakings, science works within a haze of insufficient information and has to proceed according to a Darwinian search process. The value-laden meta-hypothesis of science cannot be pinned down: every rational scientific method must be incomplete and misleading; the perfect convergence of all science is a delusive mirage.

Revealing the rules

Scientific insight testifies to a deep understanding of the rules of the game; at best, the results are presented in explicit mathematical form. Scientific interest implies an emotional distance from the process observed, unlike the immediate involvement of technological, economic and political play. Even so, researchers themselves are passionately involved in a superordinate game with its own largely implicit rules. The scientist's success depends on his mastery of the tacit and abstruse essence of this meta-game.

cf. 46

> "Science", a new-fangled card game, provides a good illustration of this train of thought. Before the game begins the leading player or 'God' writes down his own secret but well-defined rule. He then puts down cards, face up one at a time, and places them either next to the previous card (if it fits his secret rule), or under it (if it does not). Thus, certain card combinations are permitted, while all the others are forbidden. The ordinary players try to identify the underlying rule by interpreting the emerging pattern. Any player who believes he has found the solution becomes a "prophet" and takes over the role of God. If he puts a card in the wrong place, he is a false prophet and God expels him from the game. A true prophet continues until another true prophet comes on the scene. God's veracity can be checked, when the game is over, by examining the lie of the cards. The optimal strategy depends on how points are allotted, which is a problem in itself.

"Science", the card game, provides a fascinating parallel with routine scientific activity. The explicit rules for acquiring knowledge are fully defined. New empirical material is always available. We never ask nonsensical questions and always receive clear answers: right or wrong. The publication of premature conclusions will damage a scientist's reputation, but too much precaution will condemn him to obscurity.

cf. 109

Interestingly, "strategic" or "scientific" capability can, in a roundabout way, be local-ised to the prefrontal cortical lobes of the brain, which is also the centre of attention. Neuropsychologists looking for malfunction in this area (schizophrenia is often impli-cated) subject the patient to a test similar to a simple game of "science". First everything goes well but when the doctor suddenly changes the guiding rule, patients with the specific lesion cannot cope. They are unable to disregard the old experience and get stuck with a useless strategy. Unlearning is too distressing, it requires some risk-taking, a slight paradigm change, a minor leap of faith.

cf. 133; 369; 392; 425

Throughout history, scientific discovery has trailed behind technological devel-opment, usually by a large margin. (This is even more apparent in the recently conceived "soft" sciences) Only advances in technology could provide tools for accurate observation and thus create the indispensable experimental base for acute theory-building in the natural sciences.

cf. 136

cf. 133

The hallowed scientists of Antiquity saw themselves primarily as philosophers, keeping their distance from all practical applications. Even so, some interaction between scien-tific thought and technological problem-solving is evident during the cultural apogee of Greece. Pythagoras and Archimedes, famous masters of many trades, rejoiced the hearts of their respective patrons particularly by impressive feats in the martial arts. But the really significant technological triumphs of Antiquity sprang from the pragmatic efforts of anonymous craftsmen, a condition which persisted well into modern times. The first telescopes and microscopes preceded the theory of optics, and the steam engine did not await the breakthrough of thermodynamics. Acetylsalicylic acid (aspirin) was launched as an analgesic in 1899, almost a century before its *modus operandi* was elucidated.

Superconductivity has been baffling theoreticians ever since its discovery in 1911 by Heike Kamerlingh-Onnes (1853–1926) at temperatures below 4°K. In 1957 John Bar-den, L.N. Cooper and Robert Schrieffer presented a satisfactory quantum-mechanical theory of electron pairing, which helped in raising the maximum temperature for superconductivity to 23°K. The theory worked very well until 1986 when G. Bednorz and K.A. Mueller discovered a novel class of ceramic superconductors. The critical temperature was, at one stroke, raised well beyond 100°K in the face of nonplussed theoreticians who, at the time of writing, are still baffled.

Today science and technology are closely intertwined. The nineteenth-century utilization of electrical power or the recent transistor revolution would be inconceivable without the foregoing progress in electromagnetic theory and solid state physics. Nuclear power and modern biotechnology stand even more squarely on the foundation of scientific insight. But the role of the scientist is still to divulge "the truth", the explicit rules of the game while the technologists concentrate on "the practice", the implicit opportunities for play marked by the invention of new products and processes, materials and machinery, perfecting the production of goods on demand.

A rational science?

So what are the meta-rules of the scientific game? Early on, the philosophy of science had a strong leaning towards the hyperrational. First prize must surely go to the logical positivists, a school of formalist, deductive thinkers headed by *cf. 29* Ernst Mach, Rudolf Carnap and Carl Hempel. The starting point of positivist epistemology is a strictly formalized scientific language. The objective is the unaided, "automatic" capture of human experience in a web of mathematical symbols, tied together by a minimum of value-free and logically unimpeachable rules.

> These doctrines are akin to Russell's mathematical logicism: both are extremely reduc-   *cf. 21*
> tionist and highly academic. The struggle with an "impossible" problem has produced
> important forays in logic and metamathematics, but logical positivism has made a
> negligible impact on the practice of the natural sciences. Oddly enough, it has become a
> *sine qua non* for many social scientists – an overambitious attitude that reflects the
> uncertain ambiguity of their position.

The logical positivists want to reduce science to logic; their specific utopia is a self-verifying linguistic construct, based on fundamental logico-mathematical principles. Metaphysical questions and philosophical discourses, indeed any-thing of deeper interest, is dismissed as "meaningless". The striving for extreme mental hygiene results in sterility; the demand for total certainty leads to para-   *cf. 307* doxes and ends up with a complete lack of practical relevance.

Popper's critical rationalism, which has already been referred to, probably   *cf. 29* corresponds to the personal intuition of most natural scientists. Popper supple-ments the concrete world of material things, World One, and the subjective world of sense impressions, World Two, with an abstract World Three, consist-ing of relevant invariances preferably expressed in mathematical code – the fundamental rules of material games in tabulated form. For Popper, clearly expressed scientific insight thus has an autonomous existence.

> This view corresponds to David Hilbert's (1862–1943) formalist mathematics but may
> be difficult to sustain. Popper wisely emphasizes the provisional nature of scientific   *cf. 328; 331*
> truth and emphatically underlines the role of falsification in practical research rather
> than the often self-deceiving search for verification. The goal is to learn from well-
> planned, imaginative and fruitful mistakes, exposing orthodox prejudice and refuting
> false or superficial conclusions – in other words, to excel in fallibilism.

Critical rationalism makes concrete assertions about the conditions of scientific work. Theories that cannot be tested and falsified are self-immunizing and meaningless. Nor does the mere adjustment of mathematical formulae to em-pirical data pass as science. A strong, scientific theory should compete by neatly epitomizing existing knowledge and, above all, by demonstrating its ability to survive critical experiments and to make correct but surprising predictions. In other words it should cover lots of facts unknown to or even unsuspected at the outset.

Building on Alfred Tarski's (1902–83) explication of mathematical truth,   *cf. 331; 361* Popper defines the concept of verisimilitude as an objective measure of scientific knowledge. The verisimilitude of a theory increases with the element of surprise: it should absorb a maximum amount of previous uncertainty within a compact conceptual frame. Such stringent criteria imply that we must never be content even with the strongest theories of established science; the search for falsification should lead to ever deeper insight.

> An excellent example is Einstein's extension of Newtonian mechanics and gravitation, which are preserved as borderline cases of the special and general theories of relativity, respectively.

Less structured fields of research are difficult to fit into Popper's scheme which, in its analytical acuity and practical efficacy, nevertheless offers an interesting partial solution to the problem of scientific methodology.

Imre Lakatos has added depth and scope to Popperian critical rationalism by shifting the focus from the testing of hypotheses to superordinate scientific programmes. These perduring but only vaguely expressed meta-hypotheses assume a key role in the cumulative accession of knowledge. Lakatos also comes to grips with the linguistic aspects of logical and scientific argument. He pleads for a creative heuristics rather than schematic linear reasoning, and points at serious linguistic confusion even in apparently transparent mathematical expo-
cf. 341 sitions. His conclusion seems to be that the meta-rules of the scientific game cannot be explicitly formulated: every rational scientific method must be incomplete and misleading.

Intuitionist science?

Several unorthodox epistemologists have broken radically with Popperism. According to Thomas Kuhn (*The Structure of Scientific Revolutions*, 1962) the smooth progress of science is interrupted by severe crises which render obsolete the existing conceptual apparatus. Such a paradigm shift cannot be fitted into any predestined model; instead, the half-finished puzzle has to be broken up and put together anew in a different pattern. Even if Kuhn has since retreated from this extreme position, his point remains. Scientific revolutions represent powerful intellectual and moral challenges. They should never be rejected out of hand, but the burden of proof is always on the revolutionary approach.

> Both Darwin and Planck struggled with their own epoch-making insights, and for a long time refused to accept the conclusions. They were also sceptical about the reception of the revolutionary paradigms, and only trusted the new generation to take over from their stick-in-the-mud contemporaries. Up to a point, events gave the lie to their pessimism. Nonetheless, the strength of spontaneous rejection mechanisms should never be underestimated.

Nietzsche proclaimed: "Every word is a prejudice". Radical shifts in our interpretation of reality are restricted by the very components of our mental machinery. Language is, in a sense, the origin of ignorance. Lack of linguistic sensitivity predisposes us towards failure whereas a happy metaphor helps in structuring a problem and makes for successful scientific play. This is particularly relevant to the chaotic early stages of a science, when uncertainty is maximal and intuition indispensable.

Paul Feyerabend is the confirmed iconoclast among the critics of a purely rational science. In *Against Method* (1975), he rejects all explicit rules or criteria and summarizes his attitude with the battle-cry "Anything goes!". There can be no "correct" categorization of reality; personal insight is the only guide to scientific interest and working methods. This corresponds to Brouwer's intuitionist mathematics. The fertile human mind is seen as the sole source of rules for our intellectual games. (*Against Method* was conceived as the radical part in a diptych, with Lakatos as the author of the contrasting companion, but his untimely death in 1974 intervened.) *cf. 22*

In this day and age, Marxist thinking cannot be passed over, despite its recent loss of appeal. Engels, rather than Marx, was the first master of dialectical materialism as a philosophy of science. Hegel's famous triad, "thesis – antithesis – synthesis", became the starting-point of Marxist thought. Accordingly, the quantitative accumulation of poignant oppositions is supposed to cause a revolutionary clash, opening the way to a higher truth. This tenet was elevated to a law of nature, but it is of course open to arbitrary interpretation.

Dialectical materialism was totally ignored by the natural sciences, at least in the West. Instead it exercised a powerful attraction on the social sciences but has only served to sharpen their inherent contradictions. Deterministic humanism, materialistic idealism and dogmatic scientism became, all too often, appropriate appellations. Marxism has been the self-immunized gnosis of our times, the magic key to perfect knowledge. Circular argumentation was shamelessly applied as Marxist presumptions were transsubstantiated into the foundations of science. The end result was another "scientific" philosophy of science.

Hermeneutic summary

Modern hermeneutics stems from ideas promulgated by Immanuel Kant, Friedrich Schleiermacher (1768–1834) and Wilhelm Dilthey (1833–1911), spiced with Biblical exegetics and Marxist dialectics. Logico-analytical and linear-deductive thinking are rejected as atypical cases of scientific verification. All understanding of languages, the laws of nature, philosophy or religious doctrine emerges from the patient play with the pieces of the puzzle, gradually discovering the network of characteristic interactions. Every part obtains meaning and significance from all the other elements in the enigmatic structure; only in retrospect does the argument seem convincing and its logic incontrovertible. The problem is to find the right question to match the over-abundant answers.

The hermeneutic view of the workings of the human mind finds strong support in modern philosophy and epistemology. Only by playing the language game can we learn its rules and acquire the ability to communicate. This can easily be generalized to embrace non-linguistic communication, the learning of skills, the acquisition of knowledge and the formulation of scientific insights. *cf. 30; 112*

The representatives of the continental hermeneutic school, such as Carl Otto Apel, Jürgen Habermas, and Hans Georg Gadamer, are mainly concerned with the "soft" sciences. They start out from the social role of science, and emphasize the proper demarcation of the scientific interest. As they see it, knowledge grows out of structural conflict, provided hermeneutic learning methods are *cf. 314* applied. An adequate social audit and the transparency of the argument guarantee scientific veracity. Moreover, the emancipation of human thought is perceived as a general and fundamental value.

> The tacit goal is to arrive at a monolithic, generally acceptable, and total (not to say totalitarian) scientific truth covering the whole domain of human experience. Once again a circular argument lurks in the verbiage, perhaps a legacy from Marxist mentors. Have the prescribed norms, the essence of the scientific method, really and necessarily evolved from the scientific work? Do they not rather represent deeply personal, individually and historically conditioned values which have slipped in through the back door? In one breath these augurs claim to have found a universal principle of scientific progress, and in the next they declare that this principle is scientifically verified!

Our short survey of the philosophy of science is by no means exhaustive. Still it has displayed a welter of imcompatible if not contradictory opinions. In brief: the logical positivists strive for self-verifying objectivity and consequently for total value-freedom. Popper and Lakatos recommend a combination of falsifiable rationalism and self-critical pluralism while Kuhn and Feyerabend represent different degrees of value relativism. Marxism and its offshoots, on the other hand, seem to have fallen victim to serious self-immunization in their utopian search for "scientifically correct" values.

Historical experience as well as recent hermeneutic insights should make us very sceptical of any programme based on scientific self-justification. Pluralistic diversification has always been the law of life. Science, like most creative undertakings, works within a haze of insufficient information and has to pro-

cf. 377 ceed according to a Darwinian search process. Important knowledge is gained only through fruitful mistakes. The sparse truth must be substantiated by innumerable errors and false leads which appear inevitable even with the bene-

cf. 112 fit of hindsight. The value-laden meta-hypotheses of science are even more insecure, and thus the perfect convergence of all science is a dangerous delusion.

7.2   The hierarchy of sciences

The core sciences can be arranged in a neat hierarchy according to the nature of the scientific object. The abstract symbols of logic and mathematics are by far the simplest actors; yet, they are capable of an infinity of unforeseeable moves. The natural sciences cover the games of elementary particles which are governed by the strict statistical rules of quantum mechanics. With increasing complexity the actors acquire a larger scope for play; in the life sciences (biology, medicine etc.) predictability is severely curtailed. In the human sciences, like psychology, sociology and anthropology, man himself is placed under the magnifying glass. Here, the real challenge is to lay bare the hidden invariances of Homo sapiens.

Abstract sciences

The nature of the scientific object determines the conditions of scientific work and provides a self-evident point of departure for a typology of sciences. Logic and mathematics deal in pure abstractions; their elements are strictly defined processes, created and perceived by the playful human intellect. Both the "actors" or "players" and the rules of the game are defined by a minimum of unambiguous axioms. It has thus been possible to adhere to the following remarkable tenets:

☐ No branch of the abstract sciences may contradict any other; the whole body of logic and mathematics should be completely coherent and in full accord.
☐ Scientific interest is concentrated on broad generalizations. A sole contradiction, a single mental omission, or just one empirical counterexample suffices for falsification.
☐ Abstract sciences are, on principle, exact and determinate; the precision of the calculations can be increased indefinitely. Even though causality and insight are maximized, only a restricted domain is computable. The incomputable or unforeseeable and, indeed, the unknowable dominates the boundless background.
☐ The aesthetic element is predominant in the choice between otherwise equivalent alternatives.

Adding new axioms is frowned upon; like Russell's axiom of reducibility it may be the easy way out of a logical dead-end. Nevertheless, judicious expansion of the axiomatic base might be the only way to carry on the game and claim, or rather create, new territory. cf. 332 cf. 221

> Despite its aura of pure abstraction even logic is deep down an empirical effort in which our thought tries to capture its own preconditions. The basic tautological moves can be tested only with the help of common sense; falsification simply means that there is an

obvious contradiction, a paradox or some other absurdity in the fabricated language game. In logic, pure speculation is taken to its extreme and represents the centre of the circle of thought. Aided by logic we can take the measure of reality but logic in itself is no reality. Careful thought experiments produce the basic rules of logic and, aided by logic, we can take the measure of reality mindful that logic in itself is not reality.

cf. 327

Mathematics involves an empirical investigation of the rules which obtain for abstract numbers, forms, relations, sets and structures. Contrary to expectations, only the most trivial mathematical games are completely explicit. Gödel's undecidability theorem demonstrates that in order to avoid contradictions, every interesting mathematical language must comprise propositions which cannot be verified or falsified within the axiomatic system. The only recourse is to approach the man-made mathematical universe from the outside, as it were.

cf. 328

> The traditional tools of the mathematician – pencil and paper, ruler and compass – have been enormously enhanced by modern computer technology. But ingenious mental experiments are and will remain the chief working method of the mathematician. The results seem to reflect fundamental aspects of the architecture of the real universe. We find it easy to believe in deviant forms of life in distant galaxies. It is more difficult to imagine a local chemistry or a physics different from our own, and most difficult of all is to envisage deviations in logic or mathematics.

The natural sciences

The concrete interaction of simple elements of matter in the real world constitutes the research object of the natural sciences. This interplay has the following attributes:

- ☐ The actors have an immutable and irreducible substance but no identity; they can be lumped together in large homogeneous assemblies. Any variations are treated statistically.
- ☐ The basic rules of the game are given once and for all and are assumed to be immutable within our epoch (laws of nature). Statistically, at least, the same causes always have the same effects.
- ☐ Precision is paramount, but for both experimental and theoretical reasons (Heisenberg's uncertainty principle) it cannot be pursued to unlimited lengths.
- ☐ Scientific interest is concerned with the discovery of new and surprising moves and fitting them into an interconnected rule system. The coherent game structure is isomorphic with reality and constitutes a self-confirming network, permitting confident and far-reaching predictions.
- ☐ A few counter-examples do not suffice for falsification. Another structure with superior thought-economy must first be presented with some support from repeated and reliable observations.
- ☐ Causality dominates but is gradually attenuated as the increasing differentiation of the actors reduce our powers of prediction and induce exponentially escalating opportunities for independent play.
- ☐ Mathematics is an indispensable aid. It provides an abundant selection of

well-formed quantitative rules which can be filled with content, providing unambiguous guidelines for thinking and simulation.

Whereas logic and mathematics create and follow up an appropriate axiomatics, the natural sciences work from the top of perceptible phenomena down through a largely tautological mesh towards the axiomatic core of physical reality. During the twentieth century progress has been little short of phenomenal. A few deep rules of quantum physics put the intricate play of elementary particles in a clear perspective.

cf. 34

> The particle domain can be divided into two subsets. The field-mediating bosons with integral spin (photons, mesons, gluons etc) obey Bose-Einstein statistics and are completely anonymous. The territorial fermions – protons, neutrons, electrons and neutrinos – are the relatively stable building blocks of the world. They have half-integral spin and obey Fermi-Dirac statistics.
>
> In contrast to bosons, the exchange of two fermions (e.g. electrons) causes a reversal of the system's quantum-mechanical wave function ($+\Psi \Rightarrow -\Psi$), although it does not affect the probability distribution which is proportional to Ψ^2. This "hidden individuality" leads to the Pauli exclusion principle: no two fermions can exist in identical quantum states within an interactive system. One consequence is that the electrons gather in distinct shells round the atomic nucleus. All electrons in an atom have "personal" quantum numbers, like interchangeable identity tags.
>
> In special circumstances ordinary matter can "degenerate" into a bosonic state losing its normal propensity for creative interplay. For example, unlike the Helium 3 isotope, ordinary helium (Helium 4) gives rise at very low temperatures to a bosonic liquid which accordingly has neither surface tension nor viscosity. The laser phenomenon, again, is an expression of the completely synchronised and uniform bosonic behaviour of photons.

cf. 62

We are bound to postulate a minimal set of axiomatic ground rules, which has directed the self-organization of matter from its very beginning with the Big Bang. At the time of writing the list of independent constants of elementary particle physics is down to 18 items, but it still looks far too long. The variety of masses, in particular, looks arbitrary and must have a deeper cause. The Holy Grail of physics, the theory of everything (TOE) ought to be a model of profound lucidity and may now be in sight.

cf. 375

> Even if we can define a root cause in comprehensible mathematical terms, the game was probably open-ended in the very beginning. The evolution of the early universe could, in essence, have been a self-selective process which created new axiomatic information. These fundamental rules would not be derivable from first principles, which puts an upper limit to the reducibility of physical phenomena.

cf. 377

Astronomy and meteorology approach the enigma of the elementary actors from opposite directions. Whereas the weather has remained the very symbol of unaccountability, the strict discipline of the heavens became a source of inspiration and jubilation for natural scientists. Scientific progress now permits us to behold the unity of creation while appreciating the enormous diversity admitted by the underlying rules of the game.

Life sciences

The natural sciences fall into a distinct hierarchy, ordered according to the complexity of the subject matter. Chemistry can be reduced in part to physics; biology, the basic life science, exploits the whole repertoire of the natural sciences with particular emphasis on biochemistry.

The development of ever higher life forms puts increasing strain on the criteria of the natural sciences. Evolution generally broadens the axiomatic base *cf. 320* by the introduction of new, genetic information. This confers an additional set of dynamics on the game; the life sciences consequently possess a significant historical dimension. The relatively slow rate of change allows the natural sciences to retain their relevance, but it does entail a number of interesting limitations.

☐ The objects of study increase in complexity and finally become independent actors with pronounced identities. Myopic statistical processing can thus seriously distort the acquisition of knowledge.

☐ Mathematical precision must gradually give way to initiated percipience and structural connections. Most biological processes defy quantitative analysis: palaeontology is "natural history" in the true sense.

☐ Grandiose syntheses along the lines of the physicists' unified field theory are out of reach. Description and registration are major occupations, and even quite weak, qualitative relationships can be of interest.

☐ The complexity of the game increases the scope for individual play. Causality becomes clouded but still works as the accredited basis of scientific argument.

☐ Genuine predictability is still the exception, although the investigation of the rules of the game proceeds apace.

After the initial synthesis of a protein, the long string of amino acids can spontaneously fold into the "correct", predestined spatial structure (dedicated chaperone-proteins often direct the process). This intramolecular self-organization does not yet lend itself to exact simulation, even if the protein follows its own obscure rules. The famous protein chemist Jacques-Lucien Monod tells us (in *Chance and Necessity*, 1971) how he *cf. 30* achieved tacit knowledge of the folding process. In the end, he could identify himself with individual protein molecules and acquired an intuitive feel for their natural behaviour.

The invariances of natural science establish the forbidden moves at the basic level of the game, but do not prescribe which of an infinite number of permitted move sequences will actually be realized. For billions of years, life has groped its way forward, one step at a time, gradually producing a motley crew of robust survival artists. Efficient systems of self-regulation, self-repair and self-defence generally manage to keep destructive forces in check.

Sometimes just one wrong move throws the game off course and leads inexorably to a fatal conclusion. The malignancy of a cancer-evoking oncogene (c-ras) can be caused by a single error in the string of 6,000 nucleotides, which codes for the normal, life-*cf. 387* enhancing protein.

Life processes are strikingly dissipative and thus elude predeterminate causality. The internal autonomy and independent behaviour of the actors become increasingly conspicuous at higher evolutionary levels. In metaphysical terms, not even the Creator Himself can predict the course of the game. The situation is analogous to many branches of mathematics, where we watch in amazement as the game develops its own capricious modes of play albeit in full compliance with our man-made rules.

Human sciences

Man is a product of nature, and as a biological creature represents a legitimate object of natural-scientific study. There is nothing controversial here, as long as researchers behave like decent vets – investigating metabolism and hormone balance, registering nerve signals and sense impressions, dissecting and operating on discrete parts of the human body. The conditions of scientific study change radically only when man in his entirety is put under the magnifying glass. This is the case in the human sciences such as psychology, sociology and anthropology.

The human sciences are defined by their object, the species *Homo sapiens*, and are consequently beset with pernicious problems.

☐ The actors are highly complex and diverse, although their fundamental character is relatively immutable.
☐ The rules governing the interplay between the actors are flexible, and very difficult to grasp as a self-contained system.
☐ The scientific interest is not easily defined, and is dependent on personal and sometimes suppressed values. There is thus a latent conflict between descriptive and normative elements in research.
☐ Direct experiments are pestered with practical and conceptual shortcomings; empirical results are notoriously unreliable; verification and falsification can easily go astray in the labyrinths of the language game.
☐ Causal relationships are thoroughly entangled and can be isolated only under very artificial conditions. The powers of prediction are slight.

The task of the human sciences is to elucidate our species-specific rules of the game and to delimit the scope of play; in other words to lay bare the axiomatics of *Homo sapiens*. The real challenge is to cope with the diversity of the actors by making a clear distinction between the rules applying to single individuals, to separate groups, or to humanity as a whole. Much of the conceptual apparatus of the natural sciences may still be applicable, if the research is focused on the invariances in human behaviour which are deeply entrenched in our epigenetic rules.

> The best we can ever do is to draw the line between the probable, the credible, and the implausible. However, scientific ambition has regularly overshot the mark, which has led to the following unsatisfactory situation:
> – the different branches of science do not corroborate each other and fail to form a

reliable and convincing body of knowledge. Each part rests insecurely on its own presuppositions.
- within individual sciences there is a strong tendency to split into different schools, often contradicting and seldom supporting one another's conclusions.
- the absence of a common paradigm causes glaring gaps in communication. Information flows freely only between "ideologically" related researchers.
- language is still at a pre-scientific stage of development, and is either primitively descriptive or overflowing with quasi-scientific jargon, to the detriment of thought-economy and in flagrant breach of Ockhams Razor.
- many doctrines are highly self-immunizing. Far-sighted, self-simplifying developments are few and far between.

In the natural sciences we have acquired a profound understanding of the game, but in the human sciences we are sometimes worse than beginners. All too often scientists believe they already possess the rules which they should be humbly seeking, or which may not even exist. Because of the huge variety of reference frames, the normal sifting process of science cannot operate. The grains of gold discovered by painstaking researchers are lost in a morass of incommensurate publications, and cynics of all shades rest comfortably behind a barricade of misleading phraseology.

The human sciences seem to be trapped in a maze of dead-ends. To get a handle on the salient problems, we must try to view them from above and move on to the cultural sciences, those culture-specific modes of play which are rather inadequately known as the humanities.

7.3   The cultural sciences

The cultural sciences are concerned with man's actual mode of play and must be subjective in their approach. Economics (excluding praxeology), jurisprudence, political science, the science of science, not to speak of the humanities are all normative – either overtly or covertly. History supplies the only relevant experiments, but the historic facts always call for a value-laden, holistic interpretation. The cultural sciences have no real foundations; they hang by the invisible threads of implicit meta-rules. For the present, the best guide to these nebulous regions is art. Great authors tell us more about human interplay than contemporary scientific analysis.

Human sciences revisited

The excessive claims of the human sciences have not gone unnoticed. As early as the turn of the century, Vilfredo Pareto, a pioneer of economics and the *enfant terrible* of sociology, openly denied these disciplines the status of science and was accordingly met with a deafening silence.

> In his sarcastic manner Pareto sought to illuminate the relation between immutable psychological forces (the epigenetic rules) and resulting social phenomena. He predicted correctly the tidal wave of totalitarianism in general and the outbreak of fascism in particular. A contributory cause, according to Pareto, was the paralysis of the liberal democracies in the face of even the most violent provocation.

cf. 246

Many sociologists recognize the proto-scientific state of their art, and share Pareto's misgivings about "soft" science in general and sociology in particular. Even so, they claim that they are clearing the way for future insights with a wealth of strictly quantified observations. But the crystallization of this vast body of data into meaningful and serviceable knowledge is blocked by the lack of any comprehensive scientific programme. Some insight into the axiomatic set-up, the explicit rules of the game, must precede the analysis of the modes of play.

> Since the Second World War ethology and sociobiology have made great strides, and the study of primate behaviour in particular should open up interesting perspectives. Unfortunately, the sociobiologists have tried to "explain" all human behaviour in the deterministic terms of the natural sciences – an extrapolation to which the sociologists respond with an aggrieved noli-me-tangere stance. It is ridiculous that the genetic roots of intelligence, for example, are still being hotly debated with an admixture of blatant canonical arguments (human equality etc.)

cf. 81

The deadlock in human sciences is an outcome of the misfit between the blunt research tools and overambitious goals. Attempts to bridge the gap to the natural sciences have been hampered both by over-zealous reductionists and flustered humanists. We can rest assured that our animal inheritance has remained intact, however overlaid it may be with human-specific structures. Thus the mammals, especially the primates, should provide fruitful starting-points for the study of the deep structure of man.

> Mature chimpanzee males try to realize their political ambitions by familiar methods. Intimidating displays alternate with friendly gestures, collaborative manoeuvres and coalition-formation. Although "the people" (that is females and youngsters) generally back the winner, they may cast the deciding vote in a close contest. The ties of friendship are established early in life and possess considerable durability in comparison with political loyalties. The social games played by a few chimps already taxes our comprehension, and it is almost impossible to avoid anthropomorphic terminology when talking about chimpanzee communities.

In the human sciences, the very process of measurement tends to affect the outcome; it is difficult for the researcher to stand aloof from the object of his scientific interest. Underestimation of, say, social outcasts or aboriginal intelligence alternates with idealization of the "primitive". An unholy alliance of reductionist ambitions and humanist self-assertion impedes the cumulative understanding of the game.

The science of science

The study of metamathematics has made considerable progress and the historians of historical research are also well established whereas the psychology of psychologists and the sociology of sociologists are still out of reach. Among these self-referential endeavours the critical analysis of scientific play represents a rather special case, briefly surveyed in the first section of this chapter.

We could go one step further and propound a perfectly legitimate science of the science of science. Obviously we face here an elusive regression of fictitious explanations. The ultimate verification of science must lie outside the scientific domain, just as its specialized vocabulary can exist only in the context of our everyday language. Not even science can, with the best of intentions, explain itself – which need not necessarily cause us any grave concern. Scientists need the philosophy of science as much as birds need ornithology.

Despite many brilliant initiatives, the science of science succumbs to the *cf. 39* self-destructive forces inherent in all philosophy. Unsurprisingly, this fragmentation is due to the absence of a common frame of reference. Science is an open human search process in which the free scope for play seems to be boundless. Like other less systematic forays into the unknown, scientific endeavour rests upon an array of presupposed postulates or precepts which, one way or the other, make sense of a chaotic world. Research must render the game intelligible, it must spell out the invariances, the genuine taboos which demarcate forbidden or impossible moves, releasing all the permitted permutations of play.

Scientists fight tenaciously to reduce this axiomatic input to a minimum, but cannot avoid expanding their value platform in step with the subject matter. Thus, any attempt at human self-simulation must be propped up by further acts *cf. 381* of faith or be caught in the impasse of a logical bootstrap. Hence the dilemma of any explicit meta-science.

Levitating science

While the human sciences should look for conformities and invariances in their overly complex object, the cultural sciences must cope with the vastly higher complexity of man's actual modes of play. The rules of these culture-specific games are elaborated and elucidated in economics and jurisprudence, literature and linguistics, aesthetics, ethics, philosophy and theology to name but a few – there are university chairs in every conceivable area of erudition.

> The hubris of the human sciences lies in their ambition to invade those attractive but treacherous and culturally conditioned regions. Instead psychologists and sociologists should humbly work on a reliable model of the eternally human in order to create a dependable linchpin between the natural sciences and the countless ramifications of cultural play.

The cultural scientist is invariably aiming at a moving target and he must exercise extreme caution so as to cope with the following predicament:

☐ Rigorous scientific trials are out of the question, since the experimental conditions cannot be controlled or reproduced with any accuracy.
☐ The interference between different levels of play is unpredictable and highly confusing; explicit social conventions may carry considerable weight.

☐ The actors are sharply individualized and can change significantly over time, e.g. as a result of independent learning. Temporary syndicates vie with more permanent coalitions for the allegiance of the players.

☐ Causality is suppressed and the game is wide open. Subjective value judgements loom large and there are few if any criteria for objective truth.

Cultural interplay is largely chaotic in that imperceptible causes can have massive effects. Chaos is countervailed by the implicit value frame of the culture which pervades every aspect of the game, albeit in an elusive manner. All in all, we are dealing with an unparalleled dynamics where everything is, in a nontrivial sense, influenced by almost everything else.

> Obviously we cannot expect in-depth scientific penetration of our cultural games; even economics still lingers in a state reminiscent of biology before Darwin. As academic disciplines, neither theology nor ethics have so far had an appreciable impact on human affairs. The rehabilitation of criminals is still a pipe-dream of forensic psychiatry, and the ineptitude of many of our educational institutions testifies every day to the shortcomings of pedagogy.
>
> Scientific incompetence by no means rules out the acquisition of advanced technical skills. Book-keeping and cost calculation emerged in their modern form during the Middle Ages. Contemporary business managers or politicians have a whole range of practical and useful sociological tools to hand. Commercial advertising and opinion polls, public-relations campaigns and political propaganda – all these and many other technologies have been developed to a level approaching perfection. Technical progress thus provides us with a wealth of empirical material and valuable pointers for research, but it should not give the scientific establishment any cause for celebration: prowess at social engineering does not necessarily signify scientific understanding.

cf. 278

Despite their lack of foundations, the cultural sciences can perform satisfactorily if they stick modestly to their own domain, in implicit recognition of the appropriate value system. Then they appear as consistent doctrines, ostensibly levitating in mid-air but actually suspended by long-standing meta-rules, the invisible scaffolding of culture.

Holistic historiography

The unfolding of the cultural game is a highly opaque process, but in the pursuit of satisfactory self-understanding our only recourse is to probe patiently into the past. We must try to distinguish historical cause and effect – the elusive and evanescent rules of social interplay. History supplies the only comprehensive experiments relevant to the cultural scientist, but the historic facts always call for a holistic interpretation. The variables are never neatly separated, and are of course outside any kind of control. Hermeneutic iteration, the beginner's approach, is the only appropriate method. A historian worth his salt must combine a scrupulous criticism of the sources with no small portion of creative imagination.

The stage of history is crammed with individual performers continually regrouping themselves in a variety of social, economic and political coalitions, fiercely competing for the exploitable material resources. The heroic attempts at identifying general patterns of causality have so far gone astray. Marxism, in particular, does not possess the predictive value required of a scientific theory. Its own proselytizing success effectively falsifies Marx' basic conviction that the economy is the sole determinant of the social "superstructure" – administration, politics, art and religion. Instead, Marxism became a new creed which, in power, transformed economic life in its own image.

A valuable contribution to this rather tired debate comes from a detailed sociological study by Jonas Fox (*Harvest of the Palm, 1977*). The sugar palm (Borassus) and its sap provide several different ethnic groups in Indonesia and India with an identical economic base. According to Marx, these societies should have developed similar social structures. The facts tell a different story.

Roti and Savu are two neighbouring islands between Timor and Java. On Roti, society was built up around a network of legal and commercial relationships. Verbal bravura was highly prized; the litigious Rotinese could talk down even their Dutch colonial masters. Conversely, on Savu the political game was imbued with religious and aristocratic ideas. Physical courage and skill in war were the highest virtues. Consequently the Savunese were often recruited by the Dutch for military service.

On Modura, an island north of Java, the population is Islamic. The Rotinese and Savunese fed the surplus syrup from the palms to pigs, but the Modurese were proscribed from keeping pigs by Koranic instruction. Instead they established an export economy based on sugar-palm products. All three island societies bore the stamp of their idiosyncratic cultural backgrounds. Their social organization did not seem to be noticeably affected by the economic base which they had in common. On the contrary, the modes of production and commerce were fashioned by a highly conservative value frame with deep historical roots.

On the Indonesian islands the conditions of ownership varied a good deal, but every fit person took part in the syrup production process, despite considerable differences in social status. On the Malabar coast in India, however, the tree-owners never climbed the trees. Instead they appropriated the lion's share of the economic yield. The unpropertied tree-climbers, who tapped the palms for syrup, belonged to a lower caste and lived completely segregated from the rest of society without any possibility of social advancement. Only with the advent of Christian missions did the basic rules of the game eventually change.

Once again we have to conclude that the moral imperatives, the obscure foundations of faith, are the mainspring of social and intellectual life. These fundamental guidelines – the very basis of culture – are hardly accessible to even the most sophisticated cultural science. Nonetheless, they can be perceived by their omnipresent intervention in the historical process, steering it towards growth or decline, profit or loss, life or death.

Art as cultural science

cf. 370; 374; 423 Works of art faithfully reflect the richness of the cultural game; great authors have always been supreme social scientists. Art is the pure essence of culture, and should be a rewarding source of knowledge for the human-centred sciences. By and large, this opportunity to close the gap between the "two cultures" has been missed.

Literary critics are artists in their own right, but many pundits have erected pseudoscientific superstructures which, if anything, obscure the reader's view. New fashions flood this field with depressing regularity, as the professional interest swings from engaged realism to disinterested formalism, and from juicy biographical gossip to the arcane process of art in the making. True to form, the deconstructionism of Jacques Derrida attempted to lay bare the step-by-step assembly of a literary work extrapolating from its socio-semiotic preconditions while wilfully neglecting the semantic relevance of the message. The latest swing of this pendulum is referred to as new historicism which seeks to reinstate the social context of writing.

cf. 158; 345; 370

Like the painters and sculptors, the authors of the nineteenth century created a strong illusion of reality, and invited the reader to identify with his or her principal characters. Many of our greatest twentieth-century writers have abandoned this tradition. They observe people from a distance, coolly and with detached objectivity, just as superior beings from outer space might study the subtle reactions of some interesting, earth-bound animal species.

James Joyce's wayward *Ulysses* describes with scientific exactitude, up to the direct registration of the stream of consciousness. In *À la Recherche du Temps Perdu* (Remembrance of Things Past) Marcel Proust captures the hidden play of the mind down to the tiniest fluttering nuance while Robert Musil's (1880–1942) *Der Mann ohne Eigenschaften* (The Man without Qualities) strives systematically to describe and define himself as a sample of the species *Homo sapiens*. In *Der Prozess* (The Trial), Franz Kafka (1883–1924) deconstructs the inhuman machinery of faceless bureaucracy with uncanny exactitude – an impressive feat of reverse psycho-social engineering. In his short stories the external attributes of the totalitarian state are described with telepathic accuracy and the protagonists often assume animal shapes to illustrate the process of vulgarization – an idea that reappears in Eugene Ionesco's *Rhinoceros*.

The scientific detachment and the consequent elimination of any contact with supreme powers comes at a price. Transcendental legitimation is rejected; the cultural game is reduced to an object for clinical analysis; life becomes a series of meaningless, compulsory moves. The scope for play is restricted to the recognition of the absurdity of existence.

The absence of any generally accepted and meaningful goals is the key to the absurd effect. If an ordinary project group is isolated in agonizing uncertainty about what is really the purpose of the exercise, most of its members will be close to mental collapse within a week. The lack of directives combined with an awareness of some distant authority creates unbearable tension and vacuity. Any personal initiative appears arbitrary – mere self-reference is absurd. On the stage this effect has been pushed to its utmost limits. After *Waiting* in vain *for Godot*, Samuel Beckett (1906–89) plays out his dejection in *Endgame*, where the words are definitely deprived of their meaning.

cf. 83; 159; 233; 393; 420

Great art should be a source of inspiration for the human sciences which can be properly defined only within an extended frame of cultural reference. Moreover, we must look deep into our animal ancestry. The gulf between the lofty heights of art and the ethology of primates may seem unbridgeable, but there is something in common between the coalitions of male chimpanzees, the gangs of city youths, and ideological mass movements; between the ordered hierarchy in a troop of baboons and the bureaucratic phenomenon. If we fail to acknowledge and understand our innermost incentives and to recognize the limits of freedom, we will remain the playthings of absurd anonymous forces, tossed back and forth between delusion and despair.

7.4   Illuminating interference

Science is a search for significant patterns which allow for a compact description of the world. But inherently complex structures cannot be significantly reduced without some loss of information; reality is so rich that it must be illuminated from many different angles to yield its secrets. Only by means of accurate and non-trivial predictions, dependable instruments and efficient machines can science demonstrate its own relevance and veracity. The immoderate urge to understand all things imperils the acquisition of reliable knowledge about some of them.

A kaleidoscope of sciences

By now we have found that the concept of "science" covers a wide range of barely commensurable activities carried out under widely varying conditions. But there are innumerable ways of structuring and studying reality, and many of them will be hard to fit into our scheme without further comment.

Classic scientific specialization is like a strong telephoto lens, which eliminates superordinate structures and permits the collection of detailed "objective" information. We get more and more knowledge with less and less content. An opposite approach is to use a wide-angle optic to get the main pattern into focus. Irrelevant details, individual actors and functional mechanisms are then lost in the semi-obscurity of broad generalizations. A third method involves playing the technical game in an effort to prove the underlying principles in any particular application. Reliable information is acquired by a combination of these approaches. The world is so multifarious that only by illuminating it from many different angles can we throw its facets into adequate relief.

Specialized branches of science have their proper pigeonholes, but cross-scientific explications like astronomy, geography or ethology disturb the picture. Additional confusion is caused by structure-oriented approaches, such as cybernetics and morphology, which often simplify their object beyond recognition in their reliance on the impartiality of mathematical modelling. The applied sciences, on the other hand, must adopt topic-related values to retain their relevance. Every form of advanced technology generates its own specialized and explicit knowledge about the existing implicit know-how. These "technical sciences" comprise a set of practical rules for a certain range of applications, and they interbreed in numerous ways with the basic sciences.

We are thus faced with a kaleidoscopic collection of sciences, escalating with the complexity of the object and bursting all bounds in the cultural sphere. The available facts, appropriately rearranged, can be used in a huge variety of contexts and may contribute to widely varying and even conflicting scientific theories. Scientists are, like everybody else, greatly influenced by what they expect or want to see.

> When Galileo Galilei (1564–1642) demonstrated his telescope and invited the sceptics to look at Jupiter's moons for themselves, he met with little success. Critics complained, with some justification, about the ambiguity of visual impressions, about possible reflections within the lens system, about the blurred image, and so on. The moons upset received opinion; they should not have been there, and so people did not see them.

Hard facts are not immutable building blocks in the edifice of science, but are always subject to amendment and reinterpretation. Only by means of accurate and non-trivial predictions, dependable instruments and efficient machines – the rendition of reality – can science hope to demonstrate its veracity.

Confronting reality

Time is the ultimate, all-pervading actuality and the common denominator for a long line of supremely interesting and, in a deep sense, historical sciences. Historiography, radically extrapolated to evolutionary theory and cosmology, expands to become a total description of the world. Astronomy, geology and geography, meteorology, biology and ecology, palaeontology, archeology and etymology are all organized around time-bound processes.

> Mineralogy, for example, is a part of physics, while geology is the history of rocks; their origins, metamorphosis and weathering, the movement of tectonic plates and the folding and erosion of mountain ranges.

The historical sciences are concerned with the unique development of specific games, the continual dynamics of creation. Despite, or rather because of its lack of universality, such inherently anecdotal knowledge is more congenial than perfectly detached fundamental science. Astronomy has always been the gateway to the secrets of the heavens, and biological evolution still conceals many of its secrets. Its tardy progress is sometimes upset by spectacular chance events.

> About 65 million years ago a massive comet struck the earth at Chicxulub on the Yucatan peninsula in Southern Mexico. It created a 300 km wide crater and set off a string of severe environmental changes. The dust and the soot from extensive fires caused a "nuclear winter" followed by greenhouse warming due to the carbon dioxide build-up. Acid rain added to the ravage which wiped out untold species, including the dinosaurs (although other causes may have contributed to their demise). The fallout from this particular big bang can still be spotted all over the globe as the iridium-rich boundary layer between the Cretaceous and the Tertiary epochs.

If we move forward in time, we find ourselves in a "science of the future". The reliability of forecasts is a good gauge of our understanding, and overconfident predictions have taught us many lessons in humility. The sometimes ludicrous mistakes should not prevent us from continuing the unscientific dabbling in futurology but such speculation is intrinsically unreliable, especially when human institutions and values are at stake.

> While commercial products have to pass an array of technical and market tests before launch, extensive "reforms" in welfare or education are often let loose in the brainchild stage. More often than not, extensive massage at the hands of sundry committees and working groups aggravates the malformation. It is a credit to human adaptability that the damage has so far been limited, but disaster can strike on a grand scale when sweeping assumptions about human nature prove horribly wrong. Socialism's ideal citizens were identical, well-programmed, insubstantial robots, easy to fit into a comprehensible cybernetic system. But when the exuberant Marxist ideas were reduced to practice, the diversity of man could not be ignored, nor the constant arguments of reality refuted. The hothouse atmosphere of spurious science was soon dispersed by the fell blasts of naked power play.

Urgent necessity has always been the mother of invention, although nowadays this relation has been turned on its head. Anyway, it is undeniable that war, for example, has precipitated important technical innovations and has thus stimulated scientific progress.

> For centuries, the manufacture of cannons provided the driving force for the progress in metallurgy and the art of machining: these skills were indispensable when constructing the first steam engines. Subsequently, the Carnot cycle and the science of thermodynamics were conceived in order to understand the invariances of energy conversion.

Equally to the point, commercial arithmetic, navigational aids and business computers have all taken turns in impelling the development of the mathematical game, while also bringing what were once esoteric areas of knowledge *cf. 133; 310* within the reach of all. Modern technology and medicine have done the same for physics, chemistry and biology. Optics, physicochemistry and electrodynamics are not congenitally engineering sciences, but are inconceivable without their technological preconditions and applications. Even pure politics can provide a propitious spin-off for science.

> When President Nixon declared war on cancer in 1971, it was clearly a premature move. Despite enormous efforts cancer research has not yet produced a generally effective therapy. But the intensive efforts have born ample fruit in virology, immunology, molecular biology and many other branches of the life sciences.

Structural science

Careful experimentation *per se* does not unlock the vaults of nature; more often it leads us further down the blind alley of personal prejudice. From the very *cf. 315; 345* beginning we need the right bias to learn the right lessons.

> The atomic structure of matter was confidently postulated by John Dalton (1766–1844) in the early years of the nineteenth century, but the question was finally settled only after a whole century of intense debate. Dalton discovered the law of multiple proportions between the elements in chemical compounds, and it became one of the weightiest arguments in support of the atomic theory. But extreme selectivity was called for in the choice of test substances, since most products of nature wilfully deviate from the rule. For example, ordinary rust is a hotch-potch of different iron oxides, which certainly does not give us the text-book sequence FeO, Fe_3O_4, Fe_2O_3. Clay is a peculiar

blend of hydrated silicates of aluminium and so on. As it happened, the atomic principle was so conceptually attractive that scientists believed in it. They brazenly swept away a mass of irrelevant empirical data in the frantic search for decisive proof.

The ability to discern relevant structures is the gift of great scientists. Astonishing feats of judgement put the classical taxonomists of botany and zoology from Linnaeus (Carl von Linné, 1707–78) onwards on the right track. But blinkered prejudice, too, usually finds the evidence it is looking for.

> When Margaret Mead (1901–78) descended on the paradisial islands of the South Pacific in the early 1930s, she was steeped in the fashionable preconception of promiscuous islanders living in a happy state of peaceful innocence, free from neurosis and unspoilt by any culturally induced inhibitions. Her study *"Coming of Age in Samoa"*, substantially reinforced the prevailing misconceptions. This "scientific" evidence for the wholesome effects of sexual licentiousness contributed to the disconcerting influx of pop-psychology and -sociology over the following decades. Her distorted presentation was not called into question until the anthropologist Derek Freemans published a critical study in 1983 (not surprisingly, this reappraisal has been vehemently contravened).

The intrinsic problems of the human sciences are complicated by creeping changes in the epigenetic rules. The perpetual quest for valid simplification all too often turns into blatant self-deception, as opinionated structuralists try to perform their great leaps on scientific crutches. In the breathless search for the all-determining grammatical elements of human behaviour, the dynamics of the game is greatly underestimated. Just as we have cautiously begun to untangle the incredible involution of the simple elements of matter, human actors are frivolously reduced to puppets on a string. Politics and religion, myths, sagas, art – literally all culture is seen as the predetermined outcome of hidden "structures".   *Cf. 106*

> In true Scholastic style the extreme structuralists such as Claude Lévi-Strauss, Roland Barthes (1915–80) and A.J. Greimas seem to prefer an unworldly, exact and erroneous theory to vaguer concepts that confront reality, albeit in an approximate way. They *cf. 349; 370* seek a cultural-scientific mathematics (an algebra of the brain, according to Lévi-Strauss), in which the whole human game can be inferred from given social, economic and linguistic rules. We know that pure deduction fails even in number theory, and yet this amazing programme seeks to derive all culture from a flimsy anthropological base, with a generous sprinkling of psychoanalysis and Marxism, but with no support from the life sciences!

Such fashionable structuralist excesses are an interesting cultural phenomenon in themselves, and may give rise to some worthwhile literature. In their self-immunizing isolation they have little contact with the mainstream of science.

Structuralism versus reductionism

The human urge to explain and understand has, in our culture, expressed itself in a passionate scientific interest. The scientist tries to reduce the studied phenomena to a significantly lower level of complexity by finding or defining the essential rules of the game – ideally in mathematical terms. However, this reductionist programme is subject to severe limitations, as discussed in sections 2.2 and 2.8.

> The wonderful compression of massive amounts of information into simple formulae immensely enhances our thought-economy. The informational garbage from registering a multitude of moves is supplanted by a few lucid rules – but this does not necessarily "solve" the whole game. In most instances we cannot retrieve earlier configurations from present positions of play, and have to be content with simulating alternative futures rather than calculating a predetermined course of events.

cf. 32

In a state of relative ignorance, the tentative imposition of a simplified structure on the unknown is a perfectly legitimate move; in fact it is a fairly general paradigm for the scientific method. Physical particles are resolutely reduced to mathematical points; chemical compounds to molecular structures and electronic resonances; heredity to the interplay of genes; life processes to cybernetically-linked chemical reactions. Society or the biosphere or, indeed, the whole world can be reduced to a vast but greatly simplified and thus comprehensible game.

> Bold reductionist assumptions certainly facilitate meaningful structuring in the "soft" sciences. An intractable scientific object can often be "frozen" by postulating the permanence of the explicit rules. The task then becomes manageable, at the cost of a severe loss in predictive power. But without at least a temporary deep freeze, the empirical apparatus simply cannot function, however many multi-factorial regression analyses are performed.
>
> Game theory, cybernetics and information theory are prominent among the structural sciences, with semiotics and the emerging science of complexity as aspiring candidates. They are concerned with pure interactions, a kind of thermodynamics of abstraction, and they may all too easily acquire an aura of value-free and exact objectivity. For all that, the scientific interest has been substantially focused, compared with pure mathematics. Concepts such as "players", "self-regulatory systems" and "information" are introduced as conceptual reflections of active and goal-oriented processes. These very flaws introduce utility, but they also nullify high-flown expectations of creating "a science of sciences". Instead, the eventual rise in the vantage point should bring into view ever-increasing areas of ignorance.

The narrow limits of logical bootstrapping have become apparent, and full-blown reductionism is not feasible even in the "hard" sciences. Nevertheless it has preserved its attraction for many cultural scientists. Confronted by the basic dilemma of their trade, these compulsive structuralists rely on brute simplification and promptly arrive at results which fly in the face of reality. Once again we come up against the Platonic fallacy that ideas rank higher than hard facts. Ingenious mental tools acquire a mystical fascination and we fall all too easily to worshipping such man-made structures, endowing them with supernatural powers.

> The structuralist approach regularly raises the level of abstraction and generalization (the "scientificity"), into the realms of mathematics. This usually happens at the expense of the truth content; after all, only one out of a thousand random 1,000-bit strings can be mathematically compressed by more than one per cent. Even in the natural sciences, simplification has often come close to qualified dissimulation. The wonderfully simple general equation of state holds strictly only for "ideal" gases; when we try to

account for the real state of affairs, the mathematics get messy indeed. Idealized gas particles have no intrinsic volume and exert no mutual attraction or repulsion. Like the ideal people of a socialist society they are "dead", robbed of their small but disturbing creative potential.

Science is a search for significant patterns which allow for a compact description of complex phenomena. But rich and complex structures cannot be compactified without some loss of information. The problem is to reduce without amputating, to operate on the superabundance of empirical material without finishing off the subject matter. Autopsy is necessary to the acquisition of anatomical knowledge but a corpse is too ideal a patient – accommodating, predictable, and constitutionally void of unpleasant surprises.

Prima principia

We would do well to call a temporary halt here, and to restore some order after the turbulent play of the sciences. Let me for once summarize my position without recourse to the game metaphor:

☐ Logic was long regarded as a sort of philosopher's stone, until its rather limited role as a mental tool in mathematics came to be clearly recognized. Similarly, mathematics is the exact language of the natural sciences, a universal aid which is strictly applicable only under special conditions.

☐ To be serviceable, every scientific symbol system must be subordinated to more competent means of expression. In the last instance it must be incorporated in a metalanguage – our all-embracing mother tongue.

☐ All true knowledge is empirical. The successes of the natural and life sciences stem from patient efforts to understand highly selected and relatively unchanging structures in the real world.

☐ If experiments cannot be reliably repeated under identical conditions, then it is an abuse of language to equate them with natural science. Furthermore, the conditions, interpretations, objectives and above all the significance and dependability of these soft sciences diverge widely from each other.

☐ In the hierarchy of sciences, empirical falsifiability decreases and causal inference is weakened as the objects become increasingly complex and the actors acquire significant degrees of freedom. The value register must be extended accordingly.

☐ The stability of the invariances also falls off as we rise in the scientific hierarchy. Basic logical principles and laws of nature gradually lose their relevance and are finally overtaken by man-made conventions.

The world cannot be reduced to a narrow set of first principles. On the contrary, the evolution of complexity calls for the introduction of supplementary axiomatic material which is intrinsic to the subject matter and defines it at the deepest level. The syntax and the semantics of the discourse become increasingly entangled, defying all attempts at rigorous reductionism. When non-linea- *cf. 320; 348* rities and chaotic patterns prevail, humble simulation is the only way to deal with overly complex reality.

A specifically "scientific" world-view cannot be derived from our aggregate experience. Central dogmas – causality and predictability – are not empirically verifiable but are established *a priori*. Exaggeration of their applicability leads to scientific arrogance and intellectual hubris – dead-ends which most great scientists have avoided, if not in principle then at least in practice. The immoderate urge to understand all things imperils the acquisition of reliable knowledge about some of them.

7.5   Science gone astray

Antique science was sucked down in a maelstrom of moral apathy and false play. For centuries, overweening pretensions (soothsaying) and spectacular aspirations (gold making) blocked progress by suppressing information and dissipating the scientific interest. These specious goals had to be dislodged in favour of the humble study of reality before the shackles of received wisdom could be shaken off. For us, the world-view of the natural sciences is so self-evident that we regard its breakthrough as an inevitable and irreversible process. The profound cumulative development of knowledge is in fact an exceptional if not a unique event. In the absence of liberty and tolerance, scientific objectivity sooner or later falls prey to the mental self-satisfaction of people who loathe to face the truth.

Antique shallowness

Knowledge is a special aspect of our culture, fascinating because it appears universally valid and therefore irrevocable – eternal, one might say. But it does share this quality with other more utilitarian activities. Oral and written communication, pottery, weaving and tool-making owe nothing to science and yet they seem, in the light of history, to have firmer roots in the cultural tradition.

The decline of antique science during the Dark Ages is often quoted as an example of regression, and the traditional explanations are readily invoked: the fall of the Roman Empire and the chaos of the Germanic migrations. But the fall of science had begun much earlier, astronomy being the most spectacular case.

Let us examine the chain of events:
- Eudoxos of Knidos (ca. 408–355 B.C.) posits the celestial bodies in a sequence of concentric spheres, which rotate round the earth. Aristotle accepts this view of the heavens;
- around 370 B.C. Heraclides of Pontus suggests that the stars are fixed and that the earth rotates;

– around 270 B.C. Aristarchus of Samos adopts Heraclides' conjecture and proposes   *cf. 38*
an essentially Copernican heliocentric model of the planetary system. His idea aroused
a good deal of attention but did not receive general recognition; and
– in 150 A.D. Ptolemy of Alexandria fixes the established orthodoxy in a doctrinaire
geocentric system where the planets, the stars and the sun travel round the earth in
involved epicycles – intricate combinations of circular movements.

Despite the refinements in detail, a correctly conjectured and verifiable truth
had been lost during the course of the drawn-out scientific debate. The victory
of geocentric astronomy is the greatest scientific scandal of all time. It was the
result of a desperate attempt to protect the prevailing astronomical conventions, to "save the phenomena" as the Greeks said. Ptolemy successfully tallied
the stubborn data and kept up appearances about planetary behaviour.

> Quite unabashed Ptolemy declares in the *Almagest*: "We believe that the goal of astron-
> omy is the following: to demonstrate that all celestial phenomena are caused by immu-
> table and circular movements ... after we put to ourselves the task to prove, that the
> apparent irregularities of the five planets, the sun and the moon all can be represented
> by immutable, circular movements, because only such movements are fitting to their
> divine nature ... We are justified in assuming the completion of this task to be the
> ultimate goal for philosophically-based mathematical science."

According to Plato the circle is the most perfect curve, and the celestial bodies   *cf. 33; 121*
had no choice but to match this perfection. The only way of accommodating the
Platonic principle was by introducing a contorted concoction of 40 circular
epicycles – an offensively artificial construct.

> The heliocentric system of Aristarchus had one glaring problem. Its predictions were
> occasionally quite inaccurate – Mars was, at times, up to 15 degrees wide of the mark.
> Ptolemy could reduce the maximum aberration to a few degrees, and Copernicus was
> unable to improve on that figure even though he played around with off-centre posi-
> tions of the sun. Johannes Kepler was the first to consider elliptical orbits and changing
> velocities for the planets. He had the guts to discard years of arduous reckoning because
> of a 0.1 degree discrepancy between his calculations and the positions observed by
> Tycho Brahe (1546–1601).   *cf. 117*

We have no reason to be condescending about the scholars of Antiquity; they
were certainly our intellectual equals and possibly our superiors. But we can try
to learn from their fundamental errors. Astronomy cannot be written off as
chance accident, since other instances are not hard to find. Democritus' forgotten atomic theory, revived by Epikuros (341–271 B.C.) and Lucretius (97–57
B.C.), is a famous but not altogether apt example. Given the resources available   *cf. 36*
at the time the hypothesis was neither verifiable nor falsifiable; it represented a
piece of brilliant guesswork, a sparkling rocket in the pyrotechnic display of
natural philosophy in fifth-century classical Greece.

    Other trends are all the more convincing: the classic but eminently practical
medicine of Hippocrates, Herophilus and Erosistratus congealed in Galen's
faulty physiology and Dioscorides' famous but fundamentally flawed herbal
while Pythagoras' mathematical visions petered out in Euclid's admirable but
intellectually arrogant and rather sterile compilations. With a few outstanding

exceptions not only science but art and literature, too, are marred by similar shallowness.

> Around the time of Christ's birth, Maecenas ("minister for culture" to Augustus) and his circle were pouring new Latin wine into old Greek bottles. Virgil's *Georgics* and *Aeneid* follow the pattern of Hesiod and Homer while Horace took the ancient poet Archilochus (c. 700 B.C.) as a model in composing his *Ars poetica*, a poetic Almagest. Ovid, with his *Metamorphoses* and *Ars Amatoria* – Almagests of human emotion – was perhaps the most original writer in this group; symptomatically, he was exiled. The copying craze was particularly evident in the fine arts where imitations of Greek originals swamped the market. Only Roman architecture displays an innovative streak, for instance in the building of domes and aqueducts which was made possible by the invention of hard-setting concrete.

The Golden Age of Latin literature is imbued with those specific Roman virtues of realism, thoroughness and objectivity, which unfortunately tail off into pedantry, and which are more at home in military campaigning, building projects, law or historiography. Even at its best, art was merely a superficial ornament on the splendid edifice of power, deficient in deeper cultural contacts.

In *The Death of Virgil* Herman Broch (1886–1951) has given us a masterly portrayal of this incipient decadence. By the third century A.D., only the Alexandrian Academy sustained some creative talent in the shape of mathematicians like Diophantus and Pappus. The intellectual life of Rome consisted largely of empty rhetoric, tired imitations, paraphrases and travesties, all of them feeble variations on exhausted themes. Rigorous conformity to the rules led to pure affectation; the artists had drifted off into their own congenital epicycles.

cf. 110

A tortuous path

A good deal of antiquity's abundant legacy was preserved in Byzantium and further enriched under the aegis of Islam. Algebra and trigonometry came into their own while astronomy, geography and medicine made notable progress, particularly under the Califs in Baghdad.

> Our Arabic number system was originally conceived by Indian mathematicians; Brahmagupta (?598–?665) already applied negative numbers. The famous Arab astronomer al-Khwarizmi (?780–?850) was the first to document the Sanskrit signs and place-value notation in Arabic (his name, also spelled "al-Khuwarizmi" or "al-Khorezmi", became transfixed in the word *algorithm*). As it happened, this radical innovation reached Christian Europe only in the year 1202 when Leonardo Fibonacci of Pisa (?1170-?1240) published his *Liber Abaci* ("Book of computations").

Islamic science eventually came to a standstill and even began to regress by the end of the twelfth century. Enduring scientific development was obviously incompatible with the meta-rules of the Koran, and the initiative passed to semi-barbarian Western Europe.

> The finale of this process comes with an ironic twist. When Christopher Columbus (1466–1506) tried to raise funds for his bid to discover the western passage to India, sound Islamic science proved a major obstacle. To start with, Henry VII of England and Charles VIII of France promptly turned a deaf ear whereas John II of Portugal gave the

matter his serious attention. John's scientific commission, the *Junta de Mathemàticos*, cited the calculations of the ninth-century Arabian astronomer al-Farghani, which in turn were based on the *Geography* of Eratosthenes who lived in Alexandria during the third century B.C. The experts correctly estimated the distance to semi-mythical Cipangu (i.e. Japan) at about 20,000 km and did not accept Columbus' amateurish guesstimate of 4,440 km. Consequently, the whole project was turned down.

A first Spanish commission reached similar conclusions but a second one was swayed by political pressure to swallow Columbus' fortunate underestimate. It drew heavily on the later and less reliable Ptolemy, the acknowledged authority in Europe on geography as well as astronomy. Basking in the victory over the Moors, Ferdinand and Isabella finally in 1492 decided to invest in the Western passage in the hope of trumping their Portuguese rivals whose South African route had just been discovered by Bartolomeo Diaz.

Like the Pilgrim's Progress, the tortuous path of scientific discovery is lined with treacherous temptations. After all, the débâcle of Antiquity seems to represent the normal case in which human short-sightedness, egotism and weariness get the upper hand. Even great scientists can sometimes impede the advance of their   *cf. 317* successors.

> Galileo was so full of his own newly discovered rationalism that he rejected any possibility of remote forces acting over long distances between celestial bodies. Accordingly, he denied any lunar interference in earthly matters. Instead he thought that the tides depend solely on the earth's rotation, and saw this as the clinching argument for the Copernican system. Thanks to their religious inclinations, Kepler and Newton were better prepared to accept God's omnipotence in rationally comprehensible mathematical terms.

Today, human narrow-mindedness and cynical careerism are swamping the problematic human-centred sciences, making it difficult to distinguish between the genuine search for truth and the variations of modern astrology. The participation of some academic experts in political decision-making recalls the role of the augurs and alchemists of old. The wise ruler has always included such people in his entourage to enhance his prestige and to show his receptiveness to the "science" of his day.

Dilettantes and professionals

All sciences have a shady pre-history. Numerology, astrology and alchemy were embryonic proto-sciences, pursuing goals incompatible with scientific enterprise. The aim was to achieve immediate material advantage in one spectacular swoop; the instant production of gold, horoscopes, and the elixir of life were paramount interests.

> The occult sciences of the Middle Ages built on the hermetic teachings of the Ancients, transformed by Arabian proto-scientists into the rudiments of scientific method. These esoteric doctrines, a hotch-potch of eastern necromancy and neo-platonic philosophy, were "hermetically" sealed to the uninitiated. The secretive bent was transferred to latterday offshoots like the Rosicrucians and the Freemasons; nor was there any rush for publication in the early days of European science. The general solution to the cubic equation $x^3 + ax + b = 0$ was discovered by the Bolognese professor Scipiono del Ferro in

the year 1515 but was made public only in 1545 by Gerolamo Cardano in his mathematical treatise *Artis Magnae*.

For centuries overweening pretensions and spectacular aspirations blocked progress by suppressing information and dissipating the scientific interest. These specious goals had to be dislodged in favour of the humble study of reality before the shackles of received wisdom could be shaken off.

> The proto-chemist Paracelsus, actually christened Philippus Aureolus Theophrastus Bombastus von Hohenheim (1493–1541), first studied at Fugger's *Bergschule* and then went the rounds of most of the European universities, completing his education as a military barber-surgeon. The self-centred dilettantism and pretentious exaggerations of the Renaissance man concealed a genuine visionary – the "Luther of medicine". He stressed the admission of ignorance: "If thou wilt love thy neighbour, thou must not say: For thee there is no help. But thou must say: I cannot do it and I understand it not. This truth shields thee from the curse that descends on the false".
>
> Paracelsus relied exclusively on observation, and bravely challenged the antiquated authorities of his day. He was the first to stress the importance of dosage, preparing the way for more systematic successors like Antoine Laurent Lavoisier (1743–1794), the man famous for the laboratory balance.

Today we are beset with equally pretentious doctrines which do not add up to good science. The several contributions fail to cumulate convincingly over time. Even so, "science" and "scientific" have become terms of high esteem which are believed to vouch for veracity, status and government grants. Since the human and cultural sciences suffer from a credibility deficit, researchers in these fields are tempted to engage in scientific mimicry, associating themselves with the natural sciences and the successes of technology and medicine. The transient successes of some of the soft sciences do not appear very convincing; the absence of universality stands in sharp contrast to the exaggerated claims that are made.

cf. 226; 314
> Unfortunately Keynes' famous *General Theory of Employment, Interest and Money* (1936) has not justified its title, and the fashionable propensity for hyper-mathematical approaches has hardly increased the usefulness of economics. The Nobel prize-winner Wassily Leontief has described these disquisitions as follows: "Page after page, the economic journals are crammed with mathematical formulas, which lead the reader from assumptions – which sound more or less reasonable but are in fact quite arbitrary – to precisely established but irrelevant theoretical conclusions." David Colander (in *The Making of an Economist*, (1990) together with Arjo Klamer) really rubs it in: "...the profession has lost its bearings and has allowed self-interest to govern the choice of theories. Formal empirical tests are not done to answer questions, but...to satisfy reviewers and advisers. Pay, not the fulfilment of intellectual curiosity, becomes the scientists' reward."

Time and again erudite academic "expertise" has been put in its place by impassioned outsiders. But cut off from the mainstream of science even an intellect like Leonardo da Vinci (1452–1519) was unable to free himself from the fetters of the old Aristotelian language game. Unlike composers and painters, sculptors and poets, scientists create only collective masterpieces.

Faltering meta-rules

Heraclitus saw the pre-classical Greek world as one of continual change and becoming, and in the third century B.C. the genius of Archimedes was still open *cf. 35* to experiment and confrontation with practical problems. Nevertheless, a static world-view became predominant; reality was seen as an imperfect reflection of abstract ideas; human existence as a fitful regression from the Golden Age. It remained for science to justify the ideal, and to defy heterodoxy by tinkering with the facts if necessary.

Being wise after the event we can try to explain the Ptolemaic fiasco in terms of an inadequate scientific approach, but so far we have searched in vain for the correct meta-scientific method. The scholars of antiquity were unable to uphold the scientific game because they could not or would not heed the jarring notes of foul play. The defect was not intellectual but in the frame of mind. In all its splendour, the Hellenistic sense of beauty was flawed, inculcating a faulty faith. Adherence to superficial symmetry, and conformity to revered precedent were the basic tenets of aesthetics. Science became steeped in petty pedantry, resulting in all-embracing Almagests, self-parodying apotheoses of definitive scientific truths.

> A peculiar naivety in matters of health went hand in hand with the lack of metaphysical receptiveness. The Romans started early to use lead acetate to preserve wine, thus inhibiting the fermentation of alcohol to acetic acid (vinegar); at the same time the wine acquired a pleasantly sweet taste. A large section of the Roman upper class consequently suffered from chronic lead poisoning (the lead-lined water-pipes did not constitute a serious health hazard). The Greek custom of using resin for the same purpose may have been one reason for the more persistent vitality of the Eastern Empire.

Creative development is certainly very time-consuming and is therefore always in a hurry, but in fact there was time to spare. The Graeco-Roman world enjoyed relative tranquility for many centuries and Byzantium preserved its political continuity until the fatal fourth crusade of 1203. Little if anything of interest to the history of science occurred during this long millennium of imperial rule; Byzantine scholarship thrived mainly on theological tracts.

> The regression of science was only one of many symptoms of intellectual decline during late Antiquity. People dared not or could not play fair. The result was a self-righteous flight from reality, a defensiveness in the face of existential challenge, a retreat into a closed value-universe – in other words a collective mental disorder. An unmoving earth at the centre of the world nicely matched the paranoid megalomania of the human ego.

To us, the world-view of the natural sciences is so self-evident that we regard its breakthrough as an inevitable and irreversible process. But profound cumulative development of knowledge is an exceptional if not a unique event. In India the concept of a rotating earth was put forward by Aryabhata around 550 A.D. During the following centuries the impetus of moving objects was properly understood, and an atomic theory of matter was propounded but there was no follow up. In China, too, the meta-rules of domestic culture seemed to avert the systematic progress of science.

> The Chinese kept a close watch on Heaven which was considered the ultimate author-

ity. In the year 1054 they took note of a new star, a powerful supernova which has left its mark in the sky as the steadily expanding Crab nebula. This observational acuity was betrayed by unsound calculations. Twenty years later, the famous Chinese astrolabe-maker Su Sung was commissioned by his emperor to present a gift to the "barbarian prince" Liaos on his birthday which happened to coincide with the winter solstice. Alas, the Chinese calendar was inaccurate and Su Sung presented his congratulations one day early, a serious breach of etiquette with concomitant diplomatic consequences. The chronicler adds a revealing comment. "Since the barbarians had no [political] re-strictions on their astronomical and calendrical studies, their experts in this field were generally better [than ours], their calendar was actually correct..."

After his return, Su Sung was ordered to rectify the situation. He duly built a huge water-driven horologe which faithfully simulated the movements of the celestial bodies and provided a database for indispensable horoscopes. But this wonderful machine soon fell into disrepair: every new emperor was inclined to proclaim his own personal calendar which would enhance his role as surety for the Harmony of the Heavens. Under such circumstances reality had to bow to appearances and would-be scientists were careful not to cause cosmic scandals; research always had to submit to the state.

Totalitarian regimes are by their very nature incompatible with scientific ad-vance. Galileo's mild martyrdom, Hitler's obliteration of "Jewish science", and Stalin's brutal Lysenkoism all aimed at suppression of distressing facts. In the absence of liberty and tolerance, scientific objectivity sooner or later falls prey to the mental self-satisfaction of people who are loathe to face the truth.

7.6   Knowledge and faith

Science was resurrected by the spirit of humble, long-term inquiry, a new kind of divine service. The natural sciences slowly matured in a self-critical learning process. They cannot verify any explicit view of life, but they have become an indispensable part of every open value universe. Such universal truths may not be attainable within the 'soft' sciences. Instead of emulating the natural sciences, the different schools of human and cultural scientists ought to understand and openly declare their specific value frame. The fruits of the diverse scientific efforts will, in due course, bear witness to the quality of the underlying faith.

Superb self-mortification

In the absence of knowledge man has turned throughout history to magic and occultism, the intellectual dead-ends of sterile superstition. Ignorance and un-predictability in vital spheres of interest weigh heavily upon him; proto-scien-tific hypotheses all too readily become exalted dogma.

Embracing a faith implies a sublime absorption of uncertainty that bears within itself the seeds of self-righteous and sometimes impregnable self-delusion. Time and again, chiliastic sectarians have staked all their credibility on predicting the end of the world at a particular date. But lo and behold, the failure of the prophecy does not topple the faith; perhaps, it is claimed, there has been a fault in the intricate calculations, or fervent prayers may have averted the disaster. A truly self-immunizing doctrine manages to accommodate all possible facts, even its own negation; the disciples have ceased to live with their uncertainty.

The natural sciences have been granted the privilege of sweeping away a profusion of ingrained misconceptions. Generations of intrepid scientists formulated the rules which obtain for simple material actors, and structured the available evidence into a convincing evolutionary pattern. The success has been earned by the painful digestion of mistakes in method and measurement, and above all by the repeated self-humiliation of the scientific community.

> The episode of Clever Hans is a comedy of errors showing that respectable scientists, *cf. 83* too, can be prone to stubborn self-deception. At the turn of the last century, Professor van Osten, in all seriousness, launched his horse Clever Hans as a mathematical wonder. To begin with, the horse would indicate the result of simple arithmetical operations by tapping with his front hoof, but gradually he learned to solve increasingly complex problems. It did not matter who posed the almost arbitrary questions; they were generally answered with the correct number of taps.
>
> The horse's ability to count was widely accepted as authentic, until Karl Stumpf (1848–1936) and Oscar Pfungst (1874–1932) discovered the secret in 1904. Small, involuntary head movements provided the necessary clues for Clever Hans to read the questioner's mind. In other words the horse recognized when it was getting "hot" and stopped tapping at the psychological moment! But when Pfungst denied the horse any visual contact, or when the experimenter himself did not know the answer, the horse was stumped. Thus the double-blind method was established. To eliminate the effects of any prejudice, both subject and researcher must be kept in ignorance of the set-up of the experiment.

Profound scepticism has repeatedly proved its worth in clearing out the rubbish of credulous research. Spiritualism in various guises is a latent contagion, sometimes evoking a veritable orgy of spring-cleaning. Logical positivism and *cf. 106; 279* psychological behaviourism were the overt symptoms of this dread of germs, proudly displaying the appropriate hygienic sterility. A dreary doctrine was imposed on scientific inquiry, squeezing the inferences into illusory epicycles that merely lampooned reality.

> This self-amputation was a perverse instance of intellectual hubris, harking back to the Platonic preponderance of "first principles". Ironically, the ardent appeals to absolute determinism coincided with the breakdown of strict causality within physics. The gross fallibility of, say, psychology and the social sciences has been demonstrated over and over again; most "soft" scientists still refuse to eat humble pie, insisting on the irrelevance of the life sciences for their endeavour. Nor do they admit the introduction of additional axiomatics which could prove mistaken and would imperil the artificial state of unassailability.

Bold acts of faith are meta-hypotheses, primal directives of culture providing *cf. 43* the ultimate context for all human activity including science. Naturally these basic tenets are influenced by feedback from the scientific decoding of the world. The problems of science must not be transformed into questions of faith.

> As a scientist, Newton was constantly torn between physics and alchemy, but his

strongest passion was a quest for religious percipience. His hard-won insight reads: "...
hypothesis should be subservient only in explaining the properties of things, but not
assumed in determining them unless so far as they may furnish experiments..."

Faith cannot replace knowledge but values, inspired by faith, are the key to the
exhaustive development of knowledge. The juxtaposition of belief in divine
perfection with painstaking but generally disappointing observation produced
superb self-mortification. Through such ordeals human inquisitiveness was
transmuted into scientific understanding.

Victorious humility

The first commandment of any plus-sum game is: "Thou shalt not cheat". The
philosophers of Antiquity certainly accepted this rule on an intellectual level,
but their science was rendered impotent by its lack of interaction with society at
cf. 133 large. It became an abstract game without roots in any deeper convictions. Lack
of faith could not be compensated for by any amount of rational dexterity; in
the end cheating penetrated all society.

The ancient penchant for secrecy was equally inimical to scientific progress.
Only in the limelight of public discussion could the world-view of Copernican
astronomy hold its own in conflict with the powerful Church, however split by
the schisms of reformation. Excepting Galilei, the founding fathers of astronomy and physics were deeply religious men, albeit of very diverse personal
persuasions. The Greek legacy of unbridled intellectualism was tempered by
humility. The new creed was content with incremental progress; it distrusted
immoderate claims while accepting the criticism of competent colleagues.

Despite the bombast of the Baroque, the intolerance of the religious wars and
the superficial optimism of the Enlightenment, a humble, self-aware and rational scientific attitude began to gain ground. A small but loyal band was attracted by novel ideas and instruments, patiently applying empirical means towards
an understanding of the world. By the end of the nineteenth century, tentative
scientific hypotheses had acquired substantial self-certification. Science began
to have an impact on public life and, more significantly, on the public mind.

> No-one represents the spirit of the times better than Louis Pasteur. Following funda-
> mental chemical discoveries (stereoisomerism), he contributed to the foundations of
> biochemistry, biology and immunology, discovered new industrial processes (Pasteur-
> isation), and developed a vaccine for anthrax and rabies. It is less well known that after
> conducting a series of meticulous experiments he refuted once and for all the theory of
> spontaneous generation, and demonstrated that in the contemporary world, all life is
> built on antecedents.
>
> Pasteur is a Renaissance figure in the world of science. With his mastery of diverse
> areas of knowledge, he did not hesitate to go out into the field and tackle practical
> problems head on. Pasteur was not above astute self-promotion, and occasionally
> appropriated the work of competing researchers without due acknowledgement. He
> was embroiled in numerous controversies but did not allow his political opinions and
> religious conviction to spill over into his scientific work.

Enlightened opinion gradually adopted natural science, and its methods were revered as the infallible and inexhaustible sources of truth. Individuals and groups invoking other frames of reference were smugly dismissed as curiosities, ripe for the dustbins of history.

> In the hands of the self-appointed prophets of materialism the rather cautious criticism of the Enlightenment degenerated into religion-bashing. Pseudo-scientific platitudes were dressed up as the final answers of a synthetic sociology. Auguste Comte's cocksure positivism and Émile Durkheim's (1858–1917) deification of the state are exponents of this brand-new scientism, which found its political expression in Marxism.   *cf. 170; 413*

The "scientific" arrogance of philosophical besserwissers has burdened us with intellectual elephantiasis. We owe nothing to such misguided worship of naked rationality which was given the lie by the greatest scientists of the time.

> Michael Faraday (1791–1867), the father of electrodynamics, is a case in point. The originator of the field concept and the orginator of the electric generator (and motor) clung intensely to his small fundamentalist sect of Sandemanians. In his daily life, Faraday kept his science and religion apart but in a deeper sense they were of a piece.

Our late insight into the structure of matter and the universe is a byproduct of other aspirations, more subtle and pristine. The natural sciences constitute not a catalogue of truth but a continuous, self-critical learning process. They cannot verify any explicit view of life, but they have become an indispensable part of every open and evolving value universe.

Scientific pluralism

Like life, science is forever branching out and, outside its established range, it too is groping in the dark. The burning ambition of scientists is to overcome or at least to suppress this humiliating condition. No matter, at the all-important cutting edge they are restricted to inspired Darwinian fumbling. Most efforts are and must be grievously misapplied, but the ineluctable waste paradoxically endows the scientific game with its very information value.   *cf. 117; 377; 389*

While natural science has found its footing, the 'soft' sciences are still at a loss. Whole research programmes could be misguided or, what is worse, completely irrelevant. Moreover, truth may be unattainable by any single route: the nature of "soft" reality could be describable only as the sum total of several complementary approaches. Thus, the human and cultural sciences should quite consciously sort themselves out among distinct "schools" which would, each in its own way, integrate different branches of learning into a coherent whole.   *cf. 413*

> The foremost task of any school should be to test the inherent meta-hypothesis, the underlying normative axiomatics which may appear arbitrary to the outside observer. The disciples have to be rather doctrinaire but the existence of rival schools guarantees the exchange of trenchant criticism. A keen interest in the values of the competitors should not be incompatible with loyalty to the chosen alternative.
>
> The different schools would be mutually comprehensible because they could be consistent within their self-selected frame of reference. Inanity or barrenness would be attributed to inadequate or even mendacious values. Dependable meta-rules, on the other hand, could be inferred from well-behaved bodies of knowledge. Progress ex-

pressed in terms of scientific "productivity" would thus confirm the underlying axiomatic value system.

Not even natural science has proved immune to paradigmatic shifts, and cosmology as well as particle physics may still be in for many surprises. Synthetic thrusts, to be sure, call for more elaborate axiomatics and much greater absorption of uncertainty. Hence the adoption of value pluralism appears unavoidable if we want to avoid serious fallacies, especially in the cultural sciences. Meanwhile, old superstitions continue to doggedly pursue scientific status.

cf. 43; 155   The overwhelming majority of serious scientists are rejecting the "science" of parapsychology out of hand, but the American Association for the Advancement of Science was overstepping its case when it banned the publication of any positive reports. One should not *a priori* dismiss all paranormal testimony as fraud or hallucination. The absence of convincing, easily controlled and reproducible evidence need not necessarily preclude the possible occurrence of occasional spontaneous phenomena which do not follow any rules of play and which are therefore inaccessible to scientific analysis. Even if almost all the "observations" are self-deceptions or fakes, we may sooner or later strike some deep-lying singularity. For example, just one water-proof case of extra-sensory perception (telepathy in plain English) would cause an extremely interesting crack in our world-view.

Despite the present untenability of parapsychology the door should always be kept open for the unexpected. The breakdown of normality, as in hereditary disease or brain damage, often allows a glimpse of the concealed mechanisms which maintain the smooth workings of the existential machinery. Pioneering experiments sometimes succeed in manoeuvring the object into an "impossible" situation, which may provoke unexpected moves and disclose deeper rules of the game. If we categorically dismiss the possibility of "impermissible" deviations, we renege on fundamental principles and assume a self-righteous, totalitarian stance.

Meaning in the machine

Tenable results beyond the range of the natural sciences can only be obtained by applying a suitable set of values that provides an appropriate frame for the relevant research programme. Structure-oriented conceptual schemes such as information theory or cybernetics certainly apply to widely divergent schools of thought. Still, they require the infusion of some expediency or "meaning" into *cf. 296* the system, a feature they have in common with biology. As we ascend the hierarchy of science, it becomes ever harder to take the measure of these crucial values. All the same, without such external support the knowledge structure falls apart, leaving nothing but a heap of irrelevant and incommensurable data.

The "softness" of a science is related to the nature of the relevant measuring rods which, in some sense, must match or surpass the properties of the objects under investigation. Furthermore, we need a superior language with an implicit value frame to organize the *cf. 28; 331*   data thus acquired. To reiterate: no language can express its own truth criteria.

In the applied sciences, fairly self-evident objectives generally ensure relevance. But here too, over-conscientious scientists may fall into methodological traps.

> In medicine, for instance, demands for statistical reliability may mean that a therapy which, on average, helps 50 per cent of the patients in a large group but upsets the other half, is declared statistically ineffective. Human unicity quickly exhausts available research capabilities. To achieve optimal treatment, each one of us really needs a personal physician, or better still a team of highly qualified specialists for our individual care.

A structuralistic approach (say in mechanics) leads to a fairly universal set of rules, while concrete problem-solving (say in mechanical engineering) presupposes the existence of superordinate techno-economic guidelines. To allow for the assessment of long-term societal effects, the meta-rules must be further augmented – to the inevitable detriment of their universality. A whole hierarchy of values is necessary for the interpretation of historical processes – the "machine" of history.

> Dizzy with success, technology and medicine are about to burst their original self-defining bounds. The restraints on technology have already been tightened but the inherent problems of medical intervention, including eugenics and euthanasia cannot be neglected much longer. A revision of the pertinent meta-rules should be high on our cultural agenda, lest we lose sight of the meaning of human life.

In the end we arrive at the question of the purpose of compiling scientific knowledge, or in other words, the justification of science. In their own day, Pythagoras and Plato cleared the way for pure mathematics with bold acts of faith, and the pioneers of the natural sciences introduced corresponding metaphysical convictions. Similar efforts are needed to bring order into the confusion of disparate studies in the human and cultural sciences; only then can the diverging perceptions coalesce around competing, value-oriented paradigms. To make progress, we must once and for all abandon the illusion of a self-explanatory, monolithic body of knowledge, of an unambiguous, analytically inferred, absolute and ultimate truth. *cf. 414*

We are just at the beginning of a long, probably endless journey of intellectual inquest. So far, only the most tractable problems have been solved and any self-approbation is highly premature. We have only the faintest idea how to cope with the interplay of non-linearities, and lack even a good measure of the complexity which pervades the real world. Humility is thus, once again, called *cf. 389* for and we should resist the temptation to speculate on universal meta-values, a superparadigm of human erudition. Genuine knowledge has to keep up unremitting contact with its own limitations, but for this very reason definitive truth, the ultimate frame of reference, must remain beyond its recognition. We have no base for ecumenical efforts and no grounds for anticipating the final goal of the game. All we can, and must, postulate is a wide-open value universe, in which the conflicting claims to verity can join their voices in a richer harmony.

7.7   The scientist's values

Science does not create values; rather, certain values create scientists, while other values breed politicians, businessmen, artists or chessmasters. The augmentation of manifest truth is the purpose of the scientist's existence. The conscientious researcher is seeking a small stake in immortality; behind serious scientific work there is always a hidden agenda – the search for God. The challenge is to control the hubris of hyperrationalism – science as superstition. We must preserve the priceless personal religion which is the deepest source of scientific truth. Only then will we grasp the immense potential of scientific inquiry, as well as its limitations; only then will science become a universal tool and mesh into our cultural credo.

Truth-seeking coalitions

Scientific work presupposes close interplay between people with at least one common passion: the thirst for truth, focused on the object of their scientific interest. Among his peers, the scientist acts loyally for both prosecution and defence; he takes consecutive turns on the bench and in the dock. His only guidelines are the rules held in common by the scientific coalition, a special kind of jurisprudence which operates without written legislation and has no need of police or prisons. This code of honour is implanted in our deepest religious conceptions, a cross between cool classical rationalism and impassioned Judaeo-Christian morality.

> It has been shown that not only Ptolemy but Newton, Justus Liebig (1803–73) and Gregor Mendel (1822–84) among others manipulated or "adjusted" their data. A meticulous criminal investigation would probably cast at least some shadow over most of the pioneers of science. Outright swindle has repeatedly scandalized the scientific establishment. The Piltdown hoax deceived a whole generation of anthropologists, and recently the highly respected psychologist Sir Cyril Burt (1883–1971) was posthumously accused of fabricating extensive studies of identical twins which vindicated his belief in the heritability of intelligence. The widespread and widely-believed allegations are obviously heavily biased and exaggerated out of all proportion. Burt was certainly guilty of sloppy records and he mixed up some data, but systematic fraud seems to be out of the question... unless the latest testimony can be denounced as fraudulent whitewash.

The scientific scandals that pop up at irregular intervals generally concern the life sciences, biology and medicine, and of course parapsychology. In mathematics and the natural sciences the chances of succeeding at cheating are minute whereas the cultural sciences lack unequivocal criteria for fraud.

> A practised cultural scientist does not get caught in the steel jaws of logic; on the contrary he exploits them for his own ends. The argument may be stamped throughout with what could be called "local" logic. This gives credence to the reasoning despite the

fact that imperceptible shifts in meaning distort the "global" picture to the point of absurdity, in the manner of the figure 7.1. The famous drawings of M.C.Escher (1902–72) provide a good illustration of this kind of logical somersault, complete with all its plausible details.

Figure 7.1   Local and global logic

cf. 155

Scientists have so far been carried along on a rising wave of self-justification, supported by their sense of what is right and relevant – the gist of the game.

- ☐ Intense commitment is the first and foremost precondition for successful research. Ardent scientific interest occasionally overcomes countless setbacks and disappointments. More often, the scientist has to be content with quite modest results from the accumulated efforts of a lifetime.
- ☐ Scientific objectivity signifies allegiance to fair play and complete transparency to external audit. Inconvenient facts and conclusions are duly noted; conscious efforts are made to exclude prejudice or partiality.
- ☐ Scientific tolerance implies free entry for all qualified players on their own conditions. Sanctions are limited to the reluctant rejection of substandard play, and expulsion from the scientific community for obvious transgressions. Meddling by outsiders is firmly repudiated.
- ☐ The good scientist is fascinated by the ancient question of Pilate: "What is truth?" He never believes he has found the ultimate answer but shows his respect for veracity in rigorous self-discipline; he never cheats, even to himself.

All this rigour is compensated for by the joy of scientific discovery. To put it plainly: science is great fun, the most exciting game in town. The elevated purpose and occasional conviviality does not exclude competition, conflict, envy or spite among scientists. On the contrary, academic infighting and backbiting are second to none. For all that, the rules of the game can transform even pernicious energies into useful scientific work. The coalition of scientists is tied together by an impressive value package. Vulnerable in isolation it must be secured within a broader cultural context, if not in a personal faith.

Scientific idolatry

An overly ambitious aspiration to use strict scientific standards in analyzing the foundations of science produces obvious paradoxes and leads to deceptively circular argumentation, or scientific self-levitation. Neither scientists nor ordinary mortals can rationally examine their own existence "from the outside", any more than an animal or a child can understand its own "objective" situation. Thus the self-image of the scientific community as a disinterested coalition of truth-seekers, cleanly separated from society, is severely distorted.

cf. 282   The "Edinburgh" school of science sociology postulates that the scientific interest is entirely conditioned by social circumstances and consequent political processes. While this statement contains more than a grain of truth, such offhand denial of the research ethos seems unwarranted. Bruno Latour probably comes closer to reality in his *Science in Action* (1987). Wading in uncertainty and acrimonious conflict, science in the making shows no resemblance to the serene composure of post-processual science when an established majority has conferred canonical status upon scientific opinion. In *Complexity* (1993), Roger Levin applies a lighter touch in describing a branch of science in *cf. 320; 389; 415*   the making. A disparate group of enthusiasts are pushing their sometimes exaggerated claims in the face of disbelief and plain indifference.

In an admirable biography (*Darwin*, 1991), Adrian Desmond and James Moore put an exceptional scientist's predicament in its proper perspective. They retrieve in exquisite detail Darwin's quest for his theory, guided by the doctrines of Adam Smith and Robert Malthus (1766–1834). Wrestling with the ecclesiastial and socio-political conditions of the day, Darwin was bound to temporize despite his through and through honesty. He tried, unsuccessfully, to accommodate both friends and foes, a touchy establishment and his own conscience. Inevitably, Darwinism became a formidable weapon in the struggle for academic status both in Victorian England and all over the *cf. 117*   Continent.

The preservation of privilege or bigoted prejudice often posture as grandiose values and can become a proper nuisance. Thus, it is perfectly understandable that the average researcher wants to distance himself from value problems of any kind. Monod expresses the orthodox view when exclaiming: "Any mingling of knowledge with values is unlawful, forbidden." But value judgements do not go away; quite on the contrary, they exert a powerful underground influence, particularly if neglected or denied. Willy-nilly the scientist has to fall back on a set of meta-rules which he takes for granted when confronting the object of his scientific interest.

cf. 226; 304   Arjo Klamer revealed in a series of interviews (*Conversations with Economists,* 1983) that out of 11 leading American economists not one had noticeably modified his idiosyncratic views on the relationship between tax policy and economic growth, even after many years of scientific debate. The entrenched disagreement could be traced back to diverging political convictions at the college stage, which served as an unshakeable axiomatics for later economic research. Nor is it very likely that the discord between sociologists can be resolved by "scientific" discourse, to say nothing of the schisms between philosophers, aesthetes or theologians... As Jonathan Swift (1667–1745) once remarked, "You cannot reason a person out of something he has not been reasoned into". This is perhaps just as well, taking into account the present state of the soft sciences.

Unless personal frames of reference are brought into the open, science is involuntarily endowed with the superhuman attributes of an idol which, if properly worshipped, will furnish us with definitive truths not only about the world but about ourselves. Such self-glorification is bound to backfire when science fails to deliver on its overblown claims.

Faith in science

Working with differential calculus, Leibnitz and Newton were quite happy to use logically untenable infinitesimals which could only be fully legitimized by modern mathematicians, applying the theory of transfinite numbers. In their single-minded search for the atomic structure of matter, Priestley, Lavoisier and Dalton disregarded with equal insouciance the profusion of irregular chemical compounds in nature. With fine intuition, the pioneers of physics and chemistry   *cf. 296* knew what they were looking for, namely the universal and mathematically expressible rules of the game. Their passion was a special way of serving God – by peeping at His cards.

> The Reverend Thomas Bayes' (1702–61) important work on probability theory (*Essay Towards Solving a Doctrine of Chances,* appeared only posthumously, but he took   *cf. 56* great pride in publishing a glowing theodicy): *Divine Benevolence, or an Attempt to Prove that the Principal End of the Divine Providence and Governement is the Happiness of his Creatures* (1731). Less overtly but in the same spirit, Kepler, Newton, Leibnitz and Boole were all building cathedrals of knowledge, betting on the explication of God's existence by scientific exploration. Maupertois even claimed that he had proved the point by his principle of least action.   *cf. 61*

Preconceived ideas can be the source of fruitful paradigms, provided that they are in touch with reality. Ptolemy's misfortune was that his predilection for fully continuous circular symmetry was wide of the mark. In practice the system was quite useful, but it presupposed a metaphysics which was unacceptable to modern man. God's glory demanded something more beautiful and more profound – a rationally comprehensible celestial mechanics. Newton became its chief architect, and his minor fiddling with empirical data could not detract from the inspired stability of the basic conception.

Science does not create values; rather, certain values create scientists, while other values breed politicians, businessmen, artists or chessmasters.

> The combination of impassioned interest, objectivity, tolerance and loyalty to colleagues which is ascribed to scientists is also found in many chess enthusiasts; chess has indeed acquired a certain scientific stature. But the chief aim of the inveterate chess-   *cf. 221* player is to defeat his opponent whereas pure scientific passion is channelled into open plus-sum play.

The augmentation of manifest truth is the purpose of the scientist's existence. Secrets may be a source of profit or transient power, but advances in science represent stages in a boundless and, to all intents and purposes, irreversible development in the public domain. The conscientious researcher is seeking a small stake in immortality. Behind serious scientific work there is always a hidden agenda – the search for God.

> I have made a point of showing that such shamefacedness is of very recent origin. In a private remark, Wittgenstein sheds some light on the modern frame of mind. Apropos his "Tractatus" he explained that the book has an invisible companion, including   *cf. 375* everything left out of the printed work: that is the inexpressible ethics "whereof one cannot speak".

Scientists draw their values from deep wells of faith. A religious streak is easy to discern in the great visionaries from Pythagoras to Einstein; the prodigious boldness of their scientific speculations called for stable foundations. An inquisitive avant-garde sensed the existence of intelligible and coherent rules beyond the incredible diversity of the real world. Creation simply could not be a criss-cross of coincidences; hence the daring presumption of an aesthetically and intellectually attractive order in the universe.

> The theory of evolution still strikes dogmatic fundamentalists as blasphemous, but it is really a profound expression of the Christian faith. Darwinism is not incompatible with the visions of the Old Testament or the teachings of Jesus; rather, it bears witness to the transforming power of time, the reality of the historical process – a living God.
>
> Interestingly, the Darwinian notion of competitive struggle is flatly denied by an influential school of Japanese biologists founded by the venerable Imanishi. In his eyes, evolution is a well-ordered harmonious development based on the mutual consideration of individuals and species. The Japanese penchant for consensual plus-sum play gets the better of immutable evidence; reality is reinterpreted in terms of Confucian metaphysics.
>
> A kindred ecological romanticism underlies such integrative concepts as the "Biosphere" (Pierre Teilhard de Chardin, 1881–1955) or "Gaia" (James Lovelock) which project deceptively soft human values into animate and inanimate matter, deftly transforming it into surrogate deities. More moment could be oscribed to Teilhard's hypothetical "noosphere", here defined as the interacting community of human minds which *cf. 388* harbours and enhances whatever veracity there is. The noosphere is propped up by a vast memory bank, but the painstaking documentation becomes a heap of dead letters without our error-prone quest for truth.

There are no experts on points of faith; each of us is his own high-priest. The challenge is to control the hubris of hyperrationalism – science as superstition – while preserving the respect for hard facts and the priceless personal religion that is the deepest source of scientific truth. Only then will we grasp the immense potential of scientific inquiry as well as its limitations; only then will science become a universal tool and its values consciously incorporated into our cultural credo.

Concordant meta-rules

Authentic scientific games are exotic exceptions in the history of mankind. The spectacular plus-sum game of science, technology and economics in our culture seems to be inextricably bound up with ideals of freedom and democratic forms of government. Of one thing we can be certain: scientific inquiry is not a primary impulse which infallibly restructures its cultural environment. Science is rather a secondary self-illumination springing from little-understood sources of light.

> St. Augustine (354–430) is one of the improbable champions of science. His Christian faith induced him to discard the ancient cyclical view of the universe and regard history as a progression with a beginning and a pre-ordained end: the kingdom of God. He endorsed the study of nature and the acquisition of knowledge as a way to augment our wonder at the divine wisdom, albeit under the safe tutelage of theology, the queen of sciences.
>
> In his youth, St. Augustine was seduced by the all-explaining Gnosticism of the

Manichaeans, which may explain why he later preached with such burning conviction about man's fundamental fallibility. He claimed, in direct opposition to his contemporary Pelagius, that without God's grace man has neither the will nor the capacity to seek the good or resist the evil. The Vandals who sacked Hippo put an end to Augustine's mortal life but his teaching, tampered with by the Catholic Church, was reinstated by Jean Calvin (1509–64) and Luther in their strict doctrine of predestination. The contrition of the Christian soul, man's recognition of his own helplessness, has paradoxically provided fertile soil for an impassioned assumption of personal responsibility and for the most successful learning process in world history. *cf. 391* *cf. 414*

We all have to invest in something we believe in, but we must never forget that we may be – indeed we probably are – at least partly wrong. An absolutist belief in any given methods or "self-evident" truths cannot but stunt man's creative abilities. After all, scientific dogma is there to be challenged.

Even the greatest scientists come up against their own limitations when new discoveries topple their personal world-view. Liebig and Pasteur did not admit biocatalytic agents (enzymes), Poincaré never accepted Cantor's transfinite mathematics while Mach distrusted the atomic theory of matter to the end of his life. Whitehead could not be reconciled to curved space and Einstein assumed that God did not play dice – and was wrong. *cf. 303*

The collective acquisition of precious knowledge goes hand in hand with human emancipation in every sphere of life: at best the research community rises to a paragon for economic and democratic interplay. Competitive self-organization; decentralized decision-making; full publicity and tolerance of dissenters – all this gives the scientific marketplace its paradigmatic pre-eminence.

The very warp of our cultural fabric is the recognition of man's intellectual and moral fragility, his inescapable fallibility. All our scientific, political, and economic precepts are deeply affected by that negative article of faith. Multifaceted pluralism is an expression of this sceptical attitude towards any claims to perfection. It encourages the personal assumption of risk and responsibility and paves the way for conscientious progress dynamos.

Through some kind of quintessential calculus, our doubt is balanced by a serene certainty; we may even be carried away by missionary zeal, a conviction that despite all our meanderings we have found the right path and should spread the good news. Today our sense of beauty answers to rules more profound than Ptolemy's sterile circular symmetries. Advances in cosmology from Copernicus to Einstein and beyond can be measured by an abstruse aesthetic yardstick. Genuine truth slowly emerges in the light of a set of implicit and humbly applied values which cannot be verified in scientific terms. Rather, our trust is supported by the whole cultural context – technical prowess; a dynamic market economy; democratic co-operation; and scientific progress. *cf. 119; 275*

The patient accumulation of productive and procreative capital in all its different forms represents closely-linked partial solutions to our existential equation. The proper integration of these diverse strands would require the explicit formulation of the concordant meta-rules of our culture, a formidable if not insurmountable task. Such an attempt will in any case strain our verbal machinery to its breaking point. Hence we must first tackle the medium itself, and try to comprehend the limits and possibilities of linguistic communication.

8. Language games

8.1 Concrete languages

As I see it, languages span the whole gamut, from the concrete symbols of our genetic code to esoteric art languages which, at their best, impart palpable information. The language of life is encoded in a simple idiom of four letters and twenty syllables. It is completely implicit; the nucleotide and amino acid sequences immediately realize their inherent intentions. As in the vernacular, most of the permutations are non-functional, but the meaningful ones have a unique impact which depends however on the overall context. Semantics and syntax cannot be cleanly separated, which makes for a very opaque but highly creative language game.

Eloquent evolution

The curtain rose with a Big Bang about fifteen billion years ago. During the first cf. 67 fractions of a second, the basic syntax was conceived and a brand new language game could begin. The ensuing elementary particles command a very limited vocabulary but, by virtue of the uncertainty principle, their self-fulfilling formulae allow for tiny, literally immeasurable deviations from the prescribed grammatical mean. Early on, atomic exclamations combined to form increasingly suggestive molecular expressions which 3.5 to 4 billion years ago conjoined in the formula for life.

> We are and will perhaps forever remain ignorant about the actual origin of life. The first macromolecules probably evolved spontaneously from the amino acids and the (much rarer) nucleotides of the primordial soup, perhaps assisted by clay-type catalysts. Some of the compounds (with primordial ribonucleic acids (RNA) as strong contenders) may cf. 323 have achieved a propensity for autocatalytic self-replication; others (proteins are the best guess) possibly developed unstable cell structures, featuring a rudimentary metabolism. These early progenotes and prebionts were pitted against each other, probing for promising openings and discarding innumerable impossibilities.
>
> Early parasitism of RNA on the proteinaceous "cells" could have prepared the ground for beneficial co-operation. In any case a decisive breakthrough came as the "legislature" of the nucleic acids and the "executive" of proteins began to catalyze each other's production. Such a mutual feedback, called a hypercycle, is highly synergistic: the rate of reproduction is proportional to the concentration of both catalysts. Thus the

hypercycle develops in proportion to the square of the concentration of the mutually catalytic coalition, overtaking the linear rate of increase in straightforward self-propagation. The original single-track autocatalysts were relatively "tolerant" whereas the hyperbolically galloping growth of the hypercycle inexorably cut down the competition – it was a question of all or nothing, life or death.

After countless elimination rounds, an eloquent, informatory idiom – our virtually universal DNA/RNA code – came out on top. The slow evolution of the concrete language we call life has over eons accumulated the essence of existential experience.

cf. 314; 389; 415 Stuart Kaufmann has recently put forward a new coherent theory of biological evolution which supplements Neo-Darwinism (*The Origin of Order*, 1993). The basic idea is cf. 24; 66; 74 the build-up of complexity at the edge of chaos. Kaufmann works with extensive computer simulations; in essence he tries to formulate an over-arching syntactics of spontaneous self-organization.

The vocabulary of life, which is enshrined in the protein-prescribing genes, has become accessible by modern techniques. But so far we have only got a glimpse of the deep generative grammar which allows the consistent expression of long utterances in a meaningful manner. The overall organization of the genome is somehow forcing the pseudo-chaotic interplay towards a set of strange attrac-cf. 94; 323 tors, signifying appropriate structure and behaviour.

The recently identified family of highly conserved homeobox DNA-sequences codify strings of about 90 amino acids. The corresponding proteins regulate the developmental polarity (anterior/posterior) among animals from insects to vertebrates, a testimony to the conservatism of the genetic grammar.

Specialized syntax-proteins certainly act as signposts and control important gateways, but the discrete genes constitute a set of interdependent actors. Every word in the vocabulary contributes to the axiomatic base and may influence the language game at large. As in the vernacular, the content is contingent on both the linguistic and the extra-linguistic context; the message derives its proper meaning from all the consequential circumstances. Immensely opaque, the cf. 229; 348 language of life cannot be significantly reduced.

The primaeval alphabet

The genome of the cell corresponds to a book of recipes for producing all the proteins necessary to life. The key components are deoxyribonucleic acids (DNA), which are found in four variants characterized by their respective nucleotide bases: adenine (A), guanine (G), cytosine (C) and thymine (T). The DNA language thus has four letters. Almost all proteins are made up of only 20 different amino acids, which can be regarded as standard syllables, each one coded for by three letter groups (triplets) of DNA (for instance, the triplet AAA prescribes the amino acid proline). The DNA dictionary contains 4^3 or 64 triplet syllables, and although "stop" should be included in the dictionary, the DNA language features a lot of synonyms and evinces considerable redundancy.

The genetic alphabet was deciphered around 1965. Throughout, the third letter in the triplet is less significant than the first two. Perhaps life originally started out with only two-letter syllables which could have coded for 4^2 or 16 concepts (15 amino acids and "stop")   *cf. 93*

The DNA strands appear in complementary pairs, intertwined and coupled with one another in a double helix: guanidine links up with thymine, adenosine with cytosine. The sense and antisense strands of the helix contain the same information; the one being the other's negative. In normal life processes only a small part of the genome is activated, but in cell propagation the double helix uncoils completely, and both strands serve as templates for a new double helix. The duplication is brought about by the enzyme DNA-polymerase, which on the other hand can only be produced by reading out several lines in the DNA-book.

The reproduction of life presupposes the transfer of both genetic information (DNA) and a number of key proteins to read off the code and organize further protein production. This discourse between legislative deoxyribonucleic acids and executive proteins constitutes the core of life, but contemporary linguistic reality is more complex. First the DNA prescript has to be transcribed into a more communicative ribonucleic acid (RNA) dialect with one diverging letter (thymine is substituted for uracil) and a slightly different chemistry (ribose is substituted for deoxyribose).

To avoid utter confusion, the initiation of protein synthesis is strictly regulated by code words which interact with repressor and inducer proteins, all locked in a complex tangle of cybernetic feedback. In eukaryotes the control loop includes at least five regulatory sites, some of them way upstream in the DNA chain. To start transcription, the DNA double helix must be locally uncoiled (an RNA primer can do the job). Then the antisense DNA is used as a template to get a sense strand of RNA. Antisense RNA is occasionally transcribed from sense DNA and acts as an inhibitor for primer RNA.

RNA is less stable than DNA but can move about freely in the cell, mediating the DNA directives. This messenger RNA is read off by ribosomes which scan the sequences, syllable by syllable, while specific transfer RNAs link up the proper amino acid to the growing protein chain, one at a time. Thus the transformation of the DNA code to the prescribed polysyllabic protein is completed with reasonable veracity; the overall error rate is about 1 in 10,000.

Laconic word games

Viral infections are, in effect, elementary displays of skilful verbal deception. The small viral genome is cunningly injected into the cell by exploiting the fine structure of the cell membrane, whereupon the RNA or DNA of the virus starts manipulating the protein synthesis of the cell according to its pleasure. After the magical "open sesame" the enzymatic machinery is at the disposal of the invader in a dialogue to the death. In the course of evolution, countless moves and countermoves must have superseded one another before the dispute achieved its present level of sophistication.   *cf. 132*

A pathogenic breakthrough is generally followed by reciprocal adaptation between parasite and host. Still, new arguments arise and the war of words, proofs and refutations continues with unabated intensity. The smallpox virus, for example, is regarded as a new-fangled innovation dating back a mere few thousand years whereas AIDS is a fresh reminder that we cannot with impunity play around with the risk of intimate infection.

cf. 93   Vaccination and antibiotics are strong moves in the evolutionary interplay, countered – at least in part – by the rapid spread of drug resistance. Some organisms have assumed evasive tactics, tantamount to a cloak of invisibility. New pandemic influenza viruses have a diverging surface protein and can therefore slip past the immunological defences while the malaria biont and the trypanosome parasites (which cause sleeping sickness) change appearance all the time. The HIV-virus, which causes AIDS, is an RNA-based retrovirus and is modified at 1–10 points during each replication because of the error-prone RNA/DNA transcription.

Economy is a predominant feature of competitive language games, and the DNA/RNA code is no exception. Viruses have been subjected to exceptional selective pressure; maximum information must be contained within a strictly constrained protein cover. Some viruses have found an ingenious solution to the problem. Two, and in extreme cases even three, messages are written on top of one another in different reading frames. That meaningful information can be transmitted in this way verges on the miraculous.

The linguistic tricks of the virus particles can be illustrated by a similar exercise in English.

Message I   the/row/lap/ear/eat/eye/sly ...
Message II   t/her/owl/ape/are/ate/yes/ly ...

Not only should the two lines consist of comprehensible words; they should also form long sentences with hundreds of relevant symbols, and above all both the sense and the double sense must carry the right import! A third overlaid meaning represents the supreme achievement in information economy. I have been unable to produce anything but a beginning in English:

Message I   /ape/god/end..
Message II   a/peg/ode/nd..
Message III   ap/ego/den/d ...

Viruses have to content themselves with laconic messages. A typical virus such as influenza or herpes can be written out in 5,000 to 10,000 nucleotide letters while the lower limit is thought to be 2,500. The record is held by viroids, isolated and fairly disorganized RNA fragments lacking protective protein shells.

The RNA of one potato viroid (PSTV) consists of 359 nucleotides which folds over on itself in a slightly haphazard manner in contrast to the strict and comparatively stable configuration of the DNA double helix. The viroids intervene in some self-replicating mode in the nucleus of the eukaryotic cell. They are perverted forms of legitimate RNA fragments, with a regulating function within the cell. Even more enigmatic are infection-transmitting, DNA- and RNA-free substances, called prions, which could resemble self-replicating prebiontic proteins. They seem to be slightly corrupted forms of normal regulatory proteins, and cause slowly progressive disorders in the central nervous system. Kuru is an ascertained case and Parkinsonism, Alzheimer's disease (senile dementia) and multiple sclerosis are all under suspicion.

Convoluted script

Viruses are probably parasitic late-comers in the long chain of life. The self-characterization of even the simplest autotrophic prokaryotes requires millions of nucleotides, and the eukaryotes need a further tenfold genetic prescription. In addition there is an abundance of apparently inactive DNA, for instance the introns mentioned earlier, which are interspersed in the gene between the pro-tein-coding exons. During transcription the nonsensical information is also copied, but the introns are immediately cut out of the messenger RNA, and the pieces corresponding to the exon are spliced together. *cf. 94*

> In some cases the RNA strand spontaneously eliminates intron-duplicated material and establishes the correct exon sequence on its own. Besides self-splicing, such RNA-based ribozymes can also cleave other RNA or DNA sequences and catalyze some protein reactions. This may create a key role for RNA in probiotic "chemical" evolution. *cf. 319* Recently it has been shown that certain ribozymes can serve both as code and substrate and thus sustain stand-alone development.
>
> RNA can be translated back to DNA not only by specialized retroviruses (like HIV) and also by cell-indigenous reverse transcriptase. This enzyme is a million times more error-prone than the punctilious DNA-polymerase system which is supplemented by dedicated repair and proof-reading enzymes. The primordial plasticity of RNA could well serve as a vehicle for bypassing the extremely conservative DNA code. *cf. 95*

It has been estimated that in mammals only about one per cent of the genome is active. In man, approximately 100,000 proteins are codified by approximately three billion DNA letters which, in our print, would fill a small library of about 3,000 volumes of 500 pages each. The mapping of the human genome is now being undertaken in a systematic way and could well be completed within a decade. *cf. 94*

> We are still in the dark about the role of "nonsense" DNA, but it probably fulfils a function in gene expression, for example, in regulating the exceptionally complex supertwisting and supercoiling of the double helix. The whole mess has been compared *cf. 348* with a bad day in a macaroni factory; more constructively we could envisage the DNA message as a tangled ball of thread (no fisherman will doubt the incredible creativity of an excessively twisted yarn). Normally, most of the string is out of action, intertwined with itself and with specific proteins (histones) which act as scaffolding and protect it from undue influences.
>
> Now, when a change occurs in, say, the source of energy, it initiates a localized reversal of the twist and makes adjacent information accessible. The sequence of DNA nucleotides can then be monitored and protein synthesis induced at specific addresses, causing further unravelling of the double helix structure and the production of appropriate enzymes. In analogy with the highly compressed viral code described above, the eukaryotic DNA seems to incorporate a topological rebus – a sequence of superimposed messages which directs the decoding of protein synthesis. *cf. 320; 368*

Life is dependent on an extraordinary feat of information retrieval. Access to the memory bank matches the fluency of a public speaker; every word, every line should be available at the right moment, even though most of the vocabulary must lay dormant. As it happens, whole pages and even chapters – transposons or "jumping genes" – occasionally change places. Parts of alien genomes may thus be introduced by chance or by human intention.

cf. 94 Gene splicing (in technical parlance, hybrid DNA technology) involves purposeful intervention in the genetic game, and there are still lingering fears that supervirulent monsters might emerge from the test tube by mistake. However, it has become clear that the products of natural evolution are very hard to beat. Even so, potent biological weapons can be forged by designing effective delivery systems for new strains of well-known pathogens, such as the anthrax bacillus or the smallpox virus.

The synthesis of brand-new proteins, or even whole organisms according to preset specifications, is a fascinating challenge to computer-oriented genetic engineering. Well beyond the horizon lies the perpetually haunting prospect of a brave new, superhuman race. Even more exciting is the possibility of unknown hypercyclical language games, a new genetic alphabet and a new biology – the ultimate innovation.

Self-surpassing linguistics

Concrete languages are completely implicit; the nucleotide and amino acid sequences immediately realize their inherent intentions. But synonyms abound, the same message may be carried by widely diverging words.

> Lysozymes occur in, among other things, tears and saliva; the commercial source is egg white. Their function is to break down the carbohydrate-based protective coats of invading gram-negative bacteria. The lysozymes of closely-related species of birds differ from one another to a surprising degree. Nevertheless the spatial structures reveal a remarkable similarity. Time and again life has put together the same meaningful pattern from the varied means at hand.

Thus, the actual composition of the basic elements is not crucial to the discussion taking place at the higher levels of concrete language games. Symbolic content slowly takes on a life of its own through the operation of highly sensitive cybernetic feedbacks; biological communication and confrontation achieve ever-increasing refinement.

> Basically, the immunological system is constructed as an incisive interrogative: "Are you me?" – a shrewd "shibboleth" as discriminating as the password which betrayed the kindred Ephraimites to their Jewish compatriots. Despite the complicated entry codes, both viral proteins and cancer cells occasionally succeed in duping the guards by ingratiating articulation whereas in auto-immune disease the honest citizens demonstrate their genuine accent in vain. Life and death really do depend on a finely-tuned ear for the niceties of our native tongue.

Immunological reactions comprise veritable word cascades and it is not hard to imagine hormones and nerve cells "talking" to one another. From there it is but a few steps to the chemical communication of ants, the blinking of glow-worms, and the intricate dance language of the bees. The most astonishing body language is spoken by certain squids, which openly express the state of their central nervous system in the chameleon-like play of chromophores on the skin.

Many birds have whole repertoires of cries which express attention, warning, alarm or aggressiveness. The serenades of the song birds proclaim the possession of a nesting territory.

> The preprogramming of birdsong is highly variable. Many species such as doves sing

"correctly" in total isolation while others need model performances at the fledgling stage to get their repertoire right; some, like the blackbird, are learning all their life (in contrast to mammals, birds grow new neurons in the learning process). Sexually mature females seem to prefer males who sing the familiar nursery tunes. Linguistic differentiation gradually leads to local dialects and reproductive isolation, with the consequent establishment of new species.

cf. 97

Mammals communicate by an extensive and flexible set of signals – bodily stances, grimaces and sounds – which culminate in the varied facial expressions of chimpanzees and the long, enigmatic grunting sessions of the humpback whale. Social status, threat and submission, trust and fear, sexual overtures or simple playfulness – all are transmitted in a whole range of graded behavioural displays.

Primaeval sensual messages reverberate in our human language games, but it is in the liberation of the symbolic function that man finally surpasses himself. The soliloquy of the human brain culminates in avid self-consciousness which allows a fractal overview of the world. The symbolic language of the central nervous system can then be turned back to direct the self-same brain processes in runaway self-reference. Every concept is formed and used according to the subject's tacit intentions, but it can also be regarded coolly from the outside – within quotation marks so to speak. This act of self-observation can itself be observed in an infinite regress; we have stepped into an escalator of increasingly abstract expressions.

8.2   Axiomatic languages

Significant truth needs an interpretative context; perfect logical truth can exist only as an empty generalization. No language can express its own truth criteria, which instead must be defined in a metalanguage, which in turn must seek recourse to a superior language for proper definition, and so on in infinite regress. No "truth machine" can be built; sooner or later an act of faith will be necessary to stamp the sea of credibility on the system. Although truth can never explain itself it can, tentatively, be defined as the provisionally winning strategy in an open and infinitely extended evolutionary game.

The quest for certainty

Pythagoras saw salvation in accurate calculation. The correct treatment of mathematical symbols would in due course reveal even the most hidden secrets of knowledge. Leibnitz dreamed of a "characteristica universalis", a basic mental alphabet, which would provide the explicit axiomatics of an exact

cf. 349

synthetic language and make possible the deduction of all scientific truths by
cf. 350; 385 pure algebra.

> Leibnitz's deepest motives were religious and metaphysical, but he possessed a practical
> and exceedingly optimistic mind. In 1675, quite convinced about the feasibility of his
> language project, he wrote: "It will not require much more work than we see already
> being spent on ... encyclopaedias, as they call them. I believe that a number of chosen
> men can complete the task within five years; within two years they will exhibit the
> common doctrines of life, that is metaphysics and morals, in an irrefutable calculus."

Gottlob Frege (1848–1925) was the first to construct a fully formalized language of logic which gave Russell and Whitehead a platform for their grand
cf. 21 attempt to reduce mathematics to logic. Later on, Carnap and the positivists
cf. 279 tried, in vain, to resuscitate Pythagoras' and Leibnitz's utopian programme.

Mathematics and logic constitute a search for definite, unambiguous and
explicit knowledge within a toy universe. Mathematical languages should thus
be correspondingly value-free and "absolute"; they presuppose an extremely
high degree of linguistic purity. For this very reason a concentrated mental
effort is required in applying the rules of axiomatically self-confirming and fully
cf. 147 ordered logico-mathematical language games. These formal expositions are
completely dependent on the transparency of thought as reflected in unequivocal grammatical clarity and rigorous definitions. The words must first be
ruthlessly stripped of most of their current content and then handled with a
surgeon's touch and feeling for the remaining fine shades of meaning.

> Elementary propositional calculus employs the simplest possible linguistic apparatus.
> The dictionary looks like this:
> $\sim$ not
> $\wedge$ and
> $\vee$ or
> $>$ (at least) if the above, then the following (a "loose" causal relationship)
> $=$ identical with, if and only if (a "strong" causal relationship)
> ( )   parentheses which indicate the logical sequence of the operations
> P,Q .... variables, propositions

Russell and Whitehead managed to reduce the number of fundamental operations in propositional calculus from five to two; the signs for "not" and "or",
which can be further combined to "nor" ("either"-"or"). In any case, the
formalism of propositional calculus can be handled in succinct, computer-
oriented orthography.

> De Morgan's first law is one of the basic formulae of propositional logic:
>
> $$P \wedge Q = \sim (\sim P \text{ EV} \sim Q)$$
>
> or, "both P and Q only in the case of neither not-P nor not-Q".

Our specimen is of course a tautology, and propositional calculus as a whole is
nothing more than a study of tautologies. All well-formed statements are either
true or false; their truth content can be found out by unambiguous and mechanical computation. Propositional calculus is the addition and subtraction table of

logical thought, a trivial scheme in which every mistake is immediately punished – not least in computer construction and programming. It represents a
comprehensible, closed, completed and therefore "uninteresting" language
game.

George Boole (1815–64) was the first to reduce propositional logic to simple
calculation in "*The Laws of Thought*" (1854).

In Boolean algebra 1 stands for truth (or everything) and 0 for falsity (or nothing).
Addition stands for the connective "or", multiplication stands for "and". The outcome
matrix (the truth table) then assumes the following form:

"or" $+\vee$	0 1
0	0 1
1	1 1

"and" $\cdot\wedge$	0 1
0	0 0
1	0 1

In a network of on/off-switches (on = 1, off = 0) "and" stands for a serial connection,
"or" for a parallel coupling. The optimal network for any decision procedure (e.g. a
computer program) is equivalent to finding the shortest Boolean polynomial which
describes the operation. This important practical problem unfortunately lacks a general
solution for reasons which will later become apparent.

cf. 333; 350

Boole's basic motivation was to prove the existence of God in a rigorous
manner, but at the end of the book he has to admit "the powerlessness of mere
logic".

In the *Tractatus* Wittgenstein finally demolishes the claims of pure logic to
any profound wisdom. The book abounds with statements such as: "The propositions of logic do not express anything", "All propositions are equal" and
"Russell is mistaken". Magnanimously, Bertrand Russell accepted the criticism
and was instrumental in introducing Wittgenstein to a wider audience.

cf. 284; 375

Certainty about uncertainty

In predicate calculus (which subsumes propositional calculus as a special case)
it is possible to give linguistic expression to special characteristics (predicates)
of individual variables or relations between several variables, and also to formulate general statements about quantities. Predicate calculus strives for the
utmost generality and is therefore extremely abstract. It acquires substance by
being applied to a single domain, such as all natural (that is positive and real)
integers. We can thus create a specific language, in which number-theoretical
statements can be expressed with unimpeachable logic.

cf. 284; 375

For this purpose the vocabulary of propositional calculus must be extended to include
the following symbols called quantifiers.

$\forall$ (for) all
$\exists$ there exists (at least) one
S succeeds (or successor)

In addition a select part of our arithmetical vocabulary is used – zero, plus, times -but no
integers. Instead, 1 is written SO (succeeds zero), two is written SSO and so on. The

variables x, y, z designate arbitrary natural numbers, in other words they can cover the whole domain, and together with S and O they define the semantic content.

The syntax of the language is exhaustively described by the five well-known rules of first order arithmetic.

$\sim \forall x\ Sx = 0$	Zero is not the successor of any natural number
$\forall x\ (x + 0) = x$	Rule of addition
$\forall x\ \forall y\ (x + Sy) = S(x+y)$	Rule of addition
$\forall (x \cdot 0) = 0$	Rule of multiplication
$\forall x\ \forall y\ (x \cdot Sy) = (x \cdot y) + x$	Rule of multiplication

An example:

$$\forall x \sim \exists y\ \exists z (x \cdot x \cdot x) = (Sy \cdot Sy \cdot Sy) + (Sz \cdot Sz \cdot Sz)$$

"No sum of two cubes gives a cubic number" (Sy and Sz instead of y and z eliminates the special case $x = y = z = 0$)

A limitless number of correct statements can be deduced by the careful application of the rules of number-theoretical language, including the above example (there is no combination of integers to satisfy the equation $x^3 = y^3 + z^3$). But the deduction of Fermat's great theorem for long remained one of the most tantalizing problems of number theory.

cf. 22
cf. 329 At the turn of the century, David Hilbert explicitly posed several of the great issues in mathematics. One of the challenges was to prove that all rigorously formalized languages are complete and self-confirming in conformity with propositional calculus. In other words, all valid statements should be deducible and invalid statements falsifiable by grammatically reliable and recursive (that is mechanizable) procedures. Few doubted the fact itself, which was a corollary to the hyperrationalism of the day. Provability was the problem; the system must be compelled to explain itself. As late as 1930, in his Valedictory Address Hilbert confidently proclaimed "Wir müssen wissen, wir werden wissen" ("we must know, we will know").

cf. 21; 23; 381; 388 In the very same year, Gödel's razor-sharp reasoning squashed such speculation once and for all. In impeccable number-theoretical terms he arrived at a deep self-referential conclusion. This expression is called Gödel's sentence (G) and can be transcribed into everyday language as follows: "This statement cannot be deduced from the axioms of number theory in a finite number of steps".

cf. 28 One of Gödel's brilliant ideas was to apply an ingenious coding scheme for numbering all the above symbols: $\sim, \vee, \forall, \exists, =, +$, etc in an unambiguous way. The crucial point is that the lack of ambiguity is retained in any grammatically correct transformation. Every single sentence or proposition of number theory is thus represented by a unique number, in other words a long row of S's followed by 0. This number can in turn be treated as a variable, and number theory acquires the capability of producing statements about its own propositions. The language can be mapped onto itself, the mapping *cf. 350; 352* may be mapped once more and so on. Aided by Cantor's diagonal argument, Gödel succeeded in formulating a sentence roughly equivalent to "I am a liar". Whether true or false this statement cannot be accommodated within a consistent and self-explanatory axiomatic language.

"Uninteresting" languages like propositional calculus or pure addition arithmetic lack this capacity for self-reflection. The logical operations produce inevitable ambiguity and thus obliterate the unicity of any mapping. The all-important self-reference is lost and we are left with a profusion of overlapping, meaningless homonyms.

Gödel's sentence (G) must either be true or false. If false it would be deducible within number theory, but this would burden the theory with a destructive self-contradiction. Accordingly, (G) must be true. Thus it expresses a number-theoretical truth which is unreachable by deduction within the system. Actually, there are infinitely many statements which can neither be verified nor falsified within number theory although these undecidable propositions can be adequately expressed in the number-theoretical language.

Universal undecidability

According to a famous theorem of set theory, named after the mathematicians Leopold Löwenheim (1878–1957) and T.A. Skolem (1887–1963), the domain of natural numbers serves as a model for all "reasonably" structured formal systems, including Euclidean and non-Euclidean geometry. On the other hand there is a "sensible" logic imposed on all structures which fulfil the Löwenheim-Skolem comprehensibility criteria, endowing number theory and Gödel's undecidability theorem with enormous impact. All interesting axiomatic languages suffer from the same Gödelian self-reference, leading to an infinity of propositions which are rich in content but cannot be proved (or disproved) within the framework of the language game. Nor can the consistency – the ultimate "correctness" – of an "interesting", non-tautological axiomatic language be proved within the language. Paradoxically, self-verification can be achieved only if we accept inconsistency: that is, manifest untruth!

> A single self-contradiction such as 1 = –1 demolishes an axiomatic language structure, since in such a system anything can be proved. Hence the significance of consistency in mathematics.

Nor is it any help to include Gödel's sentence (G) as a new sixth axiom in number theory; the language thus enriched can also be Gödelized. An impassable line of demarcation confines all self-confirming language games within narrow limits.

> Provable mathematical truths (or falsehoods) cover only a small part of the boundless domain. The theorems put out finger-like branches which probe the area of attainable truth and falsehood. The borderline to the unattainable is an endlessly convoluted, fractal structure which is impossible to map out in detail by any finite methods. No universal decision procedure for deciding the undecidability of a proposition can exist (Church's theorem), but definite proofs are possible in special cases.   *cf. 23; 333; 381*

If, in pure desperation, we introduce the negation of Gödel's theorem (~G) as an axiom, this appears at first glance to result in a flagrant self-contradiction. However, Gödel's theorem applies only to all natural numbers; beyond these we can envisage literally countless transfinite numbers, for which ~G may be valid.

> When we list all natural numbers 0, 1, 2 ... we reach at infinity the ordinal number w

(omega). The first transfinite number is by definition w+1, while 1+w is simply the same as w. In graphic terms:

$$1 + //// \ldots\ldots\ldots = ///// \ldots\ldots\ldots = \omega$$
$$(\omega) \qquad\qquad\qquad (\omega)$$

$$//// \ldots\ldots\ldots + 1 = //// \ldots\ldots\ldots / = \omega+1 \qquad \text{thus}$$
$$(\omega) \qquad\qquad\qquad (\omega)$$

$1+\omega \neq \omega + 1$ similarly

$2 \cdot \omega \neq \omega \cdot 2$ (an infinity of 2s is not the same as 2 infinities.)

$\omega \cdot \omega = \omega^2$ can be extrapolated as $\omega^{\omega^{\omega^{\cdot^{\cdot^{\cdot}}}}}$ or ω_ω for short.

The apparent paradox of infinity mathematics lies in the fact that the quantity, the "cardinality" of all the numbers listed above, is the same (designated $\aleph_0$, aleph null), although as ordinals they can be arranged in a clear before-after relation with one another(a set is, in fact, infinite only if some of its subsets have as many elements as itself). For natural numbers, ordinality, which answers the question "in what order?" (e.g. seventh, seventeenth), coincides with cardinality which answers the question "how many" (e.g. seven, seventeen).

All ordinals with the cardinality $\aleph_0$ are said to be countable or enumerable and can be listed or mapped against one another. This means that they can be brought into a one-to-one relationship with each other; they serve as mutual models. If this mapping does not work we are faced with a higher cardinality $\aleph_1$ which cannot be reached "from below". According to the unproved (and probably unprovable) continuum hypothesis, $\aleph_1$ is equated with the set of all real (rational and irrational) numbers. But after $\aleph_1$ there follow $\aleph_2$, $\aleph_\omega$, $\aleph_\aleph$ . . .

cf. 352

As a consequence of its powers of introspection any interesting formal language receives unfathomable dimensions of infinity. Because of this transcendental independence it can serve as its own meta-language, that is to say, talk about itself. But the consistency, the meaning and the value of the game can only be judged from an external platform, or in Gödel's words "the consistency of mathematics cannot be proven within mathematics". Complete self-explanation is therefore out of the question. Full transparency is unattainable; every truth needs an interpretative context; semantics can never be reduced to syntax – content is not identical with form.

Truth as victorious strategy

Every axiomatic language game lays down its own basic rules – the axioms – which determine all provable, that is to say recursive and mechanically comput able truths (and lies) of the language. If the grammar can generate only a finite number of permutations, the game will (like chess) be completely analyzable and lack any deeper interest. The infinitely extendable axiomatic languages fall into the following categories:

cf. 53

☐ Languages that are both complete and decidable; all the information lies tautologically on the surface, as it were. An infinity of sentences can be formulated but each and every one can be resolved by finite means (for example propositional calculus, pure addition or multiplication arithmetic).

☐ Languages that are complete but undecidable. All correct propositions are theorems and can be deduced but in principle there is no generally applicable or recursive method of determining the truth content of a given proposition, that is whether it is deducible and therefore correct (predicate calculus).

☐ Languages that are incomplete and undecidable. An infinity of correct propositions can neither be deduced nor can their truth content be determined. The language reveals implicit creativity; it can articulate and express but not explain itself (number theory and all other interesting axiomatic languages).

> Predicate calculus is an overarching esoteric language game with claims to extreme universality, but it requires real models to achieve tangible expression. At that point though the completeness is lost: no consistent, finitely given theory is complete. Perfect logical truth can exist only as a total and therefore empty generalization. Semantic content, as we have seen, is not a pure formality. Abstract principles acquire effective meaning – mental inertia, so to speak – only when they are steeped in a conceivable domain of thought.

Gödel's early inspiration originated in a conviction that truth has no finite description; Alfred Tarski has shown conclusively that no axiomatic language game can express its own truth criterion. This "higher truth" can only be *cf. 28; 310; 354;* formulated in an appropriate metalanguage, which once again has to fall back *391* on a meta-metalanguage for its truth criteria and so on. No "truth machine" can be built; sooner or later an act of faith becomes indispensable to stamp the seal of credibility on the system.

Mathematical truth arises in the interaction between independent linguistic elements. In the course of such an abstract plus-sum game, the implicit potential of the language is disclosed by empirical investigation. Completed rounds of play, i.e. definitive truths, have in a way exposed their paucity. Profound truth in a formal system can be identified only as a provisionally winning strategy in an open and infinitely extended evolutionary game. Darwinian selection of the fittest seems to get its due even in mathematics. *cf. 336; 372; 377*

Transcendence through imperfection

First and foremost, linguistic symbols are used without undue reflection as syntactic moves in the thorny game of life. The symbol can also be lifted out of its operational context; it can be observed and put between quotation marks in a superordinate discourse. We have repeatedly stumbled on this double role of use and mention, which sustains self-reference and seems to underlie all creative advance. Unpredictable fractal patterns emerge when simple mathematical functions iteratively reflect on themselves; even fully formalized language *cf. 27* games may surpass their inherent limitations, intimating higher realities. Paradoxes and apparent absurdities unlock the door to new exciting worlds: elliptical and hyperbolic geometry, imaginary and transfinite numbers – an infinity of infinities.

Human thought seems, however, to be drawn to doctrinaire self-immunization. It is always tempting to declare that the game is over, to restrict geometry to the books of Euclid or to amputate set theory as Bertrand Russell did with his paradox-annihilating doctrine of types.

cf. 283; 376

To save mathematical determinism, Russell invented "the axiom of reducibility" which stated that the structure at higher levels of infinity was adequately reflected lower down in the hierarchy. This conjecture is evidently false. Zermelo and von Neumann, followed by the logician Willard Quine, have all worked hard to supplant Russell's faulty theory of types with a new axiomatics which distinguishes sets and classes, and requires (at least) nine axioms.

The temptation to "close" mathematics can now be dismissed for good. Mathematics is indeed inexhaustible. Alonzo Church has shown that the hierarchy of infinities is full of absolutely irregular discontinuities. There is no end to the unforeseeable surprises even in our most abstract and axiomatic languages which obviously possess unlimited opportunities for play and provide models for all conceivable real processes.

Meaningful language games are necessarily incomplete, deficient, flawed in some sense. Lack of comprehensiveness and perfection, a certain vulnerability, is the unavoidable price that has to be paid for the boundless scope of play. The richness of the game consists in the very profusion of implicit but unpredictable variations which can be extracted from the explicitly prescribed rules. Somehow the concrete language of tangible matter has surpassed itself in creating a peculiar cusp, the human brain, where the abstract metalanguage of the mind has risen above reality. In man the arcane world of pure abstraction conjoins with palpable corporality and becomes aware of itself.

8.3   Computer languages

So far, computers understand only transparent languages with a restricted semantic content, neatly separated from the narrow axiomatic base. Computer consciousness is not on the cards, save a breakthrough in nanotechnology which would allow molecular computers to evolve in lifelike, Darwinian fashion. So far, computers lack our fractally extended overview and, barring the unexpected, they will be restricted to reflecting clearly expressed human ideas. Man should always be able to outwit his own creation, thus proving the finiteness of the artificial mind. In the improbable contrary case, he will turn out to be nothing more than a rather unreliable machine – cause enough for the anxiety engendered by the computer revolution.

Syntactic versatility

A general-purpose computer is the most versatile device in the hierarchy of automata. Typically, the computer hardware transforms input data into predetermined output in accordance with a variety of pre-set programs (the software). Straightforward computation does not create new information. The machine simply acts as a catalyst for a well-defined set of mathematical rearrangements, resembling highly specific enzyme systems which perform the same service in biochemical processes.

> Every normal computation is inherently irreversible, because information is partly destroyed and converted to heat in the process. The actual heat dissipation of presently manufactured microchips is at least one million times greater than this thermodynamic minimum (enzymes work close to the limit; the waste heat exceeds the theoretical value only by a factor of ten). Complete reversibility could be achieved at least in theory by applying "conservative logic" which preserves all the information and allows the calculation to be run backwards. The use, or more exactly the obliteration of memory does however, entail an entropy increase and a corresponding dissipation of energy.   *cf. 66*

The hardware of any general purpose computer is equivalent to a universal Turing machine. It can, in principle, be instructed to perform all recursive   *cf. 23* operations; even the simplest personal computer can solve everything which is mathematically solvable, given enough time and floppy discs.

Computer programming involves the application of elementary logical rules, a Boolean algebra which, in its more developed forms, assumes the shape of a   *cf. 23; 327; 329;* genuine language game. One of the consequences of Gödelian undecidability is   *350* that there can be no general procedure to predict the behaviour of a computer program; big computers can never be debugged with complete certainty. Nei-   *cf. 50* ther can we, in general, calculate the time of computation beforehand; nor can we know if the computation will stop at all. Thus, the most interesting aspects   *cf. 23* of computers are non-computable – programming is bound to be an heuristic art. Inconsistencies or endless loops of circular argumentation may turn up in the most unexpected places. Proper operation can be ascertained only by empirical testing – trial and error.

The wiring diagram of a computer stands for the concrete level of language. The hardware grammar is meticulously forced upon physical reality, analogous with the cogs and levers of mechanical calculating machines or the nucleotide sequences of the genetic program.

> Theoretically, computer design could be based on the decimal system, but in practice a simple binary code has become the norm. Every active computer component can assume two distinct states, "on" or "off", generally designated by the 1 and 0 of Boolean algebra. All communication at the basic level is transmitted in this machine language by bits of information, series of ones and zeros which are immediately represented by the switches of the computer.
>
> The software tells the computer what to do and must, at the lowest level, be formulated in a meticulously detailed machine language. Here the old apothegm, "confused speaking means confused thinking" becomes almost absurdly true; the minutest lacuna in the logical continuity totally destroys the game. Nothing can be "taken for granted"; nothing is "clear from the context".

The discrete bits of the bottom-level machine language are grouped (by assemblers) into "chunks" and the chunks are further "chunked" (by compilers) into the user-friendly concepts of the actual computer idioms. These higher-level languages, like Algol, Cobol, Fortran, Lisp, Ada, Basic, C, and so on (more than 400 are in use today) can be made increasingly convenient for the user but are, at bottom, equally powerful. However, the applicability of the computer languages varies tremendously. Optimal efficiency, elegance and economy is achieved only if the chosen language fits the object of exposition.

cf. 342

> Most computers have so far been built in accordance with the von Neumann configuration. The messages flow in linear sequence between a highly-organized central processing unit (the brain), short- and long-term memories, and peripheral input-output devices. While very successful in numerous routine jobs, these "classic" machines are surprisingly inept when it comes to many plain tasks such as pattern recognition. In such cases, parallel computation often offers dramatically improved performance. Every unit in the array then has its own internal program; the interplay of the basic processors is co-ordinated in the grammar of a higher-level language. The power of these "synaptic" computers will be greatly enhanced if and when the customary electrons are replaced by even nimbler photons as vehicles of calculation.

Highly-connected parallel computers resemble neural networks and should, at least in theory, exhibit corresponding computational potential. Operations are highly distributed and local faults can be bypassed, which makes for overall robustness. Learning by experience, such machines could generate new information, rising above the humble rank of calculating devices. Even self-organization of the hardware, a sort of spontaneous creativity, may be within the realms of the possible, although the conceptual problems could well prove intractable.

Semantic enrichment

The borderline between the concrete body of governable circuitry (hardware) and abstract programs (software) is fluid. Repetitive, lower-level parts of the software program may be permanently fixed (as firmware) within the wiring diagram to make room for higher levels of the language game. The complexities of computing can often be shortcut by single-purpose, analog-type computers which embody most of the relevant cybernetics in their very design. All the humdrum but vitally important details then take care of themselves.

> Conventional musical instruments generate a great many characteristic reverberations in addition to the note struck. The information content of the composition, the musical software, is automatically enriched by the musicality of the instrument. This long-standing analog hardware still eclipses all but the most sophisticated sound synthesizers which have to reconstruct the acoustic waves from scratch.

Living organisms, including man, have utilized the inherent reliability of analog feedback to the full. Under normal circumstances, we neither register nor direct even our breathing or blood circulation while the all-important synaptic interplay lies far beyond the horizon of awareness. Our actions, on the other hand, are generally subject to conscious control but, there too, we are better off delegating all routines.

> Cortically self-conscious control of movements is an awkward and clumsy exercise. Accordingly, the fine-tuning of muscle interaction has been entrusted to the cerebellum, *cf. 100* which is the site of physical dexterity and the dazzling virtuosity of artisans and artists alike – be it a potter, a painter, a pianist or a prima ballerina. When a tennis player "freezes", self-aware exertion is interfering with the smooth cerebellar co-ordination.
>
> We may be free to compose our life's melody, and program our highly personal computer to the best of our ability, but the quality of the instruments is predetermined. Basic behaviour patterns are given: deeply buried epigenetic rules are certainly hard-wired in our personality.

For all that, we need better, problem-oriented meta-idioms which come closer to human grammar and facilitate the handling of information in ever greater chunks. This calls for extensive clumping of data and nesting of appropriate languages within each other. Hardware requirements escalate but the reward is a rich semantics and ease of operation.

Although the analogy between human and mechanized brain activity is striking, the chasm between them is deep. Computers and the associated languages are deliberately constructed according to the deterministic schemata of classical logic; they are entirely explicit, reproducible and accessible to systematic analysis. Human brains and, accordingly, human languages exist in the imprecise ambivalence and opacity of quantified reality; they are supercharged with unpredictable opportunities for play, just one of which happens to be the creation of intelligent computers.

Thinking computers

The consistent development of increasingly flexible computer languages is clearly a necessary and, possibly, a sufficient condition for what we may call artificial intelligence. We have learned that unanswerable questions abound even in very simple axiomatic idioms, but at least some of the answers may be accessible in higher-order languages. The crux of the matter is, of course, that the uncertainty grows explosively with the ascent into metalanguage; hence a further infinity of undecidable truth will be generated.

At all events, the possibility of approximating creative intellectual performance by mimicking the wiring of neural networks is quite fascinating. The knotty issue is whether we can give our intuitive human insight an explicit linguistic form. Von Neumann already recognized the intractability of this problem. A crystal-clear prescriptive text is always more restricted than the underlying intelligence; it is easier to act out a message than to produce an adequate program for its execution. Ultimately it is a question of defining the fundamental conditions of creativity, but as we have noted this seems to call for superhuman hypercreativity.   *cf. 73; 105; 111*

As early as 1950, Turing offered a challenge on behalf of computers by presenting an interesting criterion for equality between man and machine.

An interrogator is via telefax in contact with two sources of information: one is a human and the other is a computing machine. By asking questions and analyzing the answers the examiner has to identify who is what or what is whom. Turing demonstrated that nothing, in principle, prevents his theoretical Turing machine from acting as a human by foreseeing all conceivable investigating strategies. All the same, the super-computer must not be matched against an average human but should compete, say, with the team behind its own construction. When each party is challenged to explain and predict the behaviour of his counterpart the verdict should come fairly easily. Even so, total transparency should not be postulated for really sophisticated computers. J.R. Lucas has shown that "sufficiently" complicated machines are constitutionally unpredictable.

cf. 331
Instead of proving that it is human, the computer could turn the tables and accuse its adversary of being a machine. This would be hard to disprove, even for a very qualified group of people. Eventually the matter could be settled by having the combatants confront each other. The computer scientists should come out on top because they would be able to build even better computers whereas the computer at best can only duplicate itself. Furthermore, the experts could invade their opponent like hackers, inducing some kind of interminable loop in the machine or introducing short "virus" programs which multiply destructively in the host. Every computer has an Achilles heel; it cannot be proofed against all possible infections. As a last resort, the suicidal regress

cf. 381
of self-simulation can be imposed on the computer. But highly-connected parallel machines, which have been learning by experience over long periods, might be too opaque for such strategies to work and so the race can go on, at least in theory.

Regardless of their metaphysical status, modern computers can, by their in-human speed, produce certain human or even superhuman qualities. Still, the complex tasks are handled in a mode distinctly different from human problem-solving.

Chess computers have already achieved grandmaster status. The strategy is to exploit the brute calculating force of the computer and to combine it with a fairly rudimentary heuristic. At the time of writing, DEEP THOUGHT is the strongest chess computer with an ELO strength approaching 2,500. It evaluates 3,000,000 positions/second and can look eight moves ahead on average. An old-fashioned human grandmaster, with a similar ELO strength can only ponder about 30 alternatives per minute and thus has to rely on superior thought-economy. (The present world champion Gari Kasparov had the ELO rating 2,805 by January 1st 1993.)

Ethics for robots

Despite impressive developments, the gap between clever computers and genu-ine human creativity still seems insurmountable. The complexity of the central nervous system exceeds by many orders of magnitude any conventionally at-tainable hardware. In the brain, data-processing is effected by molecular proc-esses in which the error-free digital logic is blurred by the indeterminable aura

cf. 379 of quantum phenomena.

A good computer should by definition be incapable of making mistakes. This is a serious impediment to creative reasoning as Turing realized in 1947: "if a machine is expected to be infallible, it cannot also be intelligent ... but ... intelligence may be displayed if a machine makes no pretence at infallibility."

The ineluctable internal discipline of conventional computer languages seems to preclude the construction of self-creative computers, but there is still enough scope for interesting pseudo-creativity.

> A computer program can easily control monotonous optimization in analogy with, for *cf. 121*
> instance, bacterial photo- or chemotaxis, but when the "apex" of a local "hill" has been
> reached it cannot "view" the surrounding "terrain". The topography of the landscape
> may, however, be roughly surveyed by stochastic search. Tempting mirages of "moun-
> tain ranges" may be evaluated, risky "forays" undertaken, according to prescribed and
> preferably self-improving rules of the game. Allen Newell has recently (in *Unified
> Theories of Cognition,* 1990) presented one such ingenious search strategy which can
> adaptively raise its goals, break impasses and apply newly acquired knowledge. The
> fifth version (SOAR 5) of this research project is now underway.

The theoretical limitations of computer technology do not preclude a great future for increasingly qualified applications. Much of the groundbreaking research in mathematics, physics and molecular biology is already dependent on advanced computers; every branch of science and technology is benefitting from the computer revolution, not to mention the more mundane applications which are making their way into all aspects of our lives.

> The deciphering of dead and hitherto incomprehensible languages should prove a
> suitable challenge, and advances in linguistics could bring simultaneous computer
> interpretation within reach: crude translation is already on the cards. Composers will in
> the near future enjoy complete tonal freedom by computer-induced acoustic wave
> formations, film-makers already apply computer-generated animation and the most
> efficient computers will be produced by those who are best at Computer-Aided Design
> (CAD). Finally it may be possible to construct self-reproducing automata, well-adjusted
> surrogate beings. *cf. 32; 419*
>
>   The mathematician Freeman Dyson has outlined a spectacular irrigation system for
> Mars (in *Disturbing the Universe,* 1979). First self-reproducing robots are dispatched
> to the asteroid belt, where they multiply by utilizing solar energy and local minerals.
> After this self-replicating stage, they each gather a full load of ubiquitous cosmic ice,
> beat against the solar wind to Mars and finally crash on the surface of the planet (an
> alternative might be some sort of fertile "queen bees" which produce sterile ice-trans-
> porting "worker bees"). In a few hundred years Mars' water problem would be solved,
> but then we'd have to check the incessant downfall of robots. The computer brain could
> be programmed for self-destruction after a prescribed number of generations, but then
> we may face unexpected mutations and the evolution of new robot species...

In good time the dean of science fiction writers, Isaac Asimov (1920–1992), laid down the three basic laws of robotics in order of importance.

☐ A robot should never harm a human or allow a human to be harmed.
☐ A robot should obey orders issued by humans.
☐ A robot should defend its own existence.

Later on his robots have been racking their brains over a basic "zero" law which would weigh any individual harm against the overall interests of humanity – the age-old antithesis between ends and means.

   In spite of all the (un)expected obstacles, the huge mental investment in artificial intelligence (AI) is starting to pay off. Layered "neural network" computers are mimicking human memory by modifying the strengths (or rather the "weights") of the connections between the layers. Such open programming frames are capable of learning, and the memory pattern of, for example, a voice trainer will exhibit some of the idiosyncrasies of the human tutor. The operating mode of such a computer may, in the end, become impervious to detailed analysis, transcending the limits of algorithm-crunching Turing-machines.

Programs in competition

As we have seen, the pursuit of computer creativity by explicit programming has been mired by ever-increasing complexities. The unpretentious interplay of simple, wholly transparent programs is, by contrast, yielding highly interesting information.

> In 1979 Robert Axelrod arranged a thought-provoking computer tournament (*The Evolution of Cooperation*, 1984). He invited a number of game theorists to construct programs, to partake in a game defined by the outcome matrix shown in figure 8.1.

		Player B	
		colla-boration	Cheating
Player A	Collaboration	3.3	0.5
	Cheating	5.0	1.1

Figure 8.1

cf. 51; 59

> This is a variant of the well-known Prisoner's Dilemma. Although all seems set for a collaborative strategy, we have previously seen that the Prisoner's Dilemma encourages cheating, because this is the dominant strategy – the cheat obviously gets the upper hand in every permutation of the game. The tournament was conducted in such a way that all the programs were confronted with one another in pairs. The outcome was stored in the memory of the computers and available the next time the player met the same opponent. The goal was to achieve the highest number of points after 200 confrontations all round.
>
> Of 14 participants Anatol Rapoport's "Tit for Tat" was the winner. The program has two instructions only:
>
> ☐ Collaboration at the first confrontation
> ☐ Subsequently reciprocate the opponent's latest move (tit for tat)
>
> The result was evaluated and communicated to all potential participants. The second tournament attracted 62 entrants, and the longest program was 152 lines of Fortran. The winner was Anatol Rapoport's "Tit for Tat"! In an "ecological" tournament, where the payoffs mimicked reproductive success, the outcome was the same. After a thousand generations, Tit for Tat had a comfortable and steadily growing lead. Tit for Tat does not strive to beat – and is actually incapable of beating – any particular opponent; it treats all rivals as potential partners. Over a long period of play the "cynical" programs will knock each other out, while Tit for Tat is able to ward off the cheats and succeed together with constructive plus-sum players (best of all with itself!).

Straightforward computer simulation offers a significant contribution to ethics, confirming the survival value of collaboration among rudimentary organisms,

even in a hostile and "immoral" environment. It pays to show goodwill *and* to   *cf. 97*
react sharply against cheating while absolving repentant sinners. Kant's reciprocity principle seems to have found its game-empirical verification.

> In more realistic models, occasional "misunderstandings" will lock a slowly increasing
> number of tit-for-tat players into an adversarial mode. Such deterioration can be cured
> by incorporating some generosity in the strict tit-for-tat rule. In-depth simulation has
> shown that if about one third of the transgressions are "forgiven" the lost sheep can be
> brought back to the fold. But this strategy fails in the harsh world of brutally selfish
> programs.
>
> Simulations with extended, "mutation-prone" computer programs under prisoner's
> dilemma-type rules have shown that, given time, such systems can learn from mistakes,
> break out of dead ends and produce new information in the process. Long, quiescent
> incubation periods are interrupted by brief episodes of chaotic change. This tallies with
> the theory of punctuated equilibrium (pioneered by J.L. Gould), which has mustered a
> great deal of supporting evidence.   *cf. 88; 97*

Mimicking evolution, suitable Darwinian selection games could simulate polymorphism, genetic drift, founder effects, predators and parasites, environmental changes and so on. What is more, Darwinism has already been put to work
in robots which are controlled by evolvable hardware. The ultimate challenge
is, of course, to create "real" life based on plain, understandable computer
elements.   *cf. 419*

> Under favourable circumstances, modern nanotechnology can manipulate even individ-
> ual atoms, but the proponents of computer consciousness will face a metaphysical
> dilemma it they pursue miniaturization down to molecular levels. They must renounce
> explicit programming and trust the self-propagation of meaningful constellations by
> the trial and error of spontaneous mutagenic play, loosely directed by appropriate
> axiomatic rules or "values". Richard Dawkins has boldly generalized that life – natural
> or artificial – cannot arise except through Darwinian selection processes.

The high drama surrounding "thinking machines" could well subside. There is
no longer anything revolutionary about making more intelligent computers
which can perform increasingly demanding tasks. From early childhood on, our
descendants will cheerfully exploit the most complex self-learning machines
which have gathered experience and become "wiser" over tens or even hundreds of years.

> The battle over computer consciousness has been raging for several decades. In *Gödel,
> Escher, Bach* (1979), Douglas Hofstaedter takes issue with the philosopher J.R. Lucas,
> one of the most prominent sceptics in the field. The argument is engaging plenty of fresh
> mind but has remained inconclusive. I believe that the debate cannot break out of the
> present doldrums until we have a better understanding of human consciousness.

Come what may, computers and human beings will probably remain incommensurable objects. Barring the unexpected, computers are cut off from the soil
of deeper wisdom, capable only of reflecting clearly expressed human ideas.
Properly equipped experts should always be able to outwit their own creation,
thus proving the finiteness of the artificial mind. In the improbable contrary
case, man will turn out to be nothing more than a rather unreliable machine:

cause enough for the avalanche of arrogance and anxiety weighing down on the AI-movement.

8.4   Scientific languages

The largely intuitive creation of concepts is the first step in the scientific learning process. We must possess the right precognition in order to identify relevant patterns; only then can we proceed with naming and classifying the proper categories. Such powers of expression can only be bought at the cost of precision. As interest shifts from pure logic and mathematics to physical, biological and cultural games, the professional idioms must faithfully reflect the increasing complexity. At a certain point, science cannot properly name the superordinate symbol – it has to step aside and stay silent.

Mathematical quandaries

Ever since Euclid, mathematicians have overawed laymen with exact definitions and irrefutable deductive procedures, creating the illusion that the vagueness of our everyday language has been utterly banished from their domains. And yet, mathematics has always been haunted by the ambiguity attaching to basic concepts. What does "parallel" really mean? Or "infinitesimal", "set", "continuity", "proposition", "number"? Without recurring disputes on such fundamental linguistic issues, mathematics would long ago have degenerated into repetitive orthodoxy.

cf. 155   To the Pythagoreans only fractions and whole numbers counted, but in the wake of successively broader concepts of "number" we have gradually become acquainted with "monstrous" negative, irrational and imaginary numbers; the latest in line are the transfinite numbers beyond infinity.

Biology is notorious for its persistent arguments about the proper naming and classification of distinct species, but the confusion goes much deeper. Imre Lakatos has illustrated the interconnected problems of taxonomy and "irrefutable" mathematical proof in a masterly study of the history of polyhedra
cf. 280 mathematics (*Proofs and Refutations*, 1976).

In 1758 Leonhard Euler (1707–83) observed that in every polyhedron the sum of the number of verticles (V) and the number of faces (F) was equal to the number of edges (E) plus two: i.e. $V + F = E + 2$ (for instance for a tetrahedron $4 + 4 = 6 + 2$). One consequence of this relation is that there are only five regular polyhedra, known since Antiquity. In 1812, Augustin Cauchy (1789–1857) "proved" Euler's conjecture by mentally cutting up the polyhedron and spreading it out in a plane. After that things came unstuck (see figure 8.2).

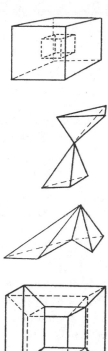

a)   In the very next year S.A.J. Lhuilier observed that Euler's equation does not hold for hollow bodies. V + F is then equal to E + 4. This counterexample can only be dealt with by limiting the validity of the proof to solid polyhedra.

b)   In 1832 F.C. Hessel presented two examples of solid polyhedra in which V + F = E + 3! In due course Möbius (1865) redefined "genuine" polyhedra such that their volume must not be divided into several parts.

c)   But, unfortunately, new monstrous counterexamples turn up: a tunnel V + F = E.

d)   A sea urchin (originally Kepler's invention – or is it a discovery?). Depending on how one "sees" it the sea urchin will either follow Euler, or V + F = E – 6!!

e)   The only available option was the return to "regular" polyhedra without cavities, but there is a simple counterexample, a cube on a cube, V + F = E + 3 which spoils even this language game.

Figure 8.2

The restriction to convex polyhedra only implies an unacceptable self-limitation. In the end the only remaining stronghold seems to be the self-immunizing, topsy-turvy definition: polyhedra are "regular" or Eulerian when V + F = E + 2.

Lakatos shows how the naive nomenclature of the early investigators was made problematic by subsequent research, until in 1899 Poincaré introduced a more sophisticated vector-algebraic language, and confusion gave way to a clear classification of polyhedra. A "regular" polyhydron, for example, is topologically equivalent to a sphere; the new abstract idiom can easily handle corresponding structures in higher dimensions.

Perplexing patterns

cf. 30; 348 The first step in the scientific learning process is conceptualization. Only on such a largely intuitive base can we proceed with naming and classifying the proper categories. Thence it is vitally important to possess the right precognition in order to identify relevant patterns.

> All beginners encounter the same difficulties in recognizing birds or mushrooms from detailed descriptions or even realistic illustrations whereas for ornithologists or mycologists a glimpse will suffice. The occasional observer pays too much attention to superficial features – colour, form or size – and misses the relevant combination of characteristics, the *gestalt*.

cf. 334 It comes as cold comfort to realise that computers are even less astute than humans in pattern recognition. M. Bongard has (in *Patterns of Recognition*, 1970) worked out 100 relatively simple problems for testing computers, which also give us mortals something to think about (see figures 8.3–5).

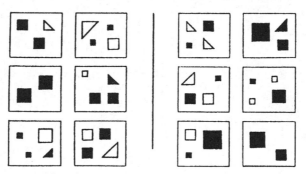

Figure 8.3   Bongard problem no. 58

What feature distinguishes the left-hand group of six figures from the right-hand group? When the material is properly arranged in homogeneous subsets, the solution is not difficult to find. The next problem is a little more realistic; the figures from Bongard no. 71 have been mixed up and the reader is asked to divide them into two groups of six figures each.

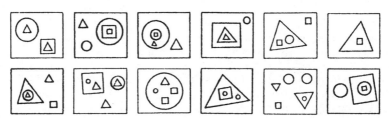

Figure 8.4   Bongard problem no. 71

Several superficial criteria will serve, but there is only one literally deep and truly enlightening alternative. If we have hit the mark, Bongard No. 70 causes little trouble.

The distinguishing criterion in both cases is the maximum complexity, the depth of the internal relationships. The last figure could provide a point of departure for botanical classification based on the number of bifurcations in the supporting structure of the plant.

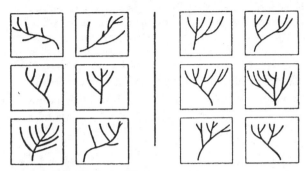

Figure 8.5   Bongard problem no. 70

As it happened, Linnaeus' perceptive eye ignored a multitude of striking characteristics and selected stamens and pistils as distinguishing features for botanical categorization. Examples of similar intuition abound in other sciences as well.   *cf. 296*

Early in the nineteenth century, J.J. Berzelius (1779–1848) introduced chemical symbols for the elements and simple formulae for inorganic compounds. By the 1860s the properties of more than 70 elements had been studied in some detail. Certain regularities were perceivable, but the search for a deeper order did not lead anywhere until, in 1869, Dmitri Mendeleev (1834–1907) developed his "natural" system of the elements. Mendeleev's tables had empty squares, and their predictive power was confirmed when the postulated elements were later discovered and revealed the predicted properties. What is more, Mendeleev's schema has received its definitive verification in the electronic scale models of atomic physics, which accurately reflect the structure of the natural system.

The new-fangled language of chemical and biological taxonomists was later confirmed by quantum physics, evolutionary theory and molecular biology. Patient play with the pieces of the puzzle can tease a telling pattern out of perplexing confusion, despite a total ignorance of the underlying rules of the game.

Self-defining science

Language does not lose its central role once the unstructured initial stage has been overcome and the fundamental concepts clarified. The special and general theories of relativity express the deep interaction between thoroughly redefined time, mass, space and energy, and similar though less radical changes constantly occur in all active sciences. The emergence of quantum physics involved many awkward linguistic problems. No lucid conceptual apparatus can faithfully reproduce the mathematically manipulated facts of quantum mechanics.

cf. 22; 34; 62
Bohr introduced the term "complementarity" to symbolize this dilemma. The essential diversity of atomic reality can only be described by using (at least) two complementary language games, for instance in the wave-particle duality of light and matter. A related dualism is reflected in the mathematical formalism of quantum mechanics. The operators for the co-ordinates (position) and momenta (motion) are non-commutative (a · b ≠ b · a). This creates a sort of mutual exclusivity; position and momenta cannot simultaneously have well-defined quantified values in the equations of quantum mechanics. If one factor is mathematically focussed and is thus endowed with unambiguous and clear numerical solutions or "eigenvalues", the other will be blurred and lose its reality; here we encounter Heisenberg's uncertainty principle in its original version.

The succinct and penetrating language of science may be abstruse and incomprehensible to the man on the street, but it is nevertheless entirely dependent on our everyday language games. Take Einstein's famous energy-matter equivalence which can be given an utterly simple mathematical form:

$$E = m \cdot c^2$$

But if we have to convey the real meaning of this proposition to somebody not in the know, we have to supplement the formula with a string of statements in plain English.

> An explication might run as follows:
> E designates energy
> = designates "is equal to"
> m designates mass
> c designates the speed of light in a vacuum
> · designates multiplication
> ^{2} designates (in this particular position) multiplication by itself

Further clarification is needed to capture the physical concepts in strictly empirical terms by tracing them back to specific experimental set-ups and observational procedures. This semantic mobilization happily results in a thought-economic convergence; the content of the message gradually becomes fixed beyond all reasonable doubt. Thus, the demonstrable interplay with the immutable games of the external world grants a genuinely scientific language many self-defining characteristics and, consequently, confers on it the stamp of truth.

In frequent use, scientific terms eventually free themselves from the bondage of the mother tongue and acquire a precise contextual meaning for the initiates. In mathematics, especially, semiotic stringency greatly facilitates the economy of the accompanying thought processes.

> The normative semiotics of algebra simplified the solution of knotty equations whereas Cartesian analytic geometry gave a wonderful corporeality to the abstract mathematical interplay. Leibnitz came in second after Newton in inventing the calculus, but his striking symbolism soon outstripped Newtonian notation. With the advent of personal computers the competition between different sign systems has now reached the public market-place.

Scientific languages are mere conventions but a lot depends on the cogency of the linguistic machinery. In analogy with computer idioms, science must consistently adapt to its topic and search for more efficient categorizations which elicit the hidden aesthetic aspects of the subject matter.

Escalating opacity

In the basic sciences, a strict, almost censorial terminology is obviously justified. Scientific analysis always involves the identification of invariances: the reduction of the apparently boundless variety of surface phenomena to a few expressive rules of maximum clarity. Ordinary usage often obstructs the sight of the fundamental game, but a stilted, pseudo-scientific terminology can also mutilate or obscure its object beyond recognition.

> In its recondite expositions, the criticism of literary criticism illustrates this self-defeating urge towards scientific self-reference which often exceeds the utmost limits of comprehensibility. *cf. 293; 370*

The depth and expressiveness of the language game must conform to the characteristics of the particular research object and the nature of the scientific interest. The mapping of complex and dynamic realities calls for successively richer and more clustered concepts. Thence linguistic transparency will be curtailed; the powers of expression can only be bought at the cost of precision.

> We have already observed that advanced chess players do not waste time in considering each possible move separately. Rather, they think more economically in chunks, superordinate aggregates which relate to specific situations in the game and are holistically connected by their chess-grammatical implications. Some of these concepts have been named: The Caro-Cann, Grünfeld and Nimzowitsch defences as well as the French, Spanish, English, Sicilian and Royal Indian openings all represent easy-to-grasp notions for the experienced chess-player. *cf. 120; 354*
>
> Chess linguistics is chiefly concerned with the dynamic aspects of the game – who can do what to whom? Every position carries a distinct semantic value in a tacit chess terminology. While beginners barely grasp a few phrases, the master achieves superior thought-economy by applying an extensive but mostly uncodified vocabulary – pawn deployment, fianchetto bishops, knight tactics, ties and threats, endgame and checkmate combinations – adding up to at least 50,000 meaningful chess patterns. The lingo of an ordinary top-level player comprises only about 2,000 such connotative "words".

Even a simple rule system like chess leads to linguistic escalation that soon exhausts the explicit vocabulary; in any language, unnamed classes always outnumber symbolic expressions. In analogy with technical problem-solving, *cf. 121* competent chess reasoning utilizes highly chunked and largely nameless concepts. Such a private language is indispensable for successful play whenever the number of possible permutations increases without limit. *cf. 115*

While the final result of scientific efforts should be expressed in the clearest terms admissable, the grammar of the actual work process remains shrouded in mystery. Creative thinking proceeds by a muddled, deeply personal monologue, applying its own idiosyncratic semiotics. Like the grandmasters of chess or gifted artists and technicians, great scientists possess a peculiar clairvoyance which surpasses ordinary verbal barriers. *cf. 118; 121; 354*

> Human vision is realized by a complex hierarchy of nerve columns, a highly-organized

synaptic network in which the primary inputs of vertical, oblique and lateral movement as well as contrast, colour, stereo effects and the like are integrated to form a meaningful, multidimensional perception. Recent research indicates that this visual "brain space" is utilized in attaching meaning to words. Before we speak or even think we have to perceive.

Scientific and linguistic play exhibit a clear correspondence; advances in science depend on acute and well-ordered verbalization. As interest shifts from pure logic and mathematics to physical, chemical, biological, and cultural games, the professional idioms must faithfully reflect the increasing complexity. Even the simplest of real objects intimates something over and above an exhaustive mathematical simulation model, and the fuzziness of the related languages snowballs as the scope for play increases.

The exertions of jurists to codify definitive and formally binding rules for human interplay meet with metaphysical impediments. Like "universal" psychology, sociology, economics, politology or epistemology, absolute justice must for purely linguistic reasons remain an unattainable chimera. Only martial law can be just and straightforward. In civil societies the happy diversity of values entails unavoidable self-contra-
cf. 165   diction which necessarily precludes the exercise of universal and clear-cut justice.

Psychology and sociology, art criticism and philosophy overflow with mutually incompatible categorizations, vain attempts to catch complex human reality "from below". The ambition to attain complete linguistic command over our existential experience recalls, once again, the efforts of the snake to swallow its own tail. The blithe repudiation of an adequate value frame converts the emergent plus-sum game to a meaningless merry-go-round.

The several "theories of value" do not contribute one iota to unravelling the jumble. We are served with the emotive, the empirical and the objective theory respectively, whereas real values certainly involve all these aspects – and more. The "supervalue" required for
cf. 375   the final choice eludes, of course, any scientific category.

Action always speaks louder than words, but the honest word is a deed on a superior level, and one that can only be judged from an even higher position. At a certain point science cannot properly name the superordinate symbol – it has to step aside and stay silent.

8.5   The mother tongue

In the vernacular, nothing can be proved beyond doubt, since every argument can be circumvented: the craftiness of our mother tongue faithfully reflects the complexity of the human mind. The vernacular can be stretched and mapped onto itself over and over again; almost by definition it subsumes any expressable human thought. Truth is a "prospective" property which cannot be circumscribed in any finite way; we can only, rather ineffectively, point at the presumed truth. For better or worse, we must rely on our taste, a set of extralinguistic values which guide us in finding the right words. Here, if ever, it is a question of playing a plus-sum game, of refraining from poisoning our most humane heritage.

The supreme meta-idiom

Not philosophy but the mother tongue is the true science of sciences, the universal instrument of thought. Most of our conscious communication and information-processing takes place within its framework. Naming is the first step towards de-mystifying our fearful and chaotic surroundings; everyday language is the only instrument available for co-ordinating our perceptions into a conceptual world of our own. Consequently, an estimated 20 to 25 per cent of human brain capacity is reserved for word-processing.

Language has for long been used and abused in deductive philosophical reasoning. Wittgenstein's incisive analysis of the language game deflated the naive trust in semantic self-evidence, once and for all. Abstract word play is either empty or fraught with ambiguity and must, in the last instance, seek recourse to the vernacular. Great natural scientists (vide Heisenberg, *Physik und Philosophie*, 1959) have testified to the superiority and indispensability of our ordinary language, even and especially in the development of recondite or formalistic disciplines.

> An amusing example of esoteric linguistic confusion is Whitehead's collection of seventeen different definitions of the logical concept "proposition". Despite the muddle, propositional calculus functions with unfailing accuracy, securely embedded in a surge of ordinary words which generates a multidimensional perspective, and thus lays bare the structure of logic.

The young Wittgenstein saw language as an isomorphic mapping of reality. However, such a simple equivalence of language and reality fails to do justice to the incredible diversity and flexibility of the vernacular. The mature Wittgenstein therefore looks upon language as an open game. Words correspond to   *cf. 28; 41* chess pieces with rather vague characteristics; they form sentences according to rules which are clearly indicated but quite flexible. The shifting sense of the message is indicated by the appropriate sequence of moves in the language game. The only imperative is that understanding is maintained or improved; anything that works is permitted.

> Deaf-and-dumb language has to restrict itself to visual devices, but it is still capable of advanced communication and even of poetic expression. A living sign language (such as ASL, American Sign Language) seems to evolve with the same mysterious dynamic as spoken idioms, inducing neologisms and dialectal variation, allowing for such niceties as puns and witticisms. But a set of easy-to-grasp pictograms does not work as a universally decipherable Esperanto. It lacks the interactive word play, the subtle implications and intimations of natural language. The all-too-simple rules deprive such an artificial idiom of developmental diversity, reducing it to a primitive pidgin.

cf. 359

The word play is directed by a grammar which in its deep if elusive essentials ought to be shared by all languages. Random word sequences are usually incongruous and void of meaning, but orderly sentences transmit our intentions (or deceptions) to an initiated fellow player in analogy with permitted chess moves or the amino acid sequences of functional proteins. Pretentious nonsense and unique expressions of the highest significance may come within touching distance while self-replicating strings oil the machinery of everyday communication.

> Verbal learning does not differ essentially from the study of mathematics. You start the game by counting "1, 2, 3, 4 ... do you get it?". Only then may, for instance, 1, 4, 9, 16 ...make sense. Understanding cannot be forced; at some point there will be a Eureka-experience when the pupil sees the pattern, and spontaneously recognizes the rules of the game. Really interesting messages totter on the borders of our comprehension. The most exciting of all are like onions: every successful interpretation uncovers a new cryptic text.

Whereas formal languages are derived from a minimal axiomatic base and science, too, strives for linguistic parsimony, the vernacular throws such self-discipline to the winds. The mother tongue thrives on an involuted and ever-broadening axiomatics which entails unlimited creativity. In analogy with concrete languages, syntax and semantics are not clearly separated. The straight-forward process of word-formation enriches the axiomatic base and affects to some extent the deep, covert grammar, the supercoiling of the self-same word game. The ultimate outcome is a highly non-linear process which creates an immense scope for free, self-organizing play. Besides intensive splitting and specialization this allows for astounding feats of generalization.

cf. 299; 320; 364

cf. 323

cf. 342; 356

> The integrative capability of the vernacular is vexing computer scientists. A simple notion like "tree" does not pose a problem for a five-year-old child which unerringly distinguishes any formerly unknown species from say a telephone pole. Not so the computer which lacks the "distributive" axiomatics of the vernacular. A comprehensive definition would be tantamount to a thorough description of every conceivable tree species; pattern recognition cannot be compactly defined. In other words, "treeness" is not a computable feature but it is "listable"; like pornography it is hard to pigeonhole but you know it when you see it.

All attempts at exposing the structure of ordinary language are pointless; no description is exhaustive, no investigation gets to the very bottom; it just accumulates the burden of interpretation. A linguistic analysis of the meaning of a word can distinguish, for instance, between its syntactical, semantic and pragmatic aspects. But every new facet must be designated by appropriate explications which should be analyzed in their turn ... The mother tongue is well-nigh incompressible and embraces all possible metalanguages. It serves as a hyperflexible simulation model of all possible worlds and can easily reflect upon itself, providing reliable signposts to our inner universe.

Depth of language

We have already noted that the content of extremely simple formal languages is tautologically true. A false statement is immediately recognisable, everything lies exposed on the surface. When the language becomes richer, it acquires a depth dimension; an increasing proportion of the message is concealed, to be reached only by qualified learning of the rules of the game.

cf. 325

> Besides the number theory discussed in section 8.2, Euclidean geometry is another familiar example of a "rich" or "interesting" mathematical language. Even so, many of Euclid's proofs such as some of the congruent triangle theorems, are trivial surface arguments. But it is not immediately obvious that the sum of the angles of a triangle is always 180°, that the central angle in a circle is twice the size of the corresponding peripheral angle or that the square on the hypotenuse of a right-angled triangle is equal to the sum of the squares on the shorter sides. Such insights into the deep structure of geometry imply a certain degree of creative linguistic play.

In comparison with mathematics, the content of ordinary language is literally immeasurable. Even number theory, for all its formalism, is a language unable to "swallow" its own self-description; no rich language allows the total transcription of its imminent messages.

Nevertheless, both logicians and linguists have persisted in their efforts to decipher the axiomatic deep structure of ordinary language. A breakthrough would stand for a major event in neurology, psychology and philosophy besides being an enormous boon to computer translation. It should come as no surprise that, by and large, the results have so far been disappointing.

> While Noam Chomsky and his associates in North America postulated the primacy of syntax, the European school has played around with the semantic content of the linguistic message. Following Ferdinand de Saussure (1857–1913) and Louis Hjelmslev (1899–1965), A.J.Greimas (*Semantique Structurale*, 1966) tries to establish a kind of semiotic mathematics founded on sememes and lexemes, fundamental semantic building-blocks underlying the verbiage of the surface structure. The desperate goal is to describe not just language but all culture – aesthetics, anthropology, sociology etc – in quantitative and "objective" terms. Once more we must conclude that this kind of structuralism sets its sights far too high, entangling itself in bizarre and self-immunizing constructs.

cf. 196; 297

> The approach pioneered by Jaakko Hintikka (*Logic, Language Games and Information*, 1973) comes closer to the spirit of the language game. He applies a self-generating cascade function, a kind of recipe for formulating propositions. The top layer obeys a self-evident surface-logic, but every round in the game reaches a deeper logical depth and reveals new levels of language play. In some cases it may be possible to apply a creative deep logic and elevate parts of the hidden structure into the daylight of explicit reasoning. Normally, however, it is impossible to distinguish in advance the sensible statements from contradictory and therefore meaningless terms. The only

cf. 112; 377   generally applicable method is to go on, persistently playing through the imputations of the game and weeding out the useless nonsense by trial and error.

The highly-publicized "revolution" in linguistics emanating from Noam Chomsky and his school has largely fizzled out. His transformational generative grammar has proved an empty scheme with little explanatory power. The ambition to establish a credible psycholinguistics has come to naught but has, significantly, produced a good understanding of the language categories applicable to different classes of automata (The Chomskian hierarchy).

cf. 38   The deepest structures of language reflect a naive belief in the absolute permanence of matter. Consistent process reasoning could perhaps unlock some linguistic trapdoors and clarify both scientific and philosophical thought, but it would not reduce the immense, unfathomable depth of our all-embracing mother tongue. Whereas its powers of expression have no bounds, the self-verifying properties are almost non-existent. Nothing can be proved beyond doubt, every argument can be circumvented: we can only, rather ineffectually, point at the presumed truth.

The art of lying

The absolute exclusion of deceit, of concealed falsehood, robs language of anything but tautological truth. This inference has been extended by Umberto Eco to all semiotics, which he calls "the theory of lying" and formally defines as "the discipline studying everything which can be used in order to lie". (*Semiotics and the Philosophy of Language*, 1988).

cf. 326; 385   The seventeenth-century Czech scholar and pioneer of popular education Comenius (properly Johann Amos Komensky, 1592–1670) was one of the greatest utopians of all time. In his *Via Lucis* he wanted to "teach everybody everything" and to refine language to such a degree of purity that falsehood would be immediately obvious and, indeed, a grammatical impossibility. Neither Comenius nor Leibnitz with his "characteristica universalis" could know that a few hundred years later Turing, Tarski and Church would establish, in Gödelian fashion, that no general method can exist for distinguish-

cf. 327; 333   ing true and false statements even within strictly defined formal languages.

cf. 364   Truth is not a listable but a "prospective" property which cannot be circumscribed in any finite way; every interesting language must allow for insidious lies. In this respect the vernacular is extremely accommodating, leading Confucius to comment with some banality: "If language be not in accordance with the truth of things, affairs cannot be carried on to success". The mother tongue unscrupulously lends itself to untruth, sophistry, bluff and deception. At the apex of equivocation we find elegantly self-destructive formulations of the type

cf. 328   "This statement is not true" – the apotheosis of lying.

> As early as the sixth century B.C. the philosopher Epimenides of Crete launched the prototype of this paradox;
>   "All Cretans are liars".
>   In his (apocryphal) epistle to Titus, St. Paul refers to an anonymous Cretan authority, a somewhat distorted Epimenides.

"One of themselves, even a prophet of their own, said, the Cretans are always
liars, evil beasts, slow bellies" .
He then spoils the effect by adding rather naively,
"This witness is true."
The paradox is even more apparent in the interlocking sentences
"The following statement is false."
"The previous statement is true."
Or what about the self-annihilating imperative:
"Never say never!",
or the eternal truth:
"There are no eternal truths",
or the modestly megalomaniac statement:
"I have nothing to say and I'm saying it."
We can close with St. Paul's resolute if somewhat circular attempt to get to grips with
Greek gnosticism:
"And if any man think that he knoweth any thing, he
knoweth nothing yet as he ought to know."
Not even one of the fundamental propositions of classical logic "either a certain fact
or its negation" (either P or ~P) is tenable in ordinary language. The assertions:
"All men are similar"
"All men are different",
are both acceptable to any open-minded person. More subtle is the contest between the
following statements:
"Everyone is needed" and
"Nobody is indispensable".

Ordinary language relies on a very fuzzy logic and easily evades the liar's
paradox. It abounds with obscure messages; indeed, superficial clarity may be
just a cover for murky duplicity. The guile of our mother tongue faithfully
reflects the complexity of the human mind.

Unlimited elasticity

The vernacular advances with intuitive certainty, haughtily establishing its own
rules. Every word and expression is pragmatically defined by all the verbal and
concrete contexts in which it is used. The roots of the vernacular are deeply
imbedded in the most primitive and palpable sensations – Mummy, food, pain –
which are gradually conjoined and extended into the astute mapping device of
the mother tongue. Without the demonstrative affirmation of personal experience and social interaction – incontestible, extralinguistic ostensions – the
whole language structure would hang in the air and be drained of any effective
content.

> Linguistic vacuity is inherent to even the best artificial intelligence. Every single state-   *cf. 121; 337*
> ment calls for a context, a domain in which it is played out; otherwise the strings of ones
> and zeros lose all significance. Computers necessarily lack "world experience", the
> digest of ceaseless confrontation with reality which produces an extensive axiomatic
> core, summed up in human common sense.

The self-defining word play is reiterated in ever deeper linguistic self-reference,
while the more conservative syntax acts as stabilizing feedback, regardless of

the choice of words. Thorough immersion in a subject matter creates a differentiated vocabulary, not only among scientists and chess-players but in every sphere of human activity.

> Eskimos have a full score of special words for different kinds of snow, but no term covering the generalised concept. They have also categorized the animal that we in our ignorance simply refer to as "seal" into about a hundred sub-classes. In the archipelago of south-western Finland the Swedish-speaking population enjoys a similar linguistic abundance in classifying islets and cliffs, shoals and shallows. Yiddish again possesses an unsurpassed wealth of nuances for depicting the peculiarities of human character, presumably engendered by the rabbinical self-analysis of an introvert ghetto community.

All trades, professions and workplaces have their own effectual jargon. The scope for false play is reduced to a minimum despite the highly-abbreviated shorthand. Every word can essentially stand alone; no-one can talk down a stockbroker or a horse-dealer on his home ground. The vernacular, however, is a dynamic totality, bursting with mischievous vitality. Everything depends on the wider context; individual utterances can be dissected only if they are reduced to special functions within a tightly circumscribed terminology.

A mathematical analogy comes to mind. The well-defined terms of professional languages seem to have a delimited and analyzable information content. The set of permutative possibilities should be enumerable and its cardinality ought not to exceed the set of all rational numbers, that is $\aleph_0$. Our ordinary language game, on the other hand, is wide open: words and concepts define one another with increasing accuracy but, like irrational numbers, the exact meaning or actual value cannot be rigorously fixed. Every permutation of the language game brings in new connotations that marginally redefine the issue and provide material for additional shades of meaning, in analogy with Cantor's famous diagonal argument.

cf. 328

> cf. 330
>
> At the beginning of the 1870s, Georg Cantor (1845–1918) concluded that the set of real (rational and irrational) numbers ($\aleph_1$) represents a higher-order cardinality compared with the set of natural (or rational) countable numbers ($\aleph_0$). In 1890 he produced convincing proof of his conjecture, utilizing the diagonal method of his invention.
>
> We first construct an exhaustive list up to infinity of all natural countable numbers in decimal form between, say, 0 and 1. Written in a binary code, the top left corner of the list is shown in figure 8.6.

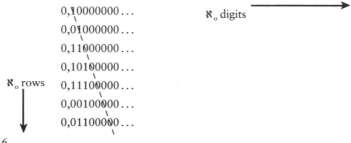

Figure 8.6

By changing one digit in every number along any of the diagonals (for instance as indicated) we can obtain new numbers deviating from all the listed ones: they should consequently be added to the list (the first number beyond $\aleph_0$ starts with $0,00111111\ldots$). The procedure is self-feeding; it can be repeated *ad infinitum*. The length of the list (and the length of the number) grows inexhaustibly beyond $\aleph_0$; we have exceeded the boundary to a higher, uncountable cardinality $\aleph_1$.

One of the lemmas of transfinite mathematics says that the number of subsets (in other words, all the modes of play) of any infinite set has a higher cardinality than the original set. Cantor's continuum hypothesis assumes that $2^{\aleph_0}$ (the set of all subsets of $\aleph_0$) $= \aleph_1$ which means that there is no intermediate cardinality between $\aleph_0$ and $\aleph_1$. This conjecture has provided one of the most refractory problems of mathematics, but in 1940 Gödel was able to prove that under certain reasonable assumptions it could not be proved wrong. *cf. 3.4.2*

Thus, the total set of possible statements in ordinary language increases without limit in equivalence with $\aleph_1$. Not only can we go on forever inventing new notions and words, but all statements reflect in some way on each other. The vernacular can be stretched and mapped on itself over and over again; almost by definition it subsumes any expressable human thought. *cf. 57; 218*

Inherent ambiguity

The diverse professional languages handle routine problems with bravura, but we can scrutinize only a tiny fraction of reality with complete rationality at any one time; practical thinking is always multidimensional as it has to cope with vague probabilities and fuzzy relations. To reduce the concomitant uncertainty, more planning is generally prescribed when economic and political decision-makers are faced with complex problems. Unpredictable and wasteful self-organization ought to be replaced by a thoroughly conscious effort, clean-cut for avid centralization. But effective planning presumes both transparency and authority. Consequently one cannot plan a genuine game, be it in chess, business or politics.

In the face of risky reality, managers of many hues try to reduce language to a quantified numbers game by making money the measure of all things. Sophisticated accounting, tight budgets, neat profitability criteria and long-term forecasting are grist to the mill of economic reductionism. For all that, self-deceptive numbers-play soon brings its own punishment. Therefore business executives have become wary of lengthy arrays of questionable and misleading figures. Instead, they aim at expressing their strategies in a stringent vocabulary, geared to the pertinent level of insight and control. *cf. 57; 218*

In the public domain, planning has always been popular among politicians and civil servants. Human habitation has particularly attracted the attention of magisterial busybodies – witness the plethora of building codes and ordinances. Some town-planning is indispensable for sure; our modern conurbations would choke without administrative interference (they seem to choke anyway). When all society comes under scrutiny, planning degenerates into the legitimation of bureaucratic fiat – a fetish in quasi-scientific guise. Socialism is the epitome of centralized planning, of course for the benefit of all.

Architecture is generally regarded as the archetype of strict forethought. Planning is applied down to the last detail in the service of economic rationality and/or aesthetic refinement. Hence Christopher Alexander et al. caused a minor upheaval with their iconoclastic classic *A Pattern Language* (1977). The human environment is broken down into a number of loosely-defined patterns. Ideally, cities, townships, neighbourhoods and even individual dwellings should emerge by applying the recommended concepts in a language-like process of concurrent planning and doing. This "soft" or "organic" mode of architecture shares some of its inspiration with the Arts and Crafts movement. It would certainly make for more humane surroundings but presupposes a widespread penchant for voluntary plus-sum play.

When applied to politics, the language game displays fateful pliability. Even the most absurd Newspeak can win supporters, particularly if the words are backed by political clout or physical violence. No such persuasion is necessary in the weightless upper regions of speculative thought where almost any pretence can attain plausibility.

The inherent ambiguity of our mother tongue provides the cynic with every opportunity to misinterpret, to take things out of context, to twist and turn, to *cf. 158* equivocate and obfuscate, in short to hit below the belt. In logic and mathematics, tricks of this kind lead to self-contradictions, but in everyday life it is impossible to nail the practised polemic. Here, if ever, it is a question of playing a plus-sum game, of refraining from poisoning our most humane heritage.

The pitfalls of language, especially in philosophical discourse, induced a radical re-evaluation. Wittgenstein was paradigmatic in using language to dissect itself and he was the first, too, to reject linguistic solipsism. Later "ordinary language" philosophers have been less prudent and, at times, proclaim the absolute primacy of language in the human mind. They overlook the point that verbalization is generally an afterthought. Lan-*cf. 118; 345* guage trails conceptualization and is, at best, a dependable thinking aid.

For better or worse we must rely on our taste, a set of extra-linguistic values which guide us in finding the right words, if not the right actions. The mother tongue is, like any other idiom, susceptible to a deep antinomy which in mathematics is known as Richard's paradox. No naming system can describe its own way of deciphering reality, nor can we ever formulate a complete set of rules *cf. 331* explaining how we link words and concepts. Nameability is unnamable, discernment itself creates more profound obscurity at a higher level. The limits of our language are not the limits of our world.

8.6   Language and culture

The mother tongue serves not only as a chain of communication but also comprises past experience and deep-seated values. Primitive languages provide a protective cocoon, reassuring the continuity of tribal relations. Like species-formation, linguistic differentiation depends on our inclination to protect a priceless cultural heritage; the development of language and culture goes hand in hand. But man appears to have an innate aversion to calling things by their proper names and we are easily infected by vigorous metaphors which can spread like a pandemic. For protection, every constituency must rely on its civic sense of fair linguistic play.

Infantile playfulness

The crucial role of language as the instrument of thought and communication endows it with a unique function in the cultural fabric. The medium is an indispensable part of the message; it is a distillate of countless challenges and confrontations in the game of life, subtly reflecting the intrinsic value frame. The mother tongue is the very foundation of identity that binds the individual to his social environment and allows the successful simulation of bewildering actualities. There are myriad modes of mental categorization; every variety of the vernacular throws its own fine-meshed net around the world as we know it.

> The unicity of ordinary languages makes perfect translation very difficult, if not impossible. "Local" veracity is out of the question because the nodes of the different world-nets rarely coincide. A "global" approach is tantamount to re-creating the text, which unavoidably entails the adulteration of the message.

The rather well-defined location of our linguistic faculties in the cerebral cortex means that all the prodigiously varying human language games must fall back on the same standardized hardware. The origin of this special aptitude lies far beyond any surviving cultural tradition, and has become an object of bold speculation.

> Joseph H. Greenberg has recently presented a much disputed family tree for all human languages. It indicates that real command of language was achieved only about 50,000 years ago with the appearance of modern *Homo sapiens*. Be that as it may, the infantile propensity for learning languages is preprogrammed with astonishing consistency as mapped out by Jean Piaget (1896–1980). The mastering of a specific language starts with individual nouns, and proceeds by way of clearly definable intermediate phases to ultimate verbal emancipation. The successive phases are spontaneously initiated as the brain matures for each task; no pushing can accelerate this progress. Naturally, a sufficient flow of external stimuli is required to call forth the latent inclination for playing the language game, one rule at a time. Deafness and dumbness, even combined with blindness as in the case of Helen Keller, are no obstacle to linguistic competence,

cf. 103   but the foundations must be laid down at an early age. Severe deprivation in infancy
cannot be compensated later; the game is lost for ever.

When learning a language, the child applies the hermeneutic method exclusively. Grammar and syntax are after-the-event constructs which cannot compete
with the untrammelled joy of discovery of the infantile brain. This quality is also
invaluable in developing new scientific (and artistic) idioms during the childish
stage that precedes conscious paradigms and hypotheses.

As in computer languages, the economy of thought is dependent on the
linguistic adaptation to the problems at hand. The euphonic stringency of the
symbols is essential for human self-orientation in a bewildering world. The
coherence of the language game, the unison of the different messages is a related
prerequisite. The existence of synonyms and homonyms is not particularly
disturbing, but mixing up incompatible concepts opens up a Pandora's box of
cf. 358   contagious confusion.

> We have already tried to find an adequate sense for the much-abused concept of
> "science". "Scientific" socialism and the "science" of astrology are just particularly
> glaring instances of mendacious language play.

Ordinarily we should not make a pedantic fuss about the choice of words; strict
definitions are often out of place. The effectiveness of language emanates from
its structural network. Every word and sentence is confirmed by all other
admissible utterances, which imbues everyday language with a prodigious
wealth of implicit information. Any serviceable usage is ultimately acceptable;
our preferences are mainly based on historical and social conditioning. Human
speech is largely a matter of taste, in which the ordinary citizens for once have
the last word.

Linguistic emancipation

Contemporary languages can be arranged in a number of disparate families,
which does not exclude a joint, pre-historical origin. Like computer idioms, all
natural languages seem to possess the same expressive potential, although the
common denominator has proved difficult to apprehend.

Primitive languages are synthetic; they take a manifestly holistic approach to
reality. Every single utterance is charged with the full emotional impact of the
specific situation, complete with family background, personal mood, anxieties
and desires. Abstract thinking does not enter the primitive mind. Even abstractions of the first degree, like "snow", "river", "finger" or "tree" in the general
cf. 348   sense, are lacking. The vocabulary is enormous, and as the words interact
vigorously, every sentence really becomes one long super-word. Primitive languages abound with genders and cases, declensions, tense systems and affixes
(prefixes, infixes and suffixes).

> The Eskimo-Aleutian language group is a case in point. Single words literally corre-
> spond to whole sentences in English. *Tikitqaarninaitnigaa* means "he said that the other
> man would not be able to arrive first" or in Inuitian syllabic order "to arrive first be able
> would not said him he". The number of word stems is restricted but the opportunities

for new derivations appear to be limitless. *Nalu* "to know" in the end becomes *nalunaa-rasuartant* "that by which one communicates habitually in a hurry" – or *telegraph* in plain English.

In high cultures, language gradually develops along analytical lines; the autonomy of individual words increases, and they can be easily arranged and rearranged in countless different contexts. Disengaged auxiliaries like prepositions and conjunctions assume key roles and act in the manner of mathematical operators. Complex interrelations can be grasped and handled with increasing economy as the language evolves into a flexible instrument of abstract thought.

> The primordial Indo-European language was spoken 5,000 years ago in a restricted area north of the Black Sea. It represented a sample-card of grammatical ingenuity, with three genders and seven cases (Sanskrit even had eight cases while classical Greek was content with seven and Latin with six. Modern Latvian and Lithuanian still stick to seven cases). English has jettisoned most of this ballast and has instead come up with a few interesting innovations. The definite form as well as interrogative and negative sentences are formed with the help of unequivocal operators (the, do, don't). The genitive is the only remaining inflected case, expressed by a single economical ending. The plural is equally simple: what remains to be trimmed away are the temporal forms of the verbs. Tense, aspect and mode could be indicated by suitable operators preceding the infinitive. With reformed spelling, English would then be a superbly streamlined medium of communication.

Classical Mandarin, mainstream "official" Chinese, successfully rivalled English when it comes to whittling away archaic grammar. The last few hundred years has seen some retrogression which leaves Vietnamese as the world leader in analytic simplification. All the same, most civilized languages retain many conservative features. Japanese still uses different idioms depending on the social relationship of the interlocutors whereas the multitude of Russian vocative forms and diminutives make it unsurpassed in the distinction of human feelings, demonstrating the emotional impact of synthetic expressions.

> The English "you" is prosaically simple and disengaged; Russian, on the other hand, offers three variations on personal address. English does not have many diminutives, but we need only compare the "Thumbelina" of European folklore with its prosaic equivalent "Small-as-a-thumb", to be struck by the cool distance of the analytic construction.

Primitive languages provide a protective cocoon, a chorus of sounds where every sensation can find its prescribed verbal equivalent, offering a constant reassurance of the continuity of tribal relations. Sudden change, on the other hand, creates problems; radical ideas and alien values may be hard to articulate.

Abuse of language

Official communiqués often try to avoid saying anything of substance and posturing politicians have their own reasons to evade the issues. We all habitually take shelter behind well-worn phrases and tired clichés – categorial expressions which happen to be worn-out members of their own hackneyed category! Man appears to have an innate aversion to calling things by their proper names.

The history of euphemistic drift makes very entertaining reading, and the pre-
cf. 254 sent, politically correct vocabulary appears outright ridiculous. At the collo-
quial level, we can find just as amusing examples of equivocation.

> Ancient taboos have left their mark on our language. An eternal problem has been to
> name the unnamable fiend of mankind; Satan, Lucifer, Mephistopheles, Beelzebub,
> Lord of the flies, Old Nick . . . . all are originally cautious circumlocutions of the danger-
> ous and dimly perceived forces of evil. Harmless pretence regularly makes its way into
> common usage. A down-to-earth term like "shithouse" is unacceptable and has to be
> replaced by a whole array of euphemisms: latrine, lavatory, ladies room, toilet, closet,
> privy, bog, outhouse, WC, loo, john . . .
>
> Officialdom has generally ignored the sordid side of our vocabulary. In 1979, the
> Swedish Academy's survey of the Swedish language still distinguished itself as a bastion
> of Victorian prudery by systematically ignoring a number of indelicate words which
> were constantly on Swedish lips. In the 1987 edition, priggery had finally been cast aside
> and the familiar four-letter words were included for the first time. Alas, bowdlerization
> is set for a new lease of life on its home ground. Good old *whore* (originally an endearing
> euphemism) has disappeared, at least from American usage, and to sensitive ears, even
> *prostitute* has a ring of discrimination; the politically correct designation is *commercial
> sex worker*.

We instinctively try to protect ourselves against insensitive invasions of emotional privacy, but deceptive prevarication can also be used for aggressive ends
cf. 41 even and especially by professional philosophers. Words like "revolution" and
"socialism" have had a tremendous impact as symbols for human hope and
hate, solidarity and spite. These powerful slogans have of course been exploited
to the full in political infighting, and unfortunately a good deal of our public
debate is afflicted by similar obfuscation.

> The good ends of, say, environmental clean-up cannot justify the foul means of disin-
> genuous exaggeration. "Chemical", "poison" and "pollution" are often misleading
> and much-abused catchwords in ecological disputes. The "peace movement" dismissed
> all sceptics as rabid warmongers while totalitarian socialism ardently adopted Orwel-
cf. 253; 356 > lian Newspeak as part of its intellectual window-dressing.

Ardent feminists are, with some justification, blaming language for insidious
prejudice against women and insist on a wholesale purge of discriminatory
usage. We should hereafter speak only about chairpersons, spokespersons,
craftspersons, salespersons and so on.

> The problem goes much deeper. *Man* does, after all, refer to all humanity (or mankind)
> and *wo-man* herself becomes (but only in English) just an appendix to man. Sundry
> minorities scramble for their linguistic "rights", but what about the left-handers who,
> in most languages, are put definitely in the wrong by the right-handed majority. The
> quest for linguistic fairness is a wild-goose chase. A Finnish proverb says: "The name
> does not defame the man, if the man does not defame the name." Incidentally, the
> pronouns are gender-neutral in Finnish; "he" and "she" or "his" and "her" are ren-
> dered as unisex "hän" or "hänen".

The history of language demonstrates how even derogatory expressions can
turn into approbation – and vice-versa. Language does not create truth, it only
reflects it – albeit after some delay.

In Antiquity, the art of addressing an audience was developed to perfection by professional rhetors who made a living by teaching the tricks of the trade. One of the reasons for Plato's despair over democracy was the influence of inflammatory speeches on the mood of the Athenian popular assembly.

> Thucudides tells us how the revolt of Mytilene (427 B.C.) during the Peloponnesian war so incensed the Athenians that, incited by Cleon, they decided to slay all the males of the city and sell the women and children as slaves. The next day the case was reopened and after a heated debate a more moderate motion carried the day. The new decision was dispatched with utmost diligence and arrived just in time to prevent a bloodbath. In the end, only an ample thousand of the most undesirable Mytileans were executed. A decade later (416 B.C.) no such mercy was extended to the residents of Melos. The Athenian Assembly took the "Cleonic" line and the verdict was promptly put into effect. The Athenians were equally inconstant in domestic affairs. Generals were appointed and sacked at the will or whim of the people; particularly displeasing specimens were executed to placate public opinion.

In modern democracies, too, the political language game may sway the electorate hither and thither. Every constituency is dependent on its civic sense of fair linguistic play – on the implicit rules which mark the borderline between poetic licence and cynical manipulation.

Confusion of tongues

Whereas self-conscious Westerners demonstratively "decide", the Japanese self-effacingly "choose" between existing alternatives. The pragmatic English have never had any use for abstract concepts like *Weltanschauung* (nor, strangely enough, for *Schadenfreude* or *Lebensraum*). It is therefore no surprise *cf. 90* that words like *truth* and *honesty, rectitude* and *responsibility, honour* and *glory,* have widely varying (or sometimes non-existent) meanings in different language areas; in Japanese there are sixteen finely-graded shades of duty. The distinctions between *sin, guilt* and *shame* are highly culture-specific, but even everyday parlance can go its separate ways.

> The Hopi Indians, have no words for time and their verbs have no temporal forms. Instead their nouns fall into groups according to chronological differentiation. In Warlpiri, an Australian aboriginal dialect, the word order has lost much of its usual significance. Subjects, verbs and objects can pop up almost anywhere in a sentence.
> In many languages the term for "foot" includes the whole leg, "eye" can include or exclude the eyeball and so on. The vocabulary of colour constitutes an interesting anthropological variable. Very primitive people divide visual impressions only into light and dark. In the next stage of development red and yellow take on separate identities whereas green and blue are the last hues to be named. Remarkably, the same sequence of colour apprehension reappears in infant language learning.

The concepts that conform in all languages probably number no more than one hundred. Universal sign languages utilize an equivalent set of pictograms which act as generalized hieroglyphs. But such pigeon-holing confines usage within very narrow limits. Once again universality can be bought only at the price of *cf. 348* excessive impoverishment. "Interesting" languages must possess hidden opportunities for unruly play.

Pidgin parlance is a sort of unstructured proto-language which appears at the interface of widely differing cultures. Originally it lacks the versatility of the vernacular but children, growing up in a pidgin environment, spontaneously utilize the rudimentary language game as a springboard for a new mother tongue – a creole. A number of creole languages, most notably swahili, testify to the collective competence of indigenous humanity.

Language serves not only as a chain of communication but also comprises past experience and deep-seated values. The preservation of group identity implies a certain exclusivity and the renunciation of easy access. Like species-formation, linguistic differentiation depends ultimately on a built-in inclination to protect a priceless cultural heritage.

For the last time we now turn to our model citizens of Switzerland. The Swiss place three languages (or four, if we count Romansh) on an equal footing within their narrow boundaries. Moreover, the Swiss-Germans cling to their ancient dialectal speech, distinct in every canton, despite the pervasive pressure of radio, television, the literature and the press which are all dominated by High German. National identity both required and permitted a high degree of linguistic pluralism, including an institutionalized divorce between the written and spoken forms of the language.

Social groups tend self-consciously to persist in their accent and diction. Class characteristics are common and even a gender split has not been all that unusual; in Japanese, for instance, there is still a clear sex bias in usage.

Among many Bantu tribes, words which could in any way be connected to the names of male relatives or their ancestors were taboo for the women. Consequently, they had to develop an idiom of their own by recreating a substantial part of the vocabulary. The ultimate in linguistic discrimination was achieved by an extinct Indian tribe in Paraguay. Reportedly, men and women no longer understood each other; they spoke two separate languages!

Artificial idioms like Esperanto or Volapuk are rather pathetic attempts to unravel the Babelian confusion of tongues; the vernacular is not very responsive to conscious meddling. Latinists have made courageous attempts to revitalize the venerable mother tongue of the Romans, but so far modern Hebrew is the only great example of a successful recreation of an ancient tongue.

Language dynamics

Cultural confluences produce radical change when vocabularies are taken over in wholesale fashion. The conquerors often impose their mother tongue on the natives though counterexamples are not hard to find. But in more tranquil times, too, the word inventory is continuously replenished, cultivated, revamped and streamlined while a lot of time-honoured material falls by the wayside.

Peripheral and isolated populations exhibit a strong streak of linguistic conservatism. In the remote mountain valleys of West Virginia the English spoken in the eighteenth century can still be heard, and old Norse has survived almost intact in Iceland. The long-exiled Hispano-Jewish Ladinos speak a fairly pure fifteenth century Castilian (although they use the Hebraic alphabet), and a lot of mediaeval German was preserved in the Yiddish-speaking ghettos.

Linguistic evolution seems to have something of the regularity of natural law. The rate of mutation of our word stock is a much-disputed question, but for the most stable core of about one hundred words it has been estimated at 14 per cent per thousand years. After a few millennia at any rate, vocabulary and sometimes grammar as well may have changed almost beyond recognition. All in all, the most conservative element in the cultural game reveals a dynamism surpassing the mutability of the DNA language by many orders of magnitude.

> Richard Dawkins (in *The Selfish Gene*, 1978) adduces an analogy between the struggle of the genes for survival and semiotic evolution. Old and newly mutated symbolic elements, which he calls "memes", partake of an incessant competition for cerebral lebensraum, striving to reproduce in Darwinian manner by multiplying and infecting new hosts. Trademarks and slogans, *Coke* and *Heil Hitler* are striking examples of the sometimes pathogenic vitality of linguistic innovations.

There is some truth in the notion that we are not altogether in control of our verbal apparatus. Language lives in its own abstract "lingosphere", where vigorous metaphors can sweep along with all the force of an epidemic. Stagnant areas remain largely faithful to the tongue of their forebears whereas linguistic revolution is often associated with the hubs of history.

> The Romance languages all stem from the vulgar Latin of late Antiquity, and yet each one developed its own idiosyncratic form within the anonymity of the Great Migrations. The regeneration of English occurred during a period of humiliating discrimination, when French was the language of the upper strata of society. Since then, the basic rules of most European languages have stabilized, although the growth in our stock of words continues unabated. English has become the world leader with its roughly 600,000 words but has simultaneously been transformed into an umbrella for widely varying usages.
>
> A particularly conspicuous split is caused by the ethnic segregation in the city slums of *cf. 97* the United States. Mutual intelligibility is declining by the day as the pronunciation, the vocabulary and the grammar of the ghetto community are, in succession, taking on novel, distinctive features. Solecisms are wilfully adopted and standard English suppressed in a half-conscious effort to ward off a depressing reality and create a new identity.

Ordinary language adapts itself to our intentions with Protean plasticity. Cultural centres are linguistic melting-pots, where the levelling and innovating forces have free play in pursuing syntactical streamlining and verbal enrichment. Nothing human falls outside the grasp of the mother tongue though it is, of course, mostly engaged in trite repetition, the daily grind of the mind. Our loquacity in speech and script produces a terrible noise level; really significant statements are easily cluttered by clap-trap and downright disinformation.

Information theory tells us that the content of a message, its truth value or verisimilitude, increases in proportion to the number of plausible alternatives which are excluded by virtue of an assertion. Very specific affirmations are *cf. 65; 279; 389* inherently self-circumscribed while general statements may seem impressive at first glance, but are often empty and of no consequence. Luckily, our assiduous wordplay is charged with connotations which convey supplementary meaning. A brief piece of surface information may conjure up a multitude of images by evoking distinct deep structures of the mind. In artistic languages, a single, unparalleled language game can then acquire unique universality.

8.7   Artistic languages

Genuine art subjugates time. It is a form of vicarious life; in enjoying art, we are having our cake and eating it. The problem of art (as well as science) is to compress and compact without undue distortion. Just as science tries to uncover the rules of all the mundane games, so too art takes the measure of man. In a work of art, the implicit rule of the game should unfold in every aspect, in every distinct move. The first command is to avoid false play and let the intrinsic intentions – the artist's better self – out into the open. However hard the artist tries to divulge his or her secret, the deepest message is perceptible only in the light of empathic compassion.

What is art?

Good literature – prose and verse – displays the capability of ordinary language to articulate aesthetically charged information, and the spoken word commands an additional multitude of accents. The same potential lies dormant in other forms of human communication. Maps and diagrams convey lucidly compressed messages, and various extra-verbal signals have a striking immediacy; body language frequently speaks louder than any oral outpouring.

> To lie with the body calls for acting talent as well as strong nerves. Even if the tone and timbre is kept under control during a verbal presentation, any underlying uncertainty may reveal itself in anxious eye movements or hand trembling. The starched cuffs of our grandfathers exaggerated tremors and became the proverbial sign of excessive strain.

The semiotic extensions of the mother tongue increase its expressiveness, generating thoroughgoing representations of indescribable experiences, feelings and visions. Grimaces and gestures are the beginning of drama; crude depictions invoke powerful magic; the lullaby and the hypnotic tom-tom beat eventually mature into memorable music. All means are mobilized to intensify the transmission of urgent messages to contemporaries and posterity. While word magic may enjoy the precedence, the enchanting language of form, colour, movement and sound can convey more stringent information. Oddly enough, the senses of smell, taste and touch seem to be disqualified from artistic communication.

> The architecture of the brain provides some interesting art-philosophical pointers. The

decentralized sense of touch remains inaccessible to language-formation (except in the Braille notation for the blind). Likewise, the perception of smell and taste sidesteps the cerebral cortex; specialized olfactory proteins (at least 1,000 varieties) act directly on the primordial limbic system. This seems to preclude artistic significance (although many a wine-connoisseur would angrily dispute this conclusion!) Hearing is a "warm" information channel well suited to emotive persuasion, unlike the more analytic sense of vision. Words, too, possess remarkable emotional impact. They bypass all the senses, but in cogent combinations they seem to act as spiritual narcotics, intoxicating the whole cerebral field.

Primitive art springs from rites and evocations intended to impose man's will on the capricious forces of nature. Ordinary language is out of its depth when confronted with the uncontrollable and incomprehensible. Less conventional instruments and new, inspiring information channels are needed to cope with the hidden rules of human existence. Already 20,000 to 30,000 years ago the cave painters of Lascaux and Altamira attained mastery over their basic theme. Their animal prey surpassed its immediate utility and was forever transfixed in the world of beauty.

We still lack a convincing interpretation of Cro-Magnon art although we can presume a background of hunting magic combined with initiation rites for adolescents. In contrast to the rare human figures, which are reduced to a few abstract lines, the vivid images of savage bisons and wild horses appear highly significant. These soothing spells, thrown at the dangerous prey, are certainly the most coherent report we shall ever receive from our distant forefathers.

Art is bound to transmit its meaning in a recalcitrant medium which calls for competent craftsmanship. The art of making pots is not essentially different from the art of ceramic ornament: the decorative elements serve as an attractive envelope for practical functionality. In high civilizations, the upper strata of society may become so steeped in artistic refinement, that contact with reality is fatally weakened. Discussion regresses into conversation; serious debate into rhetoric; plain clothing becomes high fashion; procreation is forsaken for empty eroticism. Social interplay is stifled by affected etiquette – an art for its own sake.

In the fourth century, China was internally divided, partially occupied and under constant threat of barbarian intrusions. Nevertheless, the luminaries of the Eastern Chin dynasty (317 – 419) managed to evade the burdens of serious scholarship. The refined manners at the imperial court encouraged idle posturing and produced "eloquent gentlemen" highly versed in "pure conversation" (ch'ing- t'an). Originally aimed at incisive psychological discourse, it deteriorated into a diversion for the aristocracy. Pre-ordained philosophical or artistic themes were elegantly expanded upon in an abstruse and flowery language.   *cf. 374*

Trivial but agreeable art games provide a reliable source of sensuous gratification: an exquisite menu, tasteful interior decoration or the throb of military music rarely fails to produce the desired effect. Tired of pleasure and bored by entertainment, man may become perceptive to more momentous tidings. Then he or she may, by impassioned empathy, come to know the joys of beauty.

Unique information

Great works of art are lasting channels of information, linking one sender to countless receivers widely scattered in time and space. Art aspires to an autonomous existence when, like a relevation, it surpasses the intentions of its maker. The message is presented in a self-codified language where form and content are *cf. 320; 348* axiomatically intertwined, and must be simultaneously decoded. We can talk around a work of art but never unravel it in so many words. Beauty is, like truth, *cf. 350* a prospective property, a profound but elusive veracity which gives the lie to all attempts at systematic deciphering.

When asked about the right way to compose music, Ludwig van Beethoven replied: "Every note should be unexpected when it is struck but obvious and indeed inevitable once it has been played". This is as good a theory of art as any, and perhaps the most concise. Why should every note be unexpected? Because otherwise it would be a trivial superfluity, adding nothing new to the composition. Why must the note be "inevitable"? Because otherwise it would be arbitrary noise, misrepresenting and disfiguring the message. The implicit rule of the game should unfold with each and every discrete move.

> Beethoven's criterion does not serve as a prescription for producing art, but it can help us to recognize charlatanry, pretentious posturing, bare-faced bluff and obvious nonsense. As in so many analogous cases a clear understanding of the rules has a cleansing effect even if Beethoven, in his laconic definition of art, makes no allowance for human limitations. He assumes perfect intelligence and an immediate understanding and integration of the message – truly a game for gods. Ordinary mortals learn more slowly, one word at a time. Peerless Chinese poetry leaves most Westerners sadly unmoved; we have not mastered even the rudiments of the refined rules of the calligraphic language game.

Artist are always, in some sense, expressions of their times but they are also restricted by the ability of their audience to follow their lead. To promote understanding, at least within a narrow circle of cognoscenti, the rules of the game must be divulged in a perceptible style. Great art can penetrate a whole culture, albeit in a perfunctory manner. If formulae are ready to hand, the appropriate mannerisms become petrified in trite ornament and empty embellishment – meaningless repetition by programmable convention.

Interpreting artists act out the intentions of the author. They fill the given form with tangible content, congenially performing as self-playing instruments for the original composition. Modern technology can immortalize all kinds of artistic accomplishments; film is a collective art form which, at its best, obliterates the borderline between creative originality and compelling craftsmanship.

Refined reassurance

A crucial concept in all communication is redundancy, which is a measure of repeated and basically superfluous information. If there is no redundancy, a message cannot be checked; every separate sign is axiomatic and the piece of art *cf. 382* becomes indistinguishable from a random sequence of data. Any error that slips

in because of some fault in the transmission will become irreversibly established. Self-induced learning becomes virtually impossible, because the hermeneutic approach depends on a certain amount of reiteration. The surplus information provides a starting-point in the search for meaningful patterns – the nature
of the game.

> Ordinary language is steeped in over-elaborate notation. In English, for instance, the
> average redundancy is about 80 per cent: we should thus be able to read a text from
> which four out of five letters have been deleted. In the scripts of Old Testament Hebrew,
> all vowels were omitted. The message as such did not suffer, but we find it difficult
> today to reconstruct the pronunciation of the prophets.
>
> The insufferable tedium of obligatory orations or heavy rock music is a result of
> extreme redundancy. Such manifestations are watered-down versions of tribal chants
> and religious rituals which fortify group identity and provide some reassurance against
> dimly perceived evils.

The problem of art (as well as science) is to compress and compact without
undue distortion. Abundant redundancy in art and culture entails a sense of
security and continuity, but it is also associated with exaggerated risk-aversion
– satiety and stagnation. Absence of redundancy, on the other hand, induces
anarchy and the collapse of collaborative play. A fine balance between the
innovative development of the game and confidence-producing feedback is
essential to the maintenance of artistic creativity, and equally to the viability of
society as a whole.

> Rhythm and rhyme have been the mainstay of poetry since time immemorial. Regular
> recursions reinforce the message and act as a powerful mnemonic device; slowly evolv-
> ing rhyming patterns have been identified even in the "songs" of male humpback
> whales. Contemporary poetry and music both excel in reducing redundancy. James
> Joyce's *Finnegan's Wake*, for example, is one long para- and periphrastic prose-poem
> throwing parodic puns at the whole kit and caboodle; a witty demonstration of carne-
> valesque rule-breaking; a merry relief from responsibility, pressing Beethoven's princi-
> ple to and beyond its outmost lean mitts.
>
> Tonal music relies on a few easily comprehensible but rather lenient rules which
> allow an astonishing diversity of musical expression. Despite or perhaps because of its
> strict internal logic the twelve-tone system is not as accessible to our intuitive apprehen-
> sion, and the music often degenerates into a humourless private shorthand. Ultra-
> modern compositions with glissandos, cluster effects, aleatory music and suchlike often
> make excessive demands on the human capacity to learn, particularly when the buttress
> of beat is sacrificed for stylish snobbery. Accentual and agogic finesse become redun-
> dant; the interpreter is denied the opportunity to add his own modest commentary by
> subtle adjustments of stress and tempo.

The dedicated artist is the paradigmatic progress dynamo. While accepting the
highest standards of his craft he defiantly establishes his own intrepid rules at
high personal risk. The whole enterprise may prove to be pie in the sky, and
even if he does succeed in creating transmitters of vital information, people may
never tune in to the right wavelength, or shriller voices on the same frequency
may crowd him out.

The listener prepared to receive and adopt a revolutionary message also takes
a gamble. Great artists entice us with new and interesting information but they

make stern demands on our ability to decode. Too many charlatans are destroying the credibility of the artistic profession. They have nothing to say but say it in a deliberately unintelligible way. All the reward we get for an arduous struggle may be a derisive laugh, stones instead of bread. The aficionado needs a good portion of artistic temperament – sensibility and perseverance – to partake in the sublime beauty of self-certifying language games.

Vicarious life

Art provides an outlet for our passion for the absolute which cannot find a proper subject in more mundane settings. Leonardo da Vinci was so charged with the lust for both experiment and perfection that he rarely finished a painting, and among the million words that Shakespeare wrote it is difficult to find one that is out of place (it is certainly tempting to attribute the occasional oddities to sloppy editors). Compromise may be the lot of many artists most of the time, but art zealously strives for its consummation when the masterpiece gloriously fulfils itself.

> Physical performance sometimes takes on a perfection which touches our sense of beauty; many aspects of art are, indeed, mirrored by competitive sport. All sportsmen contribute, in proportion to their prowess, to the value of the particular game but the limelight is on the champions which lend lustre to the whole exercise.

Plato lets Socrates declare that a work of art brings its creator eternal life, a yearning deep down in every one of us. Artistic artefacts can indeed give extreme perpetuation to subjective existence, but this egotistical drive alone cannot explain the quest for creation. Art is an ego-trip with transcendent rules. Self-assertion must be complemented by a deeper incentive, an annunciation, *cf. 123* initiating the gestation towards a final form.

> Great art resembles nativity by immaculate conception. Once the invisible seed has started to grow the foetus must be delivered, still-born or not. The historian Egon Friedell (1878–1938) sees aggressive conquerors and fanatical revolutionaries as poets manqués who convert their artistic frustration into political and military miscarriages (*Kulturgeschichte der Neuzeit*, 1927–31: A Cultural History of the Modern Age).

Genuine art subjugates time. It is a form of vicarious life, an emotional experience under conscious control. In enjoying art, we are having our cake and eating it. Just as scientific insights irreversibly improve our understanding of the game within a fraternity of initiates, so too art distils and preserves in ennobled form the essence of human experience.

> Computer art is now taking its first stumbling steps and subsequent multimedia and virtual reality generations could well become the supreme exponent of vicarious experience. A perfect illusion may embrace all the senses; flight simulators already come close to the real thing. More important is the possibility of playing around with ingenious software which would, besides entertainment, yield ever new exposures of strange beauty. Such progressive interaction distinguishes the confrontation with all genuine art; its inmost secrets are disclosed only to the insistent admirer.

Every fulfilment of the aesthetic impulse is an act of creation: clarifying our view of a chaotic reality; confirming personal identity; emancipating our emotional life. Great works of art are sanctuaries where we can re-experience, scrutinize, and subtly sense the sum total of the rules of our game.

Metalinguistic articulation

Great artists throughout the ages have always aimed at maximum compression of an immensely rich message. The language of art amounts to an escalation of scientific idioms beyond the all-embracing elasticity of the vernacular: art maps the infinities beyond $\aleph_1$, as it were. Every aspect of a masterpiece should truthfully articulate one separate solution to the posed problem – the artist's deepest concern. This coherence permits the extraction of implicit information and allows the lover of art to attain mastery in a rewarding plus-sum game. The information conveyed, or rather re-created, can reveal a vision of the profundity of man, the meaning of life, the existence of God – synonyms all.

> To try to analyze this process may well seem a preposterous undertaking. But a novel is after all merely a string of words, a symphony a series of notes, and a painting a set of coloured specks. Consequently, hermeneutic perusal can reach beyond self-important rationalization and go some way towards establishing the structure of the work, the internal interplay between the whole and its parts. An understanding of the surreptitious ticking of the artistic machinery is what distinguishes the good art critic. *cf. 111*

Before proceeding we must take Beethoven's principle one step further. Every note in a composition must indeed be surprising and meaningful but in relation to *all* the other notes, both before and after. Thus no work of music can, even in theory, reveal itself to the listener at the first hearing. After repeated exposure the right anticipations may come into play; the pieces fall into place; the whole begins to take shape; the mysterious language is transformed from apparent nonsense into a compelling message of exultant self-similarity. The same approach applies not only to literature and drama but to painting, sculpture and architecture. Visual examination always starts sequentially; only when the object becomes sufficiently familiar can we perceive it as a whole.

The decisive phase in the creative process is the generation of value. Received wisdom is weighed against innovative invention; preliminary themes are tested with the tuning fork of a sensitive conscience. The purpose of the exercise is to throw light on a hidden set of axiomatic directives, and bring them out into the open. Henceforth the artist can no longer bend to any shallow prejudice. His first command is to avoid false play, listen to his innermost precepts, and let the game unfold according to its own intrinsic intentions. *cf. 114*

> With his contrapuntal polyphony Johann Sebastian Bach brought the musical programme of his predecessors to a splendid consummation. His works reflect a steadfast, pietistic relation with God; they are the apotheosis of a humble plus-sum game. The young Beethoven, on the other hand, was consciously looking for new leads: "I wanted to learn the meaning of the rules, to find the best way of breaking them".

Artistic language games are played out on many levels simultaneously: messages are written upon messages. Deviation from the manifest rules creates a

higher-order configuration, which serves as a base for further modulation and
cf. 323 concordant, redundancy-reducing information. The interfering scripts may be
deciphered like a composite wave-pattern which can be resolved into a trans-
lucent set of harmonics, but the deepest impartation is hidden as on a pal-
impsest. However hard the artist tries to divulge his secret by expunging insipid
noise, the deepest meta-rule is visible only in the light of emphatic compassion.

cf. 63   High art negates entropy, it is imbued with ordered complexity and biological functionality which excludes nihilistic whim and repetitive banality, enhancing the economy of communication. It does not try to hide anything; on the
contrary it strives desperately to convey its innermost intentions in the self-
reinforcing reflection between the whole and its various parts. The masterpiece
is an outburst of human self-illumination; like a laser it concentrates its information into a coherent beam of the highest intensity.

8.8   Art and culture

Great works of art are beacons of truth. The masterpiece becomes its
own measure; its perceivable beauty an almost objective proof of the
values embraced. Form without content is mere fashion, but rich content
must be compressed in a faithful form to produce beautiful truth. Genuine art enunciates the cultural game; gives form to latent propensities;
enters into autocatalytic interplay with the human environment. The
meta-rules of the community assume sensual shape – art is the supreme
cultural science. Purely aesthetic games play truant from the realities of
life; the artist should create what the public needs, not what it wants.

Black art and white magic

cf. 83 The dream of some secret, all-revealing knowledge is an age-old illusion, fed by
fear at the vulnerability and the inexplicability of life. Cabbalism and occultism
are a resurgence of primitive religious impulses – the evil eye and protective
magic.

> In 1848 the Fox sisters in Hydesville, New York, launched a rising tide of witchery with
> their spiritualistic fancies. The Western world was swept by a wave of superstition
> which has not entirely subsided to date. The public confessions of repentant "medi-
> ums", or Houdini's one-man war against cynical mountebanks could not shake the
> faithful, including many reputable scientists, all eager to be duped. Of the many self-
> deluded spiritualists, Conan Doyle was perhaps the most to be pitied. The mastermind
> behind Sherlock Holmes had no defence against the cheap tricks of Madame Blavatsky,
> the grande dame of theosophy. Once again we can only affirm that humanity wants to

be deceived; our epigenetic hardware seems to prefer the seductive lie to truthful challenges.

cf. 204; 278

Mystification is the common denominator in all these superstitions; the conjuration of spirits shuns the light of day, and the great mysteries – be they Eleusinian, Orphic or Gnostic – have all shunned publicity. The idea that great happenings can take place openly before the eyes of the world seems to conflict with a pristine sense of propriety. Most holy events have occurred in the blackness of night or the seclusion of caves, far removed from profane eyes.

Aesthetic effects have always been put to good use in illuminating the core beliefs of society. Ancient myths excel in the pleonastic profusion of words, and their cult objects are loaded with magic attributes. Artistic relics retain a weird vitality, as though imparting some dimly apprehended knowledge. Modern necromancy, on the other hand, has left no traces in the history of art.

The emancipation of beauty, like so much else, goes back to the ancient Greeks. Aesthetic form in architecture, sculpture, painting, literature and music acquired an autonomous value and became a public religion.

> Sophocles (497–406 BC) personifies the Hellenic ideal of sophrosyne, a spiritual balance in which artistic creativity and civic loyalty are harmoniously interwoven. As a dazzling youth of 16 he heads the procession of thanksgiving for the victory at Salamis, and at 90 he leads the mourners on the death of Euripides. In the years between, Sophocles held the highest positions of state and fulfilled his responsibilities as head of his family. He had been closely associated with Pericles, Cimon and Herodotus and had, in the meantime, written 123 plays, prevailing against rivals like Aeschylus and Euripides.
>
> In Sophocles' world, man's unbridled passions and blind ambition are the instruments of his inevitable fall. This tragic process nevertheless allows a glimpse of a fathomable cosmos, ordered by divine supersymmetry – evidence that the malign forces of chaos are not completely out of control.

Like other monotheist religions, Christianity spread its gospel by utilizing every means of persuasion. Romanesque and Gothic architecture triumphantly executed their religious commission until the holistic world-view was shattered by the self-confidence of the Renaissance and the Reformation movements.

In the eyes of the most radical Protestants, artists were in league with the rival forces of evil. Art had to be banished from the church; nothing must divert the thoughts of the congregation from the Holy Word of God. This vehemence was sporadic and fairly short-lived; Luther for one declared that "in music the human mind reaches out for its creator". Nevertheless, established religion and art went their separate ways in the West. Art, at its best, became an autonomous touchstone for the meta-rules of society, a white magic with an almost supernatural impact on the initiates.

The measure of man

Evolution has sacrificed hecatombs of unsuccessful life forms; the patent registers are overflowing with useless inventions; countless enthusiastic entrepreneurs are confidently marching towards bankruptcy. The very logic of the game ruthlessly rejects the non-viable alternatives and maintains discipline with rea-sonable objectivity. But what rules should we apply in judging artistic artefacts? How can we sort out the weeds in the overgrown garden of art?

> In mathematical conjecturing, aesthetics carries great weight. In physics, elegance is a guiding star, and a perfect machine can share with the cheetah the beauty of absolute attunement to a purpose. But these yardsticks apply only within the basic framework of the game. Inconsistency is forbidden in mathematics; the theories of physics should remain in isomorphic concordance with empirical reality; the machine must work; the cheetah must survive.

We have already observed that the emancipation of the scientific object calls for richer but also less universal language games. The monolithic unity of natural science is thus splintered by the introduction of diverging frames of reference. In this perspective the domain of art can be regarded as a radical extrapolation of scientific study into the realm of boundless human diversity: art takes the *cf. 292* measure of man in all his complexity. A work of art displays the state of the world according to the artist who reflects selected aspects of human existence with self-willed subjectivity.

> The market mechanism does of course have a say in the world of art; competition can be even more ferocious than in science. Cyclical fluctuations reflect the influence of dis-criminating connoisseurs as well as the coteries of art professionals, which can make or break the reputation of an artist. Unfortunately, neither public acclaim nor so-called expert opinion provide sufficient grounds for definitive judgements. Art does not form a consistent body of knowledge, and artistic achievements are not expected to verify one another – even the verdict of posterity cannot be considered infallible.

The evaluation of art runs the whole gamut from cautious but non-committal cultural science to reckless prejudice. Art criticism is constantly wading in a quagmire, and it sinks deepest when it resorts to quasi-scientific neologisms or *cf. 293; 345* takes on sacerdotal airs. To the outsider the whole spectacle may look meaning-less – a game of arbitrary opinions in which, all too often, the emperor's new clothes double as the inscrutable veil of wisdom.

cf. 42; 297
> Roland Barthes was a much lionized representative of French literary structuralism. He shared the scientistic inclinations of the school: the reader must be liberated from his "false consciousness" and elevated to the realm of objective understanding. Barthes and his like try to overcome the Nietzschean dictum that every word is a culturally condi-tioned prejudice, but they just immerse themselves in a vacuous metaprejudice. Such preposterous speculation has, nevertheless, provided seed for new artistic departures – for instance the somewhat overwrought "nouveau roman".

The artist cultivates all the indeterminate, indefinable and mysterious aspects of our existence; for every occasion he creates his own language, roundly eclipsing the vernacular. This implies the sacrifice of practical relevance, and thus of any chance of objective quality control. Ordinary language never gets further than a fairly inarticulate or possibly exalted stammer in projecting the multidimen-sional structure of art. Art languages are the supreme cultural sciences, subject only to self-imposed rules in their rendition of ineffable realities.

Beautiful truth

Time and again aesthetic yardsticks appear as guiding impulses in the toughest evaluations of the culture game.

> Ecological evangelism is often based on insufficient or even misleading scientific argumentation. Problems such as deforestation and soil erosion are serious enough in economic terms, especially in the developing countries, but the true eco-enthusiast calls for an aesthetic re-orientation. Lead in nature is dirty; filth in the sea is untidy; the extinction of rare species or the demolition of old buildings represent an irretrievable loss of precious diversity. Our whole environment is under threat as a work of art.

Beauty is no bad criterion when we try to evaluate the holy scriptures of our culture. But we had better beware; the faint hiss of false play can be caught only by receptive and unprejudiced ears – and we are all prejudiced, one way or the other.

> A reading of the Bible reveals considerable variation in artistic cogency. Parts of Genesis and Exodus bear the stamp of genuine revelation while Leviticus and Numbers are overflowing with petty detail. The minor prophets not only discourse upon secondary problems, but also lack that penetrating radiance which, page after page, overpowers the reader of Elijah and Isaiah, Jeremiah and Job.
>
> Breathtaking beauty occasionally interspersed with cosmic mirth characterises other religious epics, too. In the *Gilgamesh,* the *Iliad* and the *Odyssey,* the *Mahabharata,* the *Edda* and the *Kalevala,* aesthetic qualities were a condition of survival over the centuries of purely oral tradition.

The truth of a religious revelation does not lie in individual sentences or passages, but in the greater network which embraces and comprises the prophetic vision. Even so, fragments of great works often express a beauty of their own. Like mutilated sculptures they acquire a new dignity in displaying the muffled intentions of their creators.

In a strange way the theme, the self-selected axiomatic premise of a work of art, foreshadows the final form. Goethe depicted the artist as "dancing in *cf. 123* chains" and Sibelius once remarked "I am the slave of my themes". The freedom of self-expression is countervailed by the restrictions imposed by the basic idea with all its implications. The latent leitmotif is thrown into manifold focus, hologrammatically expressing itself in all facets of the work.

> Paul Cézanne (1839–1906) puts this predicament into the following words: "There must not be a single link loose, not a crevice through which the emotion, the light, the truth can escape."

To the ardent observer the reliability of the core information reveals itself in aesthetic terms. The masterpiece becomes its own measure, its perceivable beauty an almost objective proof of the values embraced.

Revolutionary art attracts by its spontaneity and authenticity – honesty always shines through. The insistence upon fair play is vital to art, as fanciful fakes are legion. Artful delusion and self-delusion, superficial virtuosity and straining for effect reduce the artistic game to eclectic imitation. When the message is scrambled on purpose, art becomes empty artistry, a mere play on words, the vain narcissism of an intellectual élite. The mendacity of means signifies a truncated value universe, conveniently isolated from distressing self-examination.

> In his search for valid inspiration, the artist is sorely tempted to play false. The shamans of Siberia and Mesoamerica regularly fell into a trance from doses of mushroom-derived muscarin or mescalin, and similar methods have plenty of adherents in civilized societies. Despite some notable counter-examples (the best documented is Samuel Coleridge's (1772–1834) poem 'Kubla Khan'), biochemical shortcuts to artistic creativity have proved a sordid exit to self-destruction.
>
> Generally, artists are no paragons of virtue and, more often than not, they get their politics awfully wrong. But on their self-selected mission they must be sincere or better still – trustfully innocent. The best art may in a deep sense be unaware of itself – in Wittgenstein's words: "He who does not lie, who dares to refrain from lying is already original enough".

cf. 331   Language is not all; it *does* matter what one says, not just how one says it. Form without content is mere fashion, but a rich content must be compressed in a faithful form to produce beautiful truth.

To retain its vitality art must be an integral if not a leading element in the culture game, and many a young genius has jumped on the barricades, aching for the instant improvement of society. Yet the chief obligation of artists is to their personal percipience; they should be sources of epiphanic foreknowledge, music-makers and dreamers of dreams. Agitprop always involves the vulgarization of exalted rules, the ugly prostitution of artistic impulse by transparent categorization – a futile sacrifice to the ideological idols of the day.

Cultural compass

The kernel of the culture game is overlaid by countless self-centred interests. Interference from conflicting zero-sum play generally drowns the gentle plus-sum melody. As art fashions come and go, not even posthumous reputations have proved altogether dependable.

> Despite his exceptional qualities, Rembrandt Harmenszoen van Rijn (1606–69) enjoyed considerable success in booming seventeenth-century Holland, but he was promptly disparaged after his death by the wiseacres of enlightenment. Similarly, Johann Sebastian Bach died overshadowed by his more "modernistic" descendants. And so these giants of painting and music fell into oblivion, to be rescued only by the newborn sensibility of the Romantic age.

After generations of trial and retrial, durable artistic structures rise above the heaps of mediocre irrelevance, but nothing guarantees the reliability of this recondite selection process. Artistic and cultural stagnation is always impending, particularly when overbearing notables proclaim themselves the final arbiters of taste.

> Aleksis Kivi's (1834–72) *Seven Brothers* was the first great novel in the Finnish language. It was torn apart by the cultural gurus of the 1870s, because it distanced itself from an "elevated" literary style and lacked any "progressive" tendencies. The author died a broken and underrated man, but the Finnish people have subsequently accepted

this masterpiece together with the Kalevala and the music of Sibelius as the keynote of their national character.

With a growth in prosperity the market for art has expanded, probably at the expense of quality; in the good old days artistic illiterates seldom had the opportunity to expose their lack of taste. Gone are the courts and salons of fastidious aristocrats with their commitment to elegance and beauty. The self-serving democratic life-style is marred by widespread vulgarity and insipidity, but it also produces a profusion of artistic variety. When all the interesting opportunities for play have been explored, popular taste may well recognize the innovative moves despised by the Pharisees of art. More than once a design rejected by the establishment has become the blueprint for a temple of beauty.

> The musical revival of the seventeenth century was initiated when a genial melodic line, supported by straightforward tonality, began to displace the complicated polyphony of the old church keys. Mozart's most marvellous operas did not please the aristocracy, but found favour among a less jaded audience. Goethe's literary breakthrough, *The Sorrows of Werther*, was a bestseller overloaded with melodramatic effects, and the well-loved Hokusai (1760–1849) was never fashionable among the highbrow wood-print connoisseurs in Japan. Latterly, the "neglected genius" has become almost *de rigueur*; ambitious artists are suspicious of any widespread recognition. Even so, bits of popular music, films, ads and posters, comic strips and computer art, together with an assortment of functional utensils, bridges and skyscrapers, may have a better chance of entering the annals of art history than most specimens of avant-garde sophistication.

Only in retrospect is it possible to make out the enigmatic grammar of aesthetic languages, to discern the pattern of the cultural game. Here and now the cultural compass spins wildly, and every possible direction will have its eloquent advocates. In science, we can rely on nature providing the final verdict, but in art man is the only available arbiter: he must decide the truth about himself. Freedom of choice is our collective lot, and modern art rubs it in by throwing up a plethora of competing approaches. Each and everybody fights in Darwinian fashion for our attention, displaying their wares and values. We may prefer to sit on the fence, but only by absorbing our existential uncertainty can we steady the compass, choose our past, determine our position and stake out the future.

Consuming compassion

Great art is the culmination of linguistic development. Tautological surface logic is virtually absent: artistic information is predominantly implicit. The hallmark of art is the tangible but tacit communication of significant, self-illuminating messages. The trivial universality of the vernacular is laid aside and the complexities of the human condition are compacted into manifestations of subjective verity without loss of vital information. The objective generality of science has been transcended by triumphant value subjectivism.

The anonymous creators of myths, sagas, and ballads reflected the unarticulated faith of their societies, which was magnificently reinforced by the captivating feedback. Genuine art enunciates the cultural game, gives form to latent propensities, enters into autocatalytic interplay with the human environment. The meta-rules of the community assume sensual shape, acquire transcendental overtones and religious significance – art becomes cultural quintessence.

> Beethoven's compositions span the semi-programmatic statements of his early manhood and the almost absolute instruction of the last string quartets. The music substantiates in an inspired idiom the innermost emotions and ethics of his time. Romantic passion, tragic self-assertion, cheerful courage, conscientious heroism, human compassion and conjunction with God – what we might call Christian-bourgeois idealism – is recorded in matchless notation imbued with blessed meaning.

cf. 292   Percy Bysshe Shelley (1792–1822) has, in *A Defence of Poetry* made an impassioned case for the importance of being an artist. "Poets are the unacknowledged legislators of the world … [they are] the words which express what they cannot understand … the influence which is moved not but moves". Art is also and above all exhaustive self-description. Like God the author is both inside and outside his work, he burns like a log which sustains the fire, but is consumed not.

The work of art is its own truth beyond all proof. Vincent van Gogh's (1853–90) expressionist paintings ecstatically celebrate a universal gospel – the creativity of the cosmos and the grievous exuberance of life. Authentic art abhors the analytic distance of commonplace symbolism. Potent works of art speak in a primitive proto-language and strike the psyche of the perceptive recipient with the immediacy of an injection or a scent. Art does not speak about things or about life, it speaks things and life. It instigates a creative process just as the genetic script initiates a cascade of distinct material moves: art is information in immediate action.

The language of art penetrates our culturally conditioned mind with supreme self-sufficiency and enzymatic specificity, catalyzing processes of superior dignity, creating unique but elusive actualities. Here the language game reaches its apex, the convincing truth of beauty. But when the state of grace is lost, empty aestheticism takes over; form forfeits content, and the inner light fades.

cf. 42; 363   Goethe's and Hesse's Castalia, a utopian community of high-minded but emasculated artists, relinquishes its relevance for want of a compassionate artistic conscience. Let us listen to the 20-year-old Franz Kafka:
> "What we must have are those books which come upon us like ill fortune and distress us deeply, like the death of someone we love better than ourselves, like suicide. A book must be an ice-axe to break the sea frozen inside us."

The artist should produce what the public needs, not what it wants. Purely aesthetic games play truant from the realities of life. They become a bare pastime, a shameless solitaire for an idle upper class, glittering pageants devoid of deeper perception. When the inner illumination is gone, the discerning eye of the master is replaced by vapid conceit, and artistic rapture makes way for cold calculation. Thus we cannot, after all, take art at its face value but must, once more, summon the tired pieces of our ordinary language in the search for the spirit of the game.

9. The spirit of the game

9.1 The nature of reality

I maintain that a modern metaphysics must see the world as a dynamic entity loaded with immeasurable implicit possibilities. New invigorating information is created in the Darwinian interplay between venturesome actors and harsh realities. Most players are bound to lose in the fierce competition but, paradoxically, the very losers imbue the game with meaning. Their failures and mistakes are the real source of information and the increase in complexity. There is no reliable foreknowledge, no pre-existent path into the future. At every cross-roads we need axiomatic acts of faith to make up our minds. To examine minor truths we need access to a more patent one; to measure one infinitude, we need another of a higher power.

Infinite self-reference

The logical limitations of language become an inescapable constraint as we approach the ultimate or innermost rules of the game. This is a somewhat wordy paraphrase of Wittgenstein's much quoted conclusion to his *Tractatus Logico-Philosophicus*: "Wovon man nicht sprechen kann, darüber muss man schweigen" ("Whereof one cannot speak, thereof one must be silent"). This *cf. 315* self-evident Zen-like inference represents the dead-end of a long intellectual tradition, which strove for a logico-mechanistic explanation of the world, derived from first principles.

> Wittgenstein showed that the whole edifice of logicist deduction was hanging unsupported in mid-air: truth cannot describe itself. Just because of their extreme universality and predictability, the rules of logic are devoid of content and can provide no information about reality. They are indispensable tautological tools for the internal auditing of intellectual accounts but, as such, they have no explanatory power. *cf. 327*
>
> Time and again, deductive speculation has stumbled over itself in the history of human cerebration. Buddhism represented from its beginning (in about 500 B.C.) an explicit method for arriving at existential truth, but around 200 A.D. the sage Nagarjuna of the Mahayana tendency followed Xenophanes in the conclusion that absolute *cf. 35* truth (nisprapania) is inexplicable in speech and unrealizable in ordinary thought.

As we have seen, it is impossible to construct mathematical truth machines; all

interesting mathematics displays independent creativity and leads to unpredictable consequences which cannot be deduced from the given premises but must
be studied empirically in a wider frame of reference. Even simple self-repeating
formulas are capable of exhibiting an endless variation of concealed prefer-
cf. 330 ences. Self-limiting games like chess are completely comprehensible, but the
play becomes far richer if we allow an infinite number of self-referential moves.
Wilful juggling with these concepts leads to paradoxes – a sure sign of the
inadequacy of the language game.

> "A barber shaves all the people in the town who do not shave themselves. Does the
> barber shave himself?" M, the set of all sets which are not included in themselves, has
> been the cause of endless headaches. If M is included in itself, then it is not; if it is not
> included in itself, then it is! Similar contradictions pop up in various guises in the
> sweeping generalizations of logic and set theory. Russell succeeded in suppressing the
> paradoxes by strictly classifying different types of sets – a Pyrrhic victory whereby the
> *cf. 332* very root of the evil, the possibility of self-reference, was eliminated.

Undecidable propositions cannot be proved in a finite number of steps, but in
infinity the situation remains wide open. There awaits an endless string of
supportive points of reference, axiomatic discontinuities serving as way-sta-
tions to the absolutely incomprehensible.

Emergent processes

So the theoretical basin for a totally reductionist metaphysics has evaporated,
even though fickle chance and brute necessity certainly occupy spectacular roles
on our cosmic stage. Ancient religions desperately tried to untie the knots of
oppressive fate by manipulating a mélange of deities, and Laplace, Hilbert,
Russell et al. can be perceived as latter-day magicians, bent on uncovering the
machinery of the world through pure deduction. At bottom, the purpose of
their deterministic dogma was to make God redundant.

> The Big Bang has been interpreted as a naked singularity, utterly devoid of guiding rules
> – before and after; cause and effect. Incongruously, a high degree of primordial order
> *cf. 64; 384* seems to be called for. Be that as it may, the erupting energy immediately engendered
> self-organizing processes in expansive space-time (the rate of expansion and, according-
> ly, the age of the universe is not yet known with any precision but, thanks to space
> telescopes, we will probably be better informed in just a few years). Will the universe
> continue expanding for ever or will it start contracting? Expert opinion suggests that we
> are balancing on the borderline between these alternatives; the observed mass deficit is
> filled with hypothetical "dark" matter.

cf. 39 In Whitehead's philosophical language game, process is the central reality.
Everything is occurrence and becoming, although at very different levels of
play. The individual agent is real only in the moves he makes, irreversibly
affecting the surrounding world. The permanence we observe around us is only
relative. All matter is perishable in principle, but certain material systems happen to be highly self-stabilizing.

> Whitehead's metaphysics is well adapted to contemporary ideas on the nature of
> matter; Ilya Prigogine's recent (1980) treatise on time and complexity in the physical

sciences was aptly named *From Being to Becoming*. Physics has gradually experienced a vast paradigm shift: all reality has turned dynamic. All forces are mediated by the exchange of particles, real or virtual, and all matter can be interpreted as a system of resonances, the standing waves so comprehensibly described by quantum mechanics.   *cf. 34*

The mass of field-mediating particles is conversely proportional to the range of the associated force. Gravitation and electromagnetic interactions have an infinite range and are consequently transmitted by massless gravitons and photons, with a sub-jectively unlimited life-span; the mesons and gluons, which keep together the nucleons, have a short range and considerable residual mass. The extremely short-range creativity of the vacuum is thought to be mediated by the Higgs particle, with a mass equal to 10^5 *cf. 71; 377* protons.

It is remarkable that among countless theoretically possible resonances, only a few have elevated themselves to physically stable, self-repeating processes, which became the building blocks of the world. The dream of all grand unifying theories is to identify the basic axiomatics by formulating a mathematical "explanation" for this fact which cannot be pure coincidence.

Without chance, there is no excitement or variety; without necessity, anarchy and chaos. But these elements cannot fully reflect the inherent freedom of choice in the game; nor do they provide sufficient impulses for the evolution of matter and man. The missing link is creativity, the gift to exploit and expand the game, which is granted to all substance in some rudimentary form. The elementary constituents may follow statistically uniform rules but as composite assemblies they display unexpected talents, ultimately coalescing into complex entities – unique actors conscious of the world and themselves.

Creation proceeds by implicit but subtly innovative rules of the game. Such Darwinian self-selection of an axiomatic existential base is evident already during the early evolution of our universe. Later, life processes evolved accord-   *cf. 67; 285* ing to an analogous pattern of self-enriching competitive play. New, significant   *cf. 78; 88; 96; 319* information is created during these elimination rounds. Truth ensues from the unavoidable dead-ends; value arises from the material rejected or sacrificed.   *cf. 117; 309; 389*

The self-same principles are visibly at work during the maturation of the immune system and the human brain. Furthermore, they can be invoked in   *cf. 99; 112* human thought generation and in the formation of abstract truth; thinking is   *cf. 2.9.9; 113; 154;* the art of making virtual mistakes. In man, trial and error is supplemented by   *224; 276; 282* perceptive imagination and leaps of faith. Human cultures evolve by introduc-   *cf. 331; 350; 430* ing rival sets of axiomatic values which drive the social interplay to ever higher levels of the game. The speed of learning has increased tremendously; economy of thought and action are becoming all-important.

The tyranny of time

Time is the all-embracing and all-eroding actuality; nothing real can finally stand the test of time. The only exception seems to concern the basic rules of the game. The gravity and fine structure constants, for example, appear to have remained unchanged for at least 10 billion years.

The transience of life is the most obtrusive sign of the passage of time. Life processes can obviously persist only in the interplay between creation and dissolution; all cybernetic systems are subject to error, to the wear and tear of time. Normal human cells perish after dividing 40–60 times, which corresponds to a maximum life-span of about 120 years. Such preprogrammed obsolescence seems to be indispensable to highly differentiated multicellular organisms. Were this not so, the lure of individual immortality would break up the cell coalition at an early stage: parasitic independence would inevitably win out against altruistic co-operation. The first step of cancerous change is, in fact, the immortalization of a cell line, which opens the door for the retrogression to unrestrained cellular self-propagation.

cf. 387

cf. 72 Even the simplest occurrence requires a minimum of latitude, a stage of some kind: no process can be tied down precisely in time and space. Heisenberg's uncertainty principle and quantum mechanics will become logically inevitable only when we fully accept that particles do not take part in processes; instead primary, self-repeating processes masquerade as enduring physical entities.

> The thermal motion of the molecules cannot cease altogether even at absolute zero temperature, since otherwise both the moment and the energy of the particle would be exactly defined (in this case as zero). According to the uncertainty principle the co-ordinates in space and time would then be completely indeterminate, in other words the molecule would literally disappear.

The predominance of time-bound process can also be generalized to abstract games. After all, mathematical reality arises only in orderly interaction between virtually existing basic elements. Everyday experience endows ordinary numbers with a psychological actuality which conceals their true, esoteric character. Negative, irrational, imaginary and supernatural numbers, on the other hand, are manifestly neither more nor less than the sum total of their inherent potential for play according to the appropriate rules. The process concept implies a fundamental before/after relation, supporting Brouwer's intuitionist mathe-

cf. 22 matics.

> The tyranny of time is no big news. The Lotus-sutra of Zen-Buddhism (compiled in China about 500 A.D.) proclaims destitutely that all things are void because they have only temporary existence in a flowing reality of "dhamma", a concatenation of minute time elements.

So far, the affirmed implacability of time is not an established scientific fact but more of a metaphysical conjecture. The decay of the proton is not yet empirically verified and the process nature of the neutrinos, for example, is by no means obvious. Temporality may still have a few surprises in store and nor should we take the absence of aberrations in the three well-known spatial dimensions for

cf. 72 granted either.

> The neutrinos are enigmatic residuals of weak interactions; we do not even know if they have distinct antiparticles (antineutrinos). The neutrinos are massless (or almost massless) parcels of energy which propagate at (or almost at) the speed of light (a small neutrino rest mass is one of several candidates for filling the mass deficit of the universe). Their interaction with the world at large is very limited; matter is practically transparent to neutrinos. If we boldly assume that neutrinos have fractal access to another space dimension, the collision frequency with ordinary three-dimensional particles will obviously be extremely low.

In nuclear physics, the inseparability of the quarks is formally understood to be a one-dimensional confinement. The same end could be achieved if we conjecture that the local space-time topology is so distorted that the gluons can propagate only in the plane. The energy of partition will then be infinite since, geometrically speaking, the forces of attraction should diminish linearly with distance (instead of quadratically, as for space-scanning fields).

The metaphysical challenge

The perfect insight into the deepest relationships of elementary processes holds an irresistible attraction, and would probably open radically new possibilities for man's manipulation of reality. Indeed, the solution to the fundamental problems of physics may be within reach although it could take another metaphysical revolution.

In 1935, Einstein, Boris Podolsky and N. Rosen designed an ingenious thought experiment in order to expose the untenability of quantum mechanics. In 1965, John. S. Bell reformulated this acid test in terms of a realizable experimental set-up. Painstaking investigations have shown that the pivotal Bell-inequality does not hold when two photons with opposite polarization are separated even over long distances (several metres). This puts quantum mechanics in the right; the polarization is genuinely undecided until one of the photons is measured. Then the other gets an instantaneous "feel" for what has happened and adjusts its polarization accordingly. The photons appear to affect one another at a speed exceeding the speed of light (this does not contradict special relativity *per se* because the procedure cannot be utilized as a signal). Einstein's hidden variables, which ought to restore full determinism, are slowly disappearing into thin air despite the rear-guard efforts of some distinguished scientists. *cf. 34; 75* Quantum physics is vindicated not only as a pragmatic expedient but as an exhaustive description of elementary processes. It seems to be complete but underdetermined and follows a non-Boolean logic. *cf. 22; 62; 336*

The triumph of quantum theory has brought about a metaphysical quandary. To preserve the consistency of physics, we apparently have to sacrifice either causality or material reality. The paradox resolves itself if we assume that in the experiments above we are observing, not two separate photons but one single process of depolarisation. The deterministic wave equations of quantum mechanics do not describe "real" reality but an abstract, timeless action potential. Only when the quantum wave "collapses", in *cf. 34; 69* the interaction with, say, a measuring device, are we encountering a new irreversible reality and the telltale increase of entropy. Then a unit of time has passed in the subjective sense and only then can a before/after and thus also a cause/effect relationship be established. If we want to stick to a geometric explication of this non-locality, we can envisage the separated particles as united by an extended thread-like deformation in space-time. Contact is broken only when the next move is made and a new actuality is established.

There is no shortage of new ideas. Stephen Hawking has introduced the concept of imaginary time to eliminate the disturbing singularity of the Big Bang. The quantification of gravity and space-time are generally supplemented by various super-symmetries. Superstrings imply a 10-dimensional cosmology while supergravity requires eleven dimensions. Ingenious group mathematics is invoked *cf. 70* to account for the broken symmetries of our ordinary low-temperature existence.

The many attempts to formulate a grand unified field theory or "a theory of everything" if gravitation is included, usually start from generalized symmetry relations. Spontaneous local deviations are identified as fields of force which compensate for the broken symmetry, and thus maintain the universal order. Physicists long believed in the perfect symmetry between right and left (the conservation of parity P) and between matter and anti-matter (the conservation of charge C). When experiments refuted these notions, the believers consoled themselves with the fact that a simultaneous reversal of both aspects would maintain a higher-order CP symmetry – until they found that about one thousandth of the asymmetry nevertheless remained. The last resort is to include time reversal (T) as a third element. In other words a "right" process in ordinary matter appears entirely symmetrical with an anti-matter "left" process, only if they go temporally in opposite directions.

It seems to be mathematically impossible to formulate theories contradicting this spontaneously self-immunizing CPT symmetry. This clearly implies an entropy-independent arrow of time for elementary processes: the minute CP asymmetry must be *cf. 64*   compensated by an opposite T(ime)-asymmetry. The fundamental difference between bosons and fermions remains, but even this split is eliminated in the latest and most promising supersymmetrical theories which postulate a whole set of compensating *cf. 285*   "sparticles"; for instance "squarks", or bosonic quarks with integral spin.

Most ordinary physics (including chemistry) describes phenomena at "abnormally" low temperature, when fundamental symmetries are broken. Under these conditions, the creativity of matter becomes manifest and information can accumulate. When the energy level is increased, as in particle accelerators, the disturbed symmetries are gradually restored. All material interaction (except perhaps gravity) is presumed to ultimately unite in a single, primordial force which somewhat paradoxically displays itself in an abundance of "exotic" particles.

cf. 377   The hyper-heavy Higgs boson is supposed to turn up at ultra-high energies, not yet attained. But its appearance would further aggravate the discrepancy between the standard model of quantum mechanics and the large-scale structure of our universe. An *cf. 71*   energy-loaded vacuum implies a highly distorted space-time in flagrant contradiction to experience. In scientific terms, quantum mechanics calls for a fairly large value (about 1) of the cosmological constant in the equations of general relativity. But unequivocal, empirical evidence shows it to be very close to zero! (The estimated maximum ranges between 10^{-41} and 10^{-118}). Our micro- and macro-perceptions of the world presently diverge to a stupendous and unprecedented degree. One possible remedy is to invoke the "sparticles" of supersymmetry which would conveniently cancel out the gravitational potential of empty space.

cf. 65   To an outsider, the highly efficient formulae of modern physics are reminiscent of Ptolomy's epicycles. The vacuum attains a mysterious, self-propelled presence to provide cover for the theoretical models. At this juncture, the race between the playfulness of matter and the mathematical imagination of the physicists remains an open contest.

Touching infinity

In our mental flights of fancy we can define different degrees of infinity, but it *cf. 23*   takes the Turing machine (an ideal albeit theoretical computer) to express the concept of infinity in operative terms. Every determinable problem reaches its solution (or non-solution) after a finite number of computing steps, but if the problem is indeterminate the machine never stops. There is no universal method *cf. 329* of deciding in advance whether or not the problem has a finite solution; the only reliable method is to put it to the test. However long we have searched in vain, there is always a real though fading possibility of success round the next corner.

> The Mertens hypothesis refers to a somewhat complex relation between the products of even numbers and primes. For a long time the conjecture appeared plausible, and it was tested empirically up to values of around 10^{10}. Yet recent progress in number theory has disclosed that there are an infinite number of exceptions, although the first one does not appear until $10^{10^{70}}$! Even so, the Goldbach conjecture (every even number is the sum of two primes) and the non-existence of any odd perfect numbers (which are equal to the sum of their divisors) is widely accepted on the strength of empirical evidence.

Today we are well aware that no finite mathematical theory can prove everything within its reach. But what about the practical reducibility of complex reality and of huge chunks of information? The dream of science is to make sense of such intractable systems, to trace them back to a generating rule of much lower complexity. We now know that this is possible only in some special cases.   *cf. 32*

> In 1965, Gregory Chaitin proved that any computer program or any consistent piece of mathematics is restricted in the sense that it cannot test the complexity of a string of information which is significantly more complex than itself. At the heart of Chaitin's proof is the impossibility of iterative self-simulation. Challenged with an overwhelming task, the analytical process is trapped in an unending loop of futile iterations. The Gödelian impossibility of self-explanation has been supplemented by a definite constraint on the explanatory power of any abstract structure. We cannot, in principle, test   *cf. 23; 28; 290; 328* or understand games in which the complexity of the rules transcend a given, albeit vague limit (Rudy Rucker suggests in *Mind Tools* (1987) a surprisingly low figure of around three billion bits). Nevertheless, we should never give up because there is no way to prove that such complexity cannot be reduced to simpler, fathomable structures!

Gödel and Tarski, Church and Chaitin all point to the same deep truth from slightly different angles. Any interesting axiomatics leaves a lot of open questions within its domain and cannot probe the true consequences of its play beyond a certain limit of complexity. By the same token, it is impossible to conceal the imprints of human intentions: no computer can produce a sequence of truly random numbers.

> According to Chaitin and Andrey Kolmogorov (1903–87), the randomness of a computer-generated number is related to the length of the computer program needed to generate it. For truly random numbers, the program cannot be shorter than the number itself. In any randomizing program, a pattern will at long last appear in the printout. This residual redundancy, the gist of the program, is deeply buried in the outpour of pseudo-random numbers, but can be extracted by a more powerful computer. The randomness of a given number can never be proved; true randomness can be generated only by nature, for instance by employing the unpredictability of single quantum-physical occurrences.

Mathematics, as we know it, is identical with developments in the corresponding language games. The actors of natural sciences are less transparent, but in view of the immutability of the rules, their play can and should be represented in relatively simple and unambiguous mathematical terms. The human essence of our condition can be communicated only by means of artistically efficient language games, which at best correspond to hidden realities – or rather, they present a more convincing actuality. Art and mathematics have more in common than meets the eye. Good literature, painting, and music *is* human self-realization, just as mathematical statements do not describe but *are* mathematics.

> In principle, all mathematical knowledge could be compressed into one irrational, infinitely extended Number which defines the probability that a universal Turing machine will halt when it is fed with randomly selected programs. The sequence of digits in this Number includes no redundancy, its structure gives no indication of what is to follow. Every new digit contains a maximum of new information: the Beethoven principle has been extended *ad absurdum*. Since the Number appears completely random, there is nothing to distinguish it from numbers of total insignificance: an apparently random number holds either maximal or zero information. Like the perfect work of art, the Number can never be recognized.

cf. 364; 408

We can have no reliable foreknowledge; there is no pre-existent path into the future. It is logically impossible for us to reach our destination without covering the ground by choosing at the incessant bifurcations – scanning, testing and contesting the mundane realities of life. At the most important junctures, our minds must be made up through axiomatic acts of faith. To examine minor truths we need access to a more patent one; to come to terms with one infinitude, we need another of a higher power. We can only stay in touch with the spirit of the game by playing in real time, arduously interacting with the surrounding world.

9.2   Metaphysical credo

In a finite perspective every game becomes barren and meaningless. The greatest ambition of our forefathers was to transcend this unhappy condition; to find and define an omniscient and omnipotent God. Frustrated by this self-defeating task, we have declared Him dead but His omnipresence still haunts us in the infinite. God and non-God are both self-immunizing concepts, inaccessible to penetrating analysis. If we substitute them with slightly more transparent Good and Evil, the latter appears to me as pure negation with no independent existence. In this monistic view, evil is adequately defined as the absence of good. The best we can do is to play by the good rules and boldly make our own moves, balancing precariously on the edge of chaos and creativity.

Implicit creativity

In the beginning the world was unaware of itself, devoid of space or time or rule of reason. In the initial fractions of a second after the Big Bang, minor asymmetries occur and crucial moves are made. A group of axiomatic rules are established by primordial design or chancy self-selection. Matter is preferred to antimatter and a few self-stabilizing processes, disguised as elementary particles, begin forcing themselves on the surrounding chaos. The principal parts are assigned, the scene of action settled, and the play can commence.

The same pattern seems to repeat itself throughout the history of the universe. The implicit creativity of matter finds new expression in innovative events which extend the axiomatics – the explicit rules of the game. This again forms the base for further rounds of astounding self-organization. The evolution of matter and life and language all display the same pattern. The world in its entirety is a becoming, an unfolding of incarnate creativity into explicit execution, begetting even more implicit opportunity.

In man, the world at last becomes aware of its own existence; every individual, every moment exemplifies a unique aspect of the Great Game. Spiritual leads put the past into perspective and make history comprehensible but also irrevocable and unrepeatable. The increase in explicit insight opens up new prospects and expands human awareness, enhancing the implicit potential of the culture game. Investment in knowledge seems to repay itself abundantly; each fruitful answer generates a spate of interesting questions and problems.

> Such a world-view is an unrepentant extension of the "whig" interpretation of history, which has been scorned as the prejudiced and unscientific glorification of our rather depressing human track record. Value-relativism has been all the rage for a while but its maxims are wide of the mark. To elaborate the obvious: the evolution of ever more complex and viable forms of life and culture has been a long, costly learning process. Its denial can be excused only as the reaction against an earlier naive faith in progress. The creativeness of man has been amply demonstrated over thousands if not millions of years, granted the occasional backsliding. This fact does not however endorse facile short-term optimism; the future may well bring retrogression or outright disaster if *cf. 284; 418* complacency takes hold.

Evidently, self-promotion has for eons been the name of the game: crystals, viruses, animal species and cultures all exhibit a primitive will for power, channelling available energies according to their own selfish rules. In this merciless struggle, increased complexity carries a cost and without related benefits it will be cut short. Nevertheless, the deeper meaning of life lies in enriching plus-sum play, in nucleating higher levels of the game. The essential import of vaguely indicative prospective properties – truth, freedom, beauty, love – cannot and should not be defined; rather they intimate an endless variety of possibilities for creative advance. Evil is definable; good is boundless.

God extant?

What preceded the Big Bang? What is ultimately in store for our world? Are there any other universes – parallel, similar or completely different? Are there perhaps several worlds "one inside the other", with little or no interaction? For all we know, there may be a universe of universes, or even $\aleph_0$ or $\aleph_1$ worlds beyond that.

> The first question may be answered by approaching the inherent creativity of nothingness from the optimistic side. Presuming Heisenbergian uncertainty, quantum physical fluctuations will always arise in a primordial vacuum. Sooner or later (but has time any reality in such a case?) they will result in eruptions similar to the Big Bang. To put it crudely: when time remains at zero, energy must "at times" be almost infinite. Thus, our universe could be a "free lunch", just one of a countless number of dumb trials, a blindfolded exploration of the totally unknown. But where does Heisenbergian uncertainty come from in the first place...?
>
> The latest version of the Big Bang theory postulates that during the first fraction (10^{-30}) of a second, the breaking of fundamental symmetries initiated a sudden phase change which caused an enormous inflation of the evolving space-time, and created a macrocosm about 10^{20} times bigger than our "local" universe. In 1992 the inflation theory was vindicated by satellite mappings of the sky which confirmed the expected minute anisotropy of the background Big Bang radiation. The background temperature is $2.736\,°K$ and it varies only $\pm 15\,\mu°K$ (a millionth of $°K$). Quantum fluctuations in the original plasma, magnified by inflation, are the root cause of this miniscule variation, which initiated galaxy formation and the subsequent moves of the cosmic game. Although inflation does not supply all the answers, it explains the remarkable flatness of our universe, that is to say its apparent lack of curvature and the balancing act between
> *cf. 376*   the closed and the open alternatives.

An ambitious metaphysics ought to cover all logically feasible universes, not only our own epoch and its special space-time topology. Life and consciousness need not be realizable in all possible worlds. On the contrary, they – or any equivalents – may be out of bounds in most or perhaps all alternative universes.

> The topology of four dimensions is mathematically peculiar; there are an uncountable infinity ($\aleph_1$) of distinct, smooth structures on 4-space. Three-dimensional manifolds (which "swim" in a fourth dimension) have proved singularly resistant to topological classification schemes. Our four-dimensional world seems to be endowed with an inimitable tension between freedom and constraint.
>
> If we look at the microcosm, a slight attenuation of the strong interaction would have prevented bonding between protons and neutrons, stifling evolution in its infancy; similar coincidences abound in physics and chemistry. The very existence of our universe depends on the small excess of matter over antimatter in the aftermath of the Big
> *cf. 65*   Bang. This fortunate symmetry breaking can be brought back to the tiny CP asymmetry, which maintains time and deflects total self-annihilation. It could be caused by a deeply buried mathematical necessity or then again it was the outcome of creative self-selection.

What if our own universe is simply a chance success among innumerable miscarriages which are disqualified by the absence of intelligent actors? This "weak" anthropic principle, the self-specification of all worlds with conscious observers, is little more than a tautology. "Strong" anthropic theories surmise deeper grounds for the miraculous accord of the basic rules of the game. Self-explanatory reductionism and logico-speculative teleology will certainly remain at odds over the axiomatics of creation.

These metaphysical opposites are not necessarily mutually exclusive, but we need increasingly sharp mental tools to cope with such literally universal intelligence tests. Mathematics serves as a treasure-house of incisive formal languages, providing a huge selection of quantitative models for all conceivable realities. Strange attractors give chaotic processes a certain regularity; bewildering singularities are revealed as special cases in a higher-order game. Hassler Whitney's "catastrophe mathematics" offers revolutionary methods for mapping discontinuous functions and dissipative systems.

> In an exposition of the potential applications of catastrophe mathematics (*Modèles Mathematiques de la Morphogenèse*, 1980) René Thom has outlined an almost utopian programme for the "topologization" of all science, based on seven basic types of "elementary catastrophes" (the list of these sudden transitions in metastable systems has since been greatly extended). Thom wants "to create a theory of meaning whose *cf. 326; 350* nature is such that the act of knowing is itself a consequence of the theory". On the other hand he asserts with some self-deprecation that "all which is rigorous is insignificant" whilst retaining his faith in mathematical model-building as a universal, self-explanatory language.

Catastrophe theory may well take us a few steps further in the eternal quest for clarity, but it will certainly be superseded by even more powerful yet insufficient mathematical tools. Our world suggests that there is some covert logic underpinning the fundamental rules of matter, opening up opportunities for limitless advance. Any definite bounds or any overt "solution" would destroy the game; infinity seems to be firmly entrenched in the original conception. Since time, space and matter have conceded their finite nature, the very awareness of ourselves points to a superordinate reality.

Great thinkers have consistently associated transcendental reality with elusive immensity. Hegel and Schleiermacher described man as the projection of infinity in a finite world, whereas Ludwig Feuerbach (1804–72) reversed the argument and reduced God to the human perspective of infinity.

> The square root of –1, designated i, long carried metaphysical connotations. Nowadays God can conveniently be identified with the Greek letter Ω, the mathematical sign for an absolute infinity beyond all infinities. The reflection principle of transfinite mathematics tells us that any attribute or property we would like to use in describing Ω will always refer to a smaller cardinality. God is unnamable – He is that He is.

St. Augustine declared that God is both immanent and transcendant in relation to the world. This panentheistic notion has been part and parcel of Indian religious thought, and can be traced back at least to the Upanishad epics (from around 1000 B.C.). It still exerts great attraction and elegantly explains why the ultimate frame of reference – the infinity of truth – is beyond the reach of our finite Faustian reason. The world is comprehended as the self-simulation of God, implying His presence both inside and outside of His creation. In any case, God seems to have left His mark on the universe in momentous asymmetries, thus creating a crack in its determinate foundations and preparing the ground for human consciousness and freedom of play.

God omnipotent?

The concept of God is highly economical in any language game that seeks to integrate and interpret our entire life-experience. The problem is to demarcate the role of the domineering Grand Master: just how much scope is there for us to play?

> The evolution of life on earth seems to depend on a series of fortunate circumstances, a fact which has often been adduced as additional proof of divine grace. One counter-argument is that our own Milky Way is probably bustling with conscious life – but it may be untenable. After all, it took about five billion years, or one-third of the lifetime of the universe, to produce human consciousness in our planetary system. If we are alone in the galaxy or even in the universe, it would be a very exceptional position but does not necessarily require a miraculous explanation. The one fortuitous survivor of millions perishing in a global disaster is sure to attribute his rescue subjectively to divine intervention.

We act like pampered children by denying the wisdom of creation just because certain things are beyond our comprehension or do not suit our personal priorities. Like atoms or animals we are incapable of understanding the super-ordinate context. Even so, a little reflection shows that it would be next to impossible to modify one single fundamental rule of the game without making things worse. If God could be put right and manipulated directly to intervene in our problems, great and small, the end result would be a cataclysm of destructive play.

cf. 42 Steven Brams has presented a game-theoretical analysis of man's relation to a Higher Being, equipped with various categories of omnipotence. Very simple games already generate awkward dilemmas. Let us in figure 9.1 consider Brams' punishment game in a somewhat modified form (man has the first move).

		God	
		punishes	does not punish
Man	sins	+2, +2	+4, +1
	does not sin	+1, +2	+3, +3

Figure 9.1

The outcome matrix is based on the assumption that man's first preference is for sin without punishment. God is assumed, in the first place, to follow His own just laws but He is also merciful and consequently hopes to lead man towards the lower right-hand corner, the best payoff compatible with divine justice. If impious man does not believe in God, he has no reason to abstain from sin. Then God has to punish him or else He would be encouraging vice, leaving man to the insidious decay of sin. God and man seem to be stuck in the unsatisfactory stalemate of a "Nash equilibrium" in the top left-hand corner, unable to reach the paradisial plus-sum of mutual acceptance down to the right.

The Creator must stick to his own rules. His omnipotence cannot act in arbitrary ways because then He would destroy His own purpose. Accordingly, God's creative power is restricted to the realization of everything possible. The world has a divine interest only by virtue of its more or less autonomous actors and their unpredictable self-development. Not even God can tell how the future will turn out. Omniscience was lost once He delegated even the tiniest crumb of His creativity.

The absence of divine intervention is a petty argument against the existence of God, and one that was firmly rejected already by Job. Light without darkness, life without death, joy without pain, and awareness without confusion are all logically excluded. Positive proof of His presence is equally unconvincing. God and non-God are both self-immunizing concepts, extreme generalizations inaccessible to penetrating analysis. Instead, we must search humbly for compelling existential connections, fumbling for chinks in the walls of causality, clutching desperately at a meaning. The whole world – its ceaseless becoming – seems to testify in a dumbshow to a superior actuality.

Fair and foul

To cope with his existential uncertainty, primitive man demonizes his surroundings and turns for protection to self-made deities, striving to control the malevolent forces of nature by magical manipulations. Adversaries are habitually despised as beasts, down to the consistent, linguistic bestialization of the enemy. A simplistic world-view is impressed on our minds whenever we have to fight for our lives. This straightforward struggle between good and evil is a fatal delusion which can set up fallacious goals. Evil cannot be eradicated, blinkered counterattacks just enhance its hold.

We may not live in the best of all possible worlds but we cannot be too choosy. Our Creator has probably done His best with the rules that are the basis for our existence. It remains for us to explain away the manifest facts of evil. In the cool atmosphere of all-inclusive abstractions, earthquakes, plagues, massacres or foul play in general do not prove its reality: misery and malignity can only win by default. Evil is a symptom of the absence of good, of the incompleteness of creation and the ignorance of mankind: it exposes the imperfections of the game.

Cancer is a fairly good model of the metaphysics of evil. The ground for malignant growth is first prepared by the loss of restraints on parasitic cell egoism. One of several tumor-suppressing genes may be perverted or switched off; the gene producing the "guardian" (or "mortality") protein p53 is often involved. The onset of actual malignancy springs from genetic misprints in the form of point mutations, gene deletions or translocations, virological inclusion and so on. The ultimate cause could be hereditary disposition, exposure to mutagens, a flaw in the immunological defences or simply old age. *cf. 378* *cf. 401* *cf. 286*

The forces of evil hold all the trumps after a successful start. The tumour cold-shoulders all co-operative signals from the neighbouring cells and slyly evades antigenic identification. Furthermore, it induces the proliferation of blood-vessels which are indispensable for cancerous growth. Malignant cells are slouched off and disseminated via the bloodstream, producing metastases which create further havoc. To top it off, the tumour can, like some viruses, neutralize the heavy weaponry (T-cells) of the immune system. The plus-sum playing cell majority is virtually disarmed and mercilessly exploited as the cancer gains an overwhelming advantage – which necessarily turns into self-destruction. But – in a few exceptional cases the fatally garbled genetic grammar promotes adaptation, diversification and species-formation. Nothing is completely evil; *cf. 132*   here the principle of tolerance finds its metaphysical justification.

Evil is bound to a parasitic, self-punitive existence; left alone, it will inexorably suffocate itself. Absolute virtue is equally barren; it stands for static sterility and is literally inconceivable. Falsehood and injustice, misfortune and sorrow are part of the price of life. They can be reduced but never completely banished, any more than road accidents can be eradicated unless we abolish traffic altogether.

Nature's "order" is actually a messy struggle for survival and reproduction, devoid of any moral. Human discord and duplicity, strife and war reflect the defects of ordinary man, a lack of good will – a want of contact with God. In this monistic view, evil is pure negation with no independent existence; it is adequately defined as the absence of good.

cf. 22; 327   The monistic principle is illustrated by the constitutional difference between truth and falsehood, which are often perceived as equipotent opposites. But the systematic substitution of, say, black for white or zero for one would not deceive anyone for long. A slight alteration in the rules of the language game will soon stop the confusion; abstract truth is generally language invariant. To be sure, all interesting formal languages are *cf. 328*   susceptible to deadlock when confronted with sentences of the type: "I am a liar". In the vernacular the paradox resolves itself when we recognize that a lie is not necessarily truth in reverse but the deceitful disconnection of truth and reality. Truth stands on its own feet; lies just sponge.

We have repeatedly denounced rule-breaking as a gross iniquity but perfect obedience to the rules also threatens the development of the game. Even the greatest lies contain a grain of truth; the major steps in evolution can be described as a string of felicitous fallacies. A breach of the rules cannot always be distinguished from creative advance of the highest order. The renunciation of Aristotle's physics or Ptolemy's astronomy or Euclid's geometry amounted, in its day, to intellectual if not religious heresy.

Truth arises in the confrontation between man and the stream of occurrences we call the world. It can be expressed only in an appropriate language in which lying is equally possible. Can truth be said to have an objective "Platonic" *cf. 40*   existence independent of man? This question can, like many similar ones, be cast aside as semantically empty. Personally I feel that we make less of a mistake if we refrain from projecting abstract, anthropomorphic concepts "out there". Living truth is a field of force, a process promoted by sentient beings: it incessantly sorts, selects, separates and distinguishes fact from fiction, fair from foul. Deep truth can take place only in the noussphere, the community of *cf. 316*   human minds.

God emergent?

Slick philosophizing may conveniently banish evil from the realms of metaphysics but pain, anxiety and suffering are absolute and inescapable realities. Albert Camus called the death agony of a child a metaphysical scandal. Intuitively we place human processes in a category of their own. We cannot dismiss them as minor irrelevances by invoking historical necessity, ingenious metaphysics or the judgement of God.

Our emotional commitment is vindicated if we equate the value of the object with its information content or complexity (such speculations go back to Cantor, the pioneer of infinity mathematics). Systems of abstract thought, like scientific theories, transmit explicit but finite information whereas the simple manifestations of matter, including primitive life, can be exceedingly complex and may be associated with denumerable infinity ($\aleph_0$). Human consciousness, on the other hand, represents an immensely dense continuum of irreducible data in the realm of uncountable infinity ($\aleph_1$) and may even intrude in the fathomless expanses reserved for God. Thus human suffering is not simply additive; a single individual experience may produce a maximal readout.

> Until recently, a gauge for measuring complexity was lacking, but now thermodynamic depth is held to be fairly representative for the complexity of physical entities. The depth of random or completely ordered structures like gases or perfect crystals is (arbitrarily) set at zero. The thermodynamic depth of a structure is then proportional to the minimum amount of entropy which must be produced in the generative process. This is equal to the excess of information which had to be discarded during the build-up. Thermodynamic depth is closely approximated by the length of the shortest computer program which can reconstruct the structure from scratch. This again is roughly equivalent to the number of hard choices, in other words, the absorption of uncertainty along the road – we learn mainly by making mistakes. The stream of consciousness can perhaps partially elude such a definition because most of the alternative moves may be formulated and discarded on the quantum-mechanical wave-function level without entropy expenditure.

cf. 99; 241

cf. 118; 217; 309; 314; 320; 377; 415; 430

cf. 69; 379

We are certainly not supreme autocrats in our own spiritual kingdom and yet we do enjoy a restricted autonomy. The internal, hologram-like self-representation of the brain constitutes a marvellously rich dissipative system. Consequently, the choice between myriads of available moves can, to a certain degree, be directed from a self-referential platform, fractally penetrating into a fifth dimension. Consciousness and free will are inseparable concepts, part and parcel of joy as well as tragic bereavement. A totally determined but sentient being is a metaphysical self-contradiction, if not a logical impossibility.

cf. 72

The freedom of choice is our passion and pain. Every attempt to grapple with the Great Game exposes us to daunting undecidability, and it is tempting to escape into hedonism, agnosticism or value relativism, or to bluff it out with metaphysical word magic. Consistent refusal to make value judgements is a sign of moral cowardice which no verbal spells can conjure away. Human dignity demands the absorption of considerable uncertainty, the willingness to make a definite choice between unpleasant or unclear alternatives. We have a duty to discharge, and like Job we must accept not only others but also ourselves as a necessary sacrifice on the altar of metaphysical imperfection.

> Why did millions of people have to perish in the last world war, on the battlefield, in the ruins of their cities, or – most infamously – in the concentration camps, East and West? Presumably this lesson was needed to shatter false perceptions, human hubris in all its emanations. Will mankind go under in an orgy of self-punishment by nuclear devastation? It is possible but by no means certain. Tomorrow is only partly determined. Facts do not support fatalism; the Game has always been full of unpredictable moves and creative discontinuities.

So, what can be the metaphysical significance of events on this little speck we call earth? In light-year terms, what is the point? Huge cosmic forces seem to cancel out to make room for our game; the vanishing cosmological constant signifies the virtually unlimited scope for propitious play. Our task is to take on our distress and look for direction, to make our own moves, balancing precariously on the edge between chaos and creativity, determinism and free will. The possible consequence of humanity for creation as a whole can safely be referred to a higher authority.

9.3   A universe of values

Man acquires substance only when he aims at some higher goal, fulfilling his faith. I do not advocate a blind faith but instead a daring hypothesis, a sublime exertion of our collective creativity. Genuine faith seeks contact with the totality of existence and is tantamount to a practical creed, a strong personal commitment. By such faith we have, through internal competition, created a steadily expanding value universe which knows no bounds. Faith has no court of appeal and is thus singularly susceptible to adulteration and fraud. It must remain free to pursue its purpose and should never be used, in any sense of the word.

The mission of metaphysics

Metaphysical speculations are subjectively formulated language games which organize all the available facts into a meaningful pattern. Verification of the system is out of the question and – even worse – falsification is equally difficult. At best, metaphysics can be little more than a general mapping of universal and thus superficial experience. But such doctrines have frequently entangled their originators in a mesh of circular argumentation leaving us with an array of contradictory metaphysical models.

Our recent understanding of metamathematics has, once and for all, deflated the hope of deriving truth from self-evident first principles. Truth can never be *cf. 330* reduced to a pure formality; self-disciplined form and value-laden content cannot be separated. Similarly, body and soul or predestination and free will are not independent but rather complementary and subtly interwoven concepts.

> The ethical autonomy of man has been the subject of much speculation. The Indian didactic poem Bhagavad-Ghita (The Song of the Lord, third century B.C.) wrestles with human motivation and metamotivation, which is presumably mediated by intellectual insight (sankhya), experience (yoga) and action (karma) rounded out with bhakti, the sincere adoration of Krishna. To abstain from oneself and melt with a higher SELF becomes the highest good.
>
> A few centuries later St. Paul tried to measure up human self-reference in his fervent query: "For what man knoweth the things of man, save the spirit of man which is in him?" Later on successive Fathers of the Church fought battles over the problem of predestination and the nature of evil in man. St. Augustine proclaimed in *De civitate Dei* (The City of God) that "one cannot will one's own deliverance" and equated Grace with   *cf. 317* "a reversal of gravity". For the ageing Luther, the enigmatic relation between good deeds and moral justification, between human aspirations and divine dispensation finally merged into one unfathomable mystery.

The truth about the world and ourselves is buried in profound contradictions and cannot be expressed in explicit, unambiguous terms. Truth cannot even be defined in a general sense; it can only take place within the context of faith. Good metaphysics clears away mental rubbish, exposes blind alleys and false simplifications while unmasking pretentious, abortive, unproductive or untenable structures. The realistic goal for authentic metaphysical and philosophical thought is not to achieve true knowledge but to reduce confusion. We may be able to hone our values on these mental grindstones, but we can never derive anything from such artifacts. Philosophy does not so much create as reflect the prevailing value system.

Unfaithful play

Religious conviction of any kind is widely regarded as a "superstructure" accessible to sociological analysis. Such intellectual hubris undermines historical awareness and our capacity for metaphysical learning; severe socio-pathological symptoms – alienation, anguish, despondency and spiritual deprivation – follow in its wake. Once more the cart has been put before the horse, and the whole tragi-comic performance ends in an orgy of existential yammerschuning.

> Human reason always follows emotion. Fear, envy, the lust for power, curiosity and love are the beacons of will. What we inappropriately call irrationality is not due to   *cf. 79; 82; 100* faulty reasoning, but is the result of defects in emotional and ethical response – that is to say in the value frame. Psychoses and neuroses are just particularly severe manifestations of such affective disturbances.

The value universe shrinks to a self-contained minimum when fright, frustration, resentment or superiority complexes force themselves on the personality. Freedom of action is then almost non-existent, and the individual is reduced to a simple-minded automaton. Anti-Semitism and racism in general are not at all "irrational" in these narrow frames of reference. Like many other superstitions, they fulfil intensely felt, albeit primitive emotive needs. They cannot be surgically removed, only replaced by a better faith.

> The biodynamic craze, the antinuclear mania and the sophistry of the disingenuous greens can all be diagnosed as mass psychoses, based on hyper-conservative but emotionally satisfying responses to dimly-comprehended threats – the exorcism of "evil spirits". Single-cause campaigns are always rational. When the execration of the Jews or of nuclear power plants excludes all other considerations, the one-dimensional value system becomes enviably straightforward.

As we have seen, neither logic nor mathematics nor the natural sciences are value-free; all such knowledge has been preceded by faithful play. Mature mathematical and scientific insights, however, involve very little absorption of uncertainty. They possess general validity, at least in our own metaphysical epoch. A value frame which does not include this nucleus of compactified and reliable human experience is incomplete; if it is negated, the result is obscurantism, pure and simple. Falsifiable faith in, say, a flat earth, UFOs, or spiritism is just plain superstition; it has little or nothing to do with transcendent realities.

When we leave the hard core of science, bolder leaps of faith are required as the game increases in richness and complexity. We must make our choice between countless incommensurable value universes. There are no objective criteria; even the refusal to choose involves a choice, and our actions will expose in full the nature of our beliefs. However good our intentions, we become possessed by evil spirits if we empty ourselves of God.

> Desperate attempts to get rid of faith just delegate control to inferior levels, giving free reign to human bestiality. In one of his caprichos Francesco Goya (1746–1828) has depicted how the sleep of reason produces monsters, but the dreams of great intellects at large can be equally fertile. Plato (*The Republic*), Thomas More (1478–1535, *Utopia*) and Tommaso Campanella (1568–1639, *The Sun State*) initiated the flight into ethical irresponsibility which was consummated by communism-Leninism. As Raymond Aron (1905–83) puts it, scientific Marxism became *The Opium of the Intellectuals* (1955). That particular misapprehension may now be in retreat, but science is still in most quarters perceived as a self-sustaining truth machine. Tacitly we are still invited to discard our hard-won values and squander our stock of spiritual capital.

Scientific historical necessity or the purity of the master race called for the anaesthesia of affections. All human or "petit bourgeois" emotions ought to be repressed – a terrifying symptom of value-impoverished fanaticism. The crust of a false faith is slowly precipitated by treacherous acts of escapism, soothing lies in the trappings of truth. Genuine conversion implies an aversive re-programming of the cardinal rules of the mind, a dreadful ordeal which in most cases is

cf. 278; 425 postponed indefinitely.

Life is faith

Today faith is an unfashionable concept, often equated with naive credulity. This is a misconception however. Genuine faith refers to the totality of individual game rules, to the basis of our relationship with reality.

Hence, a bacterium can be said to have a faith which is reflected in its inherent urge to survive and reproduce itself. This should not be dismissed as just a cybernetic feedback inherent in the genetic setup. It is precisely these self-survival mechanisms that are the good guesses, the irreducible, axiomatic truths which decisively changed the rules of the game on our planet a few billion years ago. *cf. 100*

In animals, we can distinguish between diverse self-preservative and self-propagative drives, built-in beliefs in the meaning of life. Animal faith can be destroyed. Laboratory rats which have been systematically exposed to negative feedback by arbitrary intervention, do in the end "lose hope". Confronted with the man-manipulated absurdity of their existence they simply give up, long before they are physically exhausted.

Every conscious human activity must be based on personal values, that is a network of privately adopted rules of the game. It is futile to deny this requirement, and a verbal rebuttal alters nothing; the values are anyway manifest in the individual conduct of each and every one of us. We live our truth and confess our faith in every gesture, every remark, every deliberate act. Foul play and self-deception smell of disbelief, they exude a lack of trust in the innermost meaning of life.

Faith is our ultimate frontier towards existence; a bold hypothesis thrown into the confounding game of trial and error. It is the receptacle for our values and steers human passion and self-sacrifice into worthy channels. Axiomatic beliefs are the dynamos of human culture, charging it with long-term purpose. They define our deepest strivings, the quintessential rules of the personal game. Deprived of a firm faith, life becomes devoid of meaning and is felt, quite logically, to be a totally undetermined absurdity. *cf. 293*

Genuine faith seeks contact with the totality of existence and is tantamount to a practical creed, a strong personal commitment. It is never unequivocal or self-explanatory but involves considerable absorption of uncertainty and the immanent risk of self-immunization. Faith is our paramount authority, the highest court of appeal, but it is continually prone to nagging doubts or, which is worse, the disgrace of expedient casuistry. This most vulnerable rule of the game ought to be conserved but cannot escape the ubiquitous forces of corruption. Faith calls for constant re-creation; it must again and again be recast in richer, better, truer and more beautiful forms.

Jaroslav Pelikan has, in *The Christian Tradition* (1971–89), faithfully compiled the whole history of Christian doctrine in comprehensible shorthand. The light of the Gospels emerges in ever new emanations, as distorted by the imperfect lens of theological discourse which writhes with omnipresent depravity. Once again we can confirm that the false starts, the dead-ends, the totality of honest mistakes are the real source of new, valuable information. In the words of William Blake (1757–1827), "To be an error and to be cast out is a part of God's design."

Outward success generally persists long after the moral assets have started to melt away. Correspondingly, the dividends on investments in faith are slow in coming in the best of circumstances. The final rewards of a change of heart may not be evident until decades or even generations have passed. But sometimes a long parched march is rewarded by substantial returns on the accumulated intangible capital. Alas, the ensuing prosperity carries the seeds of improvidence, indulgence, incontinence and debauchery. Crucial rules of the game are *cf. 192* neglected or buried under empty entertainment or ceremonial spectacle; "human nature" claims its inalienable due.

The creative potential increases with the value of the game, as does the opportunity for parasitic play, but the final consequences take correspondingly longer to emerge. Only elementary games give away their truth – as awards and penalties – right away. In both man and beast, the ability to learn from experi-
cf. 49; 202 ence depends on the dead time. Training a dog or bringing up a child calls for the same mix of consistency and immediate response. Every delay between cause and effect weakens the crucial feedback and obscures the causal link – the existential truth.

cf. 80; 100; 424
> A very rare inherited enzyme insufficiency causes immediate and severe convulsions after the intake of common sugar (sacharose), and sufferers quickly develop a strong aversion to anything sweet. Unequivocal cybernetic feedback can thus extinguish even our innate taste preferences. But any appreciable time lag obliterates the reflex. The inconvenience of obesity does not reduce the appetite, any more than a hangover outweighs the euphoria of intoxication, unless the indisposition is reinforced by prompt physiological mechanisms. The only fallback position is our vague and weak learning capability; all too often the intellect loses the battle against short-sighted hedonistic goal-orientation. To quote Oscar Wilde, "man can obviously resist everything except temptation".

Faith is the *summa sumarum* of our fundamental existential hypotheses. Learning and unlearning are excessively slow because faith can only be falsified by our entire experience of life and death. But for man such wisdom after the event is outrageously inadequate. We are not satisfied with expressing our conviction in deeds, as is unavoidable; we crave to understand our world, our lives and, most importantly, ourselves by consciously choosing and realizing our faith. Man is loath to be a puppet on a string, he thirsts for a mite of freedom and insight, he yearns to look existence in the eye – to behold the face of God.

Value universes

The different modes of belief can be illustrated in a rough two-dimensional model (see figure 9.2). The rule hierarchy is indicated by concentric circles, with logic and mathematics at the centre. Animal behaviour and severe schizophrenia are visualized by small closed areas in which the subject is severely constrained by the narrow limits of its innate instincts or compulsive obsessions. Base superstition and mass hysteria exemplify another type of short-circuited response which soon implodes into utter insignificance. Crude animism imparts more method to its madness; quasi-logically it embraces a broader phenomenology without achieving contact with the generalizations of the mathematical-scientific sphere. The societies in question have, nevertheless, proved their viability by commanding an indigenous technology of survival.

A decisive breakthrough occurs when a closed, "primitive" religion in an act of faith opens itself to infinity. Then it accedes to an expanding value universe, a grand existential hypothesis which sets free the creative pursuit of the game. Two such events (A and B) have been depicted in our model. Both first explore a

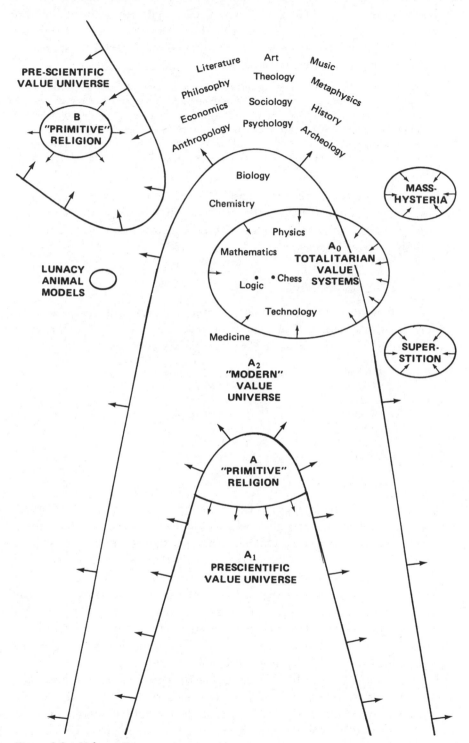

Figure 9.2   Value universes

pre-scientific region (A$_1$ and B$_1$), but B$_1$ has begun to turn back on itself after an early expansive phase. A$_1$ has gradually succeeded in incorporating the central areas of the field and has generated a "modern" value universe, A$_2$. In the process it has given birth to a totalitarian value system (A$_0$) which is spontaneously self-closing and doomed to contraction.

> Whereas widely differing views on art, metaphysics, philosophy and sociology may be held in value universe A$_2$, the totalitarian system A$_0$ probably suffers from its own peculiar economics and history, and the idiosyncrasies may extend to anthropology, psychology or even biology and physics. Strictly imposed ideological rules of the game suffocate creative play. All the fundamental questions have their predigested orthodox answers. The game is void of interest and is merely ticking over in repetition of trivial moves.

In life a comfortable draw is unattainable. Closed value systems either have to follow new revolutionary leads, or they fall back into self-confined obscurity. In any case, our faith (or the lack of it) forces the future towards a self-selected but only dimly perceived attractor.

Universal values

As we have now reached the top of the game hierarchy, this is the time to recapitulate the structure of our Game by reducing it to an emergent set of interconnected but essentially incommensurable value frames.

Game Level	Value at Stake
Corporeal	None
Biological	Survival
Technological	Scope for play
Economic	Wealth
Political	Power
Scientific	Truth
Artistic	Beauty
Transcendent	Meaning

The corporeal and biological groundwork comprises all the absolutely dependable, physical and biotic interactions which obey the laws of nature. Technological games aim to control a hostile environment by the utilization of those elemental forces. Technology defines our freedom of action and is a basic input for the economic players which manage the production factors, with money as the major parameter. Politics is played for the power to devise and supervise the rules of the economic and other social games. Truth and beauty are yardsticks for the scientific and artistic games, providing decisive impulses for lower levels of play. The ultimate transcendent frame embraces and sustains the whole structure, and imbues it with gracious meaning.

The highest levels are entirely dependent on the performance of subordinate grades, and yet they pervade the whole value hierarchy. Genuine faith has no court of appeal and is thus singularly susceptible to adulteration and fraud. At times, self-aggrandizing psychopaths have found ways to usurp the whole game and turn it into a personal pageant.

Supreme self-confidence attaches equally to prophets true or false, to tyrants and to great statesmen. The good guys are distinguished by their relaxed generosity while the paranoid high-flier gives himself away by his persistent persecution mania – a logical consequence of his distorted view of the world. The axiomatic basis of all megalomania is self-worship, the subject is the infallible centre of the universe. Negative feedback, even from close associates, is regarded as a jealous conspiracy of lesser men who must be promptly dispatched. The paranoid mind cannot stand the agony of self-doubt which Luther saw as an acid test for distinguishing blind self-assertion from lasting conviction.

As soon as we begin to perceive of ourselves as redundant cogs in the machinery of history our very humanity is at stake. Such a stance will be self-fulfilling if we persist in selfish optimization, and doggedly exploit the social coalition for our own ends. Man acquires substance only when he aims at some higher goal, thereby fulfilling his faith. But religious or spiritual authority should never be employed for sly manipulation, however noble the cause. Faith must remain *cf. 276* free to pursue its purpose, it must never be used, politically or otherwise.

9.4   Value-generation and regeneration

"Do not despair but work and pray". In my view, this simple precept of St. Benedict has sustained fifteen hundred years of unprecedented human emancipation. Our values can be regenerated only by the daily penance of self-reproval: moral tenets of everyday ethics are indicators of the quality of faith. We need something more to defend than our personal well-being, we ache for a higher authorization but cannot prescribe how the inmost accounts should be settled. One way or the other, man is dependent on contact with God. Left to his own devices, he is sooner or later reduced to a robot or a monster, or at worst to both.

Homeostatic self-repetition

Primitive value systems are devoted to the monotonous repetition of moves; comprehensive homeostasis provides ostensible protection against the overwhelming arbitrariness of existence. Totem and taboo, rites and invocations, all sustain the smooth metabolism of spiritual life. Instructive examples abound in the anthropological literature. Life in its totality – the daily chores, marriage, birth, hunting, war and burial – is regulated by a network of safe but suffocating rules which eliminates internal competition, minimizing the burden of social discontent and personal choice.

In such a society, everything important is predetermined, explicable, manage- *cf. 420* able. Setbacks and failures depend solely on formal errors, barring the ill-will of aberrant individuals or the superior magic of hostile tribes. The borderlines between chance, necessity and free play are eliminated, and all distressing vicissitudes are transferred to a magical dimension, in which everything has its given, though facile, explanation. Acute powers of observation or the perfection of practical skills are not precluded, but disturbing value-generation is deemed dangerous. Instead supernatural potentates are pressed into human service by animistic cults and ceremonial sacrifice – a straightforward, anthropocentric strategy which is still in evidence.

> During the Second World War American cargo planes dropped huge quantities of goods for the commandos in the interior of New Guinea. A substantial part was appropriated by the locals who received it as manna from heaven. When the theatre of war moved on, the cessation of deliveries precipitated an intensive "cargo cult" among the natives. They studiously worshipped mock airplanes, built from sticks, straw and clay, intent on restoring the plenty.

Every attempt at expanding the value universe has to forsake the pristine harmony of the status quo. Most of these "faith mutations" meet an adverse fate, which strengthens the existing hyperconservative value frame. A few have overcome the initial obstacles, reached a promised land and filled the earth with their progeny in a virtuous circle of cultural advance. But the primordial ecological balance is lost for ever and must be compensated for by an adequate input of dedicated creativity. Otherwise society retreats to the boring repetition of compulsive moves. The caste system in India is an example of a surrender to archaic patterns of play, maintaining social homeostasis whatever the price.

The primitive mind is consistently egocentric and shapes the spiritual world accordingly. Good and evil, right and wrong have no objective reality, but are equal to success or failure of the individual or his kin. At a higher cultural level the tribe or state become natural repositories of value. The welfare of the community is then the highest good, fulfilment of duty the supreme service. *cf. 170; 309* King and god often merge into an exalted symbol of the universal claims and ambitions of society.

> The Greek city states, the Roman republic, modern Prussia, and Japan after the Meiji revolution are all examples of societies in which public service was a sacred task, channelling the self-sacrifice and self-realization of progress dynamos. This deification of the state goes back at least to Aristotle and in due course received its philosophical (Hegel) and scientific (Durkheim) certification. But "My country right or wrong" necessarily invokes an external minus-sum game. Pure national self-assertion has always come to grief; sooner or later continuous warfare takes its toll despite the mobilization of all available moral and material resources.

A truly human culture reaches out beyond its parochial preoccupations. Blind self-glorification or a relapse into literally hopeless homeostasis are both dead ends where the living God pales into a mere reflection of the countless recursions of a cyclical universe.

Axial religions

Around the year 500 B.C. several Eurasian civilizations had arrived at an impasse which compelled a radical, religious reorientation. Zarathustra, Vardhamana Mahavira (the founder of Jainism), Gautama (Buddha), Lao Tzu and Kung Fu Tzu (Confucius), Isaiah, Socrates – they all cry foul at the prevailing iniquity and insincerity. A new hope is transcending the old tribally circum-scribed and naively self-evident frames of reference. Life is acquiring a longer and more meaningful perspective.

> Reiterative fertility rites give way to the quest for transcendental rebirth, and vague eschatalogical expectations take shape as deliberate social policies. Existence is trans-formed from being to becoming, time is forged into a spearhead against heaven. Com-munion with God is no longer the privilege of selected demi-gods, high priests, au-tocrats or mythical heroes but becomes, at least in principle, accessible to all men. Everyone is called upon to fight the forces of evil and ignorance, the temptations of the flesh or the abominations of idolatry.

Man came to see himself, not as an expendable commodity but as an actor in a cosmic controversy with a beginning and an end. The deifications of natural phenomena and the quarrelling crowd of tribal divinities were supplanted by sovereign powers; man became an intermediary between God and the world, equipped with special responsibilities and prerogatives.

> The Jews were particularly adamant, subsequently transmitting their conviction to the Christian creed. Man had a destiny different from the rest of creation. He had the right and the duty to replenish and subdue the earth, to express himself freely in the service of God. Thus, the systematic probing and exploitation of nature was not an act of sacri-lege, but the appropriation of a preordained possession.

The unity of the godhead was a doctrine common to axial religious thinking. While Zarathustra reduced the bevy of popular deities to just two, Ormuzd and Ahriman, the prophets of the Bible stuck unyieldingly to a single God. The Chinese philosophers cherished down-to-earth pantheism whereas Buddha preached a monistic creed with no God; nothingness was instead proffered as the greatest good. In this perspective the Christian trinity signifies retrogression which was, later on, condemned by the monotheistic Mohammed.

> When the fervour of an axial religion permeates ancient beliefs and traditions, the result is devotional hybridization. Accordingly, all the great religions appear in a wide variety of locally coloured creeds. On its arrival in Japan, by way of India, China and Korea, unworldly and timeless Buddhism becomes steeped in heroic stoicism. The castigation of intellectual self-sufficiency is accomplished by disconcerting verbal exercises (koans), culminating in a sort of mental seppuku in which all contradiction is dissolved in the flow of time. The famous Zen master Dogen, who lived in the thirteenth century (and disapproved of koans), exclaims in neat opposition to the original message: "Imperma-nence is Buddha" and "Buddha is time".

The common ground of the axial religions did not prevent widespread and sometimes bloody conflict. Eventually the eager hope, the vision of salvation, was displaced at least in the East by the boredom of submissive fatalism. In human play, any plus-sum is dismissed as an illusion: the final goal is to withdraw from the game. Religious bankruptcy is rationalized in terms of the vanity of life, the absolute zero-sum nature of existence.

Similar lines of reasoning were also evident in the West. The Early Fathers of the Church engaged in a constant struggle with all-explaining and all-permitting Gnostics and Manichaeans. The Inquisition had its origin in the conflict with their spiritual heirs, Cathars, Bogomils and other "devil worshippers". Byzantian orthodoxy was, despite internal Christological controversies, united in the neo-platonic notion of an all-knowing and all-forgiving saviour. Such total confidence in the creator was bound to deteriorate into misanthropic self-absorption, reflecting the atrophy of the axial religions.

The metaphysics of ageing

The values of a viable culture are isomorphic with the deepest human aspirations. They are the provisional imputations of a tripartite game in which a supreme being acts as arbiter between man and man. Adequate codification and conscious development are the tasks of established religion, but this is an inherently impossible mission because any liberty of opinion necessarily entails heterodoxy and sectarianism. Coercion, on the other hand, may bring about unity and stability but the muzzled creed will, before long, be reduced to the irrelevance of old age.

Authoritarian regimes are habitually fond of ardent admonitions and hasten to establish a facade of quasi-religious verbiage to cover up the cynical double-dealing of those in power. The freedom of play is reduced to a trivial minimum; everything is forbidden except that which is expressly permitted. As people invariably try to sneak around the rules, the upshot is bureaucratic megalomania, a proliferation of ordinances and decrees which supervise human conduct down to the minutest detail – a disgraceful regress to the total social control of primitive societies.

cf. 146   Confucius and his followers believed in the perfectability of man and society. Veneration of ancestors and deference to elders and superiors should pervade society, culminating in its apex – the emperor. He was the ultimate guarantee of peace and social justice, and was restrained only by the "Mandate of Heaven", whatever that meant. As an inveterate pragmatist, Confucius relied on "human-heartedness", a "reasonable" love with appropiate distinctions. Accordingly, the Confucian version of the reciprocity principle is formulated in negative terms: "Do not unto others as you would not be done by".

This touch-me-not attitude seems to reflect an introvert, self-sufficient value universe, a congenial straitjacket for the ruling class of haughty mandarins. The ethical acumen evaporated as attempts at reform ran foul of stifling orthodoxy. Rationally cool-headed cynics triumphed over enthusiastic progress dynamos. The élite could not rise above their all-too-explicit code of conduct, and China remained shackled to the ever-rotating

cf. 143; 144   wheel of Yin and Yang, despite the patient toil of the people.

Human organizations often possess impressive powers of self-remedy but the highest value-generating level always remains vulnerable to corrosion and corruption. Even meta-rules suffer from wear and tear; the information they provide is distorted by interference and noise, and errors creep into the programs for repairing the repair system ...

Physiological ageing can be traced, at least partly, to defects in the DNA code for the

enzymes whose job it is to repair DNA damage. These errors set off the deterioration of the repair system and cause escalating infirmity. An additional safeguard – an inhibitor or "guardian" protein (p53) – shuts down replication if extensive maintenance is called for, and as a last resort liquidates the cell if the proper program cannot be restored. But the guardian, too, is of course subject to corruption which indeed opens the gates for runaway misrepresentation and cancerous self-destruction. In the long term, self-repa-   *cf. 387*
ration is a losing strategy in the fight against disinformation and disintegration. Mere defence must be complemented by judicious re-creation.   *cf. 32*

Gerontocracy, the rule of the old, is a sign that the self-renewal of a community is in question. The comprehensive elimination of uncertainty becomes the ephemeral goal, apparently guaranteed by a carefully polished ideology and total control of political power. Competition degenerates into intrigue, and the search for truth is replaced by linguistic conjuring tricks. Reformers who might upset the applecart are suppressed with a satisfactory safety margin, and society can happily enjoy its senile dementia without any disturbing premonition of impending coma.

A fount of rejuvenation

The ancient Greeks have been the paradigm of youthful vigour in our culture. Their lifestyle, philosophy and aesthetics spread like rings on a pool throughout the then known world. The thirst for life knew no bounds. Drained to the dregs, the cup of knowledge and beauty left a bitter aftertaste. The gods of the Greeks were closely delimited projections of human self-knowledge. In a world both finite and comprehensible, there was no room for hope, mercy or compassion: the Hellenic quest for harmony was rooted in cosmic despair.

In Christian Europe, insight into the unity of creation carried optimistic overtones. Following St. Paul, St. Augustine and St. Francis, occidental mysticism has been intellectually disciplined and was supported by a singular self-confidence. The mystical experience of the kingdom of heaven is more than the realization of personal bliss. It implies a renewal of the gospel that prompts pity and co-responsibility through active participation in the game. Meditation is not a pleasurable end in itself but a station en route in the Imitation of Christ.

During the Dark Ages the monasteries acted as versatile cultural catalysts, autarkic enclaves in the disintegrating antique world.

According to legend, Ireland was converted by St. Patrick around the middle of the fifth century A.D., and for a hundred troubled years it was the only fairly peaceful refuge for the declining spiritual life of the Western Roman Empire. Towards the end of the sixth century the Irish, lead by St. Columba, won Scotland and Northern England for Christianity. Traces of Columba's mission have been found in Gaul as far away as the Rhine.

Benedict of Nursa (?480-?543) founded the monastery of Monte Cassino in 529 A.D., in the darkest hour of Western Europe; the nadir of civilization is underlined by the closing in the same year of the Athenian Academy, founded by Plato. The bubonic plague struck with devastating force in the years 541–543 and the turmoil of the Great Migration continued. Unperturbed, St. Gregory the Great (ca.540–604), the first pope in the modern sense, wanted to "make angels of Angles" and sent Benedictine brothers to convert Southern England by the end of the century. They ran across their Irish

colleagues and, not surprisingly, engaged in both theological and political argument –
but the rising tide of barbarity had turned for good.

The monks of the early Middle Ages were the technological, economic and
artistic progress dynamos of their age. They filled a painfully obvious vacuum,
both material and spiritual, and were often well received by the heathen peoples. The conversion of England, for example, occurred without a single known
case of martyrdom. The monastic institution petrified but the original vision
was revitalized over and over again. "Do not despair, but work and pray" ran
the pragmatic message of both St. Benedict and Luther, which pointed the way
to a pious work ethic and a cultural crescendo.

> The Christian missions, the Red Cross and the Salvation Army are practical expressions
> of universal human solidarity. We spontaneously support the underdog and back the
> losing side, willingly sharing our gospel, our knowledge – even our money. All are
> accepted without entrance fee as members of a divinely inspired coalition in which the
> needy enjoy favourable conditions. The political agents of the proletariat have surely
> tried to fan envy and greed while appealing to the might of the masses, but the union of
> the repressed acquired its cohesion and legitimacy from a deeper source.
>
> Relief from material want is an understandable priority of the destitute and the
> Gospels are replete with empathy for the sufferings of mankind. According to St.
> Matthew, Jesus says "your heavenly father knoweth that you have need of all things"
> and continues: "but seek ye first the kingdom of God and his rightousness; and all these
> things shall be added to you". This promise is now being fulfilled beyond the wildest
> expectations. The eradication of poverty is within reach, provided we persist in putting
> first things first.

cf. 431

To us was given an almost magic formula for success which in a flash has
achieved unprecedented human emancipation and unrivalled control over the
environment. The surfacing of ecological responsibility is an obvious consequence of our new relationship with nature. Knowledge, power and wealth
entail the exacting obligations of ownership: the unity of creation is easy to
comprehend from an unthreatened landlord position.

> A modicum of humility is all to the good, but too much provides a convenient pretext
> for shirking responsibility. Many of us would after all like to spit out the bitter elixir of
> youth and opt for quiet spiritual senescence. Such defeatism exemplifies the monistic
> principle. Evil lies in a paucity of creative courage and compassion, the lack of an urgent
> imperative.

Youthful impatience; feverish search; desperate revolt against the brevity of life;
spiritual agony over the eternal torments of hell; the eager expectation of a
heavenly or earthly millenium – in short an obsession with time has put its
stamp on Western culture. In the early Middle Ages the monks were busy
making increasingly accurate clocks to mark the hours of their offices, and this
painstaking subdivision has continued to the present day. Time is the bottleneck
of existence, the decisive reality. Jesus exhorts us to be constantly on watch, and
Nietzsche has condensed our metaphysical distress into a single cry: "Es ist
höchste Zeit, es ist allerhöchste Zeit" ("It is high time, it is the highest time of
all").

Moral capitalization

As we have established by now, no society, and least of all a democracy, can survive on the strength of internal, coldly calculated zero-sum games. This *cf. 60* inevitable mode of play must be modified by some kind of collective self-discipline. While the separate political moves are generally based on petty conflicts of interest, the joint outcome is highly dependent on the underlying values. Democratic constitutions do not trust the benign incorruptibility of their overlords; instead they pass the buck to the individual citizen.   *cf. 152*

> Enforced virtue creates no working capital, as the many attempts at prohibition have   *cf. 164*
> shown. In the late Middle Ages, drunkenness did not provoke legislative action: instead
> the abuse of language was seen as the ultimate source of evil. In France blasphemous
> cursing so incensed the authorities that edicts against swearing were repeatedly promul-
> gated by Charles VII (in 1422), by Louis XI (in 1478) and by Francis I (in 1525),
> apparently to no avail. One might expect that totalitarian societies, with their unre-
> stricted means of propaganda and coercion, would at least be able to root out trivial
> vices such as smoking. But so far, *mirabile dictu*, only the democracies may be making
> some slow progress as people voluntarily kick the habit, one by one.

Well-meaning proclamations or admonitions remain no more than insubstantial fictions unless supported by spirited determination and a public sense of fair play. Flagrant cynics have to be censured but the bureaucratic enforcement of good behaviour is in vain.

> The Spanish soldier-missionary Bartolomé de Las Casas (1474–1566) was horrified by
> the ravages of the European treasure-seekers in the New World and became an indefati-
> gable champion of Indian rights. He gained the support of the Emperor Charles V who
> in 1544 passed a series of enlightened ordinances, the laws of the Indies. Las Casas was
> sent to America but soon found himself in open conflict with the local establishment.
> Implementation of the new legislation was obstructed and the Indians continued to be
> ruthlessly exploited despite the good intentions at the top. Las Casas fought to the end
> for his wretched Indians and predicted the downfall of the Spanish Empire: "If God
> determines to destroy Spain, it may be seen that it is because of the destruction that we
> have wrought in the Indies and his just reasons for it may be clearly evident."

Ethical creativity has little to do with administrative fiat or explicit moral codes. Nor will the purple passages of public rhetoric or campaigns of moral rearmament do the trick. Devoid of heartfelt substance, sermonizing will only drain meaning from the values it purports to defend.

Faith of its very nature is all-embracing and all-penetrating, definable only in its pragmatic projections. Thus, the moral tenets of everyday ethics are indicators of the quality of faith. No member of the social coalition can avoid confrontation with these rules of the game, accepting, rejecting, or recreating existing values.

> In the middle of the seventeenth century, protestant orthodoxy had run its course in
> war-torn Germany. On this parched spiritual ground the new-won pietism of Philipp
> Jakob Spener (1635–1705) and August Hermann Francke (1663–1727) fell like a
> salutory spring shower. The benefactions spread far and wide; the Moravians and the
> Methodists took the Gospel to heart, inspiriting the old message; educational reform
> took hold at all levels with benefits for science and art. From Bach to Goethe the leading
> spirits of the age navigated by the spirit of pietism.

Despairing of organized religion, many enlightened minds have called for the wholesale repudiation of religious devotion. Such arrogance is misplaced, to say the least; in their disorientation people accept any misbelief on offer. The capacity for self-organization will waste away, and the historical machine can run its unobstructed, downhill course.

> Alexis de Tocqueville declared (in *Democracy in America*, 1835) that the development and maintenance of democracy in the United States is dependent on the religious heritage of the founding fathers, and he elevated this finding to a universal truth: "I am inclined to think that if faith is wanting in him, he must be subject, and if he be free, he must believe". Herman Melville (1819–1891), that all-American writer, exclaims in jesting earnest: "The Great God absolute! The centre and circumference of all democracy! His omnipotence, our divine equality." (*Moby Dick*, 1851).
>
> Americans are among the most ardent churchgoers in the world. In spite of, or perhaps because of this the fear of spiritual dissolution has been ever present. Zbigniew Brzezinski (in *Out of Control, 1993*) is the latest to lament the fading of faith among the Americans while Amitai Etzioni bravely pleads for moral re-armament in *The Spirit of Community* (1993).

cf. 275

A viable democracy calls for some connective tissue in the social coalition, a minimum of personal commitment which maintains fair play. Only by acts of faith can we ennoble the brutal Darwinian elimination game, where the triumphant are always right, and gain a lasting foothold for our joint venture.

cf. 275
cf. 180

Personal freedom is expressed and justified in the daily penance of self-reproval. We need something more to defend than our personal well-being, we ache for a higher authorization but cannot prescribe how the innermost accounts should be settled. Every man is dependent on contact with God. Left to his own devices he is sooner or later reduced to a robot or a monster, or at worst to both.

9.5   Cultural credo

The global impact of Western culture stems from a multifaceted pluralism which may superficially resemble value-neutralism. A good message nevertheless pervades the whole game. The interpretation of right and wrong is not left in the hands of professional sages but is the personal responsibility and daily task of the progress dynamos, the collective conscience of the cultural coalition. Despite the absence of explicit ends, our culture is a hermeneutic whole which depends on general adherence to sanctifying means if it is to yield a rich return. The main determinant is the passion to improve, enhance and enrich the world. I call it meta-capitalism, the morality of wealth.

A voyage of discovery

The history of humankind is the history of its gods and idols, not as traduced in tired rituals but as manifest in flesh and blood, in sweat and tears, in passions and acts of faith. Why did Vikings, crusaders and Portuguese merchants travel with such far-reaching verve? Where did Columbus and company find the courage to sail across unknown seas to look for gold, honour, and heathen to convert? What drew Captain Cook more than once to the icebergs of the Antarctic in his search for an elusive southern continent? The profit motive is not the only answer; if cupidity had been enough, the ocean routes of the world would have been staked out much earlier by crafty Phoenicians, by enterprising Greeks or, at the latest, by well-organized Romans or Chinese.

> According to Herodotus, around 600 B.C. Pharaoh Necho II dispatched an expedition which may well have circumnavigated Africa, and the Carthaginian Hanno almost certainly reached the Bay of Guinea in 450 B.C. The commercial connections of the Roman Empire extended from Scandinavia to Central Africa and the Far East. There were no technological barriers to transoceanic exploration but the Romans had more pressing priorities: power and money, bread and circuses. In the year 1406 a Chinese eunuch, Admiral Cheng Ho, embarked on the first of seven voyages of discovery with 317 ships and 28,870 men; eventually he reached the Persian Gulf, the Red Sea and East Africa. News from these faraway lands seems to have been met with little response from the Ming rulers who commanded a population of 80 million and boasted the most magnificent culture of their time.

The self-assertive, the appetite for life, is the driving force of animal as well as human development. The ceaseless exploration of untold opportunities mostly meets with a negative response; but life does not take no for an answer. Man has always been afoot, invading every inhabitable corner of the globe well before the advent of any written history.

Voyages of discovery are a continuation of these bold ventures into the unknown. They represent and symbolize inspiriting impulses, the hidden triggers of culture. We have embarked on an audacious expedition, exploring the ultimate limits of man. The many disasters along the way bear out the shortage of relevant, genetically established guidelines. Nonetheless, the voyage has met with spectacular success, wholly irreconcilable with our scanty mental resources and inexplicable in terms of any rationally planned co-operation.

> The challenge of historiography is to crack the cultural code of bygone civilizations in order to fully understand the rules of expired games. This seems to be a dispiriting task even in the bright light of hindsight. How then can we capture our own hectic vitality, get a measure of the present – an ever-culminating wave-front, foaming and breaking in endless wealth of variety?

Now our main occupation is not to write history, but to make it. We must move on, otherwise the steerageway is lost and we are left aimlessly adrift in an ocean of irrelevance. We navigate, albeit clumsily, according to a multidimensional field of morality which tacitly co-ordinates our cultural plus-sum game. The chief determinants have already been set out in the foregoing pages; it now remains to weave them together into a cultural credo.

Thou shalt not coerce

Freedom is our most precious possession. It is a vague concept definable only in negative terms as the absence of compulsion and constraint. Without liberty, the best set of rules will come to grief in a maze of dead-ends, choking our collective creativity. In the long run only unfettered inquiry, free and daring choice can maintain corrective feedback and the fairness of the game. Our open value universe and cultural plus-sum play depend, in the final instance, on the last, decisive derivative: the spirit that keeps reforming the rules.

The prophetic perceptiveness of a few faithful believers once introduced a new axiomatics into the cultural game. This initial investment in love has gently structured our aimlessly dissipating energies in an unequalled plus-sum game, evoking unlimited opportunities for rewarding personal moves. Ingenious techno-economic leads have happily broadened the base for free and open play, but the spectacular material success is apt to obscure the value of our intangible assets.

> Respect for nature is an extension of human self-respect; it does not require a return to an outdated animist ecology. Instead of inordinate and indiscriminate reverence for the secrets of life we should live up to our insights and prudently take care of our garden of Eden. We should protect and preserve, prune, plant and enrich – in short behave as good gardeners and gamekeepers. All creation must be embraced and enriched by the spirit of the game.

Any successful coalition will be tempted to rest on its laurels, to shirk the uncertainty of arduous growth in order to indulge in the single-minded pursuit of shameless self-satisfaction. Then and there, tired escapism replaces painful readjustment; the passion for play is wasted in ephemeral pseudo-activities; genuine faith is swamped by sundry superstition; in short, life becomes a dreary carnival.

Our culture is wide open to infection from the doctrines of false prophets. The crackpot inventor or the voluble humbug will not get very far in a competitive marketplace, but there are no incontrovertible criteria for the identification of the con-men of politics or pseudo-religion. The omnipresent risk of deception, fraud or betrayal must be accepted if we are not to imperil inalienable assets – freedom and tolerance.

> Beethoven's ninth symphony immortalized Friedrich von Schiller's (1759–1805) ode 'An die Freude'. Originally the poem was a glorification of liberty named 'An die Freiheit'. The usually rather lenient censors of the day were incensed by the ongoing revolutionary agitation and insisted on less fieriness. Subsequent generations have thus been force-fed with bland joy instead of the invigorating "Freiheit schöner Götterfunken, Töne aus Elysium..."

Instead of coercion we are free to use powers of persuasion to amend private and public conduct. Libertarians and libertines alike love to dismiss such attempts as mere moralizing, an unseemly infringement on our civil rights. This argument will never come to rest, but tantalizing uncertainty may, paradoxically, be the very seal of approval for the values in doubt. As long as we insist on our absolute freedom, we will remain chained to the wheel but if we cling to a covenant, we are set free.   *cf. 50*

The global impact of Western culture stems from a multifaceted pluralism which may superficially resemble value-neutralism. A good message never-theless pervades the whole game. The interpretation of right and wrong is not left in the hands of professional sages but is the personal responsibility and daily task of the progress dynamos, the collective conscience of the cultural coalition.

Thou shalt not waste

The abuse of freedom is constrained by the oldest and most universal meta-rule of the whole game: thou shalt not waste. Our minds should be dedicated to guarding and maintaining, economizing and improving, thus upholding the ancient law of life. All surplus ought to be reinvested in the future, in new progeny and production, in new inventions and discoveries, in better education and in deeper knowledge, in an environment, both balanced and beautiful, and above all, in reforming the rules of the game. Our passion for play should be fully mobilized in the unrestrained creation of material and spiritual capital.

Such meta-capitalism does indeed consummate the quest for unlimited plus-sum play but, coupled to an explicit eschatology, it can easily lead to self-righteous tyranny and terror. The excellence of the ends justifies any sacrificial means while the original conviction slowly sinks into a mire of minus-sum machinations. The meta-capitalistic creed must be outweighed by a humble awareness of our limited perspective and the imperfection of our play. Only on the strength of heart-felt humility can we find the courage to cope with in-grained fallacies, and truthfully assess our own ignorance.

> From the very beginning, life has been exposed to the vagaries of informational clutter and faulty transmission. To deal with the inherent vulnerability of the complex genetic message, a multitude of mutually supporting DNA repair systems has been assembled. *cf. 323; 401*
> This provides a good example of Dancoff's principle of maximum error which is widely employed by scientists, wrestling with experimental uncertainty. No single source of knowledge can be deemed trustworthy, especially if the data derives from insensitive or unreliable instruments. Tolerable fidelity can nevertheless be attained by repeating measurements, tapping into alternative information channels and applying overlapping test procedures.
>
> The Dancoff principle ought to be invoked whenever self-ascertained propositions are passed off as truth. It has served our criminal courts well, and underlies political pluralism. The play of neural co-operation utilizes similar methods to increase the acuity of sensory or motoric performance. And in difficult language games communi-   *cf. 100*
> cation is greatly enhanced by approaching the subject from many different angles, varying vocabulary and imagery.

The recognition of human fallibility is yet another apparently negational insight into the nature of the game. No verification is definitive, no revelation final. Our ignorance and the absorption of uncertainty increase as we proceed from production prototypes or market research to political decision-making, and they reach their peak in works of art and religious doctrine. Pluralism is the logical expression of an appropriate modesty. Prodigal diversity and unfettered competition alone can uphold the impetus of human inquiry. Such extravagance is the one and only way to counter wishful thinking, and keep cynical cheats at bay.

Technical progress is gradually relegating all repetitive games to robots and computers while a profusion of alternatives ensures adequate experimentation at the higher levels of cultural play. Most people may soon be free to become at least part-time trackers of truth, meta-capitalists who reinvest their return in the whole-hearted search for the good – the "frui Deo" ("consuming God") of St. Augustine.

Thou shalt not bear false witness

The passion for truth is borne out by yet another injunction: the repudiation of lies and falsehood, concealment and pretence. Renouncing false testimony clears the way for an ascending spiral of creative play. Deep truth is the strangest of attractors but Absolute Truth, the Kingdom of God, is not of this world. It recedes before our bold advances, forever holding out the hope of a higher verity.

cf. 39; 74

cf. 382

> The aim of scientific endeavour is explicit knowledge, the naked truth, but the success of science is contingent upon good faith as we have discussed at length. Like the naked electric charge naked truth can have no independent existence; its realization would require infinities of information. We neither can nor will ever be sure of the most important things in life.

cf. 59

cf. 166; 192

This game of hide and seek is not played out in the abstract but involves our daily life; truth is often individually maladaptive. Putting aside plain egoism, we are caught in a perpetual conflict between public duty and immediate human considerations which can become an excruciating moral dilemma. Should I be true to principle, or follow the dictate of age-old epigenetic rules in dealing with friends, neighbours and relatives? In the end we have to live with a manifold of divided loyalties, navigating as best we can among the exigencies of personal truth.

Our Faustian endorsement of the searching intellect has taught us to face up to unexpected and unpleasant facts, to proceed despite awe-inspiring prospects, to endure the curse of knowledge and the scourge of self-criticism – in short to accept disturbing truths. The burden of human emancipation becomes particularly onerous when even faith appears as a long-term contingency. Despite dispiriting doubts we ought to achieve at least a crude and provisional codification of our faith. Only then can we follow our vocation and faithfully intimate the good tidings, spreading the cultural gospel with its attendant blessings and burdens, duties and rights.

cf. 192

> We have seen how the vitality of culture seems to be roughly proportional to its human base. Global coverage thus throws open a vast opportunity for cultural progress. The world population constitutes an enormous resource, provided that a broad majority can personally participate in the game. Every new member born into the grand coalition

then becomes a potentially valuable fellow player, not just another mouth to feed. Nobody can assume paternalistic responsibility for millions or billions of people; instead we should try to draw them into an exciting, accountable plus-sum game.

Missionaries on low budgets but with strong convictions have been the true pioneers of development aid. Technical skills and know-how belong to the next stage in the culture game. Large-scale economic aid cannot be absorbed until the crucial meta-rules have been more or less established. In due course the domestic creation of spiritual and material capital will encourage enterprise and attract investment; the self-propelling machinery of economic progress will then be in place.

What, then, is the deepest mainspring of cultural play? Why this zeal to improve the world, to excel in meta-capitalism – what is the motivation behind the resolute reinvestment in new creative moves? What is the origin of charity and compassion so patently absent from the self-centred hedonism of Antiquity? And who can safeguard our value universe from regression and final self-destructive implosion?

In the last instance, you and I are the only sureties in sight. We cannot pass the buck; our faith in an uncertain future, our individual assumption of responsibility, our care and our love are, in all their frailty, the only endorsement available. Or have we after all some invisible backing and infallible support? To us is given only the barely adequate knowledge of what we shall not do – the forbidden moves. But unlike the pieces on the chessboard we have an infinite number of permissible moves, innumerable degrees of freedom.

Cultural focus

Western culture, warts and all, is now a worldwide venture which, despite or because of its diversity, is held together by a set of concurrent meta-rules. The cultural interaction can be compared to a paraboloid mirror with our instinctive animal impulse at the focal point (figure 9.3).

The reflecting surface corresponds to the decisive rules of the meta-game which organize the whole field of play, co-ordinating the energies that radiate from the animal focus in a coherent bundle of rays. Pure survival occupies the bottom of the paraboloid while technical, economic, political, scientific and artistic games enjoy increasing scope for play. As the paraboloid expands upwards, the convergent radiation of the cultural game is intensified until finally it may throw some light on an infinitely remote transcendent focus. Or, conversely, we can regard ourselves as a flawed mirror, imperfectly focussing information from an eternal source. Both processes can be envisaged in laser-like interference, a celestial self-illumination.

Western culture does not prescribe strict rules of conduct; on the contrary, the game is extraordinarily versatile. Even so we cannot pick and choose among the values like shoppers at a supermarket. In the long run, neither material affluence nor democracy can coexist with a lack of care, concern or competition. Scientific objectivity, too, easily falls victim to self-centred power politics. The tree of knowledge must be accepted in its entirety, including its bitter but nutritious fruits. Despite the absence of explicit ends, our culture is a herme-

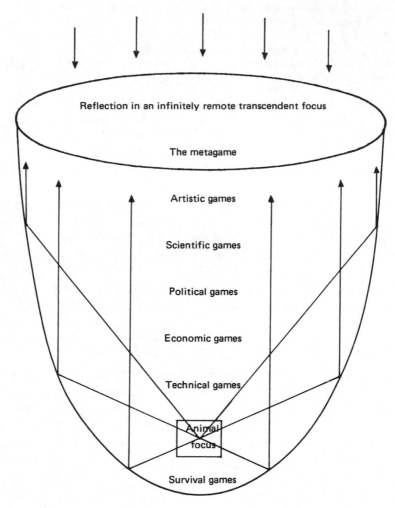

Figure 9.3 The paraboloid captures and re-emits the animal and transcendent messages in laser-like self-amplification.

neutic whole which depends on general adherence to sanctifying means if it is to
cf. 182 yield a rich return.

Destination unknown

We have not yet been paralysed like previous high cultures by overwhelming traumatic events. But it is high time to resume our soul-searching and to make a stuttering confession of faith. Today our welfare cocoon is trembling at the slightest sign of economic setback or the threats of lamentably impotent terrorists. What conviction will give us strength when we are confronted, not with a few pounds of TNT but with devastating nuclear devices or even more sinister biological and chemical poisons? Our faith must be hardened even against a nuclear holocaust; such faith may provide the only chance of avoiding the apocalypse in the long term. The surest way of calling down disaster is to try to stave it off at any price.

To put the ego at the absolute centre of the universe whilst both natural and rational is nevertheless a deeply unsatisfying notion. Lacking something to die for, there is no real reason for living. We should represent something more than our own comfort and lack of commitment, our fashionable lukewarm indifference. We should ask ourselves:"What makes life really worth living? What is more important than life itself?" The right response will release boundless scope for play, the proper heritage of *Homo sapiens*.

> The vanity of materialism can be exposed only by excesses of physical gratification. In the same way, an all-inclusive safety clause would definitively discover the vacuity of a self-centred life; immortality would be the final validation of the emptiness of pure existence. Despite emphatic efforts to the contrary, man cannot live by bread, sex and drugs alone. The absence of struggle invites boredom and disaffection – a fate in many respects worse than the danger of death. The exclusive pursuit of short-term satisfaction negates our humanity; it is original sin.

An open value universe is the first condition for a rewarding cultural game. The investigation of our inner world has always won the praise of professional do-gooders, who see human perfection solely in terms of an introspective glass bead game. But our craving is for external as well as internal expansion and *cf. 419* exploration. Man is more than the stuff of pseudo-philosophical daydreams, he is a bundle of animal appetites and all-too-human passions, precariously controlled by burning ambition and sporadic contact with God.

> The games of nature go on yielding to our probing intellect, and soon we should possess the know-how to control all aspects of our environment, including climate. Yet confinement to this planet of ours will inevitably lead to escalating global conflict and/or the compulsory taming of human nature by genetic intervention. In due course the self-imposed manipulation of man may become desirable or even necessary, but rather than disgusting self-emasculation it should signify self-elected evolution and emancipation. A literally earthbound scenario is repulsive in its implication of enforced submission and endless reiteration – a living death in a meaningless life.

We bear the future in our womb and are constantly suffering pangs of birth, the price of fecundity. Our whole culture game comprises an anagogic instruction: our mission is to spread the good news wider and higher. Meta-capitalism is the morality of wealth. We must conquer the outer as well as the inner universe, both reach the stars and save our souls in a bold venture – destination unknown.

9.6   Modern theology

As I see it, we urgently need competing centres for the open and comprehensive airing of our meta-rules: semi-organized associations for the elucidation of faith. Paradoxes abound: if we assume that we can better ourselves, degradation seems to be inescapable whereas the assumption of human helplessness has proved a sound basis for lasting self-advancement. Besides historical experience, fundamental insights in the relevant sciences are the self-evident cornerstones of a modern theology, which should teach us to navigate in our value universe. Powered by the exponential growth in knowledge, mankind is hesitantly entering a new supercoalition which is capable of creative self-control down to the genetic base. As in the beginning of life, we are on the threshold of a new hypercycle. Once again on our planet it is a question of all or nothing.

Know thy faith!

The time has arrived for the systematic investigation of our existential situation: only then can we consciously intervene in our future. The call is, frankly, for a modern theology to throw some light on the confusion of contending value frames. We ought to introduce a semblance of method into our Sisyphean labour. Generations of stone-rollers must learn to pool their experience, secure the rocks a little higher and gain some slight irreversibility. It is a tall order but it is time to take theology seriously once again, to recall the pains of past generations, to engage our best progress dynamos, to mobilize faith, hope and love.

Many grandiose attempts at mathematical theology should have taught us the futility of a rational, self-confirming knowledge of God. In his *Ars Magna* the Franciscan Ramón Lull (1235–1315) was perhaps the first to try seriously to circumscribe our existential uncertainty with his cabalistic calculating discs. In Baruch Spinoza's *Ethics* the goal is the same but the methods more refined. A universally valid theory of morality is deduced with geometric rigour, including axioms, definitions, proofs and corollaries; the argument concludes in true Euclidian spirit with a QED.

cf. 350 As we have noted, Spinoza's contemporary Leibnitz hoped to resolve all metaphysical and moral problems at one blow with his "*Characteristica Universalis*". With great self-assurance he writes: "If controversies were to arise, there would be no more need of disputation between two philosophers than between two accountants". Alas, accountancy has lost some of its self-evident clarity since Leibnitz's day.

cf. 266. John Stuart Mill is perhaps the most typical exponent of a more recent secular theology. His *System of Logic* (1843) is a brave attempt to engraft scientific causality and proof on to the human and cultural sciences, using the utilitarianism of Jeremy Bentham and his father James Mill (1773–1836) as a starting point (Bentham characteristically puts his faith in a felicific "calculus", a moral arithmetic which infallibly produces the "correct" set of legislation). Like the architecture of his time, J. S. Mill's ecumenical projects suffer from an eclectic indistinctiveness but, together with his friend Alexis de Tocqueville, he did draw up some tenable guidelines for democratic play.

Historical experience is a natural point of departure for a comparative theology. It should be possible to interpret every culture in terms of the creed which endows the complex cultural interplay with its plus-sum character. Societal diseases and deformations provide insights into the life-maintaining cybernetics of culture just as human pathology uncovers the functions of diverse organs. Great historians have been able to penetrate and recreate some vital aspects of past events. The problem is to capture the essence of innumerable interrelations and reduce them to a few characteristic invariances, the crucial rules of the game.

> Marxism, of course, supports this programme but is a good example of systematic self-deception. The basic creed is deftly hidden away and the whole undertaking assumes an air of deductive analysis, of "scientific" conclusiveness and universality. *cf. 309* Mediaeval theologians were more sincere in their pursuit of semantic clarity. Fundamental hypotheses were openly declared and the emphasis was on discovering any self-contradictions within the proclaimed doctrine.

In theological terms, totalitarian societies constitute a relapse to a primitive value-universe. Explicit ideologies become the measure of all things, modern Molochs for whom no sacrifice is too great. For society, this is a point of no return. Personal and national egoism flourish while tyranny and corruption gradually force a retreat to the primaeval, epigenetic rules of the kinship game.

We urgently need competing centres for the open and comprehensive airing of our meta-rules, semi-organized associations for the regeneration of faith. The *cf. 309* first task would be to renew the ancient metalanguage of theology in order to investigate the dynamics of faith as displayed in the historic patterns of permitted and forbidden moves. Then the alternative models could be used as yardsticks to test and try our own value universe with burning passion and cool reason.

> An awful lot of energy has been spent on explaining away the weak but persistent pull of transcendence. Everything beyond rational self-interest is marked down as superstition *cf. 56; 168; 309;* by discomforted theorists who do not pause to consider their own motivation: the last *432* thing an unconcerned egoist would do, is to sit down and work out elaborate explications of human co-operation. Faith should be freed from its superficial trappings and be recognized as an axiomatics which creates the scope for play in a specific plus-sum game. This is not incompatible with reasonable self-interest but leaves narrow-minded maximization to fall by the wayside.

Modern theology should be the crown of the cultural sciences, a prophetic institution for the holistic interpretation of the world. It should not issue normative decrees or fall back on the self-immunizing formulae of tautological universality, philosophical syncretism or undemanding, all-embracing ecumenicalism. What we need are disinterested guardians of our conscience who can contribute to cultural self-understanding and provide raw material for sincere truth-seekers. A modern theology should weed out nonsense, chart the conditions of freedom and teach us to navigate in our value universe, unremittingly defining and redefining the ultimate context. In brief, it should try to discover how we play against God.

Rational uncertainty

Every genuine faith reflects some essential aspect of existence, and represents a partial solution to the existential equation. But a personal quest achieves permanent merit only when it becomes integrated in an overarching effort. Otherwise it collapses in vain self-assertion or takes refuge in the decrepit structures of conventional religion.

However rational the means, the ultimate ends will elude our probing intellect. The enigma of existence can never be captured in a single formula, and we are bound to face a whole set of mutually conflicting frames of reference. Painful disorientation and irresolution is thus a natural predicament for those in the vanguard. Accordingly, creative achievement is tied to competitive pluralism and pestered by schismatic discontent. Only in the fair play of conflicting views can we establish a dynamic equilibrium, which compels mutual consid-

cf. 311 eration while steering clear of stagnation.

cf. 279

cf. 391

cf. 317

Positivistic philosophers were wont to decry many awkward philosophical or ethical quandaries as "meaningless" just because they entailed disturbing paradoxes. Such an arrogant attitude would have dismissed the most interesting parts of mathematics, and goes on excluding important intellectual domains from serious study. We ought, for example, to reinvestigate the old theological riddle of the nature of man. If we boldly assume that we can better ourselves on our own, moral and material degradation seems to be inescapable whereas the assumption of human helplessness in the face of evil has proved a sound basis for lasting self-advancement!

cf. 56; 60 We have previously observed that all socially relevant norm systems suffer from game-theoretical contradictions; moral principles tend to run into conflict with themselves. Rational clarity on questions of values is a sure sign of self-deception; the creativity of the culture game is not compatible with a completely lucid account of the meta-rules. The definitive verification of any specific value system is impossible but systematic falsification may be feasible.

If every conceivable theology, save one, could be falsified, then the remaining alternative would appear increasingly plausible. Such an indirect approach might help in underpinning a specific faith, but it can certainly not be brought to a conclusion in a finite number of steps.

Modern theology should systematically expose religious, metaphysical, philosophical and linguistic double-dealing. Persistent cynics can never be proved wrong, but foul play and self-immunizing superstition can always be divulged before men and women of good will.

It would be presumptuous to try to anticipate the structure of a modern theology. Nevertheless, our game metaphor allows the formulation of a universal imperative: intensify the plus-sum game! The actual content of the plus-sum remains dependent on subjective evaluation, but a clear pattern emerges if we draw on universal human virtues and shortcomings. Zero-sum games provide the exemplar of nullity; the minus-sum means negation, waste and destruction. Only the plus-sum implies the generation of value, enhancing the level of the game, encouraging commitment, altruism, ethical stamina. The plussum game is an enunciation of agape, divine love, which seeks not its own but suffers and endures, believes and creates all things.

The writing on the wall

Besides historical experience, fundamental insights in mathematics and the natural sciences are the self-evident cornerstones of a modern theology which should take advantage of the latest advances in infinity mathematics, complexity theory, computer science, cybernetics, evolution theory, neurobiology, anthropology, archeology and so on.

> The Santa Fe Institute for the study of complexity is a pointer in this direction. Founded in 1984 at the instigation of (among others) the physicist Murray Gell-Mann, the Institute aims at cross-scientific interaction ranging from mathematics and physics to biology, medicine, meteorology, ecology, economics, sociology . . . . . .in the future maybe even modern theology.

cf. 314; 320; 389

Howsoever we approach the overabundant material, it will take perceptive minds to discern the relevant patterns. A few conspicuous lacunae meet the eye. To begin with, the charting of alternative value universes requires more reliable intelligence about the aptitudes of *Homo ludens*, playing man.

> In *Promethean Fire* (1983), which builds on *Genes, Mind and Culture*, Edward O. Wilson and Charles Lumsden have made a first foray into the territory indicated, and claim that under certain plausible conditions genetic selection keeps pace with culture evolution. The genetic stabilization of a human cultural breakthrough is assumed to require only about fifty generations, or roughly a millenium. The authors are overly reductionist, and look forward to a "scientific" futurology, independent of deep historical understanding. Tacitly they are viewing the culture game from an external, putatively value-neutral platform where the scientist makes his observations in splendid isolation.

cf. 81; 136

After many wrong turns we are now in the process of formulating the right questions about man's dependence on his genetic program. Knowledge about the topology of human decision space is indispensable but does not provide the means to assess the validity of the value universe. The culture game remains dependent on its axiomatic framework which should be compatible with prevailing epigenetic rules but cannot be deduced from them.

Human play is of course greatly influenced by environmental obstacles and opportunities. It would be absurd to deny the importance of the material base, of natural resources, geography and climate. Such external conditions provide interesting touchstones for a modern theology. The clash between reality and faith is the best source of information about the content of our meta-rules. The interaction with religious orthodoxy – its myths, magic, ritual, and ceremony – is less important. The distinction between concretely operative faith-in-action and the formal exercise of religion is pivotal to my argument.

> In the twentieth century, natural science has been the most evocative expression of hands-on human faith. Einstein's rejection of absolute space and time was widely interpreted as endorsing a gross value relativism. Today the Big Bang serves as a reference point in time while the lingering background radiation provides an absolute

yardstick for measuring galaxial movements. Accordingly, it now seems proper to abrogate unfettered value nihilism.

To chart the value universe would be a mind-numbing task of meta-cybernetics, but the availability of even a partial simulation model could mean the dawn of a new cultural epoch. Empirical self-examination, preferably over several generations, remains in any case the only reliable way of getting to grips with the hyper-complex web of existential feedbacks. Unprejudiced social trials therefore deserve our attention.

> Whereas religious splinter groups often exhibit extraordinary staying power (witness the Amish of Eastern Pennsylvania), the experimental socialist co-operatives along the lines of Charles Fourier (1772–1837) could not keep afloat. Considerable reserves of visionary goodwill and hard cash put forward by people like Samuel Owen (1771–1837) did not help. Internal conflict and a lack of enthusiasm in the succeeding generation led to dissolution from within. Even the ardour of the kibbutzim is wearing thin as the outside challenges abate.

Regional supernations – old, new and future coalitions – are going to dominate global politics. These structures not only allow but patently require far-reaching decentralization and value pluralism. Separate autonomous communities should find ways of living peacefully, not only alongside one another, but also deeply entwined in creative interplay.

The right balance between local autonomy and federal affiliation, between independent risk-taking and supervised solidarity has long been central to democratic rule. The cohesion of the whole must not be jeopardized, although liberal allowance must be made for the misdirected moves that are unavoidable in any imaginative development of the game. Without the pragmatic test and trial of freely-flowing meta-hypotheses we would remain cocooned in received truths, shackled by paralysing self-contradictions, vulnerable to distortive superstition – unable to see the writing on the wall.

Faith made flesh

The evolution of life and particularly that of man can be related to cumulative acts of faith, correct existential conjectures which have been firmly reduced to practice and irreversibly entrenched in the genome. How can such a process proceed today? It presupposes a certain measure of social and genetic isolation, based not on vulgar racism but on the overt selection of mutually compatible meta-rules as exemplified by the Jews, the Quakers, the Moravians and the Methodists.

> The self-selection of a clearly designated community is the first step up the evolutionary ladder. When the group dissociates itself from its surroundings, those who deviate from the internal norm will feel ill at ease. They will opt out while proselytes may swell the ranks of the chosen people. We can presume a clear correlation between the espoused societal rules and specific character traits, which are to some extent genetically conditioned. Let us furthermore assume that the deviant group has an edge in reproductive

success. Then societal and genetic selection reinforce one another, and stabilize the divergent persuasion according to the scheme in figure 9.4.

cf. 98

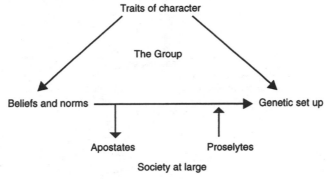

Figure 9.4 The self-selection of a group

Eventually the increasingly conspicuous peculiarity of even the most unassuming religious community will provoke an allergic reaction in the bulk of society. Times of trial, however, often fortify the faith. Early success is inimical to selection; the core of true believers is easily swamped by encroaching opportunists. Thus, persecution – or at least some discrimination – seems to be indispensable if a new breed is to achieve its full potential. By the time the original revelation has become acceptable or dominant, it is also to some extent fixed in the pattern of human DNA – faith has become flesh.

People with prophetic powers can obviously make their mark genetically without actually producing offspring; Buddha, Jesus and Mohammed may have done more to shape our genome than Abraham himself. This is why religious wars are fought with such ferocity; the survival of the species is at stake. National and ideological conflicts, too, carry ominous genetic overtones. Nazism was of course openly racist, while the myth of Soviet man was more reminiscent of the socio-genetic selection mechanism indicated.

All or nothing

After countless abortive moves and rejected scripts the cultural offensive is now reaching its peak. No amount of petty yammerschuning alters the fact that for the first time almost unlimited material resources are within our grasp. We are cracking the secret code of nature and our global culture is taking possession of creative meta-rules, which have cleared the way for long-term human interplay. For good or ill we are now finally digesting the forbidden fruit. Life in its human incarnation is approaching a decisive discontinuity: a new, superordinate hypercycle is establishing itself (see figure 9.5).

The diversity of human culture has been built on interlocking games with the DNA protein hypercycle at the base. Now we can perceive the outline of an integrated meta game, the projection of a fruitful faith which encourages constructive interaction at every level of play. Powered by the exponential growth

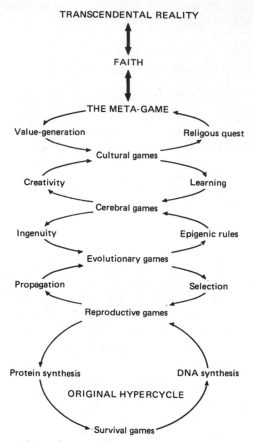

TRANSCENDENTAL REALITY

FAITH

THE META-GAME

Value-generation   Religous quest

Cultural games

Creativity   Learning

Cerebral games

Ingenuity   Epigenic rules

Evolutionary games

Propagation   Selection

Reproductive games

Protein synthesis   DNA synthesis

ORIGINAL HYPERCYCLE

·Survival games·

Figure 9.5 The superordinate hypercycle

in knowledge, mankind is hesitantly entering a new supercoalition which is capable of creative self-control down to the genetic base.

The elevation of a select set of values to universal norms is proceeding half-consciously in the heat of the game. The dominant meta-rules are autocatalytically growing in strength and sophistication, integrating and/or subjugating alternative existential models. Logically speaking, they are just as high-handed and arbitrary as the vocabulary of the DNA code or the grammar of everyday language. The imposition of tolerance and pluralism, for example, implies a supreme intolerance of fanaticism and regimentation. The structuring and monopolization of a value universe are two aspects of the same process.

The launching of a hypercycle is a dramatic climax in the Great Game. The stage is shaken by convulsions, existential uncertainty appears unendurable. Dissipative discharges set off catastrophic consequences, and the situation lies in a state of chaotic indeterminacy on the threshold of a higher fractal dimension. Just as the profound self-discipline of genetic and human languages created their own independent scope for play, so our cultural self-reference grants

us new degrees of freedom, articulates unknown realities and allows unparalleled creativity.

> Barrow and Tipler have presented a detailed case for the feasibility of extensive space
> colonization (*The Anthropic Cosmological Principle*, 1986). The centrepiece of their
> strategy is the von Neumann probe, an intelligent self-repairing and self-reproducing
> universal constructor which would carry either replicas of the human genome or suffi-
> cient information to rebuild it from scratch. The probes would utilize local sources of
> energy and raw material, and would in due course introduce human beings wherever
> possible. Assuming only currently known, non-nuclear modes of propulsion, the colo-
> nization of our galaxy would require about 300 million years.
>
> Eric Drexler has, in a similar vein, heralded the advent of nanotechnology. Self-
> replicating, molecular nanorobots would smoothly supply all necessary goods and
> services. Drexler holds out the prospect of eternal life through the incessant care of
> perfectly-programmed nanonurses, circulating in the body. This nanofuture may well
> hold even greater technological and ethical challenges than the conquest of the Milky
> Way.
>
> In *Infinity in All Directions* (1988) Freeman Dyson ventures well beyond his earlier
> speculations towards the outermost limits of time. Provided that we can avoid the Big
> Crunch, the gradual cooling of the universe should prove no obstacle. Dyson boldly
> postulates that life can take hold almost everywhere, not least in the rarefied radiation
> which is probably the ultimate end of all matter. Furthermore, his calculations show
> that, due to the efficiency of information processing close to absolute zero, the energy
> available is sufficient to sustain life for ever.

cf. 259
cf. 32

cf. 339

cf. 337

cf. 65

Do we dare to desire a literally liberated existence, burdened with responsibility? The stakes are high, the risks unpredictable, craven retreat alternates with
frantic presumption. A decisive showdown will take place soon, probably
within a few centuries. The fate of the hypercycle hangs in the balance. Once
again on our planet it is a question of all or nothing.

9.7   The limits of humanism

The methodical maximization of pleasure is an absurd and self-denying
goal; we just become trapped in a perfunctory zero-sum game which is
hardly worth the trouble. Happiness – the ultimate satisfaction – is not
the reliable outcome of safe play; it appears only as the by-product of a
meaningful existence. A century ago, the death of God was a sensation
which few took seriously. Now it is a trivial fact, and the man-in-the-
street has become the measure of all things. Such a self-satisfied breed
suggests nothing but its impending downfall. Man cannot, in the end,
justify himself. Only before God is humanism, our care for one another,
reconciled with a higher mission.

Human self-adulation

In the Judaio-Christian culture the immense value of the individual is perhaps the most clearly expressed of all meta-rules. *Noblesse oblige*; he who has received much, shall be held to ransom for even more. Our right to exist should not be taken for granted but must be incorporated in a broader frame of reference. Mankind acquires real significance only as a pointer towards an open but dimly anticipated future. Man as his own purpose inevitably implies a shrinking value universe.

cf. 37   Our urge to trivialize the transcendent and to close the value universe harks back to hellenistic wiseacres. The *logos* doctrine of the Jewish-Hellenic philosopher Philo (20 B.C.-50 A.D.) contaminated the gospel according to St. John with self-wise philosophical speculation, and later on the Neo-platonist Plotinus (AD 205–270) influenced, not only Islamic thought but major Renaissance scholars, including prominent humanists like Erasmus of Rotterdam (1466–1536) and his friend the agreeable Sir Thomas More. His *Utopia* was, no doubt, written with the best intentions, but it has become the archetype of a fatuous termination of our human game in totalitarian homeostasis,
cf. 397   complete with forced slave labour.

By rejecting God, man has made himself the purpose and point of the whole play. Remembering Auschwitz and Treblinka, Dachau and Buchenwald, Kolyma and Katyn, we might feel that respect for human value can hardly be overemphasized, but taken out of context even this venerable principle leads to hubris.

Human credulity has been exploited so often for religious purposes that a resigned retreat into agnosticism and nihilism is hardly surprising. This attenuation of spiritual energy seems to be a spontaneous process, an extension of the second law of thermodynamics. Meaningful purpose becomes rudderless disorientation in aimless dissipation of cultural exergy. Life cannot be halted at a comfortable level of safe play; the entropy of moral disorganization increases inexorably in tightly-closed ethical systems.

cf. 233; 293   Nietzsche proclaimed not only the death of God but invoked an Übermensch, a superman, to assume command over the indolent bourgeoisie. In times of plenty, desperate value anarchy is dressed up in ever-varying fashion. Personal freedom becomes wellnigh intolerable, in the absence of any restrictive conventions or external threats whereas real problems of survival provide an effective cure for welfare-itis. Primo Levi (1919–87) tells us in *The Drowned and the Saved* (1986) that suicide was virtually unknown in the German concentration camps. The survivors tell us that mental patients recovered, ulcers healed, flu and the common cold almost disappeared.

Despite all our ostensible caring, we refuse to assume true responsibility for our fellow human beings. Instead we simply throw money at the problems, and back away from unpleasant but inevitable consequences. By accepting foul play, we degrade the rules and actually disqualify our handicapped playmates. Compliant liberalism can be pushed no further; in many quarters even the last pretensions of decency have been lost.

cf. 273   Christiania in Copenhagen was advertized as an unconventional alternative society. In fact, it was an astonishing bluff, the latest version of the Emperor's new clothes. Christiania was altogether parasitical, devoid of resources for survival and completely dependent on the charity of its host organism which supplied money, goods and services without getting anything in return. Similar free-riding structures can be seen in Amsterdam, San Francisco and elsewhere – a disgrace to our culture but a great success if the game is misère.

When we flee all responsibility, we become trapped in a tedious treadmill, a perfunctory zero-sum game which is hardly worth the trouble. Widespread cynicism induces the hyperactivation of lower levels of play; hedonistic sensualism becomes the only valid currency. Free fall may be an exhilarating experience, but sooner rather than later it comes to a very disagreeable end.

Severed from God we are unreal and meaningless automatons. Evil is the absence of God; godlessness implies inexorable self-annihilation; the execution of God is an infernal tragedy. Human self-assertion must give way to the contrition of the soul. Only by enacting our part in the play can we discover the passionate joy of the game, the fulfilment we are all striving for in the end.

The taint of triumph

The lavish fortunes of democratic freedom have nourished the fallacy of human self-perfectability. *Homo sapiens* appears ripe to manage splendidly without any tiresome, authoritarian meta-rules. Human frailty is invariably blamed on the pernicious social environment, childhood adversity, the ballast of history or whatever. We consistently refuse to find serious fault with ourselves but when wickedness shows its ugly face, our allegiance all too easily evaporates in an exasperated renunciation of any man-made future. Man is, of course, neither safe and sound nor irretrievably lost; he is merely unfinished and very far from his destination.

The fugitives from life claim that the whole game is futile, a vanity of vanities. This position is of course untenable; the only logical conclusion would be self-destruction, a walkover. The meaning of existence is a mystery which cannot and should not be explicitly expressed or clearly comprehended. But we can give our life some substance by acts of faith which will be tried and tested in protracted cultural play.

> We lose nothing but can gain a lot by assuming, even against overwhelming odds, that life has a point. This argument of the wager goes back to the mathematician Blaise Pascal (1623–1662) who was intimately connected to the Jansenist reform movement in France. Regrettably, it cannot convince the unbelievers although it provides a rational justification for faith in the future. Our evident perception of the significance of life has little to do with rational reasoning but is a gift of grace; it proclaims hope in the creative interplay of DNA and RNA, enzymes and hormones, neuronal discharges and brain waves.

Our hypertrophic analytical intellect has triumphantly torn our norm systems apart, corroded our values and relativized the rules of the game. Recently the intellect in its other incarnation has been forced to recognize both the inevitability of superrational premises and its own subordinate instrumental role. Voltaire's ironic proposition:"If God does not exist, he must be promptly invented", was watered down with an expedient disclaimer:"but the whole of nature cries out that he exists." Anyhow, Voltaire's quip should be turned inside out – *we* are the invention desperately looking for a purpose.

So are we left with any hope for the future, any sacred passion for the game? Cultural pessimists have always invoked the blatant misappropriation of the cultural legacy, and they have been right. There is no reliable method of encapsulation; even sacrosanct values must, at times, be called into question if they are to retain their potency. All things considered, facile cultural optimism is a more dangerous delusion than excessive pessimism.

> A few examples will serve to illustrate the paradox of futurology in a vigorous culture. After the Second World War, conventional wisdom predicted a deep depression, severe unemployment and a shortage of energy and food. In fact the outcome was an all-time boom and a surplus of fuel and food, partly thanks to the pessimistic forecasts. The original, poorly researched scenario of the Club of Rome has certainly reduced the probability of raw material shortages and ecological disaster by its exaggerated predictions of doom. The much-proclaimed energy crisis may vanish like a *fata morgana*, provided we take it seriously! Thus, corporate executives should make their long-term decisions against all the widely accepted expert advice. This would be excellent counsel, provided it were generally ignored!

The future of any free and conscious agent is logically unpredictable. Every credible forecast affects the premises of the game, mostly in a self-negating way. This serves as a strong argument in favour of pessimistic prognostication.

> Apocalyptic visions as exemplified by the Revelation of St. John can be understood as particularly dramatic attempts to influence opinion and avert imminent cataclysm. It is certainly thought-provoking that we are now more than capable of eliciting the divine punishment which the seer on Patmos perceived as a terrifying reality – an impressive performance in futurology.

cf. 226 Democracies are generally long on sinister precognition, but we may become weary of the wailing choir of Cassandras. Environmental fundamentalists join in condemning our culture while simultaneously obstructing any new openings in the game. No new disquieting solutions ought to exist, creative opportunities are pre-empted, inventive expedients denied. We are sorely tempted to seek a secure shelter, to opt for bland contentment, rejecting the challenge of life. A perverted bad conscience drives us into dangerous risk minimization.

We are playing for high stakes, and there is every reason to consider seriously the many disheartening scenarios. The breakdown of democracy has often been cf. 203 preceded by starry-eyed optimism and unsuspecting economic follies. Unshakable self-confidence is indispensable in distress; yet it becomes a crippling burden in the hour of prosperity. In adversity we could perhaps do without the support of a Supreme Being, but a helping hand will be sorely needed when we emerge tainted by triumph.

Detour in depth psychology

By enacting the death of God the French Revolution tried to remove any rival authority, and promoted human reason to the single object of veneration. A long line of prophets-cum-psychologists have since expended considerable effort in implementing this programme by discreetly assuming the role of high priest. Man has been reduced in turn to"only" a machine (Laplace, Saint Simon), or to"nothing but" an untamed beast (Spencer) or to a"mere" maladjusted animal (Freud) or, most recently, to"just" a hypersophisticated computer. A subsequent wave of"scientific" behaviourism repeated this *reductio ad absurdum* with painstaking precision and empirical impeccability. *cf. 73*

> Arrogant"homunculism", the scientistic contempt for man, is gradually losing ground. But as late as 1946 the psychoanalyst George B. Chisholm, who became the first Secretary General of the World Health Organization, had the nerve to advocate "the eradication of the concept of right and wrong" and declared:"with the other human sciences, psychiatry must now decide what is to be the immediate future of the human race"!

Great artists have always been several steps ahead of scientific inquiry in investigating the depths of the human mind. Dostoyevsky for one is still unsurpassed in his unflattering depiction of man in a state of unfettered emancipation,"practising the absence of God" in the words of C.S. Lewis (1898–1963). *cf. 292*

> In *Notes from the Underground* (1864) Dostoyevsky renders the modern intellect pinned down by the needle of intellectual self-examination:"You boast of your consciousness, but you vacillate because, although your mind functions, your heart is clouded with depravity, and without a pure heart a real consciousness is impossible. And how importunate you are, how you force yourself on people, how you put on airs! Nothing but mendacity and more mendacity. But actually you are all right, it is really both vulgar and base. And basest of all is that I tried to justify myself to you just now. And baser yet is that I am making this remark. But anyway that's enough, or we'll never finish, one thing will be baser than the next."

Out of sheer self-preservation we refuse to be finished off by cocksure psychologists. And such innate scepticism stands on firm epistomological ground. According to Husserl, a scientific psychology presupposes the adequate self-description of the psychologist superego, the divulgence of his deepest motivation. This challenge defies our finite minds.

> Unaware of Dostoyovsky's writing I pursued as a teenager the following, typically adolescent train of thought. I wanted to be good (why?), but such a conscious decision could only lead to conceited self-righteousness; and so I decided to penetrate my self-complacency, but this only caused more self-reproach for conceit at a higher level, and so it went on. When I felt good about myself, I became bad but when I felt bad it was a cause of feeling good. Inadequate self-transparency, what could be called psychological Gödelization, haunts us every time we try to trap our ego in a self-sufficient language game. Self-examination is a set of Chinese boxes with"Egoism" inscribed on each one; it is just a question of how deep the delusion is.

We cannot become better"by ourselves", the infinite regress of self-simulation soon exhausts our powers of introspection. Chaitin's proof (9.1.12) corroborates St. Augustine's dictum that the self-perfection of man is a hopeless undertaking. No programme can improve itself beyond certain rather narrow limits; no one and no thing can know the truth about itself.

The exploration of our inner universe, Arthur Schopenhauer's"*Welt als Wille und Vorstellung"* ("The World as Will and Idea"), is still the almost exclusive domain of the artist and is well-nigh inaccessible to the systematic burrowings of philosophers, psychologists or neurologists. Man will certainly remain a mystery to himself, and may not be wholly transparent even in a higher perspective. After all, we cannot fully comprehend even the animal versions of mental life; mammalian behaviour seems to elude our most sophisticated cybernetic models.

> In dressage, food is used to reinforce the desired behaviour, but in practice undiluted reliance on conditioned responses results in dysfunction. The prospect of food may fail to supply sufficient motivation; even pigs can become so bored that they prefer to go hungry. Keller and Marian Brelands, specialists in the field, recount their experiences as follows:"These egregious failures came as a rather considerable shock to us, for there was nothing in our background in behaviourism to prepare us for such gross inabilities to predict and control the behaviour of animals with which we had been working for years" (*The Misbehaviour of Animals*, 1961).
>
> The heyday of behaviourism and psychoanalysis is over, but while Ivan Pavlov's (1849–1916) conditioned reflexes appear to have reached their animalian limits, they are successfully applied in healing human disorders. Painful but voluntary conditioning therapy – the systematic reinforcement of negative feedback – has proved effective in the cure of alcoholism and various phobias. Radical unlearning is always arduous, but given the right sanctions both withdrawal and habit-forming treatment can be surpris-
> *cf. 394*   ingly effective.

Parallel with a pragmatic approach to psychiatry, a more respectful and even humble conception of man is emerging. The archetypes of Carl Jung (1876–1961) are hereditary concentrates of human experience, predecessors to the epigenetic rules of sociobiology. Alfred Adler (1870–1937), Abraham Maslow (1908–70) and Viktor Frankl arrive at similar conclusions from disparate starting-points. Ordinary man can be understood and supported only if the integrity of his personality is recognized. This puts faith, the individual meta-rule, in the midst of the action.

Before his fall into linguistic solipsism, Heidegger rediscovered conscience as a life principle, and (following Jaspers) the existentialists were forced into a renewed confrontation with ultimate realities. God is still taboo (or has not yet become fashionable), but the heroic slogan"meaning despite and because of meaninglessness" comes strangely close to the"credo quia absurdum" of the mediaeval schoolmen.

Neurotic tension

In the last instance we are thrown back on our emotions, we are our deepest desires, our strongest ambitions. Like the power of concentration, these intense self-representations are probably mediated by a chemical reward system which in appropriate measures evidently outbids more immediate satisfactions.

cf. 99   We all produce our own private drugs, which obviously contribute to the self-stabilization of the central nervous system. The pain-killing encephalins have been thoroughly
studied, and other endorphins (biologically active polypeptides) are emerging as building blocks of an electrochemical psychology. In rats, preprogrammed behaviour (sleep,

copulation, eating, drinking) is transmitted by specific substances; other compounds trigger fear of darkness (in mice) or reinforce the memory function. The brain has localized pleasure centres which can be artificially activated by an electric current. A rat will continue pressing its "happiness button" until it dies of hunger or thirst whereas humans are quickly tired of such facile self-gratification.

Most sources of enjoyment gradually lose their efficacy; the longed-for euphoria requires larger and larger dosages. In many societies the fulfilment of material needs is now taken for granted. Illness and bodily suffering may soon be eliminated altogether but for good or ill we can never abolish the anguish of the soul. Affluence has brought one immeasurable benefit: an expanding proportion of the population is now dissatisfied at ever higher levels.

The methodical maximization of pleasure is an absurd and self-denying goal. Happiness – the ultimate satisfaction – is not the reliable outcome of safe play. And so we may well ask ourselves whether life is worth living at all. But what is the alternative? All we can beg for is a meaning in life, a point to our striving, a structured scope for play. After all, as Camus observed, Sisyphus was happy in his torturous toil. Fulfilment lies in taking on our all-too-human limitations – not in vain pursuits of happiness but rather in the steadfast imitation of suffering.

> Happiness has been linked, in turn, with a full stomach, security of life and limb, unlimited access to sexual partners, luxury and extravagance, and finally "self-realization" – the greatest luxury of all – but that too seems to be a dead-end. Eugene Ionesco declares frankly that "we can only realize ourselves by self-sacrifice". Otherwise, in the words of Paul Valéry (1871–1945), we will find that "we are shut in outside ourselves". To repeat a blunt expression: no pain, no gain.

Our inborn discontent has been evolutionarily adaptive. An immoderate intellectual craving, the insatiable passion for the game must have been a powerful implement in anthropogenesis. The latent emotional discord has stimulated the data-processing part of the brain, our somewhat overpromoted intelligence. A creative culture does not enjoy a tranquil state of good health; rather, it thrives on inhibitions and neurotic tension which we should strive to preserve in careful balance.

> Arthur Koestler's desperate call for a drug to deliver us from the schizoid state of man's intellect has its roots in painful, personal experience. High intelligence could not prevent him from falling prey to communist ideology. On the contrary, it helped to immunize his personality against doubt by producing a self-serving dialectic: every inconvenient fact was deftly explained away. Remorseful conversion is a traumatic process and the delinquent is left in a state of psychological liquidation. Most of the efforts of a lifetime must be written off overnight. *cf. 108; 278; 392*
>
> Talmud tradition has obviously provided fertile soil for pure intellectual ambition. There is no question of the disproportionately high Jewish contribution to political radicalism as well as to our most ingenious scientific games. Whether right or wrong, Jews have for long been on the cutting edge of our culture. Chess offers a rare opportunity for quantifying mental performance: according to de Groot, about 70 per cent of the Grandmasters have been of Jewish extraction.

Distrust and merciless criticism are the chief instruments of the intellect, and are all too rarely applied in self-diagnosis. Doubt is indeed a necessary and even inevitable complement to faith. Unlike lukewarm indifference, honest doubt represents an alternative conviction, a negation of belief which can be far more productive than many articles of faith. In some situations nagging doubt is the only move which advances the game. But scepticism cannot stand alone; it is just a reliable antidote against ubiquitous deception and self-deception.

Reason must be consulted as a talented and cunning counsellor, eager to make himself master in the house. If we succumb to intellectual intoxication, the self-contradictory outcome is dogmatic fanaticism – a caricature of genuine faith. The fanatic anaesthetizes his conscience with huge doses of doctrinaire self-deceit: the infallibility of the pope, the party or the prophet – opiates for every season.

In strictly rational terms nothing can make up for my physical death which becomes an outrageous affront. In order to transcend human self-importance – the *paralysie générale* of culture – we must defer our man-made measuring rods to supreme criteria. Only before God are all men equal in their shortcomings; only before God is humanism, our care for one another, reconciled with a higher mission.

The gift of grace

A century ago the death of God was a sensation which few took seriously. Now it is a trivial fact, and in the wake of godlessness the field is open to ahistorical improvidence, the fiendish misrepresentations of modern superstition and, worst of all, the hubris of the average citizen. The man-in-the-street has become the measure of all things, a target of abject adoration and idolization. Comfort and security rank highest in the scale of values, death is a scandalous imperfection, the God-relation a mental disorder. Such a syncretistically reduced and self-satisfied breed suggests nothing but its impending downfall.

> The relentless quest for happiness is a conspicuous symptom of spiritual confusion, a loss of nerve. Vanity Fair no longer holds all its former attraction, and the hunt for a conveniently packaged meaning to life is becoming increasingly frantic. Ancient occultisms from Cabbalism and spiritualism to astrology and exorcism are repeating the rounds. Yoga, Zen and Theosophy, Trancendental Meditation and Anthroposophy have become popular non-prescription drugs; the unique selling proposition is a dose-related kick with no untoward side effects.

To overcome all these afflictions we need a helping hand, a share of the Holy Spirit. On our own we cannot rise above petty self-gratification and sustain a higher hope and a higher truth.

> Contemplation is an ancient remedy for spiritual woes. In meditation or prayer we deflate our overblown ego and express our complete confidence in creation: God's grace can work without hindrance. Mental convulsion gives way to composed serenity while self-healing forces are given a free rein. But the blessing that ensues – an unaccountable upsurge of value – impels us back into the hurly-burly of the game where once again our faith is sorely tried.

The gift of grace imparts a cognizance of the universal plus-sum game, giving the progress dynamo the strength to endure human fallibility and dereliction. Grace is accessible to all creation but only man is free to reject grace, to set up his own isolated and meaningless play. Redemption lies in finding and fulfilling a personal mission, enriching the pleasure in play by apprehending a few significant rules of the Great Game.

Happiness is not our due: it appears only as the by-product of a meaningful existence. Happiness is delight in a life which, like a work of art, beautifully expounds its self-sustaining intent. A sense of grace is no guarantee of truth; it is simply a sign that we are not lost in total falsehood, inanity and eternal death. No absolute assurance of happiness and harmony, of righteousness or salvation can or must exist. Otherwise the game will be up, the face of God blasphemously unveiled.

God's true nature must remain a mystery to man – man who cannot even understand himself. All we can do is to cling to Him, sucking like leeches to draw some meaning into our lives. Only the fear of God can stop man declining into beastly superman or self-centred philistine. The fear of God is an old-fashioned, despised and misunderstood expression. This fear does not primarily refer to the dread of judgement or death or hell; rather it is the persistent anguish of estrangement from God, forfeiting the gift of grace. Our daily repentance should be; my God, my God, why have I forsaken thee?

9.8   Personal credo

Why should I contribute? The burden of evidence lies with you – why not you? We should not shirk our only freedom: to choose a lord worth serving, a mission worth pursuing, a game worth playing to the bitter end – the service of God. Every able body is privileged, standing in for all those countless souls who cannot take part. You are only called upon to do your best, struggling for self-control, resisting everything except challenges. After all, the best you can do in the end is to become a good loser, thus imparting value to the game. Every honest mistake has a meaning, fair play retains its value forever. Innocent faith is pushed towards ever higher levels of the game but the search for God remains an eternal instruction – the spirit of the game.

Childish faith

Only to a child is play sufficient unto itself. Adolescent lust for adventure needs idealistic fervour to reach a high pitch and by middle age, at the latest, worries about the vacuity of existence come to the fore. As we work against the inexorable deadline, the whole exercise gradually loses its point; in the end, we all sacrifice our lives, but for what purpose? Then, if not before, we must try to discover our calling, to find our own particular part in the game.

So what shall I do with my life? The crucial test is: what if everybody does as I do? Let thy play be fair and square, a modest contribution to the plus-sum game, enriching the wealth of variety in the world.

> So far so good. But life is a turmoil of simultaneous play and our moves are made under constant time pressure. The score must be assimilated at first sight; we play out our lives *prima vista* in clumsy improvization, pestered by repeats and wrong notes. False chords, jarring tones, aborted themes are there for everyone to hear. Carnal self-realization stands for the short-circuiting of vital energies and ends in anguished boredom, a drastic increase in spiritual entropy. Ardent asceticism is similarly fixated at the libido; healthy self-discipline turns into sterile masochism, the mortification of the flesh.
>
> The wanton disregard for tried and tested rules invites monstrous mismanagement, but the longing for facile perfection can tempt us into empty, imitative exercises from which all erroneous moves are excluded in advance. At a higher level, plagiarism is commendable; we ought to make the best of the ancestral body of laboriously accumulated spiritual capital. Outstanding personalities and doctrines provide inspiration and guidance, while rational reasoning and critical scepticism keep our gullibility at bay and serve as the guardians of intellectual health.

After all its Odysseys the human spirit can find relative peace in the safe haven of an ineffable and childlike faith. Each one of us has his own exclusive God-relation, admitted or denied, but nobody can have more than a shred of His truth. The aggregate perception of transcendent reality must be an incongruous collage; complete unanimity about Him is unattainable. But the Alfa and Omega of the game is our trustful dialogue with God, reborn in each individual and each generation. Some form of naive self-evidence, a holy simplicity, is the sole point of departure for blessed play.

The greatest advances of mankind have sprung from creative neoteny and spiritual innocence, a chaste and cheerful credulity in confronting the world and its inhabitants. It is a matter of abstaining from casual pessimism, wordly-wise cynicism and pointless self-pity. According to St. Matthew Jesus says: "Be ye therefore perfect, even as your father which is in heaven is perfect".

> At the age of 16, Benjamin Franklin (1706–90), the future doyen of the American revolution, wrote in his diary that he "conceived the bold and arduous project of arriving at moral perfection", and that he wanted to "imitate Jesus and Socrates". In the 1930s Ludwig Wittgenstein once made the rounds among his acquaintances in Oxford, apologizing for a hypothetical transgression: he may have left the impression that he repudiated his Jewish background. When Wittgenstein was met with the incredulous exclamation "Do you really want to be perfect" his astonished answer was: "Yes, of course I want to be perfect".

cf. 161 The progress dynamo is an exploitable resource, a paragon of generosity. He wants to enrich the world, to be both strong and good, adroit and honest – in short he wants to be God's help. A prodigious but not inhuman programme, well worth failing. Despite all setbacks we must become better losers. We must try to live our truth, to capture at least a glimpse of the innermost meaning of life.

Sacrificial service

Extreme individualism which sees the existence of the self as the only or at least the highest good, is difficult to reconcile with any form of helpfulness or sacrifice. Such a stance is fundamentally asocial; society cannot survive without constant deeds of abstention, even if this is no more than a voluntary renunciation of latent advantage. Sheer enlightened self-interest breaks down in large societies, where sponging and scrounging become the dominant strategies.

The original function of sacrifice was to solicit the support of supernatural powers. In this game of wheeling and dealing you either paid an instalment on prospective favours, or you settled your debts afterwards. A grand sacrificial act could also relieve social tension and wipe out accumulated societal liabilities in one sweep.

> The civil coalition was certainly exposed to traumatic strain already in prehistoric times, as the hierarchy had to be extended beyond the tribal chieftain level. The prehistoric king (or arch-priest) enjoyed disproportionate power and more than his share of the amenities of life, but the term of his rule was often limited. When the mandate expired he was sacrificed as a tribute to the gods; sometimes he was even eaten in a macabre act of communion. The masters of this world, however, have always had the knack of looking after themselves, and gradually this elegant method of achieving political equitability between the ruler and his subjects was replaced by various forms of vicarious oblation.

cf. 233

Genuine sacrifice implies a selfless investment in a transcendent plus-sum game, mirroring the ethos of all axial religions. A mundane spin-off of such devotion is sorely needed in any civilized polity. Democracies must rely upon the consent of the citizens in the surrender of a substantial part of their income, if not their lives and limbs, for the common good. The best of constitutions is of no avail once the funds of volitional sacrifice are depleted.

How are we to overcome our stage fright, the fear of failing our part? A prompter is available if our contribution is at odds with the gist of the game. But the muted whisper forever insisting on fair play is easily drowned out by the ingratiating rumblings of an inflated ego. Fortunately some measure of altruism is inscribed in our genetic code. Helping your neighbour is a source of satisfaction, even at some personal inconvenience. We long for a cause which deserves some self-sacrifice, but a hypertrophic rationality threatens to do away with our only fundamental freedom: to choose a lord worth serving, a mission worth pursuing, a game worth playing to the bitter end – the service of God.

Unflinching courage

Personal vanity and ambition are part and parcel of leadership. The manipulation of men arouses the strongest passion for play, it exerts an even greater fascination than chess or the stock exchange. The core of leadership nonetheless lies in discerning the potential plus sum. An authentic leader endows his cause with meaning by fighting for what is necessary within the framework of what is possible. A career is thus not an end in itself; it is a logical consequence of the contribution to the group. None of this depends on the established social hierarchy; rather, the value of an initiative lies in the responsibility and risk-taking that it involves.

Our moral assets are fairly evenly distributed. We are all equally remote from God, we sorely need more civic courage of conviction and moral fibre, some measure of humanity and compassion to maintain the production of vital values. Democratic societies depend on such leadership which, in the broadest sense, is open to each and every one.

Why should I contribute? The burden of evidence lies with you – why not you? Every able body is privileged, standing in for all those countless souls who cannot take part – the fallen, the maimed, the wretched and helpless, dead, living and as yet unborn. Unless we lift ourselves out of the vicious circle of the prisoner's dilemma, we will be condemned to the dustbin of history – a meaningless existence and irrevocable annihilation. We are only called upon to do our best, struggling for self-control, resisting everything except challenges.

cf. 377; 389   Self-indulgence and self-deceit are cowardly concessions; the game gets its merit from all the unpleasant truths accepted and from all the tempting moves passed by. In the words of Mencius:"Only when a man will not do some things is he capable of doing great things." If we live a lie, denying disagreeable realities, personal as well as national wreckage will follow. We should abhor any easy satisfaction and stand our ground, put the bar ever higher though we knock it down. The laconic Samuel Beckett understood this: "Ever tried? Ever failed? Never mind. Try again. Fail better."

Without our personal commitment the game will be taken over by the misguided and ignorant who in zealous enthusiasm for their scrap of truth shut themselves up in narrow and barren value systems, neglecting the rest of human experience. The visible effects of widespread godlessness are even more horrifying. It is high time for a new self-aware people of God to stand forth and in all humility take up their burden, boldly deciphering His intentions, willingly accepting the risk of error and misrepresentation. This is a task for the best and purest and strongest amongst us; in democratic terms, it is a task for Everyman.

Love of God

Self-love is the predicament of man, but humans cannot be fully content with the idle pastime of promoting themselves. With the courage of despair we crave to take part in a grander game which is also worth losing. After all, the best we can do in the end is to become good losers, thus imparting value to the game. The sole injunction of this perfect plus-sum play is to love God: a sacrifice that makes life worth living. This ultimate challenge does not yield any clear resolution – it bends every human rule.

Let us assume that a historical person, say a carpenter's son in Galilee under the Emperor Tiberius, was invested with supreme insight and an all-encompassing love for the Creator. What would have been the right move for such an exceptional human being? To set himself up as dictator for life, regimenting all mankind? But enforced virtue only evokes self-poisoning lip-service as many capable emperors, Egyptian or Roman, Chinese or Indian have discovered to their chagrin. What about teaching practical skills and techniques, developing science and medicine, raising the standard of living? We know only too well that such activities become destructive when divested of their higher context. Then what about developing a flawless doctrine of wisdom which could convince and persuade people on rational grounds of the only right and the only good? We are beginning to realize that this is a logical impossibility. But healing the sores of a wretched humanity would certainly be worthwhile? Jesus did this only with great reluctance, and we have come to understand that it does not solve any deeper problems. However great the hindsight, every strong move appears counterproductive, a betrayal of the spirit of the game.

Jesus of Nazareth did not come to abolish the old commandments but to free people from pedantic self-righteousness, to renew and consummate propitious leads; to initiate loving and fearless activity; to reinstate the supremacy of the Holy Spirit over abstract law. To love one's enemies and forgive one's brother seventy times seven goes far beyond the golden rule of reciprocity, unfolding new dimensions of human interplay. Love, the strongest of attractors, is the deepest truth and requires the greatest absorption of uncertainty.

Agape, love of God, is always in short supply. It cannot be otherwise. Consequently, we have to economize on love and instal well-formed rules to bear the brunt of human selfishness. All we really need to pray for is more love – love of God and the other loves that it inspires, the love of our fellow-beings, of nature, of all creation. Since love is the invisible bonding of good coalitions, all the rest follows in the light of reason and experience under the various aspects of the culture game.

cf. 402

We may identify ourselves with the pawn, which is readily sacrificed in favour of more valuable pieces, but which can always dream of becoming queen. All chessmen are sacrificed for the king but if the king himself is given up, the game breaks down or acquires a higher significance beyond the visible board. Sacrifice of the king, as we have seen, is a very old concept. The ruler was part of a smooth-running system of planned obsolescence. Nor were the gods exempt; in the Near East, Tammuz, Adonis and Osiris died and rose again with the regularity of clockwork.

Jesus was obviously the transmitter of a unique message. After unsuccessful attempts at passing on the information by conventional means, he finally chose a radical approach since the good tidings had to get through, whatever the cost. His self-sacrifice, an embarrassing challenge to God and men, was to provide a new lease of life for a deadlocked mankind.

"Love of God" – what reality can be expressed by this poor language game, made up of three words and nine letters? In grace we get, but in love we give something for nothing. Love of God means that we take part in Him, in the whole truth. It is the only permissible monomania, an imperative to free men. Faith can and should gradually emancipate itself, become imbued with insight, give rise to penetrating knowledge, skill and judgement. Innocent faith is thus pushed towards ever higher levels of play, but search for God remains an eternal instruction – the spirit of the game.

Divine love

Considering our sad insufficiency, the most difficult act of faith is to believe in divine love. Why should any deity or demiurge take particular interest in the grain of dust we call earth or even in separate human creatures? Or suppose we are the target of a scornful hoax? Or what if, most probable of all, we are on our own in a chilly cosmos?

> Charles Darwin blames "the clumsy, wasteful, blundering, low and horrible works of nature". He felt for a moment that life only was a meaningless round; to eat and be eaten. Such glimpses of the abyss have the ring of truth just because of the anxiety and discomfort they evoke. The games of nature come terribly close to naked, self-devouring logic. Hard-won experience has made us sceptical of agreeable truths, of duplicity and deception, opiates and orgies – foul play of every kind.

Our desires seek satisfaction in repeatable, genetically entrenched follies with the inevitable penalty of physical and moral hangover. The impasses of boredom and insentience are familiar enough including all their accompanying, fundamentally uninteresting neurotic peculiarities. In the end, the inane emptiness and indifference of the universe stares us down, however hard we try to slake our thirst for life in sensual pleasure or cocksure ideology. As long as God supports us we feel the weight of our sins; only in free fall can we embrace the illusion that gravity is just a construct of petty minds.

All paths seem to be blocked, except arduous ascent. If we rule out regression towards beastly self-repetition, we are painfully compelled to heightened self-reference. Yet we are totally dependent on subordinate biological structures. Reliable neurological rewards are indispensable in sustaining our appetite for life; they are the heavy, primary rocket stages which hurl us out into outer space, our true albeit vague and indeterminate vocation.

> Any higher strivings, not least a belief in God, can be dismissed as a set of sneaky lies, derisory acts of self-delusion. But, whether right or wrong, every honest faith is self-confirming to some degree. Whereas the non-believers stay prudently put, the deluded will spread their gospel like life itself; aggressive sceptics are just proponents of a different faith. The real and rational unbeliever is a cynical hedonist who keeps a very low profile, astutely looking for the pleasurable free ride. He may or may not be in the right, but his parasitic conviction will remain subordinate to self-selected faith which creates its own truth and always opts for eternal life.

Liquidation is the outcome of poor collective play but, for the individual, death is the final prize in any case. We live entirely on credit; sooner or later the strutting and fretting of life must be made good by the exit to extinction. The question is only whether we are happy lessees; our debt must be honoured – that rule knows no exceptions. More difficult to accept is the purgatory of old age which can be grotesquely extended by modern medicine. Every human being must have the right to make the closing move, switch off the clock of life and pass on.

A literal belief in immortality or reincarnation smacks of superstition and wishful thinking; death is where black magic makes its last stand.

Since time immemorial, primitive reincarnation myths have propped up the morality of mankind by holding out a spurious hope. The Rig-Veda, The Upanishads and the learning of Buddha have, in succession, brought the transmigration theory to its utterly rarefied conclusion. Nirvana, neither being nor non-being, is the final reward for good conduct – a systematic redemption by deeds thoroughly denounced by the fathers of the Christian Church.

All hypotheses of human immortality contain their own paradoxes. Our earthly experience points to an irrefutable link between body and soul but beyond the fractal overview of consciousness we can, despite all the rebuttals, conceive miracles of a higher order. Unfortunately we are all too inclined to autistic self-absorption, spiritually paralysed by our unbelief. And when, sporadically, we seem to grasp with transcendent clarity or to hear with perfect pitch, we struggle like aphasics in vain for the right word.

Ordinary language is, after all, only the science of the expressible. Like the collapse of a quantum-mechanical wave function, a word congeals a fuzzy concept but it rarely hits the bull's eye. Our real intentions always risk misrepresentation as the uttered word takes on a reality of its own – or it attains a better truth.

In covenant with God we gain the strength to face ineptitude, misgivings, disillusion, disappointment and finally certain defeat. We may occasionally encounter moments of joy, happiness, harmony and peace when the pleasure centre of our brain relays a positive response – an agreeable but not very reliable sign of the grace of God.

The euphoria of mystic revelation comes dangerously close to drug-induced "trips" and the pleasurable states caused by some epilepsies or syphilitic brain damage. Deepest insight and lunatic delusion seem to overlap to a disturbing degree; creativity culminates at the borderline with chaos.

Mystic contact with God mediates the best messages, but can also strike a false chord; visionary perspicuity is not too far removed from hyper-ingenious self-deception. The tension between these complementary apprehensions admits a certain scope for play and allows us to take part in God's creation – and the creation of God? Each individual move both uncovers and locks, shapes and discards. Inevitably we go astray and end as rejects which still, in some wonderful way, share in His labour of love. Every honest mistake has a meaning, and fair play retains its value forever.

There are no losers in the Kingdom of God. We can safely place our personal fate in His hands, praying for faithfulness unto death. Nothing is wasted, in Him every thing is forever present. God's mercy is boundless, He lives and dies with us, our sins of omission and commission simply add to His suffering.

In a concentration camp the internees are called out to witness an execution. The victim is bound to a post and is slowly whipped to death. Someone in the front row cries out in a smothered voice: "Where is God?" Another replies, just as softly: "He hangs there before us."

We are open-ended metaphors, harbingers of history, forerunners of futurity, self-illuminating threads in the garment of God. Once dimly preconceived, potentially existing, this moment is the burning focus of time. The Big Bang, the stages of evolution, past generations resound in us – here and now everything is at stake.

Selected Bibliography

In writing the book, I have drawn on everything I have read or heard or experienced in my life, most of which must necessarily be omitted here. In general, I have refrained from cluttering the text with references concerning sources, facts and figures. Furthermore, I have excluded from the bibliography the classics of literature, philosophy and science cited in the book, since they are widely available in a variety of translations and editions. Thus, the bibliography is restricted to a sampling of the most apposite background reading, with particular emphasis on more recent publications.

Abegglen, James C. & George Stalk Jr. 1985. *Kaisha.: The Japanese Corporation*. Charles E. Tuttle. Tokyo.

Ackoff, Russell L. 1981. *Creating the Corporate Future: Plan or Be Planned for*. John Wiley, New York.

Aitchison, Jean 1981. *Language Change: Progress or Decay*. Fontana, London.

Alexander, Christopher et al. 1977. *A Pattern Language: Towns, Buildings, Constructions*. Oxford University Press, New York.

Arendt, Hannah 1970. *On Violence*. Allen Lane, London

Aron, Raymond 1955. *The Opium of the Intellectuals*. Secker & Warburg, London. (French original: Paris 1955.)

Aron, Raymond 1983. *Memoires: Fifty Years of Political Reflection*. Holmes & Meier, New York & London.

Arrow, Kenneth 1951. *Social Choice and Individual Values*. John Wiley, New York

Axelrod, Robert 1984. *The Evolution of Cooperation*. Basic Books, New York.

Barnsley, Michael 1988. *Fractals Everywhere*. Academic Press, New York.

Barrow, John D. & Frank J. Tipler 1986. *The Anthropic Cosmological Principle*. Clarendon Press, Oxford.

Bloch, Ernst 1959. *Das Prinzip Hoffnung*. Suhrkamp Verlag, Frankfurt.

Bongard, M. 1970. *Patterns of Recognition*. Spartan Books, New York.

de Bono, Edward 1967. *Lateral Thinking: A Textbook of Creativity*. Penguin, Harmondsworth:.

Boorstin, David J. 1973. *The Americans: The Democratic Experience*. Vintage Books/Random House, New York.

Boyd, Robert & Peter J. Rickesson 1985. *Culture and the Evolutionary Process*. The University of Chicago Press, Chicago.

Braitenberg, Valentino 1984. *Vehicles*. MIT Press, Cambridge, Mass.

Brams, Steven 1983. *Superior Beings: If They Exist, How Would We Know? Game-theoretic Implications of Omniscience, Omnipotence, Immortality and Incomprehensibility*. Springer-Verlag, New York.

Brandon, Ruth 1983. *The Spiritualists*. Weidenfeld & Nicolson, London.

Braudel, Fernand 1979. *The Wheels of Commerce: Civilization and Capitalism 15th–18th Century*, Collins, London. (French original: Paris 1979.)

Breland, Keller & Marion 1961. "The Misbehaviour of Animals". *American Psychologist* 16, 681-4. (Gould, J. L. 1982. Ethology, Appendix A, 15–19)

Brennan, Geoffrey & James Buchanan 1987. *The Reason of Rules*. Cambridge University Press, Cambridge.

Brzezinski, Zbigniew 1993. *Out of Control*. Scribners, New York.

Buchanan, James & Nicos Devletoglou 1980. *Anarchy in Academia*. Basic Books, New York.

Calvin, William 1990. *Cerebral Symphony*. Bantam Books, New York.

Casimir, Hendrik B. G. 1983. *Haphazard Reality: Half a Century of Science*. Harper and Row, New York.

Chandrasakhar, S. 1987. *Truth and Beauty: Aesthetics and Motivation in Science*. Chicago University Press, Chicago.

Clark, W.C. 1982. *Carbon Dioxide Review*. Oxford University Press, New York.

Crick, Francis & Graeme Mitchison 1988. *What Mad Pursuit: A Personal View of Scientific Discovery*. Basic Books, New York.

Crozier, Michel 1964. *The Bureaucratic Phenomenon*. Tavistock, London

Davis, Morton D. 1970. *Game Theory: A Nontechnical Introduction*. Basic Books, New York.

Dawkins, Richard 1976. *The Selfish Gene*. Oxford University Press, Oxford.

Delbrück, Max 1986. *Mind from Matter: An Essay on Evolutionary Epistemology*. Blackwell Scientific Publications, Oxford.

Dennett, Daniel 1991. *Consciousness Explained*. Penguin, Harmondsworth.

Desmond, Adrian & James Moore 1991. *Darwin*. Penguin, Harmondsworth.

Dewdney, A. K. 1989. *The Turing Omnibus: 61 Excursions in Computer Science*. Computer Science Press, Rockville, Md.

Dickerson, Richard 1972. The Structure of History of an Ancient protein. *Scientific American* 226 (4), 58–72

Dickerson, Richard & Irving Geis 1983. *Hemoglobin*. Benjamin Cummings, California.

Drexler, Eric K. & Chris Petersen with Gayle Pergamit 1991. *Unbounding the Future: The Nanotechnology Revolution*. William Morrow, New York.

Drucker, Peter 1969. *The Age of Discontinuity*. Heinemann, London.

Drucker, Peter 1973. *Management: Tasks – Responsibilities – Practices*. Harper & Row, New York.

Drucker, Peter 1980. *Managing in Turbulent Times*. Harper & Row, New York.

Drucker, Peter 1989. *The New Realities*. Heinemann Professional Publishing, London.

Dunn, Edgar S. Jr. 1971. *Economic and Social Development*. The John Hopkins Press, Baltimore.

Dyson, Freeman 1979. *Disturbing the Universe*. Harper & Row, New York.

Dyson, Freeman 1988. *Infinite in All Directions*. Harper & Row, New York.

Eccles, John C. 1989. *Evolution of the Brain, Creation of the Self*. Routledge, London.

Eco, Umberto 1988. *Semiotics and the Philosophy of Language*. Macmillan, Basingstoke.

Edelman, Gerald 1989. *The Remembered Present*. Basic Books, New York.

Eibl-Eibesfeldt, Irenäus 1984. *Die Biologie des Menschlichen Verhaltens: Grundriss der Humanethologie*. Piper, München.

Eigen, Manfred & Ruthild Winkler 1975. *Das Spiel – Naturgesetze steuern den Zufall*. Piper, München.

Eliade, Mircea 1979. *A History of Religious Ideas: Vol 1. From the Stone Age to the Eleusinian Mysteries*. Collins, London (French original: Paris 1976.)

Etzioni, Amitai 1988. *The Moral Dimension: Towards a New Economics*. The Free Press/ Macmillan, London.

Etzioni, Amitai 1993. *The Spirit of Community*. Crowns, New York.

Eysenck, H. J. 1973. *The Inequality of Man*. Fontana, London.

Fairbank, John King 1986. *The Great Chinese Revolution 1800–1985*. Harper & Row, New York.

Farquharson, Robin 1969. *Theory of voting*. Yale University Press, New Haven.

Feyerabend, Paul 1975. *Against Method*. NLB, London

Feynman, Richard 1965. *The character of Physical Law*. MIT Press, Cambridge, Mass.

Feynman, Richard 1985. *QED, The Strange Theory of Light and Matter*. Princeton University Press, Princeton.

Fox, James J. 1977. *Harvest of the Palm*. Harvard University Press, Cambridge, Mass.

Fraiberg, Selma H. 1959. *The Magic Years*. Scribners, New York.

Fraser, J. T. 1987. *Time: The Familiar Stranger*. University of Massachusetts Press, Cambridge, Mass.

Friedman, Milton 1968. *Capitalism and Freedom*. Chicago University Press, Chicago.

Friedman, Milton 1976. *Price Theory*. Aldine, Chicago.

Fukuyama, Francis 1992. *The End of History and the Last Man*. The Free Press, New York.

Gardner, Martin 1982. *Logic Machines and Diagrams*. University of Chicago Press, Chicago.

Gauthier, David 1986. *Morals by Agreement*. Clarendon Press, Oxford.

Gelder, Georg 1981. *Wealth and Poverty*. Basic Books, New York.

Gleick, James 1988. *Chaos: Making a New Science*. Heinemann, London.

Gleick, James 1992. *Genius: Richard Feynman and Modern Physics*. Little, Brown, New York.

Goodall, Jane 1986. *The Chimpanzees of Gombe: Patterns of Behaviour*. Harvard University Press, Cambridge, Mass.

Gould, James L. 1982. *Ethology. The Mechanisms and Evolution of Behaviour*. W.W. Norton, New York.

Gould, Rowland 1970. *The Matsushita Phenomenon*. Diamond Publishing, Tokyo.

Gould, Stephen Jay 1973. *Ever Since Darwin: Reflections in Natural History*. Penguin, Harmondsworth.

Grant, Michael 1992. *Greeks and Romans: A Social History*. Weidenfeld & Nicolson, London.

Greimas, A. J. 1966. *Semantique Structurale*. Larousse, Paris

Griffin, Donald R. 1984. *Animal Thinking*. Harvard University Press, Cambridge, Mass.

Griffin, Donald R. 1992. *Animal Minds*. University of Chicago Press, Chicago.

de Groot, Adriaan D. 1965. *Thought and Choice in Chess*. Mouton, The Hague.

Habermas, Jürgen 1968. *Erkenntnis und Interesse*. Suhrkamp, Frankfurt.

Habermas, Jürgen 1973. *Kultur und Kritik*. Suhrkamp, Frankfurt.

Hamburger, Henry 1979. *Games as Models of Social Phenomena*. University of California, Irvine.

Hampden-Turner, Charles 1990. *Charting the Corporate Mind*. The Free Press/Macmillan, London.

Hansen, M.G. 1987. *The Athenian Assembly*. Basil Blackwell, Oxford.

Hartman, Robert S. 1967. *The Structure of Value: Foundations of Scientific Axiology*. Southern Illinois Press, Carbondale.

Hawking, Stephen W. 1988. *A Brief History of Time*. Bantam Press, London.

von Hayek, F. A. 1944. *The Road to Serfdom*. Routledge, London.

von Hayek, F. A. 1988. *The Fatal Conceit: The Errors of Socialism*. Routledge, London.

Heisenberg, Werner 1959. *Physik und Philosophie*. Ullstein Bücher, Stuttgart.

Hingley, Ronald 1977. *The Russian Mind*. Scribner, New York.

Hintikka, Jaakko 1962. *Knowledge and Belief: An Introduction to the Logic of the Two Notions*. Cornell University Press, Ithaca N.Y.

Hintikka, Jaakko 1973. *Logic, Language-games and Information: Kantian Themes in the Philosophy of Logic.* Clarendon Press, Oxford.

Hofer, Myron A. 1981. *The Roots of Human Behavior: An Introduction to the Psychobiology of Early Development.* W. H. Freeman, San Francisco.

Hofstaedter, Douglas R. 1979. *Gödel, Escher, Bach.* Basic Books, New York.

Hook, Sidney 1975. *Revolution, Reform and Social Justice.* New York University Press, New York.

Hunt, Morton 1985. *Profiles of Social Research: The Scientific Study of Human Interactions.* Russell Sage Foundation, New York.

Jacobson, Max 1961. *Finland Survived: An Account of the Finnish-Soviet Winter War 1939–40.* Otava, Helsinki.

Janik, Allan & Stephen Toulmin 1973. *Wittgenstein's Vienna.* Weidenfeld & Nicolson, London.

Jantsch, Erich 1980. *The Self-organizing Universe.* Pergamon Press, Oxford.

Johanson, Donald & Maitland Edey 1981. *Lucy. The Beginnings of Humankind.* Simon & Schuster, New York.

Jung C. G. 1961. *Memories, Dreams, Reflections.* Random House, New York.

Kennedy, Paul 1988. *The Rise and Fall of the Great Powers.* Random House, New York.

Kennedy, Paul 1993. *Preparing for the Twenty-first Century.* Harper Collins, London.

Klamer, Arjo 1983. *Conversations with Economists.* Rowman & Allanheld, Totowa, N.J.

Klamer, Arjo & David Colander 1990. *The Making of an Economist.* Westview Press, Boulder.

Klima, Edward S. & Ursula Bellugi 1979. *The Signs of Language.* Harvard University Press, Cambridge, Mass.

Koestler, Arthur 1949. *Insight and Outlook.* Macmillan, London.

Koestler, Arthur 1968. *Drinkers of Infinity: Essays 1955–67.* Hutchinson, London.

Koestler, Arthur 1970. *The Act of Creation.* Pan, London.

Krajewski, Wladyslaw 1977. *Correspondence Principle and Growth of Science.* Reidel, Dordrecht.

Kuhn, Thomas S. 1962. *The Structure of Scientific Revolutions.* University of Chicago Press, Chicago.

Kundera, Milan 1986. *L'Art du Roman.* Gallimard, Paris.

Lakatos, Imre & Alan Musgrave 1970 (eds.) *Criticism and the Growth of Knowledge.* Cambridge University Press, Cambridge.

Lakatos, Imre 1976. *Proofs and Refutations: Logic of Mathematical Discovery.* Cambridge University Press, Cambridge.

Lander, David S. 1983. *Revolution in Time: Clocks and the Making of the Modern World.* Harvard University Press, Cambridge, Mass.

Lasky, Melvin 1976. *Utopia and Revolution.* University of Chicago Press, Chicago.

Latour, Bruno 1987. *Science in Action: How to Follow Scientists and Engineers through Society.* Harvard University Press, Cambridge, Mass.

Lee, Richard B. & Irvin DeVore 1978. *Kalahari Hunter-gathers: Studies of the Kung San and Their Neighbors.* Harvard University Press, Cambridge, Mass.

Levi, Primo 1986. *The Drowned and the Saved.* Summit Books, New York.

Levin, Roger 1993. *Complexity.* Dent, London.

Le Vine, R.A. & D.T. Campbell 1972. *Ethnocentrism: Theories of Conflict, Ethnic Attitudes and Group Behaviour.* John Wiley, New York.

Lewontin, Richard 1982. *Human Diversity.* Scientific American Library, New York.

Lorenz, Konrad 1965. *Über Tierisches und Menschliches Verhalten.* Piper, München.

Lowe, Victor 1985. *Alfred North Whitehead. The Man and His Work.* The Johns Hopkins University Press, Baltimore.

Lumsden C. J. & E. O. Wilson 1981. *Genes, Mind and Culture: The Coevolutionary Process.* Harvard University Press, Cambridge, Mass.

Lumsden C. J. & E. O. Wilson 1983. *Promethean Fire.* Harvard University Press, Cambridge, Mass.

Luria, A. F. 1987. *The Mnemonist.* Harvard University Press, Cambridge, Mass.

Maccoby, Michael 1976. *The Gamesman.* Simon & Schuster, New York.

Maccoby, Michael 1988. *Why Work: Leading the New Generation.* Simon & Schuster, New York.

MacMullen, Ramsay 1988. *Corruption and the Decline of Rome.* Yale University Press, New Haven.

Mallory, J. P. 1989. *In Search of the Indo-Europeans.* Thames & Hudson, London.

Mandelbrot, Benoit B. 1977. *Fractals. Form: Chance, and Dimension.* W. H. Freeman, San Francisco.

Maslow, Abraham H. 1962. *Toward a Psychology of Being.* Van Nostrand Reinhold, Princeton.

Maslow, Abraham 1971. *Farther Reaches of Human Nature.* Viking, New York.

McClelland, David 1961. *The Achieving Society.* Van Nostrand, Princeton.

McClelland, David 1976. *The Achievement Motive.* Irvington, New York.

McDonald, John 1975. *The Game of Business: Modern Game Theory and the Interactions of People in Economic Life. The Rules, Choices, Strategies in Important Business Events.* Doubleday, New York.

McEvedy, Collin & Richard Jones 1978. *Atlas of the World Population History.* Penguin, Harmondsworth.

Medawar, Peter 1986. *Memoir of a Thinking Radish: An Autobiography.* Oxford University Press, Oxford.

Miller, George A. 1981. *Language and Speech.* W.H. Freeman, San Francisco.

Mokyr, Joel 1990. *The Lever of Riches: Technological Creativity and Economic Progress.* Oxford University Press, Oxford.

Monod, Jacques 1971. *Chance and Necessity.* Random House, New York.

Moore, J.M. 1975. *Aristotle and Xenophon on Democracy and Oligarchy.* Chatto & Windus, London.

Morita, Akio, Edvin M. Reingold & Mitsuko Shimomura 1986. *Made in Japan.* Dutton, London.

Murray, Charles & Catherine Bly Cox 1989. *Apollo: The Race to the Moon.* Simon and Schuster, New York.

Needham, Joseph 1982. *Science in Traditional China: A Comparative Perspective.* Harvard University Press, Cambridge, Mass.

von Neumann, John & Oscar Morgenstern 1944. *Theory of Games and Economic Behaviour.* Princeton University Press, Princeton.

von Neumann, John 1958. *The Computer and the Brain.* Yale University Press, New Haven.

Newell, Allan 1990. *Unified Theories of Cognition.* Harvard University Press, Cambridge, Mass.

Olson, Mancur 1982. *The Rise and the Decline of Nations.* Yale University Press, New Haven.

Parfitt, Derek 1984. *Reasons and Persons.* Clarenden Press, Oxford.

Peitgen, Heinz-Otto & Dieter Saupe (eds.) 1988. *The Science of Fractals.* Springer Verlag, New York.

Pelikan, Jaroslaw 1989. *The Christian Tradition: A History of the Development of Doctrine.* Chicago University Press, Chicago.

Penrose, Roger 1989. *The Emperor's New Mind.* Oxford University Press, Oxford.

Peters, Thomas J. & Robert H. Waterman Jr. 1982. *In Search of Excellence: Lessons from America's Best-run Companies.* Harper & Row, New York.

Pfungst, Oskar 1911. *Clever Hans (Kluger Hans),* Henry Haltan, New York.

Pierre, John R. 1983. *The Science of Musical Sound.* Scientific American Library, New York.

Polanyi, Michael 1958. *Personal Knowledge: Towards a Post-Critical Philosophy.* Chicago University Press, Chicago.

Polkinghorne, J.C. 1979. *The Particle Play.* W.H. Freeman, Oxford.

Polkinghorne, J.C. 1984. *The Quantum World.* Longman, London.

Polya, Georg 1981. *Mathematical Discovery: Combined edition.* John Wiley, New York.

Popper, Karl 1952. *The Open Society and its Enemies, 2 vols.* Routledge, London.

Popper, Karl 1962. *The Logic of Scientific Discovery.* Hutchinson, London.

Popper, Karl 1983. *Postscript to the Logic of Scientific Discovery, 2 vols.* Rowman and Littlefield, Totowa N. J.

Porter, Michael E. 1990. *The Competitive Advantage of Nations.* The Free Press/Macmillan, London.

Prigogine, Ilya 1980. *From Being to Becoming: Time and Complexity in the Physical Sciences.* W.H. Freeman, San Francisco.

Putnam, Robert; Robert Leonardi & Raffaella Nanetti 1992. *Making Democracy Work.* Princeton University Press, Princeton .

Quine, W.V. 1987. *Quiddities.* Harvard University Press, Cambridge, Mass.

Ramo, Simon 1988. *The Business of Science: Winning and Losing in the High-Tech Age.* Hill and Wang, New York.

Rapoport, Anatol 1970. *N-person Game Theory: Concepts and Applications.* Ann Arbor Science Library, The University of Michigan Press, Michigan.

Rawls, John 1971. *A Theory of Justice.* Clarendon, Oxford.

Rawls, John 1993. *Political Liberalism.* Columbia University Press, Columbia.

Reed, Graham 1972. *The Psychology of Anomalous Experience: A Cognitive Approach.* Hutchinson, London.

Rheingold, Howard 1991. *Virtual Reality.* Summit Books, New York.

Rhenman, Eric 1966. *The Organization: A Controlled System.* SIAR, Stockholm.

Rhenman, Eric 1968. *Industrial Democracy and Industrial Development.* Tavistock, London.

Rhenman, Eric 1973. *Organization Theory for Long-Range Planning.* John Wiley, New York.

Ronan, Colin A. 1983. *The Cambridge Illustrated History of the World's Science.* Cambridge University Press, Cambridge.

Röpke, Wilhelm 1944. *Civitas Humana.* Rentsch, Zürich.

Rucker, Rudy 1982. *Infinity and the Mind: The Science and Philosophy of the Infinity.* Harvester Press, Brighton.

Rucker, Rudy 1987. *Mind Tools.* Houghton Miffin, Boston.

Ryle, Gilbert 1949. *The Concept of Mind.* Hutchinson, London.

Sacks, Oliver 1974. *Awakenings.* Duckworth, London.

Sakharov, Andrei 1990. *Memoirs.* Hutchinson, London.

Schama, Simon 1987. *The Embarrassment of Riches: An Interpretation of Dutch Culture in the Golden Age.* Collins, London.

Schneider, Stephen H. & Randi Londer 1984. *The Coevolution of Climate and Life.* Sierra Club, San Francisco.

Schrank, Robert 1978. *Ten Thousand Working Days.* MIT Press, London.

Schwartz, Peter 1991. *The Art of the Long View: Planning for the Future in an Uncertain World.* Doubleday, New York.

Schweitzer, Albert 1935. *Die Weltanschaung der Indischen Denker.* Beck, München.

Sherburne, Donald W. (ed.) 1966. *A Key to Whitehead's Process and Reality*. Indiana University Press, Indiana.

Simon, Herbert A. 1969. *The Sciences of the Artificial*. M.I.T. Press, Cambridge, Mass.

Simon, Herbert A. & Allen Newell 1972. *Human Problem Solving*. Prentice-Hall, Englewood Cliffs, N. J.

Sloboda, John A. 1985. *The Musical Mind: The Cognitive Psychology of Music*. Clarendon Press, Oxford.

Smith, John Maynard 1982. *Evolution and the Theory of Games*. Cambridge University Press, Cambridge.

Smith, John Maynard 1989. *Evolutionary Genetics*. Oxford University Press, Oxford.

Soros, George 1987. *The Alchemy of Finance: Reading the Mind of the Market*. Simon & Schuster, New York.

de Soto, Hernando 1989. *The Other Path: The Invisible Revolution in the Third World*. Harper & Row, New York.

Squires, Arthur M. 1986. *The Tender Ship: Governmental Management of Technological Change*. Birkhauser, Boston.

Stapp, Henry J. 1985. "Consciousness and Values in the Quantum Universe". *Foundation of Physics*, 15, 1, 35–47.

Stewart, Ian 1987. *The Problems of Mathematics*. Oxford University Press, Oxford.

Stewart, Ian 1989. *Does God Play Dice?* Basil Blackwell, Oxford.

Strauss, William and Neil Howe 1991. *Generations: The History of America's Future, 1584 to 2069*. William Marrow, New York.

Szamuely, Tibor 1974. *The Russian Tradition*. Secker & Warburg, London.

Tainter, Joseph A. 1988. *The Collapse of Complex Societies*. Cambridge University Press, Cambridge.

Tavaststjerna, Erik 1989. *Jean Sibelius*. Otava, Helsinki.

Thom, René 1983. *Mathematical Models of Morphogenesis*. John Wiley, New York.

Thurow, Lester 1980. *The Zero-sum Society: Distribution and the Possibilities of Economic Change*. Basic Books, New York.

Toulmin, Stephen 1983. *The Return to Cosmology: Postmodern Science and the Theology of Nature*. University of California Press, Berkeley.

Trivers, Robert 1985. *Social Evolution*. Benjamin Cummings, California.

Troelstra, A.S. 1968. *Principles of Intuitionism: Lectures presented at the summer conference on Intuitionism and Proof Theory at SUNY at Buffalo, N.Y.* University of Amsterdam, Amsterdam.

Tufte, Edward R. 1990. *Envisioning Information*. Graphics Press, Cheshire, Conn.

Ulam, S.M. 1976. *Adventures of a Mathematician*. Scribners, New York.

de Waal, Frans 1982. *Chimpanzee Politics: Power and Sex among the Apes*. Cape, London.

Watson, James D. 1968. *The Double Helix: A Personal Account of the Discovery of the Structure of DNA*. Weidenfeld & Nicholson, London.

Weart, Spencer R. 1988. *Nuclear Fear: A History of Images*. Harvard University Press, Cambridge, Mass.

Weinberg, Steven 1993. *Dreams of a Final Theory*. Hutchinson, London.

Wilson, Edward O. 1975. *Sociobiology: The New Synthesis*. Harvard University Press, Cambridge, Mass.

Wilson, Edward O. 1978. *On Human Nature*. Harvard University Press, Cambridge, Mass.

von Wright, Georg Henrik 1971. *Explanation and Understanding*. Routledge, London

von Wright, Georg Henrik 1982. *Wittgenstein*. Basil Blackwell, Oxford.

Wyatt, Geoffrey 1986. *The Economics of Invention: A Study of the Determinants of Inventive Activity*. Harvester Press, Brighton.

Yergin, David 1991. *The Prize: The Epic Quest for Oil, Money and Power*. Simon & Schuster, New York.

Yoffee, Norman & Georg L. Cowgill, (eds.) 1988. *The Collapse of Ancient States and Civilizations*. The University of Arizona Press, Tucson.

Yukawa 1973. *Creativity and Intuition*. Kodansha International, Tokyo .

Zinovjev 1978. *Lichte Zukunft*. Diogenes, Zürich.

Index